PASSAGE THROUGH THE GARDEN

PASSAGE THROUGH THE GARDEN

Lewis and Clark
and the Image
of the American Northwest

JOHN LOGAN ALLEN

UNIVERSITY OF ILLINOIS PRESS
URBANA   CHICAGO   LONDON

LIBRARY OF CONGRESS CATALOGING IN PUBLICATION DATA

Allen, John Logan, 1941–
  Passage through the garden.

  Bibliography: p.
  1. Lewis and Clark Expedition. 2. The West—
Description and travel—To 1848. 3. Lewis, Meriwether,
1774–1809. 4. Clark, William, 1770–1838. I. Title.
F592.7.A48   917.8′04′20922   74-14512
ISBN 0-252-00397-7

TO MY WIFE, ANNE
AND TO MY CHILDREN,
TRACI AND JENNIFER

CONTENTS

ILLUSTRATIONS

PREFACE

This work is primarily intended to be a study of exploration, especially the great and epic trek of Lewis and Clark through the American Northwest in the years 1804–06. But it is also a study of geographical images—for Lewis and Clark, like others before and after them, were influenced by those "images" or patterns of belief about the nature and content of the Northwest that changed only gradually throughout the eighteenth and nineteenth centuries. It must be accepted as true that explorers very seldom, if ever, move into an area without having some objective that has emerged out of the religious, political, military, or commercial designs of those who would seek to have blank spaces on maps filled. Explorers and exploration, therefore, cannot be separated from the greater historical realities of their time and place. Nor can exploration be detached from what was or was believed to be geographic reality, since exploratory goals are derived from geographical knowledge. All explorers are conditioned by the geographical lore characteristic of their own milieu and by the mechanisms which exist therein for the analysis and interpretation of that lore. The consequences of this conditioning or "programming" process are the images of the regions to be explored.

Formerly, most examinations of exploration and of geographical images have been carried out separately. Neither group of studies has, therefore, reached its full potential for defining the importance of exploration for the attitudes that men have held about their environment. Numerous volumes of material on the exploration of the American Northwest exist, along with a lesser number dealing with the geographical image of the Northwest in literature and other art forms or in the general intellectual level of a given period. But nowhere, in all the work that has been done on the Northwest, is there anything dealing specifically and systematically with the relationships between exploration and geographical images. This book is intended to begin making up this deficiency by examining the Lewis and Clark Expedition from the standpoint of the basic and inherent connectivity between the exploratory process and geographical lore. In order to illustrate this relationship, I have adopted the following approach: first, to demonstrate the manner in which the store of knowledge gathered from exploration prior to Lewis and Clark was assimilated and articulated within the framework of early nineteenth-century American geographical thought to form an image of the American Northwest; second, to show how Lewis and Clark took that image and, during their expedition, modified and re-shaped it; and third, to speculate as to how the experience of the expedition served as a modifier of earlier images and as a molder of subsequent American concepts about the nature of the Northwest.

In this approach, I have relied mainly on original materials or "primary sources." French, British, and Spanish geographical journals, travel accounts, maps, newspapers, government documents, and private correspondence have been used to determine the impact of early exploration on views of the Northwest before Lewis and Clark. American newspapers, magazines, books, travel accounts, and maps have helped to indicate the nature of general American attitudes toward the Northwest at the beginning of the nineteenth century. Government documents, private correspondence, maps, and the writings of Thomas Jefferson have been used to show how Jefferson, the originator and sponsor of the expedition, viewed the Northwest. The correspondence between Jefferson and Lewis and Clark has enabled some conclusions to be drawn about the degree to which Lewis and Clark shared Jefferson's ideas about the Northwest. The original journals and maps of the first American transcontinental expedition have been used to illustrate the modifications made in the images of the West derived from earlier lore. And finally, the first published versions of the Lewis and Clark journals and maps have been used to demonstrate the impact of the expedition on American geographical thought. All these primary sources have been supplemented by the writings of modern authorities on the expedition and the Northwest and by literally thousands of miles of field research along "the Lewis and Clark Trail."

Becauses of the rather diffuse nature of the research, I am so deeply in the debt of so many persons that I hesitate to begin listing for fear of omitting someone. There are, however, a number of individuals and institutions that must be acknowledged for their courtesy and invaluable assistance:

Martyn J. Bowden of the Graduate School of Geography, Clark University, Worcester, Massachusetts, through his seminar in geographical thought and a not entirely rhetorical question about the "world view" of

Lewis and Clark, was initially responsible for the ideas that led to this undertaking and, during its various phases, provided friendship, encouragement, and advice.

The late John K. Wright of Lyme, New Hampshire, and former director of the American Geographical Society not only offered extremely helpful guidance and suggestions in the incipient stages of research but, through his published writings and unpublished ideas, has contributed immeasurably to all phases of this project.

A profound debt of gratitude is owed to Herman R. Friis of the National Archives in Washington, D.C. He opened his office and files and allowed me to pore over his notes, representing years of research in the history of exploration and cartography in North America, and saved me months and months of research time that would otherwise have been devoted to compilation of materials from the Archives and elsewhere. In addition, he offered, during many pleasant and productive conversations, a good many suggestions that have been retained in this study.

Perhaps the greatest contributor of all to this work has been a man I never had the pleasure of knowing—Bernard DeVoto. Above all who have written about Lewis and Clark, he understood their role as accepters, modifiers, and shapers of geographical lore and images. His masterpiece, *Course of Empire*, has served as the major conceptual foundation upon which I have erected this book.

Many persons have read portions or all of the manuscript and made valuable and valued recommendations. Some of them should receive special attention for that and other services:

Hugh Prince of University College, London, taught me a great deal about the nature of research methodology in historical geography;

William Koelsch of Clark University kept me straight on terminology and organization and corrected some critical mistakes in my notions on just what was or was not a "geographical image";

Saul Cohen, director of the Graduate School of Geography, Clark University, arranged a post-doctoral year which allowed me to complete the bulk of the project.

Steve Hobart, Brad Baltensperger, and Henry Aay, graduate students in my seminar on exploration in the American West at Clark, challenged my thinking on many points, offered many helpful suggestions, and kept me honest.

Most important of all, Donald Jackson, editor of the Papers of George Washington, Alderman Library at the University of Virginia in Charlottesville, assisted greatly in the revisions of the manuscript, in interpreting cartographic materials, in acquiring rare pieces of data, and in drawing my attention to some important information that I had missed in my research. Moreover, like all those who have written on Lewis and Clark in the last decade, I am grateful beyond expression for his *Letters of the Lewis and Clark Expedi-*

tion with Related Documents, 1783–1854 (Urbana, 1962), a masterful and scholarly treatment of primary material which has eliminated so much of the "legwork" in Lewis and Clark research. The importance of Jackson's contribution will be readily apparent in the pages to follow.

In addition to the above, many thanks are due the following:

In Washington, D.C.

The director and staff of the Manuscript Division and the Rare Book Division of the Library of Congress and special thanks to the staff of the Geography and Map Division of the library for their help in locating and analyzing a vast amount of seventeenth-, eighteenth-, and nineteenth-century cartographic material;

The staff of the Cartographic Records Branch of the National Archives, with particular thanks to Ralph Ehrenberg, who was most helpful and encouraging.

In Virginia

William G. Ray, Anne Freudenberg, and Francis L. Berkeley, Jr., of the Alderman Library, University of Virginia, Charlottesville, who provided tremendous assistance in uncovering data on Jefferson;

James Bear, curator, and his staff at the Thomas Jefferson Memorial Foundation (Monticello) for allowing me to roam through the estate and browse through the Jefferson materials there at my will.

In Massachusetts

Stephen T. Riley, director of the Massachusetts Historical Society, who provided help in tracking down information on Jefferson's library collections;

Marcus A. McCorison and the staff of the American Antiquarian Society in Worcester, Massachusetts, who cooperated most courteously in gathering eighteenth- and nineteenth-century newspapers and broadsides.

In Missouri

George R. Brooks, former director of the Missouri Historical Society, St. Louis, and his staff, who produced vast amounts of manuscripts on Lewis and Clark during a very limited and hurried visit;

James W. Goodrich of the State Historical Society of Missouri, Columbia, for being so efficient and courteous in obtaining manuscript maps for my use;

John Francis McDermott of the St. Louis Historical Documents Foundation, who graciously allowed me the use of published materials and provided encouragement at the very beginning of the project.

In Connecticut

Archibald Hanna, librarian, Library of Western Americana, Yale University, and his staff for their aid in compiling bibliographies and obtaining Lewis and Clark maps;

Miss Roberta K. Smith and her staff of the Reference Department of the Wilbur Cross Library, University of Connecticut, who provided kind and efficient assistance in procuring rare documents on microfilm;

My colleagues in the Department of Geology and Geography at the University of Connecticut, who provided much encouragement during the writing of this book and "picked up the slack" enough to allow me a leave of absence to complete the bulk of it;

Solomon Wollman and his staff of the University of Connecticut Laboratory, who graciously, professionally, and efficiently assisted with the preparation and reproduction of cartographic materials.

I am further grateful to Yale University Press and the University of Oklahoma Press for permission to reprint portions of copyrighted materials and to the *Western Historical Quarterly*, the *Geographical Review*, and *Montana, the Magazine of Western History*, for permission to reprint portions of articles that appeared in their pages.

I would also like to express my thanks to the numerous officials of the U.S. Forest Service, Department of Agriculture, and the Bureau of Land Management, Department of the Interior, for being so very helpful during various excursions into the Northwest on field trips. In this context I also would like to extend my deepest appreciation to my father, John M. Allen of Wheatland, Wyoming, who accompanied me on those trips and acted as driver, wrangler, cook, and chief bottle washer so I might be free for picture-taking, compass-reading, map-drawing, and other more esoteric pursuits. He also read and commented critically on the completed manuscript.

Wilma B. Fairchild, former editor of the *Geographical Review*, was invaluable in preparing the index and assisting with the proofreading.

The greatest thanks of all go to my wife, Anne, who assisted with the necessary but tedious clerical duties, endured without a single word of complaint my long and frequent absences, and kept two small children out of my notes and out of my hair when I was home and writing.

All of these people contributed immeasurably to this study. But none of them can be called to task for any errors that exist in it. Responsibility for those is mine alone.

Storrs, Connecticut
Spring, 1974

JOHN L. ALLEN

PROLOGUE:
THE PASSAGE
AND THE GARDEN

On June 20, 1803, Thomas Jefferson, President of the United States, penned a letter to Meriwether Lewis, his private secretary and personal choice to lead the first American exploration venture into the American Northwest.[1] It was to be the mission of that "Corps of Discovery of the Northwest," wrote Jefferson, "to explore the Missouri river, & such principal stream of it, as, by it's course and communication with the waters of the Pacific ocean, whether the Columbia, Oregan, Colorado or any other river may offer the most direct & practicable water communication across this continent for the purposes of commerce."[2] The key words in Jefferson's instructions were "water communication across this continent for the purposes of commerce." But although the phrasing was Jefferson's, the idea was not. Other men, at other times, had used different words to say the same thing and had called the water communication a Northwest Passage or a Passage to India.

The concept of a water route across the North American continent had

1. The term will be used herein to refer to that portion of the North American continent bounded on the east by the Mississippi River from its junction with the Missouri northward, on the south by the Platte River, on the north by the waters of the Saskatchewan system, and on the west by the Pacific Ocean.

2. Jefferson's instructions to Lewis, June 20, 1803 (Library of Congress, Manuscript Division, Jefferson Papers).

been a fundamental part of the geographical lore of North America ever since the world had first been made aware of that continent's existence. The ancients had shown the world was round, and they had pointed to the west and said that India was but a few days' sail with a favoring wind. Classical antiquity bequeathed precious few geographical doctrines to the Middle Ages, but when the commercial desires of Renaissance Europe sought a short route to the silk and spices of the Orient, Strabo, Virgil, Seneca, Aristotle, and others were pressed into service, and their tales of the Elysian Fields and the Fortunate Isles and the other wonders to be found west from Europe assumed new importance.[3] Dr. Hieronymus Muenzer, physician of Nuremberg and adviser on geography to the king of Portugal, cited the classics as proof of his contention that India was, in fact, but a few days' sail with a favoring wind: "There are countless and even conclusive proofs, from which we can see and clearly deduce that the sea in the direction of eastern Cathay can be crossed in a very few days."[4]

The presence of the New World, revealed as such by the post-Columbian voyages, was a profound surprise to men of classical learning such as Dr. Muenzer. The possibility of a short passage westward to India was a corroboration of the teaching of the ancients, and that a barrier to such a passage should exist was both unexpected and unwelcome.[5] But somewhere the Passage must exist—so said both logic and desire—and if the New World formed a barrier then a way must and could be found through it. Even before the murmurs over the rumored New World to the west had died away in Europe, theoretical geography had combined with the persistent teleological faith that man could find the answers to his hopes and dreams in the direction West.

This combination provided a solution to the problem of the obstacle lying in Europe's path to India and Cathay. Peter Martyr d'Anghiera, dean of Granada Cathedral and the first historian of America, wrote in his *De Orbe Novo* of 1515 that the new-found land to the west was indeed a new world and that it did form a barrier between Europe and Asia. But no matter—for somewhere along the coasts of that great new land would be found "great straits which provide a passage for the waters flowing from east to west, which I judge to be drawn round by the attraction of the heavens."[6]

Peter had seen the Northwest Passage; it was a salt-water strait which formed a corridor between the Seas of the North and of the South. Other theorists after him viewed it differently. It became a great inland body of water, the Western Sea, connected to the Atlantic by sea-level passages and

3. William H. Tillinghast, "The Geographical Knowledge of the Ancients Considered in Relation to the Discovery of America," in Justin Winsor, ed., *Narrative and Critical History of America* (8 vols., Boston, 1889), I, 1–33.
4. Cited in Paul Hermann, *The Great Age of Discovery* (New York, 1958), p. 12.
5. Tillinghast, "The Geographical Knowledge of the Ancients," p. 1.
6. Cited in Tryggvi J. Oleson, *Early Voyages and Northern Approaches* (New York, 1964), p. 132.

opening into the Pacific, the Sea of the South. It became a lake, resting athwart the highest lands on the continent and draining toward both the western and eastern oceans. It became a river that could be navigated upstream to a point where its waters mingled with those of a stream that flowed to another ocean. And in its final and most realistic form, it became a simple and very short portage between the navigable waters flowing to the Atlantic and some great river which flowed toward the setting sun. But the ideas were all the same; the decrees of logic and desire *would* be obeyed and a water communication *would* be found across the continent. Every stream, every river, every opening in the shore, every rumored lake in the interior might have been the Passage, and the exploration of North America was conditioned for three centuries by the logical assumptions and the teleological positiveness that would not die.[7]

2

The earliest attempts on the passage by water across or through North America were predicated on the idea that there was no room for a large land mass between Europe and Asia. Logic allied itself with desire and used the proven computations of classical and medieval geography as a foundation for the premise that North America must be narrow from east to west. Through this narrow land mass there must be a water passage leading to the fabled Orient. The Florentine pilot Giovanni da Verrazano claimed to have reached a point along the eastern shores of the New World where the land mass became so narrow that he could look across it and see the Western Sea. But he found no passage through the land barrier.

A few years after Verrazano's reported discovery of the Western Sea, Jacques Cartier believed he had found the passage which led toward it. The St. Lawrence had lighted his hope, but it, like all the other rivers which those in search of the Passage to India had entered, failed to lead to the sea whose waves washed the golden sands of Cipangu and encircled the Golden Chersonese. Yet the idea of the Western Sea persisted, and as the size of the North American continent expanded with expanding geographical knowledge, the Western Sea simply retreated farther and farther into the west.

As the migratory Western Sea shifted westward across the maps, the

7. Bernard DeVoto, *Course of Empire* (Boston, 1952), pp. 55–57. The search for the Passage has been the central theme of many works on the exploration of North America, among them: Winsor, *Narrative and Critical History;* Lawrence J. Burpee, *The Search for the Western Sea* (2 vols., Toronto, 1908); and John Bartlett Brebner, *The Explorers of North America* (London, 1933). DeVoto's *Course of Empire* is, however, the most imaginative treatment of the impact of theoretical geography and commercial incentive on North American exploration and has, along with John Kirtland Wright, *Human Nature in Geography* (Cambridge, Mass., 1966), provided the conceptual basis for the present work. If many of my statements in the following chapters often seem to resemble those of DeVoto or Wright, the similarity is far from coincidental.

rivers believed to flow from or toward it became longer. The experiences of the English and Dutch seamen who sought a passage by sea to the northwest and the observations of the Spanish search for the Straits of Anian on the western margins of the continent had shown that no easy passage from the Atlantic to the Pacific could be found by an ocean route. The emphasis then shifted to those great rivers which could provide a water communication with the Western Sea; with this shift in emphasis came continental penetration.

The explorers of England, France, and Spain pushed into the interior of North America via its great river systems, and as they expanded geographical awareness they changed some older concepts. The Western Sea, which had fled before the course of exploration, changed in nature from a mighty body of water which led to China into a land-locked inland sea that drained to both the Atlantic and Pacific oceans. This interior sea diminished to the size of a lake which occupied an area of higher lands and spawned the rivers which flowed to the east and to the west. And with one final gasp the lake disappeared altogether, leaving behind only the height-of-land. The dream of the Passage remained, however, and from this height-of-land rivers flowed to the eastern and western oceans. The way to the riches of Asia might be found to the west, up a great river which emptied into the Atlantic, up to the height-of-land, then across a short and easy portage and down the other side—down the Great River of the West which logic said must flow into the Pacific.

Experience narrowed the choices of where to look for this water communication to the blessed shores of Cathay until, in 1673, the final solution was offered. For in that year Louis Jolliet and Jacques Marquette, two explorers of New France, discovered the Missouri River and recognized in it the key to the Passage to India. Poised on the edge of the unknown, Marquette looked at the great river rushing from the heart of the west and arrived at the conclusion which was of such momentous importance. By ascending the Missouri, Marquette believed, one would reach a portage to a second great river, one which flowed toward the west of southwest.[8] Thus did the greatest and most durable misconception about the Missouri's headwaters enter geographical lore and thus was the Missouri recognized as the beacon that would dispel the mists which had hidden the Passage to India from the view of so many for so long.

3

The explorers of New France, searching for the easy passage to the Sea of the South and thus to India, had discovered the Missouri River and had recognized it as the possible key to the mystery of the water passage across

8. "The Journal of Father Marquette," *Jesuit Relations and Allied Documents,* ed. Reuben Gold Thwaites (72 vols., Cleveland, 1896–1901), LIX, 141.

the continent for the purposes of commerce. The focus of those who dreamed of the Passage was henceforth to be centered on a real and tangible geographic feature. The Missouri was a great river and it came from the west where that which was desired—the short portage and the Great River of the West—might be found. The experience of 130 years of exploration, from Jolliet and Marquette, who discovered the Missouri, to Lewis and Clark, who made it known, did not diminish the dream of the conceptual passageway.

Following the great and muddy river westward, the explorers of New France expanded the frontiers of geographical knowledge toward the Pacific until, by 1754, when the French and Indian War erupted, they had ascended many branches of the Missouri toward the mountains and had made known in a general way much of the geography of the Northwest. But they had not found the Passage, and when European politics and American military conflicts combined to oust France from the heart of the continent, the Spanish empire in North America fell heir not only to France's possessions in the trans-Missouri region but also to her desire to find, via the Missouri and those streams heading with it and flowing west, the water communications across the continent.

During the latter years of the eighteenth century, like the adventurers of French Louisiana before, explorers and fur traders sponsored by the Spanish regime in Louisiana used the Missouri as a highway to the interior and to the hoped-for water communication. And in the coastal waters of the Pacific Northwest, Spanish ships quested after the elusive Great River of the West, which, with the Missouri, would complete the Passage. But as Spain reached the upper Missouri and the waters surrounding Vancouver Island, she ran headlong into the drive of the British.

Great Britain had already attempted her own water communication in Arctic waters and, by way of rivers, in the western interior of Canada. And like Spain, Great Britain was active in the coastal waters of the Northwest. But British attempts in the Arctic and in the Canadian West had ended in discouragement, and the Great River of the West was as much a will-o'-the-wisp for England as it was for Spain. The Montreal-based fur trade, recognizing the immense economic value of a water passage that could link the rich fur lands of the Northwest and the fur-hungry Mandarins of China, therefore began to eye the Missouri as the final hope of that passage.

Yet defeat stalked the ambitions of the colonial powers and their fur-trading representatives who would go in search of the Passage to India. In 1792 Captain Robert Gray, an American, discovered the Columbia River, making reality out of theory and enhancing the possibilities of a connection between the Missouri and what had previously been only a conjectural Great River of the West. But before anyone had had a chance to act on that discovery and its implications, as New Spain and England met in conflict on the upper Missouri and in the waters of Nootka Sound, negotiations in Europe transferred most of the Northwest from Spain back to France and shortly thereafter to the new American republic. An American expedition, conceived by Thomas Jefferson and commanded by Captains Meriwether Lewis and William Clark, would make the final assault on the Passage, an assault based on the knowledge and experiences of all those who had gone before.

4

It would be unthinkable to imagine that the idea of sending an expedition to seek the water communication across the continent by way of the Missouri and Columbia sprang full-blown from the mind of Jefferson. Rather, the objective of the passage to the Pacific took shape in Jefferson's mind as he accumulated information from the geographical lore of those who had penetrated the Northwest in search of the water communication or who had sailed the shores where the Great River of the West entered the Pacific.

Contributions to regional awareness made by the French and Spanish in the territory that was known as Louisiana and by the British in the western interior of Canada had added to the store of misconception about the Missouri and had reinforced the idea of the river as a highway to the Pacific and to the Orient beyond. And as Spanish, British, and American exploration increased knowledge of the Pacific Northwest and the lower Columbia River during the closing years of the eighteenth century, the concept of the Passage grew even stronger. The Passage had always existed in the geography of the mind, and as the exploits of those who had sought it were recorded and translated by journalists, historians, geographers, cartographers, and others, it became a fixture of what was viewed as reality.

By the beginning of the nineteenth century the conjectural Passage had become such a dominant element in the geographical lore of the trans-Missouri area that anyone who might have been interested, as Thomas Jefferson was, in resolving finally its true nature and location had a wide range of source materials from which to derive geographical data. From this source material, representing the accumulated experience of exploration and the interpretations of that experience, there emerged a group of *images*—patterns of belief about the nature and content of the land lying between the Missouri River and the Pacific Ocean.

The dominating feature of these images was the persistent idea of the passage to the Orient by way of the river systems of North America. Yet while this notion played an important role in the exploration of the Northwest during the period between 1673 and 1803, it would be a mistake to assign to it a position of total dominance in an assessment of the geographical lore of the Northwest during the opening years of the nineteenth century. The concept of the water passageway through the Missouri and Columbia systems to the Pacific was an integral part of geographical knowledge; it had been and was to be the conceptual basis for geographical discovery. But supporting the concept was an even older idea: the West was a place of romance and mystery, where hopes and dreams and ambitions could come true and life would somehow be better.

5

Man has a natural desire to seek what lies toward the sunset. It is this desire that lured Europe westward as much as did the attraction of the passage to the Golden Chersonese. Ever since the first primitive man began to associate his dead with something other than the grave, the region where the sun sets has occupied man's fancy as the place to which departed souls go for blissful rest and tranquility.[9] In the imaginary geography of the ancients, West was a direction of enchantment and in the West were the lingering places of romance. To the West departed the Homeric heroes, and on the earth's extremest verge they found the Elysian Fields, "where life is easiest to man. No snow is there, nor yet storm nor any rain, but always ocean sendeth forth the breeze of the shrill west to blow cool on man."[10]

Even though the Middle Ages relegated Homer's Elysian Fields, Plato's Atlantis, and the Blessed Isles of the Latin poets to the musty realms of classical learning, medieval geography was not barren of their reflections. Medieval maps swarmed with fabulous lands of gold and spices to the west and in the medieval geographies may be found traces of the ancient longing for the delightful and fertile lands that hovered on the verge of the unknown, on the edge of the world, to the west.[11] Here it was that Sir Thomas Malory's Arthur found his Isle of Avalon, where "falls not rain, or hail, or any snow, nor ever wind blows loudly."[12] Here also were the legendary isles of the Atlantic that exerted such a powerful fascination on the medieval mind. Even into the Age of Discovery the theme held constant. Columbus believed he had found, in the Orinoco, the great river which flowed from the terrestrial paradise of the West; and Cabeza de Vaca, wandering lost across North America, "ever held it certain that going towards the sunset we must find what we desire."[13]

De Vaca was not the first to voice the faith in the West—nor was he the last. Throughout the geographical lore of the Northwest, the theme ran in nearly a continuous thread. The land was fertile and the climate benign, the vegetation lush and the mineral wealth unsurpassed. The indigenous peoples

9. For an excellent treatment of this idea, see Howard Mumford Jones, *O Strange New World* (New York, 1964), ch. 1; of further interest are Mircea Eliade, "The Yearning for Paradise in Primitive Tradition," *Daedalus*, LXXXVIII (1959), 255–67; and Loren Baritz, "The Idea of the West," *American Historical Review*, LXVI (1961), 618–40.

10. From Samuel Bryant's translation of the *Odyssey*, bk. IV, v. 561.

11. Tillinghast, "The Geographical Knowledge of the Ancients," pp. 31–33.

12. Cited in Jones, *O Strange New World*, p. 382.

13. "The Narrative of Cabeza de Vaca," *Spanish Explorers in the Southern United States*, ed. Frederick W. Hodge (New York, 1908), p. 105.

resembled heroic races more than did the eastern forest worshippers of Manitou, and surrounding them were features of myth, features that must be found to the west simply because they were a part of the West.

Thus compounded from the disparate pieces of lore that made up the source materials on the West was the first general theme of the images of the trans-Missouri region—in the American West was the Garden of the World.[14] It was a very old and a very new idea and it would be fundamental to American thought during the nineteenth century. But more important for present purposes, this first theme in the images was intimately connected to the second; the notion that the Missouri and some river heading with it and running westward would furnish the answer to the riddle of the Northwest Passage was as much a part of the teleological faith in the West as it was the process of logical deduction following the elimination of other unknowns from the map. The components of the conceptions of the geography of the Northwest fit the pattern of both logic and faith. The mountains were low and easy to cross and amply provided with short portages between the heads of navigable rivers whose drainage patterns were symmetrical and whose courses took them in the proper direction for a water communication. The Garden and the Passage to India were the twin themes that were so preponderant in the images of the American Northwest at the time of the Lewis and Clark Expedition. All the elements present in those themes combined to give hope expression in conceptual geography, and Lewis and Clark would go westward, through the Northwest, seeking a Passage through the Garden.

14. See Henry Nash Smith, *Virgin Land: The American West in Symbol and Myth* (Cambridge, Mass., 1950); and Leo Marx, *The Machine in the Garden: Technology and the Pastoral Ideal in America* (New York, 1964).

PASSAGE THROUGH THE GARDEN

CHAPTER I

THE NORTHWESTERN MYSTERY

The geographical lore that would govern the nature of the first major American attempt to solve the "Northwestern Mystery"[1] comprised many different components of knowledge. All exploration is conditioned by the geographical lore that has grown out of previous exploratory behavior, and the transcontinental journey of Lewis and Clark would prove no exception to this rule. The travel accounts and journals of earlier explorers, the records of their exploits in literature, and the cartographic results of their wanderings were the most crucial of these components, and many of them would be made available to the commanders of the forthcoming attempt on the Passage to India. Some of the components were more accurate than others, just as some colors of the spectrum outshine others in their brilliance. But the relative accuracy of the various elements that made up the geographical lore of the Northwest on the eve of the Lewis and Clark Expedition is not important. For accurate or not, all the components had an impact on exploration, the proportionate quantities of truth or fiction in them having no real bearing on their importance as shapers of the images of the Northwest. It is therefore

1. The term was first used by Bernard DeVoto (*Course of Empire*, pp. 73–75) to refer to the trans-Missouri West, "an area . . . that contained the key features of continental geography which were the last to be discovered and understood."

I

necessary to dissect the source materials for the geographical conceptions of the Northwest, in order to resolve into its constituent parts the geographical lore upon which Jefferson would base his plans for the discovery of the Passage to India and which would condition Lewis and Clark in their efforts to transform those plans into the actual establishment of the water communication across the continent for the purposes of commerce.

2

The French were the first contributors to the geographical lore of the trans-Missouri area that was available in the beginning of the nineteenth century. Operating out of posts in the Great Lakes country and in the Louisiana Territory, claimed for France in 1682 by La Salle, French missionaries, adventurers, soldiers, and fur traders had sought to find a water passage to the Pacific. Their reports and the chronicles which recorded their activities from 1673, when the Mississippi-Missouri system was discovered, to 1763, when France's ouster from North America became official, were seminal in the development of later images of the Northwest. As such, the French contributions to geographical lore laid the foundations for the themes of the Garden of the World and the Passage to India that were so basic to images of the West at the time of Lewis and Clark.

From the very beginning of French exploratory activity in the Northwest, the motif of the Garden emerged as a cardinal element in the lore which French explorers and chroniclers furnished to the general fund of knowledge about the trans-Missouri region. Illustrative of the theme in the source materials that stemmed from the period of French exploration were assessments of land quality that spoke of the West as a region of tremendous beauty and fertility; comments on soil, climate, minerals, and vegetation; observations on the nature of the indigenous peoples; and descriptions of those mythical features that were inherently part of thought about the West.

The first Frenchman to record for posterity the abundance of the northwestern lands was Marquette, who commented on reaching the Mississippi valley that "no better soil can be found either for corn, for vines, or for any other fruit whatever."[2] The Northwest was a garden and Marquette's commentary was echoed by others. A member of La Salle's first expedition into the country south of the Great Lakes reported the presence of a vast area "of exceeding great fertility and beauty. . . . There are vast Meadows, which need not to be grubb'd up but are ready for the Plow and Seed."[3] La Salle himself spoke of "vast fields of the best land in the world, all ready for cul-

2. "Jolliet's Report to the Missions," *Jesuit Relations*, ed. Thwaites, LVIII, 105–7.
3. Louis Hennepin, *Nouvelle Decouverte, a New Discovery of a Vast Country in North America*, trans. and ed. Reuben Gold Thwaites (Chicago, 1903), p. 213.

tivation,"[4] and the historians of the La Salle journeys referred to "the finest and most fertile countries in the world; the soil, which there produces two crops of every kind of grain a year, being ready to receive the plough."[5]

The French concept of the West as a garden did not diminish after the beginning of the eighteenth century. Accounts of the early 1700s described landscapes that presented charming prospects: "Oak Trees, Elms, Chestnut-Trees, Walnut-Trees, Apple-Trees, Plum-Trees, and Vines which bear their fine cluster up to the very top of the Trees, upon a sort of ground that lies as smooth as one's hand."[6] And as the expansion of exploration carried Frenchmen away from the wooded lands of the Mississippi valley into the prairies and plains to the west, the garden concept was reinforced. Virtually all the sources describing French entry into the lands west of the Mississippi evoked images of beautiful and extensive prairies upon which thousands of buffalo, elk, and deer grazed; overhead, skies were clear and the very air was scented with rich perfumes.[7]

In descriptions of this type there are few if any regional distinctions noted; the description of one area of Louisiana as a garden might be considered to apply equally to all the lands of the Northwest. Several analogies to the fertility and "salubrity" of the Northwest were common, perhaps the most popular being those that compared the western rivers to the Nile and the western soils to the soils of Egypt after the flooding of the Nile.[8] The lands to the west, although more of a grassland than the country of the Mississippi valley, were no less fertile: "The soil is so fertile that, almost without cultivation, it produces European wheat and all kinds of fruit and vegetables which are unknown in France."[9] As late as the 1750s the traditional picture was of a beneficent landscape, created by a bountiful Nature for man, a landscape in which crops would grow in profusion with limited labor.

Of the mineral wealth in the West little specific information was available although nearly all reporters agreed that the regions beyond the Mississippi must be extremely rich in minerals of various sorts. General and specific knowledge both were available for such mundane minerals as lead and salt; but even though no one had found any traces for sure, explorers related tales of deposits of gold and silver farther west. The western natives, according to one observer, carried out extensive trade in gold with nations dwelling deep

4. Pierre Margry, ed., *Decouvertes et etablissements des Français dans l'ouest et dans le sud de l'Amerique Septentrionale, 1614–1754* (6 vols., Paris, 1876–86), II, 244. Margry's volumes contain a wealth of original sources and documents on the French discoveries in North America. The citations from Margry used herein are my own translations.

5. Cited in Dorothy Anne Dondore, *The Prairie and the Making of Middle America: Four Centuries of Description* (reprint ed., New York, 1961), p. 18.

6. Baron de Lahontan, *New Voyages to North America* (2 vols., London, 1703), II, 319.

7. M. Penicaut, "The Annals of Louisiana from 1698 to 1722," in Benjamin F. French, ed., *Historical Collections of Louisiana* (5 vols., New York, 1846–55), VI, 107.

8. Jean Bernard Bossu, *Travels through That Part of North America Formerly Called Louisiana* (London, 1771), p. 131.

9. Bossu, *Travels through . . . Louisiana*, p. 61.

in the interior, and another writer supported the tradition: "It is said that there is much gold there within that country and some rubies."[10]

There was little general agreement among the French sources as to the nature of the inhabitants of the vast garden of the Northwest. The indigenous peoples were variously characterized as noble savages living in near-civilized splendor, or as rude and barbarous tribesmen little above the level of the beasts of the forest. But the farther the chroniclers attempted to carry their descriptions into the still-unknown West, the more fanciful and picturesque became the natives. Toward the interior were natives who wore clothing and sailed canoes on a large salt-water lake.[11] Many of these tribes were, in the mind's eye of the French authors, white, civilized, and living in great cities. Some of them were distinguishable by features worthy of medieval romance: "very large ears in which they wore gold hoops . . . and very long fingernails,"[12] or "large eyes, an inch apart from the nose."[13] There were not only the traditional red Indians; there were also white Indians, black Indians, bearded Indians, dwarf Indians, and even Indians whose descriptions were so strange that a Jesuit priest was moved to write: "Might they not be Tartars or stragglers from Japan?"[14]

The Northwest, in the French source material, was indeed a garden, fertile in soil, benign in climate, rich in minerals, and peopled with the hosts of fantasy. And although the more mythical elements in the French descriptions of the western interior—civilized natives living in golden cities and surrounded by mineral wealth—had been recognized as misrepresentations of reality by the beginning of the nineteenth century, the basic notions about the lushness and value of the western lands that ran throughout the French literature were still highly acceptable and contributed much to the images of the Northwest at the time of Lewis and Clark.

3

Just as the source material from the French period in Louisiana lent support to the theme of the Garden of the World in early nineteenth-century images of the trans-Missouri area, so did it contribute to the concept of the Passage to India. When French explorers moved into the western interior, they began to speculate about, report on, and draw maps of the greater geography of the Northwest. Through the exploratory activity of the French the cardinal features of western geography—the river systems, the lakes, the mountain ranges—became a part of geographical lore. Those interested in a water passage across the continent could extract from that lore enough in-

10. Margry, Decouvertes . . . des Français, VI, 745.
11. Bossu, Travels through . . . Louisiana, p. 105.
12. Bossu, Travels through . . . Louisiana, p. 213.
13. Margry, Decouvertes . . . des Français, VI, 745.
14. Thwaites, Jesuit Relations, LXVIII, 233.

formation to support the contention that the Passage to India did, in fact, exist.

The speculative geography of the Northwest and its relationship with the Passage to India had begun to take shape even before actual French penetration into the Mississippi valley. The French explorers in the Great Lakes region had heard rumors of great rivers that led to the Pacific as early as the middle of the seventeenth century; consequently, the instructions given to Marquette and Jolliet in 1672 included the admonition to discover that stream which flowed to the Gulf of California and to follow it down to its entry into the sea.[15] But the rumored great river did not lead to the Pacific. When the fact that the Mississippi flowed to the Gulf of Mexico was theoretically determined by Marquette and proved by La Salle, speculation began to revolve around the Missouri.

On the earliest maps the Missouri was only a short stream (fig. 1); such representation, however, did not match the earliest descriptions of the river. According to Marquette, it was a river "of considerable size, coming from the northwest, from a great distance."[16] It led in the direction of the Pacific and, based on information that Marquette received about the river, formed part of the desired water passage. By ascending the Missouri for only five or six days, Marquette related, one would reach a fine prairie, which, if crossed ("it is not very difficult to transport canoes through so fine a country as that prairie"), would lead to a second large river. This river flowed "toward the southwest, for ten or fifteen leagues, after which it enters a lake, small and deep, which flows toward the west, where it falls into the sea." "I have hardly any doubt," said Marquette, "that this is the Vermillion Sea, and I do not despair of discovering it some day."[17]

The idea that conditioned geographical thinking about the Northwest from Marquette's time forward was picked up immediately after his and Jolliet's return to their home base at the Jesuit mission of Sault Ste. Marie following their journey to the Mississippi in 1673. The superior of the mission, Claude Dablon, took the thread of rumor and spun it into his annual report of 1674: "By going up that river, one will perhaps arrive at some lake which discharges toward the west."[18] Marquette had recognized the Missouri as the prospective passage to the great South Sea, and the activities of the French down to the middle of the eighteenth century confirmed that recognition.

The next French explorer to assimilate rumors about the Missouri and its connections with the Pacific was the Recollect father Louis Hennepin. Hennepin was the official historian of La Salle's first expedition to the Mississippi River, the first exploring party after Marquette and Jolliet to move into the

15. Thwaites, *Jesuit Relations*, LIX, 87.
16. Thwaites, *Jesuit Relations*, LIX, 141.
17. Thwaites, *Jesuit Relations*, LIX, 143.
18. Cited in DeVoto, *Course of Empire*, p. 119.

1. Jacques Marquette's map of the Mississippi. Tracing by J. G. Kohl

Notes.

This is a copy of the fac-simile of a map of the Mississippi, which has been communicated in Part IV of Mr. French's History of Louisiana. The original of this Sketch is preserved at St. Mary's College, Montreal Canada East.

It is believed, that it is the very draught, which Father Marquette made himself at the time of his canoe-voyage on the river.

We have already given in our collection copies of different maps, which pretend to be copies from Marquette's map (for instance the map of Thevenot), or which are said to have been made by Marquette's Companion, the Sieur Joliet either on the voyage itself or soon after (for instance the map of Joliet which I found in the Dépôt de la Marine in Paris, and of which I communicated a copy in this collection).

All these maps agree in the principal features and contents. They show all a part of the Canadian Lakes the Wisconsin and Illinois-River and the Mississippi from there as far down as the mouth of the Arcansas. They have, however, all slight differences in the Latitudes and in the orthography of the names.

At first sight our present map appears to be the most incomplete of them all. It has not so many names and not so many details of riverbranches, as the other maps.

As for the course and direction of the mainchannel of the Mississippi and its principal bends and turnings it is, however, the most perfect of the whole class of maps relating to Marquette's discoveries.

In this respect I attract the attention of the reader to the following bends and angles: 1) mouth of the Wisconsin. 2) North of the Missouri. 3) at the mouth of the Missouri. 4) at the mouth of the Ohio. They correspond all very well with nature. On the other maps, (ex Thevenots) the river-channel runs nearly always one straight line.

With respect to the orthography of names, we may observe the following. The Mississippi is called on our map: "R. de la Conception" (Conception River) while it is called on the other maps: "Rivière Colbert (Colbert River) or R. Mitchisipi ou Grande Rivière". The Missouri is named on our map: "Pekittanoui", a name still afterwards to be found on other maps. The Ohio is called on our map: "Ouabou... (Wabash River), on the other maps: "Ouabouquigou". The Arcansas on our map: "Akansea", on the other "Balansea".

To the South of the Arcansas is written on our map: "Bassin de la Floride". On the other the "Golfe de Mexique" is depicted.

The Latitudes for the 4 principal points are on our map: for the mouth of the Wisconsin about 42° N.L, for the mouth of the Missouri about 38° N.L, for the mouth of the Ohio about 36° N.L, for the mouth of the Arcansas about 34° N.L, which is much nearer to the truth, than the Latitudes given on the other maps.

In the critical details of the other names we cannot enter here.

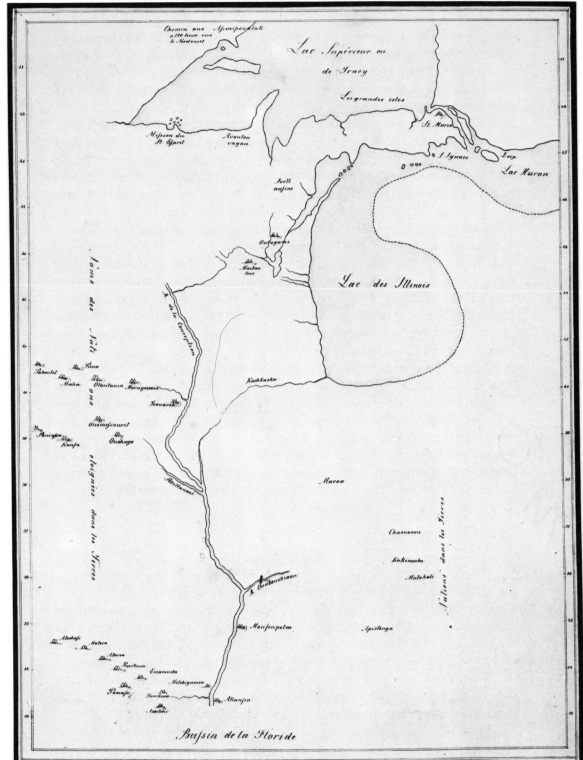

The **MISSISSIPPI** by Marquette 1673.

Mississippi valley. Early in 1680 Hennepin was dispatched by his commander from a crude fort on the Illinois River to seek information about the country to the west. From Hennepin's narratives of his wandering there emerged statements that became core segments in the geographical lore of the trans-Missouri region.

The Missouri was, wrote Hennepin, a mighty river. It was formed "from several other Rivers, which spring from a Mountain about twelve days' Journey from its Mouth." It was further related that "from this mountain one might see the Sea, and now and then some Great Ships."[19] A new element had been added to the geography of the Northwest. Not only was the Missouri a great river which flowed from the west but about its source waters were mountains, mountains which later generations would call the "Mountains of Bright Stones," the "Shining Mountains," the "Stony Mountains," and, finally, the Rockies. From these mountains the Missouri flowed; beyond them, Hennepin added, one might find "some great River running into the Pacifick-Sea, whereby . . . it will be easie to trade and have commerce with China and Japan."[20] With this statement the third critical element of the geography of the Northwest had been added: beyond the mountains of the interior was the Great River of the West.

From Marquette, from Hennepin and his commander, La Salle, there emerged the central concepts about the geographic elements of the trans-Missouri region. These concepts would be current until the time of Lewis and Clark: the Missouri was a mighty river that came from the west; it had its sources in a range of mountains somewhere in the western interior; beyond this range of mountains a mighty river ran westward to the Pacific. Later generations of explorers, narrators, and cartographers added to and enlarged and refined these concepts—but the basic structure remained the same.

4

The immediate impact of the initial activity of French explorers in the Northwest was felt most strongly in the areas of cartography and popular literature. Following the early French references to the cardinal elements of western geography, cartographers now could give specific positioning on their maps to those features which had previously been located by deduction alone, and the Missouri, the mountains of the interior, and the Great River of the West began to appear on maps of North America. And popular authors now had the geographic material to hold the fascination of their readers as they embellished the exploratory accounts of the early Louisiana French.

Some of the earliest maps of the trans-Missouri area[21] appeared in various

19. Hennepin, *Nouvelle Decouverte*, p. 188.
20. Hennepin, *Nouvelle Decouverte*, p. 373.
21. It is not my intention to give a specialized treatment of the cartography of the American Northwest. The maps selected for discussion are either highly representative of

editions of Hennepin's published accounts; they showed the Missouri River as a definite feature, with its source in a range of mountains, in a lake which, by inference, must have been close to the Pacific (fig. 2). The maps attributed to La Salle, although crude, also showed the Missouri and depicted its headwaters as lying east of a lake in which the "Rio del Norte" or Rio Grande had its head. The idea that the Missouri and the Rio Grande sprang from the same source region became from this time on a dominant fixture in geographical lore. Other early French maps depicted the Missouri as flowing directly from the west in a straight-line west-to-east direction, reinforcing the idea that the Missouri headed close to the Rio Grande somewhere in the Spanish possessions of New Mexico.

But the Rio Grande was not the only river near the Missouri's source. For on French maps of the last years of the seventeenth century there appeared the notation that to the west of the Missouri's headwaters there was "a river which flows to the south and west coming from the east and north on which people are clothed like us and of which neither source nor mouth is known."[22] The idea that there was another river west of the Missouri gained substance, and the Great River of the West made its appearance in cartographic form.

In the popular literature also there materialized allusions to those elements of the geography of the Northwest that had been established by the early French explorers. The accounts of Louis Armand de Lom d'Arce, Baron de Lahontan and a former lieutenant in the French army, were widely circulated throughout Europe and America during the eighteenth century; these typified the popular treatment of exploratory accounts.[23] Lahontan had supposedly made a series of journeys into the western parts of North America in the late seventeenth century, and from these apocryphal journeys came accounts of civilized nations living in great splendor somewhere in the western interior. More important, however, was the fact that Lahontan's marvelous Indians lived on the banks of the "Long River," a great river tributary to the Mississippi and having its source in a range of mountains. Beyond the mountains, not far removed from the headsprings of Long River, another river flowed west into the Pacific (fig. 3). In purely fictitious as well as in more or less factual accounts the major elements of western geography appeared.

---

period cartography or are connected in some way with Jefferson or Lewis and Clark. The best source for information in more detail on maps of the Northwest may be found in Carl Irving Wheat's magnificent 5-volume study *Mapping the Transmississippi West, 1540–1861* (Menlo Park, Calif., 1958–62). The first volume, *The Spanish Entrada to the Louisiana Purchase*, includes a discussion of exploration and cartography during the period with which the present work also deals.

22. Such a legend appears on a map of the Northwest drawn by Jean Baptiste Louis Franquelin in 1697 (MS, Newberry Library, Chicago).

23. Lahontan's works were very popular in France and England and went through a number of editions between 1703 and 1735. The most popular was that of 1735, printed in London, and the one that was in Jefferson's library. This edition was not changed textually from earlier versions.

2. Louis Hennepin's map of Louisiana. From *A New Discovery* (London, 1698) LIBRARY OF CONGRESS

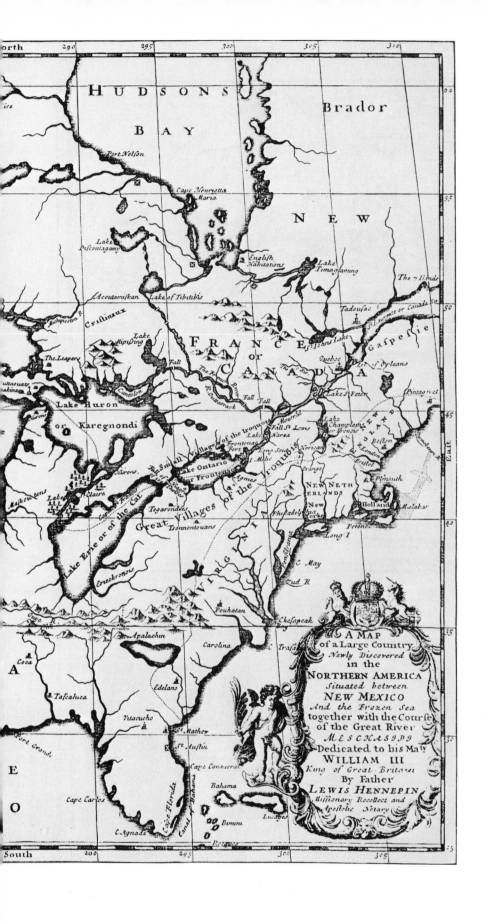

A MAP
of a Large Country
Newly Discovered
in the
NORTHERN AMERICA
Situated between
NEW MEXICO
And the Frozen Sea
together with the Course
of the Great River
MESCHASIPI
Dedicated to his Maⁱʸ
WILLIAM III
King of Great Britain
By Father
LEWIS HENNEPIN
Missionary Recollect and
Apostolic Notary

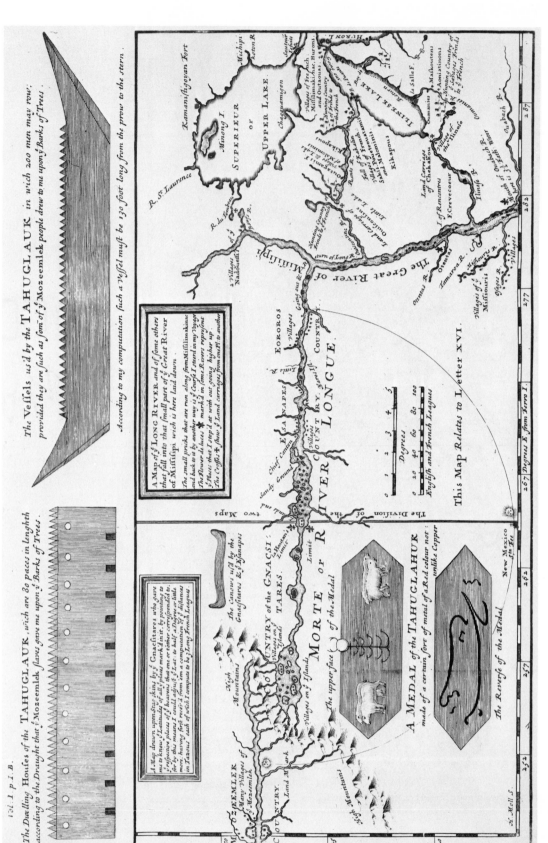

3. The Baron de Lahontan's "Rivière Longue" or Long River. Drawn by Hermann Moll for *New Voyages to North America* (London, 1735). LIBRARY OF CONGRESS

5

After the first penetration of Frenchmen from New France into the Mississippi valley, Louisiana was colonized and a French foothold was established from which still other explorations were launched that supplemented the earliest geographical knowledge about the Northwest. In the opening year of the eighteenth century a French adventurer named LeSueur moved into the trans-Mississippi area in search of mines of gold and silver and, in his ramblings, passed the Missouri and noticed that it came from the direction of the Sea of the South.[24] The reflection of a French colonial official in the infant colony of Louisiana carried the same impressions. The Missouri, one official noted, flowed from a height-of-land the other side of which gave rise to rivers that led to the Pacific.[25]

For the first few years of the eighteenth century, French exploratory activity in the Northwest was at a low ebb. But the French reports continued to mention the Missouri, although an unmapped and essentially unknown geographic quantity, as a river which flowed nearly west from New Mexico and provided a passage to the Pacific. It would, wrote one French priest, be very serviceable for Frenchmen who wished to discover the South Sea.[26] The idea gained currency as French adventurers began to make the Missouri known and established posts in its lower reaches. One such adventurer had heard of Chinese on the upper Missouri; if there were Chinese then the Missouri must lead to the Passage. Thus the definite hope which had been voiced by Marquette had not been discredited.[27]

French officialdom in Louisiana began to investigate actively the possibility that a water communication could be found via the Missouri. "This project would be very easy to execute," wrote one official, "and would not require a difficult portage, as had been feared."[28] For the Missouri went through a "magnificent pass" through a range of mountains to a river which flowed to the Pacific. "This discovery," continued the official, "should be important enough to warrant investigation."

External events continually thwarted the desire of the Louisiana French to locate the Passage, however, and it was not to be discovered during the French tenure in the heartland of the continent. Nor were the attempts of the fur-trade interests of New France successful in locating the Passage, and the endeavors of explorers such as the Vérendryes ended in failure. But

24. LeSueur's narratives are in Margry, *Decouvertes . . . des Français*, V, 416–20, and Thwaites, *Jesuit Relations*, LXVI, 337–38.
25. Margry, *Decouvertes . . . des Français*, VI, 178.
26. Thwaites, *Jesuit Relations*, LXVI, 225.
27. Other routes were being rejected, however, as geographical knowledge increased. Lahontan's "Long River" was one of the mythical elements that gradually lost acceptance among the French in Louisiana if not among the reading population of Europe and the British colonies in North America. For commentary on Lahontan's fictions by Louisiana Frenchmen, see Margry, *Decouvertes . . . des Français*, VI, 384–86.
28. Margry, *Decouvertes . . . des Français*, VI, 187–90.

throughout the period of French colonialism in North America the idea of the Passage remained current; the chroniclers and historians who preserved the events of France in the New World for later generations continually alluded to the fabled water connection between the Atlantic and Pacific. The great French Jesuit scholar Pierre F. X. Charlevoix, sent to North America by the duke of Orleans to record events in New France and Louisiana, assessed the possible and alternative routes to the Pacific from the center of the continent. The Missouri rose in mountains far west of the Mississippi valley, he reported, and behind these mountains there was "probably" another large river rising nearby that flowed westward.[29] "I have good reason to think," Charlevoix wrote to his patron, "that after sailing up the Missouri as far as it is navigable you come to a great river which runs westward and discharges into the sea."[30]

Another popular chronicler of French Louisiana, Antoine Simon le Page du Pratz, described the same geographical configuration and told of an Indian named Moncacht-Apé who had actually made the journey. Always keeping to the northwest, Moncacht-Apé had gone up the Missouri to its source, where he crossed a short portage and visited several nations who lived on the "Beautiful River," which ran in a direction opposite that of the Missouri, flowing eventually into a western ocean[31] (fig. 4). The evidence was conclusive and inescapable. The distance between the Atlantic and Pacific could be shortened immeasurably by such a short portage, and Du Pratz's relation contained the faith that nearly all other French accounts had possessed. The belief that the Missouri could be used to reach the Pacific dominated the geographical lore of the Northwest provided by the French contributors. It was the central ingredient of the geographical knowledge which, when interpreted in the light of early nineteenth-century American thought, was to form the basis of Thomas Jefferson's image of the Northwest and the chief objective of the Lewis and Clark Expedition.

6

During their years of possession of Louisiana, the French had sought the Passage to India, and from their searchings there developed the concepts that were the backbone of the geographical lore of the Northwest at the beginning of the nineteenth century. But France's search for the Passage ended in 1763 as Spain took control of former French Louisiana and Great Britain assumed dominion over what had been New France. The established objective of the

29. Pierre François Xavier de Charlevoix, *A Voyage to North America* (2 vols., Dublin, 1766), II, 180.
30. Margry, *Decouvertes . . . des Français*, VI, 534.
31. Dumont de Montigny, "Memoires Historique de la Louisiane," in French, *Historical Collections*, V, 123.

water communication across the continent was not lost, however, and during the late eighteenth century both Spain and Great Britain made their own attempts on the Passage. From those attempts, as well as from those of the French, came contributions to geographical lore.

Unlike the French and later the Spanish, the British quest for the Passage was not through the lands of the trans-Missouri area but was channeled instead through the Saskatchewan system to the Canadian Rockies and then down the Pacific slopes of British Columbia. Indeed, the British did not penetrate the upper Missouri region until the closing years of the eighteenth century. But from the English explorers in the Canadian West came knowledge about the location of the Rocky Mountains, information on the nature of the Rockies in terms of height and breadth, and understanding of the character of the Continental Divide and the connections between eastern and western rivers. Much of this data on the western interior of Canada was interpolated by the best geographical minds of the early nineteenth century and applied to the key physical elements of the geography of western North America below as well as above the 50th parallel. A significant fraction, then, of Thomas Jefferson's understanding of the trans-Missouri area as he planned the Lewis and Clark Expedition was steeped in the literature and cartography based on the English search for the Western Sea.

7

Primarily because the British had not become familiar with the lush lands of the Mississippi valley, the lore which they contributed did not include concepts of the trans-Missouri area as a garden of beauty and fertility, capable of providing future generations with unheard-of agricultural possibilities. One British observer who had pushed into the Mississippi valley did, it is true, speak of the country west of the Mississippi as promising to "produce a sufficient supply of all the necessaries of life for any number of inhabitants," and of the mountains of the interior as containing "more riches in their bowels, than those of Indostan and Malabar."[32] But these statements were less consistent with the general trend of British lore than the statement of one of the first English explorers into the upper Missouri region that "these Great Plains may be said to be barren for great spaces, even of coarse grass . . . even the several Rivers that flow through these plains do not seem to fertilise the grounds adjacent to them."[33] From the British geographical lore another

32. Jonathan Carver, *Travels through the Interior Parts of North America in the Years 1766, 1767, and 1768* (3rd ed., London, 1781), p. 536. Although Carver was actually a native-born American, he is given the appellation "British observer" since his travels were carried out within the framework of British exploration rather than being American in origin.

33. J. B. Tyrrell, ed., *David Thompson's Narrative of His Explorations in Western America, 1784–1812* (Toronto, 1916), p. 186.

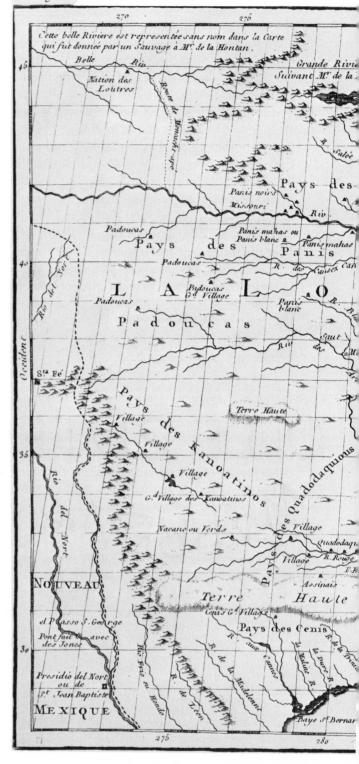

4. Antoine Simon le Page du Pratz's map of Louisiana. From *Histoire de la Louisiane* (Paris, 1758)

Septentrion — 285 — 290 — 295 — 300 — 45

Lac des HURONS

Lac ONTARIO

Sioux

Villages des Sioux

Saut de S. Antoine

Sioux

Pays des Sioux

R. des Sioux

F. de Niagara Niagara

Saut de... de Chûte

IROQUOIS ou les 6 Nations

Mascoutin ou Nation du Feu

Forre du Detroit

Lac ERIE

F. du Quesne

Vastes Prairies

Portage

R. du Rocher

Portage

Illinois

Lac de Pimiteoui

Pimiteoui

Rocher

Miamis

R. du Portage

Ohio Riv.

Mongona ou R. du Sel

Pays des

Pays des

R. des Miamis

Monts Apalaches

NOUVELLE ANGLETERRE

Virginie

Lansez Village

Missouris

Fort det.

Mine de la Mothe d'Argent

Mine de Maramec d'Argent

Mis souris

Mine de Plomb

Illinois

Fr. François Saline

Tamaroas et Kaskaquias

Ouabache Riv.

Riv.

des Chaouanons

Caroline

R. des Osages

R. des Cheraquis

Riv. des Cheraquis

Cherakis

Caouitas Nation

Riv. de S. François

Ecores à Prud'homme

Mine de Fer

Pays des Tchicachas

Kapas

F. des Tchicachas

Arkansas Ft. François

F. Tombecbec

Riv. des Alibamons

Riv. Noire

Terres Hautes

Pointe Coupée

Pays des

Mobiliens

Alibamons

B. Ste Rose B. S. André

mus Mine de Duplessis Natchitoches

Natchez det.

Les Ysles

Fort François

Rapide

Avoyels

Ft. Rosalie

chatkas

Chatkas

Apalaches

Riv. des

Fort Louis

Joseph

R. Sablonniere

Tonicas Pointe Coupée

Manchac

R. Rouge ou Riv.

Nlle

I. Dauphine

a Corne

I. aux Vaisseaux

I. de la Chandeleur

Atacapas

Tchitimachas

Fort

Passe de l'Est

Balize ou l'on passe

Embouchures du Fl. S. Louis

GOLFE DU MEXIQUE

Midi — 285 — 290 — 295

Orient — 40 — 35 — 30

CARTE DE LA LOUISIANE
Colonie Française
avec le Cours du Fleuve St. Louis,
les Rivieres Adjacentes,
les Nations des Naturels, les Etablissem.ᵗ Français
et les Mines.
Par l'Auteur de l'Histoire
de cette Province
1757.

element was added to the images of the Northwest, a contradictory element that saw parts of the trans-Missouri country not as a garden but as a desert given by Nature in perpetuity to the original Indian inhabitants.

Like the soil, the climate was considered by the British as being insufficient to support traditional European agriculture. The causative factors were the northern winds from the Arctic, which blew southward as far as the Gulf of Mexico. These gales, in the British opinion, gave to the entire western interior a winter that was unimaginable in length and severity to Europeans and made the region virtually useless as a potential area for agricultural settlement.[34] Even within this harsh image, however, a cautious note of optimism was sounded by one British author who commented that the climate of the interior was improving slowly and that the change might, in the course of time, give to America the climate of Europe.[35] A certain faith in the preordained benefits of North America was apparent; but it is unlikely that this teleologically induced point of view was widely enough held to offset the general British image of a cold and somewhat barren continental interior.

8

The same British lore which spoke pessimistically of the potential of the trans-Missouri region for agricultural development referred in glowing and optimistic terms to the cardinal elements of western geography; the mountains and rivers of the Northwest offered a means of access not only to the interior but also pointed the way to the completion of the transcontinental communication by water. Knowledge gathered during exploration was combined with theoretical geography to describe the Passage.

As early as the 1720s British promotional literature on North America had introduced the concept of symmetrical geography. It was known that rivers which flowed westward into the Mississippi had their sources in mountains that were close to the Atlantic. It was further known that those same westward-flowing streams had interlocking drainage systems with the rivers that flowed east to the Atlantic. The same set of geographical conditions, according to the tenets of symmetrical geography, should apply to the western parts of the continent. Daniel Coxe, author of the promotional tract *Carolana*, described great western rivers that flowed from interior mountains "passable by Horse, Foot, or Wagon in less than half a day." On the western

---

34. Alexander Mackenzie, *Voyages from Montreal through the Continent of North America to the Frozen and Pacific Oceans in 1789 and 1793* (London, 1801). Citations from Mackenzie herein are from a 2-volume reprint edition (Toronto, 1911), II, 344–51.

35. Mackenzie, *Voyages*, II, 351. The notion of climatic changes through human action was a prevalent one during the early years of the nineteenth century, and the author of the above quote noted: "It has been frequently advanced, that the clearing away the wood has had an astonishing influence in ameliorating the climate. . . ." The idea has a parallel in the American concept, *ca.* 1840–60, of "rain following the plow."

side of those ranges were "Rivers, which run into a great lake that empties itself by another great navigable River into the South Sea."[36] (fig. 5).

The British reasoning on symmetrical drainage patterns soon resolved itself into definite views of mountain divides in the western interior, and Samuel Hearne, one of the earliest British explorers in the Canadian West, told of mountains in the western part of the continent beyond which all rivers ran to the westward.[37] Hearne had postulated, without seeing it, the Continental Divide. His writings were popular in extract form in the periodical literature of the eighteenth and early nineteenth centuries and his notions on the dividing nature of the western mountains became fixed in British cartographical representations of the continental interior, representations which included the American as well as the Canadian West. One such map was drawn by Peter Fidler, a surveyor for the Hudson's Bay Company, who apparently followed instructions received from natives during his travels in the Canadian West and depicted the nature of the Divide in a sketch of the Northwest (fig. 6). On the eastern slope of a range of mountains labeled as the Rocky Mountains a series of rivers were shown, some flowing into the Saskatchewan system and others into the Missouri. On the western slopes of the mountains were rivers which had their heads adjacent to those of the Missouri system and flowed directly west into the Pacific. Fidler's map was available to cartographers of the last few years of the eighteenth century and was incorporated into the maps of Aaron Arrowsmith, prominent British mapmaker and creator of what Thomas Jefferson and other geographical thinkers of the early 1800s held to be the most accurate portrayals of the American Northwest.

Other British maps that illustrated the Continental Divide and the close relationship between the sources of the Missouri and streams flowing to the Pacific also became a part of the geographical lore available in the early nineteenth century. In 1784 Peter Pond, a Connecticut Yankee employed by the Northwest Company, presented the U.S. Congress with a map he had compiled during his sojourns in the Canadian West (fig. 7). On that map the Missouri was shown as heading in a single ridge of moutains which ran from north to south around longitude 113° W. The positioning of the Rockies was amazingly accurate, even though the single-ridge symbolization of them was erroneous and partly responsible for later misconceptions as to their true nature. But more important was Pond's portrayal of a river flowing into the Pacific from a source on the western side of the dividing ridge near the headwaters of the Missouri. Pond called this river the "Naberkistagon," and though the origin of the name is unknown, the river it was meant to identify

36. Daniel Coxe, *A Description of the English Province of Carolana by the Spaniards Call'd Florida and by the French, La Louisiane* (2nd ed., London, 1741), p. 63.
37. Hearne's journals were first published in pamphlet form in London in 1773 and went through several editions after that date. Used herein is a reprint edition, *A Journey from Prince of Wales Fort in Hudson's Bay to the Northern Ocean,* ed. J. B. Tyrrell (Toronto, 1911).

5. Daniel Coxe's map of the Mississippi and the province of "Carolana." Tracing by J. G. Kohl from *A Description of the English Province of Carolana* (London, 1741)

LIBRARY OF CONGRESS

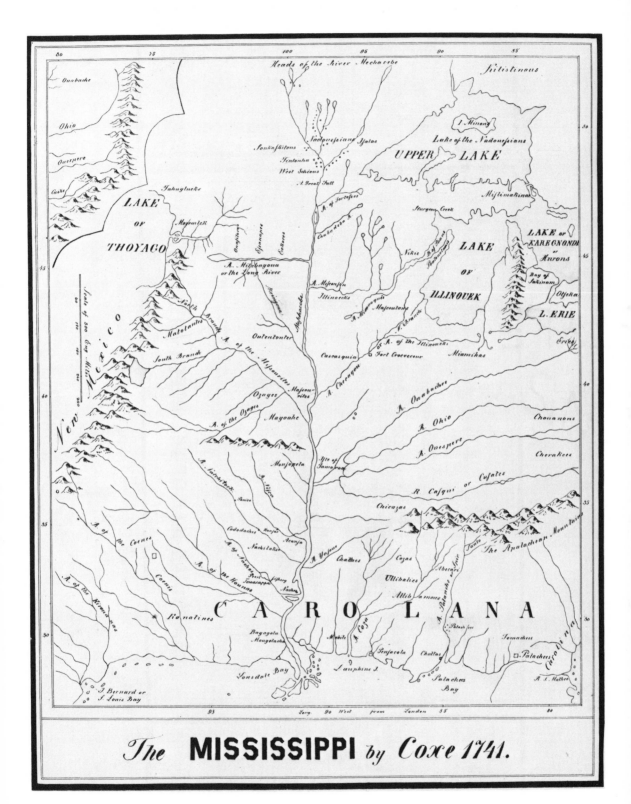

The **MISSISSIPPI** by Coxe 1741.

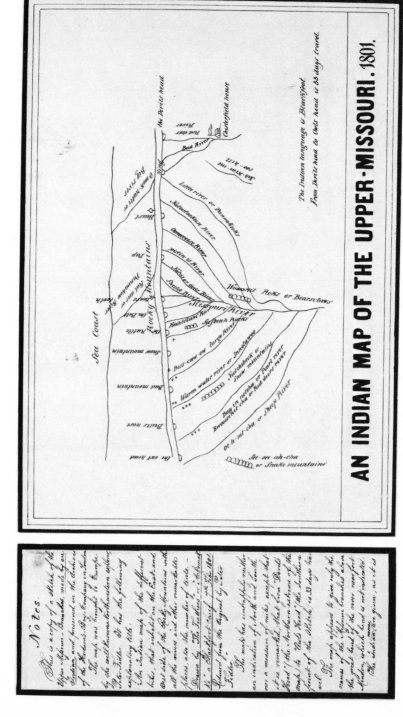

6. Peter Fidler's copy of an Indian sketch map of the upper Missouri. Tracing by J. G. Kohl   LIBRARY OF CONGRESS

is not. This was the Oregon or Great River of the West, and it headed close by the sources of the Missouri River. The route to the Pacific must have seemed obvious to some of those who viewed Pond's map.

9

The concept of a continental divide was not the only contribution to geographical lore made by the British; other important notions as well emanated from the literature of the English explorers and fur traders who sought a route to the Pacific. The first of these, the concept of a pyramidal height-of-land in the western interior, was related to the theory of a continental divide.[38] But instead of theorizing a range of mountains which ran the length of the continent and separated the waters of the Atlantic from those of the Pacific, the advocates of the pyramidal height-of-land envisaged mountains somewhere in the interior which were high and steep, the highest lands in North America.[39] From this area, the center of the drainage system of the continent, rivers flowed in four directions; the headwaters of those rivers were close together, and if one only located the central source area for the major North American river systems he could travel to all the seas surrounding the continent without abandoning water transportation.

Although the pyramidal height-of-land construction was hinted at in some of the earlier French literature, it does not seem to have entered general geographical lore until first detailed by Robert Rogers, of French and Indian War fame. In a petition he wrote to induce the British Parliament to support financially his planned expedition in search of the water passage to the Pacific, Rogers spoke of a proposed route westward from the Great Lakes to a height-of-land from which flowed several mighty rivers—among them the Mississippi and "Ouragan."[40] In a literary work of the same time—*A*

38. The concept of a pyramidal height-of-land and radial drainage patterns was a very old one in geographical theory. As early as the latter part of the sixth century clerical scholars reconstructed from scriptural references the conception of a point from which four major rivers rose and spread through the then-known world (C. R. Beazley, *The Dawn of Modern Geography* (3 vols., New York, 1949), I, ch. 6). The idea was still current at the time of the Columbian voyages, and Columbus himself wrote of discovering "one of the four rivers of Paradise" (the Orinoco) which flowed from the highest point in the world. The Elizabethan theorist Sir Humphrey Gilbert demonstrated in his "Discourse to Prove a Passage by the Northwest to Cathay and the East Indies" that continents and river systems were symmetrical and that transportation routes through continents could follow the drainage patterns of rivers with great facility. The concept also appears in some of the earliest French descriptions of North American geography. By the middle of the eighteenth century the pyramidal height-of-land was the dominant theoretical explanation for the pattern of the river systems of North America.

39. Robert Rogers, *A Concise Account of North America* (London, 1765), p. 153.

40. The origin of the name "Oregan" (and its various spellings) to refer to the Great River of the West is unknown. Rogers seems to have been the first to use the term. George Stewart, in *Names on the Land* (New York, 1945), suggests that the name Oregon derives from a spelling error on a copy of a Lahontan map in which the term "Ouisconsink" (the Wisconsin River) was modified and hyphenated into "Ouracon-sint." This explanation is probably as good as any.

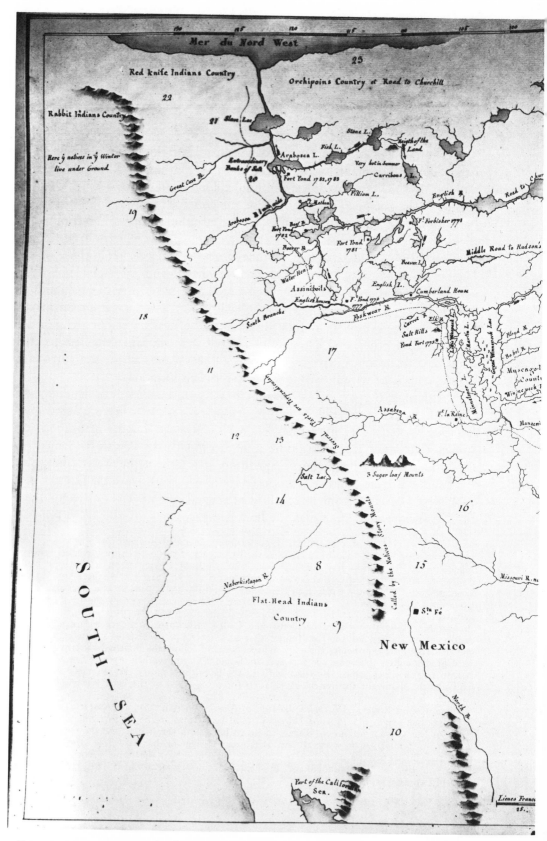

7. Peter Pond's map of a portion of western North America. Copy
made (*ca.* 1784) by St. John de Crevecoeur   LIBRARY OF CONGRESS

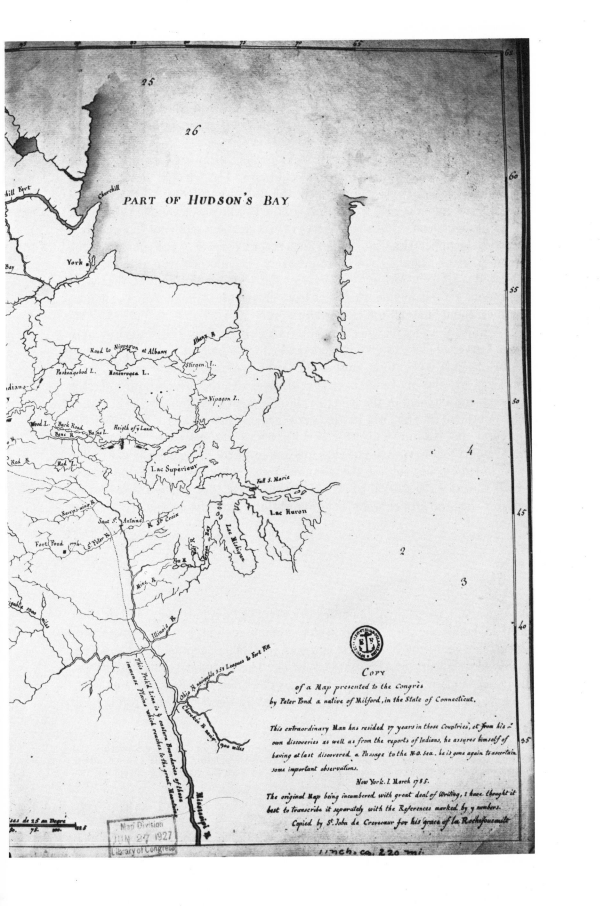

25

26

PART OF HUDSON'S BAY

ill Fort

Churchill

Bay

York

Road to Nipizeron et Albany

Albany R.

Pasheagobod L.   Monenrogea L.

Sturgen I.

Indian

Nipagon I.

Wood L.   Back Road

Bone R.   Rasue L.

Heigth of y Land

Red R.   Red L.

Lac Supérieur

Fall S. Marie

Raviyi-wing R.

Saut S. Antoine   R. St Croix

Lac Huron

Fort Pond   1776   S. Peter R.

Lac Michigan

Fox R.

Min. R.

Illinois R.

This Prick't Line is y eastern Boundaries of these immense Plains which reaches to the great Mountains

Ohio R. navigable 353 Leagues to Fort Pitt.

Charkaio R. 1000

900 miles

Mississipi R.

4

2

3

Copy

of a Map presented to the Congrès
by Peter Pond a native of Milford, in the State of Connecticut.

This extraordinary Man has resided 17 years in those Countries, et from his own discoveries as well as from the reports of Indians, he assures himself of having at last discovered a Passage to the N.O. Sea, he is gone again to ascertain some important observations.

New York, 1 March 1785.

The original Map being incumbered with great deal of Writing, I have thought it best to transcribe it separately with the References marked by y numbers.

Copied by S. John de Crevecœur for his Grace of la Rochefoucault

eas du 25 au Degré

50.   75.   100.   125.

1 Inch = ca. 220 mi.

Concise Account of North America—Rogers offered his theories in more detail to the reading public of England and her North American colonies. The mountains of the western interior, he asserted, were "situated in the center, and are the highest lands in North America." From these highlands the rivers flowed in all directions and "by those rivers the continent is divided into many departments, as it were from a center."[41]

Funding was never granted Rogers for his proposed venture, but he began on his own without financial assistance. He selected other French and Indian War veterans to aid him in the discovery of the Northwest Passage, and although the planned journey to the Pacific never was consummated, one of his lieutenants, Jonathan Carver of Connecticut, actually did make his way into the upper Mississippi valley on a reconnaissance of the country in the direction of the height-of-land. From Carver's wanderings came the journals, published as *Travels through the Interior Parts of North America*, that were to become a fundamental part of early nineteenth-century American geographical thought about the western interior.[42]

According to intelligence he gained from Indians on his western travels, wrote Carver (failing to give Rogers credit for the concept of the pyramidal height-of-land), the "four most capital rivers of the Continent of North America, viz. the St. Lawrence, the Mississippie, the River Bourbon [the Nelson], and Oregan, or the River of the West have their sources in the same neighbourhood"[43] (fig. 8). In the same general area was to be found the source of the Missouri and, proposed Carver, if one passed up a branch of the Missouri "till having discovered the source of the Oregan or River of the West, on the other side of the summit of the lands that divide the waters which run into the Gulph of Mexico from those that fall into the Pacific Ocean," then the proper water communication across the continent would be determined.[44]

10

Another critical British contribution to geographical lore still further aided in fixing the idea of the water communication in early nineteenth-century images of the Northwest and was, like the conceptual height-of-land, related to the theory of a continental divide. This additional contribution was the concept of the short portage between the heads of eastward- and westward-flowing rivers, an idea alluded to earlier by the French but refined and

41. Rogers, *A Concise Account*, p. 154.
42. Carver's geographical conceptions were assimilated by many of those who authored texts on geography, among them the "father of American geography," Jedediah Morse, whose *American Universal Geography* and *American Gazetteer* were the standard geographical reference books of the period.
43. Carver, *Travels*, p. 118.
44. Carver, *Travels*, p. 542.

stamped indelibly on the source materials for later images of the trans-Missouri area by the British.

Unlike many other features of the geographical lore of the Northwest, the British concept of the short portage was based on something other than speculation and conjecture. The short portage had been proven by exploration. In 1793 Alexander Mackenzie of the Northwest Company[45] followed the Peace River, a tributary of the Mackenzie system, westward to its source in the Canadian Rockies and found there "a beaten path leading over a low ridge of land eight hundred and seventeen paces in length."[46] By this path Mackenzie crossed the Continental Divide and made fact what had previously been speculation. The interior mountains could be crossed with a simple and short portage.

The fact was impressed upon geographical lore by the publication of Mackenzie's journals,[47] and the concept of the short portage became applied to the mountains of the western interior—below as well as above the 50th parallel. Mackenzie had crossed the Rockies near the 55th parallel over a pass that was approximately 3,000 feet above sea level; south of his crossing, he wrote, the Rockies continued "with less elevation, to divide the waters of the Atlantic from those which run into the Pacific."[48] The critical phrase was "with less elevation"; if Mackenzie had traversed the northern mountains via a low and scarcely discernible pass, how difficult could a pass through the lower southern mountains be? Supporting evidence was offered by David Thompson, a British surveyor-explorer in the upper Missouri area during the 1790s, who noted that the headwaters of the Missouri gave several passages across the mountains. And, like the mountains that Mackenzie had crossed in Canada, the mountains about the headwaters of the Missouri were comparatively low.[49]

The same information worked its way into cartography of the late eighteenth and early nineteenth centuries, and Aaron Arrowsmith's map of North America, published in 1795 and considered by many to be the most accurate rendition of western geography, noted that the Rocky Mountains were only "3520 Feet High above the Level of their Base"; other reputable sources claimed that this base was not more than "3000 feet above the sea."[50] The Rockies were, in the geographical lore provided by the British, a rela-

45. Mackenzie had made an earlier (1789) attempt to reach the Pacific but had followed the Mackenzie River (he named it the "Disappointment"), which led him into the Arctic Ocean instead.

46. Mackenzie, *Voyages*, II, 109.

47. The journals of Mackenzie were first published in London and were widely circulated in both Europe and America. Extracts from the journals were printed in many American periodicals, and the journals themselves were advertised for sale in bookstores in the major cities of the Atlantic seaboard.

48. Mackenzie, *Voyages*, II, 346.

49. Tyrrell, *David Thompson's Narrative*, p. 187.

50. *Medical Repository*, V (1st hexade, 1802), 462. This periodical, one of the most reputable published in America, was edited by Samuel Latham Mitchill, a congressman from New York and correspondent of Thomas Jefferson.

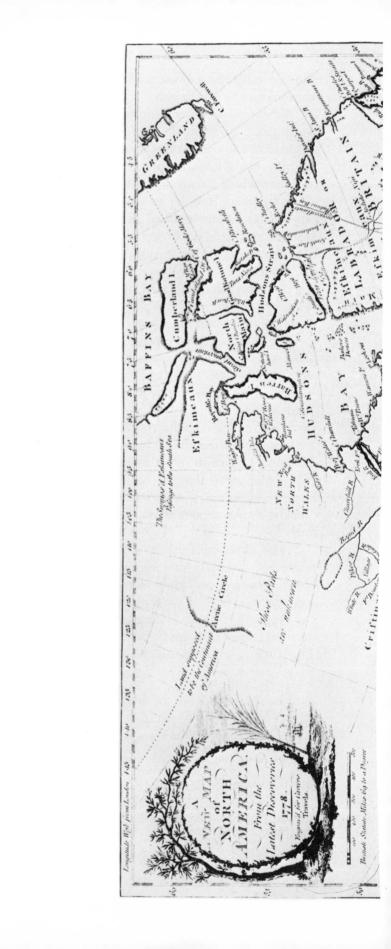

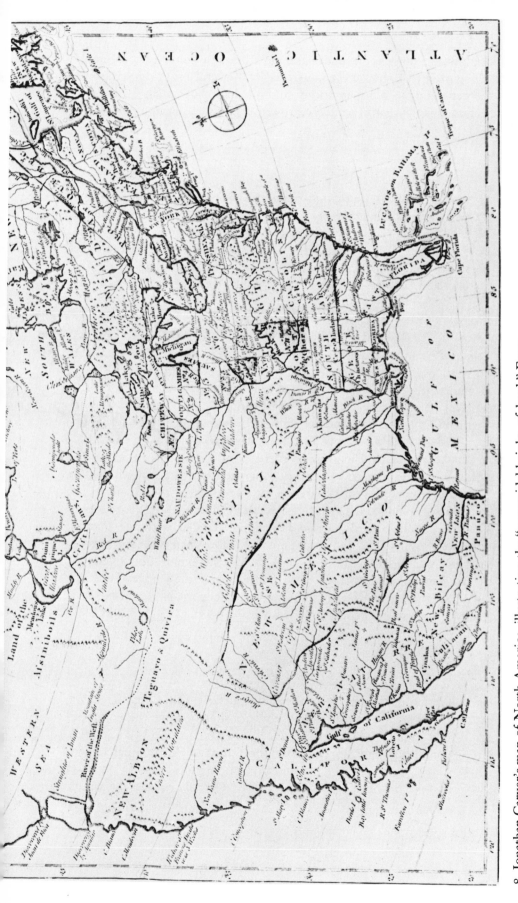

8. Jonathan Carver's map of North America, illustrating the "pyramidal height- of-land." From *Travels through the Interior Parts of North America* (London, 1781)   LIBRARY OF CONGRESS

tively insignificant range of mountains, and although some of the better sources recognized that they were composed of "several low ridges in some parts," the cartographic representations continued to show a single, narrow chain of mountains that could be easily crossed via a short portage (fig. 9).

II

Mackenzie had done more than just establish the theoretical short portage as geographical fact. For beyond his crossing of the mountains, he found a river which flowed in the direction of the setting sun, and although the Indians told him it was unnavigable for a substantial distance between the mountains and the Pacific, forcing the British explorer to complete his trek to the ocean overland, it was—in Mackenzie's mind—the Great River of the West.

Mackenzie's Great River of the West would later be named the Fraser after the first man to descend it to the sea.[51] But when he returned to London to write the journals that would be so central in geographical thought about the Northwest, Mackenzie learned that as he had been toiling across the Canadian wilderness, British and American sailors had discovered the mouth of a great river entering the Pacific near the 46th parallel. This was a good deal farther south than his first contact with his great western river, although that river, when he had been forced to leave it, was flowing in a southerly direction. Mackenzie named the great river the "Tacoutche Tesse," in accordance with the Indian term for it. But he recognized it as the Columbia, discovered by Robert Gray a year before his own crossing of the Divide. The Fraser, of course, is not the same river as the Columbia. But Mackenzie thought it was, and he saw its course as running parallel with the Pacific coast on the westward side of the mountains for "more than eight degrees of latitude before it mingled with the ocean."[52] British exploration overland from the east had linked in theory with British and American exploration from the Pacific; the Great River of the West had been given a course based on the resulting conjectural geography.

12

The exploration of the Pacific coast and the drive to the Great River of the West began with the Spanish coastal voyages shortly after the conquest of Mexico. By the middle of the eighteenth century, the Spanish had explored most of the Pacific shoreline; searching for the Straits of Anian—that fabled

51. Simon Fraser of the Northwest Company passed through the tortuous canyons of the lower Fraser to reach the sea in 1807.
52. Mackenzie, *Voyages*, II, 347.

western terminus of the Northwest Passage—and had rather accurately defined the outline of the Pacific coast. The Spanish voyages had laid the foundation for the development of the theoretical great river that was supposed to debouch somewhere along the Pacific coast. By the closing decades of the eighteenth century, the mythical Straits of Anian and the theoretical Great River of the West had fused into one central myth, for the discovery of the Great River would provide the same transcontinental crossing as the opening of the Straits would. This central myth became a part of geographical lore in 1775 when Bruno Heceta, sailing on a mission from New Spain and instructed to fortify the northern California coast against the encroachment of the Russian fur trade from the north, discovered a large bay at around latitude 46° N. The currents coming from this bay were so strong that they swept Heceta's ships out to sea.

"These currents and eddies of water cause me to believe that the place is the mouth of some great river, or of some passage to another sea,"[53] wrote Heceta, and he was right on both counts. For the currents he noted must have been coming from the Columbia River; and that river would serve as the terminus for the passage from another sea. At last someone had located quite precisely one of the mysteries of the geography of the Northwest; the "Beautiful River" of Du Pratz and the "River Oregan" of Jonathan Carver would become geographical fact. But for seventeen years after Heceta no one would enter or recognize it again as the Great River of the West which had been appearing on maps for the last half-century (fig. 10).

The final and permanent establishment of the Columbia as the Great River of the West which would provide a passage to another sea came from another beginning than Spanish geographical information. In the same year that Heceta quite possibly discovered the mouth of the Columbia, Captain James Cook of Great Britain was also exploring the coast of the Pacific Northwest in search of the passage eastward. Cook missed the mouth of the Columbia and did not find the Straits of Anian. But he did return to Europe with word of the tremendous wealth in furs along the Pacific coast. This wealth was being tapped only by the Russian fur trade, and when word of the rich fur resource reached England and America, companies were formed for the purpose of exploiting it. It was the geographical knowledge resulting from the voyages of these fur companies, when combined with Mackenzie's journals, that formed the complete image of the Great River of the West.

In 1791 Captain Robert Gray sailed from Boston in command of the *Columbia* with orders to attempt the establishment of fur-trading contacts with natives of the Northwest coast. After exploring and trading in the area during 1791 and 1792 Gray returned to Boston with news of a fundamental discovery. In April, 1792, the *Columbia* had reached latitude 46° 39′ N. on the Pacific coast, and Gray reported in the ship's log that a line of breakers

53. Thomas Russell, ed., *Voyages of the Sonora in the Second Bucareli Expedition* (San Francisco, 1920), pp. 86–87.

9. A portion of Aaron Arrowsmith's
large map of North America, 1795

Notes.

George Anson on his famous circumnavigation of the Globe captured as is well known the Spanish Manilla Galeon Nuestra Señora de Cabadonga in the Chinese Waters at the end of the year 1742. He found in her immense treasures, and amongst her papers also a Spanish map of the Northern Pacific Ocean.

The Original of this map appears unhappily to be lost to us. But after the short description, which Anson gave of it, it seems to have comprised a picture of the whole Northern Pacific as high as 39½° N. L. It was probably one of those charts, as the Manilla Galeons usually had them in crossing from Asia to America. It may have been an old Spanish map. We can give to it no other date but the year 1742 in which it was captured.

In the work: "Anson's Voyage round the World. London 1748." a reduced copy of it is communicated, in which the Longitudes appear to be taken West from the Meridian of S. Bernardino in the Philippinas, two degrees West from Cabo Spirito Sto. On this map the Coasts of California are represented, as the copy on the first of the annexed sheets shows it. We learn from it, that the Spaniards then did know more of California than our other European Geographers. The figure of the Coasts and the names appearing on them seem to indicate, that the map principally rested on the survey and exploration of Vizcayno (in 1602). "Punta de los Reyes" and "Los Farallones" indicate our S. Francisco Bay, though in a somewhat too high Latitude. "Punta de Pinos"— our Monterey harbour. The Coast round "Punta de la Concepcion" (Point Conception) is very well indicated.

The islands of the Sta Barbara Channel have only partly still the same names to day. "Pto de S. Diego" has a somewhat too high Latitude.

"Bay de S. Francisco" in 30° N. L. must not be confounded with our S. Francisco Bay in Upper California. It is a more southern bay, which was also called so on Viscayno's voyage. The Southern extremity of California: "Cabo S. Lucas" has its true Latitude: 22½° N.

This map captured by Anson at the time being seems to have excited a good deal of interest amongst the geographers. The first, who copied it, and embodied it into his larger works, filling with it a great gape in the North west Coast of America was Jefferys, then a most active chartographer in London. How he did this shows the second annexed sheet, which is a copy of his chart of the North Pacific. It was as Jefferys says, laid down chiefly from the Spanish Chart, used on board the Cabadonga, taken by Anson 1743 (ought to be 1742), which is scarce reconcilable with other charts and journals either as to the names or situation of Places.

We find on it also many groups of islands, which were probably depicted on the Spanish map. For instance the Sandwich islands, called "La Mesa" "Los Monges" etc. They have their Latitude, but are placed much too far East.

Jefferys has added to the map the routes of different navigators, and likewise his and other geographers ideas about the "River of the West." Jefferys himself thinks that the old "Opening discovered by D'Aguilar 1603," is the true great river of the West, and has it consequently in about the Latitude of our present Columbia River. He has also a nameless broad inlet in the Latitude of De Fuca strait.

Faser to the North west he writes: "Fousang of the Chinese" because many geographers of the time believed them, as Du Halde had made them believe, that the country of the East ("Fousang") of the Chinese was America, and not, as it really is, Japan.—

The map of the Indian Ochagack, of which Jefferys speaks we will communicate among our Canadian maps. (See our collections).—

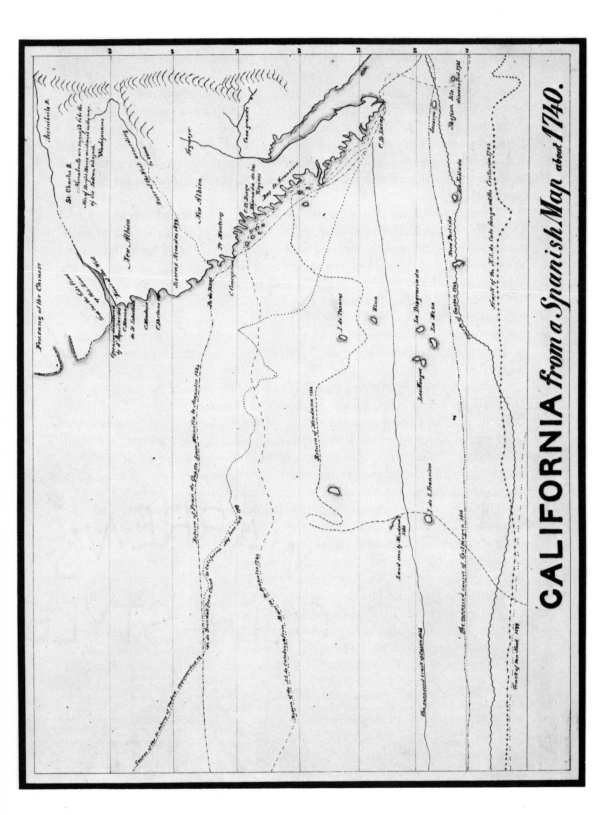

CALIFORNIA from a Spanish Map about 1740.

could be seen toward the shore and beyond them the entrance to a great river. He made an attempt to enter the river but the current prevented him from doing so.[54] Six days after sighting the mouth of the great river, Gray met two ships of "his Britannic Majesty's" under the command of Captain George Vancouver, sailing the northwestern waters to acquire information about the potential of the fur trade and to gain accurate data "with respect to the nature and extent of any water-communication which may tend, in any considerable degree, to facilitate an intercourse, for the purpose of commerce, between the northwest coast and the country upon the opposite side of the continent."[55]

Gray reported his discovery to Vancouver, who was thoroughly convinced that no such river or arm of the sea existed, in spite of the assertions of the theoretical geographers. But the American captain was of better faith and would not be dissuaded from searching for what he knew to be a river. On May 12, 1792, Captain Gray took the *Columbia* into the great river which would henceforth bear her name. The mighty river that Bruno Heceta had sighted and that theoretical geographers had for years thought proper to insert on maps had been entered. Gray did not explore the river further; but he christened it, claimed it for the United States, and returned to his home port.

It was up to Vancouver, the skeptical British captain, to complete the image of the Great River of the West. He sent one of his men, Lieutenant Broughton, across the bar at the mouth of the Columbia and upstream for more than a hundred miles. Broughton stopped at a point which he named "Vancouver"[56] and noted that to the east he could see a magnificent mountain peak which he drew on his charts as "Mount Hood." Vancouver's journals and maps and the maps of the lower Columbia provided by his lieutenant became a part of geographical lore and, when merged with the accounts of Alexander Mackenzie, offered near-conclusive proof of the possibility of a water communication across the continent (fig. 11). For the mountains visible from the coast, in the minds of many, bore a relationship to the mountains crossed by Mackenzie. And the great river discovered by Mackenzie west of the Divide could be none other than the mighty stream entered and surveyed by the British navy.

The latitude of the Columbia was virtually the same as the latitude of the Missouri's source waters; therefore if the northern branches of the Columbian system had been reached by Mackenzie then the southern branches of

54. The best primary sources for Gray's discovery of the Columbia are John Boit, "Log of the Second Voyage of the Columbia," in Frederick H. Howay, ed., *Voyages of the "Columbia" to the Northwest Coast* (Boston, 1941), pp. 363–431; and T. C. Eliot, "A Remnant of the Log of the Columbia," *Oregon Historical Quarterly*, XXII (1921), 352–56.

55. George Vancouver, *A Voyage of Discovery to the North Pacific Ocean* (3 vols., London, 1798), I, xviii.

56. Later the site of Fort Vancouver, across the Columbia River from the present-day site of Portland, Oregon. The accounts of the Broughton ascent of the Columbia are included in Vancouver, *A Voyage of Discovery*, II, ch. 3 (pp. 52–78).

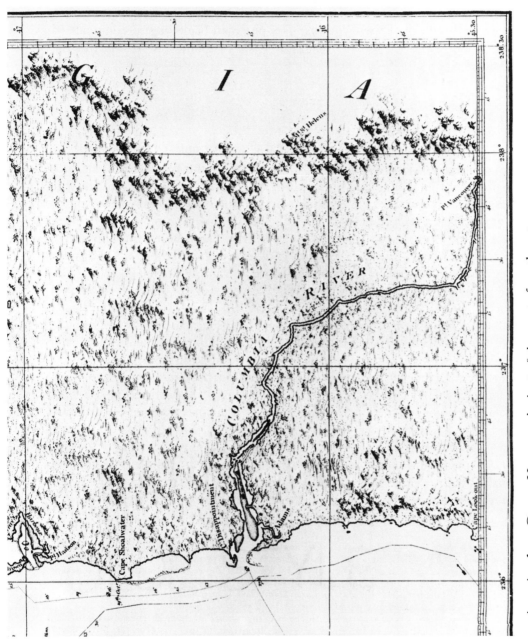

11. A section from George Vancouver's chart of the coast of northwestern America. From *A Voyage of Discovery to the North Pacific Ocean* (London, 1801)   LIBRARY OF CONGRESS

the Columbia could probably be just as easily approached through a short portage from the waters of the Missouri. This was the theoretical reasoning that American speculators during the first years of the nineteenth century applied to their formulation of a conceptual water communication. It was reasoning that became even more logical when reinforced with earlier French lore about the Missouri, with the data provided by the British in the Canadian West, and with the knowledge that was just then beginning to come out of the efforts of the Spanish Louisiana fur trade to follow the Missouri to the Pacific.

13

At the end of the Seven Years' (French and Indian) War, the Spanish government in North America was granted full authority over the territory of Louisiana as France had possessed it, that is, the entire western drainage basin of the Mississippi River sytem. And as the Spanish took possession of Louisiana they took possession also of a certain amount of the geographical lore of the French who had gone before.[57] For many years, the knowledge left by the French was the best there was. Even after the period of Spanish occupation of Louisiana most of the sources available on the geography of the trans-Missouri area were based on the works of the French chroniclers and explorers rather than on information gathered during the Spanish regime. This is not to say that significant increments to geographical knowledge were not made while Spain ruled Louisiana. But precious little of the data gathered under Spanish rule was available to the general public at the beginning of the nineteenth century.[58] Several key elements of northwestern geography were added, however, features which were to prove of importance in the final combination of geographical lore on the trans-Missouri area prior to the Lewis and Clark Expedition.

Because of an increased level of trading activity into the western portions of Louisiana during the period of Spanish rule, the Spanish lore on land quality was, on the whole, more realistic and balanced than either the British or French data. The accounts of French and British explorers and traders who were operating in Louisiana under the authority of the government of

57. A memoir was left in New Orleans by the French which dealt in part with the geography of the Northwest. The memoir stated a fact of symmetrical geography—the Missouri extended as far west as the Ohio did to the east—that shows the strength of the thinking found in the works of authors such as Daniel Coxe and Pierre F. X. Charlevoix as late as the 1760s. See Abraham P. Nasatir, *Before Lewis and Clark: Documents Illustrating the History of the Missouri, 1785-1804* (2 vols., St. Louis, 1952), I, 58–59.

58. One of the major reasons for this is that there were no Spanish counterparts of the chroniclers of French Louisiana. An even more important factor was that the government of Spanish Louisiana, with its paranoic fears of invasion of Louisiana and/or New Mexico by either the British from the north or the Americans from the east, was unlikely to let out such information as would provide data on the geography of the Northwest that might make invasions easier.

Spanish Louisiana[59] managed better than earlier reports to capture the nature of the great open and treeless expanse that stretched from the mouth of the Platte all the way to the mountains.

The more recent descriptions of the Northwest often pictured the area of the plains as at least partially barren, arid, and sterile. Some Spanish officials, perhaps still dreaming of a garden in the Northwest, paid little apparent attention. One such official wrote to the governor-general of Louisiana that the "situation" of Upper Louisiana (north and west from the mouth of the Missouri) was extremely conducive to agriculture and that "few countries unite so many advantages as this under one sky and in a very delightful climate."[60] The cold, he continued, was severe some years but there was "no winter which the fine moderation of the spring does not allow the farmer the opportune time to do his plowing. . . . It is a fact (and experience itself has shown its strength) that the soil of this country is extremely fertile."

The Northwest for some was still a garden—as it had been in the minds and lore of the French at an earlier time. But in spite of the optimism indicated by some Spanish officials, the garden image of the trans-Missouri region was qualified by the reports of explorers in the area during the closing years of the eighteenth century. One explorer had called the regions of the Northwest which were without trees "great waste lands" and mentioned that they were "completely sterile; scarcely grass grows there."[61] Another noted that although it was true that large parts of the Northwest were "even & fertile," there were many other areas which were "Mountainous & barren . . . [where] a tree can hardly be found."[62] Still another observer commented that although some of the region was "like a meadow," other parts were of "sandy soil, without wood, full of sand dunes and rocks," a sight which was "the most disagreeable that can be imagined."[63]

To the element of the garden in the geographical lore of the Northwest, then, must be added the element of the desert. As will be seen later, the latter set of concepts was less effective in shaping the early nineteenth-century American views of the trans-Missouri area than the former. This was, however, more a function of the strength of the garden concept of the Northwest than of the weakness of the images of deserts beyond the Mississippi. Both elements were present in the geographical lore; the initial American acceptance of the garden rather than the desert is simply a function of the optimism which has always crept into thought about the Northwest.

59. Although Spain controlled the government of Louisiana, the greatest proportion of the population was French. Thus, most of the explorers and traders under the command of the Spanish-commanded military and fur-trading enterprises were French. Some of the traders and adventurers were British subjects who had moved into the Mississippi-Missouri country from Canada. There were very few real "Spanish" residents or explorers operating in "Spanish" Louisiana.
60. Nasatir, *Before Lewis and Clark*, II, 543.
61. Nasatir, *Before Lewis and Clark*, II, 377.
62. "John Evans' Journal," ed. Milo M. Quaife, *Wisconsin Historical Society Proceedings*, LXIII (1915), 197.
63. Nasatir, *Before Lewis and Clark*, I, 124.

As the garden concepts of the land quality of the West had undergone a certain amount of transformation from earlier French lore, so had other elements changed slightly. The Northwest was not described by the Spanish as being filled with great mines of gold and silver, although the country was said to be "abundant in lead mines and salt deposits scattered a certain distance one from another. . . . There are also iron mines in abundance."[64] Nor were the Spanish-sponsored explorers who contributed to geographical lore, after years of trading with the tribes of the interior, liable to the French romantic notions of the noble savages of the interior. There were, in the Spanish contributions to lore, no golden cities inhabited by little people with protuberant eyes and golden buskins.

14

Spanish geographical lore did much to remove at least a part of the romance from the images of the Northwest as they took shape in the years immediately preceding Lewis and Clark. But if romance was gone, it was replaced by information of a more factual and accurate character. The pace of Spanish Louisiana in expanding the frontiers of geographical knowledge toward the Pacific during the first two decades of Spanish dominion over the continent's heartland had been slow indeed.[65] But the American war for independence and the immediate geographical results of that war—the transfer of the eastern side of the Mississippi from England to the new United States—served to heighten Spanish Louisiana's fear of the "ruffian" Americans, who, it was believed, might penetrate all the way to the colony of New Mexico via the Missouri, still believed to have its source waters near those of the Rio Grande.

This fear, coupled with the word of an occasional British trader moving from Canada into the area of the upper Missouri and with the news of possible Russian encroachment on the Spanish territories on the Pacific, made it mandatory that Spanish Louisiana fortify and control the Missouri all the way to its source and, if possible, all the way to the Pacific by way of the western rivers which connected with the Missouri at its head. This impulse was strengthened by the desire of the fur-trading interests of St. Louis to find the water passage to the Pacific. From the exploratory activity that was the response to both these sets of stimuli came a number of crucial pieces of geographical data that completed the knowledge of the trans-Missouri region

64. Nasatir, *Before Lewis and Clark*, II, 537.
65. The government of Louisiana was apparently content to view the area as a buffer between the British and Americans on the north and east and the territory of New Mexico on the south and west. The reports of Francisco Cruzat, lieutenant governor of Louisiana, indicate that as late as 1777 the Spanish traders had not ascended the Missouri beyond the mouth of the Platte River. See Louis B. Houck, *The Spanish Regime in Missouri* (2 vols., Chicago, 1909), I, 62–75, 138–48.

before Lewis and Clark. The most important increments to knowledge made during the Spanish rule in Louisiana were descriptions of some critical landmarks of the upper Missouri basin, descriptions that entered lore following Spanish penetration to the Mandan villages of the upper Missouri.

The villages of the Mandan nation, located near the Great Bend of the Missouri, were the focal point of both the Louisiana and Canadian fur trade during the late eighteenth century and formed an important point of reference for the geography of the trans-Missouri region.[66] The Mandans had been partially known since the visits to their villages by French Canadian traders and explorers beginning in the 1730s.[67] But as the Spanish Louisiana fur trade worked its way up the Missouri River in the last decade of the 1700s, the villages of the Mandans and the character of the country they occupied became firmly fixed in geographical lore.

The earliest reports on the Mandans from the Spanish-sponsored fur trade came in the early 1790s, when Jacques d'Eglise (Santiago de la Iglesia in the Spanish literature) returned to St. Louis from the interior with news that he had ascended the Missouri as far as "eight villages of a nation about which there was some knowledge under the name of Mandan, but to which no one had ever gone in this direction and by this river."[68] D'Eglise's reports on the Mandans did much to substantiate the Spanish belief that the Missouri's sources were near New Mexico, for, according to the trader-adventurer, the Mandans had "considerable trade with the Spaniards or with nations that know them."[69] Near their villages, continued d'Eglise, was "a mountain with a volcano," a phenomenon that was to prove one of the most durable myths about the upper Missouri. But more important was d'Eglise's statement that at the Mandan villages the Missouri had "sufficient water for the passage of the largest boats." If the Missouri were navigable as far up as the Mandans then it must still be a considerable distance from there to its source. And because of the supposed ease of navigation, it would provide a ready passage to the rumored rivers which flowed to the Pacific from just beyond the mountains in which the Missouri had its source.

Commenting on the geographical information brought back by d'Eglise and others, one Spanish official asserted that the Missouri was "vast and navigable in all its parts," and was known to take its rise "a short distance

66. The Mandan Indians, probably of Siouan stock, had lived in a number of locations between the mouths of the Heart and Knife rivers along the Missouri (in central North Dakota) during the eighteenth century. They were at one time a numerous people, but wars and disease had diminished their numbers; at the beginning of the nineteenth century they were living in two villages with a total population of approximately 1,250 persons. Their close relatives and neighbors were the Hidatsas or Minitaris (or Gros Ventres). Both the Mandans and the Hidatsas had frequent contact with the St. Louis and Canadian fur trade, and several representatives of various fur companies were in residence with the Mandans during the 1790s.

67. The first European to reach the Mandan villages (then located near the mouth of the Heart River) was Pierre Gaultier de Varennes, Sieur de la Vérendrye, in 1738. See Lawrence J. Burpee, ed., *The Journals and Letters of Pierre Gaultier de Varennes de la Vérendrye and His Sons* (2 vols., Toronto, 1927).

68. Nasatir, *Before Lewis and Clark*, I, 160.

69. Nasatir, *Before Lewis and Clark*, I, 161.

from a chain of very lofty mountains, which are located only forty leagues from the South Sea." At the foot of these same mountains was to be found "another large and navigable river which empties into the above-named sea."[70] This pattern of geographical thinking was, of course, nothing new. But the fact that the St. Louis fur trade had actually pushed as far west as the Mandans and had talked with Indians who could describe the country to the west lent greater validity to the old rumors about the Missouri and its connections with westward-flowing rivers.

During the 1790s other Spanish-sponsored traders pushed their way into the upper Missouri area, toward the Mandan villages, and returned with information that agreed substantially with that of d'Eglise. Jean Baptiste Truteau, in 1794, headed up the Missouri for the Mandan villages, hoping to make them a base for an assault on the passage to the Pacific. His expedition failed but was nonetheless of primary importance from the standpoint of the contributions it made to the geographical lore of the early nineteenth century.[71] The Missouri could be navigated a great distance, Truteau avowed, even beyond the Mandans all the way to the mountains. And although he did not claim to know exactly where this river had its source, the common belief among the Indians he talked with was that it came "from the great mountains of rock which they say cross, from the north to the south, this vast country unknown to civilized nations."[72] It could provide an avenue to the Pacific, Truteau asserted, for he had visited with natives who had actually crossed the mountains near the source of the Missouri and had found themselves on "the banks of a wide and deep river, well-timbered, the waters of which appeared to go in the direction of the winter sunset."[73]

Other reports returned to government officials in St. Louis by traders who had been in the Mandan country were even more explicit. A pair of traders from Canada who had visited the Mandans while in the employ of the Northwest Company gave testimony in St. Louis that the passage to the Pacific could be found not more than 500 miles above the Mandans. For there, "on the slope of a high cliff," a beautiful river had its source. Past the same mountain flowed the Missouri, and it was "as navigable on the upper part of the mountain as on its slope."[74] By inference, the "beautiful river" ran toward the Pacific, and the fact that the Missouri was navigable in its upper reaches held out the hope for Spanish Louisiana that the Pacific and the pas-

70. Houck, *The Spanish Regime in Missouri*, I, 10.
71. Two documents—"The Journal of Truteau on the Missouri River, 1794–95" and "Truteau's Description of the Upper Missouri"—came out of the travels of Jean Baptiste Truteau. Nasatir, *Before Lewis and Clark*, prints both the former (I, 259–311) and the latter (II, 376–85). Truteau's "Description" formed the bases for a number of articles about the Northwest in early nineteenth-century publications: cf. Victor Collot, *A Journey in North America* (London, 1826), pp. 271–300; François Marie Perrin du Lac, *Voyages dans les deux Louisianes* (Paris, 1805); and the article on Louisiana in the *Medical Repository*, III (2nd hexade, 1806), 314–15.
72. Nasatir, *Before Lewis and Clark*, II, 377.
73. Nasatir, *Before Lewis and Clark*, II, 380.
74. Nasatir, *Before Lewis and Clark*, II, 333.

sage to it could be found. In response to this hope the last major, and in many ways the most important, expedition before Lewis and Clark was undertaken. This was the expedition of James Mackay and John Evans; their reports added to geographical lore the final elements of northwestern geography.[75]

15

Between 1795 and 1797, Mackay and Evans were active in the portion of the Missouri between St. Louis and the Mandan villages. The stated objective of their expedition was to "ascertain the discovery of the Pacific Sea," and although they failed in that objective, they succeeded in refining and enlarging the geographical lore of the trans-Missouri region. The basic view of the Northwest as held by most thinkers before the Mackey-Evans travels included a Missouri River which ran a nearly straight west-to-east course from a single range of mountains that were parallel to and not a great distance from the Pacific coast. Such aberrations in the Missouri's course as the Grand Detour and the Great Bend were known in rough fashion; they were distorted and out of position, however, and other important landmarks of the trans-Missouri region were left completely out of most images of the Northwest in Mackay's and Evan's time.

This situation changed radically after the journeys of Mackay and Evans. The Yellowstone River and the Great Falls of the Missouri were fixed by their reports as critical landmarks of the country west of the Mandans. Their charts of the Missouri's course between the Mandan villages and St. Louis were extremely accurate and succeeded in making this portion of the river a well-known geographic quantity.[76] And from their journals came knowledge of the multiple-ridge structure of the Rocky Mountains and of the great curving course that the Missouri follows from its source to the Mississippi. Some of these features had been alluded to in earlier lore; after Mackay and Evans they became definite components of the images of the Northwest.

"After all the Information I could collect," wrote Mackay, "it appears that the Missouri takes its source in abt. the 40th deg. North latitude."[77] From its source in a mountainous country the Missouri ran northward, bounded on

75. James Mackay was a Scot who had been in the employ of the Northwest Company during the 1780s and had moved into Louisiana sometime between 1792 and 1794 (Abraham P. Nasatir, "Spanish Exploration of the Upper Missouri," *Mississippi Valley Historical Review,* XIV (1927), 47–71; and "Capt. Mackay's Journal," ed. Milo M. Quaife, *Wisconsin Historical Society Proceedings,* LXIII (1915), 190–95). John Evans was a Welshman who had originally come to America to search for a tribe of Welsh Indians thought to be living on the Missouri. He met Mackay in St. Louis and was enlisted by him to assist in an expedition to the Mandans and hopefully to the Pacific (Abraham P. Nasatir, "John Evans: Explorer and Surveyor," *Missouri Historical Review,* XXV (1930–31), 219–39, 432–60, 585–608; and David Williams, "John Evans' Strange Journey," *American Historical Review,* LIV (1949), 277–95, 508–29).

76. Both Evans and Mackay drew maps of the Missouri that were to figure prominently in the Lewis and Clark Expedition and will be discussed in chs. 5 and 6 below.

77. "Mackay's Journal," pp. 198–99.

both its east and west sides by ranges of mountains which also had north-south alignment. Somewhere near the 49th parallel, the Missouri turned toward the east, falling over the eastern range of mountains in a great cascade. This was the Great Falls of the Missouri; from this point the river ran "to the East till it reached the Mandaines." Here it bent to the southeast to join the Mississippi. Although the course of the Missouri from its source to the Great Falls was distorted in length and the twin parallel mountain ranges were highly simplistic, Mackay's description provided the first clear picture of the nature of the upper Missouri drainage basin (fig. 12).

The fact that the Mackay-Evans material placed the headwaters of the Missouri as far south as latitude 40° N. substantiated the fears of Spanish officials in Louisiana that the Missouri could be used as a highway for invasion of New Mexico.[78] But if the Missouri might serve as an invasion route into Spanish territory in the Southwest, it had other and more beneficent purposes. For Mackay had claimed that the river was navigable nearly all the way to its source in the western range of mountains. Beyond those mountains there must be "rivers which go toward the setting sun"; therefore the core of misconception retained, after Mackay and Evans, the same basic structure it had had since Marquette. By the end of the eighteenth century the idea was firmly cemented in geographical lore: if one could navigate the Missouri to its source and cross the mountains, the way to the Pacific and the Passage to India might be realized.

16

For well over a century the explorers of the colonial powers in North America had tried without success to reach the Sea of the South via the river systems of the continental interior. But as the curtain drew across the eighteenth century, so also did it draw across this period of exploratory activity. The veil of ignorance which had clouded the reaches of the upper Missouri from the eyes of Britian, France, and Spain had parted only slightly during the St. Louis fur trade's last gasping, feeble efforts to reach that which had been the goal of exploration since the end of the fifteenth century. The weak thrust of Spain had penetrated to the Mandan villages—but here it ended and would go no farther. The upper Missouri and what Thomas Jefferson called "that desideratum not yet satisfied"—the connection between the Missouri and whatever river headed with it and ran to the great South Sea—still remained in almost total geographic darkness.

But not all the Northwest was in darkness. From the experiences of

78. In *Before Lewis and Clark* (vol. II), Nasatir includes a number of documents illustrative of these fears. The Spanish in Louisiana were particularly concerned about the possible ramifications of the proposed Lewis and Clark Expedition when news of Jefferson's planning reached New Orleans and St. Louis from Washington.

those who had sought the Passage to India and who had penetrated the interior in search of furs and other wealth there came geographical information. The knowledge was sketchy and incomplete and became more so toward the interior portions of the continent. But men can shape geographical images from relatively scanty material, and the Americans, soon to possess most of the trans-Missouri region through the purchase of Louisiana and on the verge of launching their own expedition to seek a Passage through the Garden, did just that.

Using the accounts of Lahontan and Du Pratz, of Hennepin and other chroniclers of French Louisiana, Americans developed notions on the climate, soils, and land quality of the Northwest and saw a garden. From the travel accounts of the British, of Carver and Hearne and Mackenzie and Vancouver, they shaped notions on the physical geography of the interior and developed concepts of a continental divide, a pyramidal height-of-land, and recognized the feasibility of a Passage to India.[79] And although restrictions placed on information by the government of Spanish Louisiana had prevented widespread circulation of the accounts of such travelers as Truteau, Evans, and Mackay, enough Americans had moved into the Mississippi borderlands by the beginning of the century to gain some sketchy data on Spanish-sponsored exploration into the trans-Missouri area. This lore was transmitted to friends, relatives, government officials, and newspapers in the East, and in the American view of the Northwest there appeared traces of the desert concept, rumors of volcanoes and mountains of salt, and rather firm notions on the great size and navigability of the Missouri River.

American lore about the Northwest before Lewis and Clark was not, however, simply an extraction from the exploratory literature of the seventeenth and eighteenth centuries. Compounded with the conceptions of the West that came from that literature were elements which were particularly American, built upon earlier lore and experience, it is true, but built also from the hopes and desires and dreams of a new people. From those hopes and from their translation into images of the Northwest would come the proposal to send forth the expedition that would provide the final solution to the riddle of the Passage to India.

79. John L. Allen, "Geographical Knowledge and American Images of the Louisiana Territory," *Western Historical Quarterly*, II (1971), 151–70.

12. Anonymous Spanish Louisiana map (*ca.* 1798) reflecting some influences of the James Mackay–John Evans explorations LIBRARY OF CONGRESS

Longitude Ouest du Meridien de Londres

CHAPTER 2

PROPOSING THE
FINAL SOLUTION

The European colonial powers had sought a way through the continent of North America, and the United States was also interested in the Passage to India. But her motives were just as political and territorial as they were commercial, and her people viewed the West in the light of their 200-year heritage of hewing homes from the wilderness. While the European explorers had sought the ephemeral passage to the Orient, Americans had been, as Thoreau said, "realizing westward." By the beginning of the nineteenth century, as European exploration below the 50th parallel trickled to an end and as the mists rolled in across the great river Missouri, across the wild grape and briar and sod, across the fields of corn and squash and the earthen lodges of the Mandan and Hidatsa nations, the vanguard of American expansion had reached the edge of the Northwest.

The standard bearers of the American folk migration looked into the West and saw not only the future possibilities of the commercial passage to the Pacific that had concerned Europeans and Americans alike for so many generations. They saw also, mingled with optimism and desire and longing, the vision of "one happy union, the whole country from the Atlantic to the

Pacific Ocean, and from the lakes of Canada to the Gulf of Mexico."[1] The poets would record the vision:

> Towards the desert turn our anxious eyes,
> To see 'mong forest statelier cities rise;
> Where the wild beast now holds his gloomy den,
> To see shine forth the blessed abodes of men.
>
> The rich luxuriance of a teeming soil,
> Rewards with affluence the farmer's toil,
> All nature round him breathes a rich perfume,
> His harvest ripens and his orchards bloom.[2]

The water route to the Pacific was, for many Americans, a Passage through the Garden. That fact lent zest and flavor to early nineteenth-century American images of the Northwest, images out of which grew the grand designs of Jefferson and his contemporaries to unravel the Northwestern Mystery.

2

The United States in the new nineteenth century was an agricultural nation. Thomas Jefferson, who considered the independent small farmer the backbone of an ideal republic, had been elected president in the disputed election of 1800 partly because of his adherence to the agrarian tradition. It is only natural, perhaps, that American images of the Northwest should have been colored by the predominant feeling that the United States had to maintain vast areas for the expansion of an agricultural population if she were to remain a republic. The dominant portion of the Americans' images of the Northwest, in terms of land quality, could only have been based on hope and optimism—a hope that the lands to the west would provide a firm base for the agrarian republic and an optimism that this must be the case.[3]

Detractors might have written in the newspapers of the larger cities of the seaboard that the West was "an absolute barren that nobody knows the bounds of or cares."[4] Indeed, many of the reports of the later Spanish-sponsored explorers such as Truteau might have (insofar as these reports were available) substantiated this notion. But these critics were not in the majority. The Northwest was, of course, a large area with room for lands of both high and low quality. But the majority of the source materials available to Americans spoke of fertility and lushness, and the revelations were widely

1. David Ramsey, "An Oration on the Cession of Louisiana" (Charleston, S.C., 1804), p. 21.

2. W. M. P., "A Poem on the Acquisition of Louisiana" (Charleston, S.C., 1804), p. 20.

3. This statement is borne out by a survey of newspapers for the period 1801–04. Only rarely (except in the papers of the urban centers of the Northeast) do critical statements about the agricultural potential of the western interior appear.

4. *National Intelligencer* (Washington), Sept. 26, 1803, p. 2.

accepted.[5] It mattered little that the source materials were describing only the fecundity of the Mississippi valley and its immediately adjacent area. For when information on an entire region is limited, regional differences and distinctions within that area are blurred in the images that are created for it. Data on one part of a region, if it is the only information available, becomes applied to the region as a whole. Because the greatest volume of lore that Americans possessed about the Northwest depicted it as a garden, a garden it was in the mind's eye of the early nineteenth century, full of hopes and not disillusionment.[6]

3

Like the view of the land itself, the ideas on what the land contained were based on the agrarian tradition. For centuries wealth in gold, gems, and precious minerals had been sought toward the sunset, but in the American images of the Northwest in the early nineteenth century few elements of El Dorado remained. The official reports of government investigations might have set forth the notion that the lands of the trans-Missouri region contained precious minerals locked in their bowels, but the traditional emphasis on mineral wealth was more practical. To most Americans who thought about the Northwest and the future potential of the region, lead, iron, and salt—the basic needs of a frontier agricultural society—were foremost; gold, silver, and other precious metals could come later.[7]

If optimism cloaked the American images of the Northwest with regard to the quality of the land and the salubrity of the climate, so also did it permeate the nature of American thought about the native inhabitants of that area. Correspondents writing from the borderlands of the Mississippi to eastern papers had posted the news that not only was the Northwest the land of promise, with soils of great fertility and hordes of grazing beasts, but also that there were "no hostile Indians to contend with."[8] Few Americans had come in contact with the Plains tribes (the French and Spanish fur

5. Out of a total of 134 items related to the Northwest that were generally available at the time of the Lewis and Clark Expedition, 54 made direct reference to land quality. In these items (including newspaper and periodical articles, geographical texts, travelers' accounts, etc.), the words "barren," "sterile," and "waste" appeared twice, three times, and once respectively. By contrast, words such as "fertile," "benign," "lush," "salubrious," "verdant," and "beautiful" appeared between thirty-six and three times.

6. A qualification of this statement is necessary. The degree to which the elite and highly educated portions of the American society accepted such a view of the Northwest was, seemingly, less than acceptance of the garden concept by the folk elements of society. It was the folk elements, however, that were instrumental in expansion into the trans-Mississippi region, and their adherence to a garden concept was more than a minor factor in the expansionist tendencies of the nineteenth century.

7. Only five out of twenty-nine references to minerals in the Northwest in the geographical lore available prior to Lewis and Clark mentioned precious metals or stones.

8. *Federal Gazette* (Baltimore), Jan. 12, 1804, p. 3.

traders, who had, would have told a different story), and, although they should have known better, Americans tended to view the western Indians as distinct from the eastern tribes.

Like other features of the Northwest, the natives were surrounded with an aura of mystery. They were somehow different and more romantic than the general run-of-the-mill Indians. Some authorities thought it highly probable that many of the western tribes were descended from various pre-Columbian European adventurers such as the Irish, the Norse, or even the Welsh. Or perhaps the western natives were remnants of the Lost Tribes of Israel. Some of them were white and some of them were black and some of them wore beards and lived in cities of gold in conditions which approached and rivaled (if not excelled) the standards of European civilizations. The farther west one went the more likely he would be to encounter utopian civilizations and fabulous peoples.[9] This was a function of a general tendency to fill the least-known areas on a map with the least likely phenomena. It was also a function of the romanticism inherent in geographical thought about the lands toward the sunset.

In spite of these tendencies toward romantic and image-filled attitudes about the Northwest, the American views of the region contained surprisingly little of a mythical character. Many of the geographical elements of the Northwest were poorly understood; but there were few true features of myth in the components of western geography. Concepts of land fertility, notions about the size and height and location of interior mountains, theoretical ideas about symmetrical drainage patterns and common source areas for major rivers—these all had some basis in fact that was misconstrued and misunderstood. It is true that some literature of the early 1800s contained wild tales about great lakes in the interior, surrounded by civilized natives living in splendid cities. And other literary sources discussed the possibilities of discovering beasts of medieval mythic character in the mountains and plains of the Northwest.[10] But such fanciful imaginings do not seem to have been a part of general geographical lore.

Of all the features of the geography of the Northwest that might be considered mythical, only two gained any measure of popular acceptance. The first of these was a mountain of rock salt, described in articles in the most reputable periodicals and geographical writings. After the cession of Louisiana to the United States in 1803, even the government's official account of the lands encompassed in the newly acquired territory reported solemnly that there was, about a thousand miles up the Missouri, a mountain of solid rock salt, 180 miles long and 45 wide, without a single stick of vegetation

9. Two of the most popular works that depicted great civilizations in the western interior were: Don Alonzo Decalves, *Travels to the Westward or the Unknown Parts of America* (Keene, N.H., 1794); and (anon.) *Narrative of a Voyage . . . to the Western Continent* (Windsor, Conn., 1801).

10. Cf. Decalves, *Travels to the Westward;* and "The My-attic Ram" in the *Boston Weekly Magazine,* II (1803–04), 93.

on it.[11] A second popular notion dealt with the presence of great volcanoes in the interior. Travelers who had been on the Missouri had seen and brought back pieces of pumice stone found floating on the waters of the river. These were considered to have been produced by volcanic activity and proved conclusively the existence of lofty volcanoes in, as a major scientific periodical had it, "those immense and unexplored mountains which may be called 'the Northern Andes.' "[12] Beyond the widespread acceptance of these two fictions there seems to have been little else in the American images that was without some basis in fact.

The absence of mythical features in the literature and lore of the years just before Lewis and Clark notwithstanding, it must be noted that Americans had already developed the propensity to "talk tall." But this tendency meant other things than the creation of a mythical geography for the interior; rather than filling the empty spaces on the map with pure fantasy, Americans chose to exaggerate what they had learned about the Northwest from the accounts and chronicles of the seventeenth and eighteenth centuries. The soils of the West were the best in the world, the climate was gentle and kind, and the natives resembled heroic races of Homeric proportions. The West was a land of opportunity—even at this early date—and should be viewed with optimism and hope. It would provide the home for the expansion of the republic and through its vast river systems, connecting with short portages through mountains that were no barriers to the spread of American civilization, that republic might reach the Pacific and the Orient beyond.

4

In speculating on the quality of the Northwest for future occupation, Americans were operating out of a traditional and ageless faith in the West. Therefore, with few exceptions, there was general agreement about the overall potential of the trans-Missouri region. But the major physical geographical features of the Northwest—the Missouri, the Rockies, and the Columbia—are revealed as highly contradictory in the geographical lore of the early nineteenth century.

Most authorities on western geography agreed that the interior was a "well-watered" region, with many streams available for mill sites and many rivers for transportation. The major river systems of the Northwest were, however, only dimly understood, although most Americans held common concepts of their great length, breadth, and extensive navigability. Various authors referred to the Missouri, for example, as running a course of well over 2,000 miles and affording "a more extensive navigation and [being] a

11. *American State Papers* (vol. XX, "Miscellaneous"), I, 346, article entitled "An Official Account of Louisiana," authored by Thomas Jefferson. See also "The Louisiana Salt Mountains" in the *Federal Gazette* (Baltimore), Feb. 7, 1804, p. 3.
12. *Medical Repository*, IV (1st hexade, 1801), 304.

longer, broader & deeper river than the Mississippi."[13] It was believed to have its source, as did the Columbia, the Mississippi, the St. Lawrence, and the Nelson, in a common source area that lay somewhere in the interior. In this height-of-land, "the highest lands in North America," the rivers' headwaters were "within thirty miles of each other," and from here they ran courses of "above 2000 miles" and were navigable throughout.[14]

Because of this supposed symmetrical arrangement of the river systems, with major rivers rising in a common area and then flowing in their various courses to the sea, the opinion of many was that the river systems of the Northwest offered particularly good transportation possibilities. Like the notions about the quality of the land, this was an important feature of the optimism with which Americans viewed the interior. Beyond the sources of the Mississippi and Missouri, to the west and only a short distance away, would be found the source waters of other great rivers, sometimes given the name of "Oregan" or "Columbia" and at other times simply referred to as "the Great River of the West." Through these channels of communication with which the Northwest was blessed, the agricultural produce that was a necessary adjunct of the great fertility of the interior might find new outlets —even to the shores of China and Japan:

> Rejoice, ye too, rejoice ye swains,
> Increasing commerce shall reward your cares.
> A day will come if not too deep we drink
> The cup, which luxury on careless wealth
> Pernicious gift bestows; a day will come
> When through new channels we shall clothe
> The California coast, and all the realms
> That stretch from Anian's Streights to proud Japan.[15]

5

The rivers were wide, long, and great, and their sources were close together. This boded well for the possibilities of commercial contacts throughout the Northwest. But what of the nature of the source regions themselves? The highest lands on the continent, those from which the major rivers flowed, were variously seen as a range of mighty mountains or as an upland plateau area that was level and flat. Some geographical writers spoke of the "very high range of mountains separating the waters which fall into the Mississippi from those which fall into the Pacific Ocean."[16] But others referred to the source area of the Mississippi and Missouri as being an area of "very extensive

13. Thomas Hutchins, *An Historical Narrative and Topographical Description of Louisiana and West Florida* (Philadelphia, 1784), p. 26.

14. See Benjamin Workman, *Elements of Geography* (9th ed., Philadelphia, 1803), p. 8; John Pinkerton, *Modern Geography* (2 vols., Philadelphia, 1804), II, 414; and Jedediah Morse, *The American Universal Geography* (5th ed., 2 vols., Boston, 1803), I, 750–59.

15. *Royal American Magazine* (Boston), Jan., 1774.

16. John Hubbard, *The Rudiments of Geography* (Walpole, N.H., 1803), p. 14.

plains" (fig. 13), or to the interior itself as being primarily a region where "delightful and immense plains stretched to the southern ocean."[17]

It is clear that, in the American geographical views of the Northwest in the early 1800s, the mountains of the interior were misty, shifting, and illusory features—if they existed at all. Some authorities who did recognize the presence of mountains in the interior viewed them as one unbroken chain, running 3,000 miles north from Mexico; they appeared as such on many maps of the period. In many of the geographical texts, on the other hand, not one but two ranges of western mountains are described.[18] To the south were the mountains of New Mexico, and in the north were the "Shining Mountains," or Rocky Mountains, of the Canadian fur trade. The northern range had its southern terminus near the 47th or 48th parallel of latitude; here "a number of rivers rise and empty themselves into either the N. Pacific Ocean, into Hudson's Bay, into the waters which lie between them, or into the Atlantic Ocean."[19]

In this statement lies the fundamental core of misconception about western geography as it was understood on the eve of the Lewis and Clark Expedition. The drainage divide between eastward and westward-flowing streams need not necessarily be a range of mountains at all but might just as well be a high plateau, an area of extensive plains, a theoretical height-of-land. It is possible that for many Americans the mountains of the interior were viewed as a continuous range that ran without break from north to south. But even Alexander Mackenzie, whose report fixed the nature of the interior ranges in the minds of many, had indicated that he could not speculate on how far south the mountains he had crossed extended. It was therefore conceivable that breaks in the backbone of the continent might be found below the 50th parallel. The Rocky Mountains, or "Shining Mountains," or "Stony Mountains," or "Mountains of Bright Stones," were definitely a part of the American view of the Northwest. But their function as a continental divide was not clearly recognized. Neither was their barrier-like structure understood nor the fact that through them a water passage to the Pacific might be found.

Just as the true nature of the Rockies as the ultimate divider of Atlantic-from Pacific-slope streams was not fully grasped, neither was their size and location completely discerned. The altitude of the interior mountains was a matter of great conjecture; where some sources referred to "their astonishing heights" which were as great "as any in the known world," others spoke only of a slight "ridge of mountains from which the streams run due west."[20]

17. Charles B. Brown, "An Address to the Government of the United States on the Cession of Louisiana" (Philadelphia, 1803), p. 17.
18. Cf. Morse, *American Universal Geography*, pp. 750–59; and Morse, *American Gazetteer* (Boston, 1803), articles on "The Shining Mountains" and "The Mountains of New Mexico."
19. Morse, "The Shining Mountains."
20. *American Museum* (Philadelphia), Aug., 1787.

The most acceptable view was perhaps that stated in the best geographical texts and most respected periodicals: the height of the mountains was nowhere more than the 3,250 feet above the 3,000-foot base level specified in the British geographical lore. It is obvious that the true height of the Rockies, either in terms of their vertical rise or of their base height above sea level, was not even remotely understood.

Confusion also ruled the American conceptualization of the location of the western ranges. Most sources agreed that the mountains of the interior were similar in structure to the Blue Ridge of Virginia, a single ridge or series of parallel ridges transected by rivers; the true nature of the Rockies as a broad and massive alpine region was not even dreamed of. The location of this range, moreover, varied greatly according to the authority consulted. From sources in the British literature and cartography, it seemed as if the mountains were an unbroken chain that lay somewhere between the 112th and 115th meridians of longitude; this positioning was indicated by Aaron Arrowsmith's several maps of North America, the best cartographic representations of the Northwest available in the early 1800s. Other sources, however, pushed the mountains farther west, toward the Pacific. Spanish officials in Louisiana during the last decades of the eighteenth century had believed that the mountains were as close to the Pacific as approximately 100 miles; they appeared, in a sense, as mirror images of the ranges of the Atlantic coast. This type of concept worked its way onto Samuel Lewis's map of Louisiana (fig. 14), which depicted the Rockies as a series of broken north-south ranges, lying close to the Pacific coast and having one of their major breaks near the head of the Missouri. While this cartographic portrayal of the Northwest was much less accurate than those of Arrowsmith,[21] it was much more symbolic of American optimism. On it there appeared no apparent barriers across the path of the expansion of American commerce and population toward the Pacific.

6

If knowledge could be envisioned as three-dimensional, then the general American lore on the trans-Missouri region on the eve of Lewis's and Clark's trek could best be described as a basin, surrounded by ridges of better knowledge and grading into a vast, flat surface of pure conjecture, broken here and there by a peak of better understanding. Exploratory approaches had been made to the Northwest from several sides, and as a result of these approaches the periphery of the area was relatively well known. The American view of

21. Lewis's map appeared in *A New and Elegant General Atlas*, published in Boston in 1804 to accompany Morse's *American Universal Geography*. The *Atlas* was jointly authored by Lewis and Aaron Arrowsmith and it is obvious that there was little or no collusion between the two cartographers since their versions of western geography are at such variance.

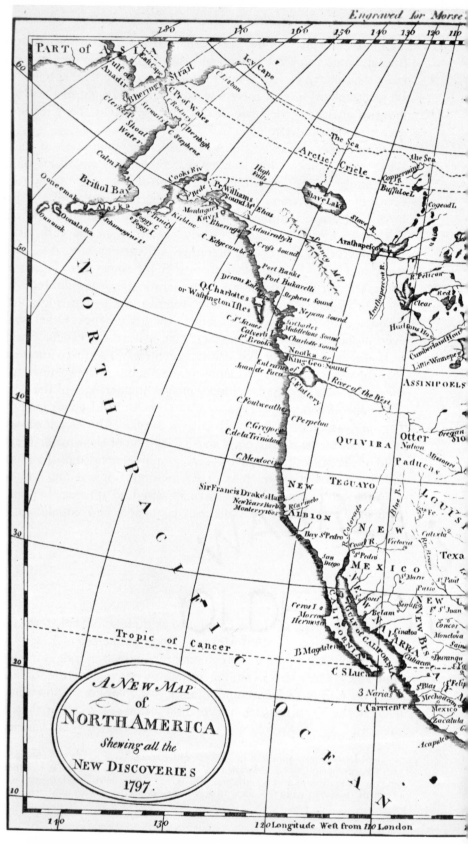

13. Jedediah Morse's map of North America, "shewing all the new discoveries." From the *American Gazetteer* (Boston, 1797)   LIBRARY OF CONGRESS

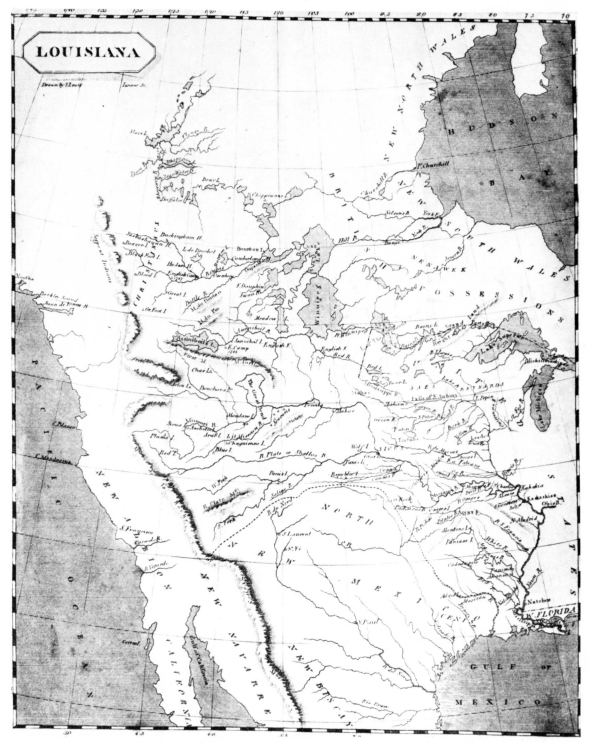

14. Samuel Lewis's map of Louisiana. From *A New and Elegant General Atlas of North America* (Boston, 1804)   LIBRARY OF CONGRESS

the lower portions of the Missouri and of the Pacific coastal area near the mouth of the Columbia was fairly accurate, derived from the costal surveys of the British in the Pacific Northwest and from the long-term French and Spanish contacts in the lower Missouri valley. But these well-known areas graded into others, such as the portion of the Missouri from the mouth of the Kansas to the Mandan villages, that were known only partially through the brief contacts of the fur traders of Spanish Louisiana. Beyond this lay only rumor and conjecture, and perhaps the single most striking feature of American geographical knowledge of the Northwest before Lewis and Clark was the almost total lack of good information on the western interior.

But lack of information does not curtail the ability to create images, and in spite of poor and inadequate data on western geography there were definite patterns of belief in the nature and content of the geographical features of the Northwest in the minds of many Americans. These images were based on American interpretations of the knowledge contributed by exploration in the trans-Missouri area from Marquette to Mackay and Evans, and in the American view appeared the twin themes of the Garden of the World and the Passage to India. Because of the confused and contradictory nature of American geographical lore, however, the images and the themes were blurred. Still, a clear image would come out of the chaos.

7

There were, in the opening years of the nineteenth century, some Americans who were possessed of better information and more complete understanding of the Northwest than most of their contemporaries. Through the articulation of the fuzzier and less specific overall American images by these individuals a plan of action was laid out. From that plan of action would come the first American expedition into the trans-Missouri area,[22] and that expedition would begin to burn off the mists and begin to light the darkness that had cloaked the American Northwest. This was the expedition of Lewis and Clark, the product of the distillation and refinement of the American views of the lands lying between the Mississippi and the Pacific.

The journey of Lewis and Clark to the great South Sea and back was aided, furthered, and made feasible by soldiers, frontier civilians, scientists, and government officials. But perhaps more than any other event in the history of exploration it was generated by the geographical understanding and

22. That the expedition of Lewis and Clark was the first American venture into the trans-Missouri region is a common historical convention. There might possibly have been, however, an earlier expedition that had at least semi-official sanction. This was the expedition of a Lieutenant John Armstrong (Colton Storm, "Lt. Armstrong's Expedition to the Missouri River, 1790," *Mid-America*, XXV (1943), 180–88). Armstrong cannot have gone far upriver (if indeed he ever went at all) and cannot, therefore, be accorded much prominence as an explorer.

imagination of one man. Towering above all other contributors to the success of the Lewis and Clark Expedition was Thomas Jefferson. It was through his formulation and implementation of the images of the Northwest that the first American transcontinental exploration became a reality. Like others of his time, Jefferson saw a garden in the Northwest, and a basic part of his desire to have the region explored was to establish firmly and scientifically that the country beyond the Mississippi was, in truth, eminently suited for occupation by the agrarian society. But another idea was even more central in Jeffersons' thinking—through the Garden lay the Passage to India.

The fascination of Thomas Jefferson with the Northwest and the possibility of a water communication across the continent, a dream for so long in the minds of so many, developed at an early date. While still a child in the Virginia piedmont Jefferson may have learned of the ambitions of a group of his father's neighbors and friends to seek by way of the Missouri River a Passage to India. Late in the year 1749, when Thomas Jefferson was only six years old, his father Peter and a group of other prominent gentlemen of Albemarle County, Virginia, had chartered a land company to be known as the Loyal Land Company.[23] The avowed purpose of this company was the "discovery and sale of western lands"—meaning lands between the Alleghenies and the Mississippi—but a deeper motive soon became apparent. Three years after the Loyal Land Company was chartered its members began to discuss and plan a western expedition on a grand scale.

The Reverend James Maury, rector of the Fredricksville parish and master of the school for boys that young Thomas Jefferson himself attended, wrote of the plans: "Some persons were to be sent in search of that river Missouri, if that be the right name of it, in order to discover whether it had any communication with the Pacific Ocean."[24] The idea for this scheme was an old one, based in the tenets of symmetrical geography. "When it is considered," continued Maury,

how far the eastern branches of that immense river, Mississippi, extend eastward, and how near they come to the navigable, or rather canoeable parts of those rivers which empty themselves into the sea that washes our shores to the east, it seems highly probable that its western branches reach as far the other way, and make as near approaches to rivers emptying themselves into the ocean to the west of us, the Pacific Ocean, across which a short and easy communication, short in comparison with the present route thither, opens itself to the navigation from the shore of the continent unto the Eastern Indies.[25]

The way to the Indies lay open. The desire of centuries, reinforced by the

23. A photostat copy of the charter of the company is in the McGregor Rare Book and Manuscript Collection of the Alderman Library, University of Virginia, Charlottesville.
24. "The Letters of James Maury," in James Fontaine Maury, *Memoirs of a Hugenot Family* (New York, 1912), p. 391.
25. Maury, *Memoirs of a Hugenot Family*, p. 388.

experiences and geographical lore of the French in Louisiana and by the theoretical symmetrical geography of early eighteenth-century British geographical thought,[26] had decreed it must be so.

If the plans of such a glorious adventure escaped the ears of young Jefferson (and the thought is unlikely), then it is more than probable that he was introduced to the idea by Reverend Maury, long a proponent of the feasibility of a water communication across the continent and Jefferson's schoolmaster after the death of Peter Jefferson in 1757. Little is known of the nature of Jefferson's geographical education under Maury, but the old master himself included a knowledge of geography as one of the essential features in the education of "the well-rounded young gentleman."[27] It seems almost certain that if Maury's most famous pupil had failed to hear anything of the projected expedition to the Pacific during the conversations at Shadwell, his father's estate, he would have learned of "these pleasing expectations" from Reverend Maury himself.

The allure of the Passage to India, thus unfolded at an early age, never left Jefferson. Throughout most of his mature life he gathered materials that would provide him with information about that transcontinental communication. From that information on the history, exploration, and geography of the western parts of North America there developed an image of the Northwest, an image that contained not only the element of the Passage to India but also many other elements that had emerged from the exploratory experiences of the French, British, and Spanish from 1673 to the cession of Louisiana to the United States.

8

By virtue of his background and training, his access to and supply of information on the geography of the Northwest, Thomas Jefferson was, at the time he proposed the Lewis and Clark Expedition, the most knowledgeable American insofar as the geographical lore of the trans-Missouri region was concerned. Following the awakening of an interest in the Northwest and the water passage during his Virginia boyhood and prior to the launching of the explorations of Lewis and Clark, Jefferson built what was probably the finest collection of published materials on the American Northwest in any North

26. The works of Daniel Coxe were central to the geographical thinking of the members of the Loyal Land Company. Maury wrote a lengthy description of the symmetry of the Mississippi drainage basin which he drew largely from Coxe's *Carolana*. He had seen the book at the house of Joshua Fry, close friend of Peter Jefferson, co-author of the Fry-Jefferson map of Virginia, and also a member of the Loyal Land Company (Maury, *Memoirs of a Hugenot Family*, pp. 389–90).

27. James Fontaine Maury, "Treatise on Practical Education" (MS, Manuscript Division, Alderman Library, University of Virginia, Charlottesville).

American library.[28] He also corresponded widely with scientists and geographers at home and abroad and with residents of Louisiana and the American settlements west of the Alleghenies. From these he derived the information that supported his belief that the Passage to India did exist and that it might be found by way of the Missouri and the streams heading with it and flowing to the Pacific.

Little is known of the geographical works in Jefferson's earliest collections since his original library was burned when the Shadwell estate was leveled by fire in 1770. But some evidence may be found in Jefferson's reply, in 1771, to a friend's request for a list of books necessary in an adequate personal library.[29] On that list there appeared several works of a geographical nature; the most important of these was Daniel Coxe's *Carolana*, quite probably the book that had stimulated the members of the Loyal Land Company to propose an expedition to the Missouri in search of a passage to the Pacific.

In 1783 Jefferson was again asked for an opinion on how to build a library, this time by a congressional committee headed by James Madison and formed for the purpose of developing a national library. Jefferson apparently complied with the committee's request, for in late January, 1783, Madison presented Congress with a book list which seems to have been based on a catalog of Jefferson's own personal library, compiled around 1783.[30] This list included several geographical volumes not mentioned in the list of 1771, including Baron Lahontan's *New Voyages to North America* and Robert Rogers's *Concise Account of North America*. Inclusion of these volumes indicates that Jefferson either owned them or was familiar with them and would certainly have gleaned from their pages the very significant geographical lore about the pyramidal height-of-land and the connections between eastward- and westward-flowing streams that was so central in his later thinking about the Northwest.

Shortly after providing this list for Congress Jefferson began the most intensive period of collecting information on western geography prior to his election to the presidency in 1800. Between July, 1784, and October, 1789, Jefferson served as the U.S. minister to France, and from all evidence much of his energy during his time in Europe was directed to purchasing materials on North American history and geography. Jefferson himself later commented on this activity: "While I was in Europe I had purchased everything I could lay my hands on which related to any part of America, and particularly had a

28. The basic reference on Jefferson's library collection is E. Millicent Sowerby, *The Library Catalogue of Thomas Jefferson* (5 vols., Washington, 1952–54).

29. Jefferson to Robert Skipwith, 3 Aug. 1771 (Library of Congress, Manuscript Division, Jefferson Papers). Unless another source is given, all Jefferson material is from the Jefferson Papers of the Library of Congress and will be cited as above, by sender, receiver, and date. An excellent published source of correspondence and documents on Jefferson is Julian Boyd, ed., *The Papers of Thomas Jefferson* (17 vols., Princeton, 1950–65). For virtually all the Jefferson correspondence relating to the Lewis and Clark Expedition, see Donald Jackson's superb *Letters of the Lewis and Clark Expedition with Related Documents, 1783–1854* (Urbana, Ill., 1962).

30. Boyd, *Papers*, VI, 216.

pretty full collection of the English & Spanish authors on the subject of Louisiana."[31] While no precise listings for Jefferson's purchases in Europe are available, his later library catalogs suggest that among those purchases were the works of Jonathan Carver, Charlevoix, and Du Pratz.[32] All of these were to be relied on heavily by Jefferson in later years as the foundation of his geographical knowledge of the Northwest.[33]

There is no evidence for any further additions to Jefferson's collection of published geographical materials on the Northwest until the year 1800. During that year, according to a list from his correspondence,[34] Jefferson purchased several more pieces of information on the West, at least one of which was to prove extremely noteworthy for the formulation of his conception of the Northwest and the Passage to India. This was Alexander Mackenzie's *Voyages from Montreal,* and it was evidently read with a great deal of interest. Mackenzie's information on the short portage between Atlantic and Pacific slope drainages was to become a dominant part of Jefferson's image of the Northwest, and Mackenzie's volume contained enough of interest to Jefferson to induce him later to purchase a less "large & cumbersome" set, quite possibly to be carried by Meriwether Lewis during his transcontinental journey.[35] The maps accompanying Mackenzie's *Voyages* were also of great importance and would later aid Jefferson and other interested officials in preparing a base map of the Northwest for use by Lewis and Clark.

Jefferson made no further purchases of published geographical materials on the Northwest before the Lewis and Clark Expedition—at least there are no evidences of such purchases. But his library collection was already quite complete and was a vital source for the knowledge on the Northwest that became available for transmission to the leaders of the still-to-be-proposed expedition. The library collection, however, cannot be considered as an isolated contributor to Jefferson's knowledge of the Northwest. The data contained in the printed volumes of his magnificent collection were instrumental in the shaping of the objectives of Lewis and Clark as set forth by Jefferson. But the published information was modified by other sources of geographical knowledge, the most meaningful of which are to be found in Jefferson's correspondence.

31. Jefferson to William Dunbar, 13 Mar. 1804.

32. Jefferson's Library Catalogue, 1783–1812 (MS, Jefferson Collection, Massachusetts Historical Society, Boston).

33. As early as 1785 Jefferson was referring to the works of Lahontan, Charlevoix, and Hennepin as being "particularly useful species of reading" (Boyd, *Papers*, VIII, 411). In later years, as Jefferson assembled data on the Northwest and wrote two documents on the exploration and history of Louisiana (an "examination into the boundaries of Louisiana" and a "chronological series of facts relating to Louisiana") he drew almost entirely on materials gathered in Europe. The documents referred to above were written in 1803–04 and published by the American Philosophical Society as part of the *Documents Relating to the Purchase and Exploration of Louisiana* (Philadelphia, 1904).

34. This list, from a note at the end of the Jefferson Papers for 1800, is in Jefferson's hand and is dated simply "notes of books purchased 1800."

35. Jefferson to James Cheetham, a New York bookseller, 17 June 1803.

9

For many years prior to the organization of the Lewis and Clark Expedition, Jefferson corresponded with both private citizens and government officials regarding the feasibility of a transcontinental water passageway and dealing with the nature of the western parts of North America through which that passageway must necessarily be routed. This correspondence, reflecting Jefferson's early interest in the Northwest and the possibilities for communication to the Pacific, was a primary source of the geographical lore available to him as he shaped his proposals for the final solution of the Northwestern Mystery.

There was only meager information on the Northwest in the Jefferson correspondence prior to 1801. But enough piecemeal testimony may be found throughout his letters, both those sent and those received, to suggest that the country west of the Mississippi was of considerable interest to him. Most references to the West dealt with the political situation in Louisiana or with the conditions among American settlers in the Mississippi valley. But there were also some items of geographical information on the farther western parts of the continent.

One major area of interest, as evidenced by the Jefferson correspondence before 1801, was the coastal area of the Pacific Northwest. Jefferson knew about the activities of Russian, Spanish, and British operatives in the fur trade of the Northwest coast and must have been aware quite early of the benefits that would accrue to anyone who could use this coast as a terminus for a transcontinental route involving the fur trade of the interior as well as the coastal regions.[36] But the western end of the passageway was not Jefferson's greatest concern. He was, it seems, more fascinated by the possible location of the passage through the interior and was in frequent contact with several interested parties regarding the benefits of such a communication. In fact, from 1782 until his election to the presidency, the vast majority of memoranda on the Northwest in Jefferson's correspondence alluded specifically to a series of proposals originating with him and respecting the establishment of the water route across the continent and the exploration of the western interior.

So far as is known, the first concrete suggestion made by Jefferson that the connections between the Missouri system and the rivers of the Pacific slope be investigated came in 1783. Late in that year Jefferson wrote to George Rogers Clark, an old friend and the brother of William Clark, who would co-command Jefferson's finally successful attempt to search for the passage: "I find they [the English] have subscribed a very large sum of money in England for exploring the country from the Missisipi to California. they pretend it is only to promote knolege. some of us have been talking here in a feeble way of making the attempt to search that country, but I doubt

36. Boyd, *Papers*, XII, 379; XVI, 392.

whether we have enough of that kind of spirit to raise the money. how would you like to lead such a party?"[37] Clark regretfully declined the tentative offer and thus failed Jefferson's first gropings toward the discovery of the Passage to India.

In less than three years after this first rejection of a proposal to discover the Pacific via the river waterways of western North America, Jefferson was to become involved in another project which, although it had little hope of success, at least indicated the persistence of Jefferson's desire to make an "attempt to search that country." While in residence in Paris in 1786 Jefferson had made the acquaintance of John Ledyard, an American citizen also interested in the water communication between the Mississippi system and the Pacific.[38] Appraised of Jefferson's willingness to provide support, Ledyard made a startling proposal. He would leave Paris and go to Russia, cross Siberia, and pick up passage on a Russian trading vessel bound for the Pacific Northwest. There he would disembark, ascend a river on the western side of the North American continent to the headwaters of the Missouri, and then travel down that river to the Mississippi and the United States.[39] Ledyard's inventive scheme, as might have been expected, was never successful.[40]

The idea of the transcontinental passage continued to ripen in Jefferson's mind, and by 1793 it had matured sufficiently for his first serious assault on the commercial water communication. This third attempt[41]—that of the French botanist André Michaux—had the official approval and support of the nation's most august body of scientists, the American Philosophical Society of Philadelphia. Michaux, who had been in Canada doing botanical research, had informed the Philosophical Society (with which he had been in frequent contact on scientific matters) of the British drive to explore the headwaters of the Missouri River and its connections with Pacific-slope streams and had suggested that the society commission him to do the job first and beat Britain

37. Jefferson to George Rogers Clark, 4 Dec. 1783.
38. Ledyard was a Connecticut Yankee who had previously served as a member of Captain Cook's exploring party in northwestern coastal waters. See Helen Auger, *Passage to Glory: John Ledyard's America* (New York, 1946) for an interesting if somewhat overenthusiastic biography of his life and travels. A more objective and more contemporary account is Jared Sparks, *Life of John Ledyard* (London, 1845).
39. John Ledyard to Jefferson, 16 Aug. 1786.
40. Although Jefferson had requested protection for Ledyard from Catherine, empress of Russia, Ledyard was prevented from crossing Siberia. Catherine had turned down the appeal for safe conduct and Ledyard was arrested and returned to Europe. He died in Cairo during the planning stages of an expedition to seek the sources of the Nile.
41. There is a tentative connection between Jefferson and a fourth attempt to explore the trans-Missouri country. John W. Harshberger in *The Botanists of Philadelphia and Their Work* (Philadelphia, 1899), p. 106, prints a letter from Dr. Caspar Wistar of the American Philosophical Society to Dr. Moses Marshall, a Philadelphia botanist, which reads in part: "I find that thee is already acquainted with the wishes of some gentlemen here to have our continent explored in a western direction. . . . Mr. Jefferson and several other gentlemen are much interested. . . . They wish the journey to be prosecuted up the Missouri, as the easiest and most interesting track. . . . If thee has any inclination, I think it would be very proper to come to town immediately and converse with Mr. Jefferson, who seems principally interested." A search has failed to turn up any correspondence between Jefferson and Moses Marshall on this point.

to the discovery of the transcontinental water route.[42] Accordingly, David Rittenhouse, president of the body, asked Jefferson to draw up a subscription paper to raise funds for such an exploration;[43] in their April meeting of 1793, the society passed a proposal agreeing to sponsor Michaux and appointed a committee, including Jefferson, to draft a set of instructions for his use.[44]

Although the drafting of Michaux's instructions was ostensibly a committee task, it is apparent from Jefferson's correspondence with the other members of the appointed group that he acted virtually alone in preparing them.[45] The instructions presented to Michaux are therefore of critical significance for two reasons: first, they illustrate the concept of the practicable water communication as Jefferson saw it in 1793, thus providing a preliminary view of his knowledge of western geography; and second, they provided a model for the instructions that Jefferson was to give Meriwether Lewis ten years later.[46] No correspondence between Jefferson and Michaux (other than the instructions) has been located, and it is not known whether Jefferson supplied further information to the French botanist. The instructions themselves, however, probably contain in summary form as much specific information on the Northwest as was available to Jefferson.

The chief objective of the proposed expedition, Jefferson informed Michaux, was "to find the shortest & most convenient route of communication between the U.S. & the Pacific ocean." Other objectives included general observations on the country—botanical, zoological, mineral, etc.—but the main purpose remained the discovery of the water passageway. The location of this passage would be found via the Missouri River. Jefferson was adamant about the Missouri as "the channel of communication between these states and the Pacific ocean," and the Missouri, he said, presented itself "under circumstances of unquestioned preference" as the transcontinental water route. The exploration of the Missouri, then, was the "fundamental object of the subscription . . . not to be disposed with." And it was further noted by Jefferson (as conjecture) that near the source of the Missouri "a river called Oregan interlocked with the Missouri for a considerable distance, & entered the Pacific ocean, not far southward of Nootka sound." Jefferson had phrased rather succinctly the core of the image of the American Northwest as derived from the exploratory experience of the eighteenth century: the Missouri and the Great River of the West had their sources in the same immediate area and therefore would form a water communication across the continent for the purposes of commerce.

42. André Michaux, *Travels into Kentucky, 1793–1796*, vol. III of *Early Western Travels*, ed. Reuben Gold Thwaites (32 vols., Cleveland, 1904–06), pp. 11–14.

43. "Agreement of Subscribers to André Michaux," 22 Jan. 1793 (Jefferson Papers).

44. Minutes for the Meeting of Apr. 19, 1793, *Proceedings of the American Philosophical Society*, vol. XXII, no. 3, p. 215.

45. From David Rittenhouse to Jefferson, 10 Apr. 1793.

46. Jefferson's file copy of the instructions to Michaux are dated 30 Apr. 1793. The citations herein are from that copy. The instructions are published in Jackson, *Letters*, pp. 669–72.

Jefferson concluded his instructions with a note of apology for not having provided the botanist with more detailed intelligence, but that this might be excused due to "ignorance of the country thro' which you are to pass." Some of the information, therefore, might be erroneous, and that being the case, the society could not expect "exacting rigorous observance" of all its instructions—with one great exception. "The first of all objects," concluded Jefferson, was "that you seek for & pursue that route which shall form the shortest & most convenient communication between the higher parts of the Missouri & Pacific ocean." That object, however, was not to be attained; Michaux's Missouri expedition, backed by the most outstanding intellects in the United States, became embroiled in international politics and was doomed to failure even before it was begun.[47]

In the wake of the failure of Michaux's proposed attempt to reach the Pacific via the Missouri and Columbia rivers, Jefferson seems to have lost interest in the project, at least temporarily. He resigned from the post of secretary of state in December, 1793, and went into retirement at Monticello, his estate near Charlottesville, Virginia. During the years 1794–96 there was a sharp drop in the total volume of Jefferson's correspondence and virtually no mention of either the Northwest or a projected water route through it. Nor did Jefferson's return to public life as vice-president of the United States in 1796 seem to have terminated this transitory lull in his interest in the Northwest and the Passage. His correspondence during his term as vice-president contained only passing reference to the West and these few items dealt exclusively with political and economic problems.

10

The halt in communication on the Northwest came to an end in 1800. Jefferson intensified his efforts in gathering information on the trans-Missouri area during the election campaign of 1800, and shortly after his election to the presidency began collecting geographical materials on the Northwest on a scale greater than anything since his acquisition of library materials during his years in Europe. Although there is no written evidence to suggest exactly when the idea of an official government-sponsored expedition to seek the water communication was translated in Jefferson's mind into the reality of the Lewis and Clark Expedition, his augmented collecting of knowledge on the Northwest was clearly part of that translation.

As early as May, 1800, Jefferson was requesting and receiving intel-

47. Michaux was involved in the "Citizen Genet conspiracy," a plot on the part of the French minister to the United States to foment rebellion among American citizens living in the territories between the Mississippi and the Alleghenies. The enterprise collapsed and Michaux was recalled "to pursue elsewhere the botanical inquiries on which he was employed." See Robert McColley, *Federalists, Republicans, and Foreign Entanglements, 1789–1815* (Englewood Cliffs, N.J., 1969), pp. 21–26.

ligence on the country west of the Mississippi from Americans living along the river or in Louisiana. In that month James Wilkinson, commanding general of the U.S. Army, responded to a request for information by writing that he was sending a letter to Jefferson by way of "P. Nolan, a man who has traveled in Louisiana." Nolan would, said Wilkinson, "feel pride in offering his details of a country, the soil, clime, population, improvements, & production of which are little known to us."[48] Later in the same year, Wilkinson sent Jefferson "a sketch of the further parts of the Mississippi territory" along with certain "modern manuscripts."[49] These manuscripts have never been located, but from the description that Wilkinson gives of them (they were said to have been made by an employee of the Missouri Fur Company on a trip to the Mandans) they quite possibly were Jean Truteau's travel accounts and descriptions of the upper Missouri, later to be made available by Jefferson to Lewis and Clark.

In addition to the information he received from Wilkinson, Jefferson obtained geographical materials from several private citizens in the West. In late May, 1800, Jefferson received a letter from Daniel Clarke of New Orleans offering to send details respecting the Indians west of the Mississippi. Clarke, like Wilkinson, wrote that he intended to send to Washington "an Inhabitant of the western Country . . . with the Idea that you might think it worthwhile to be among the first to acquire particular information of a country now almost unknown to the U.S. tho destined by nature to have at no remote period a close connexion & great intercourse with them."[50] Clarke added that this man had lived with the natives in "the heart of the finest country in the world." (No record of any visit from such an individual has been found.) In July, 1800, Jefferson received a letter from another private citizen who was later to supply a considerable volume of information and to undertake some significant explorations of his own at Jefferson's request. This was William Dunbar of Natchez, who promised to send Jefferson a set of notes that would "go to resolve your inquiries respecting the Mississippi."[51]

During the next year Jefferson corresponded further with Dunbar and Clarke, gaining from them supplemental data on the lands west of the Mississippi. But before receiving any additional knowledge from the West, Jefferson indicated rather firmly his desire to transform into reality his long-standing ambitions to find the water communication. Early in 1801 he wrote to a young Virginian then serving in the U.S. Army. "The appointment to the

48. James Wilkinson to Jefferson, 22 May 1800. Later correspondence from Wilkinson indicates that "P. Nolan" never reached Washington and Jefferson never received his information—whatever it might have been. "P. Nolan" was, of course, Philip Nolan, Wilkinson's accomplice in the western intrigues.
49. The manuscript sketch was not located. Since Wilkinson designated it as being of the Mississippi territory, it is probable that the map included a representation of the country east of the Mississippi.
50. Daniel Clarke to Jefferson, 29 May 1800.
51. William Dunbar to Jefferson, 14 July 1800. The tone of Dunbar's letter indicates that Jefferson had made specific requests for information on the trans-Mississippi region.

68

Presidency of the U.S.," read Jefferson's letter to Meriwether Lewis, "has rendered it necessary for me to have a private secretary. . . . Your knowledge of the Western country . . . has rendered it desireable for public as well as private purposes that you should be engaged in that office."[52] Just what those public and private purposes were cannot be known. But what is known is that nine years earlier Meriwether Lewis had applied to Jefferson for permission to accompany André Michaux on the abortive Missouri expedition.[53]

On March 10, 1801, Lewis responded favorably to Jefferson's invitation and by the next month had joined the President at Monticello. Thus began the close association that spanned more than two years—from April of 1801 until July of 1803, when Lewis left Washington to commence his western explorations. It is possible that in the first few months of his term Jefferson had no thoughts of informing Lewis of his plans for an expedition across the continent and no intention of selecting his private secretary for a position of leadership in such an expedition. But this is unlikely. Lewis spoke often of being in Jefferson's "complete confidence," and the information that the President was gathering on the Northwest must have been available to his aide as well. Furthermore, Lewis is known to have had access to the map and book collections at Monticello and the White House, and it is most probable that this reservoir of data aided him in building an image of the trans-Missouri area which resembled Jefferson's own views of that area. This fact would prove to be highly significant during the years of the expedition that lay just ahead.

II

Events moved rapidly throughout 1801 and 1802. Jefferson continued to receive communications on the Northwest from his correspondents and began the first steps of planning for a transcontinental journey. With Andrew Ellicott, a Pennsylvania surveyor who would later provide Lewis with a brief education in the methods of astronomical observation, the President discussed the best ways to take astronomical measurements with simple equipment that could be "easily carried over a long distance without over-much fatigue."[54] From Robert Patterson, professor of mathematics at the University of Pennsylvania, Jefferson requested and received a "cypher" for use in coding messages. Patterson's directions for a secret code were passed to Meriwether Lewis along with a sample message that read, rather wishfully, perhaps, "I am

52. Jefferson to Meriwether Lewis, 23 Feb. 1801.
53. In his "The Life of Capt. Lewis," written for the first published "official" edition of the journals of the expedition, Jefferson himself mentioned that Lewis had "warmly sollicited" the opportunity of being Michaux's companion (see Jackson, *Letters*, p. 589).
54. Ellicott had made several trips into the Mississippi valley and was well known for his surveys of the Mississippi River, which were published in 1803 (Philadelpha) as *The Journal of Andrew Ellicott*. His correspondence with Jefferson relating to preparations for the Lewis and Clark Expedition during the very first stages is found in the Jefferson Papers.

at the head of the Missouri. All well, and the Indians so far friendly."[55] And as this planning was going on, Jefferson had Lewis at Monticello, preparing an estimate of the expenses "necessary to carry into effort the Missie. expedicion."[56]

While Jefferson and Lewis continued their preparation and speculation, events far removed from Washington took place that would cause the President to remove his planning activities from the realm of theory into the sphere of reality. In November, 1802, Jefferson received word from his correspondents in the West that the Spanish intendant in New Orleans had closed the port there to American shipping,[57] and that the whole of Louisiana had been ceded back to France by Spain.[58] Perhaps feeling that the political climate which resulted from these actions would improve his chances of getting Congress to approve a western expedition, Jefferson determined to include such a proposal in his annual message to the legislature to be delivered in December.[59]

He sent the members of his cabinet a draft of this message sometime in November; although the draft has not survived, some of the responses to it have. Of these, that of Albert Gallatin, the Swiss immigrant who served as Jefferson's secretary of the treasury, was most revealing. Gallatin covered all the points made by Jefferson in the message and suggested minor revisions. But when he came to the "proposal of the Missouri expedition," he suggested that although he felt "warmly interested in this plan," it would best be included in a confidential message since it "contemplates an expedition out of our own territory."[60] Gallatin's advice was followed and the "proposal of the Missouri expedition" became the basis of a confidential message to Congress, January 18, 1803.

12

The ostensible purpose of Jefferson's confidential message of January, 1803, was the establishment of governmental policy on the Indian tribes in

---

55. Jefferson to Robert Patterson, 12 Apr. 1802; Jefferson to Meriwether Lewis, Dec. 1802.

56. "Lewis Meriwether. Missouri Estimate," undated but probably late 1802 (Jefferson Papers).

57. John Vaughn to Jefferson, 8 Nov. 1802.

58. "Notes on the Acquisition of Louisiana by the French" (Jefferson Papers). The notes are not in Jefferson's hand.

59. Jefferson had made a testing, of sorts, of the political opinion about Louisiana and a proposed expedition through it when he asked the Spanish minister to the United States, Carlos Martínez de Yrujo, if the Spanish court "would take it badly, that the Congress decree the formation of a group of travelers, who would form a small caravan and go and explore the course of the Missouri River" (Yrujo to Pedro Cevallos, minister of foreign affairs in the Spanish government; see Jackson, *Letters*, pp. 4–6). Yrujo tried to dissuade the President by asserting that all "examinations and attempts evidently prove there does not exist this passage of the Northwest."

60. Albert Gallatin to Jefferson, 21 Nov. 1802.

the portions of the United States adjacent to the Mississippi.[61] The Indians of the United States' western territories were, Jefferson claimed, "growing more and more uneasy at the constant dimunition of the territory they occupy," and were becoming more dangerous to American settlers in the lands east of the Mississippi. To remedy the situation Jefferson proposed two measures: first, to induce the Indians to "abandon hunting, to apply to the raising of stock, to agriculture and domestic manufacture," and second, to "multiply trading houses among them, & place within their reach those things which will contribute more to their domestic comfort than the possession of extensive but uncultivated wilds."

In view of the "late occurances on the Mississippi," continued the President, the most critical area for the establishment of such trading houses was among the tribes of the Mississippi valley in order that the United States might "present as firm a front on that as on our Eastern border." Extending this purpose a little further, Jefferson indicated that these trading houses could be made much more profitable if they were to draw trade from the areas west of the Mississippi, in particular the area of the Missouri which was "not as well known as is rendered desireable by their connection with the Mississippi and consequently with us." It was known, however, that the Indian tribes of the Missouri were carrying on an extensive traffic with Great Britain "in a high latitude, through an infinite number of portages and lakes, shut up by ice through a long season." Such a traffic could not compete with trade contacts down the Missouri, which traversed "a moderate climate, offering according to the best accounts a continued navigation from its source, and possibly with a single portage from the Western ocean." And here Jefferson came to what was the real purpose of his message to Congress.

The investigation of the possibilities of establishing such long-range trading contacts, extending all the way to the Pacific, might be best carried out by "an intelligent officer with ten or twelve chosen men, fit for the enterprize and willing to undertake it." These men could be taken from the western posts of the U.S. Army, where they could be spared without inconvenience, and they might explore the "whole line, even to the Western ocean." On the journey the party would "have conferences with the natives on the subject of commercial intercourse, get admission from them for our traders as others are admitted, agree on convenient deposits for an interchange of articles." The venture would not take a long time, persisted Jefferson, and it would be only two years at the most before the party could return with the "information required." And as if the reasons he had given were not firm enough to persuade Congress to appropriate the necessary funds, Jefferson added that since other civilized nations had "encountered great expense" by undertaking explorations for "literary purposes," then the United States would seem "to owe to the same object, as well as to its own interest, to

61. Jefferson's message is published in Jackson, *Letters*, pp. 10–14. All citations from Jefferson's message herein are taken from the original manuscript in the Jefferson Papers.

explore this, the only line of easy communication across the continent, and so directly traversing our own part of it."

Not only is this document a masterpice of persuasion but it also is highly revealing of the nature of Jefferson's geographical view of the Northwest—a refinement of the confused and inarticulate general American images of the area. The Missouri, he noted, was navigable to its source. Furthermore, it was a definite possiblity (and, according to the literature to which Jefferson had access, even a probability) that this navigation could be extended to the Pacific with only a single portage. It is evident that the President had studied the geographical lore of the Northwest thoroughly and had extracted from it a proposal to establish the Passage to India. A "Corps of Discovery" could proceed up the Missouri until they located a portage over a height-of-land. From here they would pass over a divide into the navigable waters of westward-flowing streams and then down to the Pacific. The idea was a simple one and all of Jefferson's geographical information-gathering, from his boyhood to 1803, reinforced the concept. The Missouri, a short portage, and a great river flowing to the Pacific formed "the only line of easy communication across the continent."

The case was well put before Congress, and on February 28, 1803, that body approved the proposal and appropriated a sum of $2,500 for the purpose of "extending the external commerce of the U.S."[62] From the American images of the Northwest and the refinement of those images there had emerged a means of clarifying the Northwestern Mystery, and the "Corps of Discovery of the Army of the United States from the mouth of the River Missouri through the interior parts of North America to the Pacific ocean" was now an official reality.

62. U.S. Congress, *Annals of the 7th–9th Congresses*, XII (1827), 103. It should not be supposed that the figure of $2,500 was the total cost of the expedition. Jackson (*Letters*, pp. 419–31) presents the complete financial records and suggests (p. 431, n. 25) a closer figure would be $38,722.25, which "can be augmented or diminished, depending on how we set the limits of the undertaking."

CHAPTER 3

PREPARING THE ATTEMPT
ON THE PASSAGE

During the months between congressional approval of Jefferson's proposal for the expedition to seek the "only easy line of communication across the continent" and July, 1803, when Lewis left Washington on the first leg of his journey to the Pacific, a great deal of planning and preparation was undertaken.[1] Jefferson and his secretary of the treasury, Albert Gallatin, engaged in involved discussion of western geography and assembled the best available cartographic data on the trans-Missouri area in the hope that they could furnish Lewis with the most accurate and detailed information on the Northwest prior to his departure. Lewis himself was busily gathering geographic and cartographic material, and although little is known about his operations in Washington during these months, it must be assumed that he and the President talked at great length about the nature of the country west of the Mississippi and the possible character of the speculative passage to Pacific

---

1. The extensive planning of the Lewis and Clark Expedition was perhaps the chief reason for its spectacular achievements. The planning included many more facets than those discussed in this chapter, but the purpose here is to provide insights into the nature of the preparations as they reflected the acquisition and interpretation of geographical knowledge. For a detailed look at the planning period, see Jackson, *Letters*, pp. 1–106.

waters. In addition to his virtually unknown activities in Washington, Lewis spent a brief period of time in Philadelphia and Lancaster, Pennsylvania, taking what amounted to "crash courses" in scientific methodology.[2] And finally, as befitted the man who would assume the tasks involved in commanding a military detachment in the field, Lewis occupied himself with many of the logistical details of the coming expedition.[3]

2

Of all the preparatory activity, perhaps no single phase of endeavor was quite so important as the assimilation of the most precise and up-to-date maps of the American Northwest then available. A good illustration of the efforts to provide Lewis with cartographic information of the highest possible caliber may be seen in a letter written by Gallatin to Jefferson near the middle of March, 1803:

> I have requested Mr. King[4] to project a blank map to extend from 88° to 126° West longitude from Greenwich & from 30° to 55° north latitude; which will give us the whole course of the Mississippi and the whole coast of the Pacific ocean within the same latitudes together with a sufficient space to the North to include all the head waters of the Port Nelson River. In this I intend to insert the course of the Mississippi as high up as the Ohio from Ellicot's,[5] the coast of the Pacific from Cook & Vancouver, the north bend of the Missouri & such other of its waters as are there delineated from the three maps of Arrowsmith & from that of Mackenzie, and the Rio Norte and other parts of the Missoury from Danville and Delisle. The most difficult point to ascertain is the latitude of the sources of the Rio Norte; and it is important, in order to know whether there would be any danger in following a more southerly branch of the Missouri than that delineated in Mackenzie's & the manuscript transcribed from Mr. Thornton's map by Cap. Lewis. I mention this because you may have some book at Monticello, which might throw some light on that subject or at least on the latitude & longitude of Santa Fe.[6]

To this letter Jefferson, who was then at Monticello, replied:

2. Paul Russell Cutright, *Lewis and Clark: Pioneering Naturalists* (Urbana, Ill., 1969), pp. 19–29.

3. Jackson, *Letters*, pp. 37–40, 51–53, and particularly 69–99.

4. Nicholas King was a Philadelphia cartographer who had moved to the United States from England in 1796. He had served as the surveyor of the city of Washington and as such had considerable contacts with both Jefferson and Gallatin. He was the author of several important American maps, including Clark's map drawn during the first winter of the expedition's journey to the Pacific and the first major cartographic contribution of the Lewis and Clark Expedition.

5. This is probably a reference to a map that Andrew Ellicott sent Jefferson during the summer of 1801. The map showed the area surveyed by Ellicott during his travels on the Mississippi in the years 1796–1800 and was published in his *Journals*.

6. Albert Gallatin to Jefferson, 14 Mar. 1803.

I do not find in my library any thing which can throw light on the geography of the Rio Norte. I do not believe that in modern times any thing has been added to the information given as to that river in early times. Of this information Mitchell[7] had the benefit. his map was made under public patronage & with all the information that could procure him. that it was made with great care we know from what is laid down in those Western parts with which we have lately become accustomed.[8] certainly his map we find much nearer the truth than could have been expected considering when it was made. hence I conclude that his delineation of the Rio Norte is more to be credited than any other, not excepting Danville & Delisle.[9]

This exchange between Gallatin and Jefferson is very significant for several reasons. It shows, for example, that on at least one occasion (and probably others) Lewis was engaged in assisting in the gathering of data on the Northwest by "transcribing" information from manuscripts or published materials. It also shows that there was a definite awareness on Gallatin's part of the scope of Jefferson's collection of lore on western America. There were few individuals in the country to whom Gallatin could have written requesting information who could even have understood the letter, let alone have any sources from which to construct a reply. In addition, the correspondence provides a good insight into the types of cartographic documents available, and which of this material was considered by the best geographical thinkers of the time to be the most accurate.

But above all, the Jefferson-Gallatin letters of March, 1803, show that Gallatin was gathering cartographic materials to construct a base map of the Northwest, and that Jefferson—with the exception of his point about Mitchell's map as the best for detail on the sources of the Rio Grande—seemed to be satisfied with Gallatin's selections. Had the President disagreed with Gallatin's choices he certainly would have so indicated in his correspondence with his cabinet officer. Quite probably, then, the base map by King, utilizing the various maps mentioned by Gallatin, was as close as any map of the time to one that Jefferson himself might have drawn to illustrate his view of the trans-Missouri region.[10] Therefore it is necessary to examine closely the proposed sources for King's base map; for the image of the Northwest held by Thomas Jefferson was essentially the image transmitted to Meriwether

7. Dr. John Mitchell, a British historian and cartographer, produced maps which were quite popular during the middle and later parts of the eighteenth century.

8. A possible reference to the surveys of the interior made by Ellicott and by Thomas Hutchins, the official geographer of the United States. Hutchins made surveys in the country north and west of the Ohio River in the years immediately after the Revolution, and his accounts were published as *A Topographical Description of Louisiana and Western Florida* (London, 1795). This work went beyond the materials that Hutchins had gathered during his official explorations.

9. Jefferson to Albert Gallatin, 20 Mar. 1803.

10. This is not to suggest that Jefferson ever did draw a map of the Northwest, either for Lewis's use or after the expedition. Given his interest in both cartography and western geography, it is rather curious that he never attempted to do so.

Lewis and the image that conditioned the beginning stages of the Lewis and Clark Expedition.

3

The first three sets of maps mentioned by Gallatin were Andrew Ellicott's map of the Mississippi valley and the maps accompanying James Cook's and George Vancouver's journals of their explorations in the Pacific Northwest. These maps were less important than some of the other cartographic sources alluded to by the Secretary but they did, nevertheless, present geographical data basic to the total view of the American Northwest at the time of Lewis and Clark.

The Ellicott map was almost positively the one published in his journals late in 1803 and probably seen by Gallatin prior to publication in the form of a manuscript copy which the Pennsylvania surveyor had sent to Jefferson earlier.[11] This map (fig. 15) was the most accurate rendition to date of the Mississippi River between the Gulf of Mexico and the Great Lakes. Although it contained little information of a highly critical or informative nature on the geography of the trans-Missouri region, it did illustrate accurately the drainage configurations of the area about the confluence of the Missouri and Mississippi and located the mouth of the Missouri more precisely than any other contemporary map.

The Cook and Vancouver maps,[12] although they provided more-than-adequate detail on the area that would serve as the terminal point of the Lewis and Clark Expedition, were of questionable value to the development of a broader view of the Northwest. Except for the representation of the lower part of the Columbia and some data on the coastal ranges on the Vancouver charts, neither set of maps made attempts to outline geographical features of the country between the Pacific coast and the interior. The Vancouver surveys, published with his *Voyage of Discovery to the North Pacific Ocean*,[13] were much more detailed than Cook's charts, made years earlier. Vancouver did place the mouth of the Columbia in the correct location and displayed, together with the course of the river to Lieutenant Broughton's farthest inland penetration, remarkably exact locational data on the major peaks of the Cascade and Olympic ranges, which were visible from the sea or the lower Columbia. The Vancouver charts were the best available on the Pacific Northwest and served as the base material for many later maps of that region.

11. See n. 5 above.
12. Gallatin had long been aware of the value of Vancouver's surveys in particular. When he responded to Jefferson's draft of his annual message to Congress in late 1802, he suggested that Jefferson immediately purchase a set of "Vancouver's Survey, one copy of which, the only one I believe in America, is advertised by F. Nichols No. 70 Chestnut St. Philadelphia. Price with all the charts 55 dollars."
13. Vancouver, *A Voyage of Discovery*, pls. 3, 5, 14.

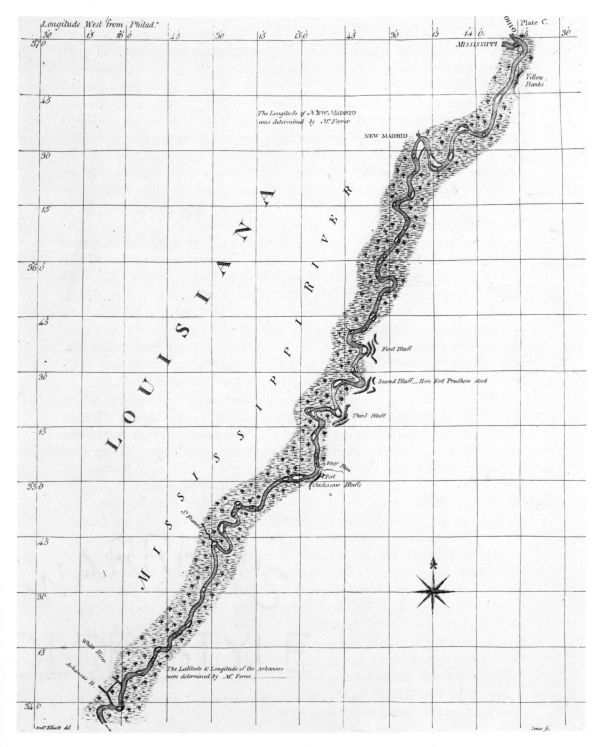

15. Detail from Andrew Ellicott's map of the Mississippi. From *The Journal of Andrew Ellicott* (Philadelphia, 1803)   LIBRARY OF CONGRESS

Of much greater importance to the determination of the geography of the interior than the above-mentioned charts was the group of maps that Gallatin called "the three maps of Arrowsmith." Aaron Arrowsmith was the most distinguished (and by far the most reliable) cartographer of his day and had produced many maps of North America that were available in the United States, either as separate sheets or as smaller versions included in many of the published works on North American geography.[14] Although it cannot be definitely known just which of Arrowsmith's many maps Gallatin was referring to, it is most likely that at least two of them were the widely circulated 1795 and 1802 editions of the British cartographer's large map of North America.

Arrowsmith's 1795 map of North America,[15] showing "all the new discoveries in the Interior Parts," is interesting for its reflection of the striking lack of knowledge of the Northwest below the 50th parallel. The map showed the discoveries made by Samuel Hearne along the Arctic shores, included the areas mapped by Peter Fidler, and detailed Mackenzie's 1789 trek down the river that bears his name to the Arctic Ocean. It did not depict Mackenzie's journey to the Pacific nor his crossing of the Canadian Rockies, although the Saskatchewan River system was reported faithfully and Peter Fidler's travels to the Canadian Rockies in 1791 and 1792 were noted.

The most relevant section on the Arrowsmith 1795 map was that which dealt with the region of the upper Missouri in the vicinity of the Mandan villages. At one point on the map, along the Assiniboine River, a dotted line was shown leading to the southwest and connecting with the Missouri near its northernmost bend. This line carried the legend "12 Hours Journey on Horse Back," apparently a misreading or misunderstanding of the legend on one of Peter Pond's maps which described the Mandans who lived on "one of the branches" of the Missouri and who were said to "bring to our factory at Fort Epinett on the Assinipoil River Indian Corn for Sale. Our People go to them with loaded Horses in twelve days." It was ostensibly this type of information that induced Gallatin to query Jefferson about the distance of the southern branches of the Missouri from the sources of the Rio Grande. It must be kept in mind that the Northwest was not yet American territory when Gallatin was making his selections of data, and he was probably concerned about the government's dispatching Lewis into an area along a river that was purportedly only twelve hours by horse from British trading establishments and was, at the same time, perhaps dangerously near to the source region of the Rio Grande in the Spanish-held territory, guarded more jealously than other colonial possessions.

14. Jedediah Morse, the foremost American geographer, consistently relied on Arrowsmith's maps to illustrate his own works.
15. See fig. 9 above.

The Arrowsmith 1795 map was also of interest by virtue of the fact that its author did not link the Missouri either to the "Stony Mountains" shown to the west or to the Mississippi on the east. The Missouri was represented simply as a fragment of a stream upon which the Mandans' villages were located. West of this fragmentary Missouri there appeared the range labeled as the "Stony Mountains," with a legend inscribed along their western side which read "3520 Feet High above the Level of their Base and according to the Indian account is five Ridges in some parts." This information was based on Peter Fidler's reports, available to Arrowsmith through the cooperation of the Hudson's Bay Company. Also from the Fidler data came the names Arrowsmith applied to some of the peaks of the interior range. The naming of the peaks, however, was of less immediate value than the fact that the Arrowsmith map added to contemporary geographical lore the suggestion that the Rockies were something other than a narrow, single ridge of mountains.

The greater part of the map below the 50th parallel was virtually blank. There was, however, a vestigial Great River of the West on the western side of the mountains. The "Great Lake R." had its source southwest of the Saskatchewan and flowed from thence to the Pacific, and although its full course to the sea was not indicated, the implication was that it flowed into the Columbia. The Columbia, or "River Oregan," was laid down, as was the Pacific coast, after the Vancouver charts, and the course of the Columbia was shown inland as far as Point Vancouver. The remaining details of the coastal regions were also adapted from the Vancouver surveys.

A second Arrowsmith map, a revision of the 1795 map of North America published in 1802, was also quite probably familiar to Gallatin and was even more crucial than the earlier version. Arrowsmith's 1802 map contained more recent and more accurate information on the Northwest, was the single most important item of cartographic data available to Jefferson and Lewis, and played an important role during the course of the expedition itself.[16] It is known that by the time Gallatin wrote his letter discussing source materials for a base map, Jefferson had already obtained a copy of the Arrowsmith 1802 map[17] and seemingly considered it important enough to later order a copy for Lewis's use in the field.[18]

The Arrowsmith 1802 map (fig. 16) was essentially a copy of the 1795 map but with several momentous supplemental details, particularly in the upper Missouri region. Rather than appearing as an isolated fragment of a

16. During the summer of 1805, when the expedition encountered the Marias River and became geographically confused as to whether the Marias or the Missouri was the proper route to Columbian waters, the information on the Arrowsmith map, as corrected in the field by Lewis and Clark, was instrumental in determining the correct course of exploration.

17. Louis Pinchon, the French minister to the United States, reported to his superiors that when Jefferson, soon after gaining congressional approval for the expedition, applied to him for a French passport for Lewis's protection, he explained the purpose of the expedition on the Arrowsmith 1802 map. This is evidence that Jefferson had a copy of the map as early as March 2, 1803 (Jackson, *Letters*, pp. 22–23).

18. Around the middle of June, 1803, Jefferson ordered another copy of the Arrowsmith map from James Cheetham (Jackson, *Letters*, pp. 55–56).

16. Detail from Aaron Arrowsmith's 1802 map of North America   LIBRARY OF CONGRESS

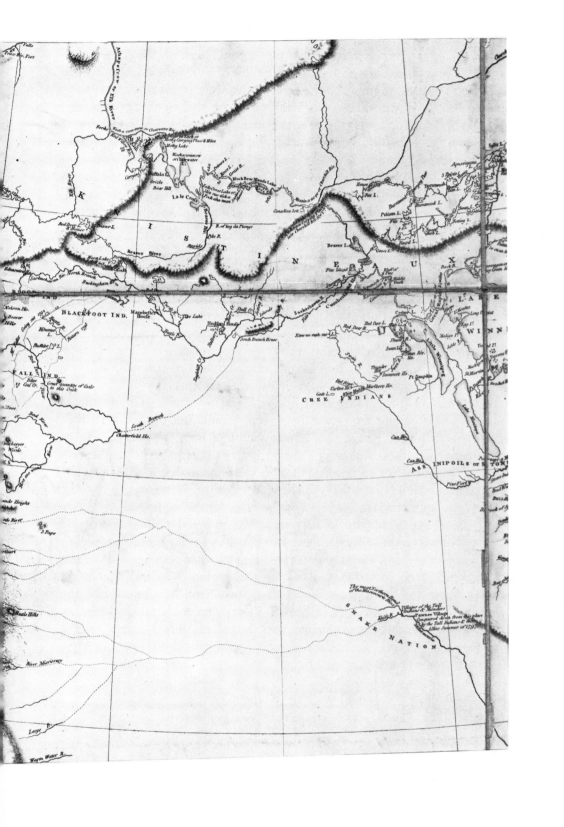

river as it did on the earlier map, the Missouri of the 1802 version connected with the Mississippi in approximately the correct location. St. Louis was, inexplicably, not shown on the map, but the ruins of Fort Orleans, built by the French adventurer Bourgmont in the early 1700s, were located by the cartographer along the lower Missouri. The course of the river, between the Mississippi and the mouth of the Kansas River, was outlined in considerable detail, although the course upstream from the Kansas to the Mandan villages was very highly generalized, indicating that Arrowsmith had no access to the cartographic results of the explorations of the Spanish-sponsored St. Louis fur trade during the last years of the eighteenth century.

By far the most notable section of the 1802 Arrowsmith production (at least for Gallatin's and Jefferson's purposes) was that which depicted the course of the Missouri from the Mandan villages to the mountains. Above the Mandan villages (shown on the map as the "Villages of the Tall Indians & Manders") the drainage system of the Missouri was rather elaborately drawn, most of the details being assimilated once again from Peter Fidler's reports in the archives of the Hudson's Bay Company. The cartographer represented the upper Missouri watershed as a huge fan or triangle with its broad base lying against the Rocky Mountains. From the mountains a number of rivers flowed east—a configuration duplicating that shown on a map drawn by Fidler[19]—and then joined to form two major rivers that came together to create the Missouri proper just west of the Mandan villages. The northernmost of these two major rivers was not given a name, but the southern fork was labeled "Knife R." near the Mandans and "River Mississury"[20] at its source in the mountains almost due west from the villages. The implication was clear that the major river, the Missouri proper, ran almost a direct west-to-east course from its headwaters to the villages of the Mandan nation.

Near the southernmost branches of this river which seemed to symbolize the real Missouri appeared the notation that "Hereabout the Mountains divide into several low ridges."[21] In the same neighborhood the headsprings region of the Rio Grande and Colorado rivers was indicated. Although no rivers were shown flowing into the Pacific from this region, a logical conclusion could be drawn by someone well versed in theoretical geography and the concept of the pyramidal height-of-land: by following the southern branches of the Missouri system, an exploring party might possibly locate a critical source region of several "low ridges" which would provide an easy access to the southern waters of the "River Oregan" and thence to the Pacific.[22]

19. See fig. 6 above.
20. This usage or that of "Missesourie" was a common convention in both maps and textual materials during the late eighteenth and early nineteenth centuries.
21. There are a number of sources from which Arrowsmith could have derived such information. The most likely was the Fidler data in the Hudson's Bay archives; the same type of information could also have been interpreted from the works of Mackenzie and (if accessible) David Thompson.
22. In the same area would also be found the headsprings of the rivers of New Mexico, the Rio Grande, and the Rio Colorado. The pyramidal height-of-land concept had originally

The 1802 map, like its predecessor, was virtually blank on the western side of the Rockies. The track of Mackenzie to the Pacific was drawn on the map, however, along with his "Tacoutche-Tesse River," which flowed south as a dotted line on the map and entered the "River Oregan" at Point Vancouver. To the east of this junction Arrowsmith placed Mt. Rainer, Mt. St. Helens, and Mt. Hood, derived from the Vancouver materials. The Great Lake River was once again depicted, but this time was definitely represented as a tributary of the Tacoutche-Tesse. A further addition was the inclusion of a legend along the course of the Great Lake River between its source in the mountains and its entry into the Columbia to the effect that "the Indians say they sleep 8 Nights in descending this River to the Sea." The country through which Great Lake River flowed was, according to another legend, "Open Country." The Great Lake River headed with the Saskatchewan and not the Missouri, but Arrowsmith's map added fuel to the theoretical fire of belief about the possible connections between the waters that ran east and those that ran west.

5

The Mackenzie map mentioned by Gallatin must have been the large map of western North America that appeared in the British explorer's *Voyages from Montreal*[23] and was, because of the obvious analogies between the exploratory experiences of Mackenzie and those hoped-for discoveries by way of the Missouri, one of the most important source materials in the geographical lore of the time. The Mackenzie map (fig. 17) concentrated on the line of his two journeys, and, although encompassing the area between the 40th and 70th parallels, it showed little detail south of the Saskatchewan system. The Missouri was extended only a short distance beyond the Mandan villages and there was no indication of the connections between the Missouri and the westward-flowing streams beyond the mountains.

The implications that might have been drawn from the map are important, even though few specifics on the American Northwest were provided on Mackenzie's chart. The map showed a very short portage between the navigable waters of eastward-flowing streams (the Peace River) and the navigable waters of a large Pacific-slope river. The large river that Mackenzie had found west of the Continental Divide was the Fraser, named for Simon Fraser, who followed it to the Pacific in 1807. But at the time Gallatin and

---

been applied to an area farther north and more toward the center of the continent. But now the theory was being used to define the drainage configuration of western North America rather than the continent as a whole (John L. Allen, "Pyramidal Height-of-Land: A Persistent Myth in the Exploration of Western Anglo-America," *International Geography 1972*, I, 395–96).

23. Alexander Mackenzie, *Voyages from Montreal through the Continent of North America to the Frozen and Pacific Oceans in 1789 and 1793* (London, 1801).

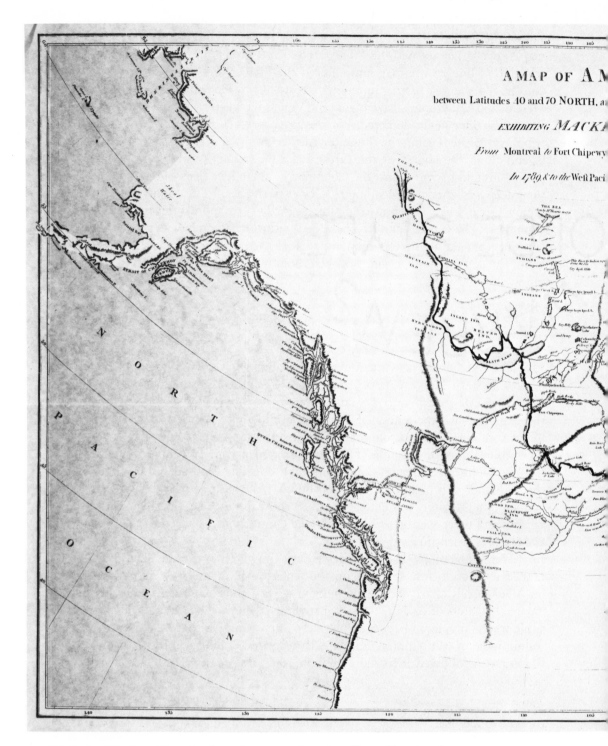

17. Alexander Mackenzie's map of northwestern America. From *Voyages from Montreal* (London, 1801)   LIBRARY OF CONGRESS

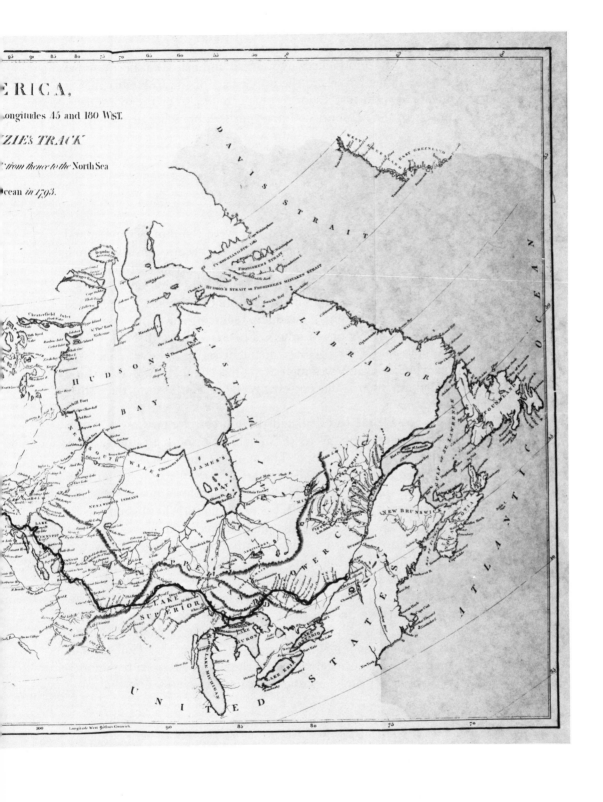

Jefferson were discussing western geography they, along with Mackenzie and nearly every other contemporary geographer, assumed it was the Columbia or "Tacoutche-Tesse" of Mackenzie's journals and map. If a short portage existed between the Peace River and the upper part of the Columbia then it was not too much to expect that a short portage could also be found connecting the headwaters of the Missouri with the southern branches of the "River Oregan."

6

The next group of maps cited by Gallatin were those of "Danville and Delisle." This was an obvious reference to the eighteenth-century French cartographers Jean d'Anville and Guillaume Delisle, authors of numerous maps of North America published in various atlases between 1703 and 1780. As was the case with the Arrowsmith maps, it cannot be definitely established which of the French cartographers' products Gallatin had in his possession or had examined in the collections of others. The exact dates of the d'Anville and Delisle maps are not as important as it might seem, however, since the critical areas in which Gallatin was interested—the connections between the Rio Grande and the Missouri—did not change significantly from the earlier to the later French maps.

As early as 1703 Delisle had depicted the sources of the Rio del Norte or Rio Grande as being very far to the north, just south of the farthest western tributaries of the Mississippi. The most popular Delisle map and presumably the one enumerated by Gallatin was the 1718 "Carte de la Louisiane et du Cours du Mississipi" (fig. 18). On this map the Missouri was variously labeled along its course as "le Missouri R." near its mouth, "le Missouri ou R. de Pekitanoni" near where the Platte should have been but wasn't, and "le Missouri R. ou Riv. Large" near its source.[24] Adjacent to the western waters of the Missouri and slightly to the south Delisle drew the sources of the Rio del Norte, beneath which appeared the legend that the Spanish forded the Missouri on horseback while going to trade with gold-mining Indians.[25] This information, combined with that on the 1795 Arrowsmith map to the effect that the upper Missouri was only twelve hours by horseback from the Assiniboine, should have been enough to reinforce any notions that Gallatin and Jefferson had relative to the critical nature of the upper Missouri region as a common source area for many important streams. The area was the theo-

24. The "Riv. Large" may have been a holdover from the "Rivière Longue" of Lahontan's narratives. Lahontan's descriptions were reflected in many of the contemporary cartographic productions and the works of Delisle were no exception.

25. This was probably a misinterpretation of the rumors prevalent in the early years of French occupation of Louisiana about the fords across the Platte River. At this time the Platte and the Missouri were often confused as being the same stream.

retical height-of-land and it was a crossroads for prospective transcontinental trade.[26]

The d'Anville map that Gallatin had seen was probably the "Carte de la Louisiane," which was included in various editions of d'Anville's *Atlas Generale* between 1737 and 1780. Nearly all of the versions of this map showed essentially the same relationship between the sources of the Rio Grande and the southern waters of the Missouri as had the charts of Delisle. The concept was firm in the contemporary lore and was consistent with the long-standing geographical concepts of the Spanish in Louisiana, who had for years assumed and feared that the Missouri would provide in its upper reaches a route to New Mexico via the northernmost portions of the Rio Grande.[27]

7

Identification of the final map mentioned by Gallatin, the one described as having been transcribed in manuscript form by Lewis, is more tentative than any of the others. Some scholars have suggested that the map "transcribed from Mr. Thornton's map" referred to a copy that Lewis might have made of a map of Louisiana in the English geographer John Thornton's *Atlas Maritimus* of 1703.[28] This Thornton map was practically a facsimile of an earlier (1701) map of Louisiana by the cartographer Hermann Moll and contained so many questionable features and so much conjuctural geography that it is difficult indeed to conclude that either Jefferson or Gallatin could have placed much faith in it. Nor has any trace of such a map copied by Lewis been located.

It is far more likely that Gallatin was describing a map of the Great Bend of the Missouri River near the Mandan villages, drawn either by David Thompson of the Northwest Company following his journeys to the Mandans in the late eighteenth century or by someone who had access to Thompson's surveys. A copy of this map might well have been in the possession of Edward Thornton, British chargé d'affaires in Washington in the early 1800s, and might have been copied by Meriwether Lewis.[29] There is a good deal of

26. It was also more or less an international "no-man's land" due to conflicting territorial claims regarding the rights to the drainage basins of certain streams. In light of this Jefferson requested, and received, passports for Lewis from both English and French (legal possessors of Louisiana although Spanish authorities were still in actual control) officials in Washington (Jackson, *Letters*, pp. 19–20).

27. Many of the documents printed in Nasatir, *Before Lewis and Clark*, show that Spanish fears were not stilled by the increases in geographical knowledge during the late 1700s. A great deal of official correspondence between St. Louis, New Orleans, and Madrid concerned itself with the threat presented to Spanish possessions in the Southwest by the party led by "Mr. Merry, Captain of the United States Armey." "Mr. Merry" is elsewhere referred to as "Merry Weather Lewis."

28. Jackson, *Letters*, p. 28.

29. Jackson offers the suggestion that the Mr. Thornton of Gallatin's letter might have been Edward Thornton but concludes that it is more likely that the reference was to John Thornton (*Letters*, p. 28, n. 5). I cannot agree with this conclusion.

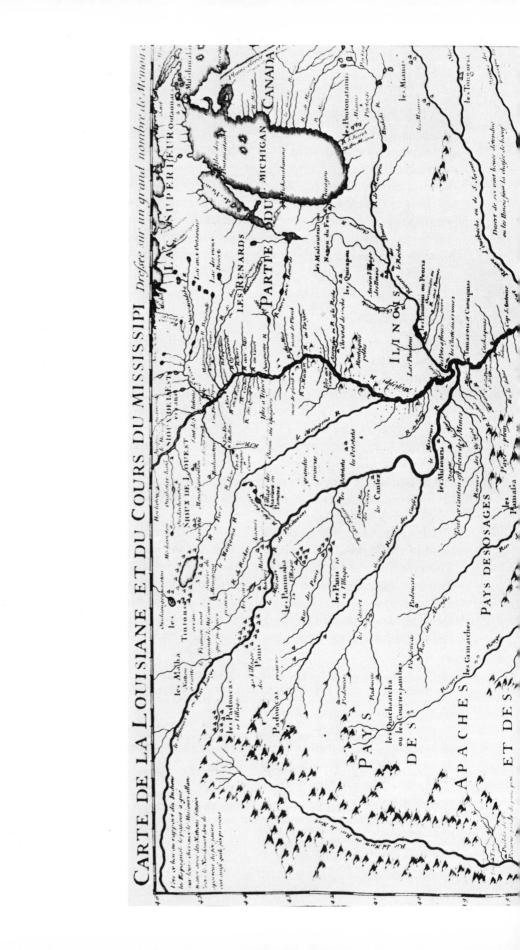

CARTE DE LA LOUISIANE ET DU COURS DU MISSISSIPI Dressée sur un grand nombre de Memoires e...

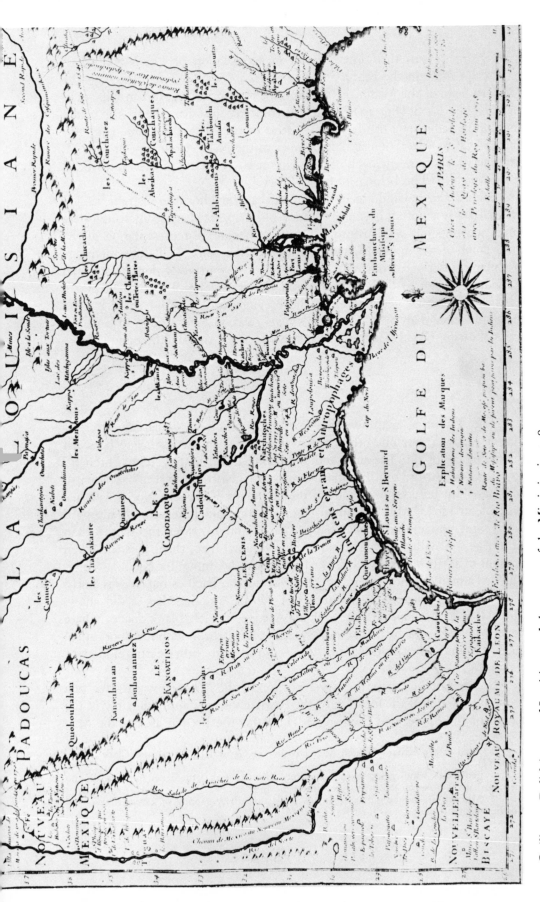

18. Guillaume Delisle's map of Louisiana and the course of the Mississippi, 1718
COURTESY, AMERICAN GEOGRAPHICAL SOCIETY OF NEW YORK

evidence to suggest this. There exists, in a collection of Lewis and Clark manuscript maps in the Library of Congress, a copy of a map showing the northern bend of the Missouri River and the location of the Indian villages in that neighborhood (fig. 19).[30] On the front of this map there is a pencil notation in Jefferson's handwriting: "Bend of the Missouri. Long. 101° 25'. Lat. 47° 32' by Mr. Thomson astronomer to the N.W. Company in 1798."[31] Another notation on the back of the map reads "A sketch of the North Bend of the Missouri. This belongs to Capn. Lewis."

Such evidence would seem to suggest that the Thornton map mentioned by Gallatin was not an obscure, century-old map based on Munchausen-like travel accounts but was, instead, a recent and accurate representation of the focal point of the upper Missouri region. Furthermore, Gallatin's reference to a map transcribed from "Mr. Thornton" is suggestive of contact with an individual known to both Jefferson and Gallatin and still living, and not a relatively unknown geographer of the previous century. But there is even firmer evidence that "Mr. Thornton's map" was, in fact, a copy of a manuscript showing David Thompson's surveys of 1798; this will be cited later.

8

The Thornton map was the last enumeration in Gallatin's letter of March 14, 1803, but one other map was included in the exchange between the Secretary of the Treasury and Jefferson. This was Dr. John Mitchell's 1755 map of "British and French Dominions in North America," apparently considered by Jefferson to be one of the best maps of western North America available in 1803.[32] Mitchell's map (fig. 20) was, said Jefferson, "Made with great care" and must be accepted as being "much nearer the truth" than either the d'Anville or Delisle maps. The Mitchell map, then, must be taken account of as the final source for the base map to be drawn by Nicholas King. Mitchell's map did not extend all the way to the Pacific, but it was fairly accurate in representing that portion of North America that it did show. Mitchell at least admitted a lack of knowledge and left blank spaces where no information was available rather than filling them in with apocryphal inland seas and other mythical features as did so many other cartographers of his time.

On the Mitchell map, the lower portion of the Missouri was drawn as a great river, and near the location of the Pawnee villages, approximately at the mouth of the Platte, was the legend "Thus far the French ascend the Mis-

30. Filed in the Geography and Map Division as G3701.M53, Lewis and Clark Manuscripts (J).
31. Jefferson's handwriting is so completely distinctive that there can be virtually no question that the notes on the map were written by him.
32. Mitchell's map was published in his book, *The Present State of Great Britain and North America* (London, 1755), p. 254.

souri." The upper Missouri area bore the legend "Missouri river is reckoned to run Westward to the Mountains of New Mexico, as far as the Ohio does Eastward." This notion was based on the logic of theoretical symmetrical geography and brings to mind the works of Daniel Coxe and the "grand scheme" of the Loyal Land Company of Jefferson's youth. Of the lands west of the Missouri's source in the mountains, Mitchell said only that they were "not well known." He thus showed no connections between the Atlantic and Pacific drainages—but once again inferences could be drawn. The drainage patterns of the eastern and western sides of the Mississippi basin were similar. This must have been of great interest to Jefferson and Gallatin, who were even then thinking of cutting canals across the height-of-land between the upper Potomac and the sources of the Ohio.[33] Might the same be possible between the Missouri and the "River Oregan"?

9

Beyond his probable acquisition of the map from Edward Thornton, little can be said of Lewis's part in the preparation activities in Washington—although he must have been quite busy. But about a month after the exchange about cartographic sources had taken place between Jefferson and Gallatin, Lewis left the capital for Pennsylvania to learn some practical field techniques for scientific method and observation.[34] In addition to the highly useful, albeit brief, exposure to natural history, mathematics, and rudimentary field medicine that he received in Philadelphia and the helpful hints for determining latitude and longitude that he picked up in Lancaster, Lewis managed to gather some valuable geographic and cartographic information.[35]

Among the items of geographical lore obtained in Philadelphia was a copy of *History of Louisiana* by Du Pratz, one of the French chroniclers upon whom Jefferson himself relied heavily for his own understanding of Louisiana. Lewis was given the book by Benjamin Smith Barton, professor of botany at the University of Pennsylvania and one of the men from whom the future explorer received his invaluable training while in Philadelphia. The *History of Louisiana* was carried with the expedition and was cited in several places

33. Such a possibility had occurred to Jefferson as early as 1784 when he wrote, "I think the opening of this navigation an object on which no time be lost" (Boyd, *Papers*, VI, 548).

34. In February and March Jefferson wrote to several members of the American Philosophical Society, indicating that Congress had approved a transcontinental expedition. He related that he had appointed "Capt. Lewis, my secretary, to conduct it," and that it would be greatly appreciated if the members of the society would assist in training Lewis. Those to whom Jefferson wrote included Benjamin Smith Barton, Caspar Wistar, Benjamin Rush, Andrew Ellicott, and Robert Patterson (Jackson, *Letters*, pp. 16–19, 21; also Cutright, *Lewis and Clark*, pp. 19–20).

35. Lewis's training in surveying and astronomy was carried out under the tutelage of Andrew Ellicott and Robert Patterson, an Irish-born mathematician. Advice on how to keep the members of his command healthy was received from Dr. Rush, training in natural history from Dr. Barton, and a brief introduction to paleontology from Dr. Wistar. Jackson reprints various items relating to this training period.

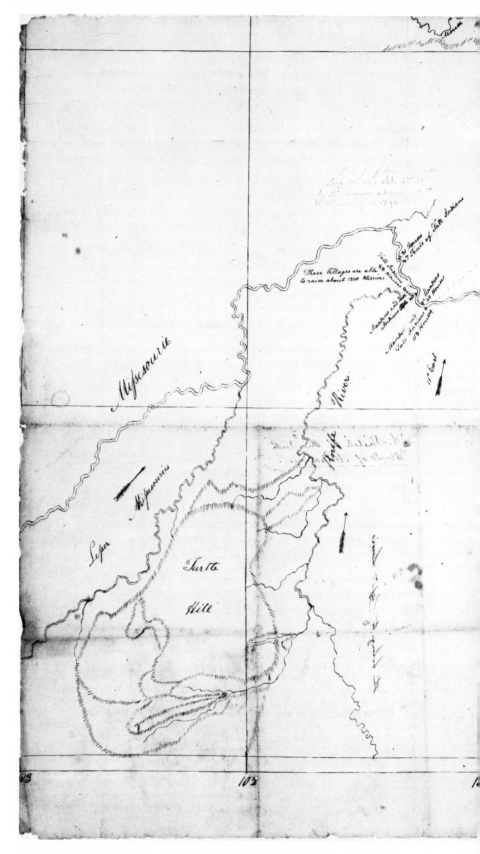

19. A copy of David Thompson's map of the Great Bend of the Missouri

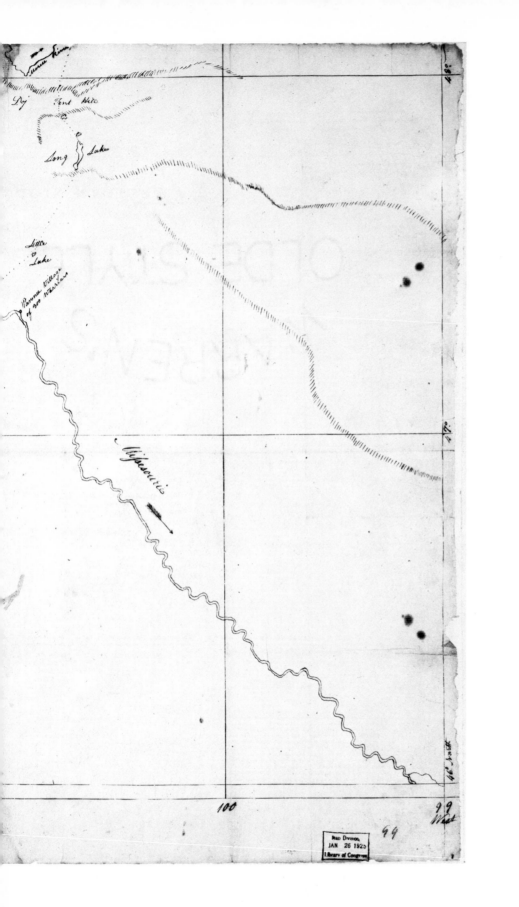

Laurens River

Dog

Fort White

Long Lake

Little Lake

Pawnee Village
of 200 Warriors

Missouri

47°

46° South

100

99
West

44

20. A section of John Mitchell's map of British possessions in North America. From *The Present State of Great Britain and North America* (London, 1755)   UNITED STATES GEOLOGICAL SURVEY

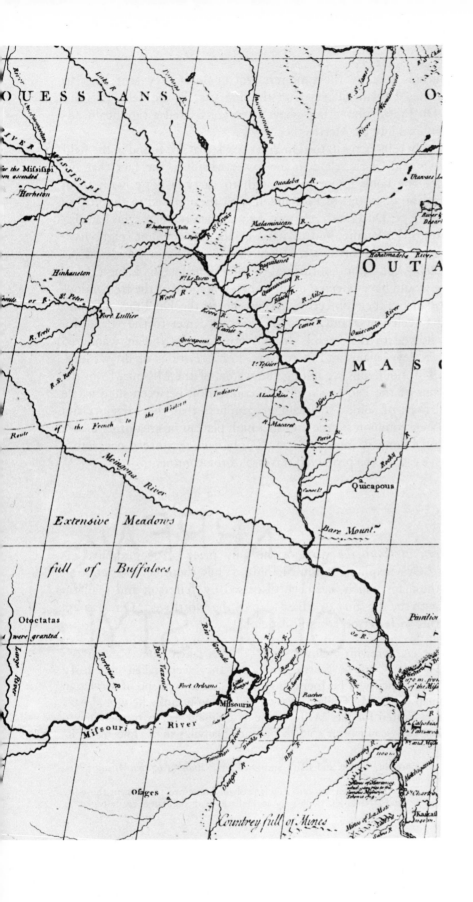

in the field journals kept by the explorers and in notes they sent back to Jefferson from the Mandan villages after the first year in the field. It is obvious that the Du Pratz volume must have been considered a significant adjunct to geographical lore by Meriwether Lewis.[36]

While the only references to the Du Pratz work that are found in the field journals of Lewis and Clark relate to the lower Missouri, the fact that the captains thought the book important enough to carry a copy with them raises the fascinating questions of how much faith they placed in the bizarre tale of Moncacht-Apé, Du Pratz's relation of the Indian traveler who had discovered a route to the Pacific, and to what extent this account might have shaped their views of the Northwest. While they could have considered the story of Moncacht-Apé's transcontinental journey fictitious, it is highly unlikely that they would have rejected it out of hand, because of the tremendous implications it had for their objective. According to the Du Pratz account, the Indian had traveled overland from the Missouri River to the "Beautiful River" which flowed to the Pacific. In this crossing the Indian wandered through open and level plains and there were, in his relations of his wandering, no mention of mountains separating the waters of the Missouri from the rivers and streams of the Pacific slope. The connection between such a tale and the speculations of some American geographers that the Missouri and Columbia had their common source area in a high plateau or area of extensive plains rather than a range of mountains could only have reinforced conjecture about the relative ease of the projected traverse of the continent.

10

The *History of Louisiana* was not the only piece of geographical information that Lewis acquired in Philadelphia. While there he also acted on the matter of the maps which had been discussed by Jefferson and Gallatin in connection with the drawing of a base map of the Northwest. On May 29, 1803, Lewis wrote to Jefferson from Philadelphia:

You will receive herewith inclosed some sketches taken from Vancouver's survey of the Western Coast of North America;[37] they were taken in a hasty manner, but I believe they will be found sufficiently accurate to be of service in composing the map which Mr. Gallatin was so good as to promise he would have projected and compleated for me. Will you be so obliging Sir, as to mention to Mr. Gallatin, that I have not been able to procure Danvill's map. The maps at-

---

36. Paul Russell Cutright, "Lewis and Clark and Du Pratz," *Bulletin of the Missouri Historical Society*, XXI (1964), 31–35.

37. These sketches have not been located. Lewis probably obtained them from the copy of Vancouver's surveys at F. Nichols's bookshop as Gallatin had suggested to Jefferson in November, 1802.

tached to Vancouver's voyage cannot be procured separately from that work, which is both too costly, and too weighty for me either to purchase or carry.[38]

This letter reveals much more than the simple fact that Lewis was gathering information. First of all it is apparent that he was sufficiently skilled in cartographic technique to have copied the charts from Vancouver's published work. If he could have done this, he could just as easily have made a copy from the manuscript of the Thompson map in Mr. Thornton's possession. More important, however, Lewis's letter shows that he was not simply a passive receptor of the geographical materials being assembled by Jefferson and Gallatin. It seems, rather, that he was active in gathering data for the purpose of taking it along on the expedition (as evidenced by his description of Vancouver's work as being "too weighty" to carry). The letter further illustrates that Lewis himself was a supplier of data for the base map to be drawn for him; consequently that map should reflect his views on the Northwest nearly as much as it did the views of Jefferson and Gallatin. Sometime in 1803 the base map was drawn and may be used as the best possible example of the state of Jefferson's and Lewis's knowledge of the Northwest prior to the expedition.

II

In a collection of papers belonging to Lewis and Clark[39] and apparently deposited in Washington sometime following their return from the West, there is a large manuscript map covering the area from the 30th to the 55th parallels and from the 86th to the 126th meridians. This map is evidently the one referred to in the Gallatin-Jefferson-Lewis correspondence, drawn by Nicholas King around 1803.[40] Annotations on the map in a hand which is clearly that of Lewis bear witness that the map might have accompanied the

38. Lewis to Jefferson, 29 May 1803.
39. During World War I, Dr. Hamblin, a clerk in the Office of Indian Affairs, unearthed a box of materials that were associated with the Lewis and Clark Expedition. These materials included both manuscript maps and journals that had been in the possession of the explorers prior to and during the overland journey. After the expedition and the death of Lewis, many of the geographical materials associated with the captains' journey were retained by Clark, then superintendent of Indian affairs in the West, for his use in preparing a map to illustrate the published journals. After Clark's death it was more or less natural for such semi-official papers to be deposited in departmental archives in Washington. The collection is now housed in the reference collection of the Geography and Map Division, Library of Congress, as "Lewis and Clark Manuscripts."
40. I first learned of the possibility that a large map in the Lewis and Clark Manuscripts might be the work of Nicholas King through conversations with Mr. Herman Friis of the National Archives. Further investigation of the map showed that the drafting techniques and the pattern and shape of the lettering, as well as some of the lettering on the map, were those of Nicholas King, the Philadelphia cartographer. Even firmer evidence is that the map was constructed from the sources discussed by Gallatin and Jefferson in March of 1803, including representation of the vicinity of the Mandan villages copied directly from the Thornton-Thompson-Lewis map. The King and Thompson maps were the only maps of the time to show exactly the same features around the north bend of the Missouri.

expedition, particularly since most of the annotations appear to be corrections made in the field.[41] Neither Lewis nor Clark ever referred to such a map in their later correspondence or field journals, however, and the notion that the map did accompany the explorers on their journey to the Pacific must remain only speculative. In fact, it is possible that Lewis never saw the map at all, as it might have been completed after his departure from Washington for the West and was, it seems, not included in the materials which Jefferson and others forwarded to Lewis during the winter and spring spent in a camp on the Mississippi's eastern shores before the actual commencement of the journey into the Northwest. But in the final analysis these facts are irrelevant. The King map was definitely the product of the cartographic materials discussed by Jefferson, Gallatin, and Lewis and was, therefore, the clearest imaginable specimen of the character of their images of the Northwest prior to the expedition.

Basically, the King map (fig. 21) was a copy of that section of the Arrowsmith 1802 map of North America showing the country between the Mississippi and the Pacific and between the Saskatchewan system on the north and the waters of the Colorado and Rio Grande on the south. There were, however, enough differences between the King map and the Arrowsmith map to suggest that Arrowsmith's representation of the Northwest was not evaluated as the best available without some reservations. King's map was a modification of Arrowsmith's and not a direct copy. By looking at the modifications, it might be possible to view the general features of the trans-Missouri region much as did Jefferson, Gallatin, and Lewis.

The easternmost portions of the map, depicting the western Great Lakes and the Mississippi, were apparently derived from Andrew Ellicott's map of the Mississippi, and they varied little in major characteristics from the representation of the same area on the Arrowsmith map. The sections of the map above the 50th parallel and along the Pacific coast seem to have come directly from Arrowsmith, who obtained his data, in turn, from the Mackenzie and Vancouver materials. But between the 95th and 120th meridians and the 50th

41. Most of the corrections were made in the drainage area of the Red and Assiniboine rivers. They were made by Lewis, probably from information he received during the winter of 1803–04 from Mr. John Hay, postmaster at Cahokia and formerly a trader operating in the Red River region. It is known that Hay did provide Lewis with information on that region (in addition to being otherwise helpful, as will be seen later), for in Lewis's own journals there is recorded a table of distances obtained from Hay, "commencing at the discharge of the Ottertail Lake, which forms the source of the Red River, to his [Hay's] winter station on the Assinneboin River" (Reuben Gold Thwaites, ed., *The Original Journals of the Lewis and Clark Expedition* (8 vols., New York, 1904–05), I, 4–6). Most of the corrections made on the King map appear between "Otter Tail L." and the western sources of the Assiniboine. Donald Jackson (personal communication, 1 Nov. 1972) has confirmed Lewis's authorship of the annotations on the map in the area enclosed by 95°–105° longitude and 45°–55° latitude and adds that at least one of the annotations could not have been made until Lewis and Clark reached the Mandan villages. This annotation refers to "Chaboillez's Ho[use] (Charles Jean Baptiste Chaboillez of the Northwest Company); since the captains had not heard of Chaboillez until reaching the Mandan villages (Jackson, *Letters*, pp. 213–14), the evidence is very strong that they carried the King map with them. For additional material on Hay's relationship with Lewis and Clark, see Jackson, *Letters*, p. 156, n. 9.

and 40th parallels, the King map illustrated meaningful modifications in the view of the American Northwest as presented by the Arrowsmith maps.

The course of the Missouri between the Mississippi and the Mandan villages on the King map resembled that on the Arrowsmith 1802 map. The King map was a little simpler, however, showing only the Kansas and Platte rivers as major tributaries of the Missouri where the Arrowsmith chart depicted a few additional streams entering the major river. Furthermore, King drew the Missouri as a dotted line from slightly above the mouth of the Platte to the Mandans. The reasons for this are unknown—Arrowsmith had used a solid line to represent the river in this area—but it might have just been an indication on the part of the cartographer that no adequate surveys of this portion of the Missouri existed.[42] But it was the area of the Mandan villages, the northern bend of the Missouri River, where King made the first real departure from the Arrowsmith map. The location of the northern bend and the villages was approximately the same on both the King and Arrowsmith charts. King, however, clearly used the map based on David Thompson's surveys of 1798 to draw this portion of the map. The representation of the area in question was, on the King map, an exact copy of the map of that area mentioned earlier as being obtained from Edward Thornton by Meriwether Lewis. This is, it would seem, nearly positive evidence as to the origin of "Mr. Thornton's map" of the Gallatin-Jefferson correspondence.[43]

Further changes made by King in the Arrowsmith view of the Northwest appeared in the sections of the map west of the Mandans. On the Arrowsmith map there were two branches of the Missouri above the Mandans. The first was a southerly fork with a source in the mountain range, where it was labeled "River Mississury," and with a course that ran nearly due east to the Mandans, where the river was labeled "Knife R." The second was an unnamed northerly fork with headwaters in the mountains near the 50th parallel and a course that ran southeast to join the southern branch near the villages. The King map, on the other hand, showed the Knife River as a small river entering the Missouri from the south at the Mandan villages (this taken from the Thompson surveys). Upstream from the junction of the Knife and Missouri, the Missouri branched as it did on the Arrowsmith production into southern and northern sections. Both of these had their sources in the mountain range as shown on the Arrowsmith map. But on the King map the northern branch, with a source near the 50th parallel, was called the "Missesourie," while the southern branch, with a source around the 46th or 47th parallel, was labeled the "Lesser Missesourie."

42. This is good evidence that the map was, in fact, drawn in 1803. By the end of 1803 Jefferson had received cartographic results of the Mackay-Evans expedition. Had such materials been available when King drew the map they would certainly have been incorporated, and the Missouri between its mouth and the Mandan villages would have been much less generalized.

43. The Thompson material was the only existing geographical data from which King could have copied the highly detailed depiction of the region of the Mandan villages.

21. Nicholas King's 1803 map of the western part of North America LIBRARY OF CONGRESS

This division of the Missouri west of the Mandans into the Missouri proper and the "Lesser" or Little Missouri was from the Thompson surveys, and the great western expansion of the Lesser or Little Missouri was perhaps a confusion of that river with rumors of the Yellowstone.[44] Slightly south of this branch of the Missouri appeared the "Sources of Rio Norte according to De lisle." This northern extension of the Rio Grande did not appear on the Arrowsmith map and was obviously a modification which grew out of the Jefferson-Gallatin correspondence on the proximity of the Missouri to the waters of New Mexico.

The aforementioned changes that King made in Arrowsmith's data were of consequence; but by far the most critical part of the King map and the area where the greatest modifications were made was the region of the mountains where both the Missouri and the southern branch of that river had their sources. On the Arrowsmith map there was, on the western side of the mountain range, a "Great Lake River" with the caption "The Indians say they sleep 8 Nights in descending this River to the Sea." The same river appeared on the King map with approximately the same legend. But King, for some reason that must remain unknown, made the Great Lake River head very close to the northern branch of the Missouri and not with the southern waters of the Saskatchewan River as on Arrowsmith's map.

The mountains themselves were laid down by King directly from the Arrowsmith map with one major exception—and this was perhaps the most unusual and important feature of the King map. Arrowsmith showed the Rocky Mountain chain running from Canada in a southeasterly direction all the way to New Mexico. The King map, on the other hand, depicted the Rockies as having a southern terminus around the 46th or 47th parallel. And even more significant, King drew a great southern branch of the Columbia running in an east-to-west direction all the way from a source near the 106th or 107th meridian to join the "River Oregan" east of Point Vancouver. The course of this unnamed river ran directly through the area where Arrowsmith had explicitly shown a major mountain range that served on his maps, and in many contemporary geographical theories, as a continental divide.

Where King might have derived his southern branch of the Columbia is not known; such a river appeared on no other map of the period. Across the portion of the King map showing this southern branch of the Columbia was written the word "conjectural," indicating that such a stream came not from definite geographical knowledge or theory but from someone's—perhaps Jefferson's and Gallatin's—interpretation of western geography. There are several possible contributing factors to such an interpretation. First, neither Jefferson, Gallatin, nor Lewis possessed the rigid concept of the nature of the Rocky Mountains as an unbroken chain like that delineated by Arrow-

44. Although the Yellowstone was named in the journals of the St. Louis fur traders and drawn on contemporary Louisiana maps based on their information, the river was not yet a part of American geographical lore. It did not become so until Truteau's descriptions of the upper Missouri were printed in the *Medical Repository*, III (2nd hexade, 1806), 314-15.

smith. Mackenzie, upon whose accounts they placed such importance, had stated that he did not know how far south of his crossing the mountains ran, and it is entirely possible that a termination of the mountains similar to that shown on the King map might have been assumed by Jefferson and the others. Such a construction would have been well within the framework of American geographical theory of the early nineteenth century.[45] And as far as the conjectural southern branch of the Columbia was concerned, the tenets of theoretical symmetrical geography might have been applied: other major rivers of the Northwest such as the Missouri and the Saskatchewan were understood to have northern and southern forks—why should the Columbia prove to be any different?

Thus was the view of the Northwest presented on the King map of cardinal importance. Jefferson and the others were well aware that the northern branches of the Missouri came dangerously close to the British territories and could have been precarious for an American expedition to follow. But a great southern river, with headwaters close to the southern waters of the Missouri, could be seen as a possible solution to the establishment of a water communication through U.S. territory that was sufficiently distant from British territory to avoid interference. As will be seen later, during the early stages of the expedition Lewis and Clark were probably thinking of just such a route—following the southern extensions of the Missouri to the mountains and to the southern branch of the Columbia.

12

The King map was a symbol of Jefferson's and Lewis's general view of the Northwest before Lewis left Washington. But it was not the only product of the planning period between January and July of 1803. At about the same time as he and Gallatin were compiling and discussing cartographic data, Jefferson began another phase of the geographical preparations necessary for the successful completion of the mission to discover the all-water connection across the continent. This stage in the preparatory activity resulted in the list of instructions, a "blueprint for discovery,"[46] presented to Lewis before he began the expedition and a remarkable document that illustrates better than anything else the precision and completeness of Jefferson's efforts to locate the passage to the Pacific.

Jefferson began drafting his instructions to Lewis sometime in the early spring of 1803 and by April had sent copies of his first draft to several of his cabinet members. Most of the comments he received on the proposed directive were unimportant, but once again the close relationship between the Presi-

45. Cf. the works of Jedediah Morse (*American Universal Geography* and *American Gazetteer*) and John Pinkerton (*Modern Geography*).
46. Cutright (*Lewis and Clark*, pp. 1–9) gives a fine analysis of the instructions to Lewis.

dent and Albert Gallatin becomes apparent. On April 13 Jefferson received Gallatin's comments on the draft copy of Lewis's instructions.[47] The Secretary began by noting that he perceived nothing needing alteration in the instructions although something might be added. He was, as has been noted, somewhat concerned about the fact that the expedition would have to travel through country that was outside of the United States' possessions (it must be remembered that the cession of Louisiana had not yet been effected). Fearing Spanish or British interference, Gallatin hoped that Jefferson would instruct Lewis to investigate completely "the present communication of the British with the Missouri" as well as acquire a "perfect knowledge of the posts, establishments & force kept by Spain in upper Louisiana."[48]

Gallatin continued his comments by saying that the "future destinies of the Missouri country are of vast importance to the United States" and that Louisiana would be the first large tract of country outside the borders of the United States to be settled by Americans. With this in mind, Gallatin recommended that Lewis's purposes be expanded to include a survey not only of the branch of the Missouri "which may be followed for the purpose of examining the communications with the Pacific Ocean" but also of all "the country drained by all the waters emptying into the river." It is clear that Gallatin was thinking, as was Jefferson, not only of the discovery of a route to the Pacific but of an assessment of the potential of the Louisiana country for American expansion.

The remainder of Gallatin's reply to the draft copy of the instructions was a rather lengthy discussion of the geography of the Louisiana area as he understood it:

> That tract of country is bounded on the north by the Waters of Hudson's bay, the extent of which southward is tolerably ascertained by Mackenzie & others; Westwardly by the Waters of the Columbia & other rivers emptying into the Pacific, which it is the principal object of this voyage to explore; and Southwardly, it is presumed by the waters of Rio Norte. How far these extend Northwardly & confine the waters of the Missouri it is important to know as their position would generally determine the extent of territory watered by the Missouri. It is presumable, from analogy that the Waters of Hudson's Bay which interlock with the many northern streams of the Missouri are divided from them by elevated lands interspersed with lakes, but not by any regular chain of mountains. By the same analogy, (for with the United States & every known part of the North American continent the spring of every river north of 42° latitude issues from a lake, and south of 41° from a mountain) it is probable that the northern branches of the Rio Norte are separated from the southern streams of the Kanses & Missouri rivers by a chain of mountains running westwardly until it unites with that chain which divides the waters of the Missouri & other rivers from those emptying into

47. Albert Gallatin to Jefferson, 13 Apr. 1803.
48. Gallatin, it would appear, was more concerned than Jefferson about potential troubles with Spain. A partial explanation for this, perhaps, is his adherence to the concept of proximal sources for the Missouri and Rio Grande as illustrated by the King map.

the Pacific. Hence it is presumable that the distance of that east & west chain from the Missouri will generally show the extent of country watered by this river. And although Cn. L. going westwardly toward his main object may not personally become acquainted with the country lying south of his track, yet so far as he may collect information on that subject & also on the communications with the Rio Norte or other southern rivers if any others, which is not probable, interlocks with the Missouri, it would be a desireable object. The great object is to ascertain whether from its extent & fertility that country is susceptible to a large population, in the same manner as the corresponding tract on the Ohio.[49]

It cannot be known to what extent Gallatin's views are a reflection of Jefferson's, for nowhere does Jefferson leave such a concise rendering of his geographical understanding of the trans-Missouri region. But whether or not Gallatin's views were similar to Jefferson's (and it can be rather safely assumed that they were since both men seem to have had access to much the same information and appear to have had a rather thorough exchange of ideas), his account of the geography of the Northwest is of great interest since it provides a look at the character of geographical knowledge as held by an educated and informed individual. Of particular interest for the implications they have for the Lewis and Clark Expedition are Gallatin's comments on the sources of North American rivers.

By stating that the rivers of North America have their heads in mountains below the 41st parallel and in lakes above the 42nd parallel, Gallatin made no provision for a definite, sharp drainage divide between eastern and western waters above the 42nd parallel. This implies that north of that parallel there could have been a general plateau or height-of-land which provided the source area for many streams and rivers. South of the 42nd parallel were the mountains of New Mexico, running in an east-west direction and terminating on the north at some point between the 41st and 42nd parallels. There was no mention whatever of any existence of a north-south chain of mountains forming a drainage divide north of these mountains of New Mexico.

Gallatin must certainly have known of the existence of the Rockies for he was familiar with both Mackenzie and Arrowsmith, each of whom presented some signs of the Rocky Mountain system on their maps. This Rocky Mountain range, however, might have been viewed by Gallatin as consisting of a series of low ridges lying between the mountains of New Mexico on the south and the mountains observed by Mackenzie and other British explorers on the north. Such a view would have been consistent with the expression of the Arrowsmith 1802 map that the mountains near the 45th parallel divided into several low ridges. The Rocky Mountains might even have terminated a short distance south of the Saskatchewan or south of Mackenzie's track across the continent, an idea that correlated with the mountains shown on the King map. If this were true, then the area between the mountains of New Mexico

49. The notion of symmetrical geography—that the western side of the Mississippi drainage basin was a mirror image of the eastern side—is quite evident in Gallatin's statement.

where the Rio Grande had its head and the Rocky Mountain chain seen by British explorers north of the 50th parallel might have been imagined as a highland plateau. There were no confirmed or reliable reports available in 1803 that described a mountain chain along the upper Missouri, and it was certainly a possibility that the Missouri had its source somewhere in a high plateau area.

It was further imaginable that somewhere in the same general plateau area might be found the source waters of the Columbia or some other westward-flowing stream, and since the area might be level or only slightly broken country, the distance between the two sources would be easily traversed. A theoretical construction of this type would not go beyond the available evidence. Theoretical geographers had for years spoken of the major rivers of western North America as having their sources in a common, pyramidal height-of-land or upland plateau.[50]

13

It was necessary that these views of Gallatin's (and possibly Jefferson's) be translated into some definite form in order to furnish Lewis with specific directives for his western expedition. Jefferson was prepared to do this by the middle of June, 1803, and on June 20 he drew up the instructions, incorporating his own ideas and Gallatin's suggestions into a document which was as close as any to a written description of the trans-Missouri area by Jefferson himself. "The object of your mission," wrote Jefferson,

is to explore the Missouri river, & such principal stream of it, as, by it's course and communication with the waters of the Pacific ocean, whether the Columbia, Oregan, Colorado or any other river may offer the most direct & practicable water communication across this continent for the purposes of commerce. . . .

The interesting points of the portage between the heads of the Missouri, & of the water offering the best communication with the Pacific ocean, should also be fixed by observation, & the courses of that water to the ocean in the same manner as that of the Missouri. . . .

Altho' your route will be along the channel of the Missouri, yet you will endeavor to inform yourself, by enquiry, of the character & extent of the country watered by it's branches, & especially on it's Southern side. The North river or Rio Bravo which runs into the gulph of Mexico, and the North river, or Rio colorado which runs into the gulph of California, are understood to be the principal streams heading opposite the waters of the Missouri, and running Southwardly. Whether the dividing grounds between the Missouri and them are mountains or flat lands, what are their distances from the Missouri, the character of the inter-

50. The height-of-land in Gallatin's and Jefferson's view was not the same height-of-land described in the contemporary geographies, i.e., was not the source region for the Mississippi, Nelson, St. Lawrence, and Columbia. But the theoretical assumptions were the same, and the new height-of-land spawned the Missouri, the southern tributaries of the Columbia, the Colorado, the Rio Grande, and other western rivers.

mediate country, & the people inhabiting it, are worthy of particular inquiry.[51] The Northern waters of the Missouri are less to be enquired after, because they have been ascertained to a considerable degree, & are still in a course of ascertainment by English traders and travellers. But if you can learn anything of the most Northern source of the Missisipi, & of it's position relatively to the lake of the woods, it will be interesting to us. . . .[52]

Should you reach the Pacific ocean, inform yourself of the circumstance which may decide whether the furs of those parts may not be collected as advantageously at the head of the Missouri (convenient as it is supposed to the waters of the Colorado & Oregan or Columbia) as at Nootka sound, or any other point of that coast; and that trade be consequently conducted throughout the Missouri and U.S. more beneficially than by the circumnavigation now practised.[53]

Although Jefferson was not in the least specific in the geographical content of his instructions to Lewis, several inferences can be made from what is contained in the document. In the first place, Jefferson's intent in proposing the expedition was quite clear; the "object" of the mission was stated most positively. If the expedition fulfilled only its major purpose—the establishment of a water communication across the continent for the purposes of commerce—then it would be a total success. And it is also clear that Jefferson considered only one river on the continent as being able to provide the Passage to India. This river was the Missouri, and it would be found to connect with the waters of the Pacific Ocean by a portage which was to be fixed by observation.

Jefferson did not care to speculate on the nature of this portage; it seems that he, like Gallatin, had no definite idea of whether the "dividing grounds" between the Missouri and the other rivers of the Northwest were composed of "mountains or flat lands." But regardless of the nature of the land which formed the divide, the waters of the Missouri were supposed to be convenient to the Pacific. It was through this convenient connection that trade from the fur regions of the Pacific Northwest and from the Orient could be conducted "more beneficially than by the circumnavigation now practised."

Although the primary purpose of the expedition and the central focus of Jefferson's instructions to Lewis revolved around the conceptual passage to the Pacific, there were other directives included, directives which not only gave Lewis the most detailed and all-inclusive orders in the history of exploration up to that time but also illustrated the full scope of Jefferson's awareness of the elements of regional geography. In addition to the purely geographical purposes of locating the Passage to India, Lewis was to make careful observa-

51. All the preceding in this paragraph did not appear in Jefferson's first draft of the instructions and seems to have been inserted after the Gallatin comments on the lands to the south side of the Missouri as being worthy of investigation.

52. This passage indicates Jefferson's access to and familiarity with the reports of the British fur trade.

53. These are only extracts from the entire instructions, which contain more complete directives. The original of the instructions is in the Jefferson Papers and is published in Jackson, *Letters*, pp. 61–66.

tions of the character of the native inhabitants of the areas through which he would pass, of the botanical and zoological features he would encounter in the unknown lands, and of the "mineral productions of every kind." And perhaps second in importance only to the primary purpose of the expedition, Lewis was to make himself fully acquainted with the quality of the lands between the Mississippi and the Pacific and record carefully soil fertility and vegetative and climatic characteristics. For there were, in Jefferson's mind and the minds of most other knowledgeable Americans of his time, two themes in the images of the Northwest. One was the Passage to India; the other was the Garden of the World. If Lewis were to find the Passage he might also find it to be located in a garden of wealth and beauty, a fertile land into which the republic could expand and increase its already burgeoning agricultural productions and population.

Jefferson's instructions were forwarded to Lewis in late June, and, armed with the detailed plans from the President, Lewis left the capital city of the new republic on July 5, 1803, to begin the first leg of his journey to the Pacific and back. But when Lewis left Washington he left with more than a set of instructions; he left with an image of the Northwest shaped during his years as Jefferson's secretary and confidant in virtually all matters respecting the western expedition. That image would shape the expedition's course during the ensuing months and years.

CHAPTER 4

IMAGE OF THE NORTHWEST, 1803

It has not been until recently that scholars of the Lewis and Clark Expedition have begun to appreciate fully the enormous importance of the years that Meriwether Lewis spent as Jefferson's private secretary.[1] The exchanges of ideas and philosophies he had with Jefferson and his circle of associates and the scope of the education and training he received in so many different areas of scientific and practical interest were indispensable elements in molding Lewis into an individual who was, by the time he began his western travels, highly qualified as an explorer. And since exploration is so purely a geographical activity, the geographical experiences and education Lewis acquired during this two-year period were more essential than anything else for the success of the expedition that he and William Clark were to lead to the Pacific and back.

Explorers must know something about the area they intend to investigate if they are to make adequate preparations for achieving the goals of their exploration. As a rule, therefore, a certain amount of time prior to exploration is spent in gathering the geographical knowledge available (even though information may be severely limited) about the regions to be explored. From

1. Cutright, *Lewis and Clark*, pp. 30–31.

this acquired knowledge explorers develop sets of preconceived ideas relative to the nature of the regional phenomena they might logically be expected to encounter during the course of their exploration. These preconceived ideas act as conditioning influences upon the process of exploration itself. Initially, the plans for an expedition are laid out according to the expectations created by the preconceptions of an area. As exploration begins, the field operations and behavior of the explorers are based on their background knowledge and the regional images derived from that knowledge. It would be impossible to comprehend fully the initial stages of the Lewis and Clark Expedition, therefore, without examining in some detail the fundamental structure of the image of the Northwest as held by Lewis when he left Washington in early summer, 1803.

2

Thus far, regional or geographical images have been described as patterns of belief about the nature and content of a land area derived from the geographical knowledge about that area. But geographical images cannot be viewed as totally objective interpretations of known facts; they are not created in a vacuum and factors other than the quality and quantity of geographical information must be taken into account. There are, in the development of an image, certain biases which impress themselves on that image. Because so little record is left of the nature of Lewis's own thoughts prior to his departure, determination of the makeup of the biases in his views of the Northwest must be made subjectively. But this task is not as difficult as it might seem. A great deal can be said about the probable biases in Jefferson's image, and because of the extremely close relationships between the two men it is more than likely that, with some exceptions that will be noted, the nature of the biases that influenced Jefferson's and Lewis's views of the Northwest was basically very similar.[2]

One very important ingredient of Jeffersonian philosophy that could have contributed heavily to Lewis's view of the Northwest, particularly with respect to the potential value of the area for future development, was the element of agrarian republicanism. As has already been noted, Jefferson's hopes for the future of the young country were part and parcel of his hopes

2. The reader must be warned that this chapter is highly speculative. When dealing with the nature and development of geographical images even today the difficulties are tremendous. They become even more so when applied to attempts to conclude anything about geographical images formed so far back in time that the individuals themselves can no longer be interviewed. The conclusions of the chapter relative to the character of Jefferson's and Lewis's view of the Northwest are, however, based on an exhaustive survey and analysis of every piece of geographical data that can definitely be said to have been in Jefferson's possession prior to Lewis's departure from Washington and every item in Jefferson's and Lewis's correspondence, journals, etc. which casts light on their views of the Northwest.

for the Northwest, and for the sake of the nation it would eventually prove necessary to expand into the interior, to build a free, republican, agrarian society in the midst of the Garden.[3] Lewis was as ardent a Republican as Jefferson and might well have held the same views with regard to agricultural expansion as did the President. Men's ambitions and desires nearly always have an impact on their geographical images,[4] and looking at the lands of the Northwest through the colored lenses of political theory, it is quite plausible that to Jefferson and Lewis those lands seemed to be a garden.

Agrarianism was not the only component of Jeffersonian philosophy that could have been a prejudicial constituent for Lewis's image of the Northwest. Just as meaningful a bias might have been that of utilitarianism, the view of science (and scientific exploration as well) as a practical contributor to the welfare of mankind. Knowledge, according to the American Philosophical Society (of which Jefferson was president and Lewis a member at the time of the expedition) was "of little use, when confined to mere speculation."[5] But when speculative truths were reduced to practice and when theories grounded upon experiments were applied to the common purposes of life, then knowledge became useful. The Lewis and Clark Expedition as planned by Jefferson was, in truth, a scientific endeavor. But it was scientific in Jefferson's terms—it had a purpose that could conceivably improve the welfare of the nation.

One of the most important manifestations of utilitarian philosophy in Jefferson's geographical thinking was his long-standing concern with the scientific aspects of drainage systems and the possibilities of linking them with canals for the improvement of navigation. Canals were most feasible, believed Jefferson, between the headwaters of rivers; if such connections could be established between the upper reaches of rivers throughout the western parts of North America, then the nation would be given the ability to "spread the field of our commerce Westwardly and Southwardly beyond any thing ever yet done by man."[6] Just as the Garden was part of the Northwest because agrarian republicanism wished it so, the Passage to India and the short portage across which canals could be built were also there in deference to the needs of utilitarianism. It is not surprising that an expedition which many have considered as one designed for purely scientific purposes should have been so imbued with the purely practical consideration of discovering a water communication across the continent for the purposes of commerce.

A final definable bias in Lewis's view of the Northwest was one that did

3. "Our governments will remain virtuous for many centuries; as long as they are chiefly agricultural; and this will be as long as there shall be vacant lands in any part of America" (Jefferson to James Madison, Dec., 1787; Boyd, *Papers*, XII, 442).

4. David Lowenthal, "Geography, Experience, and Imagination: Toward a Geographical Epistemology," *Annals of the Association of American Geographers*, LI (1961), 241-60.

5. Preface, *American Philosophical Society Transactions*, vol. I, o.s. (1743).

6. Boyd, *Papers*, VII, 558.

not depend entirely on Jefferson but was, in addition, a feature of Lewis's own experience. This bias may be termed "geographic" or "environmental." The patterns of belief about the spatial arrangement of the features of any area assume a different character in different times and different places.[7] Geographical thought about any area is highly conditioned by the environmental background and experiences of the thinker. Geographical thoughts are also greatly influenced by the general intellectual and cultural pattern of the time and place in which those thoughts or images are given form and expression. These modifiers of geographical thought are especially germane for understanding the image of the trans-Missouri area in the minds of Jefferson and Lewis.

Both men were Virginians from the Blue Ridge country. As such, their geographical ideas about mountains and rivers were given form by their observations and experiences among those mountains and rivers with which they were most familiar. The mountains of the western interior might well have been seen as mirror images of the Blue Ridge and might have been cut transversely by the western rivers just as the Potomac and other eastern streams slashed the Virginia hills. Furthermore, Jefferson and Lewis were operating within the framework of American geography of the early national period and possessed ideas that were "geoamericanistic."[8] In American geographical thought of the time, the arrangement of the physical features of the North American continent, refracted by ardent patriotism and even more ardent teleology, were viewed as a happy combination of factors which provided America with perfect conditions for human progress. The Passage to India must exist if only because of absolute faith in the ultimate perfection of America.

3

The pattern of beliefs on the geography of the Northwest that Lewis formed under Jefferson's tutelage had most of its elements in common with Jefferson's own images and was subjected to generally the same biases. This cannot, of course, be measured accurately, but considering the scope of information that must have been transmitted to Lewis by Jefferson, the possibility that the two men held common views about the trans-Missouri region seems quite strong. While he was an aide to the President, actively assisting in the planning phases of the expedition, Lewis must have had ample opportunity to survey the collection of maps and geographical works in Jefferson's possession. And it is probable that Jefferson, in private conversations, would have given Lewis even more than the formal information from maps and books. That Lewis shared a good part of the President's views seems even

7. Wright, *Human Nature in Geography*, pp. 11–23.
8. Wright, *Human Nature in Geography*, pp. 124–39.

more probable in the light of his background—social, environmental, and educational—which was so similar to Jefferson's own.[9]

And yet, if Lewis shared many elements of the image of the Northwest, his image must also have varied in some aspects from Jefferson's. Jefferson, in spite of his knowledge about the western interior, was a westerner and a wilderness traveler only vicariously. He had never been farther west than the Shenandoah, and his ideas on the relative ease of a transcontinental water passage were predicated on a notion of the Blue Ridge as a mighty mountain range and on a conception of the short distance between navigable waters of such rivers as the Potomac and Ohio as being consistent with all river systems. Lewis, with the same environmental experience, probably shared these views. But by the time he had joined Jefferson in Washington in 1801, Lewis was already a seasoned wilderness veteran and traveler as a result of his army services in the trans-Allegheny country.[10] His concept of the ease of a transcontinental passage through totally unknown territory was probably much less optimistic than Jefferson's, even if the views of the two men on the general characteristics of the unknown country were alike. This qualification of a distinction between Lewis's and Jefferson's images of the Northwest is a minor one at this point, however, and the fact remains that when Lewis left Washington in July, 1803, he held views on the trans-Missouri region that mirrored those of his sponsor.

4

The Northwest of Jefferson and Lewis was a garden of wealth and beauty. Most of the geographical lore at their disposal said as much and their agrarian bias reinforced the idea. Among all the materials on the trans-Missouri area in Jefferson's collection, the works of the French chroniclers were the greatest in number and perhaps also greatest in their influence on the understanding of the land quality of the Northwest, since the French literature included the garden concept as one of its most cardinal elements. The general geographical lore available to the literate American of the early

9. Like Jefferson, Lewis was born on a frontier plantation in the Blue Ridge country of Albemarle County, Virginia, of parents who were outstanding members of the frontier aristocracy. Lewis's relatives on both sides of his family had been neighbors and friends of Jefferson and his family for two generations. Lewis attended the same types of school as Jefferson himself had throughout his childhood. This schooling might have been significant in influencing Lewis's interpretation of geographical knowledge. During 1789–90 Lewis attended the "classical school" in Albemarle County under Reverend Matthew Maury, the son of Jefferson's old schoolmaster—heir to his father's library and perhaps some of his father's ideas on the feasibility of a western passage across North America. Good biographies of Lewis are rare; the best is Richard Dillon, *Meriwether Lewis, a Biography* (New York, 1965).

10. Lewis had joined the Army in 1794 during the "Whiskey Rebellion," found that he was "delighted with a soldier's life," and planned to make the Army his career. In 1795 he was in Greenville, Ohio, and between 1795 and 1801 he served in several different posts in the Ohio country and along the eastern bank of the Mississippi. In 1801 he was serving as regimental paymaster at Detroit when he received Jefferson's offer.

nineteenth century was also supportive of the garden concept. The information that Jefferson received from his correspondents in the western territories served to substantiate the idea further, and the President himself, in his writings on the Northwest, commented on the fertility and fruitfulness of the area.[11]

The soil of the trans-Missouri region, Jefferson wrote, was as fertile as that in the U.S. territories east of the Mississippi, and was, in fact, exceeded by no part of the world for fecundity.[12] So bounteous was the land that it would, in Jefferson's view, produce all those things necessary for the ideal agrarian civilization and "yield an abundance of all the necessaries of life, and almost spontaneously; very little labor being required in the cultivation of the earth."[13] The "one immense prairie" west of the Mississippi was, he wrote, simply "too rich for the growth of forest trees" and produced, therefore, nothing but the finest grasses in the world.[14]

That Jefferson and, by extension, Lewis probably chose to accept this view of the trans-Missouri area is an interesting commentary on their biases. They had, in compiling information, relied most heavily on the works of Alexander Mackenzie and other British writers for physiographic details on the Northwest. But it seems that they rejected Mackenzie's statements that neither the climate nor the soil of the western interior could be considered "sufficiently genial to bring the fruits of the earth to maturity."[15] And Jean Truteau, whose journals of his travels on the upper Missouri Jefferson had obtained as early as 1801 and must have recognized as the latest information on the region, had spoken of much of the trans-Missouri country as inhospitable, with barren plains devoid of timber and high winds that hindered travel and tortured the traveler. Even in the American press, comments had appeared to the effect that much of the Northwest was a "dreary tract, [where] there is little or no vegetation."[16]

These adverse representations of the land quality of the western interior seem to have had little impact on Jefferson's and Lewis's image; nowhere in Jefferson's own descriptions of the area are such discouraging phrases to be found. Nowhere in the early sections of Lewis's descriptions of his line of travel, conditioned by his preconceived ideas about the area, were there contentions that the Northwest was anything but fine and beautiful country.

11. Cf. Jefferson *et al.*, *Documents Relating to . . . Louisiana.*
12. Jefferson, "An Official Account of Louisiana," *American State Papers* (vol. XX, "Miscellaneous"), I, 346.
13. Jefferson, "Official Account," pp. 346–47.
14. Jefferson, "Official Account," p. 346.
15. Mackenzie, *Voyages*, II, 344. There was not really such a science as meteorology in Jefferson's time, although he himself was a pioneer weather observer. Because of a lack of knowledge of climatic principles, in combination with a lack of climatic data, there was no way for Americans of the early nineteenth century to evaluate the nature of the air masses which occupy the central and western portions of the North American continent at various times of the year, making those areas anything but "salubrious." But Jefferson was a firm believer in the principle (or notion) that man's activities conditioned meteorological developments, and he retained an optimism about climate and western development.
16. *National Intelligencer* (Washington), Oct. 21, 1803, pp. 1–2.

Jefferson and Lewis, agrarian Republicans, saw as necessary vast amounts of open land available for cultivation, able to sustain the growth of the system that was best suited for the human condition. This free land, fertile and well watered, would be found in the Northwest.[17]

5

Jefferson's and Lewis's view of the rivers of the trans-Missouri region is more difficult to analyze than their conception of the quality of the land. One way of approaching their conceptualization of western rivers is via the King map (fig. 22). This map showed several major streams: the Rio Norte or Rio Grande, the mythical Rio des los Apostolos, and the Rio Colorado, all flowing toward the south; the Kansas and Platte entering the Missouri from the west; the Missouri itself with its two main branches, the Missouri proper and the Lesser Missouri, above the Mandan villages; and the River Oregan or Columbia, in its upper reaches called the Tacoutche-Tesse, and also having two main branches.

The first five of these major western rivers were little known and relatively unimportant in the image. The three southward-flowing streams were in Spanish territory and significant only insofar as their sources might have been near those of the Missouri's southern waters. Of possible connections between these rivers and the Missouri, however, Jefferson and Lewis seem to have been cognizant only of the theory that the Rio Grande had its headsprings close to the Missouri's southern branch. This part of their image was a corollary of the Delisle map discussed with Gallatin. The Kansas and Platte were derived from the French and Spanish lore and cartography and there seems to have been no awareness of the length and extent of the Platte River nor of the fact that it too separated into two major branches. But this was probably due less to a lack of knowledge (although there was little available information on the Platte River) than to a lack of interest in rivers other than the Missouri and Columbia.

6

Jefferson's and Lewis's images of the Missouri must appear as somewhat contradictory partly because of the contrary nature of their information on the river. From the French chroniclers they learned that the Missouri ran a course of about 2,200 miles according to the reports of Bourgmont, who had, it was said, "ascended to its source."[18] This information would have tallied,

17. That this view is at least partly accurate cannot be denied. The point here is that the overall image of the Northwest was determined and given character by information that applied to only a relatively small proportion of the region.

18. Antoine Simon le Page du Pratz, *History of Louisiana* (2 vols., London, 1763), I, 38.

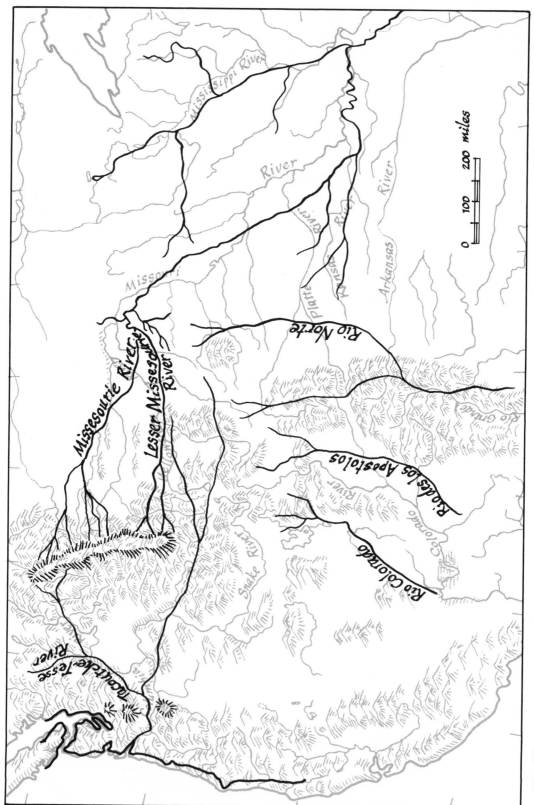

22. The King 1803 map compared with a modern base map

certainly, with all of the other data describing the Missouri as an extremely lengthy river. But such data would have conflicted with many other references in Jefferson's collected lore which depicted the Missouri as an even longer stream, with headwaters near the Pacific. Much of the geographical lore on the Missouri was based on this contention, and that the Missouri's source was near the ocean was reinforced by the concepts of Daniel Coxe's theoretical symmetry of the river basins on the eastern and western sides of the Mississippi.

In spite of the weight of information on the side of the great western extent of the Missouri, it is probable that Jefferson's and Lewis's view closely approximated that represented on the King map. The width of the continent had been well known since the Cook voyages of the 1770s, and, given the established southeasterly course of the Missouri from the Mandans to St. Louis, there was simply no way that a river which virtually all the reliable sources reported as being approximately 2,000 miles long could stretch all the way from some point near the western ocean to the Mississippi. Furthermore, Jefferson and Lewis placed more faith in British sources than in any others when it came to defining the physiographic features of the Northwest, and the British literature and cartographic materials showed the same general delineation of the length and course of the Missouri as that which appeared on the King map; it was a representation which, given the paucity of accurate data, was remarkably accurate.

The most recent explorations in the trans-Missouri area, those of Mackay and Evans, had served to implement the conception of the Missouri as having its sources close to the Pacific.[19] But the Mackay-Evans journals and maps were not accessible at the time Lewis left Washington, and he and Jefferson would, therefore, have been much more likely to accept the British descriptions on the course of the river and on the location of its source region as somewhere between the 112th and 115th meridians. The Missouri was a lengthy river in the image of 1803; its course was in the neighborhood of 2,000 miles long. But it did not, in Jefferson's and Lewis's mind, have its source waters as close to Pacific shores as many of the French and Spanish writers had speculated.

On the size and navigability of the Missouri there was much less discrepancy between the information and the probable image. Virtually all of Jefferson's source material referred to the Missouri as an extremely broad and very navigable stream. Jefferson himself wrote that the Missouri was truly

19. That Mackay and Evans had caused Spanish officials to believe in a western extension of the Missouri system was due less to their reports (which were relatively accurate) and more to misinterpretations of their positioning of the Mandan villages and their comments about the distance between the Mandans and the mountains. Because they placed the Mandans anywhere from 6° to 7° of longitude too far west and spoke of the Great Falls (or the Rocky Mountains) as being still farther west, the net impact of their reports was to decrease the distance between the Rockies and the Pacific coast. The relevant point here is that the longitudinal position of the western coast of North America had been known precisely since the Cook voyages of the 1770s. Lewis and Clark were *not*, as has so often been erroneously stated, the first to determine the width of the continent.

the major river of the entire Northwest, even larger and more important than the Mississippi.[20] This large river was navigable all the way "from its mouth to its source . . . for the largest pirogues" according to Truteau's journals, part of Jefferson's geographical collection. What is more, even the tributaries of the Missouri were navigable, and it was known that beyond the Mandan villages "many large navigable rivers discharged their waters" into the main stream.[21] It was this concept of the navigablility of the Missouri all the way to its source that was one of the major misconceptions about the river; it was an error that was to cause considerable hardship to Lewis and Clark in the months ahead.

7

The Missouri was viewed as being navigable to its source, but it was not clear just exactly where that source was. It has been noted that much of the contemporary information placed the source of the river far west of its actual position but that Jefferson and Lewis themselves probably opted for a source region somewhere near the 115th meridian as on the King map. But beyond this point there was disagreement between the British (i.e., Arrowsmith) data, which provided for two branches of the Missouri, the southern branch being the Missouri proper with headwaters near the 46th parallel, and the King map, which, although it also showed two forks of the Missouri, labeled the northern branch as the Missouri and placed its source near the 50th parallel. This could have been a reflection of the information on John Mitchell's map of 1755 (which Jefferson had described as being made "with great care") to the effect that the Missouri was supposed "to arise about the 50th degree of latitude."[22]

The Missouri, therefore, in the image of 1803, might have had its source near the 50th parallel and not the 46th parallel as shown on Arrowsmith's map. It was perhaps this view that led Jefferson to include in his instructions to Lewis the phrase which described "the Missouri river, & *such principal stream of it* [italics added]," as being the route to the Pacific.[23] The principal stream of the Missouri referred to by Jefferson could have been the southern branch of the system as shown on the King map. The northern branch might have been seen as a dangerous or worthless route to the Columbia because of its proximity to British territory.

In summary, then, the Jefferson-Lewis view of the Missouri was of a large river—even larger than the Mississippi—which ran a course of at least 2,000 miles from a northwesterly direction. It was navigable to its source, which was near 115° W. and 50° N., and it had at least one major branch

20. Thomas Jefferson, *Notes on the State of Virginia* (London, 1787), p. 10.
21. Jefferson, "Official Account," p. 350.
22. Jefferson to Albert Gallatin, 20 Mar. 1803.
23. Jackson, *Letters*, p. 61.

flowing from a source region in roughly the same meridian of longitude as the northern branch but lying some 7° of latitude (about 200 miles) farther south. And here was a critical part of the image: both the northern and southern branches of the Missouri had probable connections with waters flowing toward the Pacific. These connections had been a major feature of geographical lore since the first European contacts with the western parts of North America. Somewhere in its upper reaches, the Missouri and/or a principal branch of it passed close to the waters of a great river which ran toward the Pacific Ocean. This great western river, in the image of 1803, was the Columbia or "River Oregon."

8

The conceptualization of the Columbia was based almost exclusively on Mackenzie's accounts and maps and on the surveys of Captain Vancouver. The Columbia in 1803 was an even less known geographical quantity than the Missouri, and as a result the views of it were much less detailed. The length of the Columbia was unknown. It was assumed, according to the best information, that the Columbia was a very long river, extending from Mackenzie's contact with what he believed to be its upper portion near the 55th parallel all the way south to its entry into the Pacific at approximately 46° N. That the river Mackenzie had reached by a portage from the Peace was the Fraser instead of the Columbia was as yet unknown, and on most maps of the period the "Tacoutche-Tesse" of Mackenzie and the Columbia of Vancouver and Gray were the same stream.

The size of the Columbia had been assessed by Lieutenant Broughton of Vancouver's command at a point inland 100 miles from its mouth, and, after careful measurements, Broughton had reported that the river was a quarter of a mile wide and varied in depth from 12 to 36 feet.[24] It was further reported that the river at that point was still far from its source. The Columbia, therefore, was a long, large, and navigable river with a source at a great distance from the sea. And what was even more important, the source was represented as being close to the headsprings of the Missouri. According to Mackenzie's account, the Columbia probably headed near the 55th parallel and then ran south toward the Pacific. This would have placed the sources of the river nearly 5° of latitude (roughly 250 miles) north of the headwaters of the Missouri. But Mackenzie had also noted that the "snow-clad mountains" where the Missouri rose also provided a source area for "the Columbia emptying itself into the Pacific Ocean."[25] And both Jonathan Carver and the American geographer Jedediah Morse had spoken of the Missouri and the

24. This information appeared in Vancouver's published journals and on Arrowsmith's map, "Plan of the River Oregan from an Actual Survey" (1798).
25. Mackenzie, *Voyages*, II, 347.

"Oregan" or Columbia as having their sources "in the same neighborhood."[26]

This seeming contradiction in the proximity of the sources of the Missouri and Columbia was compensated for in the image of 1803 as illustrated by the King map. Although the Columbia itself had its source far north of the northernmost source waters of the Missouri, two major tributaries of the Columbia headed near major branches of the Missouri. Near 115° W. and 50° N., the northern branch of the Missouri had its source directly opposite the "Great Lake R.," which joined the Columbia near the Pacific. And to the south, close to the southern waters of the Missouri system, ran a conjectural great southern branch of the Columbia, providing a southern as well as a northern connection between the Missouri and the Columbia.

9

It was this interlocking nature of the waters of the Columbia and the Missouri that provided the basis for the most important section of Jefferson's and Lewis's image of the Northwest. Nearly all authorities agreed that the waters of the Columbia and the waters of the Missouri were close by at their sources. Jefferson had informed André Michaux as early as 1793 that "a river called Oregon interlocked with the Missouri for a considerable distance," and his instructions to Meriwether Lewis revealed the same general conception. The interlocking nature of the rivers was apparent on the King map; thus did the geographical knowledge provide for the only line of easy communication across the continent.

By following the waters of the Missouri River to their source, a transcontinental water route could be established. Jefferson noted in his message to Congress that the Missouri offered, "according to the best accounts a continued navigation from it's source, and, possibly with a single portage, from the Western Ocean." This was the central feature of the misconception of the geography of the Northwest. Mackenzie had found a portage of about half a mile between navigable waters that flowed into two different seas. Jefferson and Lewis applied this knowledge to the information that the Missouri and Columbia rose in the same area, added their utilitarian and "geoamerican" biases, and came up with the firm and sound conclusion that the Pacific Ocean could be reached by an easy and efficient water communication incorporating the rivers Missouri and Columbia.

10

In the image of 1803 the Missouri and Columbia waters may have been described as "interlocking," but the time was long since past when river

26. Carver, *Travels*, pp. 75–76; and Morse, *American Gazetteer*, article on "The Shining Mountains."

systems could be viewed as flowing in two directions at the same time, that is, as having the same exact source in, for example, a lake which drained through several outlets. Concepts of physical geography around 1803 necessitated, rather, that river basins be separated by heights-of-land or by mountain ranges. The nature of such a drainage divide between the waters of the Columbia and Missouri was a critical element in Jefferson's and Lewis's evaluation of the prospects of the water route to the Pacific.

It must be observed first that the traditional way of looking at the major river systems of North America was to assume that they all had their head-springs in a common source area. This was a holdover from the symmetry of theoretical geography and had been substantiated by various geographical works and travelers' accounts of the eighteenth century. Most of these works[27] had set forth the opinion that "the four most capital rivers on the continent of North America," the St. Lawrence, the Mississippi, the Nelson, and the Columbia, had their sources "in the same neighborhood." These sources were viewed as being within 30 miles of each other and lying in the highest lands of North America. According to most authorities, the Missouri also had its headwaters in the common source area. One account mentioned the Missouri as heading in an area of extensive plains a few miles west of the sources of the Mississippi,[28] and Jefferson himself had noted in the official de-scription he wrote of Louisiana that "the Missouri and Mississippi run nearly parallel courses from their heads which are relatively close to one another."[29]

But relatively close was no longer a matter of 30 miles, and by the time that Jefferson and Lewis began to put together the various pieces of informa-tion on the drainage patterns of western North America, the pyramidal height-of-land had begun to change character—not in its general configura-tion but in the conceptualization of the rivers which flowed from it. Neither the St. Lawrence nor the Mississippi could properly be said to flow from the height-of-land. The Nelson, or more accurately its western tributary the Saskatchewan, still came from the common source area. The Columbia and Missouri were also spawned in the height-of-land. But added to these streams were the waters of the Southwest, and somehow it was envisaged that the Colorado and the Rio Grande also emanated from the same general region as did the Columbia, the Missouri, and the Saskatchewan. When this view is weighed against the Jefferson-Lewis image of the Rocky Mountains, a very interesting picture emerges.

It was a curious feature of the 1803 view of the common watershed, the pyramidal height-of-land, that it bore no apparent relationship to the nature of the Rocky Mountains as they became known after the explorations of the nineteenth century. It is true that the Rockies were a feature of the Jefferson-Lewis image of the Northwest. They were known to exist somewhere in the

27. Foremost in importance was Carver's *Travels*. Nearly all the textual materials avail-able derived their descriptions of the continental drainage system from that work.
28. Hubbard, *Rudiments of Geography*, pp. 113–15.
29. Jefferson, "Official Account," p. 347.

western interior, and nearly all period maps made some attempt at showing them. The Spanish and French fur trade operating out of St. Louis had heard constant rumors of the Shining Mountains, the British fur trade in Canada had seen them, and one of the British explorers, Alexander Mackenzie, had even crossed them on his way to the Pacific. But very little was actually known about the mountains themselves. They were said to be a relatively low range. Jefferson and other American geographical theorists generally considered the Blue Ridge to be higher than the Rockies,[30] and Mackenzie, provider of the only good firsthand account of the mountains, had described them as not excessively high and as becoming even lower south of the point where the Columbia entered the sea.[31] Nor were the western ranges extensive in breadth. Nearly every period map showed them as a single ridge, and although Arrowsmith's maps had conjectured that they might divide into several low ridges in their southern portions, the multiple-ridge structure that had been visualized by Mackay and Evans was neither a part of general geographical lore nor yet available in Jefferson's store of information.

The height and breadth of the Rocky Mountains, however, was less important for the image of 1803 than the function of the range as divider of Atlantic and Pacific drainage basins. It was perhaps in evaluating this function of the mountains of the western interior that Jefferson and Lewis made their greatest conceptual errors about the geography of the Northwest. For it seems that the height-of-land which separated the Missouri, Columbia, Saskatchewan, and Rio Grande was not necessarily seen as an adjunct of the Rocky Mountains. At least a partial answer to this inconsistency lies in the nature of the information available to Lewis and Jefferson relative to the location, both in terms of north-south extent and of longitudinal positioning, of the mountains of the interior.

II

The north-south extent of the Shining Mountains was a matter of controversy. Mackenzie had viewed the mountains as far north as the shores of the Arctic Sea and as far south as about $53\frac{1}{2}°$ N., but he had commented that he did not know how far beyond that southern point the mountains continued. Peter Fidler had, according to the information supplied by Arrowsmith's maps, observed the mountains as far south as approximately the 45th parallel. And where the Arrowsmith map of 1802 showed the Rockies as a single ridge that ran unbroken from northern Canada to New Mexico, the King map gave them a southern terminus around the 46th parallel.

Arrowsmith's representation was not in great contrast with an opinion common among many American geographical writers that the Shining Moun-

30. Jefferson, *Notes on the State of Virginia*, p. 29.
31. Mackenzie, *Voyages*, II, 346.

tains were a "vast range" which ran 3,000 miles north from Mexico and which acted as a true continental divide.[32] The King map, on the other hand, reflected a cautious acceptance of the concept that the mountains may have extended only as far south as the 45th parallel. To confuse the issue further, the foremost American geographical writer of the early nineteenth century, Jedediah Morse, had dealt in terms of two mountain ranges when describing the lands between the Mississippi and the Pacific. In the south were the mountains of New Mexico, in the north the Rocky or Shining Mountains.

There were also conflicting opinions on the longitudinal position of the mountains. Mackenzie had visualized the Rockies as extending in a southeasterly direction from just west of the mouth of the Mackenzie River on the Arctic Sea and paralleling the Pacific coast to a point near the mouth of the Columbia, where they turned inland.[33] And the conjecture made by many of those who read the reports in Vancouver's published works of Lieutenant Broughton's ascent of the Columbia was that the mountains (the Cascades) seen on the eastern horizon by the British naval officer were "dependancies" of the Rocky Mountains.[34] Both Arrowsmith and King, however, had shown the Rockies farther inland, between the 115th and 113th meridians, and their views correlated with those of Fidler, who supposedly had seen the Rockies as far east as $112\frac{1}{2}°$ W.[35]

It is entirely possible that Jefferson and Lewis may have formulated an image of the western mountains which could have rationalized the conflicting reports on the location and extent of the mountains with their theories on the pyramidal height-of-land. The rationalization would have involved their viewing not one but two major western mountain ranges—the mountains seen by the British in the north and the mountains of New Mexico in the south— with the common source area for western rivers lying somewhere between the two ranges. Such a rationalization would not have gone beyond Jefferson's and Lewis's geographical information,[36] and there is some evidence to suggest that they did, indeed, conceptualize two separate ranges. The northern range, shown on the King map, would have been that range crossed by Mackenzie

32. Robert Davidson, *Geography Epitomized* (Morriston, Pa., 1803), p. 50.

33. Mackenzie, like virtually every other theorist, made the mistake of assuming that the Rockies he had crossed were somehow connected with the coastal ranges below the 50th parallel as well as above.

34. Such opinions appeared, in legend form, on maps of the Northwest drawn in England in the late 1790s, and Jefferson himself received notes on geography from a French acquaintance which included the conjecture that "Mount Hood could well be a dependance of the *Stony Mountains*" (Bernard Lacépède to Jefferson, 13 May 1803).

35. According to Mackenzie, Fidler had made contact with the mountains near the head of the Saskatchewan at about longitude 112° 30' W. (*Voyages*, II, 347).

36. In fact such a rationalization had already been provided for by Carver in his *Travels*. Although Carver viewed the Rockies as the southern range and made no comment about the nature of the mountains above the 50th parallel, he viewed somewhat the same type of configuration as Jefferson and Lewis might have. At the northern terminus of the Rockies (the mountains of New Mexico in the possible 1803 image), according to Carver, "a number of rivers arise, and empty themselves either into the South Sea, into Hudson's Bay, or into the waters that communicate between these two seas" (*Travels*, p. 121).

and surveyed and mapped (supposedly) by Peter Fidler. These were the "Stony Mountains." The southern range would have been the mountains of New Mexico which the French literature had spoken of as running northward from the lower Rio Grande.

Jefferson and Lewis knew that the southern range of mountains formed a part of the boundary of Louisiana on the west according to the original claim, and Jefferson himself always referred to that western boundary as "the mountains of New Mexico" and not the Stony Mountains.[37] The northern range might have run in a southeasterly direction from Canada to their southern end at the 46th or 47th parallel; the southern range could have run northwest from New Mexico to connect with the mountains lying just inland from the mouth of the Columbia. In his letter to Jefferson in April, 1803, Gallatin had hinted at just such an east-west range separating the waters of the Missouri from those of the Rio Grande, Colorado, and other southwestern rivers. Between the two ranges might have been an extensive high plateau or height-of-land. It was in this area that the southern waters of the Missouri and the southern branch of the Columbia as pictured on the King map might have had their sources.

That such a view could have been a part of Jefferson's and Lewis's image of the Northwest certainly seems plausible. The conflicting reports on the mountain ranges might have seemed to them to bespeak two separate ranges rather than one. And it must be noted that they had access to nearly all the available information, whereas most of the reports on the nature of the western mountains were based on partial information which precluded views of two separate ranges. Nor would a major range extending the length of the continent and acting as a continental divide have been necessary to the Jefferson-Lewis image. Such a divide did not exist in the eastern half of the continent and it could have been decided that a firm divide did not exist in the western portions of North America either.[38] The concept of an area of extensive plains or high plateau country lying between the two mountain ranges and serving as a source area for the Missouri and Columbia rivers would seem to be a credible part of the image of 1803. This might help to clarify the rationale for the great southern branch of the Columbia and its eastward extent to approximately the 106th and 107th meridians as shown on the King map.

This concept of the mountains might also explain why Jefferson, in the instructions given Lewis prior to his departure, took special care to warn the explorer away from "the northern waters of the Missouri," which would, in the image, have had their sources in the northern mountains. By following a more southerly route, the Lewis party might find a quick and easy crossing,

37. Jefferson, "Examination into the Boundaries of Louisiana," *Documents Relating to . . . Louisiana*.

38. According to the ideas of continental symmetry that were more or less in vogue, the presence of a drainage divide on the western side of the continent that ran the full length of the land mass from the Arctic to Mexico would have been unexpected.

with a single portage, through a high plains area. Finally, if this view of two mountain ranges were a part of the image, it might explain why Jefferson specifically instructed Lewis to learn whether the dividing grounds between the Missouri and other western rivers were mountainous or flat. Such instruction seems unnecessary and showed an element of doubt with respect to the more traditional view of the western ranges as extending unbroken from north to south all the way down the continent. And the concept of two mountain chains rather than one helps to explain why Jefferson himself never referred to the Missouri as having its headwaters in mountains when the majority of contemporary reports so indicated.

12

If all the elements of Jefferson's and Lewis's possible image of the geographical features of the Northwest are combined, the picture is one of a fertile, well-watered area perfectly suited for occupancy by an agrarian people. Through this garden ran mighty rivers which, by their connections, provided convenient transportation across the continent. The image of the Northwest on the eve of Lewis's departure would seem to have been truly a happy combination, a teleologically induced blend of rivers and mountains, ordered and patterned according to the concepts of universal efficiency and economy, and providing the "water communication across this continent for the purposes of commerce."

The Missouri River, wrote Jefferson in 1803, offered, "according to the best accounts a continued navigation from it's source, and, possibly with a single portage, from the Western Ocean." This statement encapsulates the Jefferson-Lewis image of the Northwest. It would not be too extreme a statement to say that nearly all elements of the image of 1803 were predicated on the ancient notion that a water communication across the continent was possible. More than a century of exploration in the trans-Missouri region had been based on the idea; Jefferson and Lewis could hardly have helped viewing the Northwest through eyes that were misted with the dreams of a Passage to India. The rivers of the trans-Missouri area were long and navigable to their sources. And these sources were in a common area, close enough to one another to allow only a short portage between navigable waters. This common source area might have been a mountain range. But if it were seen as such, then the range was certainly narrow, low, and easily crossed. Or the source might have been in a simple height-of-land; if so, the problems of a portage from the navigable waters of the eastward-flowing streams to the navigable waters of the westward-flowing streams were diminished even more.

The two greatest rivers of the Northwest, the Missouri and the Columbia, had such a connection between their upper reaches. It was this connection, in the mind of Jefferson and Lewis, that offered the last chance for the discovery of a water communication across the continent of North America. In neither content nor analysis did their image of the Northwest vary substantially from that of the Jesuit father Jacques Marquette, who looked at the Missouri one spring day in 1673 and wrote later that it led to a "fine prairie," which, if crossed, would lead to another river, which led, in turn, to the great South Sea. "I have hardly any doubt," said Marquette—and Lewis would have echoed the thought—"that this is the Vermillion Sea, and I do not despair of discovering it some day."

Thus was the image of the Northwest in 1803 a combination of fact and rumor, of theory and conjecture, with a sprinkling of hope added for seasoning. It was an image based on partial and contradictory information and therefore it had within it many areas of highly questionable accuracy. But it was an image which betokened the possibilities of a water communication across the continent. Because the image did provide for a connection between the waters of the Atlantic and Pacific drainages it would, during the years 1804–06, undergo refining and transformation by an exploratory adventure designed to establish the validity of the central premise in the conception of the Northwest: that the Missouri River and some westward-flowing river heading with it offered an easy line of communication across the continent of North America.

CHAPTER 5

TOWARD THE MARGINS
OF THE NORTHWEST

From early in 1801 until midsummer of 1803 the Lewis and Clark Expedition had taken shape in Jefferson's mind, had been approved by the U.S. Congress, and had been carefully planned by Jefferson and his private secretary, Meriwether Lewis. The preparatory stages of the transcontinental expedition were based on Jefferson's and Lewis's views of western geography, and when Lewis left Washington on July 5, 1803, he carried with him the instructions from Jefferson which reflected those views. He was to explore the Missouri River and "such principal stream of it" as offered the best connection with the waters of the Pacific Ocean and to fix the points of the portage between the Missouri and those western waters so that trade between the United States, the fur-bearing regions of the western interior, and the Orient might be "consequently conducted . . . more beneficially than by the circumnavigation now practised."[1]

Meriwether Lewis had helped to shape the image of the Northwest upon which those instructions were based. In the years between 1804 and 1806 he was to help in modifying the earlier views of the trans-Missouri area. But as he had not been alone in creating an image of the Northwest prior to his

1. Jefferson's instructions to Lewis, 20 June 1803 (Jefferson Papers).

127

explorations, he was not to be alone in modifying and refining that image. He would be aided in the process by another frontier soldier and wilderness expert, William Clark.[2] Before he left Washington, on June 19, 1803, Lewis wrote to his longtime friend and former army comrade, then living at the Clark estate across the Ohio River from Louisville, and informed him of the planned expedition and its purpose.[3] After providing Clark with a synopsis of the instructions from Jefferson, Lewis offered Clark the co-command of the expedition "with the privity of the President who expresses the anxious wish that you would consent to join me in this enterprise." A little more than a month later, Clark replied to Lewis's invitation, saying that "the enterprise &c. is such as I have long anticipated and am much pleased with."[4] Jefferson reported to a government official later that "William Clarke accepts with great glee the office of going with Capt. Lewis up the Missouri."[5].

2

Clark and Lewis were not united until the middle of October, when, after having traveled from Washington to Pittsburgh to pick up supplies and then journeying down the Ohio River, Lewis arrived at the Falls of the Ohio.[6] From there, on October 26, 1803, with a party of at least nine men engaged by Clark, "Capt Lewis and Capt Wm Clark set of on a Western tour."[7] The party reached the mouth of the Ohio on November 14, having picked up some additional volunteers on the way downriver. They remained at the confluence of the Ohio and Mississippi for nearly a week and then began the ascent of the Mississippi to the mouth of the Missouri. On December 12, 1803, at a point directly opposite the mouth of the great river that

2. Clark, like Lewis and Jefferson, had a piedmont Virginia background. Little is known of his early life or education, although an unsubstantiated family rumor has it that he was a classmate of Lewis's at Maury's school. Whether he became acquainted with Lewis during boyhood or not, it is known that the two future explorers served for a time in the same army unit in the Old Northwest. At the time of Lewis's invitation, Clark was retired from active service and was managing his family's estate near the Falls of the Ohio. It is not known whether Clark had any advance notice of the plans of Jefferson to explore the Northwest, but between 1800 and 1802 he made several trips to Washington and while there visited with Lewis and the President at the White House. The best sources for Clark's role in the early stages of the expedition are John Louis Loos, "William Clark's Part in the Preparation of the Lewis and Clark Expedition," *Bulletin of the Missouri Historical Society*, X (1954), 490–511; and Loos, "A Biography of William Clark, 1770–1813," unpublished Ph.D. dissertation, Washington University, St. Louis, 1953. Another excellent source of material on Clark may be found in the Clark Papers, Missouri Historical Society, St. Louis.

3. Jackson, *Letters*, pp. 57–60.

4. Jackson, *Letters*, pp. 110–11.

5. Jackson, *Letters*, includes various letters dealing with the acceptance by Clark of Lewis's offer.

6. Details of Lewis's Ohio River journey may be found in Milo M. Quaife, ed., *The Journals of Captain Meriwether Lewis and Sergeant John Ordway* (Madison, Wis., 1916), pp. 30–97.

7. From the "Diary of Jonathan Clark" (William Clark's brother), entry for Oct. 26, 1803 (MS, Filson Club Library, Louisville, Ky.).

Marquette and Jolliet had discovered in 1673, the "Corps of Western Discovery . . . came to in the Mouth of a littel River called Wood River."[8] Here they would camp for the winter of 1803–04.

Exactly when or how the decision was made to establish a base camp on this site is unknown. The original intention of Jefferson and Lewis had been that the expedition should travel "7. or 800 miles" up the Missouri before making their winter quarters.[9] By as early as October 3 this plan had been altered, however, for Lewis wrote Jefferson on that date and suggested that, rather than following the original plan to ascend the Missouri as far as possible, he would make camp somewhere close to the mouth of the river and "make a tour this winter on horseback of some hundred miles through the most interesting portion of the country adjoining my winter establishment; perhaps it may be up the Canceze [Kansas] River and towards Santafee."[10] Jefferson concurred in Lewis's decision not to enter the Missouri until spring but was adamant on the subject of the suggested trip along the southern side of the river. Such a journey might, said Jefferson, endanger the main purpose of the expedition. "The object of your mission is *single*, the direct water communication from sea to sea formed by the bed of the Missouri & perhaps the Oregan."[11]

Given this admonition, Lewis and Clark determined to make their winter quarters in the U.S. territory on the eastern bank of the Mississippi, and here, in what became known as "Camp Dubois," the captains made their final preparations for the journey up the Missouri. Among the most important of these preparations was the acquisition of additional geographical lore on the trans-Missouri area. Clark remained at the Wood River camp during most of the winter and occupied his time directing the activities of preparation—filling out the roster of the expedition with military and civilian personnel, and training and disciplining the men. Lewis spent most of his time in St. Louis, where he assumed the duties of securing some of the supplies still required, hiring French *engagés* to assist in the upriver journey, and gathering supplemental lore about the Missouri and the Northwest. "We are," William Clark wrote his brother-in-law, "collecting what information we can of this river and its risques so as we may make just calculations before we set out."[12]

3

The full extent of the geographical information on the trans-Missouri region gathered by Lewis and Clark during the winter in Camp Dubois, like the full extent of the lore obtained prior to Lewis's departure from Washing-

8. Quaife, *Journals of Lewis and Ordway*, pp. 70–71 (entry by William Clark).
9. From a letter of Jefferson to Benjamin Rush (Jackson, *Letters*, p. 68).
10. Lewis to Jefferson, 3 Oct. 1803.
11. Jefferson to Lewis, 16 Nov. 1803.
12. Jackson, *Letters*, p. 164.

ton, will probably never be fully determined. The nature of their contacts in the St. Louis area during the winter of 1803–04 were such that a good part of the data they received was oral rather than written and was thus, in all probability, lost to posterity forever.[13] If they did acquire informal written data on the Northwest during the Wood River period, no traces of it have been located in any of the documents or collections relating to the expedition. Problems also exist in trying to establish the acquisition of formal information—manuscript materials, published works, and manuscript or published maps. In spite of the lack of written evidence, however, it is possible to make some basic assumptions about the source materials on the geography of the Northwest gathered during the months before the embarkation from Camp Dubois in May, 1804.

These source materials are of two categories: information received from Jefferson (indicating the extent to which he was still operating as a guiding force in the expedition), and geographical lore—written, cartographic, and oral—acquired by Lewis and Clark at the Wood River camp and in St. Louis. Some of this information served to substantiate what was already known or believed known about the Northwest; some of it helped to modify the earlier image of 1803. But all of the lore gathered during the Wood River period aided in the creation of a pattern of northwestern geography as seen by Lewis and Clark prior to their journey from St. Louis to the Pacific.

4

As he had from the incipient stages of the expedition, Jefferson continued to remain active and concerned as a supplier of geographical data even after Lewis left Washington. In fact, two very important items of information were probably transmitted to Lewis on the eve of his departure. These were the Arrowsmith map of 1802 and a copy of Mackenzie's *Voyages from Montreal*. Jefferson had owned a copy of the Arrowsmith map for some time and had used it in negotiating with foreign diplomatic officials in Washington. But in June, 1803, he wrote to James Cheetham, a New York bookseller, and mentioned that he had "seen advertised in some papers that an edition of Arrowsmith's map" had been published in New York and that he would like to obtain a copy of it or of the English edition.[14] Since Jefferson was already

13. This would have been particularly true in St. Louis, where many of their informants were, at the best, semi-literate and could not have supplied information in writing. In addition, the political situation would most likely have prevented the taking of any notes on conversations with Spanish officials—still in *de facto* control of Louisiana. In a letter to Jefferson (Dec. 28, 1803), Lewis mentioned some of the difficulties encountered in obtaining information (Jackson, *Letters*, pp. 148–57).

14. Jefferson to James Cheetham, 17 June 1803. This possible attempt to get cartographic material for Lewis has been largely overlooked because of Jefferson's reference to "Arrowsmith's map of the U.S.," a wording that would seem to describe a map narrower in scope than the Arrowsmith map of North America. However, Jefferson (according to several items

in possession of a copy of the Arrowsmith map, it would seem that the acquisition of a second copy might have been intended for the use of Meriwether Lewis. This idea is supported when it is seen that, during the course of the expedition, Lewis referred to the Arrowsmith map in his daily records as if he were consulting a copy in the field.[15]

In the same letter in which he ordered a second copy of the Arrowsmith map, Jefferson noted that he understood that "there is to be had in New York an 8vo edition of McKenzie's travels with the same maps which are in the 4to edition: I will thank you to procure it for me." Jefferson had purchased a copy of *Voyages from Montreal* when it first became available, and it must be presumed that this second copy was intended for Lewis's use. The idea is reinforced by Jefferson's comment in his letter to Cheetham that he wished the new edition specifically because the older quarto was "too large & cumbersome." Like the Arrowsmith map, the Mackenzie account was referred to in the field journals of Lewis and Clark in such a manner as to indicate that the captains carried with them the copy of Mackenzie or, at the least, had made extensive notes from it.[16]

Both the Arrowsmith map and the Mackenzie journals would have been vital acquisitions, not so much for Lewis, since he must have been familiar with them, but for Clark, who had not undergone the intensive period of education in the geography of western North America. The map contained significant contemporary data on the Rocky Mountains that proved important during the course of the expedition, and Mackenzie's travel works gave quite specific details on the Missouri River near the Mandan villages. The northern bend of the river, Mackenzie had stated, was known to be in latitude 47° 32′ N. and longitude 101° 25′ W., and "according to the Indian accounts, it runs to the south of west."[17] This information was in agreement with the location given the Mandan villages in Thompson's surveys and the King map and with the course of the southern fork of the Missouri system west of the Mandans as shown on both the King and Arrowsmith maps. Perhaps even more important than the references to the upper Missouri area were Mackenzie's comments on the short portage he discovered between the Peace River and the supposed Columbia; these comments could only have supported the basic element in the view of the Northwest that the same type of portage might be found between the Missouri and the "River Oregan."

---

in the Jefferson Papers) several times referred to consulting details on the Northwest appearing in an Arrowsmith map "of the United States." It would seem that the President was not always careful about exact titles of materials in his possession; witness to this is his constant reference to Mackenzie's *Voyages from Montreal* as "Mackenzie's *Travels.*"

15. Cf. Thwaites, *Original Journals*, II, 132.

16. Cf. Thwaites, *Original Journals*, III, 60. There also appear, on a map that Lewis and Clark obtained in St. Louis during the winter of the Wood River encampment, several notes that appear to have been added by the captains after consulting Mackenzie's book and map. See Donald Jackson, "Some Books Carried by Lewis and Clark," *Bulletin of the Missouri Historical Society*, XVI (1959), 3–13.

17. Mackenzie, *Voyages*, I, xcv.

5

Unfortunately, no published geographical works other than the Arrowsmith and Mackenzie materials can be said conclusively to have been transmitted to Lewis and Clark by Jefferson. It is quite probable, however, that Lewis had taken notes from Jefferson's library; it seems very unlikely that the President would have failed to supply the man he had selected to lead a transcontinental exploration with data from the sources in his collection. But if he did so, no record of such a transmission of geographical lore before Lewis left Washington remains in either Jefferson's notes or in the records of the expedition. A burning question here is whether or not Lewis had received, from either Jefferson or Gallatin, the map drawn by Nicholas King. Certain evidences point to the fact that the King map could have been taken on the expedition;[18] the fact that it was not mentioned by either Jefferson or Lewis is not necessarily inconsistent, since nowhere does there exist an inventory list of the geographical items in Lewis's possession. It does seem unusual that the King map, if it were in the explorers' store of materials, was never alluded to in the journals of the expedition. A possible answer here is that by the time any need to consult the King map arose, that chart had already been superseded by additional material on the geography of the Northwest.[19] And in the final analysis the question is relatively unimportant. The King map did symbolize the lore of the Northwest in 1803 and probably came close to duplicating Lewis's view of the area whether he had it with him or not.

6

Although it cannot be said with certainty that Jefferson had transmitted the King map to Lewis, there are good records to show that he supplied several other critical items of information on the geography of the Northwest prior to Lewis's and Clark's final separation from civilization in the spring of 1804. The first of these was forwarded to Lewis while he was still in Pittsburgh gathering supplies for his western travels. Here he received a letter from Jefferson in which was enclosed an extract of a letter that Jefferson had just received from "Mr. La Cepede from Paris," a French naturalist to whom Jefferson had written earlier about the prospective expedition.[20] The extract read, in part:

18. See pp. 98–99 and n. 41 above.
19. The receipt of cartographic materials from the Mackay-Evans expedition to the upper Missouri prior to the departure of Lewis and Clark from Camp Dubois might have overshadowed the data on the King map since both captains surely recognized that the Mackay-Evans information was the best and most up-to-date on the trans-Missouri region.
20. On February 24, 1803, Jefferson wrote to Bernard Lacépède: "It happens that we are now actually sending off a small party to explore the Missouri to it's source, and whatever other river, heading nearest with that, runs into the Western ocean."

Mr. Broughton, one of the companions of Captain Vancouver went up the Columbia river 100 miles, in December 1792. he stopped at a point which he named Vancouver lat. 45° 27′ longitude 237° 50′ E. [archaic–he means 122°.] here the river Columbia is still a quarter of a mile wide & from 12. to 36. feet deep. it is far then to it's head. from this point Mount Hood is seen 20. leagues [50 miles] distant, which is probably a dependance of the Stony mountains, of which Mr. Fiedler saw the beginning about lat. 40° and the source of the Missouri is probably in the Stony mountains.[21]

This information was of consequence for the view of the nature of the divide between eastern and western waters and became more important when, with the passage of time and the first summer and winter spent in the North-west, Lewis and Clark began to receive lore that supported it. At the time of its receipt from Jefferson, however, it cannot be determined how the captains would have interpreted the Lacépède letter. Briefly, the letter suggested a number of things: first, that the Columbia was a considerable river, both in its breadth and length; second, that it ran to a point from which the "Stony mountains" (or at least a "dependance" of them) were visible; and third, that the Missouri had its source in these same mountains. Lewis and Clark would have known from both the Arrowsmith and (if they had it) the King map about the extent of the Columbia, and therefore the former part of Lacépède's information added little to their store of geographical knowledge.

The Frenchman's intelligence about the mountains and the source of the Missouri, however, might have been very significant. The implication in the letter was that either the Rocky Mountains were much wider than was be-lieved since both the Arrowsmith and King maps showed their eastern edge nearly 10° of longitude east of the Pacific coast, or that the mountains were much closer to the Pacific than they were represented on either the Arrow-smith or King maps, and that therefore the Missouri—known to have its source in the mountains, according to Lacépède—must extend much farther west than shown by Arrowsmith or King. The image of the Northwest as it was held by Jefferson and Lewis before July, 1803, might possibly have offered a solution to the seeming inconsistencies between the best cartographic data and the Lacépède information by hypothesizing a southern range of mountains bounding the waters of the Rio Grande, Rio des los Apostolos, and Rio Colorado on the north and running in a northwestern direction to link with the mountains near the Columbia's mouth assumed by Lacépède to be dependencies of the Rockies.

The extent to which Lewis and Clark accepted this possible solution is problematical. Some distance calculations that William Clark was to make be-fore May, 1804, on the mileage between various points in the trans-Missouri area suggest that the captains did accept the Arrowsmith-King depiction of the distance between St. Louis and the source of the Missouri. This would in-dicate that the Lacépède letter, which intimated that the Missouri extended

21. Jefferson to Lewis, 15 July 1803.

much farther west than had been suggested in the 1803 image, had little impact on the Lewis and Clark view of the Northwest immediately prior to their departure from the Wood River camp. On the other hand, if Lewis adhered to the hypothesized Gallatin-Jefferson conception of a mountain range separating the waters of the southern branches of the Missouri from the northern waters of the Rio Grande and other southwestern rivers (and perhaps channeling the great southern branch of the Columbia of King's map into a region near the Missouri's southern sources), then the Lecépède information might have seemed to support that conception. There is no substantive evidence to prop up such a suggestion—other than the simple fact that Jefferson obviously considered the letter important enough to make an extract of it for Lewis.

Any conclusions about the importance of the Lacépède letter for Lewis's and Clark's image of the Northwest before they left Camp Dubois are, however, purely conjectural. But in the months ahead, when Indian information gained in the field pushed the Rockies farther west than they should have been, the data in the French naturalist's letter may have become important and could have been interpreted as suggesting very close connections between the Rockies, the source of the Missouri, and the Pacific Ocean.

7

The letter in which Jefferson enclosed the extract from his French colleague's message was important not only from the standpoint of the geographical data it contained. "We received," wrote Jefferson in the same missive, "the treaty from Paris ceding Louisiana according to the bounds to which France had a right."[22] The news of the cession of Louisiana was made public just before Lewis left Washington,[23] therefore Jefferson's statement came as no surprise. But receipt of the treaty made the Louisiana Purchase more or less official (although it still had to be approved by the Senate) and marked the beginning of a new phase of activity in Jefferson's acquisition of geographical lore that would prove crucial for Lewis's and Clark's outlook on the Northwest.

Following the cession of Louisiana Territory to the United States, Jefferson had a twofold reason for continuing his search for the best geographical information available on the trans-Missouri area. He needed now not only to be concerned with supplying Lewis and Clark with the finest possible surveys of the area, but he also considered himself responsible for gathering enough

22. The question that Jefferson evaded in this statement was: just what were "the bounds to which France had a right?" The issue of the boundaries of the territory, particularly the western boundaries, was not to be resolved for years. An interesting contemporary treatment of the question may be found in Amos Stoddard, *Sketches, Historical and Descriptive of Louisiana* (Philadelphia, 1812).

23. Cf. Jefferson to Henri Peyroux, 3 July 1803; and the *National Intelligencer* (Washington), July 4, 1803, pp. 1–2.

evidence to support his belief that the inherent value of the acquisition of Louisiana would outweigh any criticisms that his political enemies might make about his rather cavalier interpretation of his executive powers in giving sanction to the purchase prior to congressional approval. He immediately set about acquiring additional intelligence on the Northwest, and even though Lewis had already left for the West, Jefferson continued, up through January, 1804, to transmit to the explorer the best of the geographical materials that began flowing into Washington from around the country.

The first sources to which Jefferson applied in his search for new and more complete knowledge on all features of the trans-Missouri area were members of the American Philosophical Society. During the first few days following the official release of the news of the Louisiana Purchase, he wrote to several of his colleagues at Philadelphia and appealed to them for any further details they might have. Since the majority of the individuals that the President corresponded with in the society were more knowledgeable and concerned with other fields than geography, their replies contained little information of specific geographic importance.[24]

Tucked away in some of their responses, however, were items about the geography of the Missouri country. In July, for example, Caspar Wistar raised some questions about the direction of the Missouri's course from its source to the Mississippi:[25] " 'till the publication of McKenzie's book I believed it to be nearly west, & if I am not mistaken M. Pirroux[26] spoke of it in the Same way for 2000 miles of its extent. But McKenzie's account[27] is confirmed by the Gentleman who gave the account of the Wild Sheep,[28] in his narrative he mentions the Missouri as existing no great distance from the Saskatchevine river." A few months later Wistar provided Jefferson with the encouraging news that he had learned that the Spanish had sent a party of Indians up the Missouri to the Pacific and that this party had returned in two years after having reached the coast.[29]

Wistar was one of the few society members who could offer anything substantive of a geographical nature. Of much greater value for transmission to Lewis and Clark was the information that Jefferson received from Ameri-

24. This is not surprising; the fact that Jefferson was in possession of most of the best data on Louisiana geography was probably known by his colleagues in the society. To forward what they could about western geography might have seemed, to them, a little like carrying coals to Newcastle.

25. Caspar Wistar to Jefferson, 13 July 1803.

26. Henri Peyroux, a French trader residing at St. Louis and a former government official of Upper Louisiana. Jefferson had had some contacts with Peyroux during his term as secretary of state, and the trader was to supply Lewis and Clark with some information on the Missouri region as far as the mouth of the Platte (Nasatir, *Before Lewis and Clark*, II, 598, n. 5).

27. Mackenzie (*Voyages*, I, xcv) wrote of David Thompson's surveys of the Missouri's northern bend and described the course of the river above the northern bend as being "south of West."

28. This is a reference to an article by a Duncan McGillivray in the *Medical Repository*, VI (1st hexade, 1803), 237–40. In 1800 McGillivray traveled throughout the "plains that are situated between the Sascatchevain and Misssourie Rivers, along the Rocky Mountains."

29. Caspar Wistar to Jefferson, 9 Oct. 1803.

can citizens living in or on the borders of Louisiana. In July, 1803, shortly after receiving news of the acquisition by treaty of the territory, Jefferson sent a rather lengthy questionnaire entitled "Questions on boundaries, populations, laws, etc., of Louisiana" to Daniel Clarke of New Orleans and asked Clarke to distribute it "among the different persons best qualified to answer them respectively."[30] At the same time, he sent a copy of the questions to William C. C. Claiborne, governor of the Mississippi Territory, making the same request—to distribute the questionnaire among the persons "having the best knowledge."[31]

By the end of August Jefferson had begun to receive responses to these queries, and although most of them were concerned directly with the lower portions of Louisiana, some few items of interest were obtained on the Missouri River region. The typical response was that from Governor Claiborne, who avowed that he could find no good maps of the entire area "that can be depended upon" and that although the Spanish officials had maps of the Louisiana Territory, they were "highly secretive" about these. On the boundaries of the territory, particularly the western boundaries, Claiborne was forced to admit that he had "not been able to obtain any satisfactory information." And on the subject of the geography of the trans-Missouri area, Claiborne said simply, "I can make no communication of consequence."[32]

Other correspondents, such as John Sibley of Natchitoches and William Dunbar of Natchez, returned responses to Jefferson's questionnaire that were veritable treasure troves of geographical information, but again, this information was applied only to the area of Lower Louisiana; of the upper portions of the territory—north and west of St. Louis—it was reported that "almost nothing is known."[33] This paucity of information on the trans-Missouri region was well illustrated when Jefferson issued his compilation of all the materials he had received on Louisiana.

8

In November, 1803, the U.S. Congress was presented with a document entitled "An Official Account of Louisiana."[34] Out of the thirty-six pages in this digest of geographical lore on the newly acquired territory, Jefferson de-

---

30. Jefferson to Daniel Clarke, 17 July 1803. A copy of the questionnaire is included with this letter.

31. Jefferson to W. C. C. Claiborne, 17 July 1803.

32. W. C. C. Claiborne to Jefferson, 24 Aug. 1803. Another correspondent, John Sibley of Natchitoches, made the same comment about the lack of maps, saying that no good maps were available.

33. The Jefferson Papers contain other surviving materials from the responses to Jefferson's questionnaire. With very few exceptions, these documents focus on the population, laws, governmental structures, and economy of Lower Louisiana.

34. This document was printed in numerous newspapers of the period. It is officially listed as Doc. 164, 1st Sess., 8th Cong.

voted only a little more than one page to a "General Description of Upper Louisiana," that portion of the territory from St. Louis north and west. Within that one-page description, however, was more fantasy than in all the remainder of the account, showing quite completely the speculative nature of the geographical lore of the Northwest.[35] The face of the country was seen as being "rather more broken" than in the lower portions of the territory, but it was noted that the soil was "equally fertile." Furthermore, the area of the Northwest had many advantages that were not generally "incident to those regions" occupying the same latitudinal position. It was elevated and well watered and had a "variety of large, rapid streams, calculated for mills and other water works." The soil was more fertile than anywhere else in the same latitudes and the land was said to yield its produce almost without any inputs of human labor. To the north and west, along the shores of the Missouri, the land was "one immense prairie" which produced nothing but grass since the soil was "represented as being too rich for the growth of forest trees." The land was truly a beautiful land, teeming with droves of buffalo, deer, and other kinds of game. The landscape itself was immensely pleasing; in many places it was "carved into various shapes by the hand of nature," presenting the "appearance of a multitude of antique towers."

Beyond these statements on land quality, little geographical information was contained in the section of the "Official Account" that dealt with the lands of the trans-Missouri region. There appeared no descriptions of the Missouri itself, nor of the mountains to the west. Jefferson illustrated quite well his inability to gain any knowledge of the upper Missouri beyond that which he already possessed by saying that the upper courses of the river were "but little known." And, he cautioned, no reliance could be placed on any accounts of the Missouri west of the Mandans since "no discoveries of the Missouri, beyond the Mandane nation, have been accurately detailed, though the traders have been informed that many large navigable rivers discharge their waters into it far above, and that there are many numerous nations settled thereon." Up to the time of the writing of his "Official Account," at least, Jefferson's attempts to gain additional lore on the geography of the Northwest had been almost a total failure.

9

Before the end of 1803, however, a piece of geographical lore on the trans-Missouri area was received which was to be quite important to Lewis and Clark. In December Jefferson received from William Henry Harrison, governor of the Indiana Territory, "a Copy of the manuscript map of Mr. Evans who ascended the Missouri River by order of the Spanish Government

35. Jefferson, for example, described in some detail and without qualifications the large mountain of salt that some observers had reported on the upper Missouri.

much further than any other person."[36] The greatest part of this map, drawn in several sections by John Evans of the Mackay-Evans explorations, dealt with the course of the Missouri between the Mississippi and the Mandan villages. It was later sent to Lewis and Clark and aided them in establishing the nature of the country between St. Louis and the Mandans as a firm part of their accurate geographical lore. More important, however, was the last section of the map, which showed the Missouri west of the Mandan villages and would prove of great consequence for the shaping of Lewis's and Clark's ideas on the upper Missouri and the Rocky Mountains before they left the winter camp at Wood River. With the acquisition of this map, Jefferson's role as a gatherer of information for the expedition was at an end. What remained was to transmit to the explorers everything he had acquired since Lewis left Washington.[37]

10

After Lewis and Clark went into their base camp at Wood River, they obtained some of the materials gathered by the President after Lewis's leave-taking, along with some documents Jefferson himself had written to consolidate the information he had obtained from his correspondents in Louisiana. In a letter dated November 16, 1803, Jefferson enclosed a copy of an "account of Louisiana" along with "copies of the Treaties for Louisiana, the act for taking possession, a letter from Dr. Wistar, & some information collected by myself from Truteau's journal in MS. all of which may be useful to you."[38]

The "account of Louisiana" that Jefferson sent along was a printed copy of his official account presented to Congress, already released to the press and containing little specific information that Lewis did not already have in his possession. The copies of the treaty and the "act for taking possession" were also relatively minor acquisitions and may have been forwarded by Jefferson for Lewis's use should the explorer have to perform any official functions in association with the United States' formal takeover of Louisiana. The letter from Wistar was apparently an enclosure in a letter written by the Philadelphian to the President on July 13, 1803, for in a later letter to Jefferson[39] Wistar mentioned that his earlier letter had "inclosed a letter to Major Lewis. . . ." Whatever Wistar enclosed for Lewis in his July letter to Jefferson has

36. William Henry Harrison to Jefferson, 26 Nov. 1803. Questions have been raised as to whether this map was actually an Evans map or was a copy of a map drawn by James Mackay. The controversy over the provenance of the Evans and Mackay maps associated with the expedition is discussed in my n. 50 below.
37. The fact that Jefferson's last transmission of material to Lewis and Clark was in January, 1804, makes it a near certainty that the captains did, in fact, receive all the materials he forwarded before their leave-taking in May, 1804.
38. Jefferson to Lewis, 16 Nov. 1803.
39. Jackson, *Letters*, p. 133.

not survived, although it may have been a list of "inquiries" for Lewis's use in obtaining information about Louisiana.[40]

It is possible that Jefferson, in referring to "a letter from Dr. Wistar," meant a message from Wistar to himself. Both of Wistar's letters to the President in 1803 did contain geographical information that could have been useful; the July letter dealt in part with the direction and course of the Missouri, and the October letter mentioned briefly a party of Indians sent to the Pacific by the Spanish. In any case, the Wistar material could not have been of great value. Of questionable importance as well was the extract made by Jefferson from the manuscript journals of Jean Truteau.[41] The condensation contained little in the way of geographical information other than a comment that "The soil of the Missouri is the most fertile in the Universe"; it was devoted almost entirely to a description of the location of various Indian tribes in Upper Louisiana. The extract did, it is true, make note of the fact that "In the Missouri river there is depth sufficient to carry a frigate as far up as it is known" and that the river contained no cataracts or rapids. Such comments added to the already firm conclusions on the navigability of the river, but the significance of the extract would be superseded when Jefferson later forwarded to Lewis "a translation of that journal in full."

Jefferson's role as an active supplier of information for the Lewis and Clark Expedition was nearly at an end. But before the party left Camp Dubois and began the trip up the Missouri, severing mail connections with the President, he was to submit still more articles of geographical lore which became important for Lewis's and Clark's knowledge of the Northwest. On January 13, 1804, Jefferson wrote to Lewis: "I now inclose you a map of the Missouri as far as the Mandans, 12. or 1500. miles I presume above it's mouth. it is said to be very accurate, having been done by a Mr. Evans by order of the Spanish government. but whether he corrected by astronomical observation or not we are not informed. I hope this will reach you before your final departure."[42] This map was probably the manuscript or a copy of the map drawn by John Evans in 1797[43] and acquired by Jefferson from William Henry Harrison in December, 1803.

A little more than a week after he had sent the Evans map, Jefferson made his final contribution to the geographical knowledge of Lewis and Clark. On January 22, 1804, he wrote to Lewis: "With mine of Nov. 16 I sent you some extracts made by myself from the journal of an agent

40. Wistar had promised such a list during Lewis's training period in Philadelphia, as had other members of the American Philosophical Society. It is possible that the list supplied by Wistar did survive in part, perhaps combined with a list of questions compiled by Clark sometime early in 1804 for the purpose of extracting data from the residents of St. Louis (Jackson, *Letters*, pp. 157–61).

41. Jefferson had probably received the Truteau journals from James Wilkinson in May, 1800. Jackson prints Jefferson's extract of the Truteau account (*Letters*, pp. 138–39).

42. Jefferson to Lewis, 13 Jan. 1804.

43. See my n. 50 below.

of the trading company of St. Louis up the Missouri. I now inclose a translation of that journal in full for your information."[44] Most of Truteau's journal dealt with the country between the mouth of the Missouri and the mouth of the Platte and contained little geographical intelligence of significance that had been omitted from the extract. But it is a possibility that Jefferson's transmission included not only the field journals of Truteau but his "Description of the Upper Missouri" as well.[45] If so, the captains could have obtained their first definite knowledge of the Yellowstone River in textual form and some fascinating, if speculative, knowledge of the prospective passage to the Pacific. For Truteau had met a band of Indians who had described to him a route beyond the mountains to a "wide and deep river, well-timbered, the waters of which appeared to go in the direction of the winter sunset."[46]

II

Jefferson was not the only American official to supply lore on the trans-Missouri area directly to the captains, nor was Lewis the only one to whom geographical knowledge was transmitted before the Corps of Discovery left Camp Dubois. Sometime early in November, 1803, William Clark had written to William Henry Harrison, requesting information about maps of the Northwest that he had learned were in the office of the territorial governor.[47] On November 13, 1803, Harrison replied to Clark's letter, saying that he had indeed seen a map of the trans-Missouri region and that he had "had it copied & now send it to you by the Post rider. . . . I hope it will arive safe."[48]

This map, showing the Missouri River from its mouth to just beyond the Mandan villages, apparently did arrive safely from Harrison, and it was probably the map that Lewis referred to in a letter to Jefferson, December 28, 1803, as "a map of the Missouri river, from it's mouth to the Mandane nation." Although the provenance of this map has stimulated a considerable amount of controversy among scholars of the expedition, it was almost certainly a copy of a map drawn by James Mackay during his travels on the

44. Jefferson to Lewis, 22 Jan. 1804.
45. Among a group of Lewis and Clark documents in the files of the old War Department was a handwritten manuscript entitled "Description du haut Missouri—Jean Baptiste Truteau." The "Description" was, of course, a different piece of material from Truteau's journals, but that it appeared together with other Lewis and Clark documents raises the fascinating speculation as to whether they obtained it—from Jefferson or someone else—prior to the expedition. The manuscript is now in the Jefferson Papers.
46. Nasatir, *Before Lewis and Clark*, II, 380.
47. The letter from Clark to Harrison has apparently not survived. The wording of Harrison's letter of November 13, however, suggests that Clark had written and requested help from the governor. In his letter Harrison referred to "the map mentioned in your letter of the 5th Instant."
48. Jackson, *Letters*, pp. 135–36.

Missouri in the summer of 1797, or drawn from data that resulted from those travels and supplemented with information from John Evans.[49]

12

In the Mackay map sent by Harrison and the Evans map (also originating with Harrison) forwarded by Jefferson, Lewis and Clark had cartographic sources on the area of the Northwest from the Missouri to the Mandan villages that were vast improvements over previous efforts to picture the Missouri River.[50] Although these maps covered basically only the territory

49. Jackson (*Letters*, pp. 135–36, n. 3) offers an interesting discussion of the Mackay map.

50. Confusion over the maps of Mackay and Evans has reigned supreme ever since maps said to be authored by them and found to be related to the Lewis and Clark Expedition began to turn up in the early part of this century. Some authorities have suggested that the maps sent to Clark by Harrison and to Jefferson by Harrison and thence by the President to Lewis were all copies of the same map, drawn by James Mackay (cf. Cutright, *Lewis and Clark*, p. 39). It has also been suggested that a third map exists, this one mentioned by Lewis in a letter to Jefferson of December 28, 1803, as "a map of the Missouri river, from it's mouth to the Mandane nation"; this map was supposedly also a copy of a Mackay map and was believed to have been obtained by Lewis from Antoine Soulard, surveyor-general of Spanish Louisiana (cf. Cutright, *Lewis and Clark*, p. 39; and Ernest Staples Osgood, ed., *The Field Notes of Captain William Clark, 1803–1805* (New Haven, Conn., 1964), pp. 16–17, n. 7). But these speculations do not bear up under close scrutiny. I believe that Jackson (*Letters*, pp. 135–36, 140–41, 155, and 163) has come nearest the truth by concluding that the map sent to Clark by Harrison and the one mentioned by Lewis in his letter of December 28 are the same map, drawn by James Mackay. The map sent to Jefferson by Harrison and then by Jefferson to Lewis is a different map. Jackson, however, skirts the issue of the authorship of this second map by referring to it as a "so-called Evans map," although he does add that for a convincing argument that the map was indeed an Evans product one should consult Aubrey Diller, "Maps of the Missouri River before Lewis and Clark," in *Studies and Essays . . . in Homage to George Sarton* (New York, 1946), pp. 505–19.

It is my belief that Jackson has approached the correct answer and that we are dealing with two separate maps, one by Mackay and one by Evans. The Mackay map was the one sent to Clark by Harrison and was the one mentioned by Lewis in his letter of December 28, 1803, as "a map of the Missouri river, from it's mouth to the Mandane nation." This was *not* a Soulard map. In his letter of December 28, Lewis mentioned two other maps, one of the Osage River and one a "general map of Uper Louisiana." Only one of these can be definitely identified as coming from Soulard; Lewis detailed the manner in which he obtained the map of the Osage River from the surveyor-general in his letter. The "general map of Uper Louisiana" *is* a Soulard production, but whether Lewis obtained it from him or not is not known. (Since Lewis described the acquisition of the Osage map from Soulard in detail, it seems curious that he would not do the same for the "general map of Uper Louisiana" if this chart were received from Soulard as well.) There is no reason to believe that the third map of Lewis's letter is not the Mackay map. The map had been sent by Harrison on November 13 and must have arrived at Wood River by December, having only come from Vincennes. It was an important acquisition and would have been mentioned by Lewis.

The Mackay map was brought to light in the early 1900s when it was discovered, along with other manuscript materials relating to the expedition, in some papers in the Office of Indian Affairs. It was the subject of an article written by Annie H. Abel ("A New Lewis and Clark Map," *Geographical Review*, I (1916), 329–45), who believed that it was the one drawn by John Evans and sent to Lewis by Jefferson in January, 1804. Dr. Abel based her conclusion on Jefferson's statement in his letter of January 13, 1804, that he was sending a map showing "the Missouri as far as the Mandans . . . done by a Mr. Evans by order of the Spanish government." The Indian Office map, according to Dr. Abel, was the only map found to be associated with the expedition which fit this description and must, therefore, be an Evans map. This was incorrect and hasty and stemmed partly from Dr. Abel's failure to note the hand-as far west as the northern bend of the Missouri and slightly beyond, they were highly accurate charts of the Missouri itself. Both maps showed nearly the same features and gave the same names to rivers and streams entering the Missouri. One important difference between the maps, however, was in the location they gave to the Mandan villages.

The Mackay map (fig. 23) placed the Mandan villages at around 110° W., information which compared favorably with a comment in Mackay's journal, also to come into the explorers' possession during the winter of 1803–04, that the Mandan villages were located near the 111th meridian.[51] The Evans map, on the other hand, indicated that the Mandan villages were 17° 33′ west of St. Louis or about 107° 48′ W. Both estimates were much too far west, the Mandan villages actually being located near the 101st meridian. Mackay placed the Mandans about 400 miles farther west than they should have been while Evans's estimate was about 300 miles in excess. This was a very critical error when combined with Mackay's journal information that it was 170 leagues or approximately 470 miles from the Mandans to the Great Falls of the Missouri. This latter distance estimate was amazingly accurate; the misplacing of the Mandan villages, however, had the effect of moving the Great Falls between 300 and 400 miles closer to the Pacific than they actually were. Given the captains' possession of the Thompson data, which located the Mandans "by astronomical observations" much more correctly, however, these errors in the Mackay-Evans maps may have had only a negligible impact on Lewis's and Clark's view of the Northwest.

The real importance of the cartographic results of the Mackay-Evans

---

writing on the map. On the back of the Mackay (Indian Office) map is found the notation "For Captn. William Clark or Cap. Meriwether Lewis on a voyage up the Mississippi." This is in the same hand as the letter from Harrison to Clark (in the Clark Papers at the Missouri Historical Society), and the wording compares favorably to an address on the outside of Harrison's letter to Clark ("Captain William Clark or Captain Meriwether Lewis on their way up the Mississippi supposed to be at Cahokia"). The Indian Office map was a Mackay map, sent to the explorers by William Henry Harrison.

The map sent to Jefferson by Harrison and then by Jefferson to Lewis was not a Mackay map. It was an Evans map and was specifically referred to as such by Harrison, who was close enough to the situation to know what was going on. Failure to identify such maps associated with the expedition as the Evans map stems from the fact that the real Evans map (reaching Lewis and Clark via Jefferson's transmission of January 13, 1804) remained hidden for years, being published as nos. 5–11 and 13 in the Atlas volume (VIII) of the Thwaites edition of the *Original Journals* and misidentified by Thwaites as being Clark's. Thwaites discovered the map in the collection brought back from the transcontinental journey (now in the Coe Collection at the Beinecke Library, Yale University, New Haven). He included it in the Atlas since he believed it to be Clark's work. That such is the case is impossible. The notations on the map are in neither Lewis's nor Clark's hand and the style of the map is totally unlike any of those drawn by Clark. Furthemore, the map gives the location of the Mandan villages as being 17° 33′ west of St. Louis—the same longitudinal position given by Evans in his journals. Lewis and Clark, armed with Thompson's surveys and making relatively accurate observations themselves, simply could not have made such a miscalculation. Aubrey Diller ("Maps of the Missouri River") substantiates this argument and gives other reasons for identifying the Evans map with the map found in the Coe Collection and reproduced in the Thwaites edition of the *Original Journals*.

51. Nasatir, *Before Lewis and Clark*, II, 493.

travels was on the captains' image of the area west of the Mandans. The Mackay map terminated a short distance west of the villages although it did show the mouth of the Yellowstone River, finally establishing that stream in geographical lore. Attached to the several numbered sheets which made up the main section of the Evans map, however, was an unnumbered sketch drawn by the same cartographer which depicted the course of the Missouri from the Mandans to the Rockies and was apparently based on Indian information that Evans had received during a stay with the Mandans in 1797[52] (fig. 24).

This map was of tremendous importance in its representation of the country west of the Mandans, and particularly significant was the portion of the map showing the Rocky Mountains. Whereas earlier information about the Rockies had led to a single-ridge concept of the mountains,[53] the Evans sketch clearly showed four, and possibly five, separate ridges. (This multiple-ridge configuration was in agreement with data presented on the 1795 and 1802 Arrowsmith maps, but only in caption or legend form.) Just above the mouth of the "River yellow rock" and south of the Missouri was the notation "mountain of eternal snow," possibly considered as the easternmost range of the Rockies and depicted as an isolated range. Farther to the west were four continuous north-south ranges obviously intended to represent the Rocky Mountains proper. The Missouri cut through the easternmost of the four main ranges at "the fall," bent around the northern end of the second range to the west, and then was shown as coming straight from the south between this second range and still another range on the west.

Beyond the range bordering the Missouri on the west was a fourth range labeled "montagne de roche." This last range was cut by a westward-flowing river which had its source between the third and fourth ranges. The cartographer drew a square-sided figure beside this westward-flowing stream, perhaps to indicate the existence of a European trading establishment (possibly Russian since the Louisiana Spanish of Evans's time knew of Russian posts in the Pacific Northwest). The picture presented by the Evans map was clear. The Missouri flowed through a series of mountains and had its sources to the south; west of the Missouri was a final dividing ridge and beyond that were waters flowing to the Pacific. This information was supported by the lore contained in the Mackay-Evans journals which were obtained by Lewis

52. The handwriting on the unnumbered sketch map (no. 13 in the Atlas of the Thwaites edition of the *Original Journals*) is the same as the handwriting of the numbered series (nos. 5–11 in Thwaites). The place names on the sketch also agree with place names on the numbered sheets. For example, the tribe living just upstream from the Mandans was labeled as "Wanutaries." These were the Minitari Indians, the "Minitarees" of Lewis and Clark, always referred to by that name in their journals. Both Evans and Mackay, on the other hand, consistently used the term "Wanutaries."

53. There was, it is true, some lore that spoke in terms of multiple ridges. Legends appearing on Arrowsmith maps mentioned that, according to Indian accounts, the mountains divided into a number of low ridges below the 50th parallel. But such statements were not a general feature of the geographical lore of the time.

23. James Mackay's map of the Missouri from St. Charles to the
Mandan villages (*ca.* 1797) LIRARY OF CONGRESS

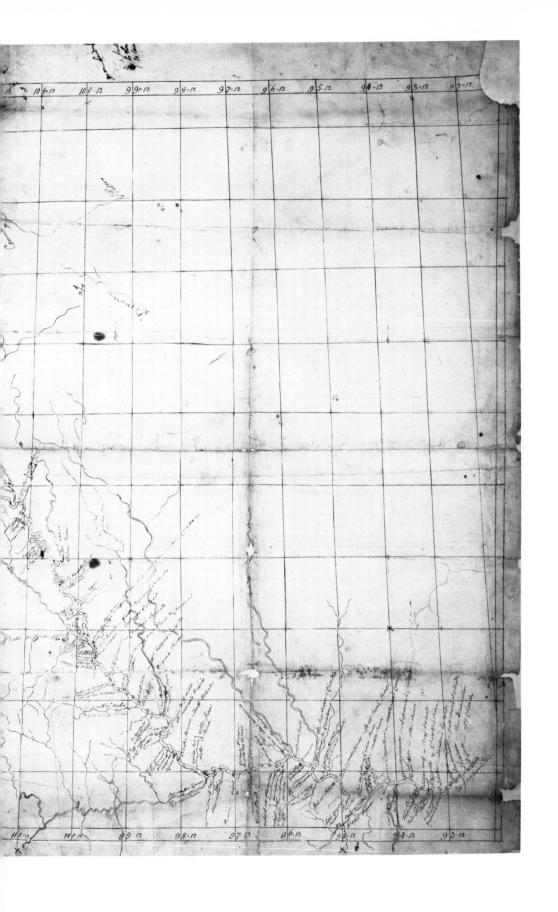

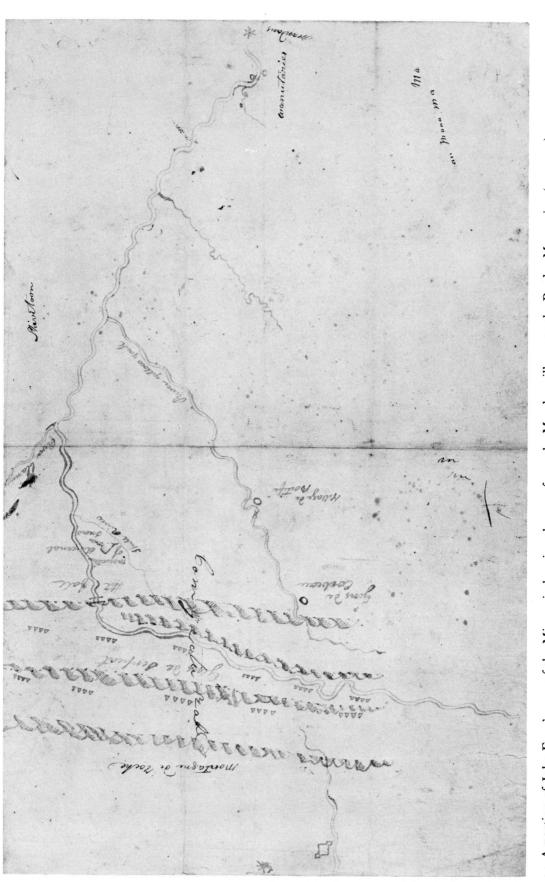

24. A portion of John Evan's map of the Missouri, showing the area from the Mandan villages to the Rocky Mountains (*ca.* 1797)
BEINECKE RARE BOOK AND MANUSCRIPT LIBRARY, YALE UNIVERSITY

and Clark, along with some other significant data on the Northwest, before the end of 1803.[54]

13

During their tenure on the margin of the Northwest in the winter of 1803–04, Lewis and Clark acquired even more geographical lore on the trans-Missouri area. This new phase of acquisition of knowledge was undertaken by the captains independently of Jefferson or other American officials in the East. It began in late November, 1803, when the explorers separated at the mouth of the Kaskaskia River, Lewis proceeding to St. Louis to present his credentials to the Spanish commandant, and Clark heading up the Mississippi to the mouth of Wood River to establish the expedition's winter quarters.

Upon his arrival in St. Louis, Meriwether Lewis wasted no time in obtaining "such information as I might consider usefull to the Government, or such as might be usefull to me in my further prosecution of my voyages."[55] On December 28, 1803, he wrote a lengthy letter to Jefferson describing his progress in the accumulation of data and relating the difficulties he had encountered in encouraging the government officials and private citizens of St. Louis to part with geographical lore on the Missouri River.[56] In spite of an obvious unwillingness on the part of many St. Louis residents to provide Lewis with assistance, he had managed to obtain several extremely important geographical documents before the end of the year. He related to Jefferson his process of gathering information and gave an inventory of those materials collected by December 28, 1803:

I have proposed many quiries under sundry heads to the best informed persons I have met with at St. Louis and within the vicinity of that place; these gentlemen[57] have promised me answers in due time, but as every thing undergoes the examination of the Commandant, you may readily conceive the restraint which exists on many points. . . .[58]

I have obtained three maps; one of the Osages river, before mentioned, a general map of Uper Louisiana, and a map of the Missouri river, from it's mouth

54. Much of the information on the Evans map was apparently used by Clark in drawing his map at the Mandan villages during the winter of 1804–05.

55. Lewis to Jefferson, 19 Dec. 1803 (Jackson, *Letters*, pp. 145–47).

56. Jackson, *Letters*, pp. 148–55.

57. Some of those with whom Lewis came in contact who could have supplied him with information were fur traders and merchants who had dealt in the Missouri trade for years, e.g. Auguste and Pierre Chouteau and Charles Gratiot. Others were government officials such as Antoine Soulard and Carlos Dehault Delassus, governor of Upper Louisiana. It is known that Lewis had contact with Soulard, and that he was on good terms with the Chouteau brothers is positive as he mentioned on several occasions that he had been entertained by them at social "balls."

58. In his letter Lewis included a lengthy passage about the nature of "the restraint." If he ever received any responses from the "quiries" he posted, none of them have ever been found. Jackson (*Letters*, pp. 161–62) prints a letter from Lewis to Auguste Chouteau that may have been typical of Lewis's "quiries."

to the Mandane nation; these I shall retain for some time yet, in order to assertain by further inquiries their accuracy or otherwise; I have also obtained Ivin's and Mac Kay's journal up the Missouri, it is in French & at present is in the hands of Mr. Hay[59] who has promised to translate it for me. . . .

The three maps mentioned by Lewis, along with the journals of Mackay and Evans, complete the list of geographical materials that can be definitely established as being in Lewis's and Clark's possession prior to their departure for the Pacific. The first map mentioned by Lewis, the map of the "Osages river," was probably a copy of a manuscript map that Lewis had seen in the office of Antoine Soulard, the official surveyor-general of Louisiana. Although the original of this Soulard map has never been found, Lewis must have received permission from Soulard to copy it, and it is likely that the material from the map was used by Clark in preparing a map of the lower Missouri later that winter. The "map of the Missouri river, from it's mouth to the Mandane nation" was probably a reference to the Mackay map that had been sent to Clark by Harrison in November. Other than the Evans map, which was not received from Jefferson until after Lewis had written this letter, the Mackay map is the only known piece of cartographic data which could fit the description.

14

The final map, referred to by Lewis as a "general map of Uper Louisiana," is one of the most important acquisitions made prior to May, 1804. This map has not been identified beyond all doubt but it is probably a copy of a map drawn by Antoine Soulard.[60] The Soulard map (fig. 25) must be given special mention for its possible impact on the geographical images of Lewis and Clark, particularly on their views respecting the distance between the headwaters of the Missouri and the Pacific Ocean.

59. Throughout Lewis's stay in St. Louis, Hay acted as his interpreter in dealing with Spanish officials and was probably instrumental in convincing government officials such as Soulard to allow Lewis to copy maps from their offices. He might also have been the person who supplied Lewis and Clark with the Mackay-Evans journals. See Osgood, *Field Notes*, p. 16, n. 7, and p. 25, n. 8; and Jackson, *Letters*, pp. 156–57, n. 9.

60. This map was discovered in the Clark manuscripts in the Coe Collection at Yale and published in the Thwaites edition of the *Original Journals* (VIII, no. 2) as "A Topographical Sketch of the Missouri and Upper Mississippi; Exhibiting the various Nations and Tribes of Indians who inhabit the Country: Copied from the Original Spanish Ms Map." How the map came to be located in Clark's papers cannot be definitely established, but it would seem reasonable that it was obtained by Lewis while in St. Louis (either from Soulard or someone else) and retained by Clark after the expedition. A special study of this Soulard map has been done by Aubrey Diller ("A New Map of the Missouri River Drawn in 1795," *Imago Mundi*, XII (1955), 175–80). Diller thinks that Lewis or Clark may have obtained the map from a G. Turner, a U.S. territorial judge in Kaskaskia, who mentioned in an article appearing first in the Cincinnati *Western Spy* in 1803 that he was in possession of a map of the western parts of North America, the original of which was in the hands of a "high official" in St. Louis. No connections between either Lewis or Clark and Turner have been established, and it is more likely that Lewis got the Soulard map from someone in St. Louis.

The single most striking feature of the Soulard map was the Missouri-Platte watershed. The Missouri was shown as nearly encircling New Mexico and running in a much more west-to-east direction throughout its course than it actually does. It flowed all the way, according to the cartographer, through a ridge of mountains labeled "The Rocky Mountains" from a source beyond those mountains and very close to a westward-flowing stream labeled "Oregan, or R. of the West." This river was much shorter than the Missouri, consequently the Missouri's head was represented as being quite close to the Pacific. Such information would have seemed to agree quite conclusively with the view of the mountains and the head of the Missouri as related in the Lacépède letter.

Since distance calculations for the expected journey between St. Louis and Pacific shores made by Clark in January, 1804, were apparently based on the idea that the Missouri's source was as shown on the Arrowsmith and King maps and not as depicted on Soulard's chart, however, it is questionable how much impact this correlation of data from the Soulard and Lacépède sources had on the Lewis and Clark image of the Northwest. But after the first summer of the expedition and the first winter spent in the Northwest, Lewis and Clark would gather data leading them to believe the mountains (and hence the source of the Missouri) were much closer to the ocean than shown by Arrowsmith or King. In this later transformation, the Soulard map, in combination with the Lacépède letter, may have been important and conclusive evidence on the spatial proximity of the Missouri to the Pacific.

Also of importance on the Soulard map was the section which depicted the nature of the Missouri's source area. Here the river was shown as flowing between two mountains on the western side of the Rocky chain, and as it broke through these mountains, the cartographer drew a straight line across it to indicate a "chute" or fall of the river. This cartographic symbolization, apparently a reference to the Great Falls of the Missouri, matched closely an account of Louisiana written in 1785 by the Spanish governor, Estevan Miró.[61] In his account, Miró described the Missouri as cutting the chain of mountains running north from New Mexico and said that at that point of transection the "cataract or cascade is formed." This was an indication that knowledge (or at least rumors) of the Great Falls were relatively common in Louisiana at the time of Lewis and Clark.

The critical information that came through on the Soulard map (and in Miró's account, although no records indicate that Lewis or Clark had access to his description) was that when the Great Falls were reached, the traveler would have traversed the mountain chain. The Rockies, then, might have been

61. Nasatir, *Before Lewis and Clark*, I, 119–27. Somewhat the same depiction appeared on a contemporary Spanish map (see fig. 12 above) which was apparently drawn after the Mackay-Evans travels and might have been in Lewis's and Clark's possession before the expedition. This map, a much cruder product than either Mackay's or Evans's maps of the Missouri River, covered all of the Northwest and showed the south-to-north course of the Missouri to what was labeled as a "chute" or fall. This map was located in the same collection of papers in the Indian Office in which the Mackay map was found.

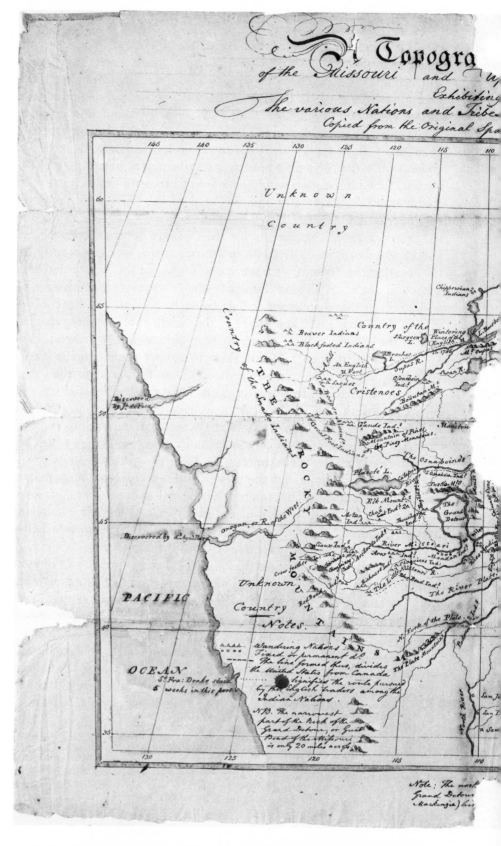

25. Copy of an Antoine Soulard map of western North America (*ca.* 1802)

Indians who inhabit the Country:
MS. Map.

PART OF

HUDSON'S BAY

Ft P. of Wales
Churchill R.

Bungi Nation
Ft York
York River

Lake Winnepeg
Maskego Indians

Lake N'ipegon

Winnebeck R.
Sauteux Indians
L. of the Woods.
Rainy Lake

Whipecoten Bay

The Grand Portage

I. SUPERIOR

English Ft
Sauteux Indians
Red L.
Sioux Ind.
Sioux Ind.

Ponca Ind.
Omaha Ind.
St. Peter's R.
The Upper Missisippi
Quiconsin R.

of Ind.
Plate
250 leagues from the Missouri Mouth
Fox R.

Oto
Little Ned Med
R. Missouri
R. des Maines
Illinois R.

Republican Ind.
Blue R. Great Ned Med
Kansey Ind.
Fork
Kanset River

Cahine R.
Kakakia
Kaskaskia
St Louis

North Fork
Great Ausage
Mesineg R.
Ste Genevieve
New Bourbon

Little Ausages
Richard R.
La Tour

River des
Arpot R.
Missisippi R.

Apacoi R.

viewed as a ridge or series of ridges somewhat similar to the Blue Ridge, and the Missouri might have been imagined as cutting through that chain in the same manner as the Potomac's passage through the Blue Ridge. Such a belief would have been at least partially shored up by the last sheet of the Evans map, which showed the Missouri cutting through ridges of mountains. Such a view might also have furthered the conceptual geography of the Jefferson-Lewis image of 1803; in that image, the source area of the Missouri was possibly seen as a high plateau, and it would have seemed conceivable for this plateau area to be located west of the mountains.

15

The final item of information that Lewis cataloged in his letter to Jefferson was a copy of "Ivin's and Mac Kay's journal up the Missouri." How this copy came into Lewis's possession is not definitely known. It may have been obtained from John Hay of Cahokia, the man whom Lewis mentioned as promising to translate it for him. There is a possibility that the Mackay-Evans journal could have been given to Lewis by Mackay himself, for the former explorer was living at St. Charles on the Missouri during the winter of 1803–04 and was mentioned several times by Clark in a journal of events that he kept at Camp Dubois.[62]

There was relatively little geographical description of the territory beyond the Mandan villages in the Mackay-Evans journals, but what there was proved to be a substantiation of the Evans and Soulard maps. In the first section of the journal, Mackay described the Great Falls and the upper course of the Missouri River:

Mr. Evans measured the Missouri near the Village of the Mandaines and he found it 500 toises [approximately 3,000 feet] large, which confirms me in my Opinion that the Sources of the Missouri is much further off than what is imagined, although the Indians who inhabit at the foot of the Rocky Mountains have but a Confused Idea of the upper parts of the Missouri; Nevertheless after all the Information I could collect it appears that the Missouri takes its source in abt. the 40th deg. North latitude from Whence it Runs to the North (between the chains of the Rocky Mountains) as far as the 49th deg. Latitude that thence running East, it falls over the East chain of the Mountains in the great plains across which it runs to the East till it reaches the Mandaines—There is no other fall, in the whole course

62. Milo M. Quaife, who edited the journals of Mackay and Evans (*Wisconsin Historical Society Proceedings*, LXIII, 1915), had this suspicion. It seems to have been confirmed by Jackson, although the possibility remains that John Hay was the agent who transferred the journals from Mackay to the explorers. In *Letters* (p. 156, n. 8) Jackson wrote: "A manuscript version of the original [Mackay–Evans journal] is in the American Philosophical Society Library. I believe that this manuscript, and another by Mackay entitled 'Notes on Indian Tribes' [in the Missouri Historical Society Library], were once carried together, folded lengthwise and bound with a paper band [also in the Missouri Historical Society Library] which bears in Lewis's hand the words 'Mr. Evin's sketches of the Missouri, present by Mr. MacKay.' "

of the Missouri, but where it falls over the Rocky Mountains, in the plains, as I have said before. This fall it is Said, is of an astonishing height, from the Situation of the Country and the Meanders of the River I suppose this fall to be 200 leagues [about 550 miles] West of the Mandans.[63]

This information from the Mackay and Evans journals was the latest available on the upper Missouri and might have exerted a considerable impact on Lewis's and Clark's impressions of the country they were to traverse. Several statements in the journals, in particular, could have proved central. The reference to the sources of the Missouri as being "much further off than what is imagined" might have substantiated the notion that the Missouri extended closer to the Pacific than it does, and that the area between the Rockies and the sea was compressed into a smaller space than the actual, vast area of the western slope of the Continental Divide. This rather vital misconception was well illustrated by Clark in a map that he was to draw at the Mandan villages during the winter of 1804–05.

Also quite important in shaping the thoughts of Lewis and Clark with regard to the Missouri's headwaters would have been Mackay's information about the latitude of origin (40° N.) and the latitude at which the river turned and headed east (49° N.). These are roughly the latitudes that were to appear on the Clark map of 1805; it is obvious that Lewis and Clark later developed an impression of the south-to-north course of the Missouri from the Three Forks to the Great Falls as being much longer than it actually is. Since this was the case, the Mackay-Evans journals were apparently an important source for the transformation of the 1803 image and the Arrowsmith-King charts. These showed two main branches of the Missouri above the Mandans, one heading in the neighborhood of the 50th parallel and the other near the 46th parallel, with each branch running in a dominantly west-to-east direction. The modification of this view into a conceptualization of the Missouri as heading in the south, then running north to a point at which it turns east, "falls over the Rocky Mountains," and then continues to run toward the east, is a closer approach to the actual course of the Missouri than that represented on the Arrowsmith and King maps—even though the extent of the north-south course is greatly magnified.

The Mackay-Evans information provided still another source for the transformation of the earlier image of the Northwest. A possible interpretation of the Jefferson-Lewis view of the trans-Missouri area had the northern branch of the Missouri heading in the Rocky Mountains near the 50th parallel and the southern branch heading near the southern terminus of the mountains around 46° N., with the great southern branch of the Columbia approachable from the southern waters of the Missouri through what might have been a high plateau country. The Mackay-Evans data, on the other hand, had the Missouri heading far in the south and then flowing north between two separate dividing ranges, the one on the west setting the Missouri apart from

63. Nasatir, *Before Lewis and Clark,* II, 497–98.

the waters of the Pacific drainages. The majority of the maps available to Lewis and Clark showed the Rocky Mountains as a single ridge.[64] But from the Mackay-Evans journals it was learned that there were not one but two ridges. The eastern ridge was cut by the Missouri after the river had flowed north for a great distance along the base of a western ridge.

The more information that Lewis and Clark gathered, the more rumors they received of the Great Falls of the Missouri. Each of these additional references to the mighty cataracts would have reinforced the Mackay-Evans view of the multiple-ridge structure of the Rockies. The view was also strongly supported by the last section of the Evans map, which also showed the south-north trend of the Missouri above the Great Falls, with the river's course confined on the west by one last ridge acting as a drainage divide between Atlantic and Pacific waters. The 1803 view of a possible portage through an open height-of-land was probably transformed into the concept of a portage over the last western ridge. But the transformation placed no insurmountable obstacle in the way to the Pacific, for the last ridge was probably imagined in the same light as the single ridge of the earlier view had been and was seen as a narrow and low range of hills. The fact that Mackenzie had found a portage across such a low ridge in the northern mountains could only lead to the conclusion that the traverse of the last dividing range would be short and fast and would lead to the waters of the great southern fork of the Columbia, which had already been provided for in the image of 1803 and in the speculations of theoretical symmetrical geography.

16

The Mackay-Evans journals were about the last items of geographical lore gathered by Lewis and Clark before May, 1804, that can be definitely identified. There remains, however, one final document which provides evidence of some additional source materials on the geography of the trans-Missouri area. This is the journal kept by Clark at the Wood River camp from December, 1803, to May, 1804.[65] There is little logical order to the

64. Again with the exception of the Arrowsmith map, which, although it showed the Rockies as a single ridge, noted in caption form that they were "according to the Indian account . . . five ridges in some parts."

65. Lewis might not have kept a journal for this period. If he did, none has been located. Clark's journal from the Wood River period is a recent find. It, along with field notes that Clark kept for the trip from the mouth of the Missouri to the Mandan villages, was discovered in 1953 in an attic trunk in St. Paul, Minnesota, along with some papers of John Henry Hammond, Civil War general and former Indian Office superintendent. How the papers came to be deposited among his records is a fascinating and as yet unanswered question. Following the discovery of Clark's field notes and the Dubois journal, there was a lengthy litigation involving the federal government, the Clark heirs, and the state of Minnesota, all claiming prior rights to the papers. The matter was finally resolved by allowing the Clark heirs to donate the materials to the collection of Western Americana at Yale University. The field notes and Dubois journal were later published as *The Field Notes of Captain William Clark*.

materials in the Clark journal, and a good deal of space is devoted to comments on the personnel of the expedition, disciplinary problems, supply acquisitions, etc. But Clark's notes for the winter of 1803–04 are more than a daily record and description of logistical difficulties. For interspersed among the daily notations are "bits of information as to the country to the north and west gathered from Visitors who came to camp."[66]

The greatest volume of geographical data was related to the immediate area of the camp, the Missouri as far as St. Charles, and the area of settlement along the Missouri, extending only to "La Charette," a French village about 70 miles up the river. There are only two recorded exceptions to this statement. On January 1, 1804, Clark noted that he had talked with a Patrick Henneberry, a blacksmith,[67] who had traveled "far to the North, & visited the Man'd Inds on the Missouris, a quiet people 6 day from [illegible word] or Red river & that the M[issouri] is about 150 yds over at this nation."[68] This information was relatively inconsequential but might have been confusing when contrasted with the information in the Mackay-Evans journals that the Missouri at the Mandans was more than a half-mile wide. Like Mackay, Lewis and Clark could have based their ideas on the length of the river and the distance from the Mandans to its source on the breadth of the river at the Mandan villages. It is a virtual certainty that Mackay's data would have loomed larger in their minds than the lore provided by Henneberry, however, and the latter's statements on the width of the Missouri were probably put by.

The second clue to geographical information in the Camp Dubois notes was Clark's entry for January 10, 1804, on the quality of the land on the upper Missouri.[69] He had derived his information from "Cap. Mackey," who had just returned from surveying some country up the Missouri and who reported that "a bountifull Countrey presents its self on the route he went & returned." No mention was made of any other information that Clark might have received from James Mackay. It is unthinkable, however, that the former Spanish-sponsored explorer would not have been questioned extensively by Clark, who was certainly aware of the fact that Mackay possessed what was the latest and most accurate data on the Northwest.

17

In addition to the above entries, there are three other sections of Clark's journal that are of interest. The first two of these relate to the information gathered prior to January, 1804, and serve to show the uses to which the cap-

66. Osgood, *Field Notes*, p. xvi.
67. Jackson (*Letters*, pp. 144–45, n. 4) identifies this man as an employee of William Morrison, a prominent merchant of Kaskaskia.
68. Osgood, *Field Notes*, p. 11.
69. Osgood, *Field Notes*, p. 16.

tains were putting some of the data they had acquired. The first entry of interest is found in Clark's notes for January 3, 1803. He wrote: "I am told that an old French fort was once built on the opsd side of the river from me, and that Some remains of the clearing is yet to be seen, this must be the fort which was built in the year 1724 by M. de Bourgmont the Comdt. The first settlement made in this quarter was made in 1679. de la Salle [blank space] then called Crevecour. arkansas was settled by 10 F. men in 1685."[70] These statements were apparently extracted from Du Pratz's *History of Louisiana* and reinforce the already firm conclusion that Lewis and Clark had a copy of that work with them prior to the commencement of their upriver journey. Moreover, the passage shows that Clark was engaged in the process of studying the information about the Missouri and the Northwest that he had available.

In the second entry, dated January 7, 1804, Clark stated: "I drew a Map for the purposes of Correcting from the information which I may get of the Countrey to the N.W."[71] This was the beginning of the first cartographic product of the expedition and was the map which Lewis was to transmit to Jefferson in May, 1804, as "A Map of a part of Upper Louisiana, complied from the best information that Capt. Clark and myself could collect, from the Inhabitants of Saint Louis, haistily corrected by the information obtained from the Osage Indians lately arrived at this place. . . . This map has but small claims to correctness, but I hope it will furnish some general ideas of the country which may be serviceable."[72]

This map (fig. 26) showed each of the settlements in Upper Louisiana and laid down the Missouri as far as the mouth of the Kansas River. It was, therefore, not of critical importance to the objectives of the expedition. But it is of interest in that it provides a certain commentary on the quality of the information gathered in St. Louis. The country of the Osage Indians was perhaps the best-known area of all of the Upper Louisiana country beyond the Missouri's mouth due to longtime contacts with French and Spanish fur traders. And yet, in spite of this, Lewis mentioned that the map—based on information received from some of those fur traders and merchants—had to be "haistily corrected" by information from the Indian inhabitants of the area. If information on this relatively well-known part of the Northwest was inaccurate, what might that information on the farther regions amount to?

The third entry in the Clark journals was a table of distances and estimated travel time between Wood River and the Pacific; this was the most significant geographical entry in the *Field Notes* and is fairly conclusive

70. Osgood, *Field Notes*, p. 11.
71. Osgood, *Field Notes*, p. 16. Here is where Clark began to come into his own. In the months and years ahead he would create many of the most important maps of the American Northwest. The map referred to here is the subject of a special study by Donald Jackson: "A New Lewis and Clark Map," *Bulletin of the Missouri Historical Society*, XVII (1961), 117–32.
72. Jackson, *Letters*, pp. 192–95.

evidence of Lewis's and Clark's view of the Northwest around January, 1804. The distance estimates were obviously based on the existing information as gathered by the captains up to that time and illustrated the nature of their image of the trans-Missouri region. By the date that Clark made his distance estimates, the captains had collected most of the information they were to gather before ascending the Missouri. But there were several central components in their store of information that had not yet been procured when Clark made his calculations, among them the very important Evans map showing the country west of the Mandans. It is also questionable whether John Hay had completed his translation of the Mackay-Evans material and given it to the explorers. But by May, 1804, the missing material would be obtained; thus it is necessary, in discussing Lewis's and Clark's image of the Northwest before they departed for the upper Missouri, to deal with two separate views—an image which was illustrated by Clark's distance calculations and which shared many elements with the earlier 1803 images, and a final image of the Northwest, containing several important modifications of the earlier view and based on all the materials gathered by the captains before May, 1804.

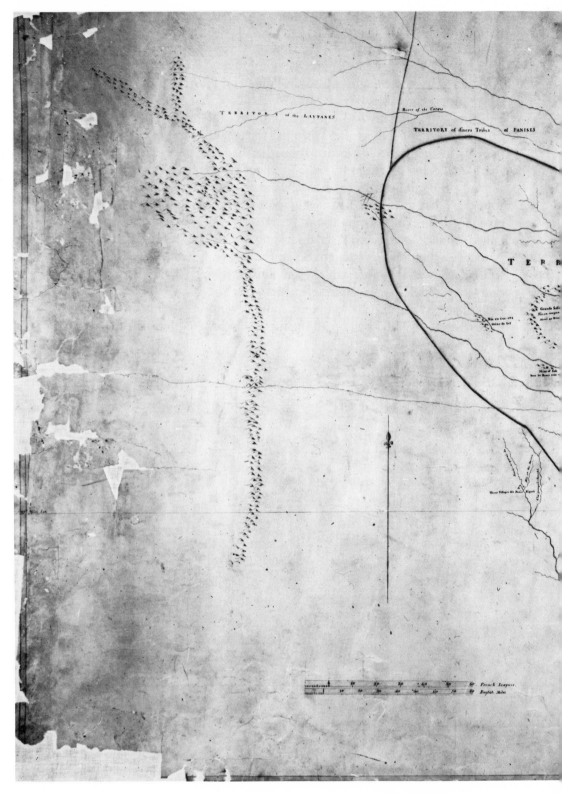

26. William Clark's map of a part of Upper Louisiana, 1804   NATIONAL ARCHIVES

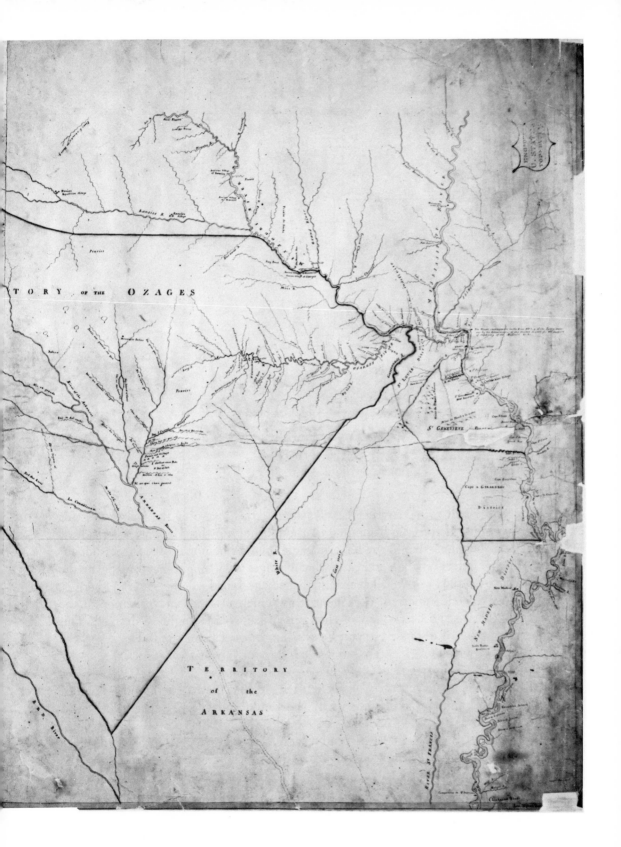

CHAPTER 6

THE VIEW
FROM WOOD RIVER

It is difficult to reconstruct Lewis's and Clark's image of the Northwest for the winter before the beginning of the journey up the Missouri. Clark drew no map comparable to the King map and neither he nor Lewis left any documents, letters, etc., to indicate what changes they might have made in the image of 1803 (or to what extent that image remained the same). There is, however, one important document from which a partial interpretation of the 1804 Lewis and Clark view of the trans-Missouri area might be derived. This is the table of distance estimates, covering the area from Camp Dubois to the Pacific, which Clark entered in his daily log for January 20, 1804.[1]

The estimates that Clark made of the distances between Wood River, the Mandan villages, the Continental Divide, and the Pacific comprise one of the most significant documents of the Lewis and Clark Expedition. These distance calculations provide good evidence of the types of geographical materials available to Lewis and Clark. But more important, the distance estimates indicate which items of geographical information were considered most accurate by the two captains as of January, 1804. Specifically, the distance calculations illustrate the importance, at this stage, of the earlier Jefferson-

1. Osgood, *Field Notes*, pp. 19–20.

Lewis image. The estimates made by Clark could well have been made by the President and his secretary before July, 1803—given their reliance on the Arrowsmith and King maps as the best representations of western geography.

2

Clark began with an estimate of the distance from Camp Dubois (the mouth of the Missouri River) to the Mandan villages, a distance he placed at 1,500 miles. The second estimate was for the distance separating the Mandan villages from the "rock Mountains," seen by Clark as approximately 900 miles from the Missouri's northern bend. The third calculation provided an estimate of the distance from the mountains to the Pacific as a total of 650 miles (Table 1). These calculations were based on Clark's estimates of the longitudinal distances between the several locations he saw as critical in the geography of the Northwest plus additional mileage added for "winding" or meanders in the river courses and other deviations from a straight-line course. Along with the distance estimates, Clark included time estimates based on a rate of travel projected at either 10 or 12 miles per day and saw the journey to the Pacific taking between 11 months and 8⅔ months.[2]

Clark's distance calculations for the return journey, from the Pacific to

TABLE 1

DISTANCE ESTIMATES—WILLIAM CLARK, JANUARY 20, 1804

	mls	months	days
From Du bois to the Manden Nation 1500 miles at 10 Mls pr Day will be 150 day Viz: May June, July Augt & Sept.——	1500 in	5	— 5
From Do. at 12 mls pr day 125 days Viz: May June July Augt & 5 days in Septr		—4	—5
From Mandens to the rock Mountains is 12° (say) is 12° W. at 41 mls Say 900 miles at 10 pr Day is 90 Days, Viz: Sept. Oct. Novr. & 4 Dy	900 in	3	—0
From Same at 12 Miles pr Day 65 Day Septr Octr & 19 of Novr		2	—15
From the Mountains to the Ocean in Longttd 123° W say 10° at 41 miles to a degree of Longtd add the windings 650 Miles at 10 Miles will take 650 in May June and July . . . . 85? . . . . . . Days		3	—0
From the Same Place at 12 mls 54 Day, May & June		2	—0
		Days	
The time to the Ocean @ 10 m pr Day		11	—0
The Time @ 12 ms pr day		8	—20 days

2. According to Osgood (*Field Notes*, p. 21, n. 6), the actual travel time—the number of days the party was on the move—between Camp Dubois and the Pacific was 376 days—not really too far off Clark's estimate of 11 months of travel at 10 miles per day.

St. Louis, were comparable to those he made for the outward journey, although he assumed that the trip from the head of the Missouri could be made at either 12 or 20 miles per day rather than the 10 or 12 of the trek westward.[3] In his chart for the return journey, however, Clark did make one change in wording which was quite significant. Rather than listing the distance from the mountains to the Pacific as in the table for the westward journey, he gave the same distance (650 miles or 410 miles plus 240 miles for the "winding" of the Columbia tributary expected to lie west of the Rockies) for the "Ocean to the river." By "the river" he was referring to the Missouri, and it is apparent that to Clark the terms "mountains" and "river" were interchangeable. In his view, the Missouri penetrated the mountains to a place where a short portage would carry the explorers into navigable Pacific-slope waters. Since the portage was so short, the distance from the mountains to the Pacific and from the Missouri to the Pacific could, for all practical purposes, be considered the same.

A comparison of Clark's distance estimates with the actual distances traveled during the years 1804–06, as recorded by Lewis and Clark in their daily records,[4] provides a fascinating commentary on both the state of the geographical knowledge available to Lewis and Clark by January, 1804, and the image of the trans-Missouri region that they constructed from that lore (Table 2).

It must be noted first that Clark's estimate of the distance from the mouth of the Missouri River to the Mandan villages was quite accurate, being short by 100 miles, an error of only 6 percent. This relative accuracy is to be expected because of the quality of the data available about this first portion of the river. Lewis and Clark must have acquired a considerable store of oral intelligence from the St. Louis fur traders who had gone up the Missouri toward the Mandans, they had Mackay's map of the Missouri, and they may have had the translation of the Mackay-Evans journals by this time. Combining all this information, some of which probably included distance data, it was possible for Clark to come up with a reasonable estimate for the first leg of the journey. The quality of his estimates for distances beyond the Mandans is much less accurate; this is a function of the less accurate nature of the geographical lore for the farther Northwest.

Clark's calculation of 900 miles (600 miles short, an error of 40 percent) for the distance from the Mandans to the "rock Mountains" is quite interesting. His estimate of the longitudinal distance from the Mandans to the mountains as being 12° is amazingly close if the distance is measured from the Mandans (101° 27′ W.) to the Continental Divide at Lemhi Pass, where

3. This assumption was based on two factors: first, on the homeward-bound journey the party would be traveling with the river rather than against the current; second, there would be less time consumed in conferences with the Indians, time lost in making observations, etc.
4. A summary table of distances traveled during the course of the expedition is in Thwaites, *Original Journals*, VI, 56–79.

TABLE 2
CLARK'S ESTIMATES AND ACTUAL DISTANCES COMPARED

Points	Actual Distance Traveled	Clark's Estimates
From Dubois to the Mandans	1,600 miles	1,500 miles
From the Mandans to the Divide (Clarks's "rock Mountains")	Mandans to Great Falls: 975 miles Great Falls to Divide: 550 miles Total=1,525 miles (690 miles straight; 835 miles "winding")	900 miles (500 miles straight; 400 miles "winding")
From the Divide to the Pacific	Lemhi Pass to Clearwater R. 375 miles Clearwater to the Pacific 650 miles Total=1,025 miles (530 miles straight; 495 miles "winding")	650 miles (410 miles straight; 240 miles "winding")
TOTAL	4,150 miles	3,050 miles

the party first crossed from the Atlantic to the Pacific drainage at about 113° 30′ W. How Clark obtained the figure of 12° of longitude between the Mandans and the mountains (or Divide—the terms are interchangeable) cannot be known for certain but it is probable that he obtained it from either the King or Arrowsmith maps.[5] A diagrammatic representation of Clark's calculations superimposed on the key points in the Arrowsmith and King charts indicates rather conclusively that Clark was indeed using those maps for his distance figures (fig. 27). Furthermore, it appears that he was figuring the distance from the Mandans to the mountains along the southern branch of the Missouri, shown on both the Arrowsmith and King maps as having its source waters near the 112th or 113th meridian, rather than along the northern branch, which Arrowsmith and King had shown as having its sources farther west, near the 115th meridian. The fact that Clark was presumably planning to travel the southern branch of the Missouri is good evidence of the dominance of the Jefferson-Lewis image of the Northwest on the captains' thinking in January, 1804.

It is difficult to assess, from the distance estimates alone, how Clark (and, by extension, Lewis) might have imagined the country between the Mandans and the "rock Mountains." Clark might have known, for example, from an examination of the Mackay-Evans notes,[6] that the Missouri was said to fall

5. Whether or not the captains did have the King chart is unimportant here since the King and Arrowsmith maps were virtually identical in representing the cardinal points of western geography that figured in Clark's distance estimates.
6. There is a possibility that Clark had not yet had the chance to examine the Mackay-

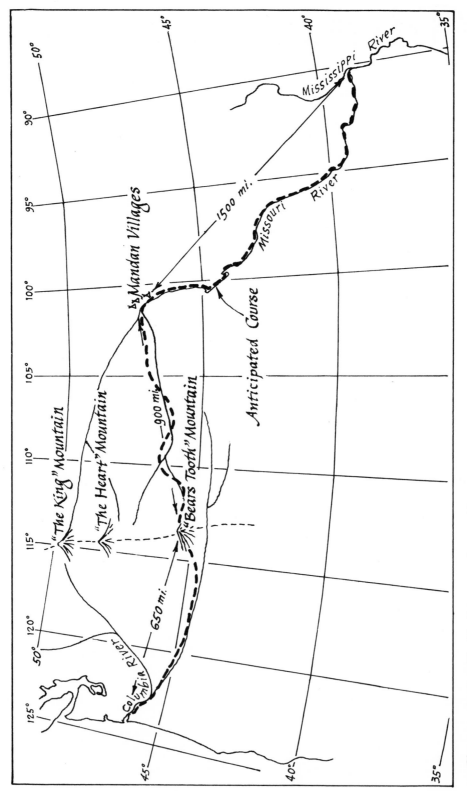

27. Chart comparing Clark's distance estimates (January, 1804) with generalized courses and mileage for the Missouri and Columbia rivers

"over the Rocky Mountains" at a great cascade, which was, according to Evans's estimates, about 200 leagues (including "Meanders" of the river) or roughly 550 miles west of the Mandans.[7] This hardly agreed with Clark's estimate of 900 miles between the Mandan villages and the mountains. It seems that the mountains where the Missouri was said to form a great cataract were not, in Clark's mind, the "rock Mountains" to which he estimated the distance from the Mandans. The "rock Mountains" of his calculations might have been the second range of mountains, which the Mackay-Evans journals mentioned as being west of the Great Falls where the eastern ridge of the mountains was breached by the Missouri. It could have been this second or western range which Clark viewed as lying about 12° or roughly 500 miles straight-line distance west of the Mandan villages.

Clark's calculation of 900 miles for the total distance between the Mandans and the mountains means that to the approximately 500 miles of longitudinal distance the explorer added 400 miles for irregularities in the Missouri's course and deviations from a straight line between the Mandans and the mountains. Since the longitudinal distance between the Mandans and the Divide is about 500 miles, it was the second part of Clark's estimate—the addition of 400 miles for irregularities in the course of the river—that was greatly in error. It would appear that Clark had no conception of the true course of the Missouri above the Mandan villages. In spite of the fact that he might have been aware of the information in the Mackay-Evans notes that the Missouri had its headwaters near the 40th parallel and then flowed north to the 49th parallel before turning east and falling over the eastern range of the Rocky Mountains, Clark apparently viewed the course of the river as being almost due east from its source to the Mandans. He had several pieces of information that would have supported this view. The Soulard map showed the Missouri flowing almost due east from its source, and the King and Arrowsmith maps showed the southern branch of the Missouri (the fork that the captains were most interested in) flowing in a generalized west-to-east course from the mountains.

Even if Clark had been aware of the Mackay-Evans information, the logic of a straight-line passage between the Mandans and the Columbia was firmly imbedded in the geographical lore of the time, particularly visible on the King and Arrowsmith maps.[8] He might, therefore, have speculated that near the point where the Missouri, according to the Mackay-Evans lore, shifted from a south-north trend to an eastern trend, a navigable branch of the Missouri could be found leading due west to the source of the Columbia's

---

Evans journals since those papers were, as late as the end of December, still in John Hay's possession. However, Clark had several occasions during which he could have talked with Mackay when the latter visited the Wood River camp and might have extracted much the same information out of the former explorer as he could have from the journals.

7. Nasatir, *Before Lewis and Clark,* II, 498.

8. See Allen, "Geographical Knowledge and American Images of Louisiana Territory," pp. 151–70.

southern waters. If this branch of the Missouri were a part of the Lewis and Clark image of the Northwest in January, 1804, then the fact that Clark persisted in figuring a direct east-west route to the Pacific—in spite of the possibility that he had information from Mackay and Evans when he was making the estimates—might be explained. It is more probable, however, that even if Clark did have the Mackay-Evans journals, he relied more, at this point, on the Arrowsmith and King maps for his distance calculations. These charts were still the most important items in the captains' geographical collection, and their significance explains the dominance of the direct-route concept for the distance between the Mandans and the Pacific Ocean. The additional distance between the Mandans and the mountains actually covered by the explorers (625 miles more than expected) was consumed by the necessary deviations from Clark's projected direct route.

The inaccuracy of 400 miles (or about 40 percent error) in Clark's estimate of the distance from the Divide or "rock Mountains" to the Pacific probably stemmed from the same type of reasoning that led to the error in the distance calculation from the Mandans to the mountains. Assuming a straight-line east-west orientation, Clark envisaged a distance of 900 miles to the Divide, then a short portage (perhaps as short as half a mile if he and Lewis could find the same type of connection as Mackenzie had), and then another straight-line or longitudinal distance of 10° or around 410 miles, plus 240 miles for the "windings," to make up a total of 650 miles from the Divide to the Pacific. Again, an examination of the diagrammatic representation of the distance estimates will show that these calculations were made for the connections between the southern branch of the Missouri with its head near the mountain that Arrowsmith and King had labeled "Bears Tooth" and the southern waters of the Columbia system, possibly the great southern branch of King's map. Clark's longitudinal calculations were relatively accurate, placing the Divide only about 50 miles too close to the Pacific. But the distance estimate of 650 miles was 400 miles short of the actual distance traveled from Lemhi Pass to the mouth of the Columbia.

Clark, using the King and Arrowsmith maps as the basis of his estimates, assumed a straight-line route (and a short portage) from the mountain to the Pacific and calculated the distance on the basis of the theoretical connection between the southern branch of the Missouri and the southern waters of the Columbia River. Because the expedition had to detour from the expected course in the journey from the Mandans to the Divide and move far south of Clark's anticipated crossing, the journey to the Pacific was nearly 400 miles longer than anticipated. Had the Corps of Discovery not been forced, in following the Missouri to its source, to travel along two legs of a triangle (from the Mandans to the Great Falls to Lemhi Pass) rather than on a straight line (from the Mandans to "Bears Tooth"), then Clark's estimate of the distance from the mountains to the Pacific would have been relatively close. But the detour to the south meant that the party had to travel a northern route to reach the approximate latitudinal position of the mouth of the Columbia—and thus get back to the straight-line route that the two explorers and Jefferson had counted on. The journey from the Divide to the navigable waters of the Columbia system (the Clearwater River) was about 350 miles long, very close indeed to Clark's underestimation of the distance between the Divide and the Pacific Ocean.

In summary, first, Clark's distance estimates indicate that he and Lewis placed more faith in the Arrowsmith and King maps of the western part of North America than in any other pieces of geographical material in January, 1804. Second, the calculations seem to have been based on the 1803 hypothesis of a connection between the southern branches of the Missouri and a conjectural southern branch of the Columbia; Clark's longitudinal estimates match almost exactly with the longitudes of key points between the Mandans and the mouth of the Columbia as shown on the King map. And perhaps most important is the retention in the Lewis and Clark image, around January, 1804, of the core of misconception in nearly all images of the trans-Missouri area. Somewhere there was a single, short portage between the heads of the streams that flowed east and the streams that flowed west, and through this short portage might be discovered a water communication across the continent for the purposes of commerce.

The short portage remained a part of the Lewis and Clark image of the Northwest throughout the months before their departure in May, 1804. But as additional information in the form of the Mackay-Evans journals and the Evans map was assimilated during the spring of 1804, the way in which the captains viewed the short portage probably changed. In their final image—their view of the Northwest as they left Camp Dubois and sailed up the Missouri—was found a mixture of elements, some of them shared with the earlier 1803 image and others the result of modifications that had taken place with the acquisition of additional geographical lore.

3

When Lewis and Clark began their transcontinental exploration in the spring of 1804, they carried with them certain elements of the 1803 image of the Northwest. During the years prior to the expedition, Jefferson had formed a pattern of beliefs about the geography of the trans-Missouri region through a long process of information-gathering and assimilation. How many of these beliefs about the nature and content of the lands they would soon enter were retained by Lewis and Clark as they prepared to depart from their winter camp on Wood River?

Lewis and Clark made few comments on the quality of the land of the trans-Missouri region prior to their journey. But it would seem that, by virtue of the geographical materials they had amassed on the area, they viewed it in much the same fashion as Jefferson had earlier, considering it a garden of beauty and plentitude. It is certain that they so viewed the lower portion of the Missouri valley, for Clark wrote in his daily journal that the country near the mouth of the Missouri was "butifull beyond description."[9] It is doubtful, however, whether the captains, after spending a winter on the edge of the Northwest, had quite as optimistic a view on land quality as had Jefferson and Lewis when the latter took his leave from Washington. Practical experience in the frontier settlements of the Mississippi valley, contact with observers of lands beyond the Mississippi, and exposure to the local lore which included within it strong elements of the desert concept[10] might have precluded strict and rigid adherence to the total garden notion. Yet if the strength of the garden as a feature in their image of the Northwest was diminished, it was there nevertheless and functioned as a conditioning factor in their observation of the lands through which they passed during the course of their explorations.

The rivers of the trans-Missouri region must have appeared to Lewis and Clark early in 1804 much as they did to Jefferson and Lewis in 1803. The Clark distance calculations are proof of the importance of the King and Arrowsmith maps in the geographical thinking of Lewis and Clark, and it is probable, therefore, that much of the pattern of rivers that appeared in the 1803 image was retained in the 1804 image. The additional information received during the winter and spring at Camp Dubois might have done relatively little to transform the basics of earlier knowledge. But the earlier knowledge was much less complete than was the lore accumulated during the months spent on the Mississippi's banks. And therefore, although the general picture of the river systems of the Northwest was probably not altered completely in the 1804 image, it became a more specific and less generalized picture. The Mackay-Evans maps and the lore on the Missouri valley that must have been acquired from those with whom Lewis came in contact in St. Louis necessarily added to the captains' view of the northwestern rivers, and although the streams of the farther West beyond the Mandans remained obscure, the Missouri and its tributaries from St. Louis to the Mandan villages came into clearer focus.[11]

But the purest essence of the image the explorers had of the western interior still remained as it had in earlier days. The Missouri, according not

9. Osgood, *Field Notes*, p. 3.
10. See G. Malcolm Lewis, "Three Centuries of Desert Concepts of the Cis-Rocky Mountain West," *Journal of the West*, IV (1965), 457–68.
11. The journals of Truteau and the journals of Mackay and Evans contained a significant amount of detail on the tributaries of the Missouri, the distances between their mouths, their navigability and length, the Indian tribes living on them, etc. (Nasatir, *Before Lewis and Clark*, I, 259–311; II, 485–99). In addition to this formal information, Lewis must have picked up supplemental data from such St. Louis residents as the Chouteau brothers.

only to the information retained from Jefferson but to nearly all other sources as well, was a long and mighty river navigable to its source. Its course, direction, and headwaters all fit within the framework of the conceptual Passage to India, for near the Missouri's source would be found the source waters of Pacific-slope streams. This was the central feature of the 1803 image of the Northwest and must also have been the core of Lewis's and Clark's view in the spring of 1804. Nearly all the information they had received substantiated the notion of the short portage, and this concept, inherited from Jefferson through countless other thinkers, probably remained at the very heart of their geographic conceptions and of the objectives of the expedition.

4

The short portage is the only portion of the geographical suppositions of Lewis and Clark that can definitely be said to have been inherited from Jefferson and retained with little or no change. Many other features of Lewis's and Clark's image of the Northwest by May, 1804, developed independently of the President. The most striking example is their probable view of the Rocky Mountain system. It has been conjecturally stated that the 1803 view of the western mountains incorporated two theoretical separate ranges, a northern chain which terminated on the south near the 46th parallel and a southern range which parted the waters of the Missouri from those of the New Mexican rivers and which ran northwest toward the Pacific.

There seems to have been considerable doubt in the earlier Jefferson-Lewis image as to whether the Missouri had its source in mountains or flat lands, whether it was separated from the Pacific streams by a ridge or by a low height-of-land. Clark's distance estimates indicated that he and Lewis thought the passage to the Pacific could be most easily reached via the southern waters of the Missouri and the southern tributaries of the Columbia, which in the image of 1803 had their sources with the Missouri's headsprings in a common height-of-land. But there is no indication that the two captains held to the possible earlier theories of two separate mountain ranges between which might lie a common source region for western streams. On the contrary, Lewis and Clark always referred to the "rock Mountains" as if they had an awareness of their existence as a divide between the eastern and western waters.[12]

Clark's distance calculations gave the impression that he imagined the Missouri's source in a mountainous area. But it is probable that both he and Lewis saw the mountain structure much as Jefferson might have. The Rocky Mountains probably appeared to them as diminutive, both in terms of height

12. This fact is apparent in Clark's distance estimates and also is visible in the daily journals during the first summer of exploration.

and breadth, in relation to their actual size.[13] Good evidence of this is Clark's reference to the "rock Mountains" and the source of the Missouri as being the same distance from the Pacific. Like Jefferson, Lewis and Clark likely saw in the Rockies only what eyes accustomed to looking at the Blue Ridge of Virginia might see. But the captains added an element to the image of the mountains that was not present in the earlier lore and the earlier images. In nearly all the geographical data available to Jefferson and Lewis in 1803, the western mountains appeared as a single ridge. Lewis and Clark in 1804, operating from the geographical lore of the Mackay-Evans experiences, probably viewed the Rocky Mountains as a series of ranges, with one final western ridge separating the Missouri from the waters flowing toward the Pacific.

Lewis and Clark were both frontier travelers and probably relied more on word-of-mouth information from St. Louis voyageurs and fur traders than on the theoretical considerations of Daniel Coxe and Jonathan Carver and Jedediah Morse that played such an important role in the shaping of earlier views of the trans-Missouri region. This means that the more information they gathered in the field, the more likely they were to reject some of the Jeffersonian concepts.[14] Even some of the material that Jefferson himself had transmitted—notably the Lacépède letter and the Evans map—served, in combination with information gathered by the captains during the winter and spring at Camp Dubois and St. Louis, to modify the theoretical geography of the period before the expedition. Thus, although major portions of the Lewis and Clark 1804 image mirrored earlier concepts—particularly the notion of land quality and the short portage—the sources for transformation of earlier lore were present and became active during the spring of 1804 and during the next two years of travel in the Northwest. Before proceeding to the transformation process that began when the explorers left Camp Dubois, however, it is necessary to outline more precisely the elements in the image of the Northwest perceived by Lewis and Clark prior to their departure in May, 1804.

13. The true size of the Rocky Mountain region was not understood even during the years following the expediton. It was not until after the activities of the American fur trade in the central and southern Rockies between 1810 and 1840 that the Rockies were recognized as a broad and extremely complex alpine region. See William H. Goetzmann, *Exploration and Empire: The Explorer and the Scientist in the Winning of the American West* (New York, 1966), chs. 1–4.

14. One of the clearest indications of this can be seen in some of the logistical details of the expedition as worked out by the captains independently of the President. Jefferson had, for example, originally suggested a party of ten or twelve men for the company. When the party left Wood River for the Pacific, it consisted of about forty-five men plus Lewis and Clark. It is apparent that the captains, as experienced frontiersmen, recognized the validity of the adage "safety in numbers" in wilderness travel. Caution must be exercised, however, in drawing correlations between the logistics of the expedition and Lewis's and Clark's image of the Northwest. It was not the image that influenced logistics; it was experience. The materiel and personnel of the party would have been selected by most knowledgeable wilderness travelers with the same financial and governmental support as Lewis and Clark. Once the expedition was under way, logistical decisions and operations in the field began to be influenced by the changing nature of Lewis's and Clark's views of the area they were traversing.

5

The element of the garden played a relatively minor role in the captains' view of western geography in the spring of 1804. Lewis and Clark did not have as great a built-in necessity to see the Northwest as a region of great agricultural wealth and overall "salubrity" as did Jefferson. And yet the Garden seems to have been visible to them; but this was a growth of vision out of their sources of information more than out of their inherent values and aspirations. Nearly all of their data spoke of the Northwest as an area of abundant wealth, with fertile soil and a salubrious and gentle climate. Jefferson had forwarded to them his "Official Account" and from it they learned that the trans-Missouri area was exceeded by no part of the world in fertility of soil and perfection of climate.[15] The land of the Northwest would yield, according to Jefferson's account, "an abundance of all the necessities of life" with only a minimum amount of effort on the part of the frontier farmer.[16]

Most of the other source materials available to the explorers spoke in the same vein about the land quality of the Northwest. They had, it is true, been exposed to the local lore of the Upper Louisiana Spanish and French, which contained strong flavoring of the desert concept of the Northwest. They might even have been in possession of the articulation of that concept in the form of Truteau's description of the upper Missouri and Evans's journal in which much of the Northwest was depicted as a "great waste land" that was often "completely sterile; scarcely grass grows there."[17] That the greater part of the region was treeless was an accepted fact, but the treelessness described by adventurers such as Truteau and Evans did not mean sterility.[18] But Lewis, the ardent Republican, must have retained in some measure the exuberance of the Jeffersonian view of the Garden.

In the final analysis, it is questionable whether Lewis and Clark accepted in full either Truteau's and Evans's pessimism or Jefferson's enthusiasm. Their view of the fertility and gentle climate of the Northwest probably lay somewhere between the two extremes. They had enough contacts with knowledgeable persons in St. Louis and on the Illinois side of the Mississippi to indicate that their opinions would probably have been more linked with the practical frontier experiences and observations of that area than with the teleological impulses of early American geography. Their own comments on the land and climate of the Northwest prior to May, 1804, relayed optimism, but a more cautious optimism than that which was probably felt by Jefferson and Lewis in the early summer of 1803.

15. Jefferson, "Official Account," pp. 344–56.
16. Jefferson, "Official Account," p. 346.
17. Nasatir, *Before Lewis and Clark*, II, 377.
18. Jefferson himself had noted in his "Official Account" that the treeless plains were devoid of trees because the soil was too rich for the growth of forests. The Great American Desert concept was, at this time, not well formed; Americans tended to think of the plains of the interior as prairie country of great value. See Henry Nash Smith, *Virgin Land*, 1; and Dorothy Dondore, *The Prairie and the Making of Middle America*, 2–3.

6

The captains' view of the river systems of the Northwest was much more important for their undertaking than their opinions on the value of the lands of the trans-Missouri area as a home for the agrarian republic. Early in 1804, the greatest sources for the river patterns of the Northwest in Lewis's and Clark's image were the King and Arrowsmith maps. Clark had based his distance calculations on those maps, and it would seem as if the two explorers initially accepted the drainage patterns shown by the cartographers and featured in the 1803 image. Clark's estimates indicated rather conclusively that he saw the head of the Missouri as being around the 112th or 113th meridian, a position that correlated with the coordinates of the Missouri's source waters as shown by King and Arrowsmith. But during the spring of 1804, Lewis and Clark came into possession of at least three items that contradicted the basic King-Arrowsmith source data.

The Lacépède letter that was sent by Jefferson and the Soulard map that had been acquired in St. Louis provided data which, although rather ephemeral, indicated a great westward extension of the Missouri by placing the river's sources near the Pacific. Lacépède had noted that Mt. Hood, visible from the Columbia only 100 miles inland, was a "dependance" of the Rocky Mountains and that in these same mountains the Missouri had its source. The Soulard map showed the Missouri coming from a position that lay within a few degrees of longitude from the Pacific coast. From Clark's distance calculations, it is clear that neither of these views was acceptable as of January, 1804.

Acquisition of the journals of Mackay and Evans, following the captains' examination of the Lacépède and Soulard materials, seemed to offer overwhelming evidence that the Missouri did, in fact, extend farther west than shown by Arrowsmith and King. The journals of Mackay and Evans implied that the Missouri's sources were "much further off than what is imagined."[19] But that information was based in part on a longitudinal error of nearly 10° in the location of the Mandan villages. Mackay had reported that the Mandans were located near the 111th meridian, and his statement that their villages were still a long way from the headwaters of the river had the function of moving the source region of the Missouri much too far west.[20] But where the captains probably accepted a great deal of Mackay and Evans data at face value, this extension of the Missouri system was less acceptable because they possessed relatively firm evidence of the correct location of the Mandan villages, obtained by "astronomical observation."[21]

19. Nasatir, *Before Lewis and Clark*, II, 498.
20. This agreed with the common belief among the officials of Spanish Louisiana that the Rockies were close to the Pacific—perhaps as close as 40 leagues or about 100 miles (Nasatir, *Before Lewis and Clark*, I, 316).
21. These words appeared on the Thompson map. In his letter which forwarded the Evans map to Lewis, Jefferson stated that he did not know whether the map had been corrected by proper astronomical sightings.

Lewis and Clark were capable and intelligent men and probably placed more faith in the accuracy of Thompson's surveys than in the conjectural data obtained from the sources which moved the Mandan villages, and thus the Missouri's source, farther west than they should have been. However, they possessed no "astronomical observations" on the course of the Missouri beyond the Mandans and probably considered the Mackay-Evans information on the direction of the Missouri's flow as the best available.[22]

Early in 1804 Lewis and Clark must have viewed the course of the upper Missouri system much as it was shown on the King and Arrowsmith maps. This was clearly indicated by the Clark distance estimates. The Missouri, in their view, had two major branches west of the Mandans, one fork with a source near the 50th parallel and the other with headwaters in the neighborhood of the 46th parallel. The fact that Clark seemed to make his distance estimates from the Mandans along a line from the villages to about 46° N. and 113° W. indicates that he and Lewis first considered the King and Arrowsmith maps as the most accurate depictions of the Missouri's course. Whether Clark assumed that the southern branch was the true Missouri (as on the Arrowsmith map) or the "Lesser Missesouri" (as on the King map) is unimportant; for either branch was viewed as being navigable to its source near the waters of Pacific-slope streams.

This supposition seemed confirmed when, by May, the two major branches of the Missouri above the Mandans were converted into something approximating reality. The northern fork was the Missouri proper; the southern fork was the Yellowstone. Lewis's connections with the members of the St. Louis–based fur trade were such that rather definite information about the Yellowstone River must have been known to him. Jean Truteau had written of "a large river, called the river of the Yellowstone," which flowed into the Missouri west of the Mandan villages, was nearly as large as the main river, and, like the Missouri, had its "source in the mountains of rocks in the western parts."[23] And contemporary maps of Spanish Louisiana, including James Mackay's map, showed the Yellowstone or "R. de roche Jaune" entering the Missouri west of the Mandan villages.[24]

The Mackay-Evans geographical lore, however, had explicitly defined the course of only one major river west of the Mandans, describing the Missouri as heading near the 40th parallel, flowing north, falling over a range of mountains near the 49th parallel, and then assuming an easterly course toward the Mandan villages. It is questionable whether Lewis and Clark

22. Although the acceptance of some data and rejection of others from the same source materials appears contradictory, it is not. The assimilation of geographical information into a coherent pattern of understanding is an eclectic process, and the captains used what information they considered best for different areas, regardless of whether other data from the same source had been rejected as being unsatisfactory.

23. Nasatir, *Before Lewis and Clark*, II, 381.

24. Evans had also mentioned, in his journals, the "Yellow Stone River, (Riviere des Roches Jaunes) . . . about 80 leagues above the Mandaines" (Nasatir, *Before Lewis and Clark*, II, 498).

would have adhered to either the King or Arrowsmith data on the Missouri's course after receipt of all this information. The addition of the Yellowstone River as a geographic factor may have seemed to support the earlier maps, but to the captains the lore obtained directly from explorers who had recently returned from the field would probably have seemed much more reliable than the cartographic sources of King and Arrowsmith, which were based on conjectural and hearsay information.[25] The image of the Missouri system in May, 1804, probably resembled the structure set forth in the journals of the Mackay and Evans travels, with the addition of the Yellowstone as a major tributary from the supplementary data obtained before May.

The navigability of the Missouri (and many other rivers of the trans-Missouri area) was another important feature of Lewis's and Clark's image as of May, 1804, that was to play an important role during the coming period of exploration. Jefferson had assumed that the Missouri and its connections with the westward-flowing streams offered "a continued navigation . . . possibly with a single portage, from the western ocean."[26] Lewis and Clark seem to have accepted this view without modification, and once again Clark's distance estimates can be used as evidence. The fact that Clark figured travel time as 10 or 12 miles per day for the entire course of the journey from the mouth of the Missouri to the Pacific indicates that he was thinking in terms of a constant transportation method throughout the length of the traverse across the continent. When Clark made his calculations all the evidence the captains possessed pointed in this direction. Nor did any of the geographical lore assimilated after January, 1804, contain anything to discourage the optimistic outlook for water travel through the Northwest.

The Truteau journals spoke of the Missouri as being navigable from its mouth to its source for even the largest pirogues.[27] The Mackay-Evans journals also spoke of the navigability of the Missouri, and the size of the river at the Mandan villages, as measured by Evans, suggested continued navigability for a great distance above the farthest penetration of the St. Louis fur trade. There was, in fact, only one exception to the unimpeded navigation of the Missouri beyond the Mandans. From the Mackay-Evans source material and from other data as well, Lewis and Clark had learned of the Great Falls of the Missouri. Although the Falls was an extremely important landmark of the upper Missouri, the addition of the great cataracts to the 1803 image was relatively unimportant in terms of the captains' projections about the ease of river travel. It was relatively certain that navigation above the falls would be as easy as below, and the uninterrupted path to the Missouri's source would be broken by only one portage around the cataract formed

25. This statement applied only to those portions of the charts which illustrated the geography of the upper Missouri beyond the Mandans. Parts of the King and Arrowsmith maps were, of course, highly accurate, being based on reliable surveys like those of Vancouver and Thompson.

26. From Jefferson's message to Congress, 18 Jan. 1803.

27. Nasatir, *Before Lewis and Clark*, I, 302.

when the Missouri passed through a range of mountains on its way to the Mandans.[28]

Much of the material on the Missouri available to Lewis and Clark had been gathered after Lewis's leave-taking from Jefferson; consequently the 1803 image of the Missouri was subject to greater modification than that of the Columbia. Information on the Columbia came from the same sources that had been consulted during the earliest planning stages of the expedition. Lewis had copied the Vancouver surveys while in Philadelphia and thus had the most accurate picture of the Columbia's lower course. Jefferson had provided the explorers with Mackenzie's, Arrowsmith's, and later Lacépède's information, and the view of the great western river derived from these sources varied little between July, 1803, and May, 1804.

The best information available to Lewis and Clark indicated that the Columbia flowed south from a source near Mackenzie's crossing of the Divide to around the 46th parallel, where it turned west toward the sea. Virtually all of their geographical material on the Columbia's distance, course, and navigability was in agreement. The general trend of the flow of the river from its source to the 46th parallel was in a line parallel with the Pacific coast. The river was known to be navigable at least as far inland as Point Vancouver and, judging from the size of the river as measured there by Lieutenant Broughton, it was probably navigable a good deal farther.[29] The Lewis and Clark view was erroneous in that it was based on Mackenzie's belief that the river he had discovered (the Fraser) was the same river that entered the Pacific near the 46th parallel. But the inaccuracy of this conception of the Columbia would not be determined until after the completion of the expedition.

The most inconclusive section of the captains' views on the Columbia were those that dealt with its tributaries having sources near those of the Missouri. The Arrowsmith map showed a "Great Lake River" heading near the 50th parallel and just across a mountain called "the King" from the sources of the northern branch of the Missouri. The King map showed the same river but added to the Columbia a southern tributary, flowing from a source area at the 45th parallel and between the 106th and 107th meridians. Whether Lewis and Clark ever fully accepted this great southern branch of the Columbia in its full extent is questionable.

The fact that Clark used the southern waters of the Missouri in making his distance estimates for the course of the river from the Mandans to the mountains indicates that he and Lewis were expecting to make contact with a southern branch of the Columbia River. But since he estimated the divide

28. This portage itself, the captains believed, would present no problems. Their view was substantiated when they learned, during the winter at the Mandan villages, that the portage around the Great Falls was only about a half-mile in length. The actual portage the expedition made in the summer of 1805 was nowhere close to a half-mile but was, rather, a tortuous 18-mile affair that consumed nearly a month of travel time.

29. According to the Lacépède letter, the Columbia 100 miles inland was "still a quarter of a mile wide, and the depth varies between 12 and thirty-six English feet" (Jackson, *Letters,* p. 46).

between the Missouri and Columbia waters to be around the 113th meridian, it is doubtful whether the great conjectural southern river of the King map was completely assimilated into the Lewis and Clark image of the Northwest. It is more probable that, by May of 1804, Lewis and Clark anticipated reaching the Divide as defined by Mackay and Evans and making contact with some stream that would flow into a major southern tributary of the Columbia west of 113°.[30] The most important reason for their probable refusal to accept the eastern extension of the southern branch of the Columbia, however, was the captains' conception of the mountains of the western interior.

7

In the geographical materials assembled by Lewis and Clark, there was more contradictory lore about the western mountains than about any other element of conjectural western geography. The Arrowsmith map showed the Rockies as a single ridge running from Canada clear to New Mexico with a diagonal direction from the 115th meridian at 50° N. southeast to the 110th meridian at 40° N. The King map showed a range located in the same position but having a southern terminus near 46° N. The Soulard map clearly showed and the Lacépède letter implied that the Rockies lay much farther to the west and ran parallel to the Pacific coast at a distance of 3° or 4° of longitude inland. And although the above sources indicated the single-ridge structure of the Rockies, the information from the Mackay-Evans journals and the Evans map added to Lewis's and Clark's store of knowledge the concept of the Rockies as a series of parallel ridges with north-south axes.

The captains' views of the mountains in terms of height and breadth most probably reflected the traditional views that the ranges of the western interior were at the most 3,500 feet above their base in height and that they were comparatively narrow ridges.[31] This view was evidenced by Clark's distance estimates, which made no provision for crossing a wide range of mountains but referred to the head of the Missouri and the mountains as the same point in calculating the distance from the Divide to the Pacific. The Missouri was navigable to a point where it was separated by only a narrow ridge from navigable waters of the Columbia. But here there was a deviation in the Lewis and Clark image of the mountains from the traditional image as illustrated by the cartographers. For the separating ridge that lay west of the Missouri's source was probably only the last of at least two and possibly more parallel ranges as hypothesized in the Mackay-Evans journals and on the Evans map.

30. This view was based on the Arrowsmith chart, which showed the upper portions of some westward-flowing rivers opposite the headwaters of the Missouri. The concept was also a feature of current notions on theoretical symmetrical geography.
31. Cf. the *Medical Repository*, V (1st hexade, 1802), 462.

The journals of Evans and Mackay spoke of two mountain ranges—an eastern range through which the Missouri flowed and created a great fall, and a western range which bounded the Missouri's course on the western side. In the Mackay-Evans information, the Missouri ran a south-to-north course between these two ranges. Lewis and Clark, as illustrated by the Clark distance estimates, did not accept this south-north course early in 1804. But lack of acceptance was due to lack of information. After the journals and Evans map had been investigated and compared, the south-north course probably became part of the captains' view, as did the concept of two or more ridges of the Rocky Mountains.

The position of the mountains (or at least of the westernmost range) in Lewis's and Clark's view was seemingly derived more from the Arrowsmith map than from any of the rest of their sources. In their view as of May, the Rockies ran as a long north-south chain which served as a continental divide, and which had a general southerly direction between the 115th and 110th meridians. Clark calculated the longitudinal position of the source of the Missouri as 113° W., and it is clear that he viewed the Missouri as having its head in mountains rather than in the plateau area that might have been hypothesized by Jefferson and Lewis earlier. Lewis and Clark always referred to the head of the Missouri as being in the mountains, and there is no evidence to indicate that either of them ever thought in terms of the possible separate ranges of the 1803 image.[32]

The Rocky Mountains, in their image of May, formed a continental divide just west of the Missouri's source, and beyond that divide the waters of the Columbia's southern tributaries could be located. Clark's conception of the Missouri's source in the divide at the 113th meridian also meant that the captains—for the present at least—rejected the implications of the Soulard map and the Lacépède letter that the mountains, and therefore the divide, were located within just a few degrees of longitude of the Pacific coast. Clark stated quite specifically in his estimates that the longitudinal distance from the Missouri's source to the mouth of the Columbia at "Longttd 123° W" was a full 10°.[33] There is no evidence to suggest that the captains moved the mountains any closer to the Pacific during the months between Clark's distance estimates and the departure from Camp Dubois.[34] The Soulard map and the Lacépède letter would become important agents for transforming the image during the ensuing months, however, and later images of the mountains,

32. Given this, it is probable that they also rejected the great eastern extension of the southern branch of the Columbia as shown on the King map.

33. Clark had very accurate information on the longitudinal position of the mouth of the Columbia from the Vancouver surveys. His positioning of 123° is more than a degree short of the actual location, and he may have been referring not to the mouth at the coast but to the inland extension of tidewater, which, according to the Vancouver surveys, was nearly a hundred miles inland.

34. Their original intent, indicated in Clark's distance estimates, was to spend the first winter near the head of the Missouri. This intention did not seem to have changed by May, 1804; if, in their view, the mountains had shifted westward then plans for the winter quartering of 1804–05 would necessarily have changed.

formed during the first summer of exploration and the first winter in the trans-Missouri region, would include ranges of the Rocky Mountains extending nearly to Pacific shores.

8

Regardless of any modifications in the geographical images of the Northwest that Lewis and Clark made prior to May, 1804, the one cardinal element of conjectural western geography remained. The Passage to India was still at the root of their thinking. The idea of the transcontinental water communication was predicated on two simple facts that appeared in all of the captains' geographical lore: first, that there were connections between the upper waters of the Missouri system and the upper waters of the Columbia (i.e., that the Missouri and the Columbia had at least some tributaries that headed in the same area); and second, that the distance between the navigable waters of these two rivers could be covered through a single, short portage.

The best cartographic sources available showed connections between the Columbia and Missouri systems. The whole basis of exploration from 1673 to the time of the Lewis and Clark Expedition had been the idea of this connection, and the fact was so firmly established in geographical lore that it would be inconceivable for the captains to have rejected the view. The single objective of their expedition as outlined by Jefferson was founded on the concept, and it is certain that the two explorers had at the core of their view of western geography the idea that the Missouri came close to waters that flowed toward the great South Sea.

Less definable are the Lewis and Clark conceptions of the nature of the connections between Atlantic and Pacific drainages. Their cartographic sources, due to lack of detail, gave them little help in establishing firm notions as to the length of the traverse by land. Some of their information, such as the Du Pratz account of the travels of Moncacht-Apé, presented a picture of a connection between eastern and western rivers that could be made only by a rather extensive overland journey.[35] Other information on western drainage systems, such as that of Alexander Mackenzie, spoke of short portages of less than half a mile between the navigable waters of different oceans. Of all their sources of data, Lewis and Clark probably selected Mackenzie's *Voyages from Montreal* as most accurate in depicting the true nature of the necessary portage between the Atlantic and Pacific slopes. The portage as seen by Lewis and Clark was a short one—so short that Clark made no provisions for it in his estimate of time and distance for the transcontinental journey. The way to the Pacific lay open and easy, and it was this simple fact of imaginary geography that gave birth to the Lewis and Clark Expedition. All other elements of their image of the trans-Missouri region were subsidiary to the theme of

35. See fig. 4 above.

the Passage to India; without the age-old dream, founded on centuries of geographical lore and exploration, that image could never have taken its full shape and structure.

The waters that ran east and the waters that ran west had a common source area. The rivers were navigable to this common source area. A transcontinental communication and transportation route might be established by utilizing the navigable streams of the Atlantic and Pacific slopes and the overland connection between their upper reaches. This overland connection—whether it was viewed as a pass over a ridge of mountains or a portage through a level plateau area—was short and easy, similar to the crossing made by Mackenzie through the Canadian Rockies. This was the central premise of the conjectural geography of the American Northwest; it was the premise that was to be tested by the Lewis and Clark Expedition. And from that testing would come a new and more complete geographical understanding of western North America and a new and more accurate image of the trans-Missouri West.

9

In spite of the geographical lore of the American Northwest that they had received and analyzed, when Lewis and Clark made ready to set forth on their great adventure it must have been obvious to them that they were entering an area about which precious little was known. Images of the Northwest had been formed—by Jefferson and by the captains themselves. But these images were based on partial information and thus were images that were of the grossest and most general nature. The Northwest was, for the most part, a void and empty conceptual region. Detailed and accurate lore was obtainable only for the region about the mouth of the Columbia and for the Missouri River itself as far upstream as the Mandan villages. The lower tributaries of the Missouri were part of this lore, but of the rivers entering the Missouri above the mouth of the Kansas little beyond rumor and conjecture was available. Even more conjectural and hypothetical were notions about the mountains of the interior and the upper drainages of the Missouri and Columbia.

But minds can fill blank spaces on maps with amazing facility. When little is known of an entire area, the little that is known or partly known is put to good use. Spot data are extrapolated and applied to the region as a whole. Therefore, if the lands of the trans-Missouri West were viewed as a garden it was because the data on land quality that was available, data that in reality could be applied only to the lower portions of the Missouri, were used to define an entire area for which data were largely absent. If the rivers of the Northwest were seen as being large and navigable it was because the recorded observations of the size and navigability of the lower Missouri and its lower tributaries were taken as applying equally to all the rivers of the region. And if the mountains of the interior were seen as low and easy to cross, it was because the mountains with which most people were familiar fit this description.

There are really three ways of knowing about areas geographically: a system of coherent knowledge based on accurate data and long acquaintance, a system of more or less coherent knowledge based on simple logical and theoretical constructions, or a system which is largely incoherent and based on desires, ambitions, long-standing myths and traditions, or pure rumor and fantasy. As a whole, the trans-Missouri area was viewed in all these different ways, some part of the area being well known from frequent contacts, another part being known through logical interpretations of assumed known facts, and still another part being known only through conjecture. The Lewis and Clark Expedition would change the nature of the American knowledge of the Northwest. The captains would replace conjecture and speculation, wild reasonings of theoretical and logical frameworks, with scientific observation. They would fill many blank spaces on the maps of the Northwest with facts recorded and verified rather than guessed at and hoped for.

As geographical observers, Lewis and Clark had few peers in American exploratory history—not only for the detail and accuracy of their recordings but for the nature of the data they recorded. During the years in the Northwest, the leaders of the Corps of Discovery assimilated data on soils, vegetation and animals, climate, mountain systems and river drainages, and on the cultures of the inhabitants of the interior. From their data would come new knowledge and new images and a more coherent understanding of a vast region. But the older images and the less coherent frameworks would not disappear altogether. For just as the nature of knowledge conditions the development of regional images, so does the nature of a regional image condition the exploratory process. When Lewis and Clark went into the Northwest, they went expecting to find certain things and to establish certain facts. Their preconceived notions had an impact on the course of their exploration, on the character of the observations they made, and on the pattern of beliefs about the geography of the Northwest that came out of their traverse to the Pacific and back.

CHAPTER 7

NORTHWEST TO
THE MANDAN VILLAGES

The long winter of preparation gave way to the damp and gusty days of spring, days that were crowded with activity as the commanders of the Corps of Discovery completed final arrangements for their departure westward to the plains, the mountains, and the Passage to the Pacific. By May, Lewis and Clark had finalized their logistics, compiled all the available information, and finished training their command for the mighty tasks that lay ahead. In the coming months these preparatory efforts would meet the severe testing of climatic extremes, the caving banks and debris-filled waters of the Missouri River, potentially hostile Indian nations, and vast and unimaginable distances. Jefferson and his associates had aided the captains immeasurably as they made ready for their journey. The "gentlemen of St. Louis" with whom so many productive hours were spent during the winter of 1803–04 had also provided invaluable advice and assistance. The help Lewis and Clark had received from these sources, the corresponding plans they had made, and the image of the Northwest they had created from information given them would partly determine the outcome of their venture. But once the captains turned their boats into the Missouri's spring flood, they would be on their own. And in the final analysis, the success of the expedition's attempt to find the Passage and reach the Pacific would depend more on the commanders' abilities to find and use new sources of information, to change their initial strategies, and to shape new images to meet the necessities presented by the trans-Missouri West itself, by a land that was still all but unknown.[1]

On May 14 everything was in readiness, and while Lewis was detained in St. Louis with a group of Osage chiefs,[2] Clark determined "to go as far as St. Charles a french Village 7 Leags. up the Missourie, and wait at that Place" until Lewis could join him. Clark's departure without Lewis reflected the impatience that both captains must have felt, and proceeding "on under a jentle brease," Clark and his men entered the Missouri River on the afternoon of May 14 (I, 16).[3] The journey from the Wood River camp to St. Charles, located some 21 miles upstream from the Missouri's confluence with the Mississippi, served as a shakedown cruise for both captain and crew, and during the three-day voyage to St. Charles Clark tested the navigability of the great muddy river and learned something of its hazards, particularly "the concealed timber which lyes in great quantities" in its bed (I, 17). The mettle of the men was tested as well, and on May 17, the day after the party had reached St. Charles, Clark convened the first court-martial of the expedition proper, trying three men for breach of military courtesy and discipline (I, 19–21).[4]

While he waited for Lewis to arrive in St. Charles, Clark examined and redistributed the loads in the keelboat and two large pirogues that were to

1. For an examination of the relationship between the captains' changing geographical conceptions and their behavior and operations in the field, see John L. Allen, "An Analysis of the Exploratory Process: The Lewis and Clark Expedition of 1804–06," *Geographical Review*, LXII (1972), 13–39.

2. See Jackson, *Letters*, pp. 195–96.

3. At this point the actual journey commenced, and a word needs to be said here about the source for the details of the trip from the mouth of the Missouri to the Pacific and back. Nearly all of the material has been taken from the *Original Journals of the Lewis and Clark Expedition*, edited by Reuben Gold Thwaites and drawn from the manuscript notes made by the captains themselves during the course of their journey. Henceforth all citations from or references to the Thwaites journals will be by volume and page number in parentheses in the text. There are two other major journals available. These will be referred to herein as the "Biddle journals" and the "Coues journals." Each of these is a full, comprehensive daily record of the entire expedition. In addition to these complete records is the journal kept by Clark during the Wood River period and the trip from St. Louis to the Mandan villages and published as the *Field Notes*, and Bernard DeVoto's masterfully condensed version of the Thwaites journals (with material added from Biddle and Coues), *The Journals of Lewis and Clark* (Boston, 1953). The "Biddle journals" consist of the "official" version of the manuscript field notes: Nicholas Biddle and Paul Allen, eds., *History of the Expedition under the Command of Captains Lewis and Clark* (2 vols., Philadelphia, 1814). As these were put together following the return of the expedition they are less satisfactory for assessing the day-to-day nature of the captains' changing geographical conceptions and consequently will seldom be referred to for data on the exploration itself. The "Coues journals" are the result of the re-editing, by Elliot Coues, of the original Biddle edition and were published in 4 volumes in New York in 1893. As these are even further from the captains' own originals, having suffered both the distortion of time and Coues's (sometimes) cavalier editorial hand, they will also seldom be referred to for details on the expedition in progress. Other journals, written by other members of the party, do exist, but since the focus here is on Lewis and Clark and their geographical ideas, these will be cited only occasionally.

4. Osgood, *Field Notes*, p. 42.

carry the expedition into the interior, making certain that "the Bow of each may be heavyer loded than the Stern" (I, 21).[5] On May 20 he was finally joined by Lewis, "accompanied by the Officers & Several Gentlemen of St. Louis," and the next day, "under three Cheers from the gentlemen on the bank" and under a gray and threatening sky, the "party destined for the discovery of the interior of the continent of North America" (I, 21) began their journey to the great South Sea.[6]

From this rainy day in mid-spring to October 26, 1804, Captains Lewis and Clark[7] would travel the first leg of their two-year trek to the Pacific, up the great river that had held for so long the key to the mystery of the Passage to India. As the Corps of Discovery proceeded upriver, the image of the trans-Missouri West that the captains had acquired before their departure would begin to take new form. The initial sources for the revision of earlier images of the Northwest and the revised plans for exploration that would emerge from that revision were found in the West itself. For the first time, Americans from a woodland environment were about to enter a total and absolute region of grasslands, and the nature of that region, as viewed and understood by Lewis and Clark, would exert a powerful influence over their geographical conceptions. And combined with the nature of the region as a wellspring for the transformation and refinement of earlier views was geographical lore and information of another sort. During their journey from the mouth of the Missouri to its Great Bend, where they would halt and spend the winter of 1804–05, the captains would derive data from fur traders who had resided in the Northwest for many years and would gather knowledge of the farther West from the Indian tribes of the Missouri valley. Lewis and Clark would blend these sources for image transformation with those obtained at the winter camp they called Fort Mandan and would, thereby, give shape and expression to a new view of the West.[8]

5. Throughout much of the more than two-year journey to the Pacific and back, Clark's experience as a riverman was to stand the expedition in good stead.

6. Jackson (*Letters*, pp. 370–73) gives a listing and brief sketch of the members of the "permanent party" (those that accompanied Lewis and Clark to the Pacific and back). In addition to these (some of whom did not enlist until the winter of 1804–05 at the Mandan villages), the party that left Wood River included nine or ten *engagés* or boatmen, most of whom returned to St. Louis from the Mandans.

7. In Clark's case the title "captain" is only an honorary and accepted one. While Lewis actually held a captain's commission in the "1st U.S. Regt. Infty.," Clark was commissioned as a lieutenant. The commission, when it arrived, highly displeased Lewis, who wrote that his friend's rank during the expedition would "by G–d . . . be equal to my own" (Jackson, *Letters*, p. 179). During the trek to the Pacific, both men shared the command responsibilities, and Clark signed his orders as "Captain." He later wrote to Nicholas Biddle that "No difficulty took place on our rout relative to this point" (Jackson, *Letters*, p. 572).

8. The purpose of this chapter is not to list or catalog the geographical discoveries of Lewis and Clark in terms of topographical features named or defined or located. This has already been done most admirably by Paul Cutright in his *Lewis and Clark: Pioneering Naturalists*. The intent is, rather, to gather the impressions and perceptions of the western environment which conditioned the image of the trans-Missouri area that the captains developed following their first season in the field.

During the first two months of the journey, the expedition wound its way up the Missouri as far as the mouth of the Platte River (fig. 28), passing through a country which, by virtue of its "fine, rich . . . & well-watered" land, exhibited all the features necessary for a quick and easy settling by an American farming population.[9] The Garden of the French chroniclers and the Garden of Jefferson's image became real in the minds of the explorers; it was visible in the landscape, and the journal entries made by Lewis and Clark from the middle of May until nearly the end of July reflected their enthusiasm and wonder over the prairie lands of the lower Missouri basin. Averaging from 10 to 20 miles a day, the Corps of Discovery worked its route up the verdant lower stretches of the Missouri valley, through lush bottomlands adjacent to the river's luxuriant banks choked with "cottonwood, sycamore, hickory, white walnut, some grapevines, and rushes."[10] On May 25 the night's camp was made near La Charette, a "Small french Village of 7 houses," and when the party passed it on their upstream journey they left behind them the final elements and traces of frontier agricultural civilization. But they did not depart from the lands "susceptible of cultivation,"[11] and from here on the explorers' journals were full of entries that reported "butifull countrey"—entries that must be read as meaning "lands available for productive American agriculture."

It was at La Charette that Lewis and Clark met the first of the many informants who would contribute to the success of their mission by providing geographical data. On their arrival at this last settlement on the Missouri, they found Regis Loisel, one of the more prominent of the Missouri River fur traders and certainly one of the trade's most knowledgeable persons with respect to the geography of the Northwest.[12] Loisel had just returned from his trading establishment, "Situated in the Country of the Scioux 400 leagues up," and graciously presented the American explorers with a "good Deel of information." What this information consisted of was not reported, but Loisel was in an excellent position to offer fairly accurate reports on the Missouri and its tributaries as far upstream as the mouth of the Teton or Bad River, having undertaken an expedition to this locality on the upper Missouri during the previous year.[13]

Loisel had been one of the original partners in the St. Louis–based Missouri Company, established in 1793 by a group of Louisiana merchants

---

9. It must be remembered that both officers were ardent Republicans and probably saw the lands they traversed in terms of the agrarianism which colored Jeffersonian political theory.

10. Coues, *History of the Expedition*, I, 10.

11. Biddle, *History of the Expedition*, I, 3.

12. For details on Loisel, see Osgood, *Field Notes*, p. 46, n. 1; and the introduction to Annie H. Abel, *Tabeau's Narrative of Loisel's Expedition to the Upper Missouri* (Norman, Okla., 1939).

13. Details in Abel, *Tabeau's Narrative;* and Nasatir, *Before Lewis and Clark*, II, 735–40.

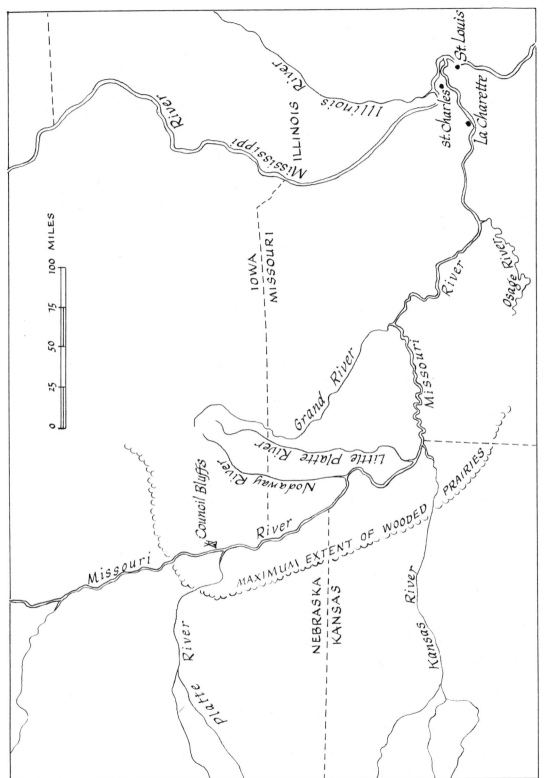

28. The route of the expedition from St. Louis to the Platte, May 14 to July 21, 1804

eager for the discovery of a route to the Pacific via the Missouri River.[14] His potential interest in the completion of the project of Lewis and Clark was probably quite high, therefore, and his assistance could have exceeded the simple providing of information. He gave the captains "Some letters," Clark noted, and these letters may have granted the captains access to further geographical data in the possession of those members of the Missouri fur trade who were in Loisel's employ and whom Lewis and Clark met during the summer's journey or during the winter sojourn near the villages of the Mandan and Minitari (or Hidatsa) Indians, situated at the Missouri's Great Bend. These men—Pierre Dorion, Jean Valle, Joseph Gravelines, and Pierre Antoine Tabeau—were all to tender bits of detail on western geography that would prove important when the captains fleshed out their views of the trans-Missouri region during the winter at Fort Mandan.

3

Before they left their winter quarters at the mouth of Wood River, Lewis and Clark had acquired maps, mileage tables, and journals derived from the most recent exploratory ventures up the Missouri by James Mackay and John Evans. The captains obviously consulted these materials during their journey; many comments in their daily logbooks from the first summer of exploration point to the American explorers' continual checking of data presented in the Mackay-Evans journals and maps. But this data, although the most detailed lore on the Missouri prior to Lewis and Clark, was lacking in basic geographical information on anything but the Missouri's course, the distances between the mouths of its major tributaries, and brief ethnological sketches of many of the Missouri River tribes. The Mackay-Evans materials had been a significant input in the process of image formation at Camp Dubois, but by the spring of 1804 Lewis and Clark had passed from the stage of image formation based on secondhand materials to the stage of data collection preparatory to new image creation. The new information that came out of the 1,600-mile journey to the Missouri's Great Bend replaced and superseded the pre-exploratory lore, even though the previous lore had long been accepted as the most complete and most accurate available.

As the expedition moved upriver from La Charette, repeated contacts were made with the Missouri River tribes and with boatloads of fur traders, coming down the Missouri to St. Louis laden with the winter pelts gathered in the lucrative Indian trade. The captains sought information whenever such contacts occurred, but many references in the daily journals suggest that seldom could (or would) either Indians or fur traders supply useful or valuable knowledge. Typical is Clark's entry for May 27, when the explorers met

---

14. The charter and background of the "Company of Explorers of the Upper Missouri" may be found in Nasatir, *Before Lewis and Clark* I, 186–93.

a total of six boats coming down from the Omahas and the Pawnees: "they informed nothing of Consequence" (I, 34). A similar situation existed when, on June 12, Lewis and Clark met two boats loaded with furs, buffalo grease, and tallow. "Those people," wrote Captain Clark, "inform nothing of much information" (I, 46). But this party was different, for, as the captains soon learned, it was part of Regis Loisel's operations, and one of its members was "old Mr. Durion."

Pierre Dorion was an old Missouri river hand who had lived (off and on) with the Sioux for at least twenty years,[15] and had served Loisel as an interpreter to this nation for several seasons. Lewis and Clark, on their first meeting with the old riverman, "questioned him untill it was too late to Go further" (I, 46), and although no inventory of the intelligence he might have supplied exists, his value as both a source of geographical accounts and as an interpreter was recognized. The captains persuaded Dorion to accompany them as a guide and translator, at least as far as the Sioux villages on the James River, and while he traveled with them, Lewis and Clark had a built-in supply of lore on the Missouri and its tributaries.

Dorion was not the only built-in data source on the expedition. The French boatmen who had been hired in St. Louis to handle the boats as far as the Missouri's Great Bend were frequently able to point out landmarks along the river itself and knew portions of the Missouri's course from earlier trips they had made in the hire of St. Louis merchants.[16] But none of them had actually lived in the region as had the doughty old interpreter, and more often than not when Lewis or Clark entered in their river journals some lengthy description of a river like the Kansas, Platte, or Niobrara, they were recording lore either derived directly from Dorion or taken from materials in the captains' possession and verified by their interpreter.

4

It continued to rain during the first days of the journey, but the damp weather and the treachery of the snags and rolling waters of the Missouri did not mar the pleasantness of the country through which they were passing. On June 1, at a distance of 133 miles from the Missouri's mouth, the party reached the mouth of the Osage River, named for the tribe whose abundant lands the expedition was traversing, and from a hill between the Osage and the Missouri Clark had what he termed a "Delightfull prospect."[17] The Osage nation claimed the beaver as their ancestor, and many of those animals were

15. Biographical and bibliographical information on Pierre Dorion may be found in Osgood, *Field Notes*, p. 55, n. 1; and Coues, *History*, I, 21, 47.

16. Details from the French and Spanish Louisiana fur-trading operations and breadth and detail of geographical information that came out of them appear in Nasatir, *Before Lewis and Clark*, I, 56–57, 73–74; and scattered through Houck, *The Spanish Regime in Missouri*.

17. Osgood, *Field Notes*, p. 48.

in evidence along the banks of the river, as were numerous waterfowl. The woods along the Missouri were full of deer and bear, and while the hunters supplied fresh meat, other members of the party supplemented the diet of the expedition by gathering the wild serviceberries, raspberries, and strawberries that grew in profusion in the Missouri's rich bottomlands.[18] Clark summed up the environment and his and Lewis's attitude toward it in one word—"Bountifull."

The view of the Garden was not restricted to just the river's banks and floodplain. Rising back from the river on both sides were the prairies, "roleing and interspursed with points of timber land" (I, 45). The prairies were predominantly grasslands, and although the traditional American opinion of treeless environments in the opening years of the nineteenth century was supposedly low, this view was apparently not held by Lewis and Clark.[19] Jefferson himself had explained the treeless character of much of the trans-Mississippi West as the consequence of soil that was too fertile for the growth of forests, and the captains' journal entries mirrored this belief. Something about the Missouri prairies or the way they were seen was different from the grasslands that early American observers in Kentucky and Ohio had classified as "the barrens." Clark noted the difference: "Those Prairies are not like those, or a number of those E. of the Mississippi void of every thing except grass, they abound with Hasel Grapes & a wild plumb of a Superior quality, Called the Osages Plumb" (I, 46).

On June 13 the expedition reached the junction of the Grand River with the Missouri and observed the site of "the ancient village" of the formerly great and numerous tribe from which the Missouri got its name.[20] Here Lewis and Clark walked to the top of a small hill between the Missouri and the Grand and from its summit "had a butifull prospect of Serounding countrey, in the open Prairie" (I, 47–48). The landscape continued to enthrall the observers, and four days later, after passing the remains of an old fort established by Etienne Bourgmont nearly a century earlier,[21] Clark revealed his fascination with the countryside: "The Countrey about this place is butifull on the river rich & well timbered on the S.S.[22] About two miles back a Prarie

18. Cutright, *Lewis and Clark*, p. 53.
19. The literature on American attitudes toward and interactions with the grassland environment is volumious. The best and most comprehensive is James C. Malin, *The Grassland of North America* (4th printing, Lawrence, Kan., 1961).
20. Coues, *History*, I, 22, n. 49.
21. Bourgmont's explorations and reports are published in Margry, *Decouvertes . . . des Francais*, VI, 398–449.
22. In the captains' journals, "S.S." usually refers to the starboard or right side of the boat. "L.S." normally means the larboard or left side. This kind of classification system was well adapted to the Missouri, for the river's meanders often made such designations as "east" side or "west" side meaningless. I have adopted a slightly different designation for use herein, referring to the right and left sides of the Missouri (as viewed from a boat traveling upstream) as, respectively, north and south as far as the mouth of the Kansas, east and west from the Kansas to the Mandan villages, north and south between the villages and the Great Falls, and west and east from the Great Falls to the Three Forks. Such a designation is more meaningful if the reader is consulting a small-scale map.

coms. [commences] which is rich and interspursed with groves of timber, the country rises at 7 or 8 miles still further back and is rolling. on the L.S. the high land & Prarie coms. in the bank of the river and continus back, well wartered and abounds in Deer Elk & Bear" (I, 51). Despite the captain's inventive spelling, his meaning came through clearly. The trans-Missouri West was a garden and exploration was simply confirming the fact.

The rainy weather persisted, and the party was finding Missouri River navigation less easy than had been expected when the plans for the expedition were being laid in faraway Washington. Nevertheless, it was a relatively easy trip, this first stretch of the river to the mouth of the Platte, and the two captains had plenty of free time to wander on the banks of the mighty stream, taking note of the lush vegetation and the "immence" herds of deer and elk, along with one of the few pests to mar the Garden, the even "immencer" clouds of "Musketors."[23] Along the Missouri's shores the wild grapes and mulberries and plums grew in abundance. The bottoms of the river were covered with growths of cottonwood and willow, and above them, on the terrace, oak and ash and walnut trees faded back into the incredibly fertile prairie lands. It was, as Lewis and Clark had been led to expect before they ever left Camp Dubois, a very bountiful and fertile country:[24]

The Country and Lands on each Side of the river is various as useal, and may be classed as follows, viz: the low or overflown points of bottom land, of the groth of Cotton & Willow, the 2nd bottom (except when it Coms to the river then from the river) about 80 or 100 foot roleing back Supplied with water (the small rivers of which loses themselves in the bottom land) and are covered with a variety of timber Such as Oake of different Kinds Blue ash, Walnut &c. &c. as far as the Butifull praries, which I am informed lie back from the river, at Some places near & others a great Distance [1, 54].

5

The expedition reached the mouth of the "great river of the Kansas" in the late afternoon of June 26, and, after pausing for three days to make the astronomical observations that were vital to their regional analysis and cartographic productions,[25] the party passed the Kansas on June 30. Lewis and Clark had some knowledge of this river from those sources collected prior to

23. The party was forced, whenever it halted for any length of time, to make large and smoky fires to "keep off the musquitrs & knats" (I, 56).
24. Other contemporary accounts agreed with Lewis and Clark in their assessment of the lower Missouri valley. Both Henry Brackenridge, *Journal of a Voyage up the Missouri River in 1811*, and John Bradbury, *Travels in the Interior of America* (vols. IV and V of *Early Western Travels*, ed. Thwaites), came to the same general conclusions about the abundance of the interior.
25. The captains carried with them a sextant, an octant, three artificial horizons, a chronometer, and a compass and with these made remarkably accurate calculations of latitude and longitude throughout the course of their journey (VI, 230–65).

their departure from Camp Dubois, but while they had their interlude near the mouth of the Kansas, they received new details about it, perhaps from Pierre Dorion: "it heads with the river Del Noird [del Norte or Rio Grande] in the black Mountain or ridge which Divides the Waters of the Kansas *Del Nord*, & Callarado & [illegible—possibly "offshoots"] from those of the Missouri" (I, 60). A new element had been added to the geographical lore of the Northwest—the "Black Mountains" or "Black Hills"—and even after the completion of their journey to the Pacific and back, Lewis and Clark would remain confused about the location and extent of that mysterious mountain range.

At the mouth of the Kansas the landscape began to change gradually to full grassland, and the captains' journal notations began to include the phrase "open and butifull plains" more frequently. The vegetation characteristics of the Mississippi valley had begun to give way to greater concentrations of that symbol of the Plains, the cottonwood, crowding closer to the water's edge and leaving behind broader expanses of the big bluestem grasses.[26] But in spite of the change in the nature of the biotic environment and the reduction of wooded land, the countryside retained its gardenlike quality. Just above the mouth of the Kansas, Clark, usually a practical and prosaic reporter, entered in his daily log what is still one of the most lyrical and picturesque descriptions of the American prairies:

The Plains of this countrey are covered with a Leek green Grass, well calculated for the sweetest and most nourishing hay—interspersed with copse of trees, Spreding ther lofty branchs over Pools Springs or Brooks of fine water. Groops of Shrubs covered with the most delecious froot is to be seen in every derection, and nature appears to have exerted herself to butify the Senery by the variety of Flours Delecately and haighly flavered raised above the Grass, which strikes & profumes the Sensation, and amuses the mind, throuws it into Conjectering the cause of So magnificent a Senery in a country situated far removed from the Sivilised world to be enjoyed by notheing but the Buffalo Elk Deer & bear in which it abounds.[27]

Clark's words can stand alone for they more than adequately express the nature of the region and the potentialities for the American agriculturalist seen in it by Lewis and Clark. Their views of the lower Missouri valley would be translated later into one of the major components of their later image of the Northwest.

Even the elements conspired to lend an aura of almost supernatural beauty to the country around the mouth of the Kansas: "at Sunset the

26. Cutright, *Lewis and Clark*, pp. 62–63.
27. Osgood, *Field Notes*, p. 69. The style of this passage is so uncharacteristic of Clark (although the spelling is unmistakably his) that there is a serious question as to whether he actually composed it. Lewis apparently did not keep a journal until the winter at Fort Mandan, but scattered throughout the daily entries are some in Lewis's hand, enough to suggest that he may have kept at least fragmentary records. The passage cited here is very similar to Lewis's distinctive style; possibly Clark copied the passage from notes made by his companion.

atmespier presented every appearance of wind, Blue & White Streeks cen-
tiring at the Sun as she disappeared and the Clouds Situated to the S.W.
Guilded in the most butifull manner" (I, 54). The Golden West of all past
centuries was coming true, and being human, Lewis and Clark could not fail
to hear and respond to the sirens' song. The valley of the Missouri between
the Mississippi and the Kansas River was a luxuriance of the mind as much as
of the landscape, and except for Clark's inspired spelling, the journal entries
for this segment of the voyage upriver differed little from those of the earliest
French explorers whose reports had done so much to shape the concept of the
Garden in the West.

6

The expedition moved on toward the mouth of the Platte River, and
that the familiarity of the St. Louis boatmen with the region became part of
the captains' compilation of geographical data was apparent when the Corps
of Discovery passed some mid-channel islands near the mouth of the Little
Platte River and Clark commented that "one of the French hands Says that
the french kept their cattle & horses on those islands at the time they had in
this quarter a fort & trading establishment" (I, 63).[28] The environmental transition that had begun near the entry of the Kansas became more apparent
when the rainy, cool weather which had plagued the party from the beginning of the journey was replaced by heat. Those of the men who manned the
oars and sweeps of the boats "were verry much over powered" with the hot,
oppressive winds that blew daily from the southeast.[29] The proportion of
grassland in the landscape became greater although the hills and valleys on
both sides of the Missouri were still "interspsd. with Coops [copses] of Timber" which gave a "pleasing deversity to the Senery" (I, 67). In many places
the scenery had "the appearance of distinct farms, divided by narrow strips
of woodland, which follow the borders of the small runs leading to the
river."[30] The gallery forest skirting the borders of the Missouri and its tributary streams, a feature so characteristic of grassland environments, had become a dominant element in the landscape.[31]

As the Corps of Discovery neared the Platte the country opened up more
and more, but the problems of navigation on the Missouri became greater,
with sandbars impeding easy progress and caving banks creating hazards for
the crude keelboat and the two clumsy pirogues. "Worthey of Remark,"
reported Clark as the party approached the great river Platte, were the "Sand
bars much more numerous and the quick or moveing Sands much worse than
they were below at the places where Praries approach the river, it is verry

28. According to the entry for this date, in Coues, *History*, I, 37, the "general outline of
the fortification" was still visible.
29. The meteorological records of the expedition are in VI, 165–229.
30. Biddle, *History*, I, 22.
31. Walter Prescott Webb, *The Great Plains* (New York, 1931), pp. 7–33.

wide those places being much easier to wash & undermine than the Wood Land's" (I, 84). The cause of the increased sediment level of the Missouri was discovered on Saturday, July 21, when the expedition reached the mouth of the Platte, 630 miles from St. Louis, and the captains observed the braided characteristics of the stream that was and is the archetype of a Great Plains river.

"This Great river being much more rapid than the Missouri forces its Current against the opposite Shore," wrote Clark. "The Current of this river comes with great velocity roleing its Sands into the Missouri, filling up its Bead & Compelling it to incroach on the North Shores. we found great dificuelty in passing around the Sand at the Mouth of this River" (I, 86–87). These notes were reminiscent of the first references to the Missouri's entry into the Mississippi in 1673, when Marquette had written nearly the same lines about the waters of the Missouri, which came rushing into the Mississippi with such "impetuosity" that he and his party "could not without great danger risk passing through it."[32] The feelings of Lewis and Clark when they encountered the Platte must have resembled in other ways those of Marquette on his discovery of the Missouri. For like the Missouri of more than a hundred years earlier, the Platte was a mystery, an exotic and anomalous stream that behaved like no other river within the frame of geographical knowledge or experience.

In 1804 the Platte River was almost completely beyond the scope of American geographical lore. It had appeared on contemporary maps as the "Rio Chato" or "Plate River," but it was normally shown as a short and unimportant tributary of the Missouri. Those few reports of the Platte which had made their way into American literature did nothing to dissolve the mystery surrounding the river since they almost universally described a land that was unimaginable and incomprehensible to Americans of the early nineteenth century: "The desart through which the Plate takes its course is said to extend a hundred miles on both sides; that it is made up of hills and plains, of arid sand—that in high winds, vast bodies of sand are taken up, and carried through the air, burying irrecoverable whatever they happen to fall upon— and that in this dreary tract, there is little or no vegetation, nor any animals to be seen excepting a species of rabbit and an animal of the goat kind—nor is it inhabited by any of the human race."[33] Such descriptions were reinforced when the Corps of Discovery reached the great river and were informed by one of the party, perhaps Dorion, who had wintered "two winters on this river, that 'it is much wider above, and does not rise more than five or six feet' Spreds verry wide (with many small islands scattered thro' it,) and from its rapidity & roleing Sands Cannot be navagated with Boats or Perogues" (I, 87). Later travelers and observers would articulate these views more

32. Louise P. Kellogg, ed., *Early Narratives of the Northwest* (New York, 1917), p. 249.
33. *National Intelligencer* (Washington), Oct. 21, 1803, pp. 1–2. This account was written by someone from Kaskaskia who used the pseudonym "Viator." It appeared in a number of American newspapers in 1803–04.

192

clearly, and among some elements of American society the concept of the Great American Desert would come to dominate images of the western interior.[34] But for Lewis and Clark in July of 1804, the inconsistency of a notion of a desert in the Garden precluded the incorporation of such elements into their geographical conceptions.

The Platte did, nevertheless, form a meridian for the explorers. Situated halfway between the mouth of the Kansas, where the tall-grass prairies started to prevail in the landscape, and the mouth of the Niobrara, where the expedition made its entry onto the High Plains, the Platte marked the beginnings of the transition to the great treeless and semi-arid plains that were not yet a full-fledged component in the American images of the Great West. This meridian, this environmental transition, is very apparent in the captains' landscape descriptions; above the mouth of the Platte, the notations of "beautiful and well-watered lands" decreased in frequency in the journals, to be replaced by "high and dry." And true to form for the Plains, the weather grew more extreme above the Platte; the rain squalls were more sudden and violent, the heat was more withering, and the strengthening northwesterly winds began to impede seriously the progress of the craft carrying Lewis and Clark and their party up the Missouri.[35]

As the Platte marked the transition from one environment to another, it marked a passage of another sort, a passage from relatively familiar territory to territory that was as yet largely known only through rumor and conjecture. For the Missouri River fur traders, the mouth of the Platte was the dividing line between the "upper" and "lower" Missouri[36] and as such was a meridian of knowledge. Below the Platte, Lewis and Clark had been operating on the sound geographical information found in their various sources and supplemented by Dorion and their French boatmen. Few of the boatmen had been beyond the mouth of the Platte, however, and the data the captains had from those explorers such as Truteau, Evans, and Mackay was insubstantial, being confined mainly to comments on the Missouri itself. West and north from the Platte was a land of mystery and misunderstanding, a land whose geography could be filled only with the knowledge gained as the expedition sailed up toward the Mandan villages.

34. Recent research findings indicate that the idea of a Great American Desert was less acceptable than many historians have believed, particularly among the rural populations of the South and West (see Martyn J. Bowden, "The Perception of the Western Interior of the United States 1800–1870," *Proceedings of the Association of American Geographers*, I (1969), 16–21). The more traditional opinion that the desert concept was widely held and therefore acted as a barrier to the westward movement is stated in R. C. Morris, "The Notion of a Great American Desert West of the Rockies," *Mississippi Valley Historical Review*, XIII (1926), 190–200.

35. Lewis and Clark were learning to accept the reports of Truteau, whose journals had stated that navigation on the Missouri was often impeded by "the winds which are frequent and very high" (Nasatir, *Before Lewis and Clark*, II, 378).

36. According to Brackenridge (*Journal of a Voyage up the Missouri*, p. 226), "the river Platte is regarded by the navigators of the Missouri as a point of as much importance as the equinoctial line amongst mariners . . . . From this we enter what is called the Upper Missouri."

7

Leaving the Platte behind, the expedition sailed on upriver, the captains busying themselves with the preparation of maps and papers that they had intended to send back downstream to Jefferson from some point above the Platte (I, 89–90). That they would do so was in compliance with the President's instructions to avail themsleves of every opportunity to send back information on western geography and their progress, as well as with their own intention to return some members of the party with one of the pirogues from a point above the Platte. Although Lewis and Clark never lagged in their collection of geographical data, the proposal to return the data collected by July was aborted sometime after the Corps of Discovery had crossed the imaginary meridian of the Platte's mouth. Just when the plans were changed is not clear, but the first mention of the matter in the captains' daily logbooks did not appear until mid-September, when the increasingly shallow channel of the Missouri had made it necessary for Clark to order the redistribution of the loads among the three boats, and consequently to keep both pirogues with the expedition as far as the "winter residence wherever that may be."[37] But the significance of the original plans to transmit geographical information to Jefferson as quickly as possible does not lie in the fact that those plans were modified. The critical point is that Lewis and Clark obviously did not consider themselves to be operating in isolation but, in accordance with their instructions, deliberately recorded data for the purposes of transmission. That they took great care in doing so is apparent from their journal notations after they entered the increasingly unfamiliar territory beyond the Platte's entry into the Missouri.

For many miles above the Platte, the captains restricted themselves to commentary on the Missouri itself, on its eastern tributaries, and on the nature of the region as observed from the river. For the first month of this segment of the voyage, the track of the expedition was through a landscape that was of "the same uniform appearance . . . rich, low ground near the river, succeeded by undulating prairies, with timber near the waters."[38] "The Countrey above the Platt R. has a great Similarity," wrote Clark, although there was no indication that the scenery had become monotonous for him or Lewis. The diversity and variety of the lower Missouri was no longer present in the perspectives on either side of the river, but the fact that the landscape was opening up and the visibility increasing with a decrease in the size and complexity of vegetation made possible observations and descriptions of botanical and topographic features that could not have been made farther downstream. On July 30, for example, while the expedition was camped near

37. See Osgood, *Field Notes*, p. 139, n. 6, and p. 144, n. 1. This was the first operational decision made by the captains as the consequence of unexpected field conditions and was the first change in plans that had been made prior to the departure from Camp Dubois.

38. Coues, *History*, I, 81.

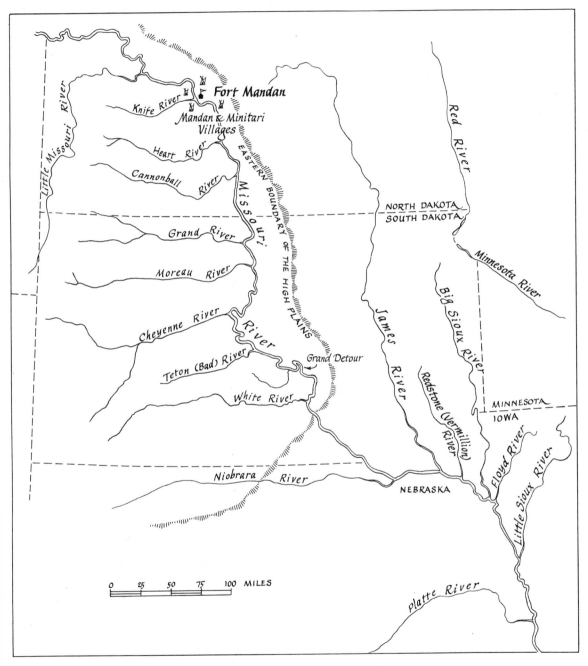

Fort Mandan

Knife River

Mandan & Minitari
Villages

Heart River

Cannonball River

Little Missouri River

EASTERN BOUNDARY OF THE HIGH PLAINS

Missouri River

Grand River

Moreau River

Cheyenne River

Teton (Bad) River

Grand Detour

White River

Niobrara River

Red River

Minnesota River

James River

Big Sioux River

Redstone (Vermillion) River

Floyd River

Little Sioux River

NORTH DAKOTA
SOUTH DAKOTA

MINNESOTA
IOWA

NEBRASKA

Platte River

| 0 | 25 | 50 | 75 | 100 MILES |

29. The route of the expedition from the Platte to the Mandan villages, July 21 to October 25, 1804

Council Bluffs,[39] Clark entered in his daily log an almost modern portrayal of the riverine environment in the Great Plains:

The Prarie [along the river] is Covered with Grass of 10 or 12 inches in hight, Soil of good quality & at the Distance of about a mile still further back the Countrey rises about 80 or 90 feet higher, and is one Continued Plain as fur as Can be seen, from the Bluff on the 2d. rise imediately above our Camp, the most butifull prospect of the River up & Down and the Countrey Opsd. presented it Self which I ever beheld; The River Meandering the open and butifull Plains, interspursed with Groves of timber, and each point Covered with Tall timber, Such as Willow Cotton sum Mulberry, Elm, Sucamore Lynn & ash (The Groves contain Hickory, Walnut, coffee nut & Oake in addition)   Two ranges of High Land parrelel to each other, and from 4 to 10 Miles Distant, between which the river & its bottoms are Contained [1, 95].[40]

A few days later, when the expedition had left Council Bluffs after a conference with the Oto and Missouri Indians had been completed, Clark recorded another typical feature of the Plains landscape, the concentration of trees in the "breaks" or small dissected valleys through which water runs off the higher elevations of the plains down to the local base level of the river. The highlands bordering the river, he wrote, "appear to be intirely clear of any thing but what is common in an open Plain, Some Scattering timber or wood is to be Seen in the reveens, and where the Creeks pass into the Hill" (I, 100). And on August 6, 1804, more than a half-century before John Wesley Powell would lay the foundations for scientific topographical analysis of river valleys, Clark set down a word picture of fluvial processes that was remarkable for its clarity and prophetic in its content. While walking through the wooded land along the Missouri's banks he came out onto a "Peninsula" almost surrounded by a great meander in the river's course, and after observing it he wrote:

The high water passes thro' this Peninsula, and agreeable to the customary changes of the river, I concld that in two years the main current of the river will pass through. In every bend the banks are falling in from the current being thrown against those bends by the Sand points which inlarges and the Soil I believe from unquestionable appearns. of the entire Bottom from one hill to the other being the Mud or Ooze of the river at Some former Period mixed with Sand and Clay easily melts and Slips into the River, and the mud mixes with the water & the Sand is washed down and lodges on the points [1, 101].

This was not the only time during their term in the field that Clark or Lewis offered such a description of landforming processes. The greater visibility of the operations of geomorphic agencies in the semi-arid western environments brought the captains to many of the same conclusions reached by the mem-

39. The Council Bluff of the journals was a location some few miles upstream and across the river from the site of present-day Council Bluffs, Iowa.
40. Clark's description illustrates his recognition of the growing confinement of the more complex biozones to the lands immediately adjacent to the river.

bers of the various geological and topographical surveys investigating the same region during the last third of the nineteenth cenutry.[41]

8

Although landscape descriptions were plentiful in the captains' journals during the months of July and August, little detail was offered on the lands to the west of the Missouri's course. This lack of data on the lay of the land was partly the result of the fact that no major western tributaries enter the Missouri between the Platte and the Niobrara, and the majority of the captains' geographical descriptions centered on the analysis and reporting of knowledge about river systems. Also partly responsible was the decreasing capability of the French boatmen to offer information—except for Pierre Dorion, who continued to be an invaluable source of geographical lore. On August 8, when the expedition reached the river shown on the Mackay and Evans maps as the "Petite Riviere des Sioux," falling into the Missouri from the east, Clark, informed by Dorion, who had (he said) been at the head of the Little Sioux, recorded the remarkably accurate intelligence that it was "navagable for Perogues Some Distance runs Parrelel to the Missouri some Distance, then falls down from N.E. thro a roleing Countrey open, the head of this river is 9 miles from the R. Demoin" (I, 103).

Dorion's familiarity with the country again proved helpful when the party reached the Big Sioux River (at the present site of Sioux City, Iowa) and the captains learned from their interpreter that it headed with one tributary of the Mississippi, the Minnesota River, and passed close by the course of another, the Des Moines (I, 115). Speculative geographies had long stated that the waters of the Missouri and the Mississippi were in close proximity to one another for a great distance into the interior,[42] and although Lewis and Clark were primarily interested in water connections through the territory west of the Missouri's course, they could not have failed to be intrigued by the apparent verification of geographical theory and the possibilities opened thereby. Even more intriguing was the knowledge gained when the party reached the James River at present-day Yankton, South Dakota: "This river . . . is navagable for Perogues a Great distance, it heads with the St. Peters [Minnesota], of the Mississippi & the *red River* which runs into Lake Winipeck and Hudsons Bay" (I, 126). The potential for long-range water travel through the continental interior must have seemed enormous, and if these conditions existed on the eastern side of the Missouri basin, Lewis and Clark might well have assumed they held for the river's western branches as well.

41. Goetzmann, *Exploration and Empire*, pp. 355–576.
42. In his "Official Account," p. 347, Jefferson himself had claimed that "the Missouri and Mississippi run nearly parallel courses from their heads which are relatively close to one another."

More immediate matters than conjecturing about future probabilities were pressing, however; among them were the necessary halts to engage in discussions related to trading rights with the various Indian nations along this section of the Missouri. Because of these delays, progress upriver from the Platte was relatively slow. It was near the end of August before the expedition had pushed as far upstream as the mouth of the Vermillion (or Redstone) River and found itself well within a Great Plains environment. The shorter grasses began to prevail over the longer varieties, the amount of mineral material washed from the soil into the waters of the river increased, the herds of animals grew in size, and on August 23 the hunters killed the first buffalo. The country was "level & open as far as can be Seen, except Some few rises at a grate Distance" (I, 121), one of these rises on the Missouri's western side forming an object of terror for the local Indians as it was supposed to be "the residence of Some unusial Sperits."[43] Lewis and Clark decided to investigate, and although they located no demons in the neighborhood, they did ascend the small chalkstone mound to gain a better perspective view of the surrounding countryside. Timber was a rarity in the landscape, and Clark remarked that "if all the timber which is on the Stone Creek [Vermillion River] was on 100 acres it would not be thickly timbered" (I, 123).[44] But even though the plains round about the mound were "open Void of Timber and leavel to a great extent," and the winds drove "with unusial force over the naked Plains and against this hill," the view was "most butifull," with numerous herds of buffalo seen feeding on the plains, which extended "without interuption as far as Can be seen" (I, 122–23). Where the prairie lands of the lower Missouri had evoked images of tilled fields and peaceful husbandmen, the plains and the vast herds that grazed thereon presented a different picture—but one of abundance nevertheless. And as the Corps of Discovery moved on upriver, these first enthusiastic responses to the biotic environment of the Great Plains waxed and the members of the party, particularly the Kentucky hunters, considered the Plains a virtual paradise.

9

On September 4 Lewis and Clark and their command reached the mouth of the Niobrara or "Que Courre" River; suffering from the absence of Dorion, their supplier of lore on the Missouri's western tributaries who had remained behind at the Sioux villages on the James, Clark was forced to report that "the heads of this river is not known" (I, 139). But the captains were not altogether without information on the country through which they were

43. This belief, Clark supposed, was the result of large congregations of birds about the hill, "a Sufficent proof to produce in the Savage Mind a Confident belief of all the properties which they ascribe [to] it" (I, 123).

44. A few weeks later the journals contained the notation that timber was "a rare object now" (Coues, *History*, I, 115).

passing. Many of the landmarks along the Missouri were mentioned in the Mackay-Evans material, and on September 8 the journals of Truteau were used to identify the site where that explorer had wintered on the Missouri in 1794–95.[45] Nearly a week later, Clark "walked on Shore the whole day" in a futile attempt to "find an old Vulcanoe, Said to be in this neighbourhood by Mr. J. McKey of St. Charles" (I, 147).[46] The Mackay-Evans data and the Truteau journals were proving singularly unsatisfactory in providing information on the country beyond the river bluffs, however, and as the expedition passed the mouths of the White and Teton (Bad) rivers the captains could only say that their courses and heads were not known.

The Niobrara symbolized more than a decline in the quantity of geographical lore; when the expedition crossed its mouth they crossed the threshold of the High Plains as well and entered a region in which the criteria used to define the Great Plains environment are found in the greatest concentration and in their most typical development. From early in November until the next summer, when they entered the broken and arid country just east of the Montana Rockies, Lewis and Clark would operate in the High Plains.[47] The journal entries containing landscape descriptions aptly characterized the elements of the High Plains region—the absence of trees except for the cottonwoods that hug the stream courses and the cedars that cluster in pockets on the few steep slopes, the essentially unbroken and featureless nature of the topography, the presence of mineral salt deposits at or near the soil surface, the continuous ground cover of short steppe grasses, the semi-arid climate with its attendant clarity and purity of atmosphere, and the high winds that blow unimpeded and almost incessantly from the west. But of all the constituents of the High Plains, the one that captured the explorers' fancy to the greatest degree was the profusion of animal life, and journal notations like "vast herds of Buffaloe deer Elk and Antilopes were seen feeding in every direction as far as the eye of the observer could reach" became commonplace (I, 151).

The animals that inhabited the region, like the physical nature of the High Plains themselves, appeared exotic to men from a woodland environment, and this is perhaps the simplest explanation for the obvious fascination the Plains fauna held for Lewis and Clark and their men. When the first prairie dog village was seen on September 7, they marveled over its extent and the seemingly organized behavior of its inhabitants. After trying to dig one of the small animals out of its burrow and failing, the captains and virtually all members of the party, acting for all the world like mischievous boys, spent

45. Nasatir, *Before Lewis and Clark*, I, 259–311.

46. The journals and accounts of most explorers in the trans-Mississippi West during the eighteenth century contained references to volcanoes somewhere in the interior. These tales were repeated in both popular and scientific literature in the opening years of the nineteenth century, and even the *Medical Repository*, the most respected scientific periodical of the day, carried articles on the volcanoes in the "immense and Unexplored mountains" of the interior (IV, 1st hexade, 1801, 304).

47. Cutright, *Lewis and Clark*, pp. 77–79.

nearly the entire day carrying water from the river to dump into the passage-ways in an attempt to drive the little creature out.[48] The previous day they had had their initial far-off glimpse of the pronghorn antelope or "goat," and when Clark finally brought in one of these animals more than a week later, he compared it to the "Gazella of Africa." Another hunter came back to camp with a jackrabbit, an "astonishing hare" that weighed a full 6¼ pounds "altho pore" (I, 147). The mule deer, another denizen of the High Plains, made his appearance, as did the coyote and the great gray prairie wolf, skulking about the herds of elk, buffalo, and antelope which grew ever more numerous. If the High Plains were drier and less well timbered than the country below, Lewis and Clark still retained definite components of the garden image of the western interior, an image that bespoke plenty and beauty and wealth.

On September 17 Lewis climbed a hill overlooking the junction of the Missouri and White rivers[49] and offered a description of the view that compares with Clark's earlier notes on the Missouri prairies in its attention to detail and clarity of vision:

The shortness and virdue of grass gave the plain the appearance throughout its whole extent of beautifull bowling-green in fine order. it's aspect is S.E. a greater number of wolves of the small kind, halks and some pole-cats were to be seen. I presume those anamals feed on the squirril. found the country in every direction for about three miles intersected with deep revenes and steep irregular hills of 100 to 200 feet high; at the tops of these hills the country breaks of as usual into a fine leavel plain extending as far as the eye can reach. from this plain I had an extensive view of the river below, and the irregular hills which border the opposite sides of the river and creek. the surrounding country had been birnt about a month before and the young grass had now sprang up to the hight of 4 Inches presenting the live green of the spring. to the West a high range of hills, strech across the country from N. to S. and appeared distant about 20 miles; they are not very extensive as I could plainly observe their rise and termination   no rock appeared on them and the sides were covered with virdue similar to that of the plains   this senery already rich and pleasing and beautifull was still farther hightened by the immence herds of Buffaloe, deer Elk and Antelopes which we saw in every direction feeding on the hills and plains [1, 152–53].

10

The general positive appraisal of the High Plains landscape and the explorers' rapture over the abundance of the faunal environment notwith-standing, there were adverse natural features encountered by the expedition

48. Cutright, *Lewis and Clark*, pp. 79–80.

49. In physiographic terms, the expedition had entered the Missouri plateau province and thus was on the true upper Missouri. But, as has been pointed out, for frontiersmen the upper Missouri began at the mouth of the Platte (DeVoto, *Journals of Lewis and Clark*, p. 26).

as it pushed on up the Missouri past the mouth of the White River. The country was neither uniformly fertile nor well watered, and although the "rich praries" still far outnumbered the tracts of "pore & broken" or "barren and sterile" country, evidences of increasing aridity were seen in the bare soils, concentrated surface mineral salts, and acres of prickly pear cactus that replaced the rich grasslands in some areas. This decrease in grassland cover magnified the effectiveness of rainfall as an agency of landform modification, and "those parts of the hills which was clear of Grass easily dissolved and washed into the river and botoms" (I, 147) [50] with two attendant results. The first was immediately visible in the greater degree of carved and sculptured topography adjacent to the river. The second was also discernible but less in a visual than in an operational sense. For as the fall rains began and the level of the river rose accordingly, navigation became more dangerous. The great complexities of the Missouri's current were augmented by the added supply of water which ran rapidly off the land, and the supply of sediment contributed by the runoff multiplied the number of sandbars in the river's twisting course. The slope wash and bank caving added to the already numerous jams of driftwood and subsurface snags, which, next to the wind, which always seemed to be blowing in the opposite direction from that in which the party wished to go, were the most significant impediments to upriver navigation. [51] Yet these regional traits did not create an image of harshness or hostility for Lewis and Clark, and the strength of the garden image did not diminish. The rains and winds and treacherous river were only inconveniences; the common scene on both sides of the river was of a "butifull inclined Plain, in which there is great numbers of Buffalow, Elk & Goats in view feeding & scipping" (I, 159).

The expedition proceeded past the Grand Detour, one of the mysteries of the Missouri that had been appearing on maps for nearly half a century but had never been measured until Lewis and Clark dispatched a member of the party to "Measure (step off) the Distance." The distance across the "gouge" or meander neck was found to be around 2,000 yards, while the course of the river through the entire meander was 30 miles; in such proportions the Grand Detour was to be represented on maps later made of the river. [52] Above the Grand Detour, the Teton or Bad River flowed into the Missouri, and here the party made a halt for a council with the Teton Sioux and did not resume their upriver journey until near the beginning of October. By this time a new season was coming to the Garden, and although the captains could hardly have been aware of the rapidity and unpredictability of

50. The Coues text says, "We had occasion here to observe the rapid undermining of these hills by the Missouri" (*History*, I, 117).

51. Somewhere along this section of the journey the captains made the decision not to send back one of the pirogues with papers and materials that had been collected—"Finding the water too Shoal Deturmind to take on the Perogue" (Osgood, *Field Notes*, p. 139).

52. Earlier charts had shown the Grand Detour as a nearly closed circle with an opening on the south; Clark's maps rotated the meander by 90° to the right and thus corrected the earlier errors.

winter's onslaught in the High Plains, they must have realized that their original plans to winter near the source of the Missouri would have to be scrapped.

II

The Cheyenne River was reached on October 1, and once again Clark stated that "the heads of this River is not known" (I, 175). This lack of knowledge was remedied when the expedition halted that evening and discovered a small trading post across the Missouri from their camp. The next morning one of the traders, a Frenchman, visited them and they discovered that he was Jean Valle, a member of a prominent Louisiana family, an employee of Regis Loisel, and a cousin of Pierre Antoine Tabeau, another Loisel associate.[53] Valle claimed that he had spent the previous winter 300 leagues (750 miles) up the Cheyenne River, and although this distance was exaggerated, he did offer several fascinating bits of lore on the country between the Missouri and the "black mountains" where the Cheyenne had its source. This river, he said, was formed from two forks that joined their waters 100 leagues or 250 miles west of the Missouri. One of the forks, the Cheyenne proper, came from the south, while the other, now called the Belle Fourche, flowed from the Black Mountains. Except for the distance exaggeration, this was accurate data, as was the notation that "the Countrey from the Missouri to the black mountains is much like the Countrey on the Missouri, less timber. & a great perpotion of Ceder" (I, 176).

Valle also added to the very fragmentary lore that the captains had received from Dorion on the Black Mountains or "Cote Noir" of earlier lore.[54] "The black mountains he [Valle] Says is verry high, and Some parts of it has Snow on it in the Summer   great quantities of Pine grow on the Mountains" (I, 176). From such details Lewis and Clark began to shape a view of the Black Hills—for this is the range that Valle was referring to—that bore little resemblance to reality. They also learned that "a great Noise is heard frequently on those Mountains," and although the cause of this phenomenon was never clear, "rumblings" from the ranges of the western interior had been mentioned in earlier lore, and the captains themselves would later contribute to the description of these curious occurrences.[55] Less puzzling were Valle's offerings about some animals that Lewis and Clark had probably heard about but had not yet seen: "on the Mountains . . . [are] a kind of anamale with

53. For details on Valle, see Osgood, *Field Notes*, p. 46; Nasatir, *Before Lewis and Clark*, I, 111; and Abel, *Tabeau's Narrative*, pp. 32–33.

54. The "Costa Negra" or "Cote Noir" had been part of lore in Louisiana for at least a decade before Lewis and Clark (Nasatir, *Before Lewis and Clark*, II, 738).

55. In some notes made following the expedition, Clark wrote that at the head of one of the Yellowstone's tributaries was "frequently herd a loud noise, like Thunder, which makes the earth Tremble" (VI, 267).

large circular horns, this animale is nearly the Size of an Elk. White bears is also plenty" (I, 176). These were the bighorn or Rocky Mountain sheep and the grizzly bear, and the men of the expedition would encounter plenty of both on their trip from the Missouri's Great Bend to the Rockies during the coming year. Finally, Valle provided support for the geographical notion, current in Louisiana in the early years of the nineteenth century, that the waters of the Missouri were in close proximity to the New Mexico settlements. For the Cheyenne River was the territory of the Indian tribe of the same name, and these natives, it was said, "Steel horses from the Spanish Settlements, to the S.W. this excurtion they make in one month" (I, 176).

After gathering as much information as Valle could give them, Lewis and Clark moved on upriver, and on October 8, near the mouth of the Grand River, met two other French fur traders in residence with the Arikara Indians. One of these, "a man well versed in the language of this nation," was Joseph Gravelines, an agent of Loisel's company; he would serve the captains well during the coming winter as an interpreter and supplier of geographical lore "relitive to the Countrey &c" (I, 184).[56] Accompanying Gravelines was Pierre Antoine Tabeau, Loisel's chief lieutenant; at the time Lewis and Clark met him he was preparing the account of Loisel's most recent expedition on the Missouri.[57] The meeting with Tabeau was momentous, for as an author and compiler of geographical information, the Frenchman was instrumental in the process of data-gathering in which the captains engaged during their winter encampment near the Mandan villages, just a short distance upstream. Lewis and Clark were already well aware of Tabeau's importance, having been given his name by Loisel and, even earlier, by Louis Labeaume, a prominent St. Louis merchant and partner of the famous Chouteaus, who had told Lewis during the winter at Camp Dubois that "Mr. Tebaux who is at present with Louasell up the Missouri can give us much information in relation to that country" (VI, 270).

12

Although Lewis and Clark were not specific as to the type of information relayed to them by Tabeau, the key to what the trader probably told them may be found in his own narratives. Much of what Tabeau knew about the Missouri and the country to the west was already a part of the lore in the possession of the captains. His statements on the sinuous course of the river and the peril of its sand- and snag-choked waters offered nothing new to the weary and experienced explorers. Nor could his descriptions of the prairie and

56. Details on Gravelines may be found in Osgood, *Field Notes*, pp. 156–57; and Abel, *Tabeau's Narrative*, p. 42.

57. Cutright (*Lewis and Clark*, p. 95) believes that Tabeau may have allowed Lewis to read part of the manuscript he was preparing during the period when the expedition was in its winter camp near the Missouri's Great Bend.

plains and their roaming herds contribute anything to the captains' already detailed view of the faunal environment. Tabeau did repeat an old myth about the Missouri country, one which had been mentioned in the Mackay-Evans sources and which Jefferson himself had inserted as near fact in his official account of the Louisiana Territory.[58] "A quantity of pumice stones which were found upon the bank indicates volcanoes," wrote Tabeau, "and the Savages know them in the Black Hills, but they could not tell me anything about the nature of the lavaas nor about time and force of the ruptions."[59] But this interesting if apocryphal information was relatively inconsequential and was overshadowed by what Tabeau knew of the country west of the Missouri.

The view he had of the Platte, the Black Mountains, and the Yellowstone might have been particularly crucial to the image of the farther West that Lewis and Clark would shape during the long winter to come:

The Rio Chato [Platte] rises west of Santa Fe, and flows between two mountains bordering the Neuve Reyno de Mexico in order to discharge its waters into the Misury under the well-known name of Rio Chato. It is impossible to open navigation with the Mexican territory by means of its channel, but there is no necessity for it, the transportation overland is easy and the distance but slight, and the road which is open so far as the savages are concerned. . . . Ascending the Missury one hundred and thirty miles above the mouth of the Rio Chato, one comes to the Rio Qui Core [Niobrara]. Its direction is the same [as the Platte's], and it rises in the first mountains known under the name of Costa Negra [Black Mountains]. That name was doubtless given those mountains because of the color of the earth. Under that earth are hidden precious minerals, as is, declared by the tribes who frequent them. They are so abundant that they are found in nuggets, scattered here and there in various places upon the Rio Chato and upon this river. . . . Continuing to ascend the Misury, one comes to the River of Rocas Paxinas or Roches Jaunes [Yellowstone] which leads also to the western region, and rises in the mountains of Neuvo Mexico, which extend farthest to the west.[60]

Whether this lore was extracted from Tabeau when Lewis and Clark first met him at the Arikara villages or whether he provided it during the winter of 1804–05 at Fort Mandan, most of it would be incorporated into the American explorers' image of the Northwest prior to their voyage from the Mandan villages to the mountains.

The Corps of Discovery had traveled far north of the Missouri's lower reaches, and as they passed into higher latitudes and the season progressed, the weather became cooler and more severe. The northwest winds intensified, bringing sudden, cold squalls of rain that threatened to overturn even the large keelboat. The river grew shallower, with greater and greater numbers of

58. Jefferson, "Official Account," p. 346. Jefferson had accepted the idea of volcanoes in the interior since the 1780s and had included "a conjecture" in his *Notes on the State of Virginia* (p. 29) that the Missouri had "a volcano on some of its waters."
59. Abel, *Tabeau's Narrative*, p. 68.
60. Abel, *Tabeau's Narrative*, pp. 235–38.

shoals and bars to negotiate. Frost began to form on the boats and gear during the hours just before sunrise, and great flocks of waterfowl on their annual southward flight etched their long, wavering arrows across the sky. On October 12 the expedition left the Arikara villages near the mouth of the Grand River; taking Joseph Gravelines with them to serve as an interpreter and supplier of information, they once again pointed their craft up the Missouri.

By now the winds had grown so strong that the men were forced to resort to hauling the boats with towlines that remained slick and stiff with ice until mid-morning. The cottonwoods along the river had already acquired their pagan hues and were now dropping their leaves, and the party experienced several of the short but intense snowstorms that are euphemistically called "flurries" in the northern Plains. As Lewis and Clark neared the villages of the fabled Mandan Indians and as large flocks of "Gees Continued to pass in gangues as also brant to the South" (I, 219), they realized that this would be about as far as they could go before the Plains winter commenced in earnest.

CHAPTER 8

WINTER
IN THE GARDEN

The Corps of Discovery moved upriver from the Arikara villages toward the Missouri's Great Bend, and as the expedition approached the place where it would winter over, the landscape characteristics typical of the northern Plains became more distinct. The herds of buffalo, elk, and antelope increased in size and number (I, 197–99), while the increasing aridity was evidenced by the greater brackishness of the water on the plains, by the higher proportions of exposed mineral salts in the bluffs bordering the river's course, and by the absence of the morning fogs and dews which the party had experienced throughout the course of the voyage (I, 177). During this part of the journey, Clark spent most of his time walking the banks of the river in order to observe the country better and in an attempt to locate those places which had been laid down in the Mackay-Evans charts or noted in the accompanying journals and tables.[1] He was joined on these strolls by Gravelines and a chief of the Arikaras who was traveling with the expedition to the Mandan villages, and from them the captain obtained bits and pieces of geographical lore to add to his own observations (I, 197).

1. "I walked on Shore in the evening with a view to see Some of those remarkable places mentioned by evins, none of which I could find" (I, 198).

The Cannonball River was passed on October 18, and it was learned that it, like many other rivers on the Missouri's western side, had its sources in "the *Court Noi* or Black Mountains" (I, 197–98). The next day the first of the old, abandoned villages of the Mandans was reached, and on the following day one of the hunters shot at but did not kill "a white Bear" or grizzly, a denizen of the Plains that the captains had yet to encounter. The air was filled with snow all throughout the morning of October 21, and in the afternoon the expedition passed another abandoned Mandan village in a plain next to the river. During the next few days more remains of ancient Mandan and Minitari settlements were viewed along the river, and the hunters had increasing difficulty in locating game—"a prof of the Indians hunting in the neighbourhood" (I, 204). Curious Mandans began to line the banks of the Missouri to see the unusually large party of whites, and on October 26, after meeting with Hugh McCracken, an Irish free trader in the employ of the Northwest Company who would supply Lewis and Clark with geographical data in the coming winter,[2] the expedition reached the first occupied Mandan villages and made a camp nearby (I, 206). The settlements of the mythic Mandans had been attained, and for Lewis and Clark, as for other earlier explorers, the simple fact was crucial.

The villages of the Mandan nation were the keystone of the upper Missouri region and had been the focal point of exploration, information interchange, and trading activity in the farther West for three-quarters of a century. In 1738 Pierre Gaultier de Varennes, sieur de La Vérendrye, had led a party of Canadian French southward from their trading establishment on the Assiniboine River, seeking a great westward-flowing stream and a tribe of fair-skinned Indians, reputedly living in a style befitting European society somewhere along its banks. Tales of white Indians on a great western river had been part of the geographical lore of the western interior since the early part of the eighteenth century, and Vérendrye thought he had found what he had been seeking when he arrived at the clustered Mandan villages near the mouth of the Heart River on the upper Missouri. After observation, however, Vérendrye learned that the Mandans were not that different from other tribes, and his successors discovered that the "river of the Mantannes" and the river that Marquette and Jolliet had discovered a half-century earlier were the same.[3] Yet myths continued to surround the mysterious Mandans throughout the remainder of the century. By the time of Lewis and Clark they had become "Welch" Indians, descendants of the twelfth-century Welsh prince Madoc og Gwynned,[4] and sought by no less an exploring duo than John Evans and James Mackay.

2. Osgood, *Field Notes*, p. 166, n. 3; and Tyrrell, *David Thompson's Narrative*, pp. 209, 243.

3. Burpee, *Journals and Letters of Vérendrye*, pp. 290–360.

4. Madoc og Gwynned was supposed to have brought Welsh colonists to North America following internecine warfare in Wales. *Gentleman's Magazine* of London ran a series of articles about the "Welch" Indians between 1789 and 1792 that placed the final descendants of

But the Mandans were not Welsh. Some of them did exhibit tendencies toward fairness of complexion, eyes, and hair—probably as the result of either genetic drift or the admixture of the blood of European traders during the eighteenth century.[5] They were completely Indian, however, and their own traditions had them springing not from the loins of the Cwmry but from an ancestral clan which had originally occupied nine subterranean villages far beneath the Missouri's waters.[6] They were different from other tribes of the Missouri River and Great Plains cultural area in the sophistication of their lifestyle and in their pursuit of a sedentary agricultural economy. But these differences were more the result of their relative geographic isolation, which had limited the number and frequency of white contacts throughout much of the eighteenth century, than the consequence of any other factor. Their relative isolation had kept them free of the cultural decline and physical disintegration which invariably followed contacts between aboriginal and European cultures; however, contacts increased during the last decade of the eighteenth century, and when Lewis and Clark reached the Mandans the decline and disintegration had begun. The nine populous villages that Vérendrye had seen around the mouth of the Heart River had, decimated by smallpox and wars with the Sioux,[7] shrunk to five villages on both sides of the Missouri near the Knife River, some 60 miles upstream from their original location. Of these villages, only two were actually inhabited by Mandans; the other three were occupied by their close relatives, the Minitari or Hidatsa peoples.[8]

2

On October 27 Lewis and Clark and their men moved upriver from their camp near the first Mandan village on the west bank of the Missouri and, passing another Mandan village on the east side of the river, made their second camp where they could hold councils with the chiefs of the Mandans and

Madoc somewhere on the upper Missouri. The myth of Madoc and the Mandans is still present in popular literature: cf. Zella Armstrong, *Who Discovered America?* (Chattanooga, 1950); Frederick J. Pohl, *Atlantic Crossings before Columbus* (New York, 1961); and Geoffrey Ashe, *Land to the West* (London, 1962).

5. Cutright, *Lewis and Clark*, p. 110.
6. Biddle, *History*, I, 139; and Coues, *History*, I, 208.
7. DeVoto, *Course of Empire*, pp. 77–79.
8. The correct ethnological term is Hidatsa, but "Minitari" will be used herein as this was the name used by Lewis and Clark. Like the Mandans, the Minitaris were of Siouan stock. One of the three Minitari villages was actually occupied by the tribe called Ahnaway or Wattasoon, which was, in nearly every way, a cultural group identical to the Hidatsa peoples. The captains' recorded lore on these and other tribes was put together during the winter at Fort Mandan and published in 1806 as *A Statistical View of the Indian Nations Inhabiting the Territory of Louisiana* (American State Papers, *Indian Affairs*, no. 113, 9th Cong., 1st Sess., Washington, 1806). The raw material for *A Statistical View* consisted of notes made by Lewis and Clark on ethnology, published in Thwaites, *Original Journals*, VI, 80–120.

Minitaris. At the second Mandan village they met René Jessaume, a French trader who had been on the upper Missouri ever since Truteau's first expedition.[9] As an employee of the Northwest Company, Jessaume had been one of the first traders after Vérendrye to reach the Mandans; his familiarity with the country and the language of the local tribes would prove invaluable to the captains in the months to come.[10] Indeed, his usefulness became apparent on the day the American explorers made his acquaintance and procured from him information "of the Chiefs of the Different Nations" (I, 209). And Jessaume was probably the "Interpreter" who accompanied Lewis and Clark on the following day as they sought to "examine the Situation & Timber for a fort" (I, 210).

"The river being very low," wrote Captain Lewis, "and the season so far advanced that it frequently shuts up with ice in this climate we determined to spend the Winter in this neighbourhood" (VI, 257). Above the Knife River the captains found the "Timber scerce, or at least Small timber such as would not answer" (I, 210). The scarcity of timber to build a fort and provide enough cooking and heating fuel to sustain a party of around fifty people for a long winter was a problem on the upper Missouri, and on October 30 Clark tried again, taking "8 men in a small perogue" up the river "as fur as the 1st Island about 7 miles to see if a Situation could be got on it for our winter quarters" (I, 213). But a "good wintering ground" could not be found above the Mandan villages, and after being informed by the white traders at the villages that both game and wood grew increasingly scanty up-river, the captains "Deturmined to drop down a fiew miles near wood and game" (I, 213).

The Garden of the West that had seemed so amiable during the voyage from St. Louis to the Mandans was proving less than hospitable to men whose environmental experiences did not include the necessity of worrying about a source of fuel. Finally, after dispatching with Hugh McCracken a letter to Charles Chaboillez, the Northwest Company's agent on the Assiniboine River, requesting "any hints in relation to the geography of the country . . . or any other information which you might conceive of utility to mankind, or which might be serviceable to us in the prosecution of our voyage,"[11] Lewis and Clark broke their camp near the second Mandan village. On November 3 they moved from the Knife River downstream about 6 miles to a site on the Missouri's east bank, where Clark had "found a place well Supld. with wood" (I, 216), and the party began the construction of Fort Mandan.

It is not possible to determine precisely when Lewis and Clark made their decision to winter near the Mandans in this historically and culturally

9. Osgood, *Field Notes*, p. 169, n. 5; and Nasatir, *Before Lewis and Clark*, I, 94–95; II, 496–97.

10. Osgood, *Field Notes*, p. 169.

11. Coues, *History*, I, 188; and Jackson, *Letters*, pp. 213–14.

significant region. The locational importance of the Mandan villages was well known to the captains before they left the East, and prior to their departure they had viewed the Missouri's Great Bend as the logical place to pare their command by sending back the French boatmen employed to accompany the expedition "to the Mandanes."[12] Thus the villages marked a projected operational change in the expedition even before the actual voyage got under way. The necessity to change the original plan of wintering near the Missouri's source must have been realized quite early in the upriver journey from St. Louis, as delays created by unexpected navigational difficulties on the Missouri and lengthy councils with the Indians hindered the rapid progress of the expedition toward the interior. In view of these delays and the established situational significance of the Mandan villages, a determination to winter there was logical, and letters received by Jefferson from correspondents in St. Louis indicate that such a decision was made as early as mid-August, 1804.[13] Jefferson wrote to Lewis's brother, Reuben, relaying the news that "it was expected" that the expedition would "winter with the Mandans" and during the ensuing summer travel to the Pacific and "return to winter again" with the upper Missouri tribe.[14]

The President's comments about the exploratory plans of Lewis and Clark were interesting, for they indicated that as of late summer, 1804, the captains still had no conception of the difficulties they would encounter beyond the Mandans and were still viewing the passage to the Pacific as something that could be accomplished with relative ease. Although it would be refined, this part of their image of the farther West would not change substantially during the winter at the Mandan villages, where, in their rude cottonwood and earthen fortification, Lewis and Clark would become *hivernants* for the first time. Nor would the captains' view of the West as a garden, reinforced by the upriver journey, be recast in a new mold, despite the severity of the northern Plains winter they were shortly to experience. And yet, if at the end of this winter of expectation the basic image components of the Passage and the Garden retained the essential characteristics developed before the expedition, the total view of the Northwest in the spring of 1805 would be much more detailed than it had been in the spring of 1804. For during the long winter of 1804–05 at Fort Mandan, a series of events took place that were unparalleled in the annals of exploration in western North America before Lewis and Clark. In the first of what was to become a lengthy series of scientific explorations sponsored by the government of the United States, Lewis and Clark, a pair of trained and intelligent observers, gathered and analyzed geographical information in what can only be described as a scientific method and documented the resulting geographical images fully in maps and regional descriptions.

12. Jackson, *Letters*, p. 90.
13. Osgood, *Field Notes*, p. xviii; and Jackson, *Letters*, pp. 218–19.
14. Jackson, *Letters*, p. 219.

3

Even before actual construction work on their winter quarters began, the American explorers met individuals who would assist them in planning their journey of the summer to come. On October 28 the camp of the explorers near the lowest Mandan villages was visited by "The Black Cat Grand Chief of the Mandans" (I, 209); he, with other headmen of the Mandan nation, would offer advice, information, and draw rough maps of the country to the west in the dirt floors of the captains' living quarters during the winter. And the next day an event of transcendent importance for the explorers' view of the farther West occurred when the "old Cheaf of the Big Bellies"[15] or Minitaris came to the expedition's camp to represent his son, a war chief of the tribe who was "then out at War against the Snake Indians who inhabit the Rockey Mountains" (I, 210). The Minitaris, virtually alone among the tribes of the Great Bend cultural area, made periodic raids toward the mountains with the purpose of stealing horses from the Shoshoni Indians, once a Plains tribe but driven by the pressures of shifting tribal territorial claims deep into the recesses of the mountains. Because of these raids, the Minitaris were able to supply Lewis and Clark with precise (if often misunderstood) geographical data on the country between the Great Bend and the mountains and even into the Rockies as far as the divide between the Missouri and Columbia drainages.[16]

The raids of the Minitaris on the mountain Indians bore other fruit as well, being directly responsible for the addition of an Indian woman of historical (although not necessarily geographical) significance to the captains' party. On November 4, the day after work on Fort Mandan had begun, the explorers were visted by Toussaint Charbonneau, a halfbreed living with the Minitaris.[17] Charbonneau indicated to Lewis and Clark his desire to hire on "as an interpiter" (I, 217). Charbonneau could contribute little in the way of information himself but he had purchased from the Minitaris and taken to wife a Shoshoni girl captured on one of their raids into the Rockies. This was Sacagawea,[18] about whom some of the most absurd and fictionalized accounts

15. The term "Big Bellies" was often applied by Lewis and Clark to the Minitaris, presumably because the French name for the tribe was "Gros Ventre," after the gesture in the sign language of the Plains tribes which referred to the Minitaris. The Minitaris of Lewis and Clark were a different group, both ethnologically and linguistically, from the Atsina Indians, also called Gros Ventre, who lived north of the southern branches of the Saskatchewan (DeVoto, *Course of Empire*, p. 452).

16. The warfare between the tribes of the Great Bend region and the Snake or Shoshoni peoples had been going on for at least two centuries before Lewis and Clark. In 1742 the sons of Vérendrye were guided by members of a tribe they called the "Gens du Arc" or "Bow Indians" toward the "high mountains which are near the sea to find the Gens du Serpent" (Burpee, *Journals and Letters of Vérendrye*, pp. 415–16).

17. Biographical information on Charbonneau may be found in Osgood, *Field Notes*, p. 174, n. 1; and L. R. Masson, *Les bourgeois de la Compagnie du Nord-Ouest* (2 vols., Quebec, 1889), I, 285.

18. The name is also spelled Sacajawea and Sakakawea. The latter form is the one closest to a phonetic rendering of the Minitari pronunciation of the woman's name, which is supposed to translate into "boat launcher."

coming out of the expedition have been written.[19] Lewis and Clark soon learned that Charbonneau had a Shoshoni squaw,[20] and they had probably also learned from the covetous Minitaris about the great horse herds owned by the Shoshonis. It is highly probable that they quickly perceived the value of adding to the permanent party an individual who could speak the language of the tribe with whom they might have to negotiate to get horses for the portage between the head of the Missouri and the head of the Columbia, and Charbonneau (with his squaw) was added to the roster.[21]

The finishing touches were put on Fort Mandan on November 25, just in time for the first major snowfall of the young winter season (VI, 179). After the huts and stockade that made up the fort were completed, the captains, the interpreters, and the men went into residence and spent the remainder of the winter making their preparations for the final assault on the Passage. While the Arctic blasts buffeted the solid walls of the crude fort and the temperatures outside hovered around the $-40°$ mark for days on end, the captains worked on the process of acquiring and assimilating geographical lore. They were visited periodically by the agents of the fur-trading companies in residence at the Mandan villages and almost daily by the chiefs and warriors of the Mandan and Minitari tribes. In formal councils held in the Mandans' earthen lodges and in talks around the warming fires of Fort Mandan, Lewis and Clark obtained detailed descriptions of the country to the west, as far as the great mountains and the passage to the Pacific which lay beyond.

4

One of the first informants to visit the fort after its completion was François Larocque, the leader of a trading party recently arrived at the Great Bend from the British establishments on the Assiniboine.[22] Along with two other members of his party, Charles Mackenzie and Hugh Heney, Larocque provided some data on what he had heard about the country to the west from

19. The Shoshoni woman was of value in the recognition of landmarks when the expedition neared the home territory of her people in the summer of 1805, and as will be seen, her relationship with the chief of the Shoshonis proved helpful in the captains' negotiations with him. However, the fact that she was the only woman on the journey has added a certain romantic interest, and she has often been accorded a place of importance that far overshadows her actual contributions. An example of an overenthusiastic biography is Grace Raymond Hebard's *Sacajawea* (Glendale, Calif., 1933). More objective are Helen Crawford, "Sakakawea," *North Dakota Historical Quarterly*, I (1927), 5–15; and C. S. Kingston, "Sacajawea as a Guide—the Evaluation of a Legend," *Pacific Northwest Quarterly*, XXXV (1944), 2–18.

20. On November 11 the American camp was visited by "two Squars of the Rock mountains, purchased from the Indians by a frenchman (Chabonneau)" (I, 219). One of these women was Sacagawea.

21. Charbonneau and both his women moved into Fort Mandan with the American party, and it was here that Sacagawea gave birth to the boy Jean Baptiste (Clark called him "Pomp"), who would accompany the expedition to the Pacific and back.

22. For details on Larocque see Osgood, *Field Notes*, pp. 176–77, 178, n. 5; and Masson, *Les Bourgeois*, I, 299–313.

the Indians with whom he traded. The nature of this information remains unknown; neither Lewis nor Clark specified what kind of details the trader may have provided, and in Larocque's own journals there is reference only to "a very grand scheme," the completion of which seemed doubtful to him and the other traders.[23]

In mid-December one of Larocque's associates, Hugh Heney, paid a visit to the American camp, and he, like many others, offered information on the territories west of the Great Bend. Heney had been in the Northwest for a long time, and in 1800, as a partner of Regis Loisel, he had led an expedition from St. Louis up the Missouri.[24] He was one of few people with whom Lewis and Clark came in contact during the winter who had information on both the country between the Mandans and the Rockies and the lands lying between the upper Missouri and the British trading posts to the northeast. He was also one of the few traders in British employ who maintained fully cordial relations with the American explorers throughout the winter.[25] After Heney's first visit to Fort Mandan, Clark noted that both he and Lewis had found the trader to be "a Verry intelligent man" and had obtained from him "Some Scetches . . . which he had obtained from the Indins. to the *West* of this place" (I, 238). Heney's information must have been considered important, for the very next day, December 18, Clark began drawing a "Small Map of Connextion &c." that was probably based on some of the British trader's data.

Armed with the sketches from Heney and whatever other data he and Lewis had been able to collect from traders and Indians, Clark was beginning to work on the cartographic projects that would consume much of his time during the winter and would be foremost among the results of the period of information assimilation and analysis. Many of these charts that were in preparation were probably only working sketches, but they would be put together to form a large map showing the entire Northwest.[26] On December 19 Clark engaged himself "in Connecting the countrey from Information" (I, 239), and two weeks later, on January 5, 1805, was still employed "drawing a Connection of the Countrey from what information I have recved" (I, 244–45). Two days later the captains were visited by "The Big White," chief of one of the Mandan villages, and were presented with a "Scetch of the Countery as far as the high Mountains, & on the South Side of the River

23. Masson, *Les Bourgeois*, I, 299–313.
24. Thwaites identifies Heney as an employee of the Hudson's Bay Company (I, 238). This is very unlikely since there were no known Hudson's Bay personnel operating in this territory, monopolized (through trade agreements) by the Northwest Company. Osgood (*Field Notes*, pp. 181–82, n. 3) and Nasatir (*Before Lewis and Clark*, I, 112–14) provide good information on Heney.
25. This relationship continued in the later stages of the expedition; on the return from the Pacific, either Lewis or Clark penned a note to Heney, requesting his aid in establishing friendly trade contacts with the Sioux (Jackson, *Letters*, pp. 309–13).
26. This map, the first accurate representation of the Northwest (although distorted in some sections), was sent downriver to Jefferson with other materials gathered during the first year of exploration and will be discussed in detail in the following chapter.

Rjone [Roche Jaune or Yellowstone], he Says that the river rejone receeves 6 small rivers on the S.Side, & that the Countrey is verry hilley and the great part Covered with Timber   Great numbers of *beaver* &c." (I, 245). Clark made a copy of this sketch to add to his collection (fig. 30) and commenced work on "a connected plott from the information of Traders, Indians & my own observations & ideas" (I, 246).

In mid-January the captains' view of the country to the west was filled out even more as "one of the 1st War Chiefs" of the Minitaris paid a visit to the American camp and presented Lewis and Clark with "a Chart in his Way of the Missourie" (I, 248).[27] In spite of the difficulties that white men in the West nearly always had in translating Indian geographical information into their own frames of reference, the contributions by the Minitaris were potentially valuable since they covered much of the Missouri's course into the Rockies, territory that the captains knew they would be traversing during the coming summer and that was absolutely crucial to the establishment of their understanding of the proper route across the mountains to Pacific waters. Clark incorporated the data from the Minitari war chief into the "Map of the Countrey on the Missouries & its water &c. &c." (I, 266).

The finishing touches were put on this map in February and March, and the completed chart, characterized as being "laid down principally from Indian information," illustrated fully the view from Fort Mandan. Lewis was also busy during February adding Minitari lore to his own efforts on behalf of the expansion of geographical lore of the Northwest— "a summary view of the rivers and creeks, which discharge themselves into the Missouri," with descriptions of the "country through which they pass" (VI, 24–55). Both Clark's map and Lewis's geographical summary were finished by March, and as the winter gradually gave way to spring, the geographical information the captains had gathered was transformed into the new image of the trans-Missouri West that would guide the expedition in its journey to the Pacific. But geographical data on the contents of the Northwest, on its rivers and mountains, were not the only inputs in the process of image formation. For images consist of patterns of belief not only about the contents of a region but about its nature as well; consequently, equally important to the captains' total image of the Northwest was the region itself—its climate, soils, mineral deposits, and suitability for agriculture.

5

Lewis and Clark had been instructed by Jefferson to observe and make careful records of

27. Just what Clark meant by "in his Way" cannot be known, but it is likely that the Minitari chief, after the fashion of many North American Indians, drew a map in the dirt floor, heaping up piles of dirt to represent mountains and tracing lines with a stick to indicate rivers. See C. H. Borlund, "American Indian Map-Makers," *Geographical Magazine*, XX (1947), 285–92.

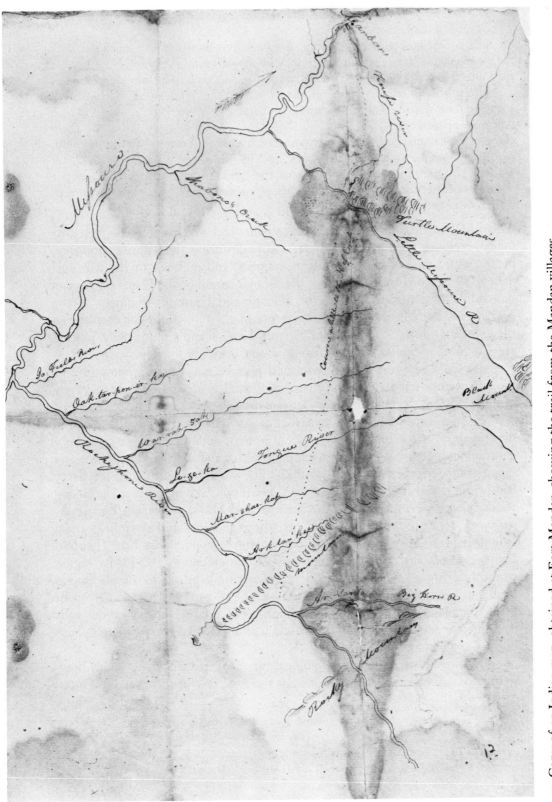

30. Copy of an Indian map, obtained at Fort Mandan, showing the trail from the Mandan villages to the Yellowstone   BEINECKE RARE BOOK AND MANUSCRIPT LIBRARY, YALE UNIVERSITY

the soil & face of the country, it's growth & vegetable productions, especially those not of the U.S.
the animals of the country generally, & especially those not known in the U.S.
the remains or accounts of any which may be deemed rare or extinct;
the mineral productions of every kind; but more particularly metals, limestone, pit coal & saltpetre; salines & mineral waters, noting the temperature of the last, & such circumstances as may indicate their character;
volcanic appearances;
climate, as characterised by the thermometer, by the proportion of rainy, cloudy, & clear days, by lightning, hail, snow, ice, by the access & recess of frost, by the winds prevailing at different seasons, the dates at which particular plants put forth or lose their flower, or leaf, times of appearance of particular birds, reptiles, or insects.[28]

According to these injunctions, the captains had taken extensive meteorological readings since January, 1804, and had, during their upriver journey, made careful note of the soils, plants, animals, and minerals of the Missouri valley.[29] The bare outlines of the captains' perception of the Plains region can be read in these first records of the climatic and biotic environment of the Northwest. But consideration of the nature of the region did not cease when the expedition halted for the winter; from Lewis's and Clark's daily journal entries at their winter camp, entries which grew progressively shorter as confinement at the fort grew tedious and preparations for the resumption of the journey occupied increasing amounts of time, evidences of their real view of the quality of the trans-Missouri lands emerge.

The constituent of the Plains environment which surfaced most often in the explorers' meteorological records and journal notations was the seemingly constant and intense wind which whipped across the short steppe grasses and raised whitecaps even on the Missouri's thick waters. Even before the party had begun construction of their winter quarters, Clark noted that the strong winds prevented councils with the Mandan and Minitari chiefs.[30] This problem was solved by removing the sails from the boats and stretching them around poles to form "a orning" under which the council was held (I, 210). But the winds that later propagandists of settlement in the Plains region would refer to as "gentle zephyrs"[31] could not be kept out by simple canvas awnings, and throughout the construction of the fort and the winter spent there, the blasts that penetrated the chinking of Fort Mandan's crude walls continued to sweep down from the Rockies and from the snow-covered plains of the Canadian interior.

On November 1 the meteorological record stated that "the winds blew so hard to day that we could not descent the river to a proper place to Camp,

28. Jackson, *Letters*, p. 63.
29. The captains' notes on meteorology, mineralogy, zoology, and botany have been consolidated and printed in Thwaites, VI, 165–229, 159–64, 121–36, and 137–58 respectively.
30. Osgood, *Field Notes*, p. 69.
31. An excellent recent study of promotional literature and images of the Great Plains is David Emmons, *Garden in the Grasslands* (Lincoln, Neb., 1971).

until after 5 P.M." (VI, 178). For the rest of the winter, comments that "The wind blew violently hard. . . . Blew verry hard last night. . . . Wind blew excessively hard this night" (I, 234, 242; VI, 180) were frequent and commonplace. The captains had ample opportunity to view the activities of the west, northwest, and the north winds in shaping the face of the Plains as the gales scoured the snow from the ground's surface and, mixing it with sand and dirt, heaped it in small piles scattered over the plains behind the river bluffs and collected along "the bead of the river, which had the appearance of hillocks of Sand on the ice, which is also covered with Sand & Snow" (I, 242).

Just as Lewis and Clark saw the winds as agents of landscape alteration, they witnessed them as modifiers of the climate: "altho' the thermometer stood at 18° above naught the violence of the wind caused a degree of could that was much more unpleasant than that of yesterday when thermometer stood at 10° only above the same point" (I, 257). Whether the wind blew or not, the temperatures dropped much lower than 18° during the winter and often hovered between −20° and −40° for days on end. In the beginning of the winter season, the temperatures dropped low enough to turn the upper levels of the Missouri's water to slush, and by the end of November the river had frozen solid enough to allow the Indians to pass back and forth between their villages on opposite banks. By mid-December the captains' thermometer had dropped to −42°, and the trees along the Missouri bottomland were fairyland white with the hoar frost "which attached itself to their boughes" (VI, 181). On many occasions Clark was forced to enter in his daily log, "little work done to day it being cold &c." (I, 226), and most of the men suffered from frostbite when it became necessary that they leave the sheltering walls of the fort. "The weather is So cold that we do not think it prudent to turn out to hunt in Such cold weather, or at least untill our Consts. are prepared to under go this Climate" (I, 237), Clark observed during a December cold snap. The very air crystallized and frost fell like snow around the American camp; by the end of December experience had conditioned the explorers to view a reading of −9° as a temperature that was "not considered Cold" (I, 242).

The new year of 1805 was ushered in by a veritable heat wave as the temeprature rose to 34° above the zero mark by the afternoon of January 1. The brief warming trend did not last, however; the next day the temperature again fell below zero and remained there for two weeks (VI, 181). But by now the captains and their men had become hardened to the severity of the climate and spent more time outside hunting. In addition to providing the meat supplies necessary to feed a large party and to prepare for the voyage in the spring,[32] hunting offered welcome relief from the boredom that had

32. "A supply of this article is at this moment peculiarly interesting as well for our immediate consumption, as that we may have time before the approach of the warm season to prepare the meat for our voyage in the spring of the year" (I, 254).

begun to set in by mid-January, boredom that appeared in Clark's journal entries: "nothing remarkable happened today" or "the accurancies of this day is as is common" (I, 242, 250). Although many of the antelope, elk, and buffalo killed on these hunts were described as "meager," the party was well enough fed throughout the winter.[33] Nor was hunting a particularly knotty problem. For even though the wind and low temperatures made life outside the shelter of Fort Mandan uncomfortable at best and hazardous at worst, movement in the relatively snow-free plains was easier than in the woodlands of the humid forest environment to which the Americans were accustomed. After one of his hunts, Clark reported that although the snow in the wooded points of land near the river was knee deep, the wind-exposed plains were often bare (I, 259–61). In fact, snow posed no problem to speak of on any occasion; the captains recorded only three major snowfalls during the months from November to March, and on at least one occasion the meteorological observations reported that the snow depths around the fort were accumulated as much "by frosts" as by actual precipitation.

6

During the deepest and coldest part of the winter, in December and January, when neither the captains nor their men strayed very far from the warming fires of Fort Mandan, the explorers' journals described almost ethereal aspects of the region, as if Lewis and Clark fully recognized the exotic and other-worldly nature of the environment in which they were living. When the sun rose in the morning its faint rays served to alter the clarity of the air, and even though the skies might have been fair at sunrise, they became "suddenly turbid, as if the sun had some chimical effect on the atmosphere" (VI, 182). And after the sun was as high in the sky as it would go in the high latitudes of the Mandan villages, it often acquired a traveling companion in the sky, the "sun dog" phenomenon used by plainsmen to predict weather changes—"the Sun Shows and reflects two imigies, the ice floating in the atmospear being So thick that the appearance is like a fog Despurceing" (I, 236). The long nights were also filled with wonder. The moon often had "a verry singaler appearance . . . as She appeared thro: the frosty atmispear," and on several occasions the night guards woke the rest of the party to see the display of the aurora borealis, "which was light, not red, and appeared to Darken and Some time nearly obscured, and open, divided about 20 degrees above horizon—various shapes—considerable space, many times appeared in light Streeks, and at other times a great Space light & containing floating colloms which appeared to approach each other & retreat leaving the lighter space" (I, 218).

33. The abundance of the environment of the upper Missouri plains would become even more meaningful to the explorers during the coming year of starvation and hardship in the mountain crossings and traverse of the barren Columbian Plain.

February and a gradual warming trend brought somewhat of a return to normalcy. The captains and their men began attempting to free their boats from the grip of the Missouri's ice so that they might be drawn up on the bank and prepared for the voyage that lay ahead. The task was incredibly difficult as the river was frozen in layers, separated by at least 8 inches of water, and as soon as the top level of ice was cut through, the water rushed upward and threatened to fill the boats themselves (I, 253). At last the February thaw solved the problem, and aided by the melting river ice and a homemade windlass, the men hauled the pirogues onshore and began to repair the ravages of the winter. By the end of the month, after a series of days described as "exceedingly pleasant," the ice in the river finally began to break up. The Mandans left their villages to consult a medicine stone which lay in the plains three days to the southwest,[34] and the American explorers began preparing in earnest for their embarkation up the river.

When March and even warmer temperatures arrived, what little snow remained soon vanished, the buds of the spicewood appeared, and the first brants and white cranes returned from their wintering grounds to the south. The air turned smoky and thick as the Indians, following the time-honored spring practice of grassland peoples everywhere, burned the prairies "for an early crop of Grass, as an enducement for the Buffalow to feed on" (I, 269, 279).[35] The captains divided the party's "Merchendize" into packages to be placed in the six dugout canoes and two larger pirogues that would carry the Corps of Discovery westward. At the same time, those "Sundery articles to be sent to the President of the U.S." (I, 280)[36] were gathered together and prepared for the return to St. Louis via the keelboat, which Lewis and Clark had already decided would only be a hindrance on the shallower waters of the upper Missouri. "All employed prepareing to Set out," Clark wrote on March 27, and in less than a week, on April 1, the captains "had the Boat Perogues & Canoes all put into the Water" (I, 279). The river craft were loaded by April 5, and two days later, "having on this day at 4 P.M. completed every arrangement necessary for our departure" (I, 283), Lewis and Clark dispatched the keelboat to St. Louis and, with the members of the Corps of

---

34. "They have great confidence in this stone, and say that it informs them of every thing which is to happen, & visit it every Spring & Sometimes in the Summer" (I, 264). Coues (*History*, I, 236–37) provides more information about the "great oracle" of the Mandans.

35. Lewis and Clark, along with many early observers in the Great Plains, attributed the treeless nature of the region to the many fires "which the natives kindle in these plains at all seasons of the year" (VII, 311). Although many modern scholars have supported climatic theories of the origin of the grasslands, a substantial body of current theory and research substantiates the original notions of fire origins. See Carl O. Sauer, "A Geographic Sketch of Early Man in North America," *Geographical Review*, XXXIV (1944), 528–73; and Omer C. Stewart, "Fire as the First Great Force Employed by Man," *Man's Role in Changing the Face of the Earth*, ed. William Thomas (Chicago, 1956), pp. 115–33.

36. Jackson (*Letters*, pp. 234–36) prints complete invoice lists of the materials sent back from Fort Mandan. Jackson's notes ((pp. 236–42) provide an excellent source of information on the disposition of the Fort Mandan materials.

Discovery who would accompany them to the Pacific and back, departed from Fort Mandan.[37] The winter in the Garden was finally over.

7

It might be supposed that the simple fact of Lewis's and Clark's tenure at Fort Mandan for five months was a major contributing factor in their image of the Northwest immediately prior to their departure from the area of the Great Bend. Their optimistic and enthusiastic geographical ideas on the land quality of the West, shaped during the upriver journey from the mouth of the Missouri, ought to have been tempered by the experience of wintering in the northern Plains. The howling winds and Arctic temperatures should have conditioned the responses of even these wilderness-hardened veterans to the western environment. As early as November 5 Clark had noted in his journals that, because of the chill and dampness, he was down with the "Rhumitism," which, aggravated by exposure and climatic extremes, was to plague both him and Lewis throughout the winter season (I, 217). And from November to April the daily weather observations made by the explorers bespoke the severity of winter in central North Dakota. But in spite of all this, the impressions gained during the years prior to the expedition and reinforced during the first leg of the journey to the Pacific were not much different after the winter at Fort Mandan than they had been before.

On their upriver journey Lewis and Clark had passed from a known woodland environment into the unknown grasslands. As they did so, they began the creation of a set of ideas about the nature of the trans-Missouri West which deviated little from their previous conception of the value of the region. The winter at Fort Mandan had done little to modify these ideas, and in the spring of 1805 Lewis wrote to his mother that "This immence river so far as we have yet ascended waters one of the fairest portions of the globe, nor do I believe that there is in the universe a similar extent of country, equally fertile, well-watered and intersected by such a number of navigable streams" (VII, 309–12).[38] Jefferson's Garden was still a definite part of the geographical lore of the trans-Missouri West.

As the Corps of Discovery had wound their way up the Missouri, the captains had noticed the transition from woodland to prairie to Great Plains or steppe environment and had recognized the mouth of the Platte River as the approximate boundary line marking the eastward edge of the great grassy expanse of the Plains proper. "The country as high up this river [the Missouri] as the Mouth of the river Platte, a distance of 630 miles is generally

---

37. The party which left Fort Mandan for the Pacific numbered thirty-two. Jackson (*Letters*, pp. 364–73) prints a roster and biographical details on the members.
38. Jackson, *Letters*, pp. 222–25.

well timbered" (VII, 310), wrote Lewis. Beyond the Platte, however, "the open or prairie country" commenced. Before they had left Camp Dubois, Lewis and Clark had learned about the grasslands from the journals of Evans and Mackay and Truteau, from contemporary newspaper accounts which had spoken of "barren tracts" of treeless land, and probably from their contacts with representatives of the St. Louis fur trade.[39]

Although their image of the Northwest in the spring of 1804 retained definite elements of the garden concept, the absorption of this data had led the captains to the conclusion that a good part of the western grassland region was "barren steril, and sandy" (VII, 310). But with respect to this "Previous information," Lewis wrote in the spring of 1805 that the nature of the open country had "agreeably disappointed" him. The West was neither barren, nor sandy, nor sterile:

On the contrary I found it fertile in the extreem, the soil being from one to 20 feet in debth, consisting of a fine black loam, intermixed with a sufficient quantity of sand only to induce a luxuriant growth of grass and other vegitable production, particularly such as are not liable to be much injured or wholy destroyed by the ravages of the fire.[40] It is also generally level yet well watered; in short there can exist no other objection to it except that of the want of timber, which is truly a very serious one. This want of timber is by no means attributeable to a deficiency in the soil to produce it, but owes it's orrigin to the ravages of the fire, which the natives kindle in these plains at all seasons of the year. The country on both sides of the river, except some of it's bottom lands, for an immence distance is one continued open plain, in which no timber is to be seen except a few detached and scattered copse, and clumps of trees, which from their moist situations, or the steep declivities of hills are sheltered from the effects of fire. The general aspect of the country is level so far as the perception of the spectator will enable him to determine, but from the rapidity of the Missoury, it must be considerably elevated as it passes to the N.West; it is broken only on the borders of the watercourses [VII, 310–11].

This evaluation of the treeless plains is little different from that of Jefferson two years earlier,[41] and it is probable that Lewis's and Clark's view of the Great Plains in the spring of 1805 was as much a feature of their preconceptions of the West based on the Jeffersonian ideal as it was on the nature of the region itself.

Not only were the great grasslands extremely fertile in the view from Fort Mandan—they were also teeming with wild game, and the herds seemed to grow larger and more varied the farther the explorers ventured westward. "Game is very abundant, and seems to increase as we progress," wrote Lewis; "our prospect for starving is therefore consequently small":

39. The desert concept of the trans-Missouri region was a basic part of the geographical lore of long-time residents of Louisiana (Lewis, "Three Centuries of Desert Concepts," pp. 460–68).

40. Lewis's comments here and immediately below reflect his belief in the fire origin of the western grasslands.

41. Jefferson, "Official Account," pp. 346–47.

On the lower part of the Missouri, from it's junction with the Mississippie, to the enterance of the Osage river, we met with some deer, bear, and turkies; from thence to the mouth of the Great river Platte, an immenc quantity of deer, some bear, Elk, turkies, geese, swan, and ducks; from thence to the river Sioux, some deer, a great number of Elk, the bear disappeared almost entirely some turkies, geese swan and ducks; from thence to the mouth of White River, vast herds of Buffaloe, Elk and some deer and a greater quantity of turkies than we had before seen. . . . From thence to Fort Mandan, the Buffaloe, Elk and deer increase in quantity, with addition of the Cabri as they are generally called by the French engages [VII, 311].

And in retrospect, the abundance of the Plains environment would become greater when, during the next year, the members of the Corps of Discovery looked back in hunger upon the rich buffalo plains from the gameless heights of the Rockies and the sterile plains of the Columbia basin.

8

It was known through experience that the richness of the land was a feature of the western environment as far into the interior as the Mandan villages. And in a geographical description of the regions west of the Mandans that Lewis wrote and sent downriver by the keelboat, the implications were that between the Mandans and the mountains much of the same would be found. For beyond the Great Bend of the Missouri, the country resembled in all respects the region upriver from the Niobrara—"open and level country generaly without timber some timber on the borders of the streams" (VI, 51). On the upper parts of the rivers which flowed into the Missouri both above and below the villages, the country was viewed as more broken and uneven, although still without significant stands of timber. But with the exception of the country of the Yellowstone River, the captains made few conjectures about the possible soil fertility west of their wintering grounds.

By this time the Yellowstone had begun to replace the Missouri as the great geographical unknown, and Lewis and Clark were intrigued by the rumors they heard about the mighty stream and its fecund valley. In its upper reaches, the natives had told them, the valley of the "Roche Jaune" was "wide in many places and the lands fertile" (VI, 52); farther down, the river descended into "a country more level, tho' still broken, fertile and well timbered" (VI, 52). It then entered an "open level and fertile country through which it continues it's route to the Missouri; even in this open country it possesses considerable bodies of well timbered land." Around the Yellowstone, then, there developed conceptions in which the best features of the Plains environment were combined with the presence of abundant timber, a natural feature which the Plains did not possess and which, in the captains' eyes, was the region's greatest deficit. The great river of the Yellowstone, claimed Lewis in his geographical account of the farther West, watered "one of the fairest portions of Louisiana, a country not yet hunted, and abounding in animals of the fur kind." Such descriptions are strangely reminiscent of the accounts of the Missouri in earlier periods and reflect the optimism with which men have viewed the unknown or little-understood West.

Past the Yellowstone and toward the head of the Missouri in the Rocky Mountains, the country continued to be "prairie" but with more and more timberland. At the Falls of the Missouri, according to the captains' informants, a change in the country took place, the landscape becoming much more "broken, mountanous, and woody" (VI, 54). The mountains themselves were thickly timbered (an illusion which was later destroyed), and beyond the mountains, to the west, were "open & level plains" like those surrounding the Mandan villages. These plains, the Indians had reported, were characterized by a number "of barren sandy nobs irregularly scatted over the face of the country" (VI, 55). This probable reference to the channeled scablands of the Columbian Plain is intriguing, for it is unlikely that the Minitaris could have penetrated that far on their horse-stealing raids into the Shoshoni country of the Rockies. The conclusions that might be drawn from the presentation of such information to Lewis and Clark are, first, that the Minitaris themselves must have been relying on information from tribes farther west in the construction of their own mental maps of the region,[42] and second, that their knowledge of the country toward the setting sun was remarkably accurate. If there were distortions in the American explorers' beliefs about the nature of the farther West, they were created more by language difficulties or inabilities to translate Indian concepts of landscape description into accepted American ones than by errors inherent in the Indian information as it had been presented.[43]

9

Although slight, the greatest variation from the captains' uniform conception of mildness, fertility, and abundance related to the Plains climate and was derived from the experiences of the upriver voyage and the winter at Fort Mandan. First, last, and always in their assessments of the weather patterns of the region was the wind; the journals from May to October of 1804 contain references to wind more than to any other weather phenomenon, and

42. Much of the Minitari information might have come from slaves taken on their western raids, and the capture of women and children might have aided the Great Bend Indians in gaining data on the territories to the west.

43. The subsistence agriculture as practiced by the tribes of the Great Bend area provided neither the conceptual tools nor the language which would have allowed the natives to describe to the American explorers just what was meant by "fertile" land. Nor could Lewis and Clark possibly have translated their concepts of land quality into a frame of reference readily understood by the Indians.

throughout the Fort Mandan journals the same holds true. The effects of the western and northwestern gales were magnified by the flatness and openness of the plains themselves, and on April 4, 1805, Lewis noted this fact: "The wind blew very hard as it dose frequently in this quarter; there is scarcely any timber to brake the wind from the river, & the country on both sides being level plains, wholy destitute of timber, the wind blows with astonishing violence. in this open country winds form a great obstruction to the navigation of this river particularly with small vessels, which can neither ascend or descend should the wind be the least violent" (VI, 187).

Like the wind, the other elements of the Plains weather seemed to the captains to come from the western quarter. Great cloud banks could be seen building up on the horizon during the afternoon; driven by the winds, these were responsible for the quick and violent squalls that attacked and retreated almost without warning and had continually threatened to capsize the explorers' craft during the upriver journey. And yet, in spite of the winds and their violence and the sub-zero winter temperatures experienced at Fort Mandan, the western weather was not considered harsh. Evidences of aridity were visible in the landscape, but neither Lewis nor Clark seemed to feel that the lack of precipitation might in any way hinder the advance of an American agricultural population into the area. In fact, in many of the meteorological records of the expedition, the dryness of the West was reported as pleasant and, in the vernacular of the time, "salubrious": "The air is remarkably dry and pure in this open country, very little rain or snow, either winter or summer, the atmosphere is more transparent than I ever observed it in any country through which I have passed" (VI, 186). In the exotic West the air itself had special properties, and the experience of the first year of exploration had confirmed what more than a century of conditioning had already established.

Indeed, there was only one set of regional characteristics observed by Lewis and Clark which did not match pre-exploratory notions on the nature of the trans-Missouri area. In their assessments of the mineral environment, the captains removed any lingering suspicions that might have remained in their image of the West that toward the setting sun might be found great wealth in precious gems, gold, or silver. Salt springs and salt deposits were found aplenty, but nowhere to be seen were the salt mountains of incredible size which even Jefferson had suspected might lie somewhere west of the Mississippi. Lewis and Clark, like later observers, were to make frequent note of the "purgative" effects of the mineral-saturated western waters, but the "salts" and other minerals of the West consisted only of the colored earths which make up the bluffs of the Missouri and its tributaries or which lie exposed in surface pan formations. Their presence was related to the drier climate, not to any special mineralogical properties of the region itself, and in the collection of minerals sent back to Jefferson from Fort Mandan were only samples of clay and shale. The West would not become the Golden West, either actually or conceptually, for nearly half a century after Lewis and Clark.

10

In summary, the element of land quality as it appeared in the image of the Northwest held by Lewis and Clark as they prepared to leave Fort Mandan was a maintenance and a reinforcement of the earlier views of the French chroniclers and of Jefferson. To them the West had clearly been a garden, and Lewis's comment that the Missouri watered "one of the fairest portions of the globe" must be considered an affirmation of that belief, a belief now backed by observation and not founded exclusively in hope and desire. Those observers who had presented contrary or derogatory details on the Great Plains were severely in error according to the captains' interpretations of what they themselves had seen; nowhere in the world, in their opinion, was there a more fertile or salubrious country than the region through which they had passed and in which they had spent their first winter in the field. Such views would not, in the years to come, be truly representative of the American explorer's view of the West,[44] and that Lewis and Clark saw a garden when later observers saw a desert may, in large measure, be attributed to the strength of their preconceived notions about what they would find.

Preconceived geographical ideas have always had an impact on exploration—if only for the simple fact that explorers do not go out in quest of nothing but have certain objectives gleaned from the geographical lore of their own and earlier times.[45] No territory is ever really *terra incognita*, since minds abhor blank spaces on maps just as nature abhors a vacuum. That the knowledge from which men create regional images of unexplored territories is invented or imagined knowledge instead of real knowledge is unimportant—for invented geography is perceived as real until proven unreal by exploration and observation. The fact that Lewis and Clark did not really find things in the western environment which caused them to change their preconceived ideas about the garden-like quality of the trans-Missouri region does not mean that such things did not, for them, exist. What it signifies, rather, is the strength and persistence of a preconception which allowed them to diminish, in their assessments of the region, those features of the western environment which did not match the pre-exploratory image of the Garden of the West.

44. Many of the elements of the myth of the Great American Desert emerged from the reports of explorers following Lewis and Clark. See Bowden, "The Perception of the Western Interior," pp. 16–21.

45. John Kirtland Wright, "Where History and Geography Meet: Recent American Studies in the History of Exploration," *Proceedings of the 8th American Scientific Congress,* IX (1943), 17–23.

CHAPTER 9

THE VIEW
FROM FORT MANDAN

The views held by Lewis and Clark with regard to the quality of the lands of the trans-Missouri West were a basic part of their image of the Northwest in the spring of 1805. But even though Jefferson had requested them to make notes on land quality and to shape ideas of agricultural potential, the central objective of the expedition remained the discovery of a water communication between the waters of the Atlantic and the waters of the Pacific. The most vital sections of their image were not those that dealt with the Garden but those that dealt with the Passage, with the structure and shape of western topography through which that Passage must be found. And just as the elements of their view from Fort Mandan which evoked images of the Garden were partly determined by their preconceived notions, so were their conceptualizations of the physiography of the Northwest conditioned by the geographical lore of earlier times.

In the first analysis of Lewis's and Clark's view from Fort Mandan it would seem that they had wiped their slates clean of any previous information on the geography of the trans-Missouri region to begin anew, creating an image of the Northwest based almost entirely on the lore obtained during the upriver journey and the winter at the Great Bend. Closer examination, however, reveals that although the extent of their knowledge of the major topographical features of the Northwest in the spring of 1805 was phenomenal in comparison with that of the previous spring, the view from Fort Mandan was characterized by many of the same distortions, inaccuracies, and misconceptions typical of earlier images. This does not diminish the captains' intelligence and capabilities, however, for when viewed in the light of the time they had spent in the field, the character of their pre-exploratory information, the general conditions they were forced to cope with, and the nature of the contacts they made, the sophistication of their image in the spring of 1805 was truly remarkable. But sophisticated or not, the view from Fort Mandan served primarily to reaffirm the conjectural geography with which the expedition had left Camp Dubois.

If the detail of the view from Fort Mandan was spectacular, the manner in which Lewis and Clark presented their image of the Northwest was equally so; out of the winter of 1804–05 came documents unlike any others in the history of geographical discovery. These reports on the progress of the expedition and the geographical lore its leaders had compiled provide full testimony to the explorers' conceptions of the Northwest prior to the completion of their traverse to the Pacific[1] and offer, therefore, an excellent source of materials with which to examine the relationship between geographical knowledge and the operations of an expedition during the course of its exploration.

The written documentary report of greatest geographical significance was that compiled by Lewis at the Mandan villages and forwarded to Jefferson in April, 1805. Its title indicated not only the content of the report itself but also the derivation of the geographical descriptions it contained:

A summary view of the rivers and creeks, which discharge themselves into the Missouri; containing a discription of their characters and peculiarities, their sources and connection with other rivers and Creeks, the quality of the lands, and the apparent face of the country through which they pass, and the width, and distance of their entrances from each other; to which is also added a short discription of some of the most remarkable points and places on the Missouri; taken from the information of Traders, Indians & others; together with our own observations, from the junction of that river with the Mississippi, to Fort Mandan [VI, 29].

The "summary view" also contained a brief description of the passage across the dividing range between Atlantic and Pacific waters and a short commentary on the lands between the divide and the western ocean. Clark's contributions supplemented Lewis's geographical essay perfectly and consisted of three items: Clark's own "summary statement of rivers, creeks, and most remarkable places," consisting of a table of distances for key points along the

1. Responsible for the voluminous materials compiled during the first year of exploration and for the captains' attempts to bring some order to the lore that they had collected was Jefferson's injunction "to communicate to us, at seasonable intervals" (Jackson, *Letters*, p. 65).

TABLE 3
CLARK'S SUMMARY STATEMENT OF RIVERS, CREEKS,
AND MOST REMARKABLE PLACES

Names of remarkable places.	The width of rivers and creeks in yᵈˢ	Side on which they are Situated	Distance from one place to another	Distances up the Missouri from the Missis-sippi	Latitude North of important places
	yards		Ms	Ms	
River Dubois { Latitude 38° 55′ 19.6″					
{ Longᵗᵈ 89° 57′ 45″					
To the Village of Sᵗ Charles		N.E.	21	21	38°54′39″
" Bon-homme Creek	—	S.W.	12	33	
" the Osage Womans River	30	N.E.	20	41	
" a Cave Called the Tavern	—	S.W.	5	47	
" " Chauretts Village & Creek	20	N.E.	27	68	
" " Shepherds Creek		S.W.	15	83	
" " Gasconnade River	157	S.W.	17	100	38°44′35.3″
" " Muddy River	50	N.E.	15	115	
" Grand Osage River	397	S.W.	18	133	38°31′16.9″
" the Murrow Creek	20	S.W.	5	138	
To the Cedar Island & Creek	20	N.E.	7	145	
" " Lead Mine Hill		S.W.	9	154	
" " Manitou Creek	20	S.W.	8	162	
" " Split rock Creek	20	N.E.	8	170	
" " Saline or Salt River	30	S.W.	3	173	
" " Manitou River	30	N.E.	9	182	
" " Good Womans River	35	N.E.	9	191	
" " Mine River	70	S.W.	9	200	
" " Arrow Prarie		S.W.	6	206	
" Two Charliton Rivers { 30 { 70		N.E.	14	220	
" " antient village of the Missouri Nation near which place Fort Orleans stood		N.E.	16	236	
" Grand River	90	N.E.	4	240	38°47′34″
" " Snake Creek	18	N.E.	6	246	
" " antient village of the little Osarge		S.W.	10	256	
" " Tiger's Island and Creek	25	N.E.	20	276	
" " Eueberts Island Creek		S.W.	12	388	
" " Fire prarie Creek		S.W.	12	300	
" " Fort point		S.W.	6	306	
" " Hay Cabin Creek	20	S.W.	6	312	
" " Coal Bank		S.W.	9	321	
" " Blue water River	30	S.W.	10	331	
" Kanzas River	230	S.W.	9	340	39° 5′25.7″
" the Little River Platt	60	N.E.	9	349	
" [point] 1½ Mˢ above Dimond Island		S.W.	—	—	39° 9′38.6″
" the Waucarba, Warconda Island opposite the 1ˢᵗ Old Kanzas Village	—	S.W.	26	377	
" 3 Mˢ below the 2ᵈ old village of the Kances	—	S.W.	—	—	39°25′47.5″
" " Independance Creek a mile below the 2ⁿᵈ old Kanzas Village		S.W.	28	405	

Names of remarkable places.	The width of rivers and creeks in y^{ds}	Side on which they are Situated	Distance from one place to another	Distances up the Missouri from the Mississippi	Latitude North of important places
	yards		Ms	Ms	
" " St Michaels prarie		N.E.	25	430	
" " Nadawa River	70	N.E.	20	450	39°39′22.4″
" Wolf or *Loup* River	60	S.W.	14	464	
" Big *Ne-me-har* River	80	S.W.	16	480	39°55′56″
" the *Tar-ki-o* Creek	23	N.E.	3	483	
opposit the center of Good Island	—	S.W.	—	—	40°20′12″
" " *Neesh-nah-ba-to-no* River	50	N.E.	25	508	
" " Little Ne-ma-har River	48	S.W.	8	516	40° 8′31.8″
To the *Bald pated prarie* the Neesh-nahbatona within 150 yards of the Missouri	yards —	N.E.	Ms 23	Ms 539	40°27′ 6.4″
Pt. opposit to a Island being the extremity of the 4th course of July 19th on L. S.	—	S.W.	—	—	40°29′38″
" " Weeping Water Creek	25	S.W.	29	568	
" " *River Platt* (or Shoal river	600	S.W.	32	600	40°54′35″
" " Butterfly or papelion Creek	18	S.W.	3		
" " Musquetor Creek	22	N.E.	7	610	
" " Camp p^t of observ^n 10 m^s N. 15° W of Platt R *White Catfish Camp*	—	S.W.	—	—	41° 3′19.4″
" " antiant Village of the Ottoes		S.W.	11		
" " antient Ayauways Village below a Bluff on the N.E. Side		N.E.	6		
" " Bowyers river	25	N.E.	11		
" Councill Bluffs (establishm^t)		S.W.	12	650	41°17′ 0″
opposit pond Inlet August 4th	—	S.W.	—	—	41°25′ 3″
on the Side of a Sand Island August 5th	—	—	—	—	41°30′ 6″
" Soldiers River	40	N.E.	39	689	
" *Ea-neah, Wau-de-pon* or Stone River Little Sieux R.	80	N.E.	44	733	41°42′34.3″
" the hill where the Late King of the Mahars was buried on a high hill		S.W.			42° 1′ 3.8″
" the *Wau-can-de* or bad Sperit Creek		S.W.	55	788	
around a bend of the river to the N. E. the Gorge of which is only 974 Yds			21	809	
To an Island 3 miles N E of the Mahar vil^g Camp *Fish* aug^t 14th			27	836	42°13′41″
" Floyds Bluff and River	35	N.E.	14	850	
" the Big Sieoux River	110	N.E.	3	853	42°23′49″
" " commencement of the Copperas cobalt, pirites and alum bluffs		S.W.	27	880	
To the Hot or burning Bluffs		S.W.	30	910	
" " White Stone River	30	N.E.	8	918	

Names of remarkable places.	The width of rivers and creeks in y^{ds}	Side on which they are Situated	Distance from one place to another	Distances up the Missouri from the Mississippi	Latitude North of important places
	yards		Ms	Ms	
" " Petite Arc an old Mahar Village. at the mouth of little bow Creek	15	S.W.	20	938	
" River Jacque or James River	90	N.E.	12	950	42°53′13″
" the Calumet Bluffs (of mineral)		S.W.	10	960	
" Antient fortification Good mans Is^d		S.W.	16	876	
" Plumb Creek	12	N.E.	10	986	
" White paint Creek	28	S.W.	8	994	
" Quicurre or rapid river	152	S.W.	6	1000	
To the Poncar River & Village	30	S.W.	10	1010	
" " Dome and village of Burrowing or barking Squirels		S.W.	20	1030	
" " Island of Cedar			45	1075	
" White River (handsom Spot)	300	S.W.	55	1130	
" the three Rivers of the Seioux pass opposit an Island	35&c.	N.E.	22	1152	
" an Island in the comencm^t of the big bend		N.E.	20	1172	
" upper part of the big bend, or "Grand de Tourte" the gorge of which is 1¼ M^s		S.W.	30	1202	
" Tylors River	35	S.W.	6	1208	
" Louisells [Loisel's] Fort on Cedar Island			18	1226	44°11′33″
" Teton River	70	S.W.	37	1263	
" the upper of five old Ricara Villages reduced by the Sieoux & abandoned		S.W.	42	1305	
" Chyenne River (place for an Estm^t)	400	S.W.	5	1310	44°19′36″
" an old ricara village on La-hoo-catts Island			47	1357	
" Otter Creek	22	S.W.	35	—	
" Sar-war-kar-na River	90	S.W.	40	1397	45°35′ 5″
" We-tar-hoo River	120	S.W.	25	1422	
" Maropa River	25	S.W.	2	—	
To 1st Ricaras Village on an Island		S.W.	4		
" 2^d Ricaras 3 Villages		S.W.	4	1430	
" the Stone Idol Creek	18	N.E.	18		
" " War-re-con-ne River	35	N.E.	40	1488	
" Cannon Ball River	140	S.W.	12	1500	46°29′ 0″
" Shy-wish or Fish Crek	28	N.E.	5		
" Chesschetar River near 6 old Mandan Vg^s	38	S.W.	40	1540	
" Hunting Creek	25	S.W.	14		
" the Old Ricara & Mandan Villages		S.W.	40	1580	
" Fort Mandan (wintering post of 1804)		N.E.	20	1600	47°21′47″

Source: Thwaites, *Original Journals*, VI, 56–59.

TABLE 4
"The Missouri and it's Subsidiary Streams higher up; are taken altogether from information collected dureing the Winter 1804, 5 of Indians &c."

	near yds		about miles	miles
To the Mouth of the little Missourior *E-máh-tark,* *Ah-Zhah*	100	S.W.	100	1730
To Ok-hah, Âh-zhah, or the White Earth River	100	N.W.	117	1847
To the Mouth of *Mee, Ah-zhah* or *Yellow stone* River	400	S.W.	3	1850
To the mouth of *Ah-mâh-tâh, ru-shush-sher,* or the River which Scolds at all others	abt. 100	North	150	2000
To the Mouth of the *Mah-tush; ah-zhah* or the Muscle Shell River	140	South	120	2120
" the Great Falls	—	—	120	2240
" *Mah-pat-puh, Ah-zhah* or Medison River	150	N.W.	15	2255
To the 1st Chain of Rockey mountains about	—	—	60	2315
To the 2nd Chain of Rockey mountains about	—	—	75	2390
To the *three* forks of the Missouri above the 3rd Chain of mountains	—	—	75	2465
To the foot of the next mountain nearly West	—	N.W.	50	2515
To a large River on the West of the mountain	—	—	15	2530

Source: Thwaites, *Original Journals*, VI, 60.

Missouri between Wood River and the Mandan villages (Table 3); a table of distance estimates for "The Missouri and it's subsidiary Streams higher up . . . taken altogether from information collected dureing the Winter 1804, 5 of Indians &c." (Table 4); and, finally, the magnificent large map of the western part of North America, "compiled from the Authorities of the best informed travellers" and with the country west of the Great Bend being "laid down principally from Indian information" (fig. 31).[2] In these four documents may be seen the detail and precision of the captains' new image of the river and mountain systems of the trans-Missouri West. The image was not new in the sense that older notions about the size, navigability, and sources of western rivers or pre-exploratory concepts of the basic structure of the mountains of the interior were drastically modified. It was new in that it was based more on conclusions made from observation, data collection, and analysis than it was on speculation and rumor. The inaccuracies and distortions present in the view from Fort Mandan were there not because of the reliance on concepts drawn from pure conjecture, but because of the deformations that appear in any geographical image, however rationally derived, that is based on less than full information and therefore subject to interpretation of and interpolation from the lore that is available.

2. This is the map that Clark had referred to in his Fort Mandan journals as "a Connection of the Countrey from what information I have recved" (I, 244–45). The manuscript map was sent to the War Department and was copied there by Nicholas King, the cartographer who had played an important role in the preparation of materials for the expedition. For an interesting discussion of the history of Clark's map, see Herman R. Friis, "Cartographic and Geographic Activities of the Lewis and Clark Expedition," *Journal of the Washington Academy of Sciences*, XLIV (1954), 348–49.

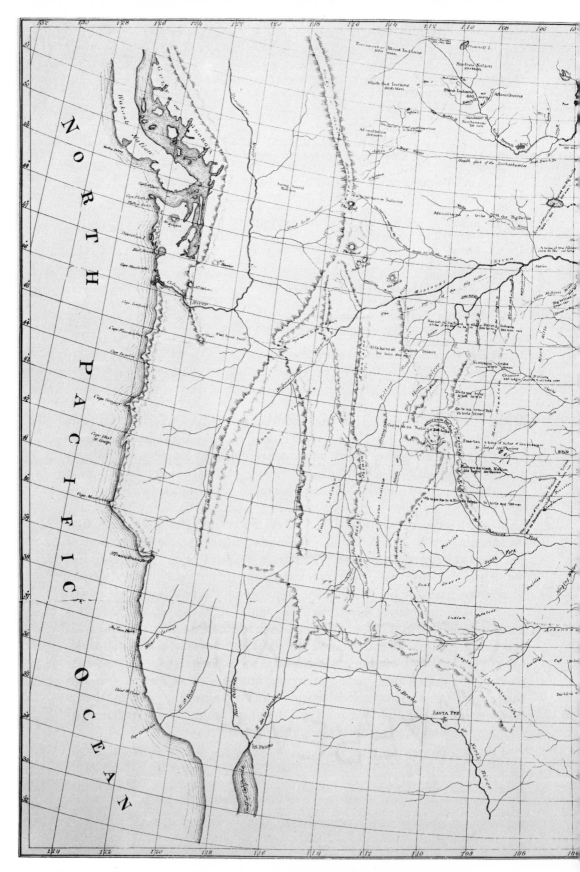

31. William Clark's 1805 map of the western part of North America. Drawn by
Nicholas King from Clark's manuscript maps and sketches   LIBRARY OF CONGRESS

The captains' view of western topography in the spring of 1805 included virtually every river and creek that fell into the Missouri between its junction with the Mississippi and the Mandan villages, along with a good many of those streams beyond the Mandans—even some conjectural streams of the Pacific slope. Combining the best previous knowledge on the area from both written and oral sources with their own firsthand observation, the American explorers came up with a highly realistic picture of the lower reaches of the rivers that flowed into the Missouri between its mouth and the Great Bend. The accuracy of their view declined toward the interior, however, for during the course of their outward journey to the Mandans, Lewis and Clark had operated for the most part only on what they could see from the river. Beyond the features visible from the deck of a small craft or from the Missouri's banks, details had been filled in from information derived from the natives and from the knowledge offered by representatives of the fur trade. And even farther beyond, past the Mandans and into the mists that still hid the upper Missouri, the Rockies, and the Great River of the West, the Indian lore and that of the fur traders had been even more critical in the captains' attempts to catalog and describe the rivers of the Northwest.

The leading components of the explorers' overall image of the lower Missouri tributaries can be identified in Lewis's summary statements and in Clark's cartographic representation of the Osage and Kansas rivers, the two most important feeder streams that entered the Missouri below the mouth of the Platte. The first of these, the Osage, was a stream well known from the experience of the St. Louis fur trade. According to Lewis, it had its source "in an open country of Plains and Praries, with some of the Northern branches of the Arkansas; some of it's tributary streams on it's North side, also have their sources in a similar country, with the southern branches of the Kanzas river. The rivers Arkansas and Kanzas circumscribe the length of this river, and interlock their branches to the West of it" (VI, 31). Like other streams which had their sources in an open plains area, Lewis wrote, the Osage experienced "an unusual depression of it's waters" during the summer months.[3] This basic characteristic of most Plains streams was not necessarily viewed by the captains as a hindrance for navigation, as the Osage was, in their view, navigable for at least "120 Leagues [320 miles] for boats and perogues of eight or ten tons burthern."[4] And the country through which it

3. This is one of the few statements found in the journals or in the Fort Mandan reports that indicate an awareness of the semi-arid nature of the Plains and of the influence of climate on stream flow.

4. Where Lewis got this information is a matter of conjecture, but it must have come from the French boatmen or contacts in St. Louis. Mackay said that the Osage River was navigable for less than 100 leagues (Nasatir, *Before Lewis and Clark*, II, 486), and official correspondence from the archives of Spanish Louisiana mentioned the river as being navigable only "for very average pirogues" (Nasatir, I, 214). Lewis's overestimation of the length and navigability of the Osage is characteristic of his entire view of the Northwest.

passed was "generally level & fertile," consisting of plains intermixed with timber which diminished in size and extent toward the west.

Most of Lewis's and Clark's information on the Osage River was quite good, particularly that dealing with the character of the source area of the river and its relationship to the branches of the Arkansas and Kansas rivers. Although Clark, on his Fort Mandan map, pushed the source waters of the river about 3° of longitude too far to the west, the error was consistent since he did the same for the sources of the Kansas and Arkansas. The resultant picture, although distorted in length, was not distorted in the relationships between the rivers, and the mistake was a common one in both Clark's map and Lewis's summary view. During the spring and summer of 1804, when the captains were making their field observations, the streams of the Missouri basin carried more water than normal.[5] This might have contributed to the captains' view of many of the main Missouri tributaries as being longer than they actually were. But it is also possible that the overestimation of the length of western rivers—as well as the optimistic calculations of the extent of possible navigation upon them—was simply a feature of the expansion of what was known. By the time of Lewis and Clark, this was a traditional approach to the formulation of images of the trans-Missouri West; in their image the river systems of the interior were stretched out toward the Pacific, filling unknown regions with recognizable features (fig. 32).

Above the Osage, the Kansas River fell into the Missouri; this great river, wrote Lewis, had its source "not very distant from the principal branch of the Arkansas in a high broken sandy country, forming the Southern extremity of the black hills" (VI, 35). To the west the rivers Platte and Arkansas interlocked their branches, presumably in much the same fashion as the Arkansas and Kansas had "circumscribed" the Osage. From the source region the Kansas took a course nearly due east, "about 300 leagues [825 miles] through fertile and level, plains & praries, intersperced with groves of timbered land." In its lower reaches, nearer its entry into the Missouri, the Kansas passed through a country equally fertile but better timbered (VI, 35–36). It had already been navigated for a distance of 550 miles and there was "good reason to believe from the appearance of the river and the country at that point," according to some unknown informant, that it was navigable "for perogues much further perhaps nearly to its source."[6]

As was the case with his summary of the Osage, Lewis's commentary on the Kansas was accurate in terms of spatial relationships with other streams and in terms of the character of the country through which it passed, al-

5. See Merlin P. Lawson, "A Dendroclimatological Interpretation of the Great American Desert," *Proceedings of the Association of American Geographers*, III (1971), 109–13.
6. Mackay's "Table of Distances" (Nasatir, *Before Lewis and Clark*, II, 487) has the navigable length of the Kansas as 60 leagues or about 150 miles, only the lower 50 miles or so being navigable for larger craft in the autumn low-water period. Tabeau did not mention the navigability of the Kansas in his narrative, nor does the daily journal of Lewis and Clark mention it. Where Lewis came by his estimate is unknown.

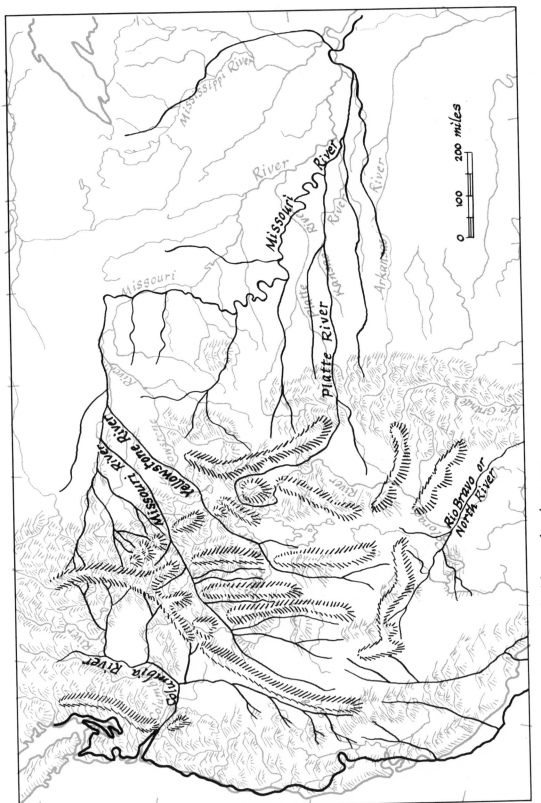

32. The Clark 1805 map compared with a modern base map

though the overestimation of the length of the river and the distance which was thought to be navigable was again considerable. On Clark's map the source of the south fork of the Kansas (later the Smoky Hill River) was shown about 3° of longitude farther west than it should have been; the northern branch (the Republican River), represented on the map as the longer branch although actually shorter than the Smoky Hill, had its source in approximately the correct location. Lewis's estimate of 880 miles for the course of the Kansas from its headwaters to the Missouri was inconsistent with Clark's map,[7] and it might have been that Lewis's calculation of the length of the Kansas considered the "windings" of the river and not the straight-line or longitudinal distance. But even so, the length of the river was unrealistic, and under no circumstances can Lewis's 550 miles of navigable water be considered as truly depicting the Kansas River's capacities for navigation.

3

The third major western tributary of the Missouri was the Platte River, and revealed in Lewis's description and Clark's cartographic representation of this river were some of the most fantastic misconceptions in their image of the trans-Missouri West, misconceptions which rested squarely on the captains' inability to comprehend the true nature of the Rocky Mountains. Their view of the lower Platte was quite accurate, however, incorporating realization of the characteristics of the Platte as a heavily silt-laden stream, braided throughout much of its course and extremely wide and shallow in many places.[8] Earlier notions that the Platte was responsible for the coloring and muddiness of the Missouri were corrected:[9] "the river Platte dose not furnish the Missouri with it's colouring matter, as has been asserted by some . . . the water of the Platte is turbid at all seasons of the year, but it is by no means as much so, as that of the Missouri" (VI, 39). And, in a surprisingly accurate piece of deduction and analysis, the captains had somehow perceived that the Platte had two main branches.[10]

7. If the Kansas were as long as Lewis thought, its headwaters would be fairly close to the junction of the Green and Colorado rivers in eastern Utah.

8. Most of the information on the Platte probably came from one of the French boatmen—"one of our engages, who is well acquainted with this river for a considerable distance" (VI, 39). Lewis further described the Platte as "from two to three miles wide, containing great numbers of small islands and sand bars. . . . the banks of this river are very low, yet it is said that it very seldom overflows them."

9. One contemporary account published in the *National Intelligencer* (Washington, Oct. 21, 1803, p. 2) claimed "The turbulence and impurities of the Plate are now communicated to the water of the Missouri. . . . Above the Plate, the stream of the Missouri is said to be clear and gentle as is that of the Mississippi above the Missouri's mouth."

10. This may have been deduction from the general knowledge in Spanish Louisiana that the Platte had "many good-sized branches" (Nasatir, *Before Lewis and Clark*, I, 123). Or it may simply have come out of the persistent tendency in contemporary geographical lore to assume that nearly all rivers had at least two main forks.

These were the south fork and the north or "Padoucas fork," and the American explorers' view of the courses of these rivers, although incorporating some amazingly precise detail, entered into the realm of fantasy:

The position of the head of the Southern, or main branch of this river is not well ascertained; on connecting the sources of the rivers better known, it appears most probable, that it takes it's rise in the Rockey or shining Mountains with the Bravo or North river [the Rio Grande], and the Yellow stone river, branch of the Missouri; from whence it takes it's course nearly East, passing the heads of the Arkansas at no great distance from Santa Fee, continues it's route to the Missouri, through immence level and fertile plains and meadows,[11] in which, no timber is to be seen except on it's own borders and those of it's tributary streams. . . . Just above the black hills, through which the Platte passes, a large river said to be nearly as large as the South Fork, falls in on the No. side, after haveing continued it's route along the Western side of the Black hills for a very considerable distance. the distance from the entrance of this river to the mouth of the Platte is not well ascertained. This is usually called the Paducas fork; it heads with the Bighorn river, branch of the Yellow Stone, in some broken ranges of the Rockey mountains. It's upper portion passes through a hilly, broken and Mountanous country, possessing considerable quantities of timber; it then descends to a plain open and level country lying between the Rockey Mounts. and the black hills, through which it passes to join the Platte. there are some considerable bodies of woodland on and near this stream [VI, 40–41].

The quality of much of this description was outstanding in its approach to the reality of the actual courses of the North and South Platte. Where the information came from is unknown, but the name "Padoucas fork" given to the North Platte suggests that it was Indian lore, received either firsthand by Lewis or secondhand through one of their boatmen or Pierre Dorion.[12] But if a modicum of accuracy prevailed in the view of the courses of the Platte's branches, the understanding of the relationships between those branches and other western rivers verged on the fantastic.

Located within an area about 20 miles square on the Clark map were the sources of the South Platte, along with the headwaters of the Rio Bravo or Rio Grande and the Yellowstone;[13] only slightly east were the headwaters of the Arkansas. This was conceptual geography of the wildest sort, and it is not sufficient to say that the feeder streams of the South Platte and the Arkansas and Rio Grande are fairly close in reality. For the sources of these rivers are separated by mountains which are higher and wider than any in the contiguous United States, and Clark showed no mountains dividing the three

11. This comment is illustrative of the captains' overall notions on fertility and land quality and is in direct opposition to contemporary Spanish Louisiana lore, which tended to picture the area through which the Platte flowed as "a sandy desart."

12. Paduca was the name given to the Plains tribe later called Comanche. Their territory during the late eighteenth century had included much of the North Platte drainage east of the Rockies.

13. The great southern extent of the Yellowstone, bringing it close to the headwaters of the South Platte, was based on the belief that it headed near a river "on which the Spanish reside," i.e., one of the rivers of the Southwest.

streams on his map. This was one of the cardinal distortions in the explorers' image of the West, and they failed, both before and after their crossing of the Continental Divide, to realize the size and extent of the Rockies.

In a second major error, the captains viewed the source region of the South Platte as being much farther west than it should have been. In a rather surprising omission, Lewis made no comment on the length or navigability of the Platte, either before or after its separation into two branches.[14] But Clark's map showed the Platte as a very large river, second only to the Missouri in size among the rivers of the Northwest;[15] the forks of the Platte were located near 105° 30′ W., roughly 4½° of longitude in excess of reality, while the farthest western sources of the Platte system were depicted as being near the 113th meridian, a longitudinal error of almost 400 miles.

Like the South Platte, the North Platte was shown on Clark's map as outsized, lying as far north and west as the 44th parallel and the 111th meridian, nearly 70 miles too far north and 200 miles too far west. The North Platte was bounded on the map throughout most of its northwardly course by a greatly elongated Black Hills, a feature that grew out of a misunderstanding of Indian information about the source regions of many other western tributaries of the Missouri. But near the northernmost extent of "Padoucas fork," Clark drew a feature which appeared on no other map of the time and was described in no period account of the Northwest. Although appearing too far west and compressed to about one-eighth its actual size, on the Clark map was clearly depicted the great bend of the North Platte, where the river, flowing northward from its source in the Colorado Rockies, curves toward the east around the northern end of the Laramie range and then turns southeast to join its sister stream, the South Platte.

Such a representation provides astonishing commentary on the quality of the information available to Lewis and Clark. Just how they might have learned about the details of the North Platte's course cannot be determined, although it is almost inconceivable that it could have simply been an accurate guess. But in spite of such approaches to truth, major portions of the captains' view of the North Platte were lacking in accuracy in terms of size of the drainage basin and relationships to other western streams. The North Platte, Lewis had written, headed with the Yellowstone, and as was the case with the South Platte, it is not enough to say that the northern waters of the North Platte are approached closely by the southernmost streams of the Yellowstone system. For although the area drained by the Sweetwater River of the North Platte system abuts the drainage basins of the Bighorn and Powder rivers of

14. The captains could have learned, in Mackay's "Table of Distances," that although navigation was impossible in the late summer and fall, during the high-water period the Platte was navigable even for large pirogues (Nasatir, *Before Lewis and Clark*, II, 489). However, Clark's journal entry for July 21, 1804, stated that the river could not be navigated by either canoes or pirogues (I, 87). This belief that the river could not be used for water travel made the Platte unique in the captains' view of major rivers of the Northwest.

15. The river was depicted by a double line on Clark's map, all the way from its mouth to the forks.

the Yellowstone system, the areas between the rivers are broad, arid, and crossed only by the dry stream channels, which fill with water during rainy periods and during the remainder of the time are absolutely empty.[16] Such a natural situation was unthinkable to Lewis and Clark, and although they had recognized a "depression of waters" in the Plains rivers during the summer months, the intermittent streams of the Wyoming basin were totally outside their geographical experience and understanding. And like the basin of the South Platte, the region drained by the north branch of the Platte was not only viewed incorrectly in terms of relationships with other drainage basins but was viewed as being larger than life-size, stretching too far into the west and compressing the area between the Continental Divide and the Pacific Ocean into a distance inconsistent with reality.

4

The Platte was the last great river that Lewis and Clark viewed as falling into the Missouri until the entry of the Yellowstone River above the Mandan villages. The streams entering the Missouri from the west between the mouth of the Platte and the Great Bend (the Niobrara, White, Cheyenne, Grand, Cannonball, and Knife rivers) can be placed together in a general classification of rivers, noted by Lewis and drawn by Clark, flowing through country that was generally described as level, fertile, and without timber in their lower reaches. But the headward portions of these streams were heavily wooded, as all of them had their sources in or near the vague range of mountains called the "black mountains" or the "black hills," running between the 41st and 48th parallels and centering approximately along the 108th meridian on Clark's map.

Lewis and Clark had received rumors of the Black Hills of South Dakota from many of their informants.[17] But the commanders of the Corps of Discovery misunderstood the size and extent of these outliers of the Rocky Mountain system, giving the Black Mountains of the view from Fort Mandan a greatly exaggerated north-south extent and placing them too far west by about 4° of longitude, or nearly 200 miles. The positioning and size of the Black Mountains on Clark's map stemmed from the information obtained relative to the lengths of the western tributaries of the Missouri (VI, 43–50). As the courses run by these streams had been magnified, their source region in the "black mountains" had been pushed toward the west.[18]

16. Cutright, *Lewis and Clark*, p. 119.
17. Loisel, Tableau, Dorion, Valle, and the Indians all presented data on the Black Hills.
18. The Black Mountains were, in addition, incorrectly assessed as a large range which formed the easternmost portions of the Rocky Mountain system rather than being separated by a large expanse of the Plains. It is probable that Lewis and Clark had heard about two separate mountain ranges—the Black Hills and the Laramie range (the northern extension of the Colorado Front range)—and had combined these two ranges into one large upland region. The term "Black Mountains" is still used by old-timers in the West to refer to the Laramie range as well as to the Black Hills of South Dakota.

The rivers which fell into the Missouri from the eastern side were much less an important part of the overall image of the Northwest than the western streams (VI, 43–50). With the single anomaly of the James River, the Missouri's major eastern tributaries (the Little Sioux, Floyd, and Big Sioux rivers) were seen by the captains as short and relatively inconsequential streams, confined in their upper reaches by the height-of-land that separated the Missouri drainage from the basins of the Mississippi and Lake Winnipeg. The country through which these rivers flowed was not viewed as being more humid, more wooded, or more fertile than the higher plains to the west; it was generally described as "an open country of plains and meadows" with only "a scant proportion of timber" found on the banks of the streams themselves (VI, 45). The central distinguishing feature of the eastern waters of the Missouri system was that they were navigable and thus offered interesting possibilities for trade between the Missouri and the Des Moines, Red, and "St. Peter's" (Minnesota) rivers. Such possibilities were mentioned by Lewis and Clark (VI, 45–46), but their cardinal objective remained the discovery of the passage to Pacific waters, and their primary interests, therefore, revolved around the western waters of the Missouri system and possible connections wtih Pacific-slope streams.

5

The image that Lewis and Clark held of the country between the Mississippi and the Mandans was, although the lengths of most of the Missouri's western tributaries were distorted, generally accurate. They had filled gaps in the pre-existing lore and had expanded the knowledge of an already partly known region. But above the Great Bend and toward the mountains and the western ocean, pre-existing lore was almost a complete cipher, and given the lack of their own experience within this region as yet, the captains had to rely nearly totally on Indian lore to complete a picture of the farther Northwest. This dependence on sketchy native data, combined with the difficulties inherent in communication and transfer of knowledge from the Indians to the explorers, was partly responsible for a degree of deformation in Lewis's and Clark's view of the uppermost portions of the Missouri basin that was even greater than the error present in their image of lower Missouri waters. In his summary of western geography, Lewis made it clear that both he and Clark recognized that such qualifications must be placed on their statements about the region west of the Mandans, although their estimation of the accuracy of their data was excessive:

As we have only ascended the Missouri, a few miles above the Mouth of Knife river, the subsequent discription of this river, and it's subsidiary streams are taken altogether from Indian information. the existence of these rivers, their connection with each other, and their relative positions with respect to the Missouri, I conceive are entitled to some confidence. information has been obtained on this subject, in the course of the winter, from a number of individuals, questioned separately and at different times. the information thus obtained has been carefully compared, and those points only in which they generally agreed, have been retained, their distance they give, by days travel, which we have estimated at 25 miles pr. day [VI, 50–51].

The first two major tributary streams which entered the Missouri above the Mandan villages, according to the Indian information, were the Little Missouri and White Earth rivers. The former was of little consequence since it, like the streams between the Platte and the Knife, had its source in the Black Hills, passed through a broken country with little timber, and was not navigable in consequence of its rapids and shoals.[19] The White Earth River, on the other hand, although it did not lead to Pacific waters, was a river of primary importance as it took its source far to the northwest, "in level open plains with the waters of the S. fork of the Saskashawin" (VI, 51). It was said to be navigable nearly to a point not far from the trading establishment of the Northwest Fur Company on the South Saskatchewan.[20]

The White Earth was a river of hope, based purely on misunderstood and conjectural information. Lewis and Clark placed the mouth of the White Earth only a short distance below the Yellowstone's embouchement into the Missouri, but in reality the only stream in that vicinity is a creek which runs a short course of about 20 miles from its head southward to the Missouri.[21] Driven by commercial desire and the theoretical probability that a Missouri tributary should come close enough to the navigable waters of the Saskatchewan to drain off the rich fur trade of that region from the British and toward St. Louis,[22] Lewis and Clark hypothesized the river they named the "White Earth." By amalgamating misconstrued data that had probably been given them regarding other northern tributaries of the Missouri, the captains "invented" a stream to match their conceptions of idealized western geography.

6

Above the mouth of the White Earth River and some 220 miles beyond the Mandan villages, according to Clark's calculations, was the Yellowstone River, "said to be nearly as large as the Missouri but is more rapid" (VI, 51). The Yellowstone was, in the view of the captains, a great and mysterious

19. This was an important modification of earlier lore. On both the King and Arrowsmith maps, the "Lesser Missouri" had been one of the two major branches of the Missouri above the Mandan villages. By obtaining definite information on the Yellowstone, the captains were able to assign the Little Missouri to a position of relative unimportance as a feeder stream of the Missouri.

20. This view was maintained when the expedition reached Little Muddy Creek near present Williston, North Dakota, during the coming summer (I, 331).

21. From observation of the Little Muddy during the summer of 1805, the captains assumed that its head might have been even farther north than the 50th parallel.

22. DeVoto, *Journals of Lewis and Clark*, pp. 89–90.

stream that took its rise "in the Rocky mountains with the waters of a river on which the Spaniards reside; but whether this stream be the N. river [Rio Grande] or the waters of the Gulph of California our information does not enable us to determine" (VI, 51). Clark did not meet the problem of the Yellowstone's source region squarely on his map, showing the mighty tributary of the Missouri in a totally unrealistic southward extension, with two major branches which interlocked their headwaters with those of both the Rio Grande and Colorado. The source waters of the Yellowstone system, in the form of the Wind River (the upper Bighorn), approach closely on the east the upper Green River, major source stream of the Colorado; the captains' notion that the Yellowstone headed near a river "on which the Spaniards reside" was, in a way, accurate. But these feeder streams of the Yellowstone and Colorado are mountain streams, unnavigable and separated by high dividing ranges, and if the captains' image was accurate in a two-dimensional sense, it was accurate in neither a three-dimensional nor a conceptual sense. To them, the statement that the heads of two rivers lay close to one another was tantamount to saying that commercial connections might be had between the areas drained by the two rivers via the navigable channels of the streams.

The critical lack, both conceptual and experiential, in the captains' background was relative familiarity with the basic distinctions between the rivers of the plains and those which flowed through the various ranges of the Rockies. Such unfamiliarity was understandable: Lewis and Clark had yet to see a mountain stream, and the Yellowstone was the first river in their image of the trans-Missouri region which was even understood to be a stream which flowed through mountains for great distances before passing out onto the plains:

from it's source it takes it's course for many miles through broken ranges of the Rocky mountains, principally broken, and stoney, and thickly timbered. the vallies said to be wide in many places and the lands fertile. after leaving the Rocky mountains it descends into a country more level, tho' still broken, fertile and well timbered. this discription of country continues as far down as the Oke-tar-pas-ah-a [Rosebud Creek] where the river enters an open level and fertile country through which it continues it's rout to the Missouri; even in this open country it possesses considerable bodies of well-timbered land [VI, 51–52].

In spite of the mountainous terrain through which the Yellowstone flowed, Lewis, incapable of comprehending the nature of a mountain stream, asserted that "the Yellow Stone river is navigable at all seasons of the year" (VI, 52). This navigability was presumed to hold for the entire course of the river from source to mouth; consequently Lewis and Clark assumed that the river would offer easy contacts with New Mexico via the "Rio Bravo" or with lower California via the Colorado.[23]

23. Essentially, what Lewis and Clark had done was to resurrect the old concept of the pyramidal height-of-land and apply it to a region in which the Yellowstone, Platte, Arkansas, Colorado, and Rio Grande originated. This conception was one of the most durable myths of western geographical lore, surviving the expedition by nearly forty years.

An overenthusiastic evaluation of the Yellowstone's navigational potential was only part of the error that allowed the captains to view the Missouri's major tributary as a highway to the Southwest. Also a contributing factor was the fantasy-tinged southward extension of the Yellowstone drainage basin, pushed nearly 300 miles too far south on Clark's map. The Yellowstone was expanded toward the west as well, distorted by the same influences that had enlarged the systems of the Missouri's western tributaries below the Great Bend. The Southwest and the Great Basin were compressed almost to nothingness because nothing was known about them, and the spaces that are filled in reality by the then-unknown Colorado Rockies were filled in the imagination of Lewis and Clark by the better-known, if still misunderstood, waters of the Missouri drainage basin.

7

Beyond the Yellowstone at a distance of 150 miles was the stream which the natives at Fort Mandan had called "the river which scolds at all others," falling into the Missouri from the north. This was the Milk River of reality, which does enter the Missouri just about 100 miles upriver from the mouth of the Yellowstone.[24] Like many of his distance estimates, Clark's calculation of the distance between the Yellowstone and the Milk was excessive and thus contributive to a western extension of the Missouri proper. And an even greater discrepancy between the captains' image and the actual location of the Milk River's mouth appeared on Clark's map, which showed "the river which scolds at all others" entering the Missouri near the 109th meridian, nearly 3° or over 130 miles too far west.[25]

The Milk River was important to the American explorers' view of the trans-Missouri region as it was the only stream of any magnitude that they saw as falling into the Missouri from the north between the mouth of the Yellowstone and the Missouri's Great Falls. When Lewis and Clark first heard about the "river which scolds" during the winter of 1804–05, their conception of the upper Missouri as presented by the King and Arrowsmith maps might have been reaffirmed, as those charts both showed the Missouri

24. This distance is straight-line or longitudinal distance and does not include actual travel miles following the course of the river.

25. Most authorities on the expedition have asserted that the Minitaris' "river which scolds at all others" was really the Marias River, entering the Missouri just a few miles below the Great Falls. This was not the case. Both Lewis's summary and Clark's map placed the entry of the "river which scolds" between the Yellowstone and the Musselshell, whereas the Marias falls into the Missouri a considerable distance above the Musselshell. Although the location of the "river which scolds" on Clark's map and as given in the distance estimates does come close to the actual location of the Marias River, this location is meaningless without reference to other key points along the Missouri. The captains checked all their various sources of data before recording them in summary statements or cartographic form, and that the "river which scolds" is clearly shown between the Yellowstone and Musselshell means that it can only have been the Milk River—and definitely not the Marias.

splitting into a northern and southern branch near the 109th meridian (near the location of the junction between the Missouri and the "river which scolds" on Clark's map). By the end of the winter at Fort Mandan, however, the captains had recognized that the southern branch on the King-Arrow-smith maps was probably represented in reality by the Yellowstone, whereas the northern fork from those charts was the Missouri itself. The bifurcation of the Missouri above the Great Bend was no longer accepted by the spring of 1805; three major channels were understood as funneling the waters of the mountains into the Missouri system. The southern reaches of the farther West were drained by the Yellowstone, with headwater connections to the Rio Grande and/or the Colorado. The central portions of the region were tapped by the Missouri itself, the river described by the Indians as leading to the waters of the Columbia. And through the northern sections of the territory west of the Mandans ran the Milk River, the channel "through which, those small streams, on the E side of the Rocky mountins laid down by Mr. Fidler, pass to the Missouri" (VI, 53). This was a crucial rearrangement of the alignment of the Missouri and its tributary streams, but the real significance of this refinement of earlier lore was not to be felt until the exploration of the coming summer.[26]

Beyond the mouth of the "river which scolds" the Musselshell River entered the Missouri from the south after heading in a range of mountains "which commence about the falls of the Missouri, and extending themselves nearly South terminate near the yellow stone river. this stream passes through a broken and woody country . . . [which] commences on the Missouri just above the mouth of this river" (VI, 54). The mouth of the Musselshell was, Clark calculated, 120 miles upstream from the "river which scolds," and once again his estimate was excessive, this time by about 45 miles. Combining this error with earlier overestimates for distances west of the Mandan villages and modifying the cumulative error by a slight directional change in the course of the Missouri above the "river which scolds," the captains placed the Mussel-shell River about 150 miles farther west than it ought to have been.[27] The consequence for their broader view of the Missouri basin was that the Missouri itself was pushed westward, in the direction of the Pacific.

8

Above the Musselshell, at an estimated distance of 120 miles, lay one of the great landmarks of the West, the Great Falls of the Missouri. Here, in the

26. When the Marias River was reached in June, 1805, the captains were assured by their readjustments of the Fidler data that this unexpected river was not the Missouri as most of their party believed but was only another channel which, like the Milk, carried water from the mountains north of the Missouri into the main river.

27. The error was not as great as it might have been since the captains saw the Missouri as trending more southward above the mouth of the "river which scolds," and therefore their estimates were no longer for a river running a due west-to-east course.

captains' view, the general directional trend of the Missouri shifted from west-east to southwest-northeast, and on this belief balanced the greatest single misconception in the image created at Fort Mandan, a misconception in which the headwaters of the Missouri River were seen as being located somewhere in what is now north central Nevada. Part of this titanic error lay in the overestimations of distances along the Missouri between the Great Bend and the Great Falls which had resulted in the positioning of the cascades, in the view from Fort Mandan, about 100 miles farther west than they should have been.[28] But much more pivotal was the captains' understanding of the course of the Missouri above the Falls.

The geographical information that Lewis and Clark had received from the Minitaris relative to the course of the Missouri between the Great Bend and the Great Falls would prove, on inspection during the journey of the summer of 1805, to be fairly reliable. The natives' data on the country above the Falls was also accurate, but in the process of translating Indian concepts of distance and direction into their own frame of reference and applying the Indian information to the Missouri's course beyond the Falls, Lewis and Clark made their greatest miscalculations. From the Mackay-Evans material the captains had extracted the information that the Missouri came from nearly a due south direction above the Great Falls.[29] Although this data was closer to reality than the view they adopted, it was rejected in favor of the belief that the river ran a southwest-northeast course from a point near the Pacific all the way to the Falls.

It is apparent from Clark's map that the Mackay-Evans statements about the source of the Missouri being located near the 40th parallel were acceptable to the captains and therefore, in the view from Fort Mandan, the Missouri proper extended far to the south.[30] But their misinterpretations of Indian lore on the western extension of the Missouri system placed the westernmost sources of that river near the 119th meridian, a full 6° beyond the actual location of the Continental Divide, bounding the Missouri basin on the west and hence almost 300 miles too close to Pacific shores. The proximity of the Missouri to the Pacific Ocean was, of course, a very old idea, having its origins in the theoretical constructions and teleological assumptions of seventeenth-century French geography. But the view of Lewis and Clark was based less on pure theory and hope than it was on misconstrued lore received in the field. The nature of their misconstructions of data relative to the proximity of the Missouri and the western ocean becomes clear when their conceptions of

28. This was not the only error with regard to the captains' view of the Great Falls. The Indians had assured them that the portage around the Falls was "not greater than half a mile" and that they therefore should not be viewed as an impediment to navigation (VI, 54). The actual portage was more on the order of 18 miles.

29. Nasatir, *Before Lewis and Clark*, II, 498.

30. Why Lewis and Clark would have accepted the Mackay-Evans conception of the latitudinal position of the Missouri's source and rejected the notion of the south-to-north course as presented in the Mackay-Evans journals is a puzzling question.

the course of the Missouri from the Great Falls, through the Rockies, to the Three Forks and the Continental Divide are examined.

Their Minitari informants had provided Lewis and Clark with rather precise directions for the route from the Falls to a point where the "Missouri divides itself into three nearly equal branches," and from thence to the height-of-land separating the Missouri from the Columbia. These directions were couched in terms of both distance or travel time, estimated by the captains at 25 miles a day (VI, 50–1), and direction, given by the natives not with reference to the cardinal points of the compass but with reference to the points on the western horizon where the sun set at different times of the year.[31] The explorers' deductions of distance were remarkably accurate, and their estimate of 275 miles for the course of travel between the Great Falls and the Three Forks was close to the 250 miles that actually separate the two landmarks. Their understanding of Indian-given direction was much less accurate, however, and where the actual course of the Missouri is northwest from the Three Forks to a point just above the Falls, Lewis and Clark mistakenly assumed that the river ran in a straight northeast line from its farthest source at the foot of the final dividing ridge to the Great Falls, where it emerged from the mountains onto the plains.

The critical error made by the captains with regard to the direction of the Missouri's course between its source and the Falls, in combination with the overestimations in distance between the Falls and the Mandan villages which had resulted in the westward displacement of the cascades by nearly 100 miles, had the cumulative effect of moving the source of the river much too far toward the Pacific (see fig. 32). But massive error in the extension of the Missouri basin notwithstanding, the explorers' image of the portion of the Northwest between the Great Falls and the Divide contained amazing detail and some elements of considerable accuracy.

9

The major constituents of the region above the Great Falls were the Missouri itself and five separate ranges of the Rocky Mountain system. The first or easternmost range of the Rockies, in the captains' view, commenced "about the falls of the Missouri" and extended "nearly South [to] terminate near the yellow stone river" (VI, 54). The Missouri, then, was understood to flow around the northern end of this first chain of mountains, and about 15 miles above the river's passage around the range at the Great Falls, the Medicine (Sun) River entered the Missouri from the west. According to Lewis's summary, this river headed "in the rocky Mountains opposite to a

31. Indian directions were customarily couched in terms of "above" or "below" the sunset, that is, right or left of the sun's setting position as the observer faced the west.

river which also takes it's rise in the same mountains and which running West discharges itself into a large river, which passes at no great distance from the Rocky mountains, runing from N. to South. it passes through a mountanous, broken and woody country; not navigable in consequence of it's rapidity and shoals" (VI, 54). The river heading across the mountains from the Medicine River was the Great Lake River of the King-Arrowsmith charts, and the river into which it flowed was the Tacoutche-Tesse or Columbia. This opinion corresponded with the information from previous sources, but the Medicine–Great Lake River route to the Columbia was disallowed by Lewis and Clark because of the lack of navigation on the Medicine River.[32]

The proper route to the Columbia, the captains had learned, was up the Missouri itself. Sixty miles beyond the mouth of the Medicine River (75 miles above the Falls), the Missouri passed through the second range of the Rockies or what Lewis called "the first connected chain." From this range of mountains the Missouri was said to be "rapid and shoaly" as far as "the second [connected] chain of the rocky Mountains a distance of 75 miles further, about the same course last mentioned [southwest]" (VI, 54). Past this second "connected" range, the current of the river again became smooth and gentle, and "still proceeding S.W. about 75 miles further the Missouri divides itself into three nearly equal branches just above a third chain of very high mountains, all these streams are navigable for some distance" (VI, 55).

Beyond the Missouri's Three Forks, the route to the Columbia lay up the Missouri's westernmost branch to the last dividing range. This branch of the river was, the explorers had been told, the largest branch of the Missouri above the Forks and was "navigable to the foot of a chain of high mountains, being the ridge which divides the waters of the Atlantic from those of the Pacific Ocean" (VI, 55). Beyond this ridge "the Indians assert that they can pass in half a day from the foot of this mountain on its east side to a large river which washes it's Western base, running from S. to No." Like nearly all of the earlier explorers in the trans-Missouri West, Lewis and Clark had received information on the classical short portage between the waters of the eastern and western seas. This had always been the core of misconception, and the Indian information was highly acceptable to Lewis and Clark, not only because it fitted so perfectly the objectives of their expedition but because it was backed up by so much previous geographical lore. The south-north river beyond the divide must have been, in the captains' image, the great southern branch of the Columbia that had appeared on the King map and that had been slightly shortened and placed behind a divide during the winter at Camp Dubois. The river beyond the divide was the Great River of the West, and it would lead to the shores of the Sea of the South and the ultimate goal of western exploration.

32. This route was actually the shortest and easiest across the Divide from where the captains were—but this fact would not be realized until after the re-evaluation of data during the winter of 1805–06, spent on the shores of the Pacific.

10

Basically, the view of the country from the Falls to the Columbian waters was accurate in its major details, and much of the information received by the captains had been of the highest quality. They had heard about the Three Forks of the Missouri and about the passage of the Missouri around the northern end of the Little Belt and Highwood ranges and through the Big Belt, Tobacco Root, and Pioneer ranges to the source of the Jefferson River in the Beaverhead range of southwestern Montana. They had learned, moreover, that across the last dividing range a tributary of the Columbia ran from south to north and had therefore received information on either the Lemhi River of Salmon River drainage or the Bitterroot River of Clark Fork drainage. Or even more likely, they had heard from the Minitaris about both of these streams of the Columbia basin and had combined them into one major river. But in spite of the fact that there are more rivers across the Divide from the Missouri's westernmost sources than they believed, the general outline of the captains' view of the relationships between the rivers and mountains of this key portion of the Northwest was remarkably accurate.

Blended in the view from Fort Mandan, however, were fact and fiction, near-comprehension and mammoth misunderstanding, and by the time Lewis and Clark were ready to depart for the mountains and the Passage, two major misconceptions still existed in their view of the farther West. The first persistent error was in the size of the drainage system of the Missouri. Basing their view of the upper portions of the Missouri on an erroneous assumption about the course of the river between its source and the Great Falls, Lewis and Clark envisaged a drainage region which was overextended toward the south and west. The second persistent error was the captains' inability to see the Missouri and its tributaries as anything but navigable streams. Partly responsible for the shaping of this error were the Minitaris, horse Indians who could not possibly have known the difference between a navigable river and an unnavigable one and therefore could not have given the explorers any accurate data on this point. More responsible for Lewis's and Clark's view of the mountain streams as navigable, however, was their conception of the nature of the mountains themselves.

Rather than being a simple, isolated ridge of hills forming a drainage divide between eastern and western waters as they had been seen earlier, the Rockies of the Fort Mandan image were viewed as a complex association of ranges. But neither of the captains had yet realized the true nature of the western cordillera as a wide and massive upland region, and this deficiency in the image of the spring of 1805 contributed to other errors. Lewis and Clark looked upon the Rockies as a series of isloated ranges that were separated by broad valleys through which ran the mighty rivers that were, it was believed (and hoped), navigable all the way to their sources "at the base of the mountains." That the captains had received relatively precise data on the Montana

Rockies is irrelevant, for, conditioned by their experiences and knowledge of what mountains were and ought to be, Lewis and Clark perceived the Rockies within a conceptual framework of mountain geography based on the model of the Virginia Blue Ridge.[33]

The one short range and the first three "connected" chains of the Rocky Mountains were understood as isolated parallel ridges aligned more or less transversely to the Missouri's course, while the fourth and final range paralleled the Missouri on the west, separating it from waters of the Pacific slope. Although the river did not penetrate the last range, it flowed through the others in the same manner as the Potomac and Shenandoah cut through the Blue Ridge and then passed through the wide and fertile valleys between the separate ranges. There seems to have been no room in the captains' geographical imagination for the massive structural deformation of the real Rockies; there was no room, in the view from Fort Mandan, for mountains of such tremendous height and breadth that the first sight of them during the summer of 1805 would be a startling and unexpected revelation. And finally, in the view from Fort Mandan, there was no room for the Southwest, the Great Basin, or the country between the Divide and the Pacific. For the northern Rockies, although not seen as being large in terms of the size of the individual ranges, covered a tremendous amount of territory, and the Continental Divide itself, pushed by the overextension of the Missouri system, lay close to the Pacific shores.

II

During the winter at Wood River, the spring and summer and fall of travel up the Missouri, and the winter at Fort Mandan, Lewis and Clark had learned more from observation, had recorded more of their thoughts and opinions, and had gathered more complete information on the trans-Missouri West than any explorers before them. As a result, their recognition of specific details relative to the major geographic components of the Northwest was far superior to all previous geographical knowledge. Yet it was the very breadth of their knowledge and their grasp of details of western geography that contributed most to the misconceived size of the entire Missouri system, the central distinguishing feature of the view from Fort Mandan. The overextension of the Missouri basin toward the Pacific was the consequence more of the expansion of known or partly known geography to fill areas of *terra incognita* than of any other single factor, including the captains' fundamental inability to transfer Indian distance and direction data onto their maps.

If that portion of Clark's map of the Northwest which shows the region

33. The process of image formation here was a perfectly normal one; all images must be created out of what is known or has been experienced (Lowenthal, "Geography, Experience, and Imagination," pp. 241–45).

drained by the Missouri could be separated from the remainder of the map and transformed to a smaller scale, it would be seen that the shape of the Missouri basin and the relationships between most of the rivers and mountains within the area come close to reality. But when the Missouri basin is viewed as an integral part of the map, it is clearly outsized, magnified out of any proportion to an accurate scale, almost as if it had been drawn as an inset on the map but in much larger scale than the remainder of the trans-Mississippi West. The terrific distortion of the Missouri basin was partly the result of the captains' attempts to blend features from previous maps with Indian lore[34] and partly the result of misunderstood distance and direction data. But underlying the distorted image of the size and scale of the Missouri system was the even more elemental fact that Lewis and Clark had learned virtually nothing of the Southwest and the country between the Rockies and the Pacific and, following a time-honored practice of conceptual and theoretical geography, had simply used the known to fill those areas still outside experience and knowledge.

In the final analysis, the view from Fort Mandan, in all its detail and complexity, was little more than a reaffirmation of the conjectures of earlier times. Many new features had been added to the geography of the Northwest —the forks of the Platte, the Black Hills, the multiple-range structure of the Rocky Mountains, the Great Falls of the Missouri, the Three Forks. But in spite of the added detail, in many ways the image of 1805 represented a regression to the type of images created during the period of French control of Louisiana. The Missouri once again flowed from the base of a mountain that was close to the shores of the great South Sea. The river systems of North America were once again symmetrical—the Missouri approached the Pacific as the Ohio approached the Atlantic. Only a half-day's travel separated the Missouri from the Great River of the West, and the logic of the short and easy Passage to India could not be shaken. The image of the trans-Missouri West in the spring of 1805 reflected this fact, and when Lewis and Clark departed from Fort Mandan, they went with the faith that ahead of them lay only the glory of the Passage and all it promised.

34. The captains had recognized that Peter Fidler, the supplier of data for the Arrowsmith map, could not have gone farther south than the 47th parallel. Therefore, they took the details on the Rockies from the Arrowsmith-King maps and placed them north of the Missouri's course. The mountains south of the Missouri's generally west-to-east course were laid down from Indian data, but rather than following the northwest-southeast alignment of the mountains above the 47th parallel (as shown on the earlier maps), Clark twisted the ranges in a southwest direction to match his understanding of the direction and distance of the Missouri's course above the Great Falls.

WEST TO THE GREAT
ROCKY MOUNTAINS

"Our vessels," wrote Meriwether Lewis as he, Clark, and the members of the Corps of Discovery departed from their fortified winter encampment on April 7, 1805, "consisted of six small canoes, and two large perogues":[1]

This little fleet altho' not quite as rispectable as those of Columbus or Capt. Cook were still viewed by us with as much pleasure as those deservedly famed adventurers ever beheld theirs; and I dare say with quite as much anxiety for their safety and preservation. we were now about to penetrate a country at least two thousand miles in width, on which the foot of civilized man had never trodden; the good or evil it had in store for us was for experiment yet to determine, and these little vessells contained every article by which we were to expect to subsist or defend ourselves. however, as the state of mind in which we are, generally gives the colouring to events, when the imagination is suffered to wander into futurity, the picture which now presented itself to me was a most pleasing one. enterta[in]ing as I do, the most confident hope of succeeding in a voyage which had formed a da[r]ling project of mine for the last ten years, I could but esteem this moment of my departure as among the most happy of my life [I, 285].

1. The pirogues had been used during the upriver journey from Camp Dubois, but the six smaller dugouts were made from cottonwoods that came from a grove just a few miles below Fort Mandan.

The "darling project" of Lewis was the discovery of a water route to the Pacific via the Missouri River; such a discovery had been Jefferson's "primary objective" and the moving force, stated or implied, behind most explorers in the American Northwest since Marquette had discovered the Missouri in 1673. But where all others had failed, Lewis and Clark would be successful—and essential to their success was the geographical knowledge which had shaped their image of the trans-Missouri West.

It was true, as Lewis stated, that the country beyond the Mandan villages was country "on which the foot of civilized man had never trodden," land which had not yet known the white man or, in turn, been known by him.[2] But separating Lewis and Clark from all previous seekers after the Passage to India was their geographical knowledge, compiled during the arduous but fruitful winter at Fort Mandan. The captains did not know all there was to know about the farther West, and much of what they did know was imperfectly understood. Unlike lesser men and less capable explorers, however, during the course of their journey across the Great Divide to the Pacific shores, they were able to separate what they would come to understand through observation from what they had only thought they knew before leaving Fort Mandan.

There are two kinds of geographical knowledge that condition exploration.[3] The first is "real knowledge," or actual information obtained through active commercial, diplomatic, military, or scholarly enterprises or from the accounts of travelers and observers, evaluated in the light of what is presently accepted as geographical reality.[4] The second and more important kind of knowledge is "perceived knowledge," or lore which is evaluated on the basis of accuracy as it is understood by the explorers themselves. In most cases explorers believe that the quality of the information they possess is better than it actually is; this fact is of prime importance in understanding the exploratory process, since explorers in the field function according to their conceptions of the quality of their knowledge. When exploration begins, an explorer has certain preconceived notions about the accuracy of his information concerning lands to be investigated. He bases his field operations on these preconceptions. As the exploration proceeds, the explorer may begin to change his conceptions about the quality of his knowledge and may make accordant changes in his field behavior, changes that are the result of the explorer's recognition of discrepancy between the geographical realities he encounters and the conditions he had expected to find.

An explorer may, for example, pass from an area that is actually well known into one that is less known (in a "real" or empirical sense). The

2. There were a few traders who had ventured beyond the Mandan villages (Nasatir, *Before Lewis and Clark*, I, 110), but the very scanty knowledge they collected was not a part of general geographical lore.
3. See Allen, "An Analysis of the Exploratory Process," p. 14.
4. John Kirtland Wright, *Geographical Lore of the Time of the Crusades* (New York, 1925), pp. 256–57.

boundary between these different areas or zones of qualitatively different knowledge may not be immediately recognized, and the explorer continues to function as if his information were of the highest quality and continues to base his field operations on what may be termed "macro-geographical information," or that lore accumulated prior to exploration. Gradually, however, the explorer begins to realize the inadequacy of his data and consequently shifts from a reliance on the macro-geographical lore to "micro-geographical information," the detailed and local lore obtained from natives and from field observations by the explorer himself during the course of his journey.

This newer lore replaces the previous data as the basis for the explorer's field decisions whenever it is realized that the original assessments of data quality were faulty. The quicker the recognition of the inadequacy of one type of data and the swifter the response to such recognition, the shorter will be the time lag between the failure of one information class to assist in making field decisions and the replacing of that class with another, possibly more adequate, informational framework. The more successful explorers are those who are capable of seeing inaccuracies in older lore and supplanting it with what they begin to observe as reality, thus becoming more effective in their operational behavior within the territories they are endeavoring to make known in a real or empirical sense.

On their trip from the Missouri's mouth to the Mandan villages, Lewis and Clark were traversing a portion of the trans-Missouri West which was both known in a real sense and understood by them to be a region for which the available geographical information was reliable. The journals of Truteau and the maps and journals of Mackay and Evans had proven accurate during the upriver journey,[5] and when the captains arrived at the Great Bend their faith in the quality of their macro-geographical lore was still high. As they learned more about the country west of the Mandans during the winter of 1804–05, however, they began to replace the older lore with more detailed and more specific information. When they left Fort Mandan, although they were still functioning (in a broad sense) within the macro-geographic framework which had at its heart the conception of the short portage between the headwaters of the Columbia and Missouri, most of their field operations and decisions would be based on the image shaped from information obtained during the winter. And as they penetrated the Northwest even further, this micro-geographical lore, like the more generalized lore before it, would be found wanting and would be replaced with still newer and more detailed informational sources. The success of the Lewis and Clark Expedition in reach-

5. The Mackay and Evans maps, in particular, were so accurate that Clark may have felt no need to make charts of his own for the course of the Missouri between the Mississippi and the Mandan villages. At least such maps by Clark have never been found. In the holdings of the Joslyn Art Museum in Omaha, however, there are maps which certainly appear to have been traced from charts made by Clark of the Missouri below the Mandans. If this is the case, then future search may eventually turn up the originals. I am grateful to Donald Jackson for drawing my attention to the maps in the Joslyn Museum.

ing the Pacific was, in large measure, attributable to the ability of its commanders to make such replacements.

2

The region immediately north and west of the Mandan villages varied little from that below the expedition's winter campsite, and as the party passed upriver, seeing on all sides the evidences of the spring reawakening, the garden-like characteristics of the Northwest were still apparent. The hills along the Missouri were somewhat more broken, bearing more traces of the alkali flats and springs and showing appearances of "having been on fire at some former period" (I, 290).[6] But beyond the high bluffs of the river were the "continued level fertile" plains that the explorers had come to know. Navigation of the Missouri was seemingly better than it had been in the fall, the current was moderate, "at least not greater than that of the Ohio in high tide" (I, 293), and travel on the stream was "comparatively with it's lower portion easy and safe."[7] The plains and the lowlands along the river teemed with returning migratory waterfowl, and although the larger game was scarce in consequence of the constant pressure of the Minitari hunters, the expedition's own hunters kept the party supplied with venison and beaver, the latter being a great delicacy.[8]

On April 12, at a distance of 93 miles above their winter camp, the expedition reached the Little Missouri, located just where it should have been according to the Indian information,[9] and as the captains called a halt to make astronomical observations at this point, Lewis repeated in his daily log the data he had received on that stream from the natives. It had its sources, he said, in a heavily dissected region west of the Black Mountains near the waters of the Yellowstone River and from thence flowed northeast to join the Missouri (I, 298). Using the same kind of physical geographical logic that would prove critical in a later stage of the journey, Lewis reasoned that since the "colour of the water, the bed of the river, and it's appearance in every respect, resembled the Missouri" (I, 299), the Little Missouri must be a plains stream, rising in and flowing through a country similar to that about the Missouri itself. His description of the character of the river, the direction of its course,[10] and the nature of the region through which it passed was quite accurate, and

6. Coues (*History*, I, 264) notes that on April 10, the expedition passed a bluff that was actually burning and throwing out "quantities of smoke." It was probably lignite, set afire by the grass fires started by the natives.

7. The Missouri was still a month away from flood stage and had been falling rather steadily during the first week of April (VI, 185–86).

8. "The men prefer the flesh of this anamal, to that of any other which we have, or are able to procure at this moment. I eat very heartily of the beaver myself, and think it excellent" (Lewis, I, 318).

9. Clark's distance estimates of the winter had placed the entry of the Little Missouri into the Missouri at approximately 100 miles above Fort Mandan (VI, 60).

10. See Coues, *History*, I, p. 267, n. 25.

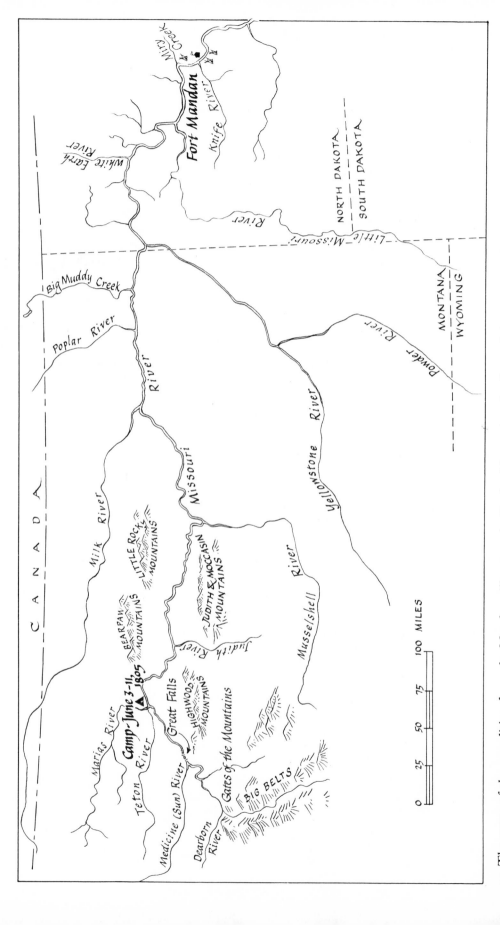

33. The route of the expedition from the Mandan villages to the Rocky Mountains, April 8 to July 19, 1805

no one was to add much more complete detail on the Little Missouri until near the end of the nineteenth century.[11]

But the captains were interested in more than simple description, and here at the mouth of the Little Missouri they began the first of what were to be many changes in their image and cartographic representation of the Northwest. From one of the French boatmen who had signed on as a member of the permanent party and who had been up the Little Missouri, Lewis and Clark learned that this stream passed within a few miles of the "Turtle Hills," which lay nearly south of the Mandan villages.[12] The location of these hills had been determined quite accurately by David Thompson,[13] and if, as the captains believed, the Little Missouri approached the small range closely on the west, then the course of the river as shown on Clark's Fort Mandan map was "laid down too far S.W." (I, 299). The same held true for the course of the Knife River, separated from the Little Missouri by the Turtle Hills. The modification thus made in the explorers' earlier view was a minor one—but it was the first glimpse of truth and foreshadowed the captains' eventual realization of their error in pushing the courses of so many Missouri tributaries too far toward the south and west.

3

The signs of spring increased as the expedition moved upstream, although evidences of the long, cold winter remained in the frozen strata of earth, visible when chunks of the Missouri's bank broke away to fall into the river (VI, 188). The river continued to be easily navigable "and not more rapid than the Ohio in an average state of it's current" (I, 307). On both sides of the stream the bluffs grew larger and took on more of the appearance of the carved landforms common to arid regions. Beyond the bluffs were still the beautiful plains, however, "uniformly fertile consisting of a dark loam intermixed with a proportion of fine sand" and generally "covered with a short grass resembling very much the blue grass" (I, 307). The Garden of Plenty still existed and the captains' daily journals during the first part of the journey toward the mountains were filled with descriptions of the "handsom high extencive rich Plains on each side" and the "immence herds of Buffaloe, Elk, deer & Antelopes feeding in one common and boundless pasture" (I, 329). As below the Mandans, only three regional characteristics marred the view of the explorers: the "Musketors" which made their appearance on the second day out from Fort Mandan and soon grew troublesome; the intense west and northwest winds which blew "with some violence almost every day" (I, 333),

11. Cutright, *Lewis and Clark*, p. 125.
12. The Turtle Hills should not be confused with the Turtle Mountains, which straddle the North Dakota–Manitoba border northeast of Minot, North Dakota.
13. See fig. 19 above.

stinging the faces of the men and obscuring the far shores of the Missouri with clouds of dust and sand;[14] and the brackish streams of the Plains, made unpotable by the concentration of mineral salts in their waters (I, 314).

One week and 127 miles beyond the Mandan villages, the party reached the point which, they believed, "was the highest point to which any whiteman had ever ascended" (I, 308) and gave to a small creek which entered the Missouri there the name of "Chabono's Creek" after Toussaint Charbonneau, their interpreter, who had camped in the vicinity with a party of Minitari hunters. Two other Frenchmen, Lewis noted, had straggled some very few miles farther upstream, but for the captains the mouth of "Chabono's Creek"[15] marked the farthest advance of the white man. It was not, however, the farthest penetration of his cultural impact; on the day after passing the mouth of the creek, Captain Lewis found the remains of a hunting camp of some Assiniboine Indians and in those remains the metal hoops once used to bind the small kegs of "Spiritous licquer" of which the Assiniboines were so passionately fond.[16] Nor was it, in absolute terms, the farthest advance of the white man himself, for an occasional Canadian or Louisianan fur trader had accompanied roving bands of Minitaris at least as far as the Yellowstone.[17] In terms of empirical geographical knowledge, however, it was much farther than any white had gone, and the observations the captains made as they passed up the Missouri toward the mountains were the first of their kind.

As the cottonwood trees began to put on their first frail and lacy coats of green and the third week of April neared its end, the Corps of Discovery reached the river upon which Lewis, writing at Fort Mandan, had based such hopes for the expansion northward of the American fur trade. This was the "White Earth River," located, like the Little Missouri, remarkably close to where the Indians had said it would be.[18] In fact, it was probably the distance estimates they had made prior to their departure from Fort Mandan that led the captains to believe they had discovered the White Earth River. For the stream they gave that name was only Little Muddy Creek, a short and inconsequential stream entering the Missouri where Williston, North Dakota, now sits.[19] It was spring and the plains streams that would be dry or nearly dry in three months were now carrying their peak loads; Little Muddy Creek was "a

14. Henry Brackenridge, in his *Views of Louisiana* (Philadelphia, 1814, p. 29), says of the upper Missouri plains: "There are extensive tracts of moving sands similar to those of the African deserts."

15. This creek was probably only a channel which carried runoff during the spring but was normally dry. The only streams in this area are intermittent.

16. The Assiniboines had been in contact with white men longer than any other of the western tribes (DeVoto, *Course of Empire*, pp. 162–64).

17. In his journals Truteau had asserted that a Canadian halfbreed named Menard had traveled as far west as the mouth of the Yellowstone (Nasatir, *Before Lewis and Clark*, II, 381).

18. There was a discrepancy of only 7 miles between Clark's estimate of the distance between the Mandans and the White Earth and the actual distance as calculated during the journey (VI, 60–61).

19. A river now named the White Earth enters the Missouri farther downstream near Stanley, North Dakota. This river is not the same as the White Earth of Lewis and Clark.

boald stream of sixty yards wide and is deep and navigable" (I, 326).[20] But the captains could not have known that this stream was not the White Earth River, for that stream never really existed. Lewis and Clark had invented (or distorted from Indian lore) the information to describe the river, and the strength of their preconviction that it existed caused Lewis to conclude about it that "this river is said to be navigable nearly to it's source, which is at no great distance from the Saskashawan, and I think from it's size the direction which it seems to take, and the latitude of it's mouth, that there is very good ground to believe that it extends as far North as latitude 50°" (I, 328). The White Earth River possessed an entirely different form in the imagination from that which it possessed in reality.

4

Once past the White Earth River, Lewis and Clark, basing their views on the distance estimates provided them by the natives, believed that they must be nearing the confluence of the Missouri and Yellowstone rivers. On the morning of April 25, therefore, Lewis separated himself from the bulk of the party and traveled overland with a small detachment to find "the entrance of that river and make the necessary observations to determine it's position" (I, 344). He had his first glimpse of the mighty, mysterious "Roche Jaune" or Yellowstone River[21] from some hills south of the Missouri. Climbing one of those hills, he gained "a most pleasing view of the country, particularly of the wide and fertile valleys formed by the Missouri and yellowstone rivers, which occasionally unmasked by the wood on their borders disclose their meanderings for many miles in their passage through these delightful tracts of country" (I, 335). After camping on the banks of the Yellowstone River two miles above its junction with the Missouri, Lewis performed the necessary astronomical observations on April 26 and found the Yellowstone's mouth to lie almost precisely at the 48th parallel, substantiating the positioning given the Yellowstone on Clark's Fort Mandan map. Moreover, the river's mouth was found to be about 280 miles above Fort Mandan, a distance quite close to the estimates obtained from the Minitaris.[22]

Lewis had no way of knowing that he was probably not the first white

20. The captains found that the White Earth "contained more water than streams of it's size generally do at this season" (I, 328). The main reason for this was the shortness of the stream and the fact that they were viewing most of the runoff coming all at once. They recognized these properties of the upper Missouri drainage system later (II, 3–4) but never applied their recognition to the White Earth River.

21. Thwaites (I, 339) says that the name "Yellowstone is simply the English of the French name Roche Jaune, itself without doubt translated from an earlier Indian appelation." See also Coues (*History*, I, 283, n. 47). According to Hiram M. Chittenden in *Yellowstone National Park* (Cincinnati, 1895), pp. 1–7, the name was probably derived from the Indian descriptions of the colored walls of the Grand Canyon of the Yellowstone River.

22. Based on Indian information, Clark had estimated (during the Fort Mandan winter) a distance of slightly more than 250 miles from the villages to the Yellowstone's mouth.

man to view the junction of the Yellowstone and Missouri; believing that he beheld a scene heretofore hidden from "civilized eyes," he felt a sense of elation in "having arrived at this long wished for spot" (I, 338). After joining forces with Clark near the junction of the two mighty streams, Lewis ordered a "dram to be issued to each person" in order to "add in some measure to the general pleasure which seemed to pervade our little community," and the evening of April 26 was spent with "much hilarity, singing & dancing." The party had good reason to be delighted. The discovery of the Yellowstone, like the White Earth located remarkably near where they had thought it would be, confirmed the reliability of the Fort Mandan lore. The prospects for continued confirmation of the Indian data, including that relative to the easy passage across the mountains to the west, must have seemed bright.

Clinging to the reinforced Indian lore from the previous winter, the captains inserted in their journals the information that the Yellowstone headed in mountainous, rocky country and flowed through a "delightfull rich and fertile country, well covered with timber, intersperced with plains and meadows and well watered" (I, 339).[23] The extreme sources of the river were, Lewis reported, "adjacent to those of the Missouri, river platte, and I think probably with some of the South branch of the Columbia river" (I, 339). In its course from the mountains to the Missouri, the Yellowstone was joined by "many large tributary streams[24] principally from the S.E. of which the most considerable are the Tongue and bighorn rivers . . . the former is much the largest . . . and heads with the river Platte and Bighorn river, as dose the latter with the Tongue river and the river Platte" (I, 340). Much of this information was accurate in general terms and some of it was totally new.

Lewis and Clark had obviously learned of such major tributaries of the Yellowstone as the Powder, Tongue, Bighorn, and Clarks Fork rivers, many of these being laid down on an Indian chart obtained during the winter (see fig. 30). The Tongue is not the largest tributary of the Yellowstone, and it is the Powder River rather than the Tongue which has sources close to those of the Platte. But the waters of the Tongue and the eastern feeder streams of the Bighorn do lie in the same vicinity, while the small southern tributaries of the upper Bighorn or Wind River approach the Sweetwater River, the westernmost tributary of the North Platte.[25] The most interesting piece of data, however, was Lewis's comment about the proximity between the source of the Yellowstone and the source of the "South branch of the Columbia river," for it was a major departure from the image of the previous winter.

Clark's Fort Mandan map showed the Yellowstone as being separated by

23. Basically the same information had already been recorded by Truteau, Mackay, and Evans (Nasatir, *Before Lewis and Clark*, II, 381, 416, 498).

24. A chart made by Clark during the previous winter (VI, 60) lists six tributary streams falling into the Yellowstone from the south. Three of these were given the names they now possess (the Powder, Tongue, and Bighorn rivers). The other three were given Indian names but are now identifiable as O'Fallon Creek, Rosebud Creek, and Clarks Fork River.

25. See pp. 239–40 above.

a full 6° of longitude (nearly 300 miles) from the southern branch of the Columbia River. How the captains arrived at the conclusion that the Yellowstone and the Columbia's southern fork headed in the same region is unknown. It may have simply been guesswork, although it was more probably an assumption based on the old hydrographical theory of the pyramidal height-of-land.[26] Whatever the basis for the statement it was remarkably accurate, since Yellowstone Lake lies only about 5 miles east of the lake in which the Lewis River, a major tributary of the upper Snake River, has its source. Because of their belief in the connections between the Yellowstone and so many other western rivers, the captains thought the confluence of that stream and the Missouri would be a highly appropriate location for a trading establishment, and before moving on up the Missouri they sought for and found a "most eligible site for an establishment" (I, 344). The connections they believed in were not really there—but the "establishment" they envisaged would be built very shortly.[27]

5

Beyond the Yellowstone the country was "open as usual and very broken on both sides near the river hills, the bottoms are level fertile and partially covered with timber" (I, 348). But the landscape contained more and more traces of the semi-arid climate of the eastern Montana plains, and for a time the expedition passed through a heavily dissected country in which the ground was so incrusted with alkali deposits that it appeared "perfectly white as if covered with snow or frost" (I, 348). Even the higher plains in back of the river hills were perceptibly less abundant than farther downstream, and although great quantities of game were seen roving the open plains, the plains themselves lacked "the verdure those below exhibited some days past"(I, 348).[28] But the decline in the apparent quality of the land was not a permanent one, and on May 1 the captains noted that the land on both sides of the river was "much more pleasant and fertile than that we have passed for several days" (I, 357).

The herds grew ever larger, and soon the hunters found it only "amusement" to secure "whatever species of meat the country affords in as large quantity as we wish" (II, 12). One of the species afforded by the country was the grizzly, a new entry on the scene, and after their first encounters with this beast the explorers might have wished that the game upon which

26. Allen, "Pyramidal Height-of-Land," p. 396.

27. Coues, *History*, I, 284; and Cutright, *Lewis and Clark*, p. 134. The first fort at the Yellowstone's mouth was built by the partnership of Ashley and Henry in 1822 and was replaced in 1829 by the famous Fort Union. The site of Fort Union is now being restored by the National Park Service.

28. This same area would later become known as the "All-Year Grazing Country" and the "Great Winter Grazing Region." See R. E. Strahorn, *To the Rockies and Beyond* (Omaha, 1879), p. 9.

the grizzly subsisted was not quite so abundant.[29] But the "white bear," although a dangerous nuisance that would torment the explorers for months, did not detract from the beauty and abundance of the Northwest, once again a garden, "one vast plain, intirely destitute of timber, but is apparently fertile, consisting of a dark rich mellow looking lome" (I, 357). The climate was remarkable; although a few light snows fell during the first few days of May, the explorers could still "behold the trees Green & flowers spred on the plain, & Snow an inch deep" (I, 361). It was a beautiful spring, and though the winds continued to blow and ice often formed on the cooking utensils during the nights, by May 4, near the mouth of the Milk River, the few remaining pockets of snow had disappeared and the open grassy plains showed the light green of spring in the High Plains.

After passing "one of the handsomest plains we have yet seen on the river" (II, 8), on May 8 the Corps of Discovery came to the mouth of the river that they named the Milk after the color of its waters, laden with the grey-brown prairie soils washed by spring rains into its current. The Milk River lay 2,090 miles up the Missouri from the Mississippi and 490 miles upstream from Fort Mandan, close enough to the distance estimate provided by the natives at the winter camp so that both captains were "willing to believe that this is the River the Minitarres call the river which Scolds at all others" (II, 13).[30] This stream, by far the largest northern tributary of the Missouri, was a critical landmark. Finding it where they did, the captains were further assured that the Indian lore with which they had left the Mandan villages was accurate. It was probably the river which the natives had described to them as heading with the southern waters of the Saskatchewan, a description which they had applied to their partly mythical White Earth. But the description applied equally well to the Milk, and, ever optimistic of finding a route to the waters north of the 49th parallel, Lewis and Clark reported that the Milk watered a "large extent of country" and that it might have its sources near those of the Saskatchewan.

Their view of the course and size of the Milk was accurate,[31] but Lewis's opinion that the river "might furnish a practicable and advantageous communication with the Saskashiwan river" (II, 9) was more illustrative of faith and optimism than it was of reality. According to the delineation of the northern waters of the Missouri on the King and Arrowsmith maps and on Clark's Fort Mandan chart, the captains must also have been aware of the possibility that the Milk might provide a connection to the Columbia as well, via the Great Lake River which entered the "Tacoutche-Tesse" or Columbia after flowing a short course west from the vicinity of the sources of the Missouri's northern feeder streams. But the Indians had told them nothing of a potential route in this direction, and since their information had proved to be

29. Cutright, *Lewis and Clark*, pp. 140–42.
30. See n. 25, ch. 9 above.
31. Coues, *History*, I, 301.

reliable thus far, a better chance for the passage across the mountains should be gained by following the Minitaris' specific directions, traveling up the Missouri past the Falls, the Three Forks, and to the very westernmost source of the river.

6

The character of the Missouri above the Milk River changed rather abruptly, as did the nature of the country through which it flowed. Navigation was still relatively easy, and in spite of the fact that the river was almost as wide as it had been where the expedition, after crossing the Mississippi's spring flood, had entered it, it was much shallower than it had been below, and its waters were clearing. Both these signs were interpreted by the captains as evidence that they need not despair of "ever reaching its source," and they began "to feel extremely anxious to get in view of the rocky mountains" (II, 17). The new and different landscapes that Lewis and Clark began to observe along the river led them to believe that they were, indeed, "fast approaching a hilly or mountainous country" (II, 20). The herds of mule deer increased in size,[32] the party began to encounter large numbers of "Bighorned anamals" or Rocky Mountain sheep, and the bluffs and cliffs along the Missouri grew more precipitous and spectacular.

The "hilly and mountainous country" was not the desired Rockies, however, but rather the lower reaches of the incredibly beautiful Breaks of the Missouri, rugged and colorful country where the marvelously carved bluffs close in upon the river on both sides and create a landscape of pure delight.[33] And in any case, the captains' desire to see the Rockies was founded more on wishful thinking than on the geographical lore in their possession. They knew from the Minitari lore that more than 200 miles of country lay between the Milk or "Scolding" River and the Missouri's Great Falls, where the first chain of mountains was said to begin,[34] and none of the data in the explorers' possession mentioned any mountain ranges between the Great Bend and the Great Falls. The Indian lore had been reinforced repeatedly during the first month of the journey from the Mandan villages, and since neither of the captains had any reason to doubt that data or to expect to encounter mountains along this stretch of the river, the expressed anxiety "to get in view" of the Rockies was literary license on the part of the journalist (Lewis) and not an indication of an actual belief in the proximity of the mountains.

32. The presence of the mule deer was important as the explorers "rarely found the mule deer in any except a rough country" (II, 20).

33. Bernard DeVoto (*Course of Empire*, p. 476) has written: "In the Journals [of Lewis and Clark] almost for the first time the word 'beautiful' means something other than fine country for settlement."

34. Clark's distance estimates postulated 240 miles between the mouth of the Milk River and the Great Falls (VI, 60).

Because of the firmness of their ideas regarding the location of the first range of the Rockies, the captains were somewhat confused when, on May 19, Clark climbed a hill on the north side of the Missouri and, looking toward the west, saw "a high mountain in a westerly direction, bearing S.SW. about 40 or 50 miles distant" (II, 50).[35] It was possible that this range on the western horizon was the first range spoken of by the Indians at Fort Mandan. If so, the captains' distance calculations were off by more than 100 miles, and the Great Falls of the Missouri would be reached very shortly. From his vantage point above the Missouri, however, Clark had seen not only the "high mountain" but had also glimpsed the mouth of a river entering the Missouri from the south. The Party reached the mouth of that river just before noon on the following day, and, comparing their own distance calculations for the length of their upriver journey to this point with the Indian-provided lore, the captains entertained little doubt that this river was the one "called by the Minnetarees the [blank space] or Muscleshell River" (II, 51), and that, therefore, a goodly distance remained between their present location and the Great Falls.

The Musselshell River, according to the Indian lore, headed near the Yellowstone River in the first chain of the Rockies and then flowed through a country that was "pretty well timbered . . . and intersperced with handsome fertile plains and medows" (II, 51). But Lewis and Clark had learned to interpret the Indian-given data a little more precisely, and since the country through which the Missouri was flowing was increasingly more arid, Lewis put forth the opinion that the timbered country of which the Indians had spoken was "similar to that we have passed for a day or two . . . which consists of nothing more than a few scattering small scrubby pine and dwarf cedar on the summits of some of the highest hills nine tenths of the country being wholy destitute of timber of any kind, covered with a short grass, arromatic herbs and the prickley pear" (II, 51). In the mind's eye of the American explorers, accustomed to humid woodlands, the presence of forested lands meant abundant precipitation, and if one generalization could be made about the climate of the country between the Great Bend and the beginning of the Breaks country it was that precipitation was anything but abundant.

It was not until the middle of May that the party experienced "the first shower that deserves the appellation of *rain*, which we have seen since we left Fort Mandan" (VI, 190).[36] The lack of rainfall also diminished the num-

35. A note on the manner in which the captains gave their compass reading is necessary for an interpretation of the bearing transcribed in their journals. Clark described the compass bearing correctly—his reading refers to the azimuth from the point of the observer to the point observed. Lewis, on the other hand, used the terms "bearing" or "bore" to refer to the directional alignment of the topographical feature observed. Thus, a mountain range that Lewis might have described as bearing 65° west of north had a directional alignment from southeast to northwest—but did not necessarily lie to the northwest of the observer.

36. Foreshadowing the Great American Desert myth of the 1830s and 1840s, Brackenridge (*Views of Louisiana*, p. 33) apparently used some of Lewis's and Clark's manuscript notes in describing the lack of rainfall in this area as "another amongst the impediments to the settlement of that vast waste."

bers of springs, a natural feature of the humid east, and both captains noted that "a fountain in this plain country is a great novelty" (II, 52) and that what few springs did exist were "impregnated with the salts which abound in this country" (II, 52). The constant winds carried fine dust which so enveloped the men that they "could neither cook, eat, nor sleep" (II, 57). The "scantey proportion" of vegetation on the hills along the river "would indicate no great fertility" (II, 59), and game was not as abundant as below. The desert that was part of the late nineteenth-century Spanish Louisianan conception of the western interior was coming true for the American explorers.[37]

7

The range of mountains which Clark had first seen on May 19 (the Little Rocky Mountains) remained in sight for several days beyond the mouth of the Musselshell; Lewis thought that they were only about 15 miles distant but "the air is so pure in this open country that mountains and other elivated objects appear much nearer than they really are" (II, 68). The captains gave the name of "North Mountain" to this first range; on May 24 a second range was sighted (the Judith and Moccasin ranges near Lewistown, Montana) south of the river, and to this range was given the appellation of "South Mountain" (II, 68). The next day, following a walk along the higher portions of the Missouri bluffs, Clark noted that he had seen mountains on both sides of the river (the Little Rocky Mountains and the Bearpaws on the north, the Judith and Moccasin ranges on the south). After observing that "those mountains appeared to be detached, and not ranges as laid down by the Minnetarees" (II, 77), the captains invented geography to match their preconceived image based on Indian lore and to rationalize the presence of mountains where there should be none.

The mountains that Lewis and Clark were viewing were not the Rockies of the Fort Mandan lore since they were neither connected chains nor, according to the captains' distance calculations, close enough to the Falls of the Missouri. Therefore, wrote Lewis,

the high country in which we are at present and have been passing for some days I take to be a continuation of what the Indians as well as the French Engages call the Black hills. This tract of country so called consists of a collection of high broken and irregular hills and short chain[s] of mountains sometimes 120 miles in width and again becoming much narrower, but always much higher than the country on either side; they commence about the head of the Kanzas river and to

37. The reports of Lewis and Clark were far less effective in shaping the desert myth than the reports of later observers, however. Richard Dillon, in "Stephen Long's Great American Desert," *Proceedings of the American Philosophical Society*, CXI (1967), pp. 93–108, has written that "the concept of the Great American Desert—largely, but not entirely, a myth—had to wait for less talented explorers and cartographers than Lewis and his able executive officer, William Clark."

the West of that river near the Arkansas, from whence they take their course a little to the W. of N.W. approaching the rockey Mountains obliquely, passing the river platte above the forks and intercepting the Yellowstone river near the bigbend and passing the Missouri at this place and probably continuing to swell the country as far North as the Saskashawan river. tho' they are lower here than they are discribed to the Sth. and may therefore probably terminate before they reach the Suskashawan. the black hills in their course no[r]thwardly appear to approach more nearly to the Rocky Mountains [II, 67].

This deduction fit not only the supposed geography as laid down on Clark's Fort Mandan map but also balanced that geography with the reality of the rugged Missouri Breaks and the detached, outlying ranges of north central Montana.

Clark had observed more than just detached ranges on May 25, however, and in addition to the view of the North and South mountains, he thought he had seen "a range of high Mounts. at a great distance to the S.W. but am not certain as the horozon was not clear enough to view it with certainty" (II, 77). A better sighting was made the following day when Lewis, intrigued by Clark's report of the distant mountain range, went on shore and from the summit of one of the highest bluffs along the river "beheld the Rocky Mountains for the first time" (II, 79):

I could only discover a few of the most elivated points above the horizon, the most remarkable of which by my pocket compass I found bore N.65° W. being a little to the N. of the N.W. extremity of the range of broken mountains seen this morning by Capt. C. these points of the Rocky Mountains were covered with snow and the sun shone on it in such manner as to give me the most plain and satisfactory view. while I viewed these mountains I felt a secret pleasure in finding myself so near the head of the heretofore conceived boundless Missouri [II, 79].

Lewis was seeing the Highwood Mountains, east of Great Falls, Montana,[38] and although he knew full well that he was not really that near the head of the Missouri, the distant range represented the "unconnected chain" which the Minitaris had described to him and Clark as beginning near the Great Falls. The observation of this chain reconfirmed, in the captains' minds, their earlier conjecture that the broken country and detached mountains they had been passing through were truly "a continuation of the black hills" (II, 80). The expedition had already traveled nearly 800 miles by river since leaving Fort Mandan, and the captains' view of the distant ranges to the southwest, coupled with their deduction that the northern portions of the Black Mountains (through which they assumed they were passing) approached the Rockies closely and their interpretations of the Minitari distance estimates, led

38. In his magnificently edited condensation of the journals, Bernard DeVoto identified the range seen on May 26 as the Little Rocky Mountains. This is a rare error by DeVoto and stems from a misinterpretation of the captains' methods of giving compass bearings. The Little Rocky Mountains are northeast of the point of Lewis's observation on May 26 and could not have been the mountains whose peaks were visible to the west.

them to the conclusion that the Rockies and the Great Falls could not be too far away.[39]

8

From the first sighting of the outlying ranges of the Little Rocky Mountains and the Bearpaws and the entry of the expedition into the heart of the Breaks country, progress upriver had been tedious and tiring. For hours at a time the party was compelled to beach their craft, waiting for the wind to stop blowing. The river became more and more choked with shoals and sandbars, and the rocks of the bluffs closed in on either side, making the towing of the boats by lines an extremely fatiguing and hazardous operation. The perceived barren nature of the landscape did little to relieve the oppression. Lewis considered much of the country beyond the mouth of the Musselshell River a "desert barren country" (II, 80), while Clark noted that "this Countrey may with propriety I think be termed the Deserts of America, as I do not conceive any part can ever be settled, as it is deficient in water, Timber, & too steep to be tilled" (II, 84). The element of the Desert had crept into the image of the Garden.[40]

Barrenness notwithstanding, the scenery was still beautiful to the explorers. The color of the bluffs was otherworldly and the structure of the river cliffs themselves was awe-inspiring. Writing about the landscapes of the upper Missouri, Jefferson, without having seen them, spoke of "multitudes of antique towers,"[41] and Lewis went his sponsor one better by describing the "seens of visionary inchantment" proffered by the Breaks landscape:

The hills and river Clifts which we passed today exhibit a most romantic appearance. The bluffs of the river rise to the hight of from 2 to 300 feet and in most places nearly preperdicular; they are formed of remarkable white sandstone which is sufficiently soft to give way readily to the impression of water; two or three thin horizontal stratas of white freestone, on which the rains or water make no impression, lie imbeded in these clifts of soft stone near the upper part of them; the earth on the top of these Clifts is a dark rich loam, which forming a gradualy

39. During the winter at Fort Mandan, Clark had learned that "from the best information, the Great Falls is about (800) miles nearly West" (I, 246).

40. Clark was apparently the first to formalize the description into the "Deserts of America," but the formalization did not hold as it was not included in the first official edition of the journals published in 1814. It was not until the publication of Edwin James's account of the Stephen Long Expedition that the "Great American Desert" became a part of the national geographical vocabulary. See Edwin James, *Account of an Expedition from Pittsburgh to the Rocky Mountains* (2 vols., Philadelphia, 1823), II, 350.

41. John Bradbury (*Travels in the Interior of America*, p. 241) explained the broken country near the mountains as the result of increasing elevation which "gives an increased velocity to the currents of water, and produces a more powerful attrition on their beds. The consequence is, the valleys in that part are deeper, and the surface more rugged and broken." The explanation is basically accurate.

ascending plain extends back from ½ a mile to a mile where the hills commence and rise abruptly to the hight of about 300 feet more. The water in the course of time in decending from those hills and plains on either side of the river has trickled down the soft sand clifts and woarn it into a thousand grotesque figures, which with the help of a little immagination and an oblique view, at a distance are made to represent eligant ranges of lofty freestone buildings, having their parapets well stocked with statuary; collumns of various sculpture both grooved and plain, are also seen supporting long galleries in front of those buildings; in other places on a much nearer approach and with the help of less immagination we see the remains or ruins of eligant buildings; some collumns standing and almost entire with their pedestals and capitals; others retaining their pedestals but deprived by time or accident of their capitals, some lying prostrate and broken others in the form of vast pyramids of conic structure bearing a serees of other pyramids on their tops becoming less as they ascend and finally terminating in a sharp point [II, 100–101].

Lewis's prose was worthy of the landscape; never has a better description of the Breaks and their glory been penned. And not until John Wesley Powell, more than a half-century later, made his celebrated first trip down the Colorado River would any observer come so close to describing the landforming processes so characteristic of arid environments.[42]

These scenes of "visionary inchantment" were not to last, nor was the "desert barren country" to continue to dominate the captains' image of the western regions. After the expedition had passed the mouth of the unexpected Judith River, not provided for in the Indian lore, the country began to change gradually. By the end of May, the hills had receded from the river and the country again became fertile, with wide and level plains extending to the horizon, the view broken only by various detached ranges. "These appearances were quite reviving after the drairy country through which we had been passing" (II, 88), wrote Lewis. Anticipation ran high as the captains discerned that their force had now passed "completely above the black hills" (II, 109), and that, judging from their distance calculations and the proximity of the mountain range (the Highwoods) which they were now fully convinced was the "unconnected" range the Minitaris had spoken of, the Great Falls of the Missouri could not be any great distance away.

9

Before reaching the Great Falls, however, the Lewis and Clark Expedition encountered one of the greatest obstacles in the course of their two-year journey, a problem that they would spend more than a week in solving completely. In the late afternoon of June 2, the party came to and camped in a

42. See Wallace Stegner, ed., *Powell Report on the Lands of the Arid Regions of the United States* (Cambridge, Mass., 1962).

grove of small cottonwoods on the Missouri's left bank, opposite the mouth of a "very considerable river" which entered the Missouri from the north and almost equaled it in size.[43] This river was the Marias, and its presence was puzzling. In the explorers' store of geographical information there was agreement that the Missouri had only one major northern tributary. That was "the river which scolds at all others," and they had passed the river fitting that description more than three weeks before. What, then, was to be made of this second northern river? Or, if the northern branch were the true Missouri, what was to be made of the southern branch? Their information contained no account of a large southern tributary stream above the mouth of the Yellowstone.

The true Missouri was the river, according to their conceptions of western geography, that had its sources within portaging distance of the navigable waters of the Columbia River. It was, therefore, the river that must be followed to its uppermost reaches if the Passage to India were to be found. But the unexpected division of the Missouri into two streams of nearly equal size necessitated a major decision: "which of these rivers was the Missouri, or that river which the Minetares call *Amahte Arz-zha* or Missouri, and which they had described to us as approaching very near to the Columbia river?" (II, 112–13). For the purpose of answering this question, the party crossed the Missouri below the junction early on the morning of June 3 and "formed a camp on the point formed by the junction of the two large rivers" (II, 112). Here the decision that would determine the success or failure of the entire enterprise would be made:

to mistake the stream at this period of the season, two months of the traveling season having now elapsed, and to ascend such stream to the rocky Mountain or perhaps much further before we could inform ourselves whether it did approach the Columbia or not, and then be obliged to return and take the other stream would not only loose us the whole of this season but would probably so dishearten the party that it might defeat the expedition altogether. convinced we were that the utmost circumspection and caution was necessary in deciding on the stream to be taken (III, 113).

The process of making this critical decision was not a simple one based on field observation alone, nor was the decision itself just a lucky guess. Instead, the decision-making procedure was a complex and well-calculated series of operations lasting more than a week. The captains had come across the first major disjunction between the geography of reality and the image shaped during the previous winter, and their field operations and behavior reflected their recognition of that disjunction.

43. Once again the explorers were viewing a river in flood stage and were misled into thinking that the Marias was a bigger river than it actually was. It would appear that the moisture conditions during the winter of 1804–05 and the spring of 1805 were above normal (Lawson, "A Dendroclimatological Interpretation," fig. 3).

10

On the first day at the junction, the captains decided to make a preliminary investigation of the width, depth, and speed of flow of the two rivers in
order to determine which was the major stream. To this end they sent a light
canoe manned by three men up each branch. In an attempt to get some kind
of long-range bearing on the direction from which the two forks came, they
also sent several small parties by land to travel as far as possible and still
return by nightfall (fig. 34). Meanwhile, the captains themselves remained at
the campsite between the two rivers and made observations in the immediate
area. During the morning they strolled to the highest ground between the
Missouri and Marias and from this observation point had what Lewis termed
an "inchanting view" of the Highwood Mountains and, beyond them, of the
Little Belt and Big Belt ranges, which from this distance and angle appeared
to be one single chain:

to the South we saw a range of lofty mountains which we supposed to be a continuation of the S. Mountains, stretching themselves from S.E. to N.W. terminating
abruptly about S.West from us; these were partially covered with snow; behind these Mountains and at a great distance, a second and more lofty range of
mountains appeared to stretch across the country in the same direction with the
others, reaching from West, to the N. of N.W., where their snowey tops lost
themselves beneath the horizon. this last range was perfectly covered with snow
[II, 113–14].

But although the view was sublime, it was inconclusive. Little could be
learned about the courses of the rivers, their channels being obscured by the
convolutions of the countryside.

From the high ground the captains wandered down into the lovely
little valley of the Teton River,[44] through chokecherry and gooseberry and
wild rose, thence back to the junction of the Missouri and Marias. Here they
examined the nature of the two main rivers more closely:

we took the width of the two rivers, found the left hand or S. fork 372 yards and
the N. fork 200. The no[r]th fork is deeper than the other but it's courant not so
swift; it's waters run in the same boiling and roling manner which has uniformly
characterized the Missouri throughout it's whole course so far; it's waters are of a
whitish brown colour very thick and terbid, also characteristic of the Missouri;
while the South fork is perfectly transparent runds very rappid but with a smoth
unriffled surface it's bottom composed of round and flat smooth stones like most
rivers issuing from a mountainous country. the bed of the N. fork composed of
some gravel but principally mud [II, 114].

"In short," wrote Lewis, "the air and character of this river [the Marias] is so

44. The explorers named this river the "Tanzey" after the quantities of a shrub of the
same name that Clark found growing in its bottoms. A detailed discussion of Lewis and Clark
at the Missouri-Marias junction may be found in John L. Allen, "Lewis and Clark on the
Upper Missouri: Decision at the Marias," *Montana, the Magazine of Western History,* XXI
(Summer, 1971), 2–17.

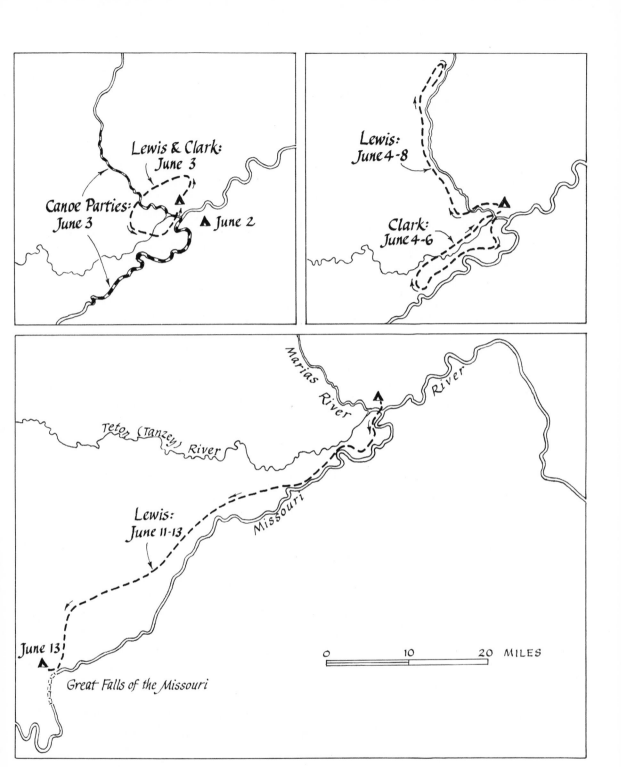

34. The decision at the Marias: map showing the routes of Lewis and Clark,
June 3–12, 1805, in their field reconnaissance around the Missouri-Marias junction

precisely that of the Missouri below that the party with very few exceptions have already pronounced the N. fork to be the Missouri."

But at this point, sometime in the afternoon of June 3, Lewis and Clark showed their competence as field observers and anlyzers of geographical information and made the initial assessment that further study would prove to be correct. "If we were to give our opinions I believe we should be in the minority," noted Lewis; nevertheless, in the captains' considered opinion the southern river was the one the Indians had described to them as approaching the waters of the Columbia. The limited and brief reconnaissance undertaken that morning was responsible for this tentative conclusion. But the conclusion was possible only because the things observed during the morning's field work were analyzed in the light of what were, to Lewis and Clark, the "known" geographical facts.

When the captains returned from their reconnaissance of the morning of June 3, they returned with a perspective that was crucial for their decision. From the height-of-land separating the Missouri and Marias they had not been able to see the course of either river beyond the junction—but they had seen mountain ranges to the south and southwest. The nearest range of mountains (the Highwoods) had been in view for over a week and was probably not, by this time, considered to be the first range of the Rockies that was believed to begin near the Great Falls. But behind these ranges, to the south and southwest and at a great distance, the lofty snow-covered peaks of the Little Belt and Big Belt mountains were visible, and these might well have seemed to be the range near the Falls. If so, and if the southern branch continued its southwesterly trend above the junction, then it was the river which lay in the proper geographical relationship with the mountains and was, consequently, the river leading to Columbian waters.

Furthermore, their examination of the characteristics of the rivers upon their return to the base camp at the junction had shown the waters of the southern fork to be transparent, running over a bottom of round and flat smooth stones. It was "like most rivers issuing from a mountainous country," and the true Missouri, according to the captains' image, ran through mountains for a considerable distance from its source, all the way to its entrance into the plains at the Great Falls. The northern fork, their examination showed, was a muddy and silty river, and although it was very similar to the Missouri below the junction, Lewis and Clark were inclined to view it only as a tributary stream. It might well have been part of the drainage system indicated in their re-evaluation of the Arrowsmith map during the previous winter[45] and probably passed through the plains north of the Missouri without penetrating the mountains far enough to interlock with the Columbia.

45. "We did take the liberty," noted Lewis, "of placing his [Fidler's] discoveries or at least the Southern extremity of them about a degree further N. in the sket[c]h which we sent on to the government this spring mearly from the Indian information of the bearing from Fort Mandan of the entrance of the Missouri into the Rocky Mountains, and I reather suspect that actual observation will take him at least one other degree further North" (II, 132).

On the evening of June 3 Lewis wrote: "I am confident that this river [the Marias] rises in and passes a great distance through an open plain country. . . . convinced I am that if it penetrated the Rocky Mountains to any great distance it's waters would be clearer unless it should run an immence distance indeed after leaving those mountains through these level plains in order to acquire it's turbid hue" (II, 114–15). The river whose transparent waters flowed from the southwest, from the mountains, was probably the Missouri and therefore the proper route to the Pacific. But this assumption was only tentative. The parties that had been sent by land and water up both branches had returned with no conclusive information, and the captains were still puzzled by the failure of their Indian informants to mention the junction of the Missouri and a large tributary stream.[46] Furthermore, it is apparent, from the tone of the captains' journals for June 3, that they were the only members of the party who did not adhere to the belief that the northern fork, because of its similarities with the Missouri below, was the proper river to follow.

Two factors played a role in shaping the events of the week to follow. First, Lewis and Clark were good enough officers to realize the potential deterioration of their command situation should they go against the opinions of their men—some of whom were trained wilderness experts and rivermen—and then be proved wrong. And second, although the captains might have been firm in the belief that the lefthand fork was the Missouri and had the geographical evidence to support this view, they were too competent not to recognize the tactical dangers of a hasty decision without more definite proof of their preliminary assessment. Accordingly, it was concluded that each officer should take a small party and "ascend these rivers untill we could perfectly satisfy ourselves of the one, which it would be most expedient for us to take on our main journey to the Pacific" (II, 116).

II

On the cool and cloudy morning of June 4, Captains Lewis and Clark departed from the camp at the junction of the Missouri and Marias rivers. Clark and a party of five men set out up the righthand side of the Missouri, keeping to the higher lands well back from the river in an attempt to get the best views possible. By the end of a rainy afternoon they had traveled

46. "What astonishes us a little is that the Indians who appeared to be so well acquainted with the geography of this country should not have mentioned this river" (II, 115). There are two possible explanations for the failure of the Indians to mention the Marias: (1) the natives did describe the river but the distortions inherent in the information transmission caused Lewis and Clark to combine Indian data on the Missouri's two major northern tributaries (the Milk and the Marias) into one river; or (2) the delineation of the Indian "war path to the mountains" as laid down by Clark on his Fort Mandan map is well south of the Missouri and the Indians may not have described the Marias because they were not familiar with it.

nearly 30 miles and made camp in an abandoned Indian shelter somewhere near the later site of Fort Benton.[47] Except for an encounter with a couple of grizzlies, the small party spent an uneventful night alongside the Missouri, the waters of which continued to run transparently over a gravelly bed. It rained and snowed intermittently throughout the night, and when the party prepared to break camp on the morning of June 5, they noted considerable amounts of snow on the mountains southeast of their campsite (the Highwoods). By around noon they had come in sight of other snow-covered mountains to the southwest (the Little Belts and Big Belts), and Clark had seen enough to convince him that the river they were following was the true Missouri.

From a ridge high above the river, Clark could see its waters running deep and swift and coming from the southwest, from those mountains that he assumed to be those near the Falls. To proceed any further would be useless, and Clark and his men struck out overland for the main camp at the junction, reaching the Teton River in the late afternoon and making camp in its valley. At five o'clock on the next afternoon, June 6, the party led by Clark arrived at the junction of the Missouri and Marias, where they expected to find Lewis waiting for them.

But Lewis was taking a little bit longer to reach a firm conclusion. He and his party of six men had crossed the Marias from the camp at the junction on the morning of June 4 and had proceeded on foot up that river along its right bank. At a distance of about 5 miles from the main camp, Lewis climbed a hill from which he viewed the "North Mountains" (the Bearpaws) lying toward the northeast and saw the northwesterly trend of the Marias. To the northwest, along the course of the river he was following, he could see nothing but a range of hills, and since this view was inconclusive he determined to proceed farther. The river continued its course to the north and west, and for the remainder of the day Lewis and his party traveled through the plains behind the river bluffs and, when the ravines grew too steep and numerous, along the bottomlands of the Marias. The evening encampment was made amidst clumps of willows, which provided protection against the wind but did little to keep out the rain that continued to fall most of the night.

The men awoke cold and wet on the morning of June 5 and broke camp early, hoping to keep warmer by walking. The river kept to its north-by-west direction and before noon had led the party to a site from which they could see a high mountain (the main peak of the Sweetgrass Hills on the Montana-Alberta border) toward the northwest and at a great distance. Late afternoon brought them in sight of still more mountains (the other peaks of the Sweetgrass Hills) in the northwest; here they made camp in a grove of cottonwoods, and the ever-inquisitive Lewis experimented by roasting some prairie dogs for supper. He found them "well flavored and tender" (II, 124).

47. Coues, *History*, II, 354, n. 3.

Had it not been for his systematic method of observation and analysis, the view of the mountains to the northwest could have led Lewis to the erroneous conclusion that this range was the one represented as starting near the Great Falls, and that this northern river was therefore the Missouri. But the mountains were, Lewis perceived, at least 80 or 100 miles away, too distant to have been the ranges near the Falls; according to the captains' mileage calculations, the Falls could not be very far above the junction on whichever river was the true Missouri. Also, the course of the river that Lewis was following ran so far north that it, in his thinking, must have drained a vast plains area and be part of the northern waters of the Missouri as shown on his and Clark's reinterpretations of the data from the Arrowsmith map. By the morning of June 6 Lewis had become "well convinced that this branch of the Missouri had it's direction too much to the North for our route to the Pacific" (II, 125) and determined, therefore, to return to the main camp.

While Lewis and four of his men engaged themselves in constructing rafts to descend the Marias, two others traveled farther up the river in order to get a more precise bearing on its course. They returned around noon with the report that the river did continue its northerly course as far as they could see, and after lunching on elk killed the night before, the small force embarked on their two clumsily constructed rafts for the mouth of the Marias. But attempted navigation of the Marias was unsuccessful, and the rafts were soon abandoned for a less comfortable but more secure land route.[48] This took them along the river bottoms where possible and across the exposed plains, which offered little protection from the wind and rain that began soon after they left the rafts and continued through the afternoon and evening.

After a night spent in an unsheltered spot, Lewis and his cold, exhausted men broke camp early and resumed their trek across plains grown slippery and treacherous from the prolonged rains. On the evening of June 7 they bivouacked comfortably in an old Indian shelter and resumed their return journey to the main camp on the cloudy and cool morning that followed. By ten o'clock on the morning of June 8 the clouds had broken under a warming spring sun, and as the weather improved so did Lewis's spirits as the party passed through "one of the most beautifully picteresque countries I ever beheld" (II, 131). But he had little else to be enthusiastic about, for although he had fully concluded that the Marias was neither "the main stream, nor that which it would be advisable for us to take" and gave it the name it now bears, the whole of his party was "fully persuaided that this river was the Missouri"

48. There was an underlying motive for the attempt at navigation. Although Lewis had concluded that the Marias was not the Missouri, it was "a noble river; one destined to become in my opinion an object of contention between the two great powers of America and Great Britain with respict to the adjustment of the Northwestwardly boundary of the former; and that it will become one of the most interesting branches of the Missouri in a commercial point of view" (II, 131). Like the Milk, the Marias might drain the rich fur country of the Saskatchewan, and if it were navigable then so much the better. The idea was intriguing enough to cause Lewis to return to the Marias during the homeward journey of 1806 and investigate it further.

(II, 130). This was a potentially serious problem and one that he and Clark would have to work out when, at five o'clock on the afternoon of June 8, the two captains were reunited at the junction of the Missouri and the river that was now officially the Marias.

12

While Lewis and his men relaxed with a "drink of grog" during the evening of June 8, Clark began plotting the courses of the two rivers as far as he and Lewis had ascended them. Looking at the crude charts, both captains were more convinced than ever that their initial supposition about which stream was the Missouri was correct. They also came to the conclusion that they had been fully justified in making corrections in the Arrowsmith map during the winter at Fort Mandan. In his journal for June 8, Lewis wrote:

I now began more than ever to suspect the varacity of Mr. Fidler[49] or the correctness of his instruments. . . . we are now within a hundred miles of the Rocky Mountains, and I find from my observations of the 3rd. Inst that the latitude of this place is 47°.24′12″.8. the river must therefore turn much to the South between this place and the rocky Mountains to have permitted Mr. Fidler to have passed along the Eastern border of these mountains as far S. as nearly 45° without even seeing it. but from hence as far as Capt. C. had ascended the S. fork or Missouri being the distance of 55 (45 miles in straight line) Milles it's course is S. 29°W. and it still appeared to bear considerably to the W. of South as far as he could see it. I think therefore that we shall find that the Missouri enters the rocky mountains to the North of 45° [II, 131–32].

Analysis of the geographical data derived from all sources, including the captains' own separate field reconnaissances, continued on June 9 and further settled in the minds of Lewis and Clark "the propryety of addopting the South fork for the Missouri, as that which it would be expedient for us to take" (II, 134). The captains determined that the Arrowsmith map, incorrect as it was, provided a strong argument against the north branch or Marias as the true Missouri. Even if Arrowsmith's informant, Fidler, had penetrated as far south as the 47th parallel and had seen only small streams running east, then the presumption was that "those little streams do not penetrate the rocky mountains to such distance as would afford rational grownds for a conjecture that they had their sources near any navigable branch of the

49. From the discoveries of Fidler, Arrowsmith had "laid down a remarkable mountain in the chain of the Rocky mountains called the tooth nearly as South as Latitude 45°" (II, 132). Clark's Fort Mandan map had moved this mountain north of the Missouri to the 48th parallel. When Lewis saw the Sweetgrass Hills, he probably believed them to be the "tooth" mountain, further confirmation of the correctness of his and Clark's revisions of Arrowsmith.

Columbia" (II, 134–35). This eliminated the Marias from consideration as the true Missouri or route to the Pacific.[50]

On the other hand, the Indian information obtained during the previous winter, combined with the Mackay journal and the Evans map, argued strongly in favor of the southern branch:

they [the Mintaris] informed us that the water of the Missouri was nearly transparent at the great falls, this is the case with the water of the South fork; that the falls lay a little to the South of sunset from them; this is also probable as we are only a few minutes [of latitude] North of Fort Mandan and the South fork bears considerably South from hence to the Mountains; that the falls are below the rocky mountains and near the No[r]thern termineation of one range of those Mountains. a range of mountains [the Little and Big Belt ranges] which apear behind the S. mountains [the Highwoods] which appear to terminate S.W. from this place and on this side of the unbroken chain of the Rocky Mountains gives us hope that this part of their information is also correct, and there is sufficient distance between this and the mountains for many and I fear for us much too many falls. another impression on my mind is that if the Indians had passed any stream as large as the South fork on their way to the Missouri that they would not have omitted mentioning it;[51] and the South fork from it's size and complexion of it's waters must enter the Ry. Mountains and in my opinion penetrates them to a great distance, or els whence such an immence body of water as it discharges; it cannot procede from the dry plains to the N.W. of the Yellow Stone river on the East side of the Rocky Mountains for those numberous large dry channels which we witnessed on that side as we ascended the Missouri forbid such a conjecture; and that it should take it's sources to the N.W. under those mountains the travels of Mr. Fidler fo[r]bid us to believe [II, 135–36].

This was a brilliant piece of deduction from a fuzzy set of facts and illustrates, as well as any other even during the course of the expedition, the competence and intelligence of its commanders.

13

Investigation had borne out the tentative conclusion made by Lewis and Clark on the very first day at the junction, but as before the men remained obdurate in their belief that the northern branch was the true Missouri. The captains tried to impress their geographical concepts and reasoning on the

50. The Marias might have provided a shorter route than the one they eventually followed. By crossing the Continental Divide at Marias Pass, they would have dropped into the Flathead Lake country, draining into the Clark Fork of the Columbia (Coues, *History*, I, 350, n. 38). This route was later that of the Great Northern Railroad (Issac I. Stevens, "Narrative and Final Report of Explorations for a Route for a Pacific Railroad near the Forty-seventh and Forty-ninth Parallels of North Latitude from St. Paul to Puget Sound," *Pacific Railroad Reports*, XII, House and Senate Document series).

51. See my n. 46 above.

men, but Peter Cruzatte, an old Missouri hand and the party's most expert riverman, "had acquired the confidence of every individual of the party [and] declared it as his opinion that the N. fork was the true genuine Missouri and could be no other" (II, 136). The situation was delicate even though discipline had been remarkably good on the trek from the Mandan villages to the Missouri-Marias junction. The men "were ready to follow us any wher we thought proper to direct" (II, 136), noted Lewis, but no good field officer could have failed to recognize the seeds of a possible breakdown in command. "Finding them so determined in this belief," wrote Lewis, "and wishing that if we were in an error to be able to detect it and rectify it as soon as possible it was agreed between Capt. C. and myself that one of us should set out with a small party by land up the South fork and continue our rout up it untill we found the falls or reached the snowy Mountains by which mean we should be enabled to determine this question prety accurately" (II, 136). This decision to split the party again does not indicate the captains' lack of assurance in their conclusions nearly as much as it indicates the necessity to maintain the confidence of their men.

The afternoon of June 9 was spent in making preparations for caching equipment prior to a departure from the junction, an operational decision necessitated by the captains' wish to increase their mobility and compensate for the delay. In the evening the party enjoyed a ration of grog distributed by the captains and danced and sang to the rhythms of Cruzatte's fiddle. June 10 was a fair, dry day and work on the cache continued. Although he was down with dysentery, Lewis decided that he and four men would depart from the camp early the following morning, leaving Clark and the remainder of the party to complete the cache and the repair of the canoes and then to follow Lewis by water up the lefthand fork. Hopefully, before Clark and the main body could proceed too far up the south fork, Lewis would have found the proof they all desired. At eight o'clock on the morning of June 11, Lewis and his men swung their packs onto their shoulders and proceeded along the right bank of the Missouri, following Clark's earlier route.

The march of that day was a short one, camp being made early when Lewis's illness grew too severe for him to proceed. But he healed himself with a concoction made from the bark of chokecherry bushes,[52] and by morning, feeling quite revived, he resumed the ascent of the Missouri. The route of June 12 carried Lewis and his party through level and open plains above the river, and after a side trip to the river for rest and refreshment during the morning, they reached a ridge of land considerably higher than the rest of the plains. From here they saw the "august spectacle" of the Little Belt and Big Belt ranges to the south and southwest, and Lewis's suspicions that they were

52. D. W. Will, "Lewis and Clark: Westering Physicians," *Montana, the Magazine of Western History*, XXI (Fall, 1971), 11.

nearing the Great Falls were confirmed. His party did not reach that vital landmark on the 12th, however, and camp was made before sunset in a clump of cottonwoods along the Missouri.

After breakfasting on venison and fish, Lewis and his small band again ascended the hills beyond the river and continued their travel across the open plains. When the river took a sharp bend to the south, Lewis, fearing that he would miss the Falls if he continued through the plains, altered his south-westerly course and headed directly for the river. About noon on June 13, Captain Meriwether Lewis found the proof he sought. After moving through a beautiful meadow above the Missouri, his ears were met with the sound of falling water and his eyes with a column of spray that rose like smoke above the plains. The roaring noise increased and became too great "to be mistaken for any cause short of the great falls of the Missouri" (II, 147). Lewis hurried down the hills to "gaze on this sublimely grand specticle," and from a position atop some rocks he came in sight of one of the great unknowns of the Northwest. Here at the Great Falls of the Missouri all the information he and Clark had collected, all the assumptions they had made, must have seemed correct. The presence of the Falls fulfilled Lewis's dreams and ambitions, and, unwilling to leave before having a look at what lay beyond the cataracts, he determined to make camp in the vicinity for the remainder of the afternoon and evening. His hunters killed buffalo during the afternoon while one of the men fished in the Missouri, and that evening they feasted sumptuously on buffalo hump and fresh trout.

The next morning Lewis dispatched a courier to Clark with a message headed elatedly "from the Great falls of the Missouri," and set out himself up the river to find the extent of the break in navigation created by the Falls. Cascade after cascade met his eyes, and, apparently not worrying about the difficulties the long and extensive rapids would place in the way of their progress toward the Passage, Lewis wrote glowingly of the views that presented themselves. He passed an eagle's nest which the Indians had told him lay near the upper end of the Falls (II, 159), and once beyond he climbed to the top of a hill and toward the south saw the Missouri's meandering course through wide and beautiful plains, flowing from the mountains that lay to the southwest. From the west came the "Medicine" or Sun River the Indians had described to him, and on the horizon was the first "connected" snow-clad chain of the Rockies. All the components of the image and of the Passage to India were there, and Lewis turned back to rejoin Clark and prepare for the glory that must be beyond. Their geographical lore had, they now believed, proved accurate; the Great Falls, the mountains, the "Medicine" River—all were as the captains had expected to find them. When, on June 16, Lewis and Clark met at the camp Clark had made at the base of the Falls in preparation for the portage around them, they must have been convinced that the easy passage across the Rockies would also be accomplished.

14

During the next few days, while Lewis remained at the camp near the base of the Falls to direct the unloading of the boats preparatory to the portage that both captains knew was necessary, Clark and a small party set out to survey the best portage route around the impassable rapids and cascades. The Indians at Fort Mandan had assured Lewis and Clark that the portage around the Falls was no longer than a half-mile (VI, 54), but here, as in the case of their failure to mention the Marias River, the Indian information broke down. Lewis had his first inkling of this when Clark did not return after the first day out surveying the portage, and when his companion had not returned by the morning of June 20, Lewis expressed his fears "that the portage is longer than we had calculated on" (II, 173). Late that evening Clark returned, and the descriptions and maps he presented confirmed those fears (fig. 35). The portage would be no easy half-mile carry but, in the captains' revised opinion, "the most perilous and difficuelt part of our Voyage" (II, 175).

While not the most perilous part of the journey perhaps, the portage was certainly one of the most difficult. From June 21 to July 14 the men of the expedition struggled over huge rocks and across steep slopes, hauling and pulling and pushing the heavy pirogues and the goods with which they had been loaded. Nor did the weather cooperate; violent thunderstorms and wind and hailstones "the size of pigions eggs" (VI, 193) hampered the efforts of the captains and their men. The surrounding mountains were covered with snow, so much snow that Clark thought they "might have derived their appelation of *Shineing Mountains*, from their glittering appearance when the sun shines in certain directions on the snow which cover them" (II, 176).[53] In every way the climate about the Falls of the Missouri appeared to be "Singular," with rain, snow, sleet, hail, and wind coming from all directions. Lewis correctly explained the unusual and highly variable climate in terms of interaction between the air masses lying over the mountains and those above the adjacent plains (II, 204). But both he and Clark were at a loss to explain the "rumbling like Cannon" which emanated from the mountains, blending mystery with the fury of the thunder and lightning.[54] But the mysterious rumblings and the fury of the storms were minor inconveniences when compared with the more concrete hardships of prickly pear cactus, which lacerated both moccasins and feet, clouds of mosquitos which the men were too busy to drive off during the day and too weary to evade at night, and the ever-present dangers of rattlesnakes, grizzly bears, and the rugged terrain itself.

The portage was barely a third completed when Lewis, chafing impa-

53. Carver and Mackenzie had penned almost the same description about the origin of the name "Shining Mountains."

54. "This phenomenon the philosophy of the engages readily accounts for; they state it to be the bursting of the rich mines of silver which these mountains contain" (II, 223).

35. Clark's field sketch of the Great
Falls and portage of the Missouri.
From *The Original Journals of the
Lewis and Clark Expedition*
(New York, 1904)

tiently at the unexpected delays posed by the Marias and the Falls, was forced to admit that the Passage might be less easy than so many earlier generations had believed and hoped. "Nearly three months have now elapsed since we left Fort Mandan and not yet reached the Rocky Mountains" (II, 200), he wrote, and because of the delays he realized that the original plans to reach the Pacific and return to the Mandans within one traveling season must necessarily be scrapped. This was an important operational decision, and it illustrated the growing ability of the captains to differentiate between the geography as it had been imagined during the previous winter and the geography as it actually was. The matter-of-fact way in which both Lewis and Clark took setbacks such as that presented by the Falls and the rational way in which they attempted to resolve the increasingly obvious disparities between what they expected to find and what they really found were at the very core of their exploratory genius.[55]

In spite of the disappointment and hardship of the month-long portage around the Falls, however, there was nothing to do but push onward, and optimism returned when the last loads were deposited in the portaged vessels on the upstream side of the last Missouri cascades. From a conspicuous eminence above the Missouri near the mouth of the Sun or "Medicine" River, Lewis had a fine view of the various ranges of the Rockies, stretching all around him and continuing, he believed, "probably to Mexico" (II, 229). He also saw the Missouri, and the direction from which it came seemed to match his and Clark's preconceptions—the passage to the Pacific once again seemed possible. It was delightful to be back on a gently flowing stream, and between the Sun River and the "first connected chain" of the Rockies the current of the river continued "gentle, bottoms low and extensive" (II, 236). But the pleasant scenery and navigable waters did not last long. On July 18, after passing the mouth of the Dearborn River,[56] the expedition entered the narrow gorge where a spur of the Big Belt Mountains confined the Missouri to a bare 150 yards in width. "From the singular appearance of this place," wrote Lewis, "I called it the *gates of the rocky mountains*" (II, 248).

55. Their skill becomes even more apparent when the nature of their field decisions and geographical analysis are compared with those of other explorers—for example, John Frémont on his fourth expedition (Goetzmann, *Exploration and Empire*, pp. 266–70).

56. Named for General Henry Dearborn, then secretary of war, the river would figure prominently in the return journey (Coues, *History*, II, 421, n. 9).

CHAPTER II

THE SEARCH
FOR THE PASSAGE

The Corps of Discovery had reached the Rocky Mountains and for the next three months would endeavor to untangle the mazes of those massive ranges, so different from all other mountains within the framework of early nineteenth-century American environmental experience and imagination. The wide and beautiful plains were no more, and Lewis and Clark and their command would struggle through nearly impossible terrain until they reached the Pacific slopes and the navigable waters of the Columbia system. In their search for the passage through the Rockies, Lewis and Clark would come to realize more and more the discrepancy between the image with which they had left Fort Mandan and the actuality of western geography.

The expedition had traveled all the way from the Mandan villages to the Gates of the Mountains using directions provided by the Minitaris. For the most part, the quality of that data had been confirmed and reinforced as the party passed the mouths of the Little Missouri, White Earth, Yellowstone, Milk, and Musselshell rivers, all located approximately where they should have been according to the Indian lore. The failure of the Indians to mention the outliers of the Rockies or to tell them about the Marias River had sown the seeds of disillusionment, however, and the captains had learned to be somewhat skeptical of their image based on the Fort Mandan data collection.

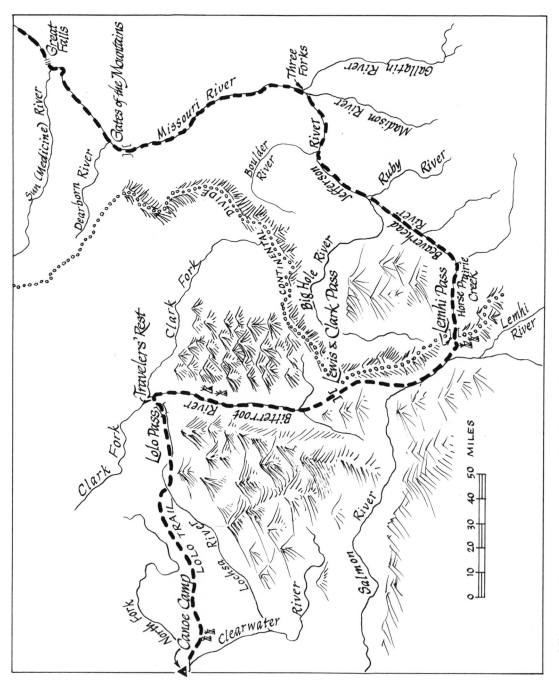

36. The route of the expedition from the Great Falls to the forks of the Clearwater, July 15 to October 7, 1805

Discovery of the Great Falls reconfirmed, for a time, the accuracy and reliability of the Minitaris' conceptions of western geography. But the portage that the men were forced to make around those cascades bore little resemblance to the natives' descriptions, and although the river above the Falls lay in the proper geographic relationship to the mountains (the captains viewed the Big Belt range as the first "connected" chain of the Rockies), the direction of the river itself was not as they had anticipated. Additionally, the mountains that hemmed the Missouri in on both sides were not the narrow, parallel ridges that the natives at Fort Mandan had drawn on buffalo-hide maps or represented by heaps of sand piled on the dirt floors of the crude log huts at the winter encampment. As they struggled upstream through the rocky gorge of the long Missouri canyon through the Big Belts, both captains began to despair of reaching the Missouri's ultimate source and locating the passage to the Columbian waters that lay beyond.

The timber which they had expected to encounter in the mountains was "still but thinly scattered," and although they encountered some "Ibex" or mountain sheep, there was "no other game whatever and indeed there is but little appearance of any" (II, 241). The times of plenty in the Garden were over and the times of hardship were to begin. Game grew ever more scarce, and navigation of the Missouri through the long canyon above the Gates of the Mountains was incredibly difficult and dangerous.[1] Moreover, the river was not leading the party in the direction the captains had supposed it would but was veering in a southeasterly rather than a southwesterly direction. Lewis and Clark grew fearful and became extremely anxious to meet with the Shoshoni Indians who, they knew from the Minitaris' information, frequented the vicinity during the summer months.[2] Contact with this mountain tribe, wrote Lewis worriedly, must be made "as soon as possible in order to obtain information relative to the geography of the country" (II, 244), and to procure the horses that would probably be necessary for the expected short portage across the Divide.

2

By the evening of July 21, the expedition had passed the worst stretch of the canyon of the Missouri and the valley again widened, although not, as

1. A series of dams above and below the Gates of the Mountains has considerably changed the character of the Missouri's flow through this spectacular gorge. Tourist and pleasure craft now pass through the area without difficulty or danger.

2. At the time of initial white contact in the 1750s, the Shoshoni (or Snake) Indians were a Plains tribe, roaming at will between the Wyoming Rockies and the South Saskatchewan River. But other tribes were closer to centers of trade, and these, having procured firearms from whites, drove the Shoshonis back toward the mountains (see L. J. Burpee, ed., "The Journal of Anthony Hendry, 1754-55," in *Proceedings and Transactions of the Royal Society of Canada*, 3rd ser., II (1908), 307-64; and Alvin M. Josephy, Jr., *The Indian Heritage of America* (New York, 1968), pp. 117-30). By the time of Lewis and Clark the Shoshonis occupied a position intermediate between the Plains culture to the east and the Plateau culture to the west.

Lewis and Clark might have expected, into a broad and flat intermountain region like the Shenandoah valley. The river was still surrounded by mountains of astonishing height, with characteristics that were difficult to comprehend: "this valley is bound by two nearly parallel ranges of high mountains which have their summits partially covered with snow. below the snowey region pine succeeds and reaches down their sides in some parts to the plain but much the greater portion of their surfaces is uncovered with timber and expose either a barren sterile soil covered with dry parched grass or black and rugged rocks" (II, 255). The mountains were neither timbered heavily nor were their slopes fertile. They were nothing like any mountains the American explorers had ever seen, and the first realization of their size and extent was one of the greatest refinements in the earlier images and a shattering blow to the ancient hopes for an easy passage from sea to sea through the western interior.[3] And the farther the explorers penetrated into the mountainous country, the more awesome the mighty ranges became, "one range above another as they recede from the river untill the most distant and lofty have their tops clad with snow. the adjacent mountains commonly rise so high as to conceal the more distant and lofty mountains from our view" (II, 265).[4]

Above the Gates of the Mountains the Missouri became a shallow "braided" stream; navigation was now a matter of towing and poling the boats through the narrow channels between innumerable mid-river islands and sand bars. The insect pests were almost unbearable, and the progress of the party upstream was hampered not only by the tedious and slow method of river travel but by the general physical condition of the men, fatigued and with feet lacerated by the prickly pear cactus and blistered by the alternation between cold waters and the hard, hot rocks of the river's banks. The only consolation offered to either officers or men was that Indian signs grew more frequent[5] and Sacagawea began to recognize landmarks, assuring the captains "that this is the river on which her people live, and that the three forks are at no great distance" (II, 260). "This piece of information," reported Lewis, "has cheered the sperits of the party who now begin to console themselves with the anticipation of shortly seeing the head of the Missouri yet unknown to the civilized world" (II, 260). Notwithstanding the information of the "Indian woman," Lewis himself could "scarcely form an idea" of a river running through such mountainous country without numerous impediments in the form of falls or rapids, and the fear of failure was ever with him and with Clark.

His worst fears, however, were not realized, and on July 25 Clark and a

3. Not all images of the western interior in the early nineteenth century pictured the mountains as low and easy to cross. But the materials and descriptions that formed the basis of the captain's geographical lore uniformly pictured the interior ranges as low, according to Jefferson even lower than the Alleghenies (Jefferson, *Notes on the State of Virginia*, p. 29).

4. The adjacent mountains were the Big Belts on the east, the Bridger range on the southeast, and the Elkhorn range on the west.

5. Cutright, *Lewis and Clark*, p. 174.

small party, traveling ahead of the main body of the expedition in a vain attempt to contact the Shoshonis before the natives could be frightened away by the larger contingent, arrived at the Three Forks of the Missouri. After two fruitless days spent in trying to locate the elusive Indians in the vicinity of the Three Forks, Clark was joined by Lewis at this "essential point in the geography of this western part of the Continent" (II, 277). Here, where the country opened suddenly "to extensive and beatiful plains and meadows which appear to be surrounded in every direction with distant and lofty mountains" (II, 275–76),[6] the captains were forced to make a decision every bit as critical as the one they had made at the junction of the Missouri and Marias.

And as they had at the time of that decision, the captains turned to the Minitari lore for the answer to the question posed by the junction of the three rivers they named (from east to west) the Gallatin, the Madison, and, "after the author of our enterprize," the Jefferson.[7] Unlike their decision at the Marias, however, there was never really any question in the captains' minds as to which river to follow to the Continental Divide and the passage to Pacific waters. The natives at Fort Mandan had specifically instructed them to follow the most western and northern branch of the river above the Three Forks, a river that was "navigable to the foot of a high chain of mountains, being the ridge which divides the waters of the Atlantic from those of the Pacific ocean" (VI, 55). For this westernmost branch of the Missouri above the Three Forks headed directly across the dividing ridge from the waters "of no other river but the Columbia" (II, 279).

3

Before following the Jefferson River toward the southwest and the hoped-for passage across the mountains, however, the captains decided to remain in the Three Forks area for a few days, making astronomical calculations and resting the men from the arduous struggles they had undertaken since early June. Observations made on July 28 and 29 of the altitudes of the sun, moon, and North Star roughly confirmed the Three Forks' latitudinal position of $44\frac{1}{2}°$ N. as shown on Clark's Fort Mandan map.[8] But the critical measurements were those specifying longitude from the known meridional

6. The beautiful intermontane basin of the Three Forks is surrounded by the Bridger range on the east, the Tobacco Root Mountains on the west, and to the southeast, south, and southwest respectively, the Gallatin, Madison, and Jefferson ranges.

7. James Madison was Jefferson's secretary of state and Albert Gallatin his secretary of the treasury. The latter had been particularly important during the planning and preparation stages of the expedition. Unlike many of the names applied by Lewis and Clark to topographical features, the names given the Missouri's source rivers that join at the Three Forks have, fortunately, survived.

8. Lewis's astronomical measurements gave about $45\frac{1}{2}°$ N. for the Forks, about 15' of latitude off in a southerly direction.

position of the Mandan villages to the Three Forks and thus indicating the distance between that landmark and the known longitude of the Columbia's mouth. Clark's map had shown the longitude of the Three Forks as approximately the 117th meridian, nearly 6° or about 300 miles too far west. But the captains' astronomical observations in late July, 1805, combined with their calculations for course and distance since leaving the Great Bend, proved that the actual location was nearer the 111th meridian.[9]

The Indian information and their image of the previous winter had led Lewis and Clark to believe that they should have traveled about 225 miles in a direct southwesterly direction from the Great Falls to the Three Forks. They had, in fact, covered approximately 250 miles from the head of the Falls to the junction of the Gallatin, Madison, and Jefferson. But this distance had been south-by-west for only a few miles above the Falls before the Missouri began a southeasterly trend. Consequently, although the expedition had traveled about the same distance that Lewis and Clark had supposed necessary to reach the Forks of the Missouri, that journey, in terms of longitudinal position, had moved them only a few miles closer to their goal than they had been at the Falls. By the time they arrived at the Three Forks, the captains were becoming aware of this fact; the calculations confirmed their worst suspicions and, realizing the inadequacy of their previous geographical knowledge, they felt the pinch of distances yet to traverse and rugged terrain to overcome: "We are now several hundred miles within the bosom of this wild and mountanous country, where game may rationally be expected shortly to become scarce and subsistence precarious without any information with rispect to the country not knowing how far these mountains continue, or wher to direct our course to pass them to advantage or intersept a navigable branch of the Columbia" (II, 279). This journal entry by Lewis was perhaps overly romantic. But the point he wanted to convey came across clearly—the optimism in the concept of a simple Passage to India was fading, and the earlier compulsion to believe that the route across the mountains was easy was weakening.

4

The expedition left the Three Forks on the morning of July 30 and began the final ascent of the Atlantic slope, up the Jefferson River and toward the ultimate source of that stream, which the captains were still confident would bring them to the short portage to the Columbian system. The mountains on either side of the Jefferson's valley were "very lofty," and Lewis and Clark and their men were getting a final lesson in the navigability of a mountain river. The canoes had to be poled and pulled by towlines over slippery rocks in ice-cold water, and the cactus on the shore pierced even the toughest buffalo-hide moccassins. At the end of each day the men dropped from

9. Correct longitudinal position of the Forks is 111° 27' W.

exhaustion; passage across the mountains was proving incredibly difficult. The mountains hemmed in the river, and although their peaks were "yet covered partially with snow . . . we in the valley are nearly suffocated with the intense heat of the midday sun [while] the nights are so cold that two blankets are not more than sufficient covering" (II, 299).

Charbonneau's Shoshoni wife began recognizing landmarks that meant they were in the Snake territory, but still there was no sign of the necessary Indians with their horses and, hopefully, their information on how to cross the mountains. Following only a couple of days' struggle up the Jefferson, it was determined that Lewis, with a small party, would separate from the main body and proceed on upstream in an effort to establish contact with the natives. But after passing the junction of the Ruby, Beaverhead, and Big Hole rivers[10] that join to form the Jefferson near Twin Bridges, Montana, and having been unsuccessful in his efforts to find the Shoshonis, Lewis turned back to join Clark at the "three forks of the Jefferson" on August 6.[11]

Believing that the rivers that entered the Jefferson (now called the Beaverhead from this point upstream) from the west—the "Wisdom" or Big Hole River—and from the east—the "Philanthropy" or Ruby River—could not be navigated, the captains determined to pursue their course up the Jefferson River. How any river could have been considered any less navigable than the Jefferson/Beaverhead this far upstream is baffling—"the river which we are now ascending is so inconsiderable and the current so much of a stand that I relinquished paying further attention to it's state" (VI, 196), wrote Lewis. It is probable that the captains' decision to follow the middle branch of the river was based less on its assumed navigability than on the fact that it led toward the southwest, the direction they had been conditioned by their information to follow.[12] On August 8, only two days up the Jefferson or Beaverhead, Sacagawea recognized a landmark that her people called "the beaver's head from a conceived re[se]mblance of it's figure to the head of that animal" (II, 321).[13] This landmark was "not very distant from the summer retreat of her nation on a river beyond the mountains which runs to the west" (II, 321), and Lewis, out of patience and weary of searching for the Shoshonis east of the Divide, decided to continue on foot "to the source of

10. To the Big Hole and Ruby rivers the explorers gave the names "Wisdom" and "Philanthropy" in commemoration "of two of those cardinal virtues, which have so eminently marked that deservedly selibrated character [Jefferson] through life (Coues, *History*, II, 467, n. 17, makes some interesting comments on the naming process).

11. Clark, meanwhile, had missed a note left at the Forks by Lewis, and with the main party had struggled for some miles up the Big Hole River before learning of the error and turning back (Coues, *History*, II, 463–65). Had Clark continued up the Big Hole he might have found Gibbons Pass into the Bitterroot valley and shortened the westward journey considerably. He would use this route on the return trip of 1806.

12. Holding to a southwesterly direction seems inconsistent, but it must be remembered that the explorers were still following what they believed were very explicit directions about the crossing of the Divide.

13. Coues, *History*, II, 469, n. 19. The famous landmark is an isolated outcrop which bears the name "Beaver Head" and which has given the name to the river, the Montana county, and the mountain range to the west.

the principal stream of this river and pass the mountains to the Columbia; and down that river untill I found the Indians . . . if it should take me a trip of one month" (II, 321).

5

On the morning of August 9, Lewis and three of the party began the trek up the treeless valley of the Beaverhead or "Jefferson" River and, following a "plain Indian road" that angled across the barren hills flanking the river, arrived at the junction of the Beaverhead and Horse Prairie Creek on August 10.[14] Beyond this point, concluded Lewis, "it would be vain to attempt the navigation any further" (II, 325), but the streams would, at least, provide alternate lines of travel to the final dividing ridge. The Indian path Lewis and his men had been following branched at the junction of the two streams, and the captain sent a man up each of the branches to discover which of the paths to the Divide was the most practical. Their reconnaissance told him what he had already anticipated—that the route up Horse Prairie Creek, the western fork, was the best, being "more in the direction I wished to pursue" (II, 326). Accordingly, he left a note for Clark at the junction, instructing him to cache the canoes there and to await the return of the advance party.

Navigation of the Missouri was ended and for all practical purposes had been since the Three Forks. But Lewis's optimism did not flag; he still envisioned the future commercial prospects of a route up the Missouri and across the mountains, a route to the great river that could not now be too far distant: "I do not believe that the world can furnish an example of a river runing to the extent which the Missouri and Jefferson's rivers do through such a mountainous country and at the same time as navigable as they are. if the Columbia furnishes us such another example, a communication across the continent by water will be practicable and safe" (II, 326). But the captain's growing awareness of the physical realities of the Rocky Mountains made him modify the enthusiasm that was such an integral part of earlier images of the Passage. For many of the mountains surrounding the junction of the Beaverhead and Horse Prairie Creek, although they did not appear to be high, were partly covered with snow. Lewis was thus convinced that, in spite of the gradual ascent they had made since entering the Gates of the Mountains, the expedition had "ascended to a great hight" (II, 326). And since the calculations that he and Clark had made at the Three Forks gave him a fairly precise idea about the distance to the Pacific from the divide he was approaching, he knew that the Columbian system ran "a comparatively short course to the ocean" and

14. This is the site of what used to be Armistead, Montana, now covered by the waters of Clark Canyon Reservoir.

that navigation upon it might be obstructed by numerous falls and rapids.[15]

Yet the logic of desire was powerful, and as Lewis and his companions followed Horse Prairie Creek and the country opened out to become a wide and treeless plain, the older notions about the ease of crossing the mountains flowed back. The fourth and final ridge of the mountains was very near and the way to the Pacific would soon be opened. On August 12, following some tracks that must have been made by a small party of Shoshoni Indians, Lewis and his men came to the "most distant fountain of the waters of the Mighty Missouri in surch of which we have spent so many toilsome days and wristless nights" (II, 335). The Missouri, highway to the Pacific in so many minds for so many generations, had been explored to its source, and—just as all the conjectural geography of the past 130 years had said—it issued "from the base of a low mountain or hill of a gentle ascent" (II, 335).[16]

After refreshing themselves at this ultimate spring of the Missouri,[17] Lewis and his men proceeded expectantly "to the top of the dividing ridge." But from the summit they saw neither the great river that had been promised nor the open plains extending to the shores of the South Sea. To the west stretched only "immence ranges of high mountains . . . their tops partially covered with snow" (II, 335). The presence of the peaks of the Lemhi range on the western horizon must have come as a great shock, for no geographical lore extant provided for them.[18] At the top of Lemhi Pass, in the Beaverhead range of western Montana, the cumulative effect of all the small erosions in the quality of geographical lore became complete.

6

As Lewis and his men descended the western slope of the mountain toward the small stream they had seen below, their dreams of reaching navigable Columbian waters within easy portage of the Missouri were no more. But they had come too far to be discouraged, and the pull toward the west was still great. At the bottom of the long slope west of the pass, in what is now

15. This was a remarkably prescient observation, was absolutely correct, and indicates the sophisticated level of Lewis's hydrographical conceptions.

16. Considering that the approach up Horse Prairie and Trail creeks does lead to the Continental Divide, the ascent is very gentle indeed, one of the easiest passes across the Divide anywhere north or south of the Wyoming basin and South Pass.

17. In terms of the distance from this point to the mouth of the Missouri, the source of Horse Prairie Creek is not the "ultimate spring" of the river—although it was considered so by Lewis. The farthest source waters are those of the Red Rock lakes, near the western border of Yellowstone National Park, in which the Red Rock River (the Beaverhead above its junction with Horse Prairie Creek) originates.

18. Clark's Fort Mandan map makes it quite clear that the only mountains the captains expected to encounter beyond the final dividing range were those visible from the Pacific coast and appearing on the charts of Vancouver and others (including the Arrowsmith and King maps).

Lemhi County, Idaho, they knelt and "first tasted the water of the great Columbia River" (II, 335). It was a statement of pure faith; for the view from the ridge had been anything but what Lewis had expected and for all he knew the small river (the Lemhi) that flowed north along the western slopes of the mountain was not of the Columbian system at all.[19] Yet the head of the Missouri had been reached and the collective geographical lore of the past century could not be totally erased—the waters heading opposite the Missouri's westernmost source must flow to the Great River of the West.

If this feature of earlier images and information was retained, other components of the data the captains had collected were not, and Lewis recognized, probably as soon as he had seen those "immence ranges" still to the west, that the picture of the western slope that he and Clark had derived from the Minitari information was sadly inaccurate. The short portage, fixed for so long in geographical theory, simply did not exist, and with this realization came the prospect of a long overland journey to reach navigable waters. The discovery of the Shoshoni nation with their horse herds and their geographical data became critical, and Lewis led his men northward, down the valley of the Lemhi River, hoping to locate the elusive tribe.[20] In this search for the Shoshonis Lewis was no longer guided by the Fort Mandan lore but followed his own geographical intuition and awareness. The distinction between the geography of hope and the geography of reality had been made at the top of Lemhi Pass; from here on the expedition's commanders would operate without regard for the Minitari lore. They had now entered a new operational zone, one in which the image of the previous winter would be largely forgotten and in which some elements gleaned from the data they had possessed before leaving Camp Dubois would be combined with new data sources to guide them to the Pacific.

The day after Lewis and his three men had crossed the Continental Divide, the first new source of lore since Fort Mandan appeared when contact was finally made with the Shoshonis in their summer camp on the Lemhi River.[21] After overcoming the Indians' initial fear and suspicion, Lewis began extracting the geographical lore which he hoped would allow him to orient himself in totally unknown territory. His faith that the Lemhi was a part of the Pacific drainage was confirmed when he was given a freshly roasted piece

19. Lewis's identification of the Lemhi as part of the Columbian system is also an excellent example of the tendency to retreat to macrogeographical concepts following the failure of microgeographical lore to match observable reality. The Lemhi had to be part of the Columbia because all the pre-exploratory knowledge Lewis had possessed claimed that waters beyond the Missouri's source and in this line of latitude flowed to the Columbia (Allen, "An Analysis of the Exploratory Process," p. 31).

20. Lewis had, in fact, seen a Shoshoni mounted on horseback the previous day, but the Indian became alarmed and fled before the explorer could converse with him (Coues, *History*, II, 477–80).

21. Lewis was the first white man to make contact with this group, and his detailed ethnological notes on them (scattered throughout the journals from II, 339, to III, 43) are extensive and highly informative. Cutright (*Lewis and Clark*, pp. 187–93) provides an excellent analysis and synopsis of Lewis's data on the Shoshonis' life-style.

of salmon and became "perfectly convinced" that he was truly "on the waters of the Pacific Ocean" (II, 343).

Just what river system of the western sea the Lemhi belonged to, however, he was not able to discover. The chief of the Shoshonis informed him that the small river "discharged itself into another doubly as large at the distance of half a days march" (II, 342). But this second stream (the Salmon River) was confined by inaccessible mountains and was so swift and rock-choked that navigation on it was unthinkable. "It was impossible for us to pass either by land or water down this river to the great lake where the white men lived" (II, 342), the Shoshoni warned Lewis. The American explorer had heard the same kind of geographical lore about the Salmon that Alexander Mackenzie, a decade earlier, had heard about the Fraser. And like Mackenzie, who attributed such information confidently to his Indian informant's "ignorance of the country," Lewis qualified the Shoshoni's statements about the Salmon—"this was unwelcome information but I still hoped that this account had been exaggerated with a view to detain us among them" (II, 342).[22]

Before examining the situation any further, Lewis and his scouts, accompanied by some of the Shoshonis, traveled back over the Divide to link up with Clark and the main party and to lead the expedition across the height-of-land. On August 17, in the willow-choked bottomlands where Horse Prairie Creek flows into the Beaverhead from the west, the two captains were reunited.[23] Clark was greeted with "great cordiallity" by the Shoshoni companions of Lewis, and one of the natives presented the captain with "Six small pieces of Shells resembling *perl* which is highly Valued by those people and is procured from the nations resideing near the *Sea* Coast" (II, 365).[24] If the Shoshonis had seashells then the way to the Pacific must be easy, and the captains continued to press the natives for information on that passage. "The

22. Cf Mackenzie, *Voyages*, II, 127–69. Mackenzie spent a great amount of time getting information on the impassability of the Fraser, and whenever he was told that it was unnavigable, he would inpute the data confidently to his informant's "lack of knowledge about the country." Lewis's response upon being told of the impassability of the Salmon by land or water was to begin the search immediately, in the vicinity of the Shoshoni camp, for big enough trees from which to fashion dugout canoes.

23. There was another reunion at the junction, one which may have aided the American party considerably in acquiring the Shoshonis' confidence, friendship, and assistance. Of this reunion Bernard DeVoto has written: "a dramatic contrivance not permitted dramatists revealed that Lewis had met the very band from which Sacajawea had been raped and that its chief [Cameahwait] was her brother" (*Course of Empire*, p. 496). The original journals do not mention this incident in detail, but the full story was told in the Biddle text (pp. 382–83).

24. Not as much is known of trade between this region and the Pacific as is known about other regions. But as one of the foremost ethnologists has pointed out, the trade routes between widely separated areas were well defined long before contact between Indians and whites in the West (John C. Ewers, "The Indian Trade of the Upper Missouri before Lewis and Clark: An Interpretation," *Bulletin of the Missouri Historical Society*, X (1954), 429–46. Trade goods often moved for great distances, and the fact that the Shoshonis had seashells and some items (bridles, etc.) of New Mexican origin did not mean, as Lewis and many other explorers believed, that the Shoshonis had made journeys (and therefore knew the route) to either New Mexico or the Pacific. The trade items were more probably derived from Spanish traders working their way northward in the late 1700s (Goetzmann, *Exploration and Empire*, p. 20).

account they gave us," reported Clark, "was verry unfavourable": "that the River abounded in emence falls, one perticularly much higher than the falls of the Missouri & at the place the mountains Closed so Close that it was impracticable to pass, & that the ridge Continued on each Side of perpendicular Clifts impenetrable, and that no Deer Elk or any game was to be found in that Countrey, aded to that they informed us that there was no timber on the river Sufficiently large to make Small Canoes, This information (if true is alarming)" (II, 366). Because the Shoshonis were so adamant, neither Lewis nor Clark could "avoid yealding confidence to what they said" (II, 364), but after the disappointing discovery of the inaccuracies in the Fort Mandan lore, the word of "saviges" could not be accepted without a test.

It was determined, therefore, that Lewis would remain on the Atlantic slope to tend to the caching of canoes and supplies and, using horses purchased from the Shoshonis, to portage the materials needed for the remainder of the journey across the pass to the Indian camp. In the meantime Clark, with a party of eleven men, would cross the Divide to the Pacific slope and "proceede himself with the eleven men down the Columbia [the Lemhi and the Salmon] in order to examine the river and if he found it navigable and could obtain timber to set about making canoes immediately" (II, 364). Since earlier Indian lore had proven, finally, to be unreliable, any local lore obtained by the explorers must now be examined and tested within the structure of earlier, more generalized knowledge and the captains' own physical-geographical lore.[25]

7

Clark and his party crossed the scantily timbered pass in the company of most of the Shoshonis, including the chief, who had traveled eastward with Lewis several days before. When the detachment arrived at the Shoshoni village on the Lemhi River,[26] Clark requested the services of a guide to lead him down the Salmon and beyond, and once again prevailed on the Shoshoni chief to "instruct me with rispect to the geography of his country" (II, 380). The Indian now attempted to convince Clark of the difficulty of the terrain by tracing lines on the bare earth of the encampment grounds to represent rivers and piling up heaps of dirt to indicate mountain ranges. Clark, who should have expected disappointment given what he and Lewis had already learned from the Shoshonis, found that the chief's cartographic delineation of the regional topography fell far short of his "expectation or wishes":

He drew the river on which we now are [the Lemhi] to which he placed two

25. Allen, "An Analysis of the Exploratory Process," pp. 32–35.
26. The Shoshonis had moved their village about 2 miles upstream from its location when Lewis first contacted them (II, 379).

branches just above us,[27] which he shewed me from the openings of the mountains were in view; he next made it discharge itself into a large river which flowed from the S.W. about ten miles below us [the Salmon], then continued this joint stream in the same direction of this valley or N.W. for one days march and then inclined it to the West for 2 more days march.[28] here he placed a number of heaps of sand on each side which he informed me represented the vast mountains of rock eternally covered with snow through which the river passed [II, 380].[29]

The river below the junction, the chief added, was beaten to a froth by its rapidity and the innumerable sharp and jagged rocks which filled its bed; the mountains themselves were "also inaccessible to man or horse" (II, 380). Beyond the point of their summer camp on the Lemhi, the Shoshoni continued, he and his nation rarely, if ever, traveled. The terrain was simply too difficult. But the Shoshonis had learned (and this information must have made Clark's heart leap) from the "persed nosed Indians" (the Nez Percé), who lived farther down the Salmon and beyond the great mountains, that the river "ran a great way toward the setting sun and finally lost itself in a great lake of water which was illy taisted, and where the white men lived" (III, 380).

The information that the American explorer received from the Shoshoni chief was basically correct, for the Lemhi flows to the Salmon which flows to the Snake and thence, in turn, to the Columbia and into the Pacific. And the information confirmed, at least partially, the Minitari lore that a northward-flowing river opposite the Missouri's source would lead to the western sea. In Clark's mind the Lemhi-Salmon must have been this river and therefore must have been the southern branch of the Columbia that he had hypothesized on his Fort Mandan map. But the error remaining in the Minitari information was critical—for according to the natives of the western slope, the southern branch of the Columbia was not navigable to the western ocean as the Fort Mandan lore had promised. If that stream were truly unnavigable (and Clark reserved his final judgment until he could go and see for himself), then some alternate means of getting to the Pacific must be found, and the explorer turned to other members of the Shoshoni band for additional data on the country south, west, and north of the village on the Lemhi.

The most revealing lore was offered by an old man who was living at the Lemhi village but belonged to a band of Shoshonis who roved the territory southwest of the Lemhi valley. When asked by Clark if a route to the ocean might possibly lie in that direction, the old man responded by depicting the country to the south and west "with horrors and obstructions scarcely inferior

27. Probably the junction of Hawley Creek and Texas Creek with the Lemhi near the modern hamlet of Leadore, Idaho.

28. This was an accurate description of the junction of the Lemhi and Salmon rivers at present-day Salmon, Idaho, and then of the course of the Salmon—first north and then west —until it enters its tremendous canyon through the Salmon River Mountain section of the Idaho batholith.

29. Clark's memoranda on his conversations with the Shoshonis were apparently rewritten by Lewis (II, 397, n. 2).

to that just mentioned" relative to the impassability of the Salmon River country (II, 381). But listening to the old man's account, Clark learned of a new way to get to the Pacific, one that he and Lewis had never really even speculated upon. This route turned south from the Shoshoni camp on the Lemhi for twenty days, the first seven over "steep and rocky mountains where we could find no game to kill nor anything but roots" (II, 381). The next ten days' travel would lead "through a dry parched sandy desart in which there is no food at this season for either man or horse, and in which we must suffer if not perish for want of water" (II, 381).[30] At the center of this plain, the old Shoshoni informed Clark, there was a large river flowing in a south-east-to-northwest direction. For the first time the American explorers were getting data on the Snake River, the true southern branch of the Columbia. But neither then nor later would either Clark or Lewis arrive at anything approaching a complete understanding of the Columbia's major tributary.

Three or four days beyond the Snake River, related the old man, was a country "tolerable fertile and partially covered with timber [and] another large river which ran in the same direction as the former" (II, 381). This second river (probably the Owyhee, south of the Snake), the one on which the old man's relatives lived, discharged into a third large river, again the Snake, although neither Clark nor the old native recognized it as such. Whether or not this third river ran to the western ocean the old man did not know. For the route used by his people to reach a country inhabited by "white people with whom they traded for horses mules cloth metal beads and the shells which they woar as orniment" (II, 381) lay in a different direction, not to the northwest but to the south.[31]

Following the Owyhee upstream, the southern Shoshonis found a pass between its headwaters and those of a river which discharged itself into the "Stinking lake." "This was the way which he would advise me to travel if I was deturmined to procede to the Ocean," wrote Clark (II, 382). The information was charged with inaccuracy, for the Owyhee heads near no river flowing to the Pacific but only near the upper reaches of the Humboldt, which essentially flows nowhere. Clark, however, basing his ideas on the King and Arrowsmith maps and on his own rendering of western geography at Fort Mandan, thought that he was being told of a route to reach the Gulf of California: "I was convinced that the streams of which he had spoken as runing through the plains and that on which his relations lived were southern

30. This data, never confirmed by Lewis and Clark, was the first accurate description of the barrenness of the Snake River plains and was depicted in more detail (and with horror) in the reports of Wilson Price Hunt's overland Astorians in 1811. See Kenneth Spaulding, ed., *The Fur Hunters of the Far West by Alexander Ross* (Norman, Okla., 1956), pp. 135–38.

31. Once again, the reference to trade with whites did not imply Indian visits to Spanish settlements but Spanish trader visits to the natives of the Great Basin and, perhaps, the Snake River itself. An interesting discussion of this trade may be found in Joseph J. Hill, "Spanish and Mexican Exploration and Trade Northwest from New Mexico into the Great Basin," *Utah Historical Quarterly*, III (1930), 30–46.

branches of the Columbia, heading with the rivers Apostles[32] and Collorado, and that the route he had pointed out was to the Vermillion Sea or gulph of Callifornia. . . . this rout was more to the South than I wished to travel" (II, 382).[33] Although he pressed the old native for further information, Clark could learn nothing more of either the country to the south or of any possible route across the mountains west of the Lemhi to intercept the Salmon (in his mind the same river as the Lemhi) "below the mountains."

8

The explorer had learned of two alternate passages to the Pacific and had tentatively rejected them both—the one which led down the Salmon because of the impassable waters and terrain, and the one which went south over the Lemhi and Lost River ranges of eastern Idaho to the Snake plateau because it led ultimately (he thought) to the Gulf of California and Spanish territory. Finally, after drawing all he could from the Shoshoni chief, Clark learned of the passage across the mountains that he and Lewis would eventually settle upon. Asking the chief about the route used by the Nez Percé Indians to get to the rich buffalo grounds of the Atlantic side of the Divide, he was told of a trail from the Pacific slope of the ranges west of the Lemhi, a trail across mountains which were "broken rockey and so thickly covered with timber that they could scarcely" be negotiated. Any party which attempted to cross them would be "obliged to subsist for many days on berries alone as there was no game in that part of the mountains" (II, 382). But after Clark had assimilated and analyzed the native descriptions of the other two avenues to the South Sea, this third route seemed the most feasible, and even though it was a far cry from the short portage that he and Lewis and generations of geographical theorists had expected, "if the Indians could pass these mountains with their women and Children . . . we could also pass them" (II, 382).

Clark had, of course, heard about the Lolo Trail across the Bitterroot range athwart the Montana-Idaho border and across the massive convolutions of the Clearwater Mountain section of the Idaho batholith. But the captain's interpretation of the complex river and mountain systems of eastern Idaho and western Montana was still distorted and fuzzy. He knew that the Nez Percé nation lived in the Salmon beyond the point where it emerged from the mountains to the west. A trail from their territory passing eastward over the mountains should, he believed, lead into the valley of the upper Missouri—for in his image of western physiography there was only one north-south river

32. The Rio des los Apostolos was a mythical river appearing on both the King map and on Clark's Fort Mandan map and probably originated from misinterpretations of early Spanish reports on the exploration of the lower Colorado.

33. This data was of critical importance for the captains' final image of the West. The lore contributed directly to the "compression of the Southwest," a tendency on the part of Lewis and Clark to squeeze the region now consisting of Colorado, Utah, New Mexico, and Arizona into an area about one-fifth of its actual size.

beyond the Divide and that river was the Lemhi-Salmon. There was no room in his regional conceptions for the Bitterroot River, a second north-south river west of the Continental Divide. Nor was there room in his conception of this third route he had learned of for a double mountain crossing—one traverse of the ranges between the country of the Nez Percé and the Bitterroot valley and another traverse of the ranges between the Bitterroot and the Missouri. And even more critical was the fact that Clark assumed that he could pick up the Nez Percé route somewhere along the line between the lower Salmon and the upper Missouri and was not yet aware of the fact that to reach the Nez Percé route he would have to cross still another range lying between the Lemhi-Salmon and the Bitterroot valley.

It would take a brutal field reconnaissance before Clark could begin to clear up his hazy image—for the short and direct route to the Pacific was too firmly ingrained to allow him to accept fully the Indian information on the impassability of the Salmon without checking. Furthermore, the fact that portions of the Minitari information had proved faulty might have made him suspicious about any information obtained from Indians. Accordingly, he and his men, accompanied by an elderly Shoshoni "well acquainted with country to the North," proceeded down the Lemhi to the Salmon in order to evaluate the Indian lore regarding the impassability of the direct route before selecting the alternate route used by the Nez Percé. On August 21 Clark arrived at the junction of the Lemhi and Salmon and named the "Westerly fork of the Columbia" after his friend Meriwether Lewis, in justice to the first "white man ever on this fork of the Columbia" (III, 10).[34]

Proceeding down the narrow gorge of the Salmon River by horseback, Clark found that the Salmon River country was filled with massive and tortured mountains whose "Rocks were So sharp large and unsettled and the hill sides Steep that the horses could with the greatest risque and difficulty get on" (III, 25). On August 23 he found the terrain so impossible that to proceed further on horseback was futile, and he concluded to leave most of his force at a temporary camp and, with three of his best men, travel by foot down the Salmon "to examine if the river continued bad or was practicable" (III, 25). Toward the west he found the river "almost one continued rapid, five very considerable rapids the passage of either with Canoes is entirely impossible, as the water is Confined between huge Rocks & the Current beeting from one against another for Some distance below &c. &c." (III, 25). In many places the sides of the gorge closed in on the river so tightly that even a portage would have been impossible. Furthermore, "not an animal of any kind" was to be found, and the only evidence of game was the track of a black bear—the food supply in this rugged country could probably not support a force as large as the one he and Lewis commanded.

34. While in this neighborhood Clark learned of the Indian route across Big Hole Pass to the Big Hole or "Wisdom" River. This route is now crossed by a dirt road between Gibbonsville, Idaho, and Wisdom, Montana.

Old "Toby," the Shoshoni guide, told Clark that the rapids he had viewed slashing through the black canyon of the Salmon were but "Small & trifling in comparrison to the rocks and rapids below, at no great distance & the Hills or mountains were not like those I had Seen but like the Side of a tree Streight up" (III, 26).[35] But Toby had other information to offer, information that would enable Clark to begin to make some sense of the Nez Percé route that he had heard rumors of while still on the Lemhi. At a point about 50 miles downstream from the confluence of the Lemhi and the Salmon, the old Shoshoni guide pointed out a route to the north which, he said, "went to a large river which runs to the north on which was a nation he called Tushapaws" (III, 27). The Tushapaws were the Flathead Indians, and the river they lived on was the Bitterroot of western Montana, an important tributary of the Clark Fork of the Columbia. Whether Clark believed this new river to be a totally new stream of the Columbia system or simply the lower portion of the Salmon after it emerged from the mountains is unclear.[36] But he did decide that the northward route his guide had pointed out was the best possible solution to the dilemma.

On August 24, having gone far enough down the Salmon to satisfy his own curiosity and reaffirm the Shoshoni information on the hopelessness of a passage in that direction, Clark began the return to Lewis at the camp on the Lemhi.[37] He sent one of his men[38] ahead with a message to Lewis suggesting the two alternate plans he had worked out for the final journey to the Pacific. The first possibility was to buy as many horses from the Shoshonis as possible and follow the route that Toby had pointed out—"by land to some navagable part of the *Columbia* River, or to the Ocean" (III, 33).[39] However, the attraction of the direct route they had hoped for at Camp Dubois and Fort Mandan was hard to shake off; Clark's second alternative was to make an attack on the Salmon, no matter how difficult that attack might prove. According to this plan the party would separate into two groups, one to make an attempt down the river by canoe and the other to proceed on horseback over the tops of the mountains which paralleled the river's course.

The geography of the area was still a puzzle to Clark, and he did not really understand the precise nature of either of the routes he suggested. But

35. Coues (*History*, II, 533–34) gives a much more detailed description of the "difficulties and dangers" of the terrain.

36. Clark's journal entry suggests that he viewed the river on which the Flatheads lived as the Salmon below the mountains: the Indians, he wrote, crossed the mountains "at this season on that side of this river to the same below the mountains" (II, 382).

37. During Clark's absence, Lewis had engaged in making pack saddles, caching unnecessary materials, and portaging the remaining goods across Lemhi Pass to the Shoshoni village. While with the Shoshonis in their camp, Lewis compiled his detailed ethnological notes.

38. This man was John Colter, later to become a very important figure in the shaping of geographical images of the Northwest after the expedition.

39. The wording suggests that Clark felt the same desperation and willingness to abandon the search for a water route that Alexander Mackenzie, more than a decade earlier, had felt when he abandoned the Fraser River and struck out overland for the Pacific (Mackenzie, *Voyages*, II, 160–69).

of the two plans he proposed,[40] the first one—even though still hazy—was immensely preferable. Clark had seen the Salmon River country and wanted no part of it. Lewis received Clark's message on August 26 and concurred in the choice of the northern route as the most likely, although he too had little conception of the difficulties that lay ahead. Pleased that a decision had finally been made, Lewis began arranging for the purchase of more horses from the Shoshonis, directed the fiddle to be played and the men to dance, and gleefully informed the Shoshoni chief that the Corps of Discovery would shortly proceed overland "to the great river which lay in the plains beyond the mountains" (III, 43). But the "great" river to which they would travel did not lie beyond the mountains. It lay to the east of a range higher and more massive than any they had yet seen. When Clark rejoined Lewis on August 29, two and a half weeks had passed since the first tasting of Columbian waters, and it would be over a month more before the expedition would finally reach Columbian waters that could be navigated safely.

9

The long struggle up the Missouri from the Great Falls and the tedious portage across the Divide had taxed the men of the expedition severely, and the Shoshoni camp on the Lemhi had offered a resting place. But after only a few days among the poor western slope natives, both captains and men were anxious to resume their journey. The Lemhi valley was virtually devoid of game, and for men used to eating heartily of buffalo, elk, mountain sheep, and deer, the few salmon and handfuls of berries available did little to stave off the pangs of hunger.[41] The starving time was to come upon the expedition shortly; when the morning frosts on the high grasses bordering the Lemhi River began to linger on past sunrise every morning, Lewis and Clark decided to leave the hospitable but impoverished Shoshonis and begin what they believed would be their final trek across mountain country.

They left the Shoshoni camp early on August 30 and by the end of the next day found themselves at the base of the massive uplands north of the Lemhi-Salmon junction, mountains that were barren in some places and thickly timbered in others and that tied the southern end of the Bitterroot range to the northern extremity of the Beaverheads. The way up those moun-

40. In the original manuscript field books of the expedition (in the American Philosophical Society Library) there is evidence that Clark was thinking about a third alternative —although not a viable enough one to suggest. Written and then crossed out in the manuscript is the following: "A third to devide. one party to attempt to pass the mountains by turns, and the other to return to the Missouri collect provisions & go up Medeson [Medicine or Sun] river &c."

41. Clark wrote, "my party hourly Complaining of their retched Situation and [illegible word] doubts of Starveing in a Countrey where no game of any kind except a fiew fish can be found" (III, 45).

300

tains was very difficult, "some of the worst roads that ever horses passed" (III, 51), and their animals found hard going over rocks made slippery and treacherous by the early fall snows which came with increasing frequency.[42] But by September 4 they had made the crossing to the Bitterroot valley and made contact with the Tushapaw or Flathead Indians.[43] Here an old and almost forgotten myth was resurrected. The Flatheads, wrote Clark, "are Stout & light complected more so than Common for Indians" (III, 53), and their language was "a gugling kind of language spoken much thro the throught." Lewis took "down the names of everry thing in their Language, in order that it may be found out whether they are or whether they Sprang or origenated first from the welch or not."[44]

If the Flatheads were believed to be the Welsh Indians nothing more was said of it, for the captains had more pressing matters on their minds. The natives had horses to replace some of those worn out and used up on the crossing from the Salmon, and after purchasing "two fine horses," Lewis and Clark resumed their journey down the lovely valley of the Bitterroot or "Clark's River" on September 6. As they traveled down that "handsome stream" they derived from their Shoshoni guide the information that it continued its course northward for a great distance, although whether or not it fell into the Columbia the old Shoshoni could not tell them. Lewis and Clark, however, operating out of faith and what was beginning to emerge as a coherent picture of the drainage patterns of the western slope, rightly assumed that it did and named it after Clark, "the first white man who ever wer on the waters of this river" (III, 53). The Bitterroot might provide the long-sought passage to a navigable part of the Columbia, but noting the lack of salmon in its clear waters, the captains concluded that "there must be a considerable fall in it below" (III, 58). If so, it probably could not be considered navigable, and their options were limited to only one choice—the crossing of the immense snow-clad range that paralleled the valley on the west.

Just before the expedition reached the point from which they would leave the Bitterroot and begin the long traverse of the mountains to the west, they obtained the piece of lore that was to be one of the most significant additions of their entire journey and would prove to be the key to the riddle of the shortest route across the Rockies. As the party neared the site where

42. A great misfortune occurred on this crossing when the last of the party's thermometers was broken. The loss of this valuable instrument greatly hampered their meterorological efforts during the remainder of the expedition, particularly any kind of comparative readings they might have wished to acquire.

43. The Flatheads were a member of the Salish linguistic stock and although were culturally members of the Plateau province, they often crossed over into the Plains to hunt buffalo and were, in fact, possessors of many traits of the Plains culture. Like the Shoshonis, they had been driven into the mountains by the more aggressive (and gun-owning) tribes. See Josephy, *Indian Heritage of America*, pp. 131–36.

44. This note is from Private Whitehouse's journal (VII, 150–51). Another of the enlisted men's journals, that of Sergeant Ordway, says "these natives have the Stranges language of any we have ever yet seen. . . . we think perhaps that they are the welch Indians, &c" (Quaife, *Journals of Lewis and Ordway*, p. 282).

Missoula, Montana, would later stand, their Shoshoni guide informed the captains that "not very far distant from where we then were" the Bitterroot was joined by "a stream nearly as large as itself which took it's rise in the mountains near the Missouri to the East of us and passed through an extensive valley generally open prarie which forms an excellent pass to the Missouri. the point of the Missouri where this Indian pass intersects it, is about 30 miles above the *Gates of the rocky Mountains*" (III, 58). A journey of only four days would take them from the Bitterroot to the Missouri, and although this was not quite the half-day portage that had been expected and hoped for, and although another mountain crossing still lay ahead of them before reaching navigable waters, this trail was much better than the way they had come. For the first time the data they had acquired about the road of the Nez Percé to the Missouri made sense. Lewis and Clark now realized that the mountain crossing of which Clark had been told involved two separate traverses and that the northward-flowing river the Minitaris had described was the Bitterroot rather than the Lemhi.[45]

This new knowledge transformed their general conception of the passage across the mountains, and testing it would be one of the foremost objectives of the return journey in 1806. Right now, however, on September 9, 1805, they could do little about it. The season was lengthening into fall, the snows were falling on the ridges to the west, and they had not yet escaped the tortuous mountain travel they now knew to be necessary before the expedition would find itself once again on navigable waters. Moving on down the Bitterroot, Lewis and Clark and their men came to the mouth of a large creek entering the river from the west and learned from their guide that the Nez Percé road across the western mountains lay up this stream. Some Flatheads they encountered confirmed this information and added the sheer fantasy that the journey from the Bitterroot to "the plain below the mountains on the columbia river" could be made in only "five sleeps" (III, 61).[46] It would take the Corps of Discovery more than twice that long to make the crossing, and because of the severity of the trek, the eleven days on the Lolo Trail must have seemed even more time-consuming.[47]

45. The Bitterroot River, wrote Lewis, continued its route northwardly "as far or perhaps beyond the sources of Medecine river. . . . The Minetares informed us that there was a large river west of, and at no great distance from the sources of Medicine river, which passed along the Rocky Mountains from S. to N." (III, 60).

46. This information was offered by an old native who claimed that some of his relatives "were at the sea last fall and saw an old whiteman who resided there by himself and who had given them some handkerchiefs such as he saw in our possession" (III, 61). The old man's relations were probably Nez Percé rather than Flathead, but even so, it is unlikely that they had actually traveled as far as the Pacific.

47. Later investigators following the same route found it as difficult and time-consuming as did Lewis and Clark. Lieutenant Mullan, searching for a route for a transcontinental railway, used the Lolo Trail and found it "thoroughly and utterly impracticable for a railroad route" (Issac I. Stevens, *Reports on Explorations and Surveys from the Mississippi River to the Pacific Ocean* (Washington, 1859), pp. 156–57). Cutright (*Lewis and Clark*, pp. 197–211) presents an excellent account of the expedition on the Lolo Trail.

Near the mouth of the creek which would lead them toward the Lolo Trail and across the "Great Rocky Mountains" (the Bitterroot range), the expedition paused for rest, astronomical observation, and, since their guide reported "that no game is to be found on our rout for a long ways" (III, 61), procurement of as much meat as possible. They named the creek "Travelers' rest" (now Lolo Creek), and in mid-afternoon of September 11 resumed their march toward the west, through a thickly timbered country that was extremely difficult for travel on horseback. Before them were the vast ranges of mountains that should not have been there, high and covered with snow and throwing still more barriers in their passage to the Pacific. As they began to wind their way up the eastern flanks of those mountains Clark reported that the road was "most intolerable" and by the end of each day's travel the "Party and horses much fatigued" (III, 63).

On September 13, after struggling through down timber and across talus fields of sharp, jagged stones, they crossed over Lolo Pass and entered the drainage basin of the Snake River, falling onto the waters of the Lochsa or "Kooskooskee" River.[48] The trail improved greatly once across the pass— "verry fine leavel open & firm"—but the valley of the Lochsa was, like the valley of the Salmon, virtually impassable, and toward the southwest and west the captains could see the huge snowy mountains that they would have to cross. They left the upper reaches of the "Kooskooskee" on September 15 and fought their way northward through "emence quantity of falling timber," the horses slipping and rolling and the men with nothing to eat but the meager flesh of a colt they had been forced to kill. Lewis and Clark and their companions in discovery were getting deeper into country that is as difficult as anything the continent has to offer; from the top of a ridge all that could be seen were "high ruged mountains in every direction" (III, 68).

The next day (September 16) found the party caught by a perfectly seasonable snowstorm which chilled and soaked them, adding to the ever-present difficulties of the downed timber, steep slopes, expanses of bruising and cutting rocks and—perhaps the worst of all—hunger.[49] Any lingering belief that the entire Northwest could be classified as a garden was now totally smashed. In desperation Clark and a small party of hunters finally detached themselves from the main body on September 18 to "proceed on in advance to Some leavel Country, where there was game Kill Some meat & send it back &c" (III, 72). After pushing himself and his men for 20 miles, Clark caught a glimpse of "an emence Plain and *leavel* Country to the S.W. & West" (III, 72).

48. Lewis and Clark initially called this river the "Flathead" River—not to be confused with the present Flathead River of Montana to the north—but later the term "Kooskooskee" was used for both the Lochsa and the Clearwater, into which it flowed.

49. "There is no living creature in these mountains, except a few small pheasants, a small species of gray squirrel, and a blue bird of the vulture kind about the size of a turtle-dove or jay; even these are difficult to shoot" (Coues, *History*, II, 600).

Hoping to reach that plain for the game it promised, Clark and his men drove onward for 12 more hungry miles but, finding nothing, were forced to camp for the night alongside a tributary of the Lochsa that they named "Hungery Creek as at that place we had nothing to eate."

Lewis, following with the main party, got his first view of the Idaho Camas Prairie country on the next day, and his journal entry describing his reaction is more revealing than that of Clark (who, stoically, merely underlined the word "leavel"): "we to our inexpressable joy discovered a large tract of Prairie country lying to the S.W. and widening as it appeared to extend to the W. through that plain the Indian [guide] informed us that the Columbia river, (in which we were in surch) run. . . . the appearance of this country, our only hope for subsistance greately revived the sperits of the party already reduced and much weakened for the want of food" (III, 73). The river running through the plain was not, of course, the Columbia. But it was the Clearwater, and it flowed to the Snake and thence to the Columbia. And most important of all, when the expedition reached the Clearwater they would once again be on navigable waters.

Still leading the advance group, Clark came out into Weippe Prairie on September 20 and there encountered a band of Nez Percé, the Indians about whom he and Lewis had been receiving rumors for over a month. The gracious Nez Percé[50] gave the explorers a small piece of buffalo meat (the first they had tasted in months), some dried salmon, berries and roots, and bread made from the camas root—"all of which," reported Clark, "we eate hartily" (III, 78).[51] Early the next day he dispatched his hunters to find meat while he delayed with the chief of the Nez Percé to collect information on the country to the west. The chief presented Clark with some amazingly accurate data, although the explorer could not as yet make much out of it. West of the Nez Percé village, the chief told him, the Clearwater was joined by another river (the North Fork of the Clearwater) and from the junction flowed toward the setting sun. After running a considerable distance westward, the river was joined by two larger streams, one from the left (the Snake) and one from the right (the Columbia), and below the second junction the combined stream passed "thro' the mountains at which place was a great fall of the Water passing through the rocks" (III, 82).

50. The Nez Percé, members of the Sahaptin linguistic group, belonged to the Plateau culture of the Columbian Plain and were noted for their fine horses. Practicers of selective breeding, they raised excellent saddle stock—one of which, the Appaloosa, is still a favorite among horse fanciers. There have been few better examples of Indian-white relations in the United States where the Indians have been so consistently friendly and the whites so treacherous than the long history of Nez Percé and American contacts. An excellent study is Alvin M. Josephy, *The Nez Percé Indians and the Opening of the Northwest* (New Haven, Conn., 1965).

51. Too heartily, perhaps, for the diet of camas root is disrupting even to healthy digestive systems and would be particularly disturbing to stomachs shrunken by hunger. From the time they arrived at the Nez Percé camp and began to consume the roots, the men of the expedition suffered from digestive complaints, stemming from the overeating of the camas and possibly from bacteria in the dried salmon (Cutright, *Lewis and Clark*, pp. 217-19).

Clark assumed that the first river the "Kooskookee" entered was the Salmon after it had passed through the mountains west of the place where he and Lewis had first seen it near the Shoshoni camp on the Lemhi. The second river, coming from the right or north, he rightly took for the Columbia,[52] and he now knew that this major stream passed through yet another mountain range (the Cascades) between him and the Pacific. But at least he now was sure that he was on the right path, and his immediate task was not to dwell on the farther west but to learn whether the Clearwater could be navigated west of the Nez Percé camp. Accordingly, he spent the latter part of the afternoon of September 21 and a good part of September 22 investigating and evaluating the Clearwater River in the vicinity of its junction with the North Fork. Late on September 22, having convinced himself that the river was navigable for dugout canoes and that a sufficient quantity of timber was available near the forks of the Clearwater for the construction of those craft, Clark returned to the Nez Percé camp on Weippe Prairie. Here he found Lewis and the remainder of the command anxiously awaiting his arrival.

Lewis and Clark and the Corps of Discovery had found the passage through the seemingly interminable ranges, and Lewis, on learning of the nearness of navigable waters, expressed his pleasure at "having tryumphed over the rockey Mountains" (III, 83). But that triumph was far from complete. The party left the Nez Percé camp and proceeded on to the junction of the Clearwater or "Kooskooskee" and its North Fork, or "Chopunnish" River, and from here on they would again be water-borne in their journey to the Pacific. But the short portage, the long-desired and long-anticipated brief interruption in water travel across North America, had turned into a month-and-a-half trek of almost 400 miles over some of the wildest terrain imaginable. Shorter routes were available and they had already heard of the one from the Bitterroot to the Missouri. But the route which had been so firmly fixed in the logic of geography, the route from the head of the Missouri to the west, had been the one that they had followed. The geography of logic and theory and desire had been tried and tested and found wanting.

52. The large river from the north, noted Clark, was the river into which "The Clarks river [he was thinking of the Bitterroot and its downstream extension, the Clark Fork of the Columbia] empties itself" (III, 85) and thus could only be the Columbia.

CHAPTER 12

DOWN TO THE
SOUTH SEA

Lewis and Clark and their Corps of Discovery spent a week and a half in their canoe camp at the forks of the Clearwater. Here they hewed and burned out the cores of huge ponderosa pine to make the rugged craft that would carry them to the Pacific. Here they dried the gear made sodden by the snows of the mountain crossing, tended the sick, and hunted futilely for meat to replace the Nez Percé diet of salmon and camas root that had contributed to the general ill health of the entire party. The horses which had served them so well in the traverse of the great mountains were caught up, branded with the words "U.S. Capt. M. Lewis," and left in the care of the Nez Percé until the expedition could return from the coast. By October 6 the dugouts had been completed, a cache of saddles, tack, and ammunition made, and two Nez Percé chiefs persuaded to travel down the Clearwater and serve as guides and interpreters.[1] And on October 7, 1805, the Lewis and Clark Expedition once again took to the water and began the final leg of their trek to the Pacific. They were about to enter a region that was as totally unknown to the white man as any other area of the continent.

The camp occupied from September 26 to October 6 was perched on the

1. Old Toby, the Shoshoni who had guided them all the way from the Lemhi, left the American camp with his son, having not "even received his pay for guiding us" (Coues, *History*, III, 618).

inner rim of what the captains would come to call "the Great Columbian Plain," a region that did not exist in the geographical lore of the early nineteenth century and that possessed a landscape as exotic as it was unknown.[2] Sharply defined on all its borders by heavily timbered mountains, the Columbian Plain is a vast inland sea of treeless and undulating (Clark used the charming term "wavering") sedimentary plains resting on top of a thick base of lava outpourings from the surrounding ranges. Properly speaking, the Columbian Plain is not a plain at all—in the same sense as the term is used to describe the Great Plains region east of the Rockies. Rather, the plain of the Columbia takes the shape of a huge bowl with the lowest part toward the center. The bowl is traversed by the mighty Snake and Columbia rivers, which leave the region through deep gashes cut through the higher surrounding rimlands. In the core of the region the banks of the rivers are low; the water travelers could see for great distances across the empty land. But elsewhere the streams are closed in by high bluffs; when the observers left the river craft to clamber up the bluffs for a better perspective, they saw not the vast and level lands which faded away into the distance from the bluffs of the Missouri, but a grainy and textured country, heavily dissected by the great outwash of Pleistocene glacial meltwater and wrinkled here and there by the warpings of ancient geological forces.[3] Landscape descriptions by either Lewis or Clark are relatively rare for the section of their journey that lay through the Columbian Plain. The reason, perhaps, is that they simply did not have the vocabulary to cope with the unusual and otherworldly physiography.

During no part of their journey did Lewis and Clark and their men make such an abrupt environmental transition as they did upon entering and leaving the Columbian Plain, not only in physiographic but in climatic, biotic, and cultural characteristics. For the upthrust of the Cascade Mountains to the west cuts off the flow of moisture-bearing air masses from the Pacific, and the shift from humid to arid climatic patterns is rapid indeed. The climatic transition means a biotic transition as well, and the rolling bunch wheat grasslands and immense sagebrush flats that met the explorers' eyes were great contrasts to the huge trees of both the eastern and western ranges surrounding the Plain. What one observer termed "the barren monotony"[4] of the landscape was heightened, for Lewis and Clark, by an almost total absence of wildlife; the Columbian Plain did not teem with the herds of buffalo, deer, elk, and antelope that made the Great Plains of the Missouri and Platte such a paradise for the expedition's hunters.[5] And finally, the dirty, poor, surly, and pest-ridden

2. Donald W. Meinig, *The Great Columbian Plain: A Historical Geography, 1805–1910* (Seattle, 1968), pp. 3–25.

3. R. L. Lupher, "Physiographic Divisions of the Columbia Intemontane Province," *Annals of the Association of American Geographers*, XXXV (1945), 53–75; and William D. Thornbury, *Regional Geomorphology of the United States* (New York, 1965), pp. 442–59.

4. Meinig, *The Great Columbian Plain*, p. 19.

5. Lewis and Clark had been forewarned by both the Shoshonis and the Flatheads that they would find no buffalo once they entered the basin of the Columbia. Recent findings

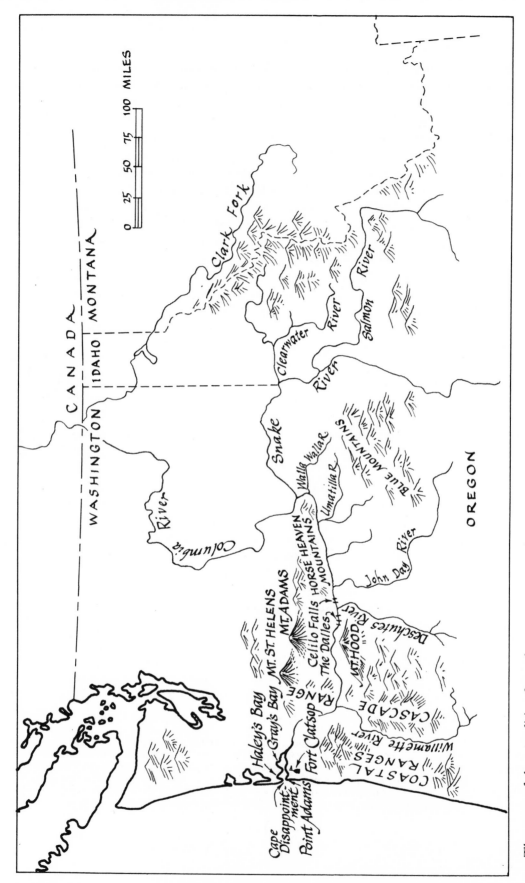

37. The route of the expedition from the canoe camp on the Clearwater to the mouth of the Columbia and Fort Clatsop, October 7 to December 7, 1805

natives of the Plain, bound to the salmon rather than the buffalo, made quite a contrast with the Indians of the eastern side of the Divide[6] and with the declining brilliance of the culturally sophisticated nations of the Northwest coastal region to the west. Lewis and Clark passed through this region rapidly, covering the 350 miles between their canoe camp and the Cascades of the Columbia in about three weeks. But they observed enough to allow them to define the Columbian Plain as a distinct region in the image of western geography that they framed after their return to civilization in September, 1806.

2

Three days down the Clearwater from the canoe camp, the expedition arrived at the junction of that river with the Snake, and Clark, in a masterful bit of geographic deduction, noted that this "large southerly fork" was "the one we were on with the *Snake* or *So-So-nee* nation" (III, 103). In a sense it was the same river, the Salmon having entered the Snake about 50 miles above the junction with the Clearwater, and it was remarkable that the explorer was able to see the river as the same one that had formed the first hope of the short portage. But the accuracy was only partial, for the captains never got the Snake River and its long, twisting course from the Yellowstone plateau quite right in their representation of western geography. While the party paused briefly at the confluence of the Snake and Clearwater, Clark learned from his Nez Percé guides that "This South fork [of the Columbia] or Lewis's River"[7] received two tributary streams above the Clearwater's entry. The first of these was a small river which entered "Lewis's River" from the west (the Grande Ronde River of northeastern Oregon), and the second was a large stream "called by those Indians *Par-nash-te*" (III, 104) which Clark mistakenly assumed also entered from the west. What neither of the captains realized—and would not even begin to realize until the return trip of the next spring—was that the second river was the Salmon, only a branch of the main stream and a much shorter and less important river than the Snake itself.

The junction of the Clearwater and Snake rivers was in level and open plains country, and "worthey of remark," noted Clark, was that there was "not one stick of timber on the river near the forks" (III, 104). This condition

---

indicate that the mountain buffalo (*Bison bison athabascae*) at one time ranged into the Divide country and even beyond into the Columbian Plateau, although Indian hunting pressure had eliminated these animals just before Lewis's and Clark's entry into the region (G. M. Christman, "The Mountain Bison," *The American West*, VIII (May, 1971), 44–47.

6. The Shoshoni, Flathead, and Nez Percé Indians occupied a position intermediate between the Plains and Columbian tribes, and despite their distinctiveness were more familiar to the American explorers than the (to them) unusual tribes of the Plateau region. A good source for the general pattern of native culture in the Columbian Plain is Verne F. Ray, "Cultural Relations in the Plateau of Northwestern America," *Publications of the Frederick Webb Hodge Anniversary Publications Fund*, III (Los Angeles, 1939).

7. The fact that the captains continued to call the Snake by the name they had given the Lemhi-Salmon when they first crossed the Divide west of the Jefferson's headwaters is a good indication that they viewed the Salmon and not the Snake as the major river.

was to continue: as the expedition proceeded down the Snake, the hills bordering its course grew higher, and after ascending them, the explorers obtained a view of more open country with "not a tree of any kind to be Seen" (III, 109). The river hills themselves often assumed fantastic shapes where erosion had removed the soil covering, exposing the "dark ruged Stone" of the basaltic platform upon which the entire Columbian Plain rests. The weather alternated between mild and fair days and cooler, windier, and rainier nights. The Snake, like the Columbia when they joined it, was in a period of low water, and even in those places where its waters were normally placid, the river had become transformed into a series of raging rapids, the water level having dropped near the jumbled rocks of the river bed.[8] As they passed the rapids near the mouth of the Palouse River, Clark commented, "This must be a verry bad place in high water" (III, 112)—but he and Lewis were driving their crude boats through the barren canyonlands of the Snake at about the worst possible time. They fought their way through one stretch of white water after another, stretches which should have been portaged and would have been "if the season was not so far advanced and time precious with us" (III, 111).[9]

It was a relatively rapid trip but it was anything and everything except pleasant. Each morning, if they could be spared, the hunters were sent out to get meat, only to return and inform the captains that "They could not See any Signs of game of any kind" (III, 117), forcing the party to continue their subsistence on salmon and roots. The lack of wood for fuel to provide warmth during the increasingly cool nights finally forced them to raid house timbers left by Indians against their return from antelope hunts in the plains. "We were obliged for the first time to take the property of the Indians without the consent or approbation of the owner" (III, 117)—at least along the Missouri there had been cottonwoods. But no trees broke the monotony of the Snake's barren and drab banks, and the even greater monotony of the lands receding from the river was relieved only by brief glimpses of the northern spurs of the Blue Mountains far to the south.[10]

3

On Friday, October 16, 1805, after having passed a series of bad rapids, the Corps of Discovery reached the goal of trans-Missouri exploration since

8. Bouldery rubble washed down by glacial outwash fills the channels of virtually all major streams of the area. See J. Harlan Bretz, "The Channeled Scablands of the Columbia Plateau," *Journal of Geology*, XXXI (1923), 617–49.

9. The captains had long since abandoned their initial intention of reaching the Pacific and returning to winter with the Mandans. All they were trying to accomplish now was to escape the Plain before the winter snows the Indians had warned them about trapped them within that inhospitable region.

10. On October 15 "Capt. Lewis walked on the plains and informs that he could plainly See a rainge of mountains which bore S.W. & N.W. the nearest point south about 60 miles, and becoms high toward the N.W." (III, 117).

1673 when, 3,714 miles distant from their starting point at Camp Dubois, they sailed their dugouts into the whirling waters of the Columbia—the Great River of the West. The journals which recorded the event were singularly unemotional, and it is obvious that for the members of the expedition, and particularly for its commanders, the final discovery of the river that had existed so long in fable was an anticlimax. The impetus had gone out of the drive to the sea. The Columbia was not close to the Missouri and the route between the two master components of western geography was not easy. When the Columbia was finally attained it had already become perfectly clear to Lewis and Clark that the way they had come was no perfect "water communication across the continent for the purposes of commerce."

The event of reaching the Columbia was, however, of enough significance for the captains to call a halt for a day and a half in order to calculate the latitudinal position[11] of the junction of the Snake and Columbia rivers and to reconnoiter the vicinity. Here the river hills were lower and the explorers saw farther than they had been able to see since leaving their camp on the Clearwater's forks. "In every direction from the junction of those rivers," wrote Clark, "the countrey is one continued plain low and rises from the water gradually" (III, 119). But other than the low Horse Heaven Mountains to the west and the distant Blue Mountains to the southeast, there was little else to be seen—except "great quantities of a kind of prickley pares, much worst than any I have before seen" (III, 120). It was a far different view than he or Lewis had commanded from eminences they had ascended during the journey up the Missouri.

On the day following the arrival at the Columbia, Clark took two men and a small canoe up the Columbia. The run of the king salmon was in its last stages, and large numbers of Indians were in the vicinity of the Columbia-Snake junction, taking the fish and drying them to furnish a food supply for the coming winter.[12] Several of these natives took Clark to a point on a mid-channel island from which he could see the mouth of the Yakima or "Tap teel" River, entering the Columbia from the west. Far away to the southeast, the tips of the Blue Mountains shone above the horizon, made glimmering and indistinct by the heat waves rising from the baked earth. But what Clark could see was of little importance anyway. For by arriving at the Columbia he and Lewis had nearly closed the traverse line across the continent. Virtually all those features they had seen and mapped between the mouth of the Platte and the junction of the Columbia and Snake were features new or at least newly defined in geographical lore. The Columbia, however, was on the maps they had brought with them, and it had been cartographically represented as "the Great River of the West" since the early Spanish forays along the coast, as the "Tacoutche-Tesse" since Mackenzie's crossing, and as the

11. The observations yielded a latitude of slightly more than 46° N., quite accurate reckoning. Apparently no calculations for longitude were attempted (VI, 263–65).

12. Cutright, *Lewis and Clark*, pp. 224–25.

"Columbia" since Gray's monumental discovery. The expedition would soon be leaving a region that was totally unknown and entering one that was partly known. When they left the junction and proceeded down the Columbia on the afternoon of October 18, they began to meet with increasing evidences of their entry into territory which, if environmentally unfamiliar, was at least not a blank in their pre-exploratory knowledge.

Indeed, on the very day they left the confluence of the Columbia and "Lewis's River," the captains received the first proof that they were approaching territory which had been carefully surveyed by explorers before them. Just after passing the mouth of the Walla Walla River,[13] the black and rugged rocks bordering the Columbia parted briefly and they viewed "a mountain bearing S.W. conocal form Covered with Snow" (III, 131). Clark climbed the basalt cliffs the next morning for a better look and from this vantage point saw for the first time another "mountain of emence hight covered with Snow, this must be one of the mountains laid down by Vancouver, as seen from the mouth of the Columbia River, from the course which it bears which is *West* I take it to be Mt. St. Helens, destant about 120 miles" (III, 135). A second mountain, the one seen the previous day, was still visible to the southwest. This peak, seen first on October 18, was Mt. Hood,[14] and the one to the west, first viewed on the following day, was Mt. Adams rather than Mt. St. Helens.[15] But the captains' misidentification was inconsequential. Exploration through the interior was linking up with exploration along the coast, and Lewis and Clark were leaving the fantasy of geographical unknowns to enter the real world of geographical knowledge, as mapped and surveyed and described by those who had preceded them from a different direction.

4

Beyond the point where the captains had their first view of the peaks of the Cascade range, the Columbia turned west and entered the long series of canyons from which the expedition would not emerge until it arrived at tidewater. The walls of those canyons were not white and gleaming like the Breaks of the Missouri but were bleak and black, and the country beyond

13. The Walla Walla was at a very low stage and was recognized only as a "Small riverlet" (III, 131). When they again passed its mouth the following spring, the captains would identify it as a major tributary of the Columbia.

14. Mt. Hood had been named after the British admiral Sir Samuel Hood by Lieutenant Broughton of Vancouver's command, the discoverer of the peak: "Mr. Broughton honored it with Lord Hood's name; its appearance was magnificent; and it was clothed in snow from its summit, as low down as the high land, by which it was intercepted, rendered it visible" (Vancouver, *A Voyage of Discovery*, II, 65).

15. Coues (*History*, II, 646, n. 21) claimed that the captains' identification was correct. However, Mt. St. Helens is west of the main range and could not possibly have been seen from any point close to the river. Mt. Adams, some 2,500 feet higher and east of the main range of the Cascades, must have been the mountain in view to the west.

the canyon rim on either side of the river was painfully barren—"not a tree to be Seen in any Direction except a fiew Small willow bushes" (III, 140). The river itself was incredibly deep and greenly transparent, but still the huge basaltic chunks nearly choked up its course and the men fought their way through rapid after rapid. On October 21 the captains' ever-growing recognition of the nearness of the Pacific was accented when, near the mouth of the John Day River,[16] they saw Indians wearing blankets made of trade goods and one wearing a sailor's jacket. But just below the entry of the Deschutes River,[17] with Mt. Hood still in view to the southwest, the greatest series of obstacles yet to their safe passage to the Pacific was met. Walking on shore to inspect the native processes of catching and preparing the salmon, Lewis and Clark came upon the hard rock barrier over which the Columbia poured its billions of gallons of water at Celilo Falls.

Large numbers of Indians were in residence at Celilo Falls,[18] and they assisted the men of the expedition in portaging the canoes and goods without mishap around the two massive drops of water which the Falls consisted of. And just below Celilo lay other obstacles: the Short and Long Narrows of the Columbia, which, as the Dalles of the Columbia, would later be such a vital landmark for the American folk migration to Oregon.[19] Here the lava basement of the Columbian Plain compressed the river's width to less than 50 yards, and as Clark viewed the tremendous volume of the Columbia's flow passing through the narrow channel, he described it better than anyone— "the horrid appearance of this agitated gut swelling, boiling & whorling in every direction" (III, 154). But the "agitated gut" notwithstanding, the captains decided to take a chance, portaging only the baggage and taking the canoes themselves through the Narrows while the astonished Indians looked down from the cliffs lining the river. It was a brave, if foolhardy, thing to do but all men and craft passed through safely.

The ride through the Dalles must have been wild and exhilarating, and if Lewis had a chance to think about it, he could not have helped but feel some self-gratification about the prescience and geographical sense he had dis-

16. This river was named later for a member of Robert Stuart's party of Astorians, who went mad near the mouth of another river of the same name, about 90 miles up the Columbia from its mouth. The tale is related in Bradbury, *Travels in the Interior*, p. 181, and in the *Missouri Gazette* (St. Louis), May 15, 1813, p. 3.

17. The Deschutes was, according to Clark, about one-quarter the size of the Columbia. That neither he nor Lewis entered any description of the stream in the journals is primary evidence of their impatience to negotiate the Celilo Falls and proceed downstream.

18. The Indians were engaged in preparing fish by drying, pounding, and stacking the flesh in layers which were bundled; this food source could be kept for several years (Coues, *History*, II, 659). According to Washington Irving in *Astoria, or Anecdotes of an Enterprise beyond the Rocky Mountains* (New York, 1849), pp. 81–82, Celilo Falls was a major trade center where Indians from the coast and from the Rockies exchanged goods for the pounded salmon.

19. The author of one of the first emigrants' guides to the Oregon country wrote: "These dalles, seriously interrupt the navigation of the river, and detract very much from the importance of the surrounding country" (Lansford W. Hastings, *The Emigrants' Guide to Oregon and California* (Cincinnati, 1845), p. 27).

played while still on the upper waters of the Jefferson River. The comparatively short distance from the Divide to the Pacific, he had written, meant that the waters of the Columbia had "the same number of feet to decend which the Missouri and Mississippi have from this point to the Gulph of Mexico"; therefore the same degree of "practicable and safe" navigation experienced on the Missouri could not be expected on the great western river (II, 327). Lewis had been right—as he and Clark so often were. And their battle with white water was not over yet. They were entering the long passage of the Columbia through the Cascade range, and although things improved in many respects—the hunters began to report signs of game and more and more timber began to line the banks of the river—the expedition still had to pass that stretch of water that the Indians they spoke with called "the great rapids." Could anything be greater than that the exhausted men and their beaten dugouts had already passed through?

Below the Dalles the expedition's commanders began to encounter increased evidence of their entry into a new region influenced directly by proximity to the great South Sea itself. An Indian they met on October 28 was wearing the jacket and hat of a Royal Navy tar and even had his hair queued.[20] The native canoes, made of cedar and with carved heads on bow and stern, were upriver diffusions from the sea-going culture that dominated the coastal area,[21] and the Indians whose villages lined the banks of the Columbia erected totem poles to extoll their family history. The country began to be "thinly timbered with Pine & low white Oake" and, behind the river, looked as if it might be good for game and hunting. The mountains continued higher on both sides of the Gorge of the Columbia through the Cascades, and from time to time the captains were able to see the snow-covered volcanic cone of Mt. Hood gleaming in the sunlight. The dryness and clarity of the Columbian Plain gave way to fog and a moister climate. The country became richer and more fertile, having "every appearance of haveing been at some distant period cultivated" (III, 179). On October 30 the party reached the first of the long series of cascades from which the range they were transecting derived its name. By November 2 the explorers had completed a long and arduous portage of the upper and lower Cascades, and when they put their boats once more into the quiet waters of the river below the rapids, they learned that, although still 100 miles from the sea, the river rose and fell rythmically. Here, after having passed through high and densely timbered mountains,[22] they reached the farthest eastward penetration of Lieutenant Broughton of His Majesty's Royal Navy, made more than ten years

20. Coues, *History*, II, 673.
21. Marian W. Smith, "The Cultural Development of the Northwest Coast," *Southwestern Journal of Anthropology*, XII (1956), 272–94.
22. "After being so long accustomed to the dreary nakedness of the country above, the change is as grateful to the eye as it is useful in supplying us with fuel" (Coues, *History*, II, 688).

earlier.[23] The traverse line across the continent of North America by way of the Missouri and Columbia rivers had been closed.

5

Below the Columbian Cascades, the country was low and rich and heavily wooded with the most massive conifers imaginable. Looking back, the explorers could see Mt. Hood behind them, "covered with Snow and in the range of mountains which we have passed through and is of a conical form but rugid" (III, 192). Coming to the mouth of the Sandy or "Quick Sand" River, they noted that it had "much the appearance of the *River Platt.* roleing its quick sands into the bottoms with great velocity after which it is divided into 2 chanels by a large sand bar" (III, 192). But in no other respect did the territory below the Cascades resemble that about the mouth of the Platte River, for the environmental transition on the western margin of the Great Columbian Plain was nearly as abrupt as it had been on the eastern margin of that barren and arid land. The moisture-laden winds that are prevented from reaching the desert interior by the Cascades are piled up by those mountains along the relatively narrow coastal strip, and the heavy and nearly constant precipitation is a classical example of orographic or topographically induced rainfall. It is truly a region with a marine climate, and the proximity to the ocean ameliorates the temperatures, making even the heart of the winters relatively mild (if damp and disagreeable). The high level of humidity and the excessive precipitation contribute to a vegetative association which is tangled and dense beyond belief[24] with fir, spruce, cedar, and hemlock growing to heights and breadths that are equaled in few other places in the world. These features of the coastal region—the dampness and the rains, the jungle-like vegetation, and the mighty forests—were the regional characteristics that dominated the explorers' journals during their tenure on and near the Pacific shores.

As the Corps of Discovery proceeded down the immense Columbia they found few signs of large game and were still forced to subsist on the pounded salmon they had acquired from Indians farther upriver. There were vast numbers of waterfowl, however, and at one point Clark noted that neither he nor other members of the party slept well at night "for the noise Kept [up] dureing the whole of the night by the Swans, Geese, white & Grey Brant Ducks &c. on a Small Sand Island close under the Lard. Side; they were emensely noumerous, and their noise horid" (III, 201). The valley through which they were passing extended "a great Distance to the right & left, rich thickly covered with tall timber, with a fiew Small Praries bordering on the

23. Vancouver, *A Voyage of Discovery*, II, 65–66.
24. The temperate or laurel rain forest of the Pacific Northwest is one of the few examples in the world of true rain-forest vegetative communities outside of the tropics.

river. . . . This is certainly a fertill and a handsom valley" (III, 202). It was also "crouded with Indians,"[25] and these tribes of the coastal region, dirty and ill-formed and untrustworthy, came off much the worse in the captains' conscious or unconscious comparisons between them and the "noble" tribes of the buffalo plains east of the Divide.

Mountains were still visible, and while the narrow and low coastal ranges restricted the view to the west, the pinnacles of the Cascades still loomed on the eastern horizon. But mountains had, by this time, become commonplace, and although Lewis and Clark dutifully noted their presence in their journals, no note of hope was attached to them as was first attached to the Rockies, which, it had been believed, hid within their vastnesses the Passage to India. It was too late for any hope of the easy passage now; the only hope left was to see the breakers and expanse of the great South Sea. By November 6 the captains knew they were close when the Indians they spoke to related tales (usually apocryphal) of direct contact with traders at the river's mouth.[26]

When the fogs lifted early next morning, November 7, 1805, Clark inscribed the words that generations of explorers had hoped to be able to write: "Great joy in camp we are in *view* of the *Ocian* . . . this great Pacific Octean which we been so long anxious to See. and the roreing or noise made by the waves brakeing on the rockey Shores (as I suppose) may be heard disti[n]ctly" (III, 210). He was acutely aware of the significance of the moment, and although he and his companions were looking at Gray's Bay rather than the Pacific proper, the fact and the accomplishment were there. The West toward which the explorers of three centuries had groped through darkness was now brought to light. But it was the light of reality and the shattering of a dream, because the road thither had been long and hard, not swift and easy. The West was not golden, it was gray. And in the grayness of that coast the captains began to think about a site for their winter camp.[27]

6

On November 8, hugging the northern shores of the Columbia (or Gray's Bay), the expedition proceeded farther toward the west, finally com-

25. According to Brackenridge (*Views of Louisiana*, p. 96), Clark estimated the regional population at "eighty thousand souls." Recent demographic evidence indicates that Clark's estimate might have been too conservative. Bolstered by an abundant resource base, the indigenous peoples of the Northwest coast reached levels of population density unmatched among nearly all other pre-agricultural peoples in the world.

26. In January, 1806, while at Fort Clatsop, Clark made a list of the ships and captains described by the natives as having recently visited the coast (III, 305–07). According to various sources (cf. DeVoto, *Course of Empire*, p. 550) an American ship, the *Lydia* out of Boston, was in the vicinity while Lewis and Clark were descending the river.

27. The decision to remain along the coast may have been made in the hopes of contacting an American ship. In his instructions to Lewis, Jefferson had suggested that a copy of the journals and notes made on the outward journey might be sent back to the United States by sea, provided a trading vessel could be located (Jackson, *Letters*, p. 65).

ing to a point opposite the later site of Astoria, where the huge waves rolling in from Cathay made further progress impossible. Here, during the 8th and 9th, they camped on a narrow strand that was only a small storm beach, rimmed inland by precipitous sea cliffs and entirely under water during high tide. The canoes were in danger of being smashed by driftwood logs, "maney of them nearly 200 feet long and from 4 to 7 feet through," but the wind and the waves were "too high to proceed" (III, 214). Finally, on November 10, the storms subsided enough to allow the captains to move their camp a little farther west along the Washington shore of the Columbia's widening mouth, but the site they selected on the east side of Ellice's Point (just south of Chinook, Washington) was little better than the one they had left—"a Small nitch at the mouth of a Small run on a pile of drift logs . . . the only situation we could find to lee" (III, 215).

"Our situation is truly a disagreeable one," wrote Clark, "our canoes in one place at the mercy of the waves our baggage in another and our selves & party scattered on drift trees of emence size & are on what dry land they can find in the crevices of the rocks & hill sides" (III, 216). There was nothing else to do and nowhere else to go, for the high winds raised tremendous seas which broke "with great force and fury against the rocks & trees on which we lie" (III, 217). A person with feelings, noted Clark, would be distressed to view their situation, the men wet and cold and hungry with nothing but pounded salmon for food and with clothing made rotten by the continual dampness and the driving rains. It was fruitless to try to move toward the interior, as the sea cliffs were so steep and choked with undergrowth that a person moving through them had to haul himself along by grasping the boughs of the smaller trees, scarce daring to put his feet on ground made so slippery by the incessant rains and the permeating dampness. At every flood tide the waves came in with more violence, pounding and breaking against the driftwood flooring of their precarious campsite.

Since they had arrived at the Nez Percé camp (it must have seemed so long ago) the Indians had continually lied to them about the presence of a white settlement at the mouth of the Columbia, and although they had seen no signs of such a settlement, Lewis decided on November 14 to take a small group and move on toward the west. Consulting his Vancouver charts, he tried to make for a small bay of the ocean just north of the Columbia's final entry into the Pacific, hoping to find there the "white people the Indians say is below" (III, 222). While he was gone Clark chafed bitterly: "from the 5th in the morng. untill the 16th is *eleven* days rain, and the most disagreeable time I have experenced confined on a tempiest coast wet, where I can neither git out to hunt, return to a better situation, or proceed on" (III, 223).

On the afternoon of November 15 the seas abated somewhat, and, in great haste lest they rise again, Clark had the canoes loaded and set out from the "dismal nitch" where he and his men had been confined. He and the bulk of the party moved on around "the blustering point" (Ellice's Point) to its western side and, finding that this "would be the extent of our journey by water, as the waves were too high at any stage for our Canoes to proceed further down" (III, 226), decided to camp on a beach near an old Indian village "uninhabited by anything except flees" (III, 225). Here, looking toward the Pacific and with Cape Disappointment and Point Adams clearly in view, they would spend another nine rain-soaked and fully miserable days.[28]

During the first day at this camp, Clark directed that the baggage and "articles of every discription" be examined for water damage and laid out to dry, taking advantage of a brief improvement in the weather although the waves continued high and looked "dismal indeed breaking with great fury on our beech" (II, 228). Lewis returned from his reconnaissance early on the afternoon of November 17, having been all around Cape Disappointment for the first view of the Pacific unobstructed by any land points whatsoever but having failed to discover either a trading vessel or the promised settlement of whites. With his companion once again in camp, Clark decided to leave the morning of the 18th with those men "who wished to see more of the Ocean" (III, 229).[29] His purpose was not to find ships or villages but only to see the vast ocean which he and Lewis and their men had traveled, by his reckoning, 4,162 miles to view.

When he and his party reached Cape Disappointment (and how meaningful that name really was), Clark reported that his men appeared "much Satisfied with their trip beholding with estonishment the high waves dashing against the rocks & this emence Ocian" (III, 234). Clark himself did not record his emotions, and his feelings must have been mixed—the Pacific was attained but the expedition's central objective of the commercially practicable water route had failed. Nevertheless, in the heading of his journal for the next day (November 19), Captain William Clark let a note of pride show through—"Cape Disapointment at the Enterance of the Columbia River into the Great South Sea or Pacific Ocean" (III, 235).

7

Clark rejoined Lewis on November 20, and for the next several days the captains debated what their course of action ought to be. It seemed futile to

28. Lewis and Clark named the bay on which this camp was made "Haley's bay from a favourite trader with the Indians which they Say comes into this Bay and trades with them" (III, 226). Point Adams, the southern cape at the mouth of the Columbia, was named by Captain Gray, the river's discoverer. Gray named the northern cape Point Hancock, but Captain John Meares, who had explored the coast in 1788, named the northern cape "Disappointment" and the bay behind it "Deception" as he believed it to be only a bay and not the entrance of a mighty river—"The name of Cape Disappointment was given to the promontory, and the bay obtained the title of Deception Bay. . . . We can now with safety assert, that there is no such river" (John Meares, *Voyages to the North West Coast of America* (London, 1790), pp. 167-68).

29. Eleven men accompanied Clark, including the halfbreed interpreter, Charbonneau, and his black "servant," York (Coues, *History*, II, 712).

remain on the coast as game was scarce, and the Chinook Indians who lived in the vicinity told them there was little likelihood of the food situation improving. Each morning dawned dark and disagreeable, and although it was "a supriseing climat" with no cold weather and only an alternation between brief spells of fair weather and more dominant rainy and windy periods, to stay much longer might prove to be unendurable. Perhaps their decision to move elsewhere was made on November 22, when the wind, accompanied by sheets of rain, blew with such violence that their camp was nearly awash—"O! how horriable is the day waves brakeing with great violence against the Shore throwing the water into our Camp &c. all wet and confined to our Shelters" (III, 243).

A small group of Clatsop Indians visited the American camp on November 23, and after learning of the kind of country occupied by that tribe on the Oregon shores of the Columbia, the captains and their men came to a conclusion—they would leave this miserable camp, cross the river to the Clatsop territory, where (the natives said) there were plenty of elk, and locate there a site for their winter camp.[30] On November 25 the entire command moved back up the Columbia and, as the waves on the great river were too high for them to negotiate, made a camp near their first Pacific coastal camp on November 7. The next day they took advantage of a short break in the weather to cross the broad, 15-mile-wide channel of the river and make another camp near the site of the future Astoria. The weather was not better on the south shore, the hunters tried without success to find deer or elk, and once again there was nothing to eat but their now-familiar diet of pounded salmon. "This is our present situation!" wrote Clark, "Truly disagreeable." And disagreeable it was, with the clothing, bedding, and tents full of holes and rotten, the men without any way to keep warm or dry, and the violent weather abating not at all—"O! how Tremendious is the day. This dredfull wind and rain continued with intervales of fair weather, the greater part of the evening and night" (III, 254).

On November 29, almost in desperation, Lewis took a small party of five men out "in surch of an eligible place for our winters residence" (III, 255). Heading west from the expedition's temporary encampment, Lewis found little to encourage him, the country being tangled with huge trees and thick laurel undergrowth and with "no fresh appearance of Elk or deer in our rout" (III, 258). Coming to the small bay where the Lewis and Clark or "Netul" River enters the Columbia, Lewis expected to find the Clatsop Indians, who "have tantalized us with their being much game in their neighbourhood. this information in fact was the cause of my present resurch, for where there is most game is for us the most eligible winter station" (III, 258).

30. The captains apparently held a consultation with their men and the near-unanimous decision was to cross over and form a permanent establishment, since "by proceeding on [upriver] at any distance would not inhance our journey in passing the Rockey Mountains, &c." (III, 247).

Lewis was not able to locate the Clatsops, however, and, forced to scout around without benefit of their information or assistance, he did not return to rejoin Clark until December 5.

Clark, meanwhile, was waiting impatiently, and as he bided his time he fretted about the safety of Lewis and his party and pondered the untenability of the situation in which he found himself: "The emence Seas and waves which breake on the rocks & Coasts to the S.W. & N.W. roars like an emence fall at a distance, and this roaring has continued ever Since our arrival in the neighbourhood of the Sea Coast which has been 24 days Since we arrived in Sight of the Great Western; (for I cannot Say Pacific) Ocian as I have not Seen one pacific day Since my arrival in its vicinity, and its waters are forming petially [perpetually] breake with emenc waves on the Sands and rockey coasts, tempestous and horiable" (III, 263). But when Lewis returned on December 5, he returned with the welcome information that he had found "a good situation and Elk sufficient to winter on" (III, 266). On December 7 the entire party moved into the mouth of the small bay on the Columbia's southern shore and up the small river which flowed into it; at the first point of high land on the west side of that river they halted at the site which Lewis had selected. Here, on high and relatively well-drained ground, they began to cut down the lofty trees with which to erect their winter fortification, and Clark's journal entry for Sunday, December 8, 1805, was headed "Fort Clatsop."

8

The crude huts and stockade begun on December 8 were not completed until December 30. During the interval the patterns of living that were to prevail throughout the winter established themselves. The rain and chill and wind that Lewis and Clark and their men had already experienced continued,[31] the only variations being from merely bad, "cool and disagreeable" to almost intolerable—"the winds violent   Trees falling in every derection, whorl winds, with gusts of rain Hail & Thunder, this kind of weather lasted all day, Certainly one of the worst days that ever was!" (III, 281). The food was scarce and poor and the party lived on elk meat made rotten by the dampness and on the soggy root crops of the coastal tribes. Even Christmas dinner was miserable: "we would have Spent this day the nativity of Christ in feasting, had we any thing either to raise our Sperits or even gratify our appetites, our Diner concisted of pore Elk, so much Spoiled that we eate it thro' mear necessity, Some Spoiled pounded fish and a fiew roots" (III, 291).

31. The weather records and meteorological observations for the winter at Fort Clatsop are in VI, 198–208, but the details are nowhere near as precise as those at Fort Mandan owing to the loss of the thermometer while crossing from the Salmon to the Bitterroot River.

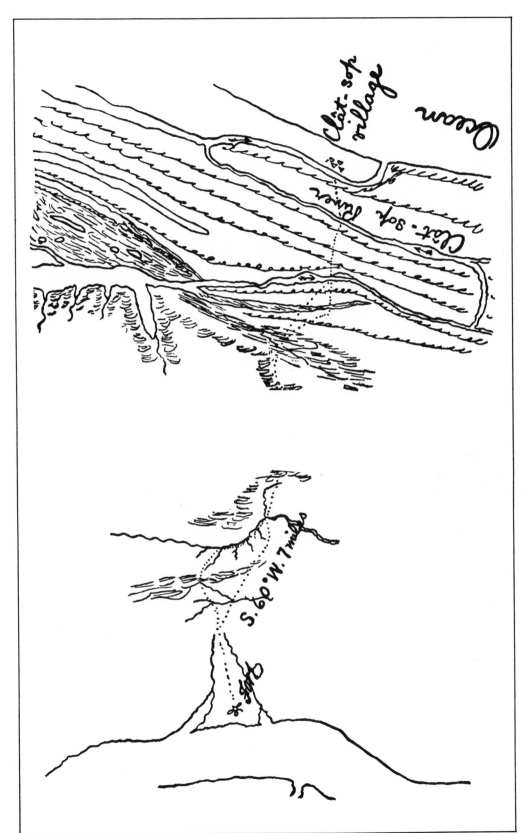

Clat-sop village

Ocean

Clat-sop River

S. 60° W. 7 m

↓ fort

38. Field sketch by Clark showing location of Fort Clatsop and a trail to the ocean. From *The Original Journals of the Lewis and Clark Expedition* (New York, 1904)

December 30, the day the fortification was finally completed, proved to be "the best we have had since at this place, only 3 Showers of rain today" (III, 298), but conditions did not improve insofar as either the weather or the diet were concerned. Added to these discomforts were the hordes of fleas, an "intolerably troublsom vermin," and an even more troublesome variety of pests, the "forward and disagreeable" natives who continually hovered about the American camp, begging and soliciting and pilfering anything that was not either closely guarded or nailed down.[32] The natives told of white traders in the vicinity but the captains were unable to make contact with any vessels, and the only reasons they had to believe the Indian tales were the wide variety of English and American trade goods possessed by the natives, along with the ability of some of the Indians to utter such elegant phrases as "sun of a bitch &c." (III, 327).[33]

The dense vegetation made hunting difficult but there were large elk herds along the coast, and the men of the Corps of Discovery, if uncomfortable, were at least in no immediate danger of starving. Remembering the barrenness of the Columbian Plain, with no fuel and no game, the presence of the assured food and wood supply along the coast prevented the captains from abandoning their soggy and dismal camp and moving inland:

it is true that we could even travel now on our return as far as the timbered country reaches, or to the falls of the river; but further it would be madness for us to attempt to proceed untill April, as the indians inform us that the snows lye knee deep in the plains of Columbia during the winter, and in these plains we could scarcely get as much fuel of any kind as would cook our provision as we descended the river; and even were we happyly over these plains and again in the woody country at the foot of the Rocky Mountains we could not possibly pass that immence barrier of mountains on which the snows ly in winter to the debth in many places of 20 feet; in short the Indians inform us that they are impracticable until about the 1st of June, at which time even there is an abundance of snow but a scanty subsistence may be obtained for the horses. we should not therefore forward ourselves on our homeward journey by reaching the rocky mountains. early than the 1st of June, which we can easily effect by seting out from hence on the 1st of April [III, 350].

So the men of the Lewis and Clark Expedition became *hivernants* for a second time, wintering over in a new wilderness. That wintering, like the one at Fort Mandan, was vastly important for their image of the American Northwest.

32. The coastal natives, particularly those near the mouth of the Columbia, presented a perfect example of the culture disintegration that normally set in after repeated contact with whites.

33. The frequency of trading voyages to the Pacific Northwest coast cannot be measured precisely, but based on the number of recorded voyages, it is apparent that the white-Indian contact was intensive during the decade prceeding Lewis's and Clark's arrival on the coast. See Dorothy O. Johansen, *Empire of the Columbia* (New York, 1967), pp. 34–62.

9

The differences between the winter at Fort Mandan and the winter at Fort Clatsop were vast—in environmental, operational, and conceptual terms. Lewis's comments about the lack of precipitation during the Fort Mandan period could never have applied to the winter on the Pacific, where, from December 7 to March 23, the rains came every day but twelve and only six days were fair. The captains had broken their thermometer on the outward journey and had no accurate basis for comparison of the temperature differential between Mandan and Clatsop, but the Pacific winter was obviously remarkably mild when contrasted with the intense cold of the northern Great Plains.[34] Perhaps the only similarity in environmental terms was the wind, which had blown with such intensity across the open plains near the Great Bend and with equal force roared through the massive timber surrounding Fort Clatsop. But the winds of the Plains had swept the skies clean and clear while the Pacific gales brought fogs across the cold offshore currents and drove rain against the Pacific encampment's log stockade. No longer did the night guards wake the party in wonderment to view the display of the aurora borealis; surrounding Fort Clatsop at night was only the small, wet blackness of night in the Pacific Northwest's rainy season.

Such environmental differences evoked perceptual differences, and the changing scale of perception, in turn, created new operational procedures. Fort Clatsop, surrounded by tall timber and closed in by fog and mist and rain, stimulated a range of thought and activity that was distinct from the operations partly inspired by Fort Mandan and the encircling vastnesses of the open plains. For the view from Fort Clatsop was introspective; where there had been expectancy and anticipation at the winter camp of 1804–05, during the winter of 1805–06 there was reappraisal and inventory.[35] At Fort Mandan there had been planning for the Passage to India and eager formation of new geographical images. At Fort Clatsop there was only the disheartening evaluation of the inaccuracy of the older images and the agonizing retrospective view of a Passage which was now nonexistent.

It had become obvious to Lewis and Clark, partly from their comprehension of how they had misinterpreted earlier geographical lore and partly from their gathering of new information during the summer and fall of 1805, that the route they had taken from the Missouri to the Columbia was not the

34. "I am confident that the climate here is much warmer than in the same parallel of Latitude on the Atlantic Ocean tho' how many degrees is now out of my power to determine" (VI, 203).

35. Although the length of time spent at Fort Mandan was nearly twice that of the expedition's tenure at Fort Clatsop, the length of the Clatsop journals is nearly four times that of the Mandan journals. Although the captains used much of their time in recording valuable ethnographic, botanical, and zoological data during the winter of 1805–06, many of the daily entries begin with the phrase "not any occurrence today worthy of notice" and then proceed to relate the most trivial details—almost as if the captains were engaging in copybook exercises in an attempt to stave off the tedium by keeping their hands and eyes busy.

best. The task they set for themselves during the winter on the Pacific was to determine how best to rationalize their final realization that the Passage did not exist in the form in which it was originally conceived with their desire to fulfill the central objective of their expedition—the discovery of "the most direct & practicable water communication across this continent for the purposes of commerce."[36] By the middle of February, after nearly two months of summing up their geographical data and trying to make some sense out of the lands through which they passed, the captains came to the conclusion which, in many ways, was the most important product of their winter on the Pacific.

"We now discover," wrote Clark on February 14, 1806, "that we have found the most practicable and navigable passage across the Continent of North America" (IV, 70). For all its positive sound, this statement was a negative one, based on the final realization of the disparity between imaginary and real geography and containing within it the ultimate destruction of the age-old myth of the water passageway. Clark's "most practicable and navigable passage" had not been found by exploration. It had been found by combining the lore from Fort Mandan, the past summer's observations in the field, and the geographical knowledge gathered from the Shoshoni, Flathead, and Nez Percé Indians. The key to the mystery of the most practicable passage to the Pacific was the route between the Missouri and the Bitterroot valleys that the explorers had heard about from natives in early September, 1805.[37] And in that key was the recognition, at long last, that passage through the Rocky Mountains must be by land travel and not by water.

The best route from the waters of the Atlantic to those of the Pacific was, wrote Clark, "that which we have traveled with the exception of that part of our route from the foot of the Falls of the Missouri, or in neighbourhood of the enterance of the Rocky Mountains untill we arive on Clarks river [the Bitterroot] at the enterance of *Travelers-rest* Creek":

The distance between those two points would be traveled more advantagiously by land as the navigation of the Missouri above the *Falls* is crooked laborious and 521 miles distant by which no advantage is gained as the rout which we are compelled to travel by land from the source of Jeffersons River to the enterance of *Travellers rest* Creek is 220 miles being further by abt. 600 miles than that from the Falls of the Missourie to the last mentioned point (Travellers rest Creek) and a much worse route if indian information is to be relied on which is from the *Sosonee* or Snake Indians, and the Flatheads of the Columbia [Bitterroot] West of the rocky mountains [IV, 70].

The core of misconception—the short portage from the navigable streams of the Atlantic to the navigable streams of the Pacific—had been effectively demolished.

The water communication across the continent no longer applied; fur-

36. Jackson, *Letters*, p. 61.
37. See pp. 301–2 above.

thermore, the final crossing must be made, according to the captains' re-evaluations, by not one but two long overland journeys. For neither "Lewis's River" (the Snake or "S.E. branch of the Columbia") nor "Clark's River" (the Bitterroot or "N.E. branch of the Columbia") could be "navagated thro' the rocky mountains in consequence of falls and rapids" (IV, 70).[38] From their experiences and from Indian information received on the Pacific side of the Divide, Lewis and Clark reached a central premise about the easiest route across the continent:

the best and most practicable rout across the Continent is by way of the Missouri to the *Falls;* thence to *Clarks* river at the enterance of Travellers rest Creek, from thence up travillers rest Creek to the forks, from whence you prosue a range of mountains which divides the waters of the two forks of this Creek, and which still continues it's westwardly course on [across] the Mountains which divides the waters of the two forks of the Kooskooskee [Clearwater] river to their junction; from thence to descend this river to the S.E. branch of the Columbia, thence down that river to the Columbia and down the Latter to the Pacific Ocian [IV, 71].

This negation of the Passage to India, the feature of all images of the American Northwest since Marquette, was the greatest single transformation of geographical lore for which the journey of Lewis and Clark was responsible.

10

The captains' final conclusion about the "best and most practicable route" across North America was not the only major geographical product of the winter at Fort Clatsop. There were other refinements in geographical knowledge as the captains consolidated their regional views of the different areas through which they had passed and added many new elements to the lore of the Northwest.[39] And for the first time the majority of those elements were based on observation and experience rather than deduction. The captains had completed the traverse line and could now base their views on what they had seen. The country on either side of their traverse line had to be filled in, it is true, with information obtained from Indians or extrapolated from what had been observed. But even the extrapolations had a greater chance of being accurate since they came from empirically derived geographical lore and not from pure imagination.

When the Corps of Discovery had left the Mandan villages in the spring of 1805, they had carried with them an identifiable set of beliefs about the Northwest. One major component of these beliefs related to the Passage to

38. This information was based partly on Indian lore and partly on the captains' own observations.

39. To include a full discussion of the captains' new image of the Northwest would be premature at this point. The subject will be treated fully in ch. 14 below.

India and was modified severely. A second major component of the view from Fort Mandan related to the concept of the Northwest as a garden; it, like the first set of elements, was also changed by the exploratory experience. In looking beyond Fort Mandan Lewis and Clark had persisted in their opinion that the land quality of the western regions was high. With the exception of the small portion of desert-like country near the mouth of the Musselshell, the country confirmed their expectations, and even into the Rockies the captains' journals carried the connotations of "fertile and well-watered" land. But when the expedition crossed the Divide the image of the Garden began to change, and as the explorers sat in their winter camp on the Pacific, looking back at the rich buffalo plains east of the Divide, the trans-formation became complete. In the view from Fort Clatsop the Northwest was still a garden. But that garden stopped at the Rockies; beyond the moun-tains, themselves not much good for anything, were the treeless and barren plains of the Columbia. To the south and east were deserts of rock; beyond, to the west, were the Cascades, too heavily timbered for agricultural occupa-tion. Finally, beyond the last range of mountains, was the Pacific coast, dank and choked with timber and underbrush. If the Passage no longer existed in its original form, neither did the Garden.

The captains' notions on western physiography east of the Continental Divide had not been changed extensively as the result of the completion of their traverse to the Pacific. The basic patterns of the river and mountain systems as laid down on Clark's Fort Mandan map were, with one major exception, still a feature of Lewis's and Clark's concepts during the winter of 1805–06. The major exception was, of course, the southward and westward extension of most rivers of the Missouri system illustrated by the Fort Man-dan map. Exploration had proven that such extension did not exist, and ob-servation had allowed the captains to rectify their earlier errors by placing the Continental Divide in its correct longitudinal position. Other errors were not corrected by exploration, and although the detail and texture of the image of the Missouri system was made finer by the addition of previously unknown streams such as the Marias, the White Earth still headed near the Saskatche-wan and the Yellowstone and Bighorn near the Rio Grande and Colorado.

The greatest transformations in the views of western physiography were made for the lands west of the Continental Divide, presented quite simply on Clark's Fort Mandan map as open plains country traversed by the Columbia and a major southern fork of that river and bounded on the west by the mountains laid down in the Vancouver charts. The first refinement in earlier views was the recognition that the final dividing ridge west of the Missouri's source was by no means the last range of mountains between the upper Mis-souri and the Pacific. The second refinement was in the view of the Colum-bian system, which, after the completion of the journey to the Pacific, was seen as having more than the one major tributary shown on the Fort Mandan map. One of these major feeder streams was the one first contacted opposite the source of the Jefferson. This stream they knew as "Lewis's River," and although they saw it as part of the same system as the Snake, they persisted in viewing the latter river as a tributary of the Salmon. The second major tributary of the Columbia was "Clark's River" or the Bitterroot, and although they knew less about it in absolute terms than they did about the Salmon and Snake, their view of it from Fort Clatsop was quite accurate. No such accuracy prevailed in the captains' conception of still another major tributary of the Columbia, however—in the view from the Pacific a third great stream of the Columbian system that the explorers had not even seen.

II

While at Fort Clatsop, Lewis and Clark had heard from some Indian visitors about a major river that they had somehow missed seeing on their downriver journey to the sea. That river was named the "Multnomah," and behind the mists of ignorance it was probably the Willamette and by no means as great and important a stream as the captains made it. According to Clark's summary of his geographical efforts during the winter of 1805–06 (IV, 70–72), the Multnomah was a large river which fell into the Columbia from the south side at some indeterminate point below the Cascades of the Columbia. One fork of the Multnomah had its source "in the mountains South of the head of Jefferson's River and at no great distance from the Spanish settlements" (IV, 71).[40] Another fork of the Multnomah headed with "North River [the Rio Grande] or the waters of Callifornia [the Colorado]." After the waters of these two branches merged, the river passed through the Columbian Plain and, breaching the Cascade range in the same fashion as the Columbia, entered that river not too far from the coast.

The Willamette River, of course, heads far from the Missouri, the Rio Grande, and the Colorado. Some of the notions on the Multnomah were probably misinterpretations of the information relayed by coastal and Columbia River Indians about the course of the Snake above its junction with the Columbia. But the greater part of the captains' view of the Multnomah stemmed from something even more important and fundamental and more characteristic in their view of western rivers as a whole. Lewis and Clark had traveled the Missouri to its source and then across the Divide to the Columbia's waters. In so doing they had amended their previous notion about both the extension of the Missouri toward the west and south and the compression of the land area between the Divide and the Pacific. But these amendments

40. A major reason for the belief in the proximity of these waters with New Mexican rivers was the fact that the Shoshonis (who supposedly inhabited the upper parts of the Multnomah) were believed to possess "a great number of mules . . . the mules in the possession of the Indians are principally stolen from the Spaniards of Mexeco." Furthermore, Clark remarked that "Among the Sosones of the upper part of the S.E. fork of the Columbia [the Lemhi] we saw several horses with spanish brands on them which we supposed had been stolen from the inhabitants of Mexeco" (IV, 74).

held for the Missouri-Columbia connections only. Those rivers which still remained outside the explorers' area of experience and observation—the Yellowstone, Snake, Colorado, Rio Grande, and mythical Multnomah—were still seen as flowing from a pyramidal height-of-land, and their courses were still overextended.

Within a small area of about 400 square miles to the south of Lewis's and Clark's traverse, the pyramidal height-of-land still existed. From that common source area the Missouri (in the form of the Jefferson and Madison), the Yellowstone and its major tributary the Bighorn, the Rio del Norte or Rio Grande, the Platte, the Arkansas, the south fork of "Lewis's River" or the Snake, and the Multnomah (a necessity of geography, needed to complete the symmetry) all had their sources. The theoretical geography of Jonathan Carver and early nineteenth-century speculators such as Thomas Jefferson had not been confirmed by exploration in the area of the Missouri-Columbia interlocking drainage. But to the south, toward the still-unknown and unseen, it was very much a part of Lewis's and Clark's conception of the West in the winter of 1805–06.

If the pyramidal height-of-land or core drainage region still persisted in geographical theory, however, it was no longer thought of in the same way as it had been prior to the Lewis and Clark journey. For experience had proved to the American explorers that many of the rivers of the West were not navigable, and where Jefferson had believed in the navigability of streams all the way from their mouths to their sources in the core drainage area, Lewis's and Clark's observation had proven that the short portage did not exist. In their Fort Clatsop journals both captains concluded that a transcontinental route by way of the newly conceptualized core drainage region would only "lengthen the distance greatly and incounter the same difficulties in passing the Rocky Mountains" (IV, 72) as they themselves had met on their outward journey. For the first time in geographical lore the concept of the pyramidal height-of-land, the core drainage region, was being merged (if fuzzily and inarticulately) with the concept of a continental divide. Wherever a crossing of the mountains was made, in Lewis's and Clark's view, that crossing was bound to be a difficult one. This was the final denunciation of the Passage to India worked out by Lewis and Clark on that gray Pacific coast during the dismal winter at Fort Clatsop. The winter was dismal not only in that the sun continually hid behind leaden clouds but also in that the sun of hope which had shone on the Passage for so long had finally set.

12

For the last part of the winter, from the middle of February, when Lewis and Clark were finalizing their geographical theories, to the end of March, the two explorers crammed their journals with notes on the flora and fauna of the country between the Divide and the Pacific and with detailed ethnological descriptions of the unique native culture of the coastal region.[41] There was no further mention of the Passage, and with nowhere else to go and nothing else to do, it may have been that the captains were trying to fill the blankness of their days by filling the blankness of the pages of their elkskin-bound field books. The dripping and shrouded days merged into one another and, interminably, into sodden weeks. The hunters began to have difficulty finding elk during the first few days of March, and the captains, although they had earlier determined not to leave their Pacific quarters until at least the first of April, began to re-evaluate the projected departure date—"if we find that the Elk have left us, we have determined to ascend the river slowly and indeavour to procure subsistence on the way, consuming the Month of March in the woody country" (IV, 135).

The impatience that the captains and their men felt to get away from Fort Mandan had been created by the desire to get on about the business of discovery and reach their objective. The impatience to get away from Fort Clatsop was a wish to escape, a fleeing from rather than a running toward. By the middle of March none of them could take the local environment any longer, and, earlier decisions to remain until April 1 notwithstanding, Lewis noted as early as March 17 that "we have had our perogues prepared for our departure, and shall set out as soon as the weather will permit" (IV, 176). The next day he prepared a list of the members of the Corps of Discovery to be given to one of the Clatsop chiefs and, hopefully, to find its way into the hands of "some civilized person who may see the same" in order that

it may be made known to the informed world, that the party consisting of the persons whose names are hereunto annexed, and who were sent out by the government of the U'States in May 1804. to explore the interior of the Continent of North America, did penetrate the same by way of the Missouri and Columbia Rivers, to the discharge of the latter into the Pacific Ocean, where they arrived on the 14th of November 1805, and from whence they departed the [blank space] day of March 1806 on their return to the United States by the same rout they had come out [IV, 181].[42]

Almost by the same route but not quite. For when the expedition, delayed by several days of rain, finally turned their backs on Fort Clatsop and again placed their canoes in the Columbia River, the captains knew that the central objective of their return trip would be to deviate enough from their outward-bound journey in order to test their deductions about the best route to the waters of the Missouri.

---

41. Cutright (*Lewis and Clark*, pp. 257–73) presents a very valuable condensation of the Fort Clatsop journals.

42. According to the Biddle edition of the journals (*History*, II, 204), this list was presented by the natives to Captain Hill of the Boston ship *Lydia*. Captain Hill gave the note to an acquaintance in Canton, China, who in turn sent a copy of it to Philadelphia in January, 1807, several months after Lewis and Clark had made their return to St. Louis.

When the members of the Corps of Discovery turned their backs on Fort Clatsop they also turned their backs to the Pacific and faced the east. For the first time in the exploration of the American Northwest, men had faced away from the glitter of the promised Golden Chersonese, and the breezes of the Spice Islands no longer smelled so sweet. The westward trek of Lewis and Clark to the Pacific was an end to the centuries of search for the Northwest Passage. The return of the Corps of Discovery was an inward journey and a beginning. Lewis and Clark would return to civilization with a new image of the West, and as they came away from the dreary coast and faced the mountains they became not the last seekers after the Passage to India but the first mountain men. In their new image there would be many dreams of the fertility and beauty and vastness of the West. But the dream was no longer the Passage to India.

CHAPTER 13

THE RETURN:
TESTING A
REVISED GEOGRAPHY

The sunrise of Sunday, March 23, 1806, was hidden by the same thick clouds and sheets of rain which had obscured every dawn for more than a week, hampering the captains and men of the Corps of Discovery in their efforts to prepare for the departure from Fort Clatsop. But having accomplished virtually everything which induced their remaining on the Pacific coast[1] and being heartily tired of the bleak coastal climate, Lewis and Clark decided to load their meager baggage into the canoes and, despite the high winds, to bid their "final adieu to Fort Clatsop" (IV, 197). When the rain ceased and the noonday sun burned away the clouds, the party pushed their craft into the Lewis and Clark River and headed downstream for the Columbia and for home. All members of the command must have exulted at leaving the soggy winter quarters, and Clark, who had grumbled throughout the winter about the rain and chill dampness, expressed the exultation by looking back at Fort Clatsop and concluding—now that they were leaving—that it might not have

1. The only objective unfulfilled, remarked Lewis, was "that of meeting with the traders who visit the entrance of this river" (IV, 192).

been such a bad place after all: "we . . . have lived as well as we had any right to expect, and we can say that we were never one day without 3 meals of some kind a day either pore Elk meat or roots, notwithstanding the repeated fall of rain which has fallen almost constantly" (IV, 197).

The Lewis and Clark Expedition was finally homeward-bound. The journey of exploration which had been conceived by Thomas Jefferson so long ago—or so it must have seemed to the wilderness-weary veterans of the company—had already accomplished a great deal. On their return Lewis and Clark would accomplish a great deal more. As soon as the captains had worked out the new assumptions on western geography during the Fort Clatsop winter, the decision had been made to separate the party into several smaller groups. "We shall be necessarily divided into three or four parties on our return in order to accomplish the objects we have in view" (IV, 180), wrote Meriwether Lewis, and those objectives, the trying out of the new assumptions, would be fulfilled. Just because a short portage had not been discovered between the Missouri and Columbia, the efforts of the expedition need not be a loss. Consequently Lewis was to attempt the short passage between the Bitterroot and the Missouri and to explore the Marias, the river he believed and hoped would rise near enough to the Saskatchewan to provide an American entry to the rich Canadian fur country. Clark was to explore the mighty Yellowstone, whose waters headed far to the south, perhaps offering connections with the "Spanish rivers" and the potentially lucrative fur and silver trade of New Mexico. Following these separate surveys, the captains would return to the United States with additional geographical lore and with a new and much more complete image of the entire West. But most important of all, they would return. In doing so they would give to the American nation a West "with which the mind could deal."[2]

2

The expedition moved slowly up the Columbia's spring flood, and the currents which had borne the canoes down from the Cascades so rapidly now worked against their upriver progress. Averaging only 16 miles of hard paddling into the current every day, the members of the Corps of Discovery passed the mouth of the Cowlitz River, flowing into the Columbia from the north, on March 27. They had missed the Cowlitz on their downriver voyage the previous November, and now, when they obtained descriptions of it from natives near its mouth, they were able to fill in one of the few remaining gaps in the geography of the coastal area. "I suspect," wrote Lewis, "that this river waters the country lying West of the range of mountains [the Cascades] which pass the columbia between the great falls and rapids, and north of the

2. DeVoto, *Journals of Lewis and Clark*, p. lii.

same nearly to the low country which commences on the N.W. coast" south of Puget Sound (IV, 206).[3] While the Cowlitz was not as important a river as the captains made it, their commentary on it was significant. During the downriver journey their observations had been brief and inconclusive as the result of the relative speed at which they had been traveling and their impatience to get within view of the ocean. And although the most important of the increments Lewis and Clark made to geographical knowledge had already been added before the departure from Fort Clatsop, many empty spaces in the image of western geography would be filled with features like the Cowlitz as the expedition slowly moved up the Columbia.

The weather continued windy, rainy, and disagreeable, and the hunters ranging ahead of the main command found little game, those few deer they did manage to kill being "remarkably pore." The level of the Columbia rose persistently, retarding progress upstream as the men were forced to keep their craft close to mid-channel to avoid the brushy tangles and trees washed down by early spring runoff. By March 29 the party had arrived at the western margin of "the Columbian valley" (IV, 213), a feature that the captains had come to recognize as a major topographic division of the coastal region. "This valley," Lewis observed, "is terminated on it's lower [western] side by the mountanous country which borders the coast, and above [eastward] by the range of mountains [the Cascades] which pass the Columbia between the great falls and rapids of the Columbia river" (IV, 22).[4] The width or east-west extent of the valley was estimated to be around 70 miles, and although its north-south length was indeterminate, the captains believed it "to be very extensive." Their conceptions of physiographic regions were still based on the Blue Ridge–Shenandoah model, and the "Columbian valley," like the Shenandoah, ran at right angles to the Columbia, bounded on the west by the coastal ranges and on the east by the "most noble looking peaks" of the Cascades. Furthermore, the Columbian valley duplicated the richness and fertility of the Shenandoah and, according to the captains' estimates, was capable of maintaining an agricultural population of 40,000 to 50,000 persons. It was, wrote Lewis, "the only desireable situation for a settlement which I have seen on the West side of the Rocky mountains" (IV, 220).[5]

In order to complete the symmetry of this fertile region, the captains believed it necessary that some river enter the Columbia from the south,

3. The Indian name for the river and the one used by Lewis in his journals was "Coweliskee."

4. The captains had originally called this valley "Wappato" after the plant that was such an important part of the regional native diet (Coues, *History*, III, 916, n. 27).

5. Given the initial destination of the Oregon migrations of the 1840s, Lewis's words seem highly prophetic. It was largely on the strength of his description that such advocates of American settlement in Oregon as Hall Jackson Kelley, founder of the American Society for Encouraging the Settlement of Oregon Territory, claimed in his "Geographical Sketch of That Part of North America Called Oregon" that the Willamette valley, if "improved and embellished" by American agriculturalists, would become "the lovliest and most envied country on earth." Kelley's published works have been collected and re-issued as *Hall J. Kelley on Oregon*, ed. F. W. Powell (Princeton, 1932).

draining the southern portions of the valley as the Cowlitz drained the north. On their seaward journey of the previous year they thought they had found such a river, and during their evaluations of western geography at Fort Clatsop had come to recognize the "Quicksand" (Sandy) River as the stream "watering the Country to the Sth."[6] But when they reached the Sandy River on March 31 and halted to make observations near the mouth of this potentially important stream, Lewis and Clark received information from Indians that caused them to make a major modification in their image of the Pacific Northwest.

While the captains and their command were forming their camp in a small clearing on the Columbia's north shore, immediately opposite the mouth of the Sandy, they entered into discussions with three natives encamped nearby. The Indians informed them by sign language that the "quick sand river was short only headed in Mt. Hood which is in view. . . . this is a circumstance we did not expect as we had heretofore deemed [it] a considerable river" (IV, 226). This data was corroborated on the following day by other Indians; the captains were now convinced "that there must be some other considerable river which flowed into the Columbia on it's south side below us which we have not yet seen, as the extensive valley on that side of the river lying between the mountainous country of the Coast and the Western mountains must be watered by some stream which we heretofore supposed was the quicksand river" (IV, 227). The expedition could not leave the vicinity until the puzzle was cleared up, and Clark, remembering the rumored river called "Multnomah" by natives at Fort Clatsop, decided that it would be necessary to conduct a search for that stream. And when Sergeant Pryor, who had been dispatched up the Sandy River on a brief reconnaissance, confirmed the Indian information that it was indeed a relatively short stream, the resolution to find and investigate the Multnomah became even stronger.

On April 2 several natives who lived near the mouth of the Willamette visited the American camp and drew a sketch of that river ("which they called Mult-no-mah") on a grass mat with lumps of coal (fig. 39). The Multnomah River, it was learned, emptied into the Columbia below the party's present position, and since its mouth was obscured by several large islands, the explorers had missed seeing it on both the downriver and upriver journeys. After being informed that it "was a large river and run a considerable distance to the South between the mountains," Clark took one of the pirogues and seven men and headed back down the Columbia. Late in the afternoon of April 2, with Mts. Hood, Jefferson, St. Helens, and Adams shining on the eastern horizon, Clark and his party entered the river "which the native had informed us of, called *Multnomah* River" and found it to be a noble stream, fully one-quarter the size of the Columbia and deep enough

6. Apparently, by the time the party reached the Sandy River, Clark's geographical intuition had already told him that some other river drained the southern portion of the region—"Capt. Clark could not believe [the "Quicksand" River] to be the river watering the Country to the Sth." (V, 225).

39. Sketch map by Clark showing the Multnomah River according to information from the Indians. From *The Original Journals of the Lewis and Clark Expedition* (New York, 1904)

for the largest ocean-going vessels (IV, 238).[7] After camping near the mouth of the Multnomah or Willamette for the night, Clark took his command up the river a short distance during the morning of April 3. He proceeded far enough to learn that the Multnomah came from the east of southeast, that navigation on it was obstructed by great falls above which the river passed high mountains, and that beyond these mountains was "an open plain of great extent." "Being perfectly satisfied of the size and magnitude of this great river which must water that vast tract of Country between the western range of mountains [the Rockies] and those on the sea coast and as far S. as the Waters of Callifornia" (IV, 239), Clark determined to return to join Lewis at the camp near the mouth of the Sandy.[8]

3

When the captains were reunited on the afternoon of April 3, Clark found that his companion and the rest of the party had been busy—for the rumors of the Multnomah had not been the only reason for halting opposite the Sandy River. During the first day at the temporary camp, the captains had been visited by natives coming down the Columbia from fishing camps at the Cascades and the Dalles. These Indians brought the disturbing news that the salmon had not yet reached the great rapids and that the Indians resident there were "much streightened . . . for want of food" (IV, 228). Since the captains had intended to procure pounded salmon from the tribes at the Cascades in order to get their command across the Columbian Plain where "there are no deer Antelope nor Elk on which we can depend for subsistence" (IV, 228), this intelligence necessitated a change of plans. Accordingly, Lewis and Clark decided to remain at this site until their hunters could kill enough game and enough meat could be dried to last the party as far as the Clearwater. In addition, the captains concluded that it would be wise to try to purchase as many of the fine native canoes as possible. These canoes could be traded for horses when the party arrived among the horse Indians of the Columbian Plain, and the speed of travel toward the Rockies, the Missouri, and home could thereby be increased. The necessity of water travel would soon be eliminated as part of the operational procedure of the expedition.

The meat supply soon reached sufficient proportions so that the captains felt they could reach the Clearwater safely—"provided we can obtain a fiew

7. Clark's assumption about the potential port facilities of the mouth of the Willamette were basically correct, and the major port city of Portland, Oregon, grew up later near the river's entrance into the Columbia.

8. On his return to meet Lewis, Clark received additional information about the Multnomah from various Indians, one of whom "drew with his finger, in the dust, a sketch of Multnomah river" (Coues, *History*, III, 927). The copy of this sketch made by Clark is printed facing p. 242 in vol. IV of Thwaites.

dogs, horses and roots by the way" (IV, 254). On April 6, "the most perfectly fair day that we have seen for a Some time," the canoes were once
again loaded and set into the Columbia. The signs of spring became more
frequent, and as the captains and their men pushed toward the interior, the
deciduous trees strung along the river and scattered across the surrounding
hills began to present a delicate green contrast to the near black of the spruce
and fir. The weather exhibited its traditional spring capriciousness, however,
and on one occasion the expedition was forced to delay a day in an uncomfortable camp because the high winds and waves made travel on the river
impossible. The gentle hills of the "Columbian valley" gradually gave way to
steep and rocky heights upon which snow fell during the cold nights, and on
April 10 the party reached the lower end of the Cascades and began the
arduous portage around those mighty rapids.

The portage around the Cascades was marred only by the loss of one of
the large canoes and by petty troubles with the thieving and quarrelsome
Indians that resided on both banks of the Columbia. By April 13 the passage
was completed and the party once again moved eastward, past the high and
rocky river hills which exhibited in many places "very romantic seenes" (IV,
279). On both sides of the Columbia spring freshets tumbled from these
heights to fall into the river, and the spruce and fir of the coastal region gave
way to the long-leafed pine of the uplands. Near the mouth of the Hood
River, above the Cascades, the party met with horse Indians for the first time
since the preceding fall, but the Americans' meager and depleted trading
goods did not entice the natives sufficiently to part them from their animals.[9]

On April 16 the party reached the westernmost margin of the Columbian
Plain—"the last point at which there is a single stick of timber on the river for
a great distance and is the commencement of the open plains which extend
nearly to the base of the rocky Mts" (IV, 287). But still they had not acquired mounts with which to cross those plains, and although both captains
had become skilled traders, Lewis began to fret that "we shall not be enabled
to obtain as many horses at this place as will convey our baggage and unless
we do obtain a sufficient number for that purpose we shall not hasten our
progress as a part of our baggage must still be conveyed by waters" (IV,
291). In spite of the difficulties in obtaining stock and the pessimism with
which he viewed his future prospects, however, Lewis was glad to leave the
fog-shrouded and vegetation-cloaked coastal region and come once again to
plains country. "Even at this place which is merely on the border of the
plains of Columbia the climate seems to have changed the air feels dryer and
more pure. the earth is dry and seems as if there had been no rain for a week
or ten days" (IV, 290). The Columbian Plain, viewed with distrust on first

9. Even before they had left Fort Clatsop, Lewis remarked that "two handerkerchiefs
would not contain all the small articles of merchandize which we possess . . . on this stock
we have wholly to depend for the purchase of horses and such portion of our subsistence
from the Indians as it will be in our powers to obtain" (IV, 173).

contact the previous fall, was evaluated differently after the damp months on the Pacific—"the plain is covered with a rich virdure of grass and herbs from four to nine inches high and exhibits a beautifull seen particularly pleasing after having been so long imprisoned in mountains and those almost impenetrably thick forrests of the seacoast" (IV, 290). The woodsman had become plainsman, and in conceptual terms it was one of the most important events of the expedition.[10]

4

At the lower end of the Dalles the captains separated once again and began to move up the river in a leap-frogging fashion, Lewis seeing to the safe portage of the boats and cargoes around the rapids and Clark on shore attempting to procure horses from the natives. By April 19 the captains were still short of the horses they would need if they were to leave the river, although they had acquired a sufficient quantity of pack animals to allow the largest canoes to be cut up for fuel.[11] The fruitlessness of Clark's attempts to buy horses led Lewis to describe the Indians residing at the Dalles as "poor, dirty, proud, haughty, inhospitable, parsimonious and faithless in every rispect" (IV, 304). But in spite of the difficulties he encountered in horse-trading with the "parsimonious" natives, Clark did secure information which confirmed his evaluation of the Multnomah as the major stream draining the country south of the Columbia. From Indians who lived near the mouth of the Deschutes River just above Celilo Falls he learned that the Deschutes had its sources in the Cascade range and therefore did "not water that extensive country we have heretofore calculated on. a great portion of the Columbia and Lewis's river and between the same and the waters of Callifornia must be watered by the Multnomah river" (IV, 308).

Once the Dalles and Celilo Falls had been passed and quiet water lay ahead of them, the captains made a decision designed to speed up the march toward the Clearwater. From here on some of the party, in two canoes loaded with baggage, would travel by water while the remainder of the force would walk onshore, using the ten horses purchased thus far to transport all those goods not carried by water. The men traveling by river had the better of it, for the level of the Columbia, higher than it had been in the fall, covered "most of the rocks in the bed in the river" (IV, 318) and obscured the most dangerous rapids. But the land party, forced to travel across the loose soil and pebbles of the river strands, found each day's march "very fatigueing" and complained nightly "of the soarness of their feet" (IV, 419–20). The relative

10. Lewis's enthusiastic initial reaction to the plains probably resulted from two factors —relief at being away from the coast and a retention (perhaps unconscious) of an overall favorable impression of plains country developed on the Missouri and not completely lost in spite of the generally negative view of the Columbian Plain in the fall of 1805.

11. Coues, *History*, III, 956.

hardships of travel by land notwithstanding, the captains had decided that mode of travel would get them to the mountains more quickly, and finally, after enough horses had been purchased to carry all the baggage, the entire command left the river.[12]

As the men of the Corps struck out across the rough terraces lying between the river and the higher bluffs and escarpments of the plains, the initial enthusiasm the captains had felt about entering the drier regions began to wane. Cold winds from the Cascade range swept across the plains, and no fresh meat was available to augment the tiresome diet of dried flesh, dogmeat, and salmon. The rains of the coast did not reach the interior, and the infertile, drought-parched plains stretched out on both sides of the river, although the short grass which covered those plains was, in spite of the season, excellent feed for the horses (IV, 323). By April 27 the party had reached a point on the Columbia's northern side immediately opposite the mouth of the Walla Walla River, and here they found a village of Walla Walla Indians whose cordial chief they had met the October before.[13]

The friendly Walla Wallas provided the American explorers with food and shelter, and in addition presented them with horses and the loan of canoes to transport loads across the south side of the Columbia. More important, however, was the geographical lore offered by the natives (fig. 40). "The indians informed us," wrote Lewis, "that there was a good road which passed from the columbia opposite to this village to the entrance of the Kooskooskee [Clearwater] on the S. side of Lewis's river" (IV, 329). This route was well stocked with deer, antelope, and good water and grass for the horses, according to the Walla Wallas, and would shorten the distance from their village to the Clearwater by more than 80 miles—"under these circumstances we did not hesitate in pursuing the route recommended" (IV, 329).

The Walla Wallas also substantiated the captains' conjectures about the drainage patterns of the entire Pacific Northwest and added new data on the Columbian Plain. The Walla Walla River, the Indians reported, had its sources in the range of mountains visible toward the southeast, and these mountains, running from southwest to northeast, terminated near a "Southe[r]n branch of Lewis's river short of the Rocky mountains" (IV, 336). This was the first accurate rendering of the alignment of the Blue Mountains and of the Grande Ronde River flowing along their eastern flanks to join the Snake. Other major streams of the Columbian Plain (the Deschutes, Umatilla, and John Day), reported the Walla Wallas, had their sources in this same range of mountains or in the Cascade range, which separated "the waters of the Multnomah from those of the Columbia river" (IV, 336). A Shoshoni Indian

12. This operational decision was based on the desire to reach the United States before the onset of another winter and on the fact that travel by water was no longer necessary since the objective of the all-water journey had already been recognized as unrealistic.

13. Cutright, *Lewis and Clark*, p. 283. The chief's name was Yellept, and the captains noted that his friendliness was most welcome after the "cold, inhospitable treatment" the explorers had received from the Columbia River natives (Coues, *History*, III, 971).

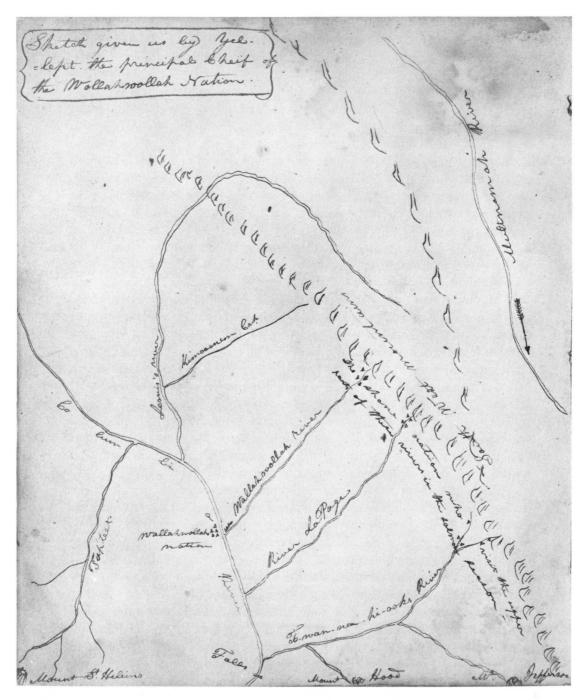

40. Sketch map by Lewis from information provided by Chief Yellept of the
Walla Walla nation   COURTESY, STATE HISTORICAL SOCIETY OF MISSOURI, COLUMBIA

prisoner of the Walla Wallas added the information that far to the south, in the plains beyond the Cascade and Blue ranges, there was a "large river runing to the N.W. which was as wide as the Columbia at this place which is nearly one mile."

One more time Lewis and Clark were hearing about the course of the Snake above its junction with the Clearwater and Columbia—and once more they misinterpreted the information. In their image the large river to the south was the Multnomah, and although the account the Shoshoni had given of it was "no doubt somewhat exagurated," the rumors of a great river south of the Cascade and Blue mountains evinced "the certainty of the Multnomah being a very large river and that it's waters are seperated from the Columbia by those mountains, and that with the aid of a Southwardly branch of Lewis's river which pass around the Eastern extremity of those mountains, it must water that vast tract of country extending from those mountains to the Waters of the Gulf of Callifornia. and no doubt it heads with the Rochejhone [Yellowstone] and Del Nord [Rio Grande]" (IV, 339). It was a grand geography—if altogether erroneous—and the magnificient distortion of the relatively inconsequential Willamette into the mighty-but-fictional Mult-nomah, one of the major rivers of the entire West, was the most critical of Lewis's and Clark's rare geographical errors. It was, however, an error most logically derived. For nothing in their geographical imagination allowed for the vast region of interior drainage that actually separates the Columbian basin from the waters of the Gulf of California; the Great Basin would not become a feature of western physiography until a good guess by Jedediah Smith in the 1830s and scientific proof by John Frémont in the 1840s made it so.[14]

5

On April 30 Lewis and Clark and their men, accompanied by a Walla Walla guide and a Nez Percé family that had joined them downriver, left the Columbia and angled almost due east across the sandy sagebrush plains of the Walla Walla valley toward the mouth of the Clearwater. The route the In-dians had recommended to them proved to be a good one, eliminating the windings and treacherous rapids of the Snake River and leading through a country in which the sand and sage gradually merged into lands of darker and richer soil and "a plenty of wood water and game quite to the Kooskooskee" (IV, 345). The open plains reminded the captains of the plains of the Mis-souri—with one cardinal exception: "these are not enlivened by the vast herds of buffaloe Elk &c. which ornament the other" (IV, 345). There was enough game to feed the party, however, and as the explorers neared the Snake River

14. Goetzmann, *Exploration and Empire*, pp. 141–44.

the plains became even more fertile and were covered with higher grasses and less sagebrush.

After passing through fertile lands "consisting of a dark rich loam" (IV, 354), the expedition reached the Snake River on May 4, and here the captains found a small village of Nez Percé. One of the residents of this village had been a trustworthy guide for the party during the journey from the Clearwater to the Dalles the previous fall, and on the strength of his recommendations the captains determined to cross the Snake at this point and ascend the Clearwater along its northern bank. Here, their former guide reported, they would find the Nez Percé band to whom they had entrusted their horses and gear before beginning the descent of the Clearwater to the Columbia. The American explorers forded the Snake immediately and began their trek up the deep canyon of the Clearwater early on the morning of May 5.

As they proceeded up the Clearwater River, the captains obtained the kind of geographical information which, although relatively inconsequential, was indicative of the function of their return journey in filling the geographic gaps left after the outward trek of the year before. Not too far west of their old canoe camp at the forks of the Clearwater, Lewis and Clark met a group of Coeur d'Alêne Indians who resided "at the falls of a large river dis[c]harging itself into the Columbia on it's East side to the North of the entrance of Clark's river" (IV, 363). This river, the Indians told them, headed in a large lake in the mountains, and turning to their Arrowsmith chart for the first time in a long while, the captains concluded that the river of which the Coeur d'Alênes spoke was probably that "which Fidler calls the great lake river."[15] The attempt to blend new and old geographies was obvious, but in the blending was the inherent recognition that the "great lake river" was not, as Arrowsmith had shown it, separated by a narrow ridge of mountains from the Missouri. The features of pre-exploratory geographical lore were still occasionally recognizable, but their juxtaposition was totally new.

On May 7, guided by a brother of the Nez Percé chief with whom they had left their horses, Lewis and Clark and their command crossed over the Clearwater and proceeded up the south side of the river across a section of the Camas Prairie country. The landscape was impressive: "the face of the country when you once have ascended the river hills is perfectly level and partially covered with the long-leafed pine. The soil is a dark rich loam thickly covered with grass and herbatious plants which afford a delightful pasture for horses. In short it is a beautifull fertile and picturesque country" (IV, 368). Much less pleasing was the news received when the American party reached the Nez Percé camp where their horses were supposed to have been kept and discovered that the intratribal squabbles during the winter had

15. The natives were probably describing the Spokane River, although it enters the Columbia from the south and not north of the entry of the Clark Fork. Clark's notes "from the Chopunnish information" (V, 93–94) seem to indicate that the journal entry referring to the mouth of this river north of the Clark Fork may have been an error. See Coues, *History*, III, 991–92.

diverted the Nez Percé chief, and as a consequence their horses had been left untended and had scattered.

But even more staggering intelligence was forthcoming: "The Spurs of the Rocky Mountains which were in view from the high plain today were perfectly covered with snow. the Indians inform us that the snow is yet so deep on the mountains that we shall not be able to pass them untill the next full moon or about the first of June; others set the time at still a more distant period. this [is] unwelcom inteligence to men confined to a diet of horsebeef and roots, and who are as anxious as we are to return to the fat plains of the Missouri and thence to our native homes" (IV, 369). The news was disquieting at best, and about the only plus that came out of the first day at the Nez Percé camp was an Indian sketch "of the principall watercourse West of the Rocky Mountains" which made the "main Southwardly branch of Lewis's river much more extensive than the other [Salmon]" (V, 5). Although the captains' plans and timetable for crossing the mountains were going awry, they were at least beginning to clear up the gross inaccuracies surrounding the course and importance of the Snake River.

While several members of the party and a number of Nez Percé searched for the branded American horses, Lewis took the opportunity to make observations he had been unable to make the previous fall. After surveying the high prairies along the Clearwater, he revised his earlier estimations of the Pacific slopes and added the immediate westward margins of the Rockies to the Willamette and Cowlitz valleys as a "desireable situation for a settlement":

The country along the rocky mountains for several hundred miles in length and about 50 in width is level extreemly fertile and in many parts covered with a tall and open growth of the longleafed pine, near the watercourses the hills are steep and lofty tho' are covered with a good soil not remarkably stony and possess more timber than the level country. the bottom lands on the watercou[r]ses are rather narrow and confined tho' fertile & seldom inundated. this country would form an extensive settlement; the climate appears quite as mild as that of similar latitude on the Atlantic coast if not more so and it cannot be otherwise than healthy; it possesses a fine dry pure air. the grass and many plants are now upwards of knee high. I have no doubt but this tract of country if cultivated would produce in great abundance every article essentially necessary to the comfort and subsistence of civillized man [V, 11].[16]

Such musings were important to the long-range purposes of the expedition. But a much more critical matter was facing the captains. They could not force the snow-clad heights of the mountains for nearly a month and must, therefore, find some temporary campsite with game, fuel, and shelter from the unpredictable spring weather.

16. It would be many years before "any positive response" to Lewis's enthusiastic description of the Idaho prairie country would be made (Meinig, *The Great Columbian Plain*, p. 31).

6

On May 14, after having caught up nearly all their horses and transported their baggage across the Clearwater to its north shore, Lewis and Clark and their men selected a campsite near the present location of Kamiah, Idaho. Here, in an "extensive level bottom thinly timbered with the long-leafed pine" (V, 33), they were compelled to reside until the snows left the mountains to the east. This camp (Camp Chopunnish)[17] was near what the Indians had told them was the best hunting in the entire region and, being on the river, was "convenient to the salmon which we expect daily." From May 14 until June 10 the restless explorers remained in their bivouac by the Clearwater, with the exception of the winters at Fort Mandan and Fort Clatsop a longer time than they spent in any other place during the two and a half years of the expedition. But conditions were considerably different at Camp Chopunnish than at those other two encampments—for where Fort Mandan had been a place of planning and expectation and Fort Clatsop one of re-evaluation, Camp Chopunnish was simply impatience and waiting.

Daily existence at Camp Chopunnish was normally just a matter of finding enough food to keep the party alive and healthy. While Lewis compiled lengthy botanical and zoological entries in his journals, Clark was kept busy ministering to the numerous ailments of both his own men and the local Indians, who set great store by his medical talents.[18] The weather was rainy and disagreeable, but the location of the camp in the bottom of the Clearwater canyon protected the party from the snows which continued to fall on the plains beyond the river hills:

the air on the top of the river hills or high plains forms a distinct climate, the air is much colder, and vegitation is not as forward by at least 15 or perhaps 20 days. the rains which fall in the river bottoms are snows on the plain. at the distance of fifteen miles from the river and on the Eastern border of this plain the Rocky Mountains commence and present us with winter at it's utmost extreem. the snow is yet many feet deep even near the base of these mountains here we have summer spring and winter within the short space of 15 or 20 miles [V, 39].

The captains kept a close watch on the level of the river, despairing when it fell and exulting when it rose, for they attributed rising water to the melting of snow in the mountains—"that icy barier which seperates me from my friends and Country, from all which makes life esteemable.—patience, patience" (V, 45). Well might Lewis have needed to obey his own exhortation

17. The captains themselves did not give the name to this camp. It was originally applied by Coues and has been accepted by later writers (cf. Cutright, *Lewis and Clark*, p. 287; and Coues, *History*, III, 1010, n. 2).

18. Descriptions of Clark's medical expertise are scattered throughout many works dealing with the expedition. Cutright (*Lewis and Clark*) describes many of Clark's medical procedures. Dr. E. G. Chuinard ("The Medical Aspects of the Lewis and Clark Expedition," Friends of the Library, Corvallis, Ore., 1965) is presently working on a book-length study of Lewis and Clark as pioneer medical practitioners.

of "patience"—for the natives he and Clark consulted all agreed that the mountains could not be passed until at least the middle of June (V, 46).

After only a week at Camp Chopunnish, the captains were beginning to chafe at the forced delay in their homeward journey, and since game was scarce they began to consider moving their camp farther toward the mountains. But the hunters who roved the plains above the river every day reported that the snows still lay deep on the spurs of the Rockies visible to the east (V, 60). Game grew progressively harder to find, and when the salmon failed to appear when the natives thought it should, Lewis and Clark in desperation sent one of the sergeants and two men overland to the Snake River to take advantage of the reported salmon run in that stream. The men returned with seventeen large fish, but the journey had been so long that the fish were spoiled and putrid. The side trip to the Snake was not without value, however, for it added one of the few items of geographical interest. The three soldiers had seen both the Salmon and Snake rivers on their brief expedition, and their observations allowed the captains to correct a major misconception of the outward journey—from here on the Snake or "S. branch of Lewis's river" would be viewed as "the principal fork" of that stream.[19]

By June 3 the explorers had lost all hope of the salmon arriving in time to allow enough fish to be caught and dried before crossing the Rockies. Consequently, a decision was made to leave the Clearwater and head for Weippe Prairie "on the 10th to hunt in that neighbourhood a few days, if possible lay in a stock of meat and then attempt the mountains about the middle of this month" (V, 104). The final remnants of the expedition's meat supply was consumed on June 9, and on the following day, "much elated with the idea of moving on towards their friends and country" (V, 119), Lewis and Clark and their men abandoned Camp Chopunnish and ascended the rugged north side of the Clearwater canyon to the plains above.

7

The lovely pale blue blossoms of the camas lily covered the prairies near present-day Weippe, Idaho, and as the captains and their men viewed the scene from their temporary camp in the prairie, Lewis commented that the covering of camas flowers so resembled "lakes of fine clear water . . . that on first sight I could have swoarn it was water" (V, 132). While the hunters brought in meat and most of the party set to work drying venison, Lewis and Clark worked on their "digest of the Indian Nations West of the Rocky Mountains which we have seen and of whom we have been repeated[ly] informed by those with whom we were conversant" (V, 133).[20] On June

19. The Salmon River, originally referred to as the "east fork" of "Lewis's River," became the "north fork" after this brief reconnaissance.
20. This "Estimate of the Western Indians" has been published in the appendices of the Biddle and Coues editions of the *History* and in the appendix of Thwaites.

14 the captains informed their command of their intent to assault the mighty ranges to the east as soon as possible, "convinced that we have not now any time to delay if the calculation is to reach the United States this season" (V, 134). And on the rainy morning of June 15, after rounding up their large herd of sixty-five horses, Lewis and Clark and their men set forth into the thick forests covering the flanks of the Rockies. When they paused and looked back over their shoulders at the country from which they had come, they "had an extensive view of the rocky Mountains to the South and the Columbian plains for [a] great extent also the SW. Mountains and a range of high Mountains which divides the waters of Lewis's & Clarks rivers and seems to termonate nearly a West cours[e]" (V, 136–37).

On the following day the altitudinal zonation of climate which they had observed while at Camp Chopunnish became painfully evident. The vegetation in the foothills was "proportionably backward" when compared with that in the plains below, and the dogtooth violet, honeysuckle, huckleberry, and white maple were showing the first tiny leaves of a new season. Such appearances in a comparatively low region, wrote Lewis, augured "but unfavourably with rispect to the practibility of passing the mountains" (V, 137), but the captains determined to push eastward nevertheless. By the afternoon of June 16, however, after passing through thick forests choked with fallen timber, the party encountered snow of such depth that it completely obscured the trail they wished to follow. And when, on the following day, Lewis and Clark found themselves "invelloped in snow from 12 to 15 feet deep even on the south sides of the hills with the fairest exposure to the sun" (V, 140), they realized that the mountains they were attempting to traverse were still locked in "winter with all it's rigors."[21]

Fearing the loss of their valuable baggage, instruments, specimens of flora and fauna, and—most important of all—their precious journals if they should try to press any farther into the snowy regions, Lewis and Clark decided to retreat, the first retrograde march during the entire expedition. Down through the thick obstructing timber they trailed until they came to a glade a few miles east of their Weippe Prairie camp. Here they found adequate grass for their horses, and when the hunters reported "much appearance of deer" a camp was made. Two men were dispatched to the Nez Percé villages to find guides capable of locating the road across the mountains in spite of the deep snows. By the afternoon of June 20, with provisions growing extremely low, the captains devised new plans out of sheer frustration and desperation.

They would move their camp back down into the Weippe Prairie and await the men dispatched to the Nez Percé. If no guides could be found, the command would be divided and the mountains passed in stages, one of the

21. It is probable that either the snowfall of the winter of 1805–06 had been exceptional or the coming of the spring unusually late. Even though the Idaho mountain climate is a rigorous one, the snow has normally melted by early June. See Ralph Space, "Lewis and Clark through Idaho" (Lewiston, Idaho, 1964), p. 15.

officers, accompanied by "four of our most expert woodsmen with three or four of our best horses" (V, 149), forging ahead to blaze a trail. Two of the advance party would then return to the main body to lead them across the mountains. If the advance party should fail in finding the road, they would return to the main command and the entire force would strike out in an entirely new direction—"through the country of the Shoshones further to the South by way of the main S. Westerly fork of Lewis's river [the Snake] and Madison or Gallatin's rivers" (V, 150). Harking back to the information obtained at the Shoshoni camp on the Lemhi, Lewis and Clark remembered that such a route—although perhaps the only one open to them at this time of year—would be much more difficult than the route across the Bitterroots.[22]

Luckily, the long and circuitous route via the Snake did not have to be attempted, since the men that had been sent to the Nez Percé village returned on the afternoon of June 23, bringing with them three Indians who had consented to accompany the expedition across the Bitterroots and then guide Lewis over the direct route between the Bitterroot River and the Falls of the Missouri. And so, on the morning of June 24, the men of the expedition once more collected and loaded their horses and headed for the snow-covered ridges of the Bitterroot range. This time they were successful, and although the snow on the heights was still over 10 feet deep in places, it was so packed that the horses could cross safely, and the Nez Percé guides had no trouble finding the easiest route.[23] Finally, just before sunset on June 30, Lewis and Clark and their men came down into their old camp at Travelers' Rest near the confluence of Lolo Creek and the Bitterroot River.

The Lewis and Clark Expedition had returned to a focal location in western geography as understood by the captains.[24] Here at Travelers' Rest converged a number of routes from the Missouri to the Columbia—none of them as simplistic as the route that Thomas Jefferson and other geographical thinkers had envisaged—but routes nevertheless (fig. 41). Behind the party lay the Lolo Trail, the tortuous but shortest possible route to navigable Columbian waters; toward the south lay the passage to the headwaters of the Jefferson, to the Three Forks, and thence to the Yellowstone across the divide between that river and the Missouri; and eastward lay the route to the Great Falls of the Missouri via the Big Blackfoot River (tributary of the Clark Fork of the Columbia) and the Sun River (tributary of the Missouri). The latter two routes would be tested when the expedition split into two main parties

22. "The Shoshones informed us when we first met with them that there was a passage across the mountains in that quarter but represented the difficulties arrising from steep high and rugged mountains and also an extensive and barren plain which was to be passed without game, as infinitely more difficult than the rout by which we came" (V, 150).

23. The Indian guides proved to be crucial factors in the success of the expedition in crossing the mountains—"without the assistance of our guides I doubt much whether we who had once passed them [the mountains] could find our way to Travellers rest" (V, 164).

24. "The several war routs of the Minetarees which fall into this valy of Clark's river concenter at traveller's rest. . . . all the nations also on the west side of the mountains with whom we are acquainted inhabiting the waters of Lewis's river & who visit the plains of the Missouri pass by this rout" (V, 188).

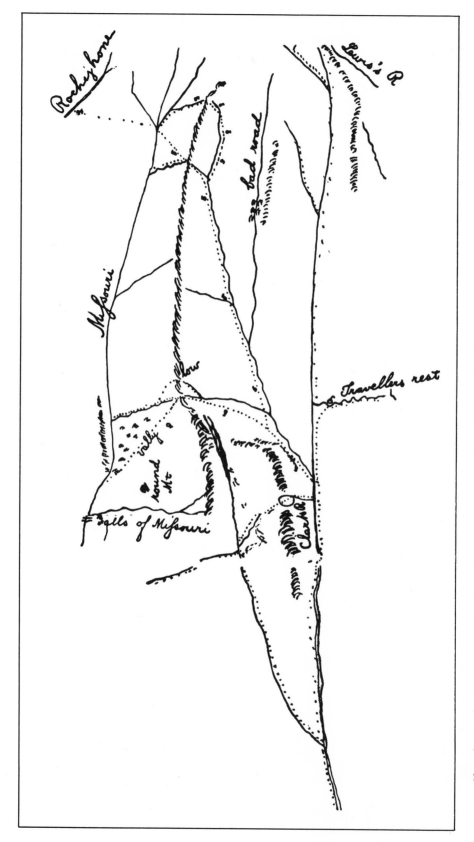

41. Sketch map by Clark showing the various routes centered on the Travelers' Rest camp. From *The Original Journals of the Lewis and Clark Expedition* (New York, 1904)

at Travelers' Rest and the most important work of the return journey began as the plans formulated at Fort Clatsop were put into operation.

Lewis and nine men would cross the mountains to the east and head for the Great Falls via the short, direct-line route that the Flatheads, the Nez Percé, and a winter of deduction had told them was the quickest way from the Bitterroot to the Missouri.[25] At the Falls Lewis would leave three men to portage canoes and baggage while he, with the remaining six members of his party, moved north to the Marias and ascended it in order to ascertain "whether any branch of that river lies as far north as Lat. 50. and again return and join the party who are to decend the Missouri, at the entrance of Maria's river" (V, 175–76). Clark and the remainder of the force were to head south up the Bitterroot valley, retracing their steps of the previous summer, until they struck another Indian trail across the Continental Divide that would lead them to the Big Hole River and then to Horse Prairie Creek, where canoes and supplies had been cached prior to the first crossing of the Divide. From the cache on Horse Prairie Creek, Clark's detachment would proceed to the Three Forks, where one of the sergeants, with a detachment of nine men, would take the canoes and supplies on down the Great Falls and link up with Lewis's command near the mouth of the Marias. With the remainder of his party, Clark was to cross the passes between the Missouri and the Yellowstone and follow that river down to its mouth, rejoining Lewis near the Missouri-Yellowstone confluence.[26] With few exceptions, these plans would be followed to the letter, and the resulting exploration would add significant items to the captains' increasing knowledge of western geography (fig. 42).[27]

8

On Thursday, July 3, 1806, "all arrangements being now compleated for carrying into effect the several scheemes we had planed for execution on our return" (V, 183), Captains Lewis and Clark separated. Lewis, with his force of nine men and five Nez Percé guides, traveled down the willow-lined western bank of the Bitterroot River until he came to the point (near the present location of Missoula, Montana) where the combined waters of the Clark Fork and Big Blackfoot rivers flow into it from the east.[28] Here the

25. Maps published in the atlas volume (VIII, nos. 41–43) of Thwaites illustrate the various Indian depictions of the routes across the Divide from the Bitterroot valley.

26. One of the men in Clark's detachment, Sergeant Ordway, was to undertake an advance journey, traveling to the Mandan villages to deliver a letter to Hugh Heney, "whom we wish to engage to prevail on the Sioux Ch[i]efs to join us on the Missouri, and accompany them with us to the seat of the general government" (V, 176).

27. Coues, *History*, III, 1064, n. 5.

28. The modern names of the rivers in this area are confusing and vary according to local usage and with the map consulted. Officially, the Clark Fork is the proper name for the main stream but in the Missoula area it is known as the Missoula or the Hellgate. Shortly

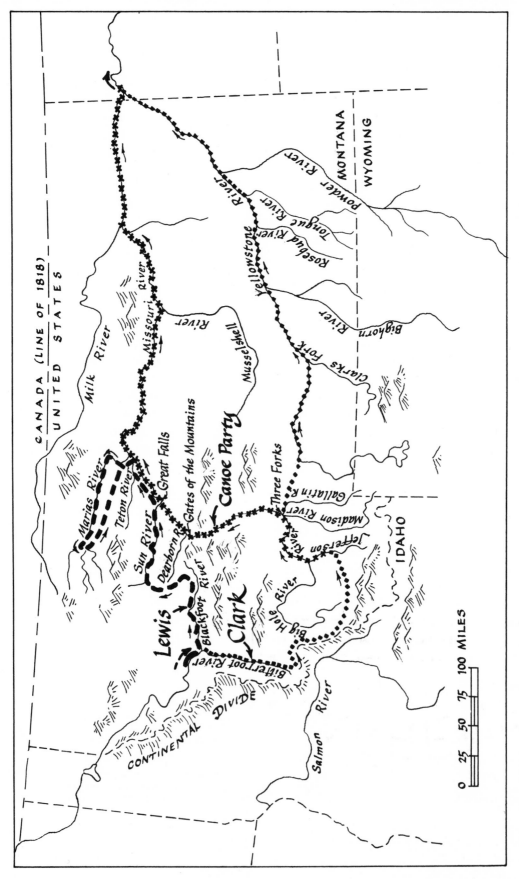

42. The return routes of Lewis and Clark from Travelers' Rest to the mouth of the Yellowstone, July 3 to August 12, 1806

explorers constructed crude rafts from driftwood and brush, crossed over the rapid stream, and made camp for the evening in the beautiful valley of the Clark Fork, surrounded by pine and fir-clad hills. In this encampment Lewis learned that the Nez Percé offers of assistance in finding the proper road across to the Great Falls of the Missouri were being withdrawn. Fearing an encounter with their traditional enemies the Minitaris, who frequently raided this far west of the Divide, the Nez Percé departed early the following morning after having pointed out to Lewis the direction to "the *river of the road to buffaloe* and thence to medicine river and the falls of the Missouri where we wish to go" (V, 184). Lewis would have to find the short route across the mountains without direct Indian help—but the direction could hardly have been less explicit: "not far from the dividing ridge between the waters of this [Clark Fork] and the Missouri rivers the roads forked they recommended the left hand as the best rout but said they would both lead us to the falls of the Missouri" (V, 185).[29]

After the erstwhile guides had made their departure, Lewis and his men pushed overland through the treeless plains surrounding the Clark Fork above its junction with the Bitterroot until they came to the entrance of "the river of the road to buffaloe," the Big Blackfoot, joining the Clark Fork from the east. Turning up this stream, they trailed through thickly timbered country along its northern bank until evening and camped in a "handsom bottom on the river where there was an abundance of excellent grass for our horses" (V, 189). The march of July 5 and 6 carried Lewis's party through the alternating prairie and timber country drained by the Big Blackfoot River, and by now Lewis should have realized that he was finally on the short road between the Columbian system and the Missouri described by the Minitaris at Fort Mandan so many months before. For part of his course during these two days led through "an extensive high prarie rendered very uneven by a vast number of little hillucks and sink-holes. . . . these plains I called the prarie of the knobs from a number of knobs being irregularly scattered through it" (V, 191).[30] The Minitaris at Fort Mandan had described the country west of the Continental Divide in much the same terms,[31] but if Lewis recognized the similarity between his journal entries for July, 1806, and his description based

downstream from its junction with the Big Blackfoot River it is joined by the Bitterroot from the south and then becomes the Clark Fork as far as Lake Pend Oreille. Downstream from the lake until its junction with the Columbia it is called the Pend Oreille River.

29. A number of excellent passes across the Continental Divide may be found in the vicinity, including Dearborn Pass lying northwest of Lewis's route across the mountains (Lewis and Clark Pass) and Cadotte or Blackfoot Pass to the south. An excellent study of Rocky Mountain passes is Marshall Sprague, *The Great Gates* (Boston, 1964); see pp. 42–43 and 419–37 for descriptions of passes used by Lewis and Clark.

30. Later observers gave essentially the same description of this area (now known as Blackfoot Prairie); see, for example, the reports of the Stevens Expedition in *Pacific Railroad Reports*, XII, 121, 212.

31. For example, "a number of barren sandy nobs irregularly scattered over the face of the country" (VI, 55).

on Indian information written well over a year earlier, he made no commentary on it.

The evening of July 6 found Lewis's detachment camped near the headwaters of Lander's Fork of the Big Blackfoot,[32] and on the following day, via Lewis and Clark Pass, they crossed over "the dividing ridge between the waters of the Columbia and Missouri rivers" (V, 194). In the distance Lewis had a clear view of "the fort mountain" or Square Butte, first seen over a year before during Lewis's desperate search for the Great Falls of the Missouri. The captain and his men were now in familiar territory, and although they had yet to find the first eagerly awaited buffalo, there was "much old appearance of dung, tracks &c" (V, 195). July 8 brought the American explorers down out of the mountains for the last time and then north along their base, across the upper reaches of the Dearborn River to the "Medicine" (Sun) River. Down that stream they trekked into the plains of the Missouri, and Lewis joyfully proclaimed: "much rejoiced at finding ourselves in the plains of the Missouri which abound with game" (V, 196).

A "very fat buffaloe bull" was killed on July 9, and the party halted practically on the site of the kill to dine on the first succulent buffalo flesh they had tasted for almost a full year. Lewis determined to remain at this site for the rest of the day since the cold and the rain made traveling extremely uncomfortable. By late afternoon the rain clouds had cleared and the party saw behind them fresh snow on the ranges they had just crossed; when they arose the following morning the clouds had closed in again.[33] After proceeding down the south bank of the Sun and across plains which, although "beautiful level and smooth," were "rendered so miry by the rain which fell yesterday that it is excessively fatigueing to the horses to travel" (V, 198), the Lewis party camped for the night of July 10 in a small grove of cottonwoods just a few miles from the Missouri. The morning of the 11th was fair, and as Lewis neared the Missouri his spirits rose—"the plain looked beatifull the grass much improved by the late rain. the air was pleasant and a vast assemblage of little birds which croud to the groves on the river sung most enchantingly" (V, 199). The Americans were once again in the Garden of the World—the hunters killed eleven buffalo before noon—and when Lewis got his first glimpse of the Missouri's waters, he knew that he had just completed what would have to answer for the Passage to India. The road from the Clearwater to the Missouri was not the half-day portage that he and Jefferson had believed in and hoped for, but a lengthy overland journey of 340 miles between the navigable waters of the Atlantic and those of the Pacific. Nevertheless, it was nearly 600 miles shorter than the route that had been followed

32. Coues (*History*, III, 1076, n. 27) gives a detailed description of the pass itself, including later crossings made during the railroad surveys of the 1860s.
33. Although evidence suggests that the overall climatic picture in the Northwest in the summer of 1806 was well within normal limits (cf. H. C. Fritts, "Tree-Ring Evidence for Climatic Changes in Western North America," *Monthly Weather Review*, XCIII (1965), 421–43), Lewis's weather journals for the month of July (VI, 221–22) indicated a pattern of precipitation and temperature that was more like April than midsummer.

on the westward-bound trek, and Lewis's role in fulfilling the exploratory objectives of the return was nearly over.

9

Lewis made his first camp on the Missouri opposite the White Bear Islands just above the head of the Great Falls. He immediately sent out all hands to assist in the killing, skinning, and butchering of buffalo and the bringing in of the buffalo meat to feed men heartily tired of the past year's diet of camas root, salmon, and "horse beef"; the hides of the great shaggy beasts were to be used for tents, clothing, and canoes to be "made after the mandan fassion" (V, 200).[34] In the late afternoon of July 12, after a stiff wind had died down and the skin canoes were completed, Lewis and his men crossed over to the river's eastern shore, where they found the mosquitos, their old nemesis along the Missouri, "extremely troublesome" (V, 200). The next day they moved their camp to the place where the cache had been made following the portage of the Great Falls the year before; unfortunately, nearly everything except a large map of the Missouri was either destroyed or severely water-damaged.[35] The party remained at this site until July 16, when Lewis, his original plans somewhat modified, departed for his reconnaissance of the Marias. Somehow the Indians, signs of whom they had seen since crossing the Divide, had run off with seven horses, reducing the captain to only ten animals, and he decided to take only three men with him instead of the intended six. After choosing his three best men (George Drouillard, Reuben and Joseph Fields) to accompany him and leaving the rest of the men under the command of Sergeant Patrick Gass to portage the Falls, Lewis headed northward past the "sublimely grand" Great Falls of the Missouri.

Early on the morning of July 17, Lewis and his detachment steered a course through the plains west of the Falls. As they rode across this wide and level area, Lewis became one of the first observers of the western landscape to discover an analogy that became so popular later in the century—"those plains have somewhat the appearance of an ocean, not a tree nor a shrub to be seen" (V, 205).[36] The whole face of the country through which they rode on their way toward the north was, although not as fertile as the plains country farther east, "like a well shaved bowling green, in which immence and numerous herds of buffaloe were seen feeding" (V, 206). At five o'clock in the afternoon, Lewis and his men reached the Teton ("Tanzey" or

34. Lewis's reference is to the "bullboat," a buffalo hide stretched tautly across a frame of willow branches to make a buoyant but unpredictable tub-shaped craft. Clark gives a good description of these skin boats in V, 325–26.

35. The items destroyed included Lewis's entire collection of botanical specimens collected between the Great Bend and Great Falls (Cutright, *Lewis and Clark*, p. 312).

36. Many travelers remarked upon the visual similarities between the Great Plains and the ocean. Dr. F. A. Wislizenous, a St. Louis scientist, referred in 1846 to the "constant undulations . . . resembling the waves of the oceans," while Captain R. B. March of the U.S. Army called the Plains "an ocean of barren prairie" or "a region almost as vast and trackless as the ocean" in 1849 (cited in Malin, *Grassland of North America*, pp. 113, 85–86).

"Rose") River, and having decided that he could not reach the Marias before nightfall, the captain determined to make camp in a grove of cottonwoods on the north bank of the Teton. Signs of a wounded buffalo bull discovered near the river provided further inducements to remain, for such signs were evidence of Indian activity in the area. And as both the "Minnetares of Fort de prarie" (Atsina Indians) and their cousins the Blackfeet[37] were, in Lewis's opinion, "a vicious lawless and reather an abandoned set of wretches" (V, 206), contact with them was to be avoided if at all possible.

Although Lewis and two of the men looked further for Indian signs on the evening of the 17th, they found nothing, and shortly before sunrise on July 18, with all senses alert for the potentially hostile natives, Lewis's small command "ascended the river hills and continued our rout as yesterday through the open plains" (V, 207). When they reached the height-of-land separating the Teton basin from that of the Marias, Lewis had a spectacular view of the surrounding countryside: "from hence the North mountains [the Bearpaws], the South mountains [the Highwoods], the falls mountains [the Little Belt and Big Belt ranges] and the tower mountain [Sweetgrass Hills] and those arround and to the East of the latter were visible" (V, 208). By early evening the party had reached the Marias above Lewis's farthest ascent of the previous spring, and they made their camp in a small grove of cottonwoods on the river's western bank—still without having seen the Indians they now believed to be in the area.

Lewis's party continued the ascent of the Marias on the following day, across the treeless tablelands covered with the curly dry bunchgrass and the prickly pear. The evidence of increasing aridity was everywhere—the topsoil had grown thinner, occasionally giving way completely before vast stretches of glacially deposited gravelly till, and the "mineral salts common to the plains of the missouri" were more abundant than usual. The Sweetgrass Hills looming on the northern skyline were, Lewis believed, "destitute of timber" (V, 209), and the only break in the monotony of the region was the narrow ribbon of cottonwood trees, willow, and greasewood that lined the banks of the Marias. But the relative sterility of the region was unimportant, for the purposes of Lewis's reconnaissance were related to things other than land quality. As he and his men moved across the river hills north of the Marias, the captain maintained his faith in the proximity of the Marias and the southern reaches of the Saskatchewan: "from the apparent decent of the country to the North and above the broken mountains [Sweetgrass Hills] I am induced to believe that the South branch of the Suskashawan receives a part of it's waters from the plain even to the borders of this river and from the brakes

37. The Atsina were also called Fall Indians and were no relation to the Minitaris who lived at the Great Bend. Both they and the Blackfeet spoke Algonquin tongues, and although the Atsina were not members of the "Blackfoot confederacy" of Blackfeet, Piegan, and Blood Indians, they were allies of the Blackfeet and by the early nineteenth century had already attained a reputation for belligerence (see Josephy, *Indian Heritage of America*, pp. 116–18).

visible in the plains in a no[r]thern direction think that a branch of that river decending from the rocky mountains passes at no great distance from Maria's river and to the N.E. of the broken mountains" (V, 211). Lewis's image was based on optimism and desire—for the lands to the north were part of the Milk River drainage rather than that of the Saskatchewan.

By the early afternoon of July 21, when he and his men arrived at the junction of the two creeks (Cut Bank Creek and Two Medicine Creek) which join to form the Marias, Lewis's enthusiasm began to fade as the size and course of these two streams led him to the conclusion that the source region of the Marias "I now fear will not be as far north as I wished and expected" (V, 212). Clinging grimly to his old hopes, however, Lewis decided to push up Cut Bank Creek, the northernmost of the two forks, hoping it would lead him "to the most no[r]thern point to which the waters of Maria's river extend" (V, 212). But by late the next day, as the snow-covered peaks of the Lewis range hove into sight on the western horizon and the valley of Cut Bank Creek was seen coming from that range, the captain lost "all hope of the waters of this river ever extending to N. Latitude 50°" (V, 214). But old ideas die hard; if not the Marias then some other northern tributary of the Missouri would lead to the Saskatchewan: "I still hope and think it more than probable that both *white earth* river and milk river extend as far north as latd. 50°" (V, 214).

10

After reaching these conclusions, Lewis decided that he had pursued his northward march far enough, and in a grove of cottonwoods along Cut Bank Creek he and his men made the camp they called "Camp Disappointment."[38] Here they remained for four frustrating days during which rain and clouds obscured the skies and made impossible Lewis's attempts at astronomical observations, while the game virtually disappeared and the party was forced to resort to a diet of roots and rancid grease. With signs of Indians becoming increasingly abundant, Lewis, perhaps believing the old frontier adage that the most dangerous Indians were those you couldn't see, became more and more apprehensive "that I shall not reach the United States within this season" (V, 217). On July 26 the small detachment began the return journey across the heavily dissected plains of the upper Marias basin, but their march toward the southeast was abruptly terminated when, from the high plain above Two Medicine Creek, Lewis saw a band of eight Piegan Blackfoot Indians.[39] Resolving to "make the best of our situation," Lewis approached the natives, and after cautious but relatively cordial conversations he and his men made

38. Paul Russell Cutright has located this site as being about 12 miles northeast of Browning, Montana ("Lewis on the Marias—1806," *Montana, the Magazine of Western History*, XVIII (Fall, 1968), 35).
39. Cutright, "Lewis on the Marias," p. 35.

camp with the Blackfeet near "three solitary trees" (V, 221)[40] in the bottom of Two Medicine Creek.

The next morning, shortly after Lewis was awakened at dawn by sounds of conflict, there began what was probably the most dramatic and critical episode of the entire expedition. At the same time as one of the Blackfeet attempted to carry off the guns of Reuben and Joseph Fields, "two others advanced and seized the guns" of Drouillard and Lewis. Reuben Fields apprehended the native attempting to steal his and his brother's weapons and stabbed him in the chest, killing him almost instantly. Drouillard succeeded in wrestling his gun from the grasp of the Indian trying to steal it, and Lewis, drawing his pistol, forced the native carrying away his weapon to drop it. Just then the Fields brothers came up with their guns ready to fire, and the Americans turned their attention to the horses, which the Blackfeet were trying to drive off. Lewis, in pursuit of the fleeing natives, fired on and hit an Indian, who returned his fire—"being bearheaded I felt the wind of his bullet very distinctly" (V, 225). Many horses were still milling about in the clouds of dust raised by the brief melee, and the Americans, saddling and mounting rapidly, rode up the steep cliffs south of Two Medicine Creek. Once on the open plains above the stream, they whipped their horses into a gallop and headed southeast toward the Missouri. They reached the Teton River by midafternoon and, wishing to put still more distance between themselves and any possible pursuit, pushed on toward the Missouri. At two o'clock in the morning they halted and camped near the Missouri, close to the modern site of Fort Benton. Their wild ride had taken them nearly 100 miles from the site of the conflict with the Blackfeet.[41]

After only a short night's rest, Lewis and his bone-weary men again mounted their horses and headed for the mouth of the Marias and the rendezvous with the remainder of the party under Lewis's command. By midmorning, from a high point on the Missouri's north shore, Lewis and his exhausted companions "had the unspeakable satisfaction to see our canoes coming down" (V, 228). In the canoes were the party commanded by Sergeant Gass that Lewis had left at the Great Falls and the party commanded by Sergeant Ordway that had, after separating from Clark, made the descent of the Missouri from the Three Forks. Turning the horses loose and gleefully throwing the saddles in the river, Lewis and his three men boarded the canoes, and the expedition that had begun as an all-water trek was water-borne once more.[42]

40. This site has also been located by Cutright and by Mrs. Helen B. West of Cut Bank, Montana. Mrs. West's efforts to pinpoint the site are detailed in Helen B. West, "Meriwether Lewis in Blackfeet Country" (Museum of the Plains Indian, Browning, Mont., 1964).

41. The feat was accomplished over a period of about eighteen hours, and the fact that Lewis and his companions rode 100 miles directly across the grain of a heavily dissected country with numerous deep dry washes and small creek beds during that time is almost unbelievable.

42. Lewis had been traveling by horse since leaving the Columbia at the end of April, nearly three months earlier.

Lewis's command, now numbering twenty men, moved down through the spectacular Missouri Breaks with great rapidity, and the captain's journal entries were brief—"as I have been very particular in my discription of the country as I ascended this river I presume it is unneccessasary here to add any-thing further on that subject" (V, 230). By August 1 they had passed the mouth of the Musselshell River, and, being "extreemly anxious to reach the entrance of the Yellowstone river where we expect to join Capt. Clark and party" (V, 233), Lewis directed that the men should cook enough meat during the evenings to last them throughout the following day, thus eliminating any necessity of halting during the day for food preparation. Passing the mouth of the Milk River on August 4, Lewis's optimism about the possible connections between the Missouri and Saskatchewan systems again asserted itself: "this stream . . . affords as much water at present as Maria's river and I have no doubt extends itself to a considerable distance North" (V, 234). But no time remained for a reconnaissance of the Milk, and Lewis's detachment hurried downstream, reaching the mouth of the Yellowstone on August 7 only to find that Clark and his men had been there and departed.

Believing that Clark could not be too far downstream, Lewis proceeded only as far as the mouth of the White Earth River, where he halted for three days to repair the canoes and allow the men to make themselves some new leather clothing as most of them were "extreemly bare." On August 11, after having broken camp and moved on down the Missouri to find Clark, Lewis met with an unfortunate accident while he and one of his men were on shore hunting elk. The captain, who had traveled for so many thousands of miles without suffering any serious injury, was wounded in the thigh by a ball from the gun of Peter Cruzatte, who mistook the buckskin-clad officer for an elk in the thick cover. Although the wound was not extremely dangerous, it was painful, and when Lewis's command caught up with Clark on the following day, the injured man was probably not only pleased to find his friend well but was relieved to be in the hands of the highly competent field physician that Clark was. And here, after the reunion with Clark, Meriwether Lewis concluded his entries in the journals which would eventually bring the expedition to the literate world and make him immortal—"as wrighting in my present situation is extreemly painfull to me I shall desist until I recover and leave to my fri[e]nd Capt. C. the continuation of our journal" (V, 243).

II

Once reunited with Clark and his party, Lewis soon discovered that his partner in discovery had also carried out a successful, if slightly less dramatic, reconnaissance. When the force had split at Travelers' Rest on July 3 and Lewis had pointed northward down the Bitterroot, Clark and a party of twenty (including Sergeants Ordway and Pryor, fifteen enlisted men, Clark's

357

"servant" York, and Charbonneau with his squaw and child) had trailed southward along the western side of the Bitterroot valley, "boutifully versified with small open plains covered with a great variety of Sweet cented plants, flowers & grass" (V, 245). By nightfall Clark and his command had covered a total of 36 miles, and with the snow-covered peaks of the Bitterroots to the west and the Sapphire range to the east glowing in the last light of day, they made their camp just north of the present location of Hamilton, Montana.

The following day being "the day of the decleration of Independence of the United States and a Day commonly scelebrated by my Country" (V, 246), a halt was called early to partake of a "Sumptious Dinner," after which Clark and his party marched a few more miles to a place where they could ford the Bitterroot. The river was passed safely on July 5, whereupon Clark began the first of several planned deviations from the outward-bound route. In conversations with natives during the previous fall, he had learned that the pass he and Lewis had used to cross from the Salmon to the Bitterroot (Lost Trail Pass) was far from the best road across the mountains and that a more satisfactory pass lay slightly east. This trail was used by the Flatheads to get to the Missouri drainage, and as it would shorten his route to the cache on Horse Prairie Creek by at least two days, Clark "deturmined to make the attempt." Ascending "a ridge with a gentle slope" on July 6, the Clark party crossed Gibbons Pass[43] and dropped down into the basin of the Big Hole ("Wisdom") River—they were once again on Missouri waters.

The trail from the eastern side of Gibbons Pass to Horse Prairie Creek was clear and bore evidence of use by buffalo and Indians—"proving that formerly Buffs. roved there & also that this is the best route, for the Buffs. and the Indians always have the best route & here both were joined" (V, 249–50). Once again in her home territory, Sacagawea began recognizing landmarks and pointed out a gap in the mountains between the Big Hole and Beaverhead rivers that her people often used. Following her directions and the clear trail, Clark steered a southeasterly course toward the cache where the party had left their canoes prior to the first crossing of the Divide at Lemhi Pass. After an easy march through "high dry and uneaven stoney open plains and low bottoms very boggy with high mountains on the tops and North sides of which there was snow" (V, 254), Clark and his party reached the cache at the junction of Horse Prairie Creek and the Beaverhead on July 8. In words reminiscent of Charlevoix and Coxe,[44] Clark proclaimed: "[This] road and with only a few trees being cut out of the way would be an excellent waggon road one Mountain of about 4 miles over excepted which would

43. On some maps and charts of the late nineteenth century, this pass is called (as it ought to be) "Clark's Pass." The name it now bears commemorates General John Gibbon, commander of the U.S. Army forces against the Nez Percé in the Battle of the Big Hole in 1877 (Coues, *History*, III, 1122–23, n. 7).

44. Early eighteenth-century speculators on the potential routes across the western interior, Charlevoix and Coxe among them, had discussed the possibility of wagon roads across the heights-of-land.

require a little digging   The distance is 164 Miles [from Travelers' Rest]" (V, 255).

The cache on Horse Prairie Creek was opened and found to have weathered well; the tobacco was distributed among the users of that item, and Clark set the men to cleaning and repairing the canoes preparatory to setting out for the Three Forks. On July 10 the party under Clark's command moved down into "that butifull and extensive Vally open and fertile which we call the beaver head Vally which is the Indian name" (V, 256). When the river widened and became "not so sholl," Clark decided to transfer all the baggage for his Yellowstone trip into the canoes and proceed to the Three Forks, leaving Sergeant Pryor and six men to drive the large herd of fifty horses through the valley. With great speed[45] the force moved down the Beaverhead, past the junctions of the Ruby and Big Hole rivers, and shortly after noon on July 12 reached the Three Forks of the Missouri, that "essential point in the geography of this western part of the Continent" (II, 277). Here the command split, the six canoes and a party of ten men under the direction of Sergeant Ordway bound down the Missouri for the Falls and a reunion with Lewis's detachment, and Clark and the remaining members of the Corps bound for the Yellowstone.

Passing to the east through the lovely mountain-ringed basin where the waters of the Gallatin, Madison, and Jefferson rivers mingle to become the Missouri, Clark and the Yellowstone party made their evening camp of July 13 on the banks of the Gallatin River, near the present site of the hamlet of Logan, Montana. From this camp Sacagawea pointed out the various passes in the surrounding mountains and recommended the gap at the southern end of the Bridger range as the best route to the Yellowstone. On the following day the Clark party moved toward this gap and, after striking an old buffalo trail, moved eastward up a gentle slope and pitched camp on the western terminus of Bozeman Pass.[46] Clark's use of the Virginia-Kentucky term "gap" to describe Bozeman Pass was appropriate, for the gentleness of the ascent and descent of the divide between the Gallatin and the Yellowstone was more typical of the Appalachians than the Rockies. The passage from the Missouri to the Yellowstone basin was accomplished, "an excellent high dry firm road with very incon[si]derable hills" (V, 262), declared Clark, and at two o'clock in the afternoon on July 15, he and his party arrived at the Yellowstone River near where Livingston, Montana, now stands.

12

Once down into the lovely valley of the Yellowstone, with the mighty snow peaks of the Absaroka massif gleaming on the southern horizon, Clark

45. The trip from Horse Prairie Creek to the Three Forks, consuming two days of travel time on the homeward journey, took two and a half weeks to complete when the party was traveling by water on the Pacific-bound trek.

46. Coues, *History*, III, 1133, n. 19.

set about finding trees large enough from which to construct dugout canoes. But although the river bottom abounded in cottonwoods, none of them were "sufficiently large for canoes," and the currents of the Yellowstone were, the captain adjudged, too treacherous for the Mandan-style buffalo-skin craft. "No other alternative for me," concluded Clark, "but to proceed on down untill I can find a tree Sufficiently large &c. to make a canoe" (V, 267). Clark and his command wound their way down the valley, alternating their march between the level but brushy bottomlands and the open, exposed plains back of the river. They were once again in the violent and unpredictable High Plains climate, and although the days were comfortably warm, frost gathered on the grasses before sunrise, and the rains, accompanied by high winds, soaked the shelterless explorers during the night. Game was ever more abundant, but still no trees that would answer for the purpose of canoe construction could be found.

On July 18 the first signs of Indians were seen on the Yellowstone as a column of smoke was observed toward the southeast. But Clark was less concerned about Indians than he was about the speed of land travel. "There being no timber on this part of the Rochejhone sufficiently large for a Canoe and time is pracious as it is our wish to get to the U States this Season" (V, 275), Clark decided on July 19 to ride ahead of the main body until he found a tree large enough for his purpose. Finally, somewhere between the present towns of Columbus and Laurel, Montana, the captain found a cottonwood grove in which the trees, although not large enough to make a single dugout, were of a size that could be used to make two smaller craft which could be lashed together. Such a craft, reported Clark, would be sturdy and "fully sufficient to take my small party & Self with what little baggage we have down this river" (V, 278). Work on the canoes commenced, and by July 23 Clark and his men were ready to resume river travel once again.

Work on the canoes was finished just in time, for during the interval Crow horse thieves had made off with about half of the detachment's stock, and although Clark sent two men to track the thieves, the horses were lost irrevocably. But the captain was not particularly alarmed. He was "in the beginning of the buffalow Country" (V, 279), and with an assured food supply and the knowledge that the Indians would not be likely to attack a force the size of his, and that his downriver travel would be speeded up when he once again took to the water, Clark proceeded with confidence. Before leaving the canoe camp of the Yellowstone, the captain dispatched Sergeant Pryor to take the remaining horses and proceed overland with a letter to Hugh Heney at the Mandan villages.[47] And on the morning of July 24, Clark

47. The text of the letter to Heney is printed in Jackson, *Letters*, pp. 309–13. Pryor never made it to the Mandan villages ahead of the rest of the command. The Crows stole the remainder of his horses and he and the three men with him were forced to build bullboats to descend the Yellowstone. In the meantime, Clark's party had passed them and Pryor didn't catch up with the main party until August 8 (V, 325–26).

and his command, with their lashed-together dugout canoes loaded, "Set out and proceeded on very well" (V, 288).

Early in the morning of July 24, Clark passed the mouth of a bold stream entering the Yellowstone from the south (the Clarks Fork of the Yellowstone) and "thought it probable that this might be the big horn river" (V, 288). He revised his view two days later when, after passing through herds of buffalo, elk, deer, and antelope so numerous that he swore to be "silent on the subject further" (V, 290), and after passing the unique erosional remnant he named "Pompey's Tower,"[48] he arrived at "the enterance of Big Horn River on the Stard. Side" (V, 296). The Bighorn was very shortly to become an important river in the development of the Northwest, and Clark recognized its importance:

I am informed by the *Menetarres* Indians and others that this River takes its rise in the Rocky mountains with the heads of the river plate and at no great distance from the river Rochejhone and passes between the *Coat* Nor [Côte Noir] or Black Mountains and the Most Easterly range of Rocky Mountains. it is very long and contains a great perportion of timber on which there is a variety of wild animals, perticulary the big horn which are to be found in great numbers on this river. . . . This river is said to be navagable a long way for perogues without falls and waters a fine rich open Country [V, 297].[49]

When Clark and his detachment crossed the mouth of the Bighorn, they crossed a meridian of geographical significance. For just as the Platte had marked the line between the upper and lower Missouri, the Bighorn marked the transition from the mountain Yellowstone to the Yellowstone of the plains. Beyond the Bighorn Clark remarked, "I take my leave of the View of the tremendious chain of Rocky Mountains white with Snow in View of which I have been since the 1st of May last" (V, 302); the Yellowstone below the mouth of the Bighorn was now a Plains river, resembling the Missouri "in almost every perticular."

Clark's party moved swiftly down the Yellowstone, past the mouths of Rosebud Creek and the Tongue River[50] and across the rapids near the mouth of the Powder, then through the badlands extending from present-day Miles City to Glendive, Montana. And on Tuesday, August 3, at eight o'clock in the morning, Clark and his command arrived at the junction of the Yellowstone and Missouri and formed camp immediately "in the point between the two river[s] at which place the party had all encamped the 26th. of April 1805" (V, 318). They had closed the circle of exploration and had, or so

48. Named after Baptiste or "Pompey," the child of Charbonneau and Sacagawea. The landmark (now known as Pompey's Pillar) bears the only still-visible evidence of the expedition: carved in the soft rock near the top of the pillar is "Wm. Clark   July 25 1806."

49. One of the most critical features of later images of western geography, the Bighorn will be discussed in detail in the concluding chapter below.

50. Clark was able to recognize the feeder streams of the Yellowstone from descriptions and sketches given him by natives at Fort Mandan (cf. fig. 30 above and VI, 51-53).

Clark believed, confirmed many of the deductions made about the Yellow-stone: it was a mighty river; it flowed through a delightful country; it was navigable for a great distance; it headed with the Platte, Bighorn, Snake, and perhaps the Multnomah and waters of the Gulf of California; most important, "a good road passes up this river to it's extreem source from whence it is but a short distance to the Spanish settlements" (V, 320).[51] The Yellowstone had taken over from the Missouri as a river of mystery and speculation and promise.

The mosquitos were so vicious in the vicinity of the Yellowstone-Missouri confluence that they drove Clark and his party farther down the Missouri. Consequently, the meeting with Lewis was delayed, and it was not until August 12, more than a week later, that "Capt Lewis hove in Sight with the party which went by way of the Missouri as well as that which accom-panied him from Travellers rest on Clarks river" (V, 330).[52] The reunion was joyful, marred only by Clark's apprehension over Lewis's painful wound, and the captains soon formed a happy camp about 30 miles east of the present Montana–North Dakota border. The Corps of Discovery was whole again, having accomplished the tasks assigned by the captains when they took leave of their soggy quarters on the Pacific more than four months earlier. The new assumptions about western geography had been tested and, with the exception of the Marias disappointment and the still-unproven conjectures about the proximity of the Yellowstone's sources to those of the Rio Grande or Colo-rado, had been found to be correct.

51. These notes, in the manuscript journals, are in Lewis's hand, presumably copied from field notes made by Clark. An interesting entry in these notes reads: "there is also a con-siderable fall on this river within the mountains but at what distance from it's source we never could learn" (V, 320). But this statement is set apart by asterisks and an explicit "(no)" is written after it. Apparently the captains had heard of the falls of the river in the Grand Canyon of the Yellowstone but either mistrusted their information or received contrary data on the falls.

52. Here Clark inserted in his own journals a summary of Lewis's explorations (V, 331–35).

CHAPTER 14

A NEW WEST:
THE PASSAGE
AND THE GARDEN

Even before Lewis and Clark were reunited on the Missouri's muddy waters below the mouth of the Yellowstone, they received the first indications that the West which they had been the first to penetrate was changing. On August 11, the day prior to his reunion with Lewis, Clark met "two men from the illinoies Jos. Dixon, and [blank space] Handcock those men are on a trapping expedition up the River Rochejhone" (V, 329). At eight o'clock the next morning, Lewis, traveling down the Missouri virtually on Clark's heels, discovered a camp of "two hunters from the Illinois by name Joseph Dickson and Forest Hancock. these men informed me that Capt. C. had passed them about noon the day before" (V, 243).[1] Lewis tarried with the Illinois trappers longer than Clark had and gave them "a short discription of the Missouri, a list of distances to the most conspicuous streams and remarkable places on the river above and pointed out to them the places where the beaver most abounded."

1. Virtually nothing is known of these two earliest American trappers in the Yellowstone country or of Colter's experiences with them other than that contained in the journals or in Thwaites (V, 242, n. 1).

This was the first transmission of the geographical information gathered during the expedition and signaled the beginning of Lewis's and Clark's role as shapers of new American conceptions of western geography. When their epic exploration was nearly complete, the captains must have been well aware of the part they were now to play in future developments in the trans-Missouri region. They had left behind them the old West of Marquette and Vérendrye, of Pierre Charlevoix and Daniel Coxe, of Jonathan Carver and John Evans and James Mackay, and of Thomas Jefferson. A new West of Lewis and Clark, of Manuel Lisa and Robert Stuart and John Jacob Astor, of Bridger and Carson and Jedediah Smith, of John Frémont and of many, many others lay ahead. And as the Corps of Discovery swept down the Missouri, past the mouth of the Little Missouri toward a reunion with old friends at the Mandan and Minitari villages, past the mouths of the Grand and White and Niobrara and Platte, the captains would be met with ever-increasing evidence that the West they had passed through on their outward-bound journey was not and never would be operationally and conceptually the same as it had been.[2]

2

"Those people were extreamly pleased to See us," wrote Clark of the Mandans and Minitaris upon the expedition's arrival at the upper villages on August 14, and after forming a camp some 4 miles upriver from their former winter encampment site, he and Lewis called the natives (and their former interpreter, René Jessaume) to council. Remembering Jefferson's injunctions relative to the western Indians—"If a few of their influential chiefs, within practicable distance, wish to visit us, arrange such a visit with them"[3]—and remembering too the role they were playing in the imperial struggle for the American Northwest,[4] the captains attempted to persuade the several Mandan and Minitari chiefs to accompany the American party downriver. Following lengthy discussions, one of the Mandan chiefs[5] agreed to travel down the Missouri "to See our Great Father," and by midday on August 17 the captains were ready to depart from the Mandans on the last leg of their homeward voyage.

At two o'clock in the afternoon of the 17th, the Corps of Discovery left their encampment at the Mandans, leaving behind several members of their

2. Goetzmann, *Exploration and Empire*, p. 8.
3. This order was within the instructions Jefferson had given Lewis preparatory to the explorer's departure from Washington in 1803 (Jackson, *Letters*, p. 64).
4. Excellent analyses of the imperial struggle between the United States and Great Britain for western North America may be found in ch. 12 of DeVoto, *Course of Empire*, and in ch. 1 of Goetzmann, *Exploration and Empire*.
5. The Mandan chief was Sheheke or "the Big White." Details on his visit to Washington may be found in Jackson, *Letters*, pp. 325 (n. 7), 351, 362, *et passim*.

permanent party. Toussaint Charbonneau, with his squaw Sacagawea and their child, elected to remain with the Minitaris, "observing that he had no acquaintance or prospects of makeing a liveing below, and must continue to live in the way that he had done" (V, 344). And since John Colter, one of the young men from Kentucky who had been with the expedition from the very beginning, had "expressed a desire" to join the trappers Dickson and Hancock in their Yellowstone venture, Lewis and Clark relieved him of his duties and the Kentuckian returned to the mountains. Colter would shortly be heard from again when, after a series of the most amazing adventures in the history of the Rocky Mountain region, he would furnish Clark with important geographical information to be included on the captain's forthcoming master map of the American West.

From the Mandan villages the trip was downhill all the way—both literally and figuratively. The current of the Missouri carried the dugouts downstream rapidly, and as the men "plyed their ores" with a will, the craft sped down the river at a rate more than twice that achieved on the upriver pull against the current. Lewis's wound continued to heal, and although winds still hampered navigation at times and the Missouri was as full of snags and sand bars as it had been two summers before, this was the easiest section of the entire journey. Through the plains with their teeming grasslands curing to a yellow gold, the officers and men of the expedition sped, fighting the mosquitos and snags and tricky currents as they went and passing in sequence those sites they had noted in the summer of 1804. The expedition was almost over and most of the participants must have felt a pardonable pride, a pride which occasionally crept into the journals—"I informed them," stated Clark after a conference with the chiefs of the Cheyenne and Arikara nations above the mouth of the Grand River, "where we had been, what we had done" (V, 351).

The dugouts of the expedition passed the mouth of the Niobrara River on Monday, September 1, and the following morning, just beyond the mouth of the James, the captains observed the first specific instance of change in the Missouri country. "I observed the remains of a house which had been built since we passed up, this most probably was McClellins tradeing house with the Yanktons in the Winter of 1804 & 5" (V, 373).[6] On the next afternoon the evidence of increased American activity in the valley became concrete when two boats with several men were hailed—"[these] boats Saluted us with their Small arms" (V, 374). In the lead boat was James Aird,[7] a Scot trader in the employ of a St. Louis firm, and the captains eagerly plied him with

6. Apparently both Lewis and Clark had known Robert McClellan when he served as a scout under the command of General Wayne in 1794-95 in the Ohio country; he later became a member of the Astoria party and is mentioned in various contemporary accounts of the Astorians.

7. Bradbury (*Travels in the Interior*, p. 87) also mentions having met Aird on his Missouri River voyage of 1810.

questions about events in the United States—"our first enquirey was after the President of our country and then our friends and the State of the politicks of our country &C" (V, 374). Aird informed the captains "of maney changes." Many changes indeed, and absolutely the first word from home that the explorers had received in nearly thirty months: James Wilkinson was governor of Louisiana, the Spanish were acting up near Natchitoches, British ships had fired on an American vessel near New York, and Alexander Hamilton had been killed in a duel with Aaron Burr.

Just above the Little Sioux River, on September 6, one of Auguste Chouteau's[8] trading boats was met and the captains obtained—actually attempted to purchase but the commander of the boat would take no pay—the "first spiritous licquor which had been tasted by any of them since the 4 of July 1805" (V, 378). Two days later the mouth of the Platte was passed— "our party appears extreamly anxious to get on, and every day appears [to] produce new anxieties in them to get to their country and friends" (V, 380). On the next day the expedition met a trader who informed the captains that they had not been the only American explorers operating in the West—"Mr. Pike and young Mr. Wilkinson had Set out on an expedition up the Arkansaw river or in that direction" (V, 381).[9] Two days later Robert McClellan, whose trading post had been seen more than a week before, met the expedition, and accompanying him were Joseph Gravelines and the elder Dorion, who had served Lewis and Clark so well two years earlier.[10]

More traders were met near the mouth of the Kansas, and the enthusiasm Americans felt for the return of the men who would become their epic heroes was apparent—"those young men received us with great friendship and pressed on us Some whisky for our men, Bisquet, Pork and Onions, & part of the Stores" (V, 384). Beyond the mouth of the Kansas the heat grew intolerable, particularly difficult for men who had been in "a northern Country open and Cool" for nearly two years, but the expedition pressed onward. Below the mouth of the Osage River, on September 20, the men "saw some cows on the bank which was a joyfull Sight to the party and caused a Shout to be raised for joy" (V, 389). Shortly thereafter the small village of La Charrette came into view, and "every person, both French and Americans seems to express great pleasure at our return, and acknowledged themselves much astonished in seeing us return. they informed us that we were supposed to have been lost long since, and were entirely given out by every person &c." (V,

8. Chouteau was one of the founders of St. Louis and one of the "St. Louis gentlemen" to whom Lewis had addressed queries about the West prior to the expedition's departure in the spring of 1804 (Jackson, *Letters*, pp. 161–63).

9. Captain Zebulon Montgomery Pike was sent by General James Wilkinson, then governor of Louisiana Territory, in 1806 to locate the western boundary of the territory around the sources of the Red and Arkansas rivers. He was accompanied by James B. Wilkinson, a son of the general (Goetzmann, *Exploration and Empire*, pp. 44–53).

10. Gravelines had just returned from Washington, where he had journeyed with a chief of the Arikaras (Jackson, *Letters*, pp. 303–05).

390).[11] St. Charles was reached on the following day, the captains noting their astonishment at the number of settlements that had sprung up between La Charrette and this place during their absence. And about noon on Tuesday, September 23, 1806, the Corps of Discovery under the command of Captains William Clark and Meriwether Lewis brought their boats into the river town of St. Louis. They were received with joy and amazement and celebration—America had crossed to the South Sea and had come back.

3

After receiving the "harty welcom" of the inhabitants of St. Louis who lined the banks of the river and after accepting Peter Chouteau's[12] gracious offer of quarters more luxurious than anything they had known for nearly two and a half years, Lewis and Clark began the initial stages of what, in later years and following even more far-flung explorations, would be called "debriefing." The baggage was examined and stored for transshipment, clothing was purchased to replace the worn and greasy buckskins, "visits of form, to the gentlemen of St. Louis" were made, and the explorers were feted on the evening of September 25 at a "dinner & Ball" given in their honor. There were more important events within the summary stages of the expedition, however, and Clark's final succinct journal entry is instructive—"Friday 25th [26] of Septr. 1806 a fine morning we commenced writing &c." The process that would culminate in the greatest transformation of the geographical images of the American Northwest since Marquette's discovery of the Missouri River had begun.

In their first communications with the people of the United States since the spring of 1805 from Fort Mandan, Lewis and Clark sounded the death knell of the all-water Passage to India that had formed the central objective of their journey. "In obedience to your orders," wrote Lewis to Jefferson, "we have penitrated the Continent of North America to the Pacific Ocean, and sufficiently explored the interior of the country to affirm with confidence that we have discovered the most practicable rout which dose exist across the continent by means of the navigable branches of the Missouri and Columbia rivers."[13] This "most practicable rout" was that traveled by Lewis on the return, and his description of it ended 130 years of speculation on the short portage. For between the upper end of feasible navigation on the Missouri

11. As early as December, 1805, Dr. Benjamin Smith Barton had written Jefferson: "We are made uneasy here by a report, that Capt. Lewis and his party have been cut off. I hope this is not true" (Jackson, *Letters*, p. 276). The longer the expedition was gone, the greater the fears for their safety among the members of the eastern establishment.

12. Pierre (Peter) Chouteau of St. Louis had acted as the agent for Lewis and Clark during their absence in the Northwest and accompanied them to Washington after their return (Jackson, *Letters*, p. 325).

13. Jackson, *Letters*, p. 319.

("five miles below the great falls of that river") and the navigable part of the "Kooskooskee" or Clearwater, there lay a "passage by land of 340 miles . . . the most formidable part of the tract proposed across the Continent; of this distance 200 miles is along a good road, and 140 of tremendious mountains which for 60 mls. are covered with eternal snows."

The grand geography of Jefferson's 1803 vision was not to be—but Lewis's letter went beyond the simple statements of fact and became daring in its "inferences, implications, and recommendations."[14] The route that he and Clark had pioneered, claimed Lewis, although it would never equal ocean routes for the transport of goods between "the East Indies" and the United States, could be used to convey "many articles not bulky brittle nor of a very perishable nature" from the Orient to North America and could, therefore, be viewed "as affording immence advantages to the fur trade":

The Missouri and all it's branches from the Chyenne upwards abound more in beaver and Common Otter, than any other streams on earth, particularly that proportion of them lying within the Rocky Mountains. The furs of all this immence tract of country including such as may be collected on the upper portion of the River St. Peters, Red river and the Assiniboin with the immence country watered by the Columbia, may be conveyed to the mouth of the Columbia by the 1st of August in each year and from thence be shiped to, and arrive in Canton earlier than the furs at present shiped from Montreal annually arrive in London. The British N.West Company of Canada were they permitted by the United States might also convey their furs collected in the Athabaske, on the Saskashawan, and South and West of Lake Winnipic by that rout within the period before mentioned. Thus the productions [of] nine tenths of the most valuable fur country of America could be conveyed by the rout proposed to the East Indies.[15]

It was a great design, made greater by the additional suggestion that establishments be "made on the Columbia, and a sufficient number of men employed at them to convey annually the productions of the East Indies to the upper establishment on the Kooskooskee, and there exchange them with the men of the Missouri for their furs. . . . By this means the furs not only of the Missouri but those also of the Columbia may be shiped to the East indies by the season before mentioned, and the comodities of the East indies arrive at St. Louis or the mouth of the Ohio by the last of September in each year."[16] The plans were equal to those of history's most sophisticated geopolitical strategists, "an open, explicit form of trade imperialism"[17] designed to destroy the economic viability of the British fur trade and, above all, to add the country west of the Continental Divide to the United States. Lewis's

14. DeVoto, *Course of Empire*, p. 526.
15. Lewis's commentary on the potential of the fur trade and its relationships to the imperial ambitions of both the United States and Great Britain, when compared with Alexander Mackenzie's introductory remarks in his *Voyages*, seems to have been a direct response to the Scot's proposals for the establishment of a route through Canada to the fur region of the Rocky Mountains and Pacific coast.
16. Jackson, *Letters*, pp. 321–22.
17. DeVoto, *Course of Empire*, p. 528.

suggestions were prophetic—not in that the route he proposed would ever become "undertaken by individuals with as little concern as a voyage across the Atlantic is at present," but in that the initial American response led to the Astorians, the Rocky Mountain fur trade, and ultimate American victory in the imperial conflict over the Oregon country.[18] And as early as January of 1807, Thomas Jefferson would refer to "our country, from the Missisipi to the Pacific."[19]

While Lewis was recommending the establishment of an extensive commercial empire that would eventually make the United States a continental nation, Clark was penning the letter upon which the initial fame of the expedition rested.[20] In a missive directed to his brother, George Rogers Clark, the captain told the story of discovery that would spread throughout the country as fast as the communication technologies of the day allowed. Of the operations of the Corps of Discovery, Clark wrote: "we were completely successfull and have therefore no hesitation in declaring that such as nature has permited it we have discovered the best rout which does exist across the continent of North America in that direction."[21] Like Lewis's letter to Jefferson, Clark's message carried the word of the "emence advantage to the fur trade" of the expedition's discoveries while playing down the fact that the long-hoped-for all-water route simply did not exist. But where Lewis's letter was for the eyes of the President, Clark's was for the public. It contained a synopsis of the great adventure and a promise of more to come—"As I shall shortly be with you and the post is now waiting I deem it unnecessary here to attempt minutely to detail the Occurencies of the last 18 months."

4

The American public would wait until 1814 for the detailed "Occurencies" pledged by Clark,[22] and it is perhaps for this reason that the initial American response to the expedition focused on the glamor and romance of the feat rather than on the wealth of geographical, ethnological, botanical, zoological, and other data that Lewis and Clark added to the store of scientific knowledge. Jefferson himself, in his annual message to Congress in late 1806, could say little other than that "The expedition of Messrs. Lewis & Clarke for exploring the river Missouri, and the best communication from that to the

18. Goetzmann, *Exploration and Empire*, pp. 8–35.
19. Jackson, *Letters*, p. 361.
20. Jackson, *Letters*, pp. 325–30, particularly the note on p. 330.
21. Jackson, *Letters*, p. 326.
22. The process of getting the journals before the public is related in the introduction to the Thwaites edition of the *Original Journals* (I, xxxiii–xlvi) and in the bibliographical notes in the Coues edition of the *History* (I, cvii–cxxxii); documents in Jackson (*Letters*, beginning with no. 301) also contain material bearing on the preparation and publication of the 1814 edition of the *History*.

Pacific ocean, has had all the success which could have been expected."[23] In his original draft of the message Jefferson had referred to the "important channel of communication with the Pacific" that Lewis and Clark had discovered, but this passage was deleted from the final version of the address—had the President decided that the captains' enthusiasm over "the most practicable rout" across the continent was unfounded?

Even if Jefferson had not so decided, many other citizens of the country began to look upon the reality of the Passage to India with something less than optimism and ecstasy. The official report released to the Washington *National Intelligencer* and subsequently published in numerous newspapers spoke only quietly and in a matter-of-fact vein about the completion of a heroic event but made no reference to the potential trade route.[24] Other news items were openly critical of the expense to which the government of the United States had gone for such a limited return. The "direct course" across the continent, commented a New York paper dourly, "will probably never be traveled."[25] Such reaction was far from atypical among the newspapers and periodicals of the cities along the seaboard. It is true that some Americans, like the intensely nationalistic Republican poet and essayist Joel Barlow, eulogized Lewis and Clark as new Columbuses, openers of extensive trading routes to Cathay:

> Let the Nile cloak his head in the clouds, and defy
> The researches of science and time;
> Let the Niger escape the keen traveller's eye,
> By plunging, or changing his clime.
>
> Columbus, not so shall thy boundless domain
> Defraud thy brave sons of their right;
> Streams, midlands, and shorelands elude us in vain,
> We shall drag their dark regions to light.[26]

But more representative of the public reaction in the eastern portions of the United States was the parody by John Quincy Adams:

> Good people, listen to my tale,
>   'Tis nothing but what true is;
> I'll tell you of the mighty deeds
>   Achieved by Captain Lewis—
> How starting from the Atlantick shore
>   By fair and easy motion,
> He journied, *all the way by land*,
>   Until he met the ocean.[27]

23. Jackson, *Letters*, p. 352.
24. *National Intelligencer* (Washington), Oct. 27, 1806; summarized in Thwaites (VII, 349).
25. *New York Gazette*, Nov. 25, 1806; reprinted in Thwaites (VII, 349).
26. Jackson, *Letters*, p. 362.
27. Jackson, *Letters*, p. 363.

In the small towns and on the farms of the South and Old Northwest, however, the men that would respond to Lewis's and Clark's exploits most directly by following them into the wilderness had a different reaction. Such men thought little of the Passage to India, for geopolitics and long-range commercial and imperial objectives were simply not a part of their frame of reference. Instead, they thought of the promised Garden that had been proclaimed, and, being frontiersmen themselves and knowing what had actually been accomplished, they hailed the captains as the heralds of a new destiny: "you have navigated bold & unknown rivers, traversed Mountains, which had never before been impressed with the footsteps of civilized man, and surmounted every obstacle, which climate, Nature or ferocious Savages could throw in your way. You have the further satisfaction to reflect that, you have extended the knowledge of the Geography of your country; in other respects enriched Science; and opened to the United States a source of inexhaustible wealth."[28] To Lewis and Clark the rights "to disclose to the world" the glories of the trans-Missouri West had been given, and in the eyes of men from the states of Kentucky and Tennessee and Ohio, from the territories of Indiana and Illinois and Missouri, the rights to use those glories had been awarded. And when the journals of Lewis and Clark were finally made available, the source of "inexhaustible wealth" would become even more apparent. If the original version of the all-water Passage were gone from American images, the Garden was not and would endure.

5

The first series of works about the expedition that circulated among the general public came from Jefferson's official message to Congress in February, 1806, and were not, properly speaking, derived from the reports of the explorers themselves. From the progress reports that Lewis and Clark had sent down the Missouri from the Mandan villages in the spring of 1805, the President extracted the most significant details on the country between St. Louis and Fort Mandan. These data, combined with reports of contemporary explorations of the lower Mississippi tributaries,[29] were printed in pamphlet form in a number of American cities and were available for sale even before the captains and their men had returned to St. Louis.[30] A number of apocry-

28. From an address of the citizens of Fincastle, Virginia, to Lewis and Clark; printed in Jackson, *Letters*, pp. 358–59.

29. Mr. William Dunbar of Natchez had, at Jefferson's request, explored the Red and Washita rivers in late 1804 and early 1805. His reports, notes on the Indians in the lower portions of Louisiana by Dr. John Sibley of Natchitoches, and the reports sent back by Lewis and Clark from Fort Mandan were presented to Congress by Jefferson (Jackson, *Letters*, pp. 298–300) and were subsequently published as *Message from the President of the United States Communicating Discoveries Made in Exploring the Missouri, Red River and Washita* . . . (Washington, 1806).

30. The "Prodrome," as Coues termed it, was published in several subsequent editions following the original Washington printing (Coues, *History*, I, cvii–cxi).

phal works quickly emerged from these first available sources of information on the Northwest, and in these "Apocrypha," data lifted almost directly from Jonathan Carver and Alexander Mackenzie were blended with the accurate but incomplete material in Jefferson's message and presented with such titles as "An Interesting Account of the Voyages and Travels of Captains Lewis and Clark, in the years 1804, 1805, and 1806."[31]

These spurious publications have made evaluations of the impact of Lewis and Clark on geographical images extremely difficult. It would appear, however, that the lack of detailed information in the "Apocrypha" prevented their incorporation into the formal geographical lore as found in "scientific" geographies.[32] Less formal sources of geographical data such as articles in American periodicals and newspapers also contained little material from the fictitious works, and any significant increments in general American geographical knowledge about the Northwest, therefore, waited upon the publication of more authentic and detailed versions of the exploits and adventures of the Corps of Discovery.

The first attempt to place such a work before the American public was made in October, 1806, possibly even before Lewis and Clark and a small party had departed from St. Louis for Washington to receive the accolades they so richly deserved.[33] In September and October of 1806, one of the privates in the corps, Robert Frazer of Vermont, circulated by hand in the St. Louis area a prospectus for publishing by subscription his own journals of the trek "From St. Louis in Louisiana to the Pacific Ocean Containing An accurate description of the Missouri and its several branches; of the mountains separating the Eastern from the Western waters; of the Columbia river and the Bay it forms on the Pacific Ocean. . . ."[34] Frazer's journal, if it ever existed in manuscript form at all, has never been found,[35] and although his proposals for publication appeared in several eastern newspapers in late 1806 and early 1807, no Frazer work was ever published. But another of the enlisted men of the command would beat his captains to the punch by getting his journals to the press and the public long before theirs.

The *Pittsburgh Gazette*, March 24, 1807, informed the public that Sergeant Patrick Gass would soon publish his own edition of "a Journal of the Voyages & Travels of a Corps of Discovery."[36] The Gass journal, edited by

31. The term "Apocrypha" is Coues's; publication details on these spurious works are in Coues, *History*, I, cxi–cxvii.
32. For an examination of the nature and content of the nineteenth-century geographies, see Martyn J. Bowden, "The Great American Desert and the American Frontier, 1800–1882: Popular Images of the Plains," in *Anonymous Americans: Explorations in Nineteenth Century Social History*, ed. Temara K. Haraven (Englewood Cliffs, N.J., 1971), pp. 48–79.
33. Jackson, *Letters*, p. 325, n. 7.
34. Jackson, *Letters*, p. 345.
35. A manuscript drawn by Frazer does exist, however, and is preserved in the Geography and Map Division of the Library of Congress. Although much simpler and cruder, the map resembles Clark's famous chart that accompanied the first edition of the *History of the Expedition*.
36. Jackson, *Letters*, pp. 390–91.

Pittsburgh bookseller David McKeehan, was published in a one-volume edition in Pittsburgh shortly after the prospectus was circulated and was reprinted in a London edition in 1808 and three Philadelphia editions in 1810, 1811, and 1812. The Gass journal told the story of the Corps of Discovery well, if rather unimaginatively, but the wealth of geographic and other scientific data, along with the maps, found in the captains' own journals was absent from that of their sergeant.[37] Consequently, although occasional extracts of landscape descriptions or geographical commentary from Gass appeared in periodical literature and material probably based on the Gass journal worked its way into grammar-school geographies, the publication of the Gass account had little real impact on American geographical lore.

6

During his first few months back in the United States, Lewis became increasingly concerned about the "several unauthorized and probably some spurious publications now preparing for the press, on the subject of my late tour to the Pacific Ocean" and began, therefore, to circulate a prospectus of his own.[38] This work would be the only "genuine" record of the expedition, claimed Lewis, and the first volume—containing "a narrative of the voyage with a description of some of the most remarkable places in those hitherto unknown wilds of America . . . together with an itinerary of the most direct and practicable route across the continent"—was projected as being available by January 1, 1808. A second volume containing "WHATEVER properly appertains to geography, embracing a description of the rivers, mountains, climate, soil and face of the country" with additional commentary on the "direct trade to the East Indies through the continent of North America" and a third volume confined "exclusively to scientific research" would be available shortly after the publication of the first volume. Detached from the work and to be available by October, 1807, added Lewis, was a large map of North America embracing the captains' discoveries in "that part of the continent heretofore the least known."[39]

37. Coues gives an interesting "Memoir of Patrick Gass" (*History*, I, xcix–cvi) and offers publication details of various editions of the Gass journals (I, cxvii–cxxiii). A reprint of the original McKeehan edition of the Gass journals (*A Journal of the Voyages and Travels of a Corps of Discovery, under the Command of Capt. Lewis and Capt. Clark of the Army of the United States*) has recently been reissued (Minneapolis, 1958).

38. Jackson (*Letters*, pp. 385–86) includes Lewis's letter putting the public "on their guard" against "spurious publications . . . on the subject of my late tour to the Pacific Ocean." See pp. 394–97 for the prospectus. Lewis's letter provoked what Jackson has called "a stinging reply" from David McKeehan, the editor of the Gass journals. This reply was printed in the *Pittsburgh Gazette*, Apr. 14, 1807, and reprinted in Jackson (*Letters*, pp. 399–408).

39. Lewis's comment here suggests that Clark may already have begun work on the large map illustrating their discoveries. In the prospectus, however, Lewis gives no credit to Clark, saying only that the map "will be compiled from the best maps now extant, as well published as in manuscript, from the collective information of the best informed travellers through the various portions of that region, and corrected by a series of several hundred celestial observations, made by Captain Lewis during his late tour."

Had Lewis's plans for publication been fulfilled, the impact of the Lewis and Clark Expedition on American geographical thought (and science in general) would undoubtedly have been different. But as Lewis, appointed by Jefferson to serve as governor of Louisiana Territory, and Clark, designated as the territory's superintendent of Indian affairs, grew more and more involved in official duties and responsibilities in St. Louis, the work on their journals was pushed aside. Lewis's untimely and tragic death in October, 1809, while en route to Washington on government business, further delayed the completion and release of the official account.[40] Lewis's death could have been more than a tragedy for his friends and country, however, for in his baggage were the field notes and maps of the expedition, and had they been lost or destroyed, the cost to history would have been incalculable. Fortunately they were returned to Clark, who traveled east in 1809–10 in order to make arrangements for the writing and publication of the narratives of the expedition.

Difficulty upon difficulty beset Clark in his attempts to complete work upon the papers he and his deceased friend had compiled. Although more competent in many areas than Lewis, Clark was not the scientist that Lewis had been, and, recognizing that fact, he searched fruitlessly for "a proper scientifcul Charrutor to Compile that part of the work relitive"[41] to the scientific achievements of the expedition. It was finally determined that Nicholas Biddle of Philadelphia[42] would undertake the job of editing the narrative portions of the manuscript notes while the scientific content of the field journals would be compiled and edited by Dr. Benjamin Smith Barton.[43] But when, in May of 1810, the proposals for the new version of the "detailed and authentic history of the expedition" were published, it became clear that the integrity of Lewis's original design was at least partly destroyed.

Rather than the three volumes encompassing the narrative, western geography, and scientific data that Lewis had intended, the Biddle edition was to contain two volumes, the first being narrative and descriptive and the second devoted to botany, mineralogy, zoology, meteorology, and Indian vocabularies. Even these intentions were subverted, however, and the first authentic "History of the Expedition," published in Philadelphia in 1814 after an almost unbelievable three years of confusion and delay, consisted of two volumes

40. After more than 160 years, Lewis's death still remains a mystery, with scholarly opinion about equally divided between those who believe he was murdered in a settler's cabin in Tennessee and those who hold that he died by his own hand. The people who knew him best—Jefferson and Clark—both held the opinion that his death was a suicide. Donald Jackson, the foremost contemporary authority on the expedition, is also "inclined to believe that Lewis died by his own hand" (Jackson, *Letters*, p. 575).

41. Jackson, *Letters*, p. 490.

42. Biddle was a prominent Philadelphia lawyer and financier who had served as a diplomat prior to 1807 and was later named as president of the Bank of the United States. His papers and correspondence are in the Manuscript Division of the Library of Congress and in the American Philosophical Society Library in Philadelphia. An excellent biography of Biddle is Thomas P. Govan, *Nicholas Biddle, Nationalist and Public Banker* (Chicago, 1959).

43. Dr. Barton had been involved in the work of the expedition from the beginning and was a logical choice to edit the scientific data. It is curious that an even more competent scientist, Thomas Jefferson himself, did not become involved in the project.

devoted almost entirely to the narrative itself, with a meager amount of scientific data appended to the second volume.[44] It was certainly not the work that Lewis had projected, but it offered to the American public their first opportunity to assess the New West. And although later generations of scientists and historians may lament the deviations from Lewis's proposals, the Biddle edition was "a treasury of knowledge" from which Americans could create new images of an area that had previously been an "area of rumor, guess, and fantasy."[45]

7

Although the textual materials of the Biddle edition of the Lewis and Clark journals did not fulfill expectations completely, the first official history of the expedition did include an item of superlative craftsmanship and analysis. This was the master map of the American Northwest, drawn in manuscript form by William Clark and copied for engraving and printing by the Philadelphia cartographer Samuel Lewis.[46] From the very early stages of the transcontinental trek, Clark had proven himself to be a cartographer of unusual skill, and as he applied his talents to the consolidation of the maps he had drawn during the course of the journey to the Pacific and back, a remarkable cartographic masterpiece began to take form.[47] Before the publication of the Biddle history and the Clark map, American cartographic representations of the West were of three general derivations: from the maps published in Morse's *American Geography*, illustrating a narrow single-ridge chain of mountains in the interior with a short Missouri River on the east side of the chain and a lengthy "River of the West" or "Oregan River" on the west; from various published copies of Antoine Soulard's map of Louisiana, depicting the Rockies as lying close to the Pacific and showing the Missouri as a stream heading close to the western ocean; and from the various editions of Arrowsmith maps with the narrow Rockies and double-branch Missouri that had been the most accurate symbolizations of the West before Lewis and Clark.[48] Vestigial features from these maps would appear on charts even after

44. Details of the publication and editing process may be found in various documents printed in Jackson (*Letters*) and in the bibliographical introduction in Coues (*History*). Although Biddle had done the bulk of the work in completing the volumes for publication, his name did not appear in the finished version. Since Biddle had been elected to the legislature in 1812 and had no time for the final revision, Paul Allen of Philadelphia took his place and supervised the last stages of getting the *History* through the press.

45. Bernard DeVoto, *Journals of Lewis and Clark*, p. lii.

46. There are actually two maps—Clark's manuscript, completed in 1810, and the version published in 1814. Unless the manuscript version is specifically referred to (as "Clark's 1810 map" or "Clark's manuscript"), the commentary below may be taken as referring to the final published version.

47. Clark's map has been called "a major contribution to the geographic knowledge of Western North America" by Herman Friis of the National Archives ("Cartographic and Geographic Activities of the Lewis and Clark Expedition," p. 351).

48. Wheat, *Mapping the Transmississippi West*, II, ch. 1.

the publication of the Biddle history, but the Clark chart and those of other observers who followed him and Lewis into the West were the first representatives of an entirely new generation of American maps.

Clark's manuscript map of 1810 was made even more important by the addition of data from sources other than the explorations he and his lamented companion had made. In his capacity as superintendent of Indian affairs of Louisiana Territory, Clark was in a position to acquire information from all those explorers, traders, and trappers who began to pass through his office on their way to or from the West. Therefore, aside from its importance as the first accurate rendering of many critical features of western geography, the Clark map was indicative of the flurry of exploratory activity that took place between the return of the expedition and the publication of the journals in 1814. The master map was, then, a precise symbol of the nature of informed American geographical lore of the Northwest and the images that began to take shape following the publication of the map and the *History*.

8

One of the most important sources of data for Clark's map (aside from his own experiences) was the expedition of Zebulon M. Pike into the upper Arkansas and upper Rio Grande basins between 1805 and 1807.[49] Several specific features of Clark's 1810 map—for example, the "Highest Peak" of the Rockies (Pike's Peak) and Pike's winter camp of 1806 in the area between the westernmost waters of the Platte and Arkansas systems—were derived directly from the reports and maps of Pike. Much more important, however, were descriptions and cartographic representation of Pike's "grand reservoir of snows and fountains" in which headed the Yellowstone, Platte, Arkansas, Rio Grande, and Colorado rivers.[50] Such data confirmed Clark's erroneous conclusion about the proximity of the Missouri's source streams to those of the "Spanish" rivers, and the retention of the mythical pyramidal height-of-land on Clark's map was not only a major immediate error but one that marred the American image of the Rockies until the explorations of John C. Frémont in the 1840s.[51]

Zebulon Pike was, like Lewis and Clark, a military man, a new breed in western exploration. But another new breed, the fur trapper, was coming into being as well, and from a number of individuals in their rapidly growing ranks, William Clark acquired the geographical lore that was to be assimilated into his master map. The traditional pattern in the North American fur trade had been for the white traders to move into a rich fur region and exchange articles of European, Canadian, or American manufacture for fur trapped by

49. For details on Pike see Donald Jackson, ed., *The Journals of Zebulon Montgomery Pike with Letters and Related Documents* (2 vols., Norman, Okla., 1966).
50. Jackson, *Journals of Pike*, II, 26.
51. Goetzmann, *Exploration and Empire*, pp. 25, 142–44.

the natives. After the expedition this pattern began to change, and the Illinois trappers that the captains had met near the mouth of the Yellowstone signaled the transition. Henceforth the whites themselves would take to the beaver streams of the mountains and the plains, and in the process they would, directly or indirectly, contribute much to the geographical knowledge of the western interior.

During the years between the return of Lewis and Clark and the publication of Clark's map, the central figure in the Missouri River fur trade was a New Orleans Spaniard named Manuel Lisa.[52] Grasping almost immediately the significance of the captains' accomplishments for the future of the St. Louis–based fur trade, Lisa had gathered an expeditionary brigade of more than forty men within six months of Lewis's and Clark's return, and in April of 1807 he headed for the upper Missouri with the intention of building a string of forts to serve as operational bases for trapping and trading in the interior. Although a rascally character by nearly all accounts of his contemporaries, Lisa succeeded in bringing under his leadership two veterans of the Lewis and Clark party who would carry out exploratory feats second only to those of the expedition itself. Accompanying Lisa as guide and junior partner was the same George Drouillard who had served Lewis and Clark so well as a hunter and interpreter, and as the Lisa party pushed up the Missouri beyond the mouth of the Platte, another Lewis and Clark man, John Colter, joined the fur brigade.

Colter had left Lewis and Clark to join the Illinois trappers in the late summer of 1806 and as the result of a winter of trapping in the region had already become well acquainted with the area drained by the Yellowstone and Bighorn. His knowledge increased after he joined Lisa's command and undertook, while in Lisa's employ, an exploratory journey that was not only mythic in its proportions but immensely significant for the geographical details it added to the Clark map. No one can be exactly sure of the precise route Colter followed on his trek during the winter of 1807–08 since he kept no journals and drew no maps (other than a possible rough sketch that he might have given Clark).[53] From the dotted line representing Colter's travels that Clark inserted on his manuscript, however, it would appear that the erstwhile member of the Corps of Discovery, leaving from Manuel's Fort, the post that Lisa had established at the Bighorn-Yellowstone junction, made, completely alone, the first reconnaissance of the northwestern quarter of what is now the state of Wyoming. Conjecturally, Colter's route from the mouth of the Bighorn was west across the Bighorn Mountains into the basin of the same name that was drained by the Shoshone River (a tributary of the Bighorn), and

52. Richard Oglesby, *Manuel Lisa and the Opening of the Missouri Fur Trade* (Norman, Okla., 1963) is the best source on Lisa and his activities.
53. This is only conjecture on my part. Since Colter was living in the St. Louis area when Clark was preparing his map (cf. Bradbury, *Travels in the Interior*, pp. 44–46), it is logical to assume that he would have visited Clark and might well have, at Clark's request, made some rough sketches illustrating his travels.

thence south and southwest around the eastern margins of the Absaroka massif into the valley of the Wind River or upper Bighorn.

Colter moved west from the Wind River valley, across a pass between the sources of the Wind River and the Gros Ventres (a branch of the Snake) and down into Jackson's Hole and the Teton country. After crossing the Teton range via Teton Pass into Pierre's Hole, he backtracked into Jackson's Hole and proceeded northward to Yellowstone Lake ("Lake Eustis" on the Clark map) in what is now Yellowstone National Park. Following the Yellowstone River north out of the lake, Colter crossed over the wall of mountains ringing the eastern edge of the park and once again came out onto the Shoshone River, down which he passed to the Bighorn and Manuel's Fort.[54] Colter's journey was a remarkable achievement, even more remarkable since it was accomplished alone and in the dead of the Rocky Mountain winter. More important, the geographical knowledge acquired by Colter on his travels was combined by Clark with the data from Pike and evaluated in the light of a map drawn by George Drouillard. Such a combination gave form and substance to thousands of square miles of previously unknown territory, and the resulting view was essential in the overall view of western geography.

Drouillard's explorations were neither as lengthy nor as hazardous as Colter's and covered territory that had, for the most part, already been explored by the latter.[55] But Drouillard made a map (fig. 43) depicting the Bighorn drainage area, and when he returned to St. Louis in August of 1808 this map was presented to William Clark,[56] was copied by him, and was later incorporated into Clark's master map. The major role of the Drouillard map as a shaper of later views of the West that would be based on the Clark map was its embodiment and seemingly conclusive proof of the theory of the pyramidal height-of-land upon which was based Clark's firm conviction that the upper waters of the Yellowstone and the Bighorn lay in close proximity to the sources of the "Spanish" rivers. The critical section of the Drouillard-Clark maps was that depicting the Shoshone or "Stinking Water" River, particularly the area about the headwaters of its southwestern branch (the modern South Fork of the Shoshone).[57] On the upper portion of this "princi-

54. This route is hypothetical but based on the sound analysis in Burton Harris, *John Colter* (New York, 1952), pp. 73–114.

55. For details on Drouillard and his travels, see M. O. Skarsten, *George Drouillard, Hunter and Interpreter for Lewis and Clark and Fur Trader, 1807–1810* (Glendale, Calif., 1964).

56. The Drouillard map is preserved in the Lewis and Clark Manuscripts in the Geography and Map Division of the Library of Congress. The copy of the map that was made by Clark from the original, along with Clark's notes on information given him by Drouillard, is in the Missouri Historical Society, St. Louis, and published in Skarsten, *George Drouillard*.

57. Drouillard's map showed the country around present-day Cody, Wyoming, with amazing detail, including a notation on the hot springs of the Shoshone River that were seen by both Drouillard and Colter and were the springs referred to as "Colter's Hell" rather than the thermal regions in the Yellowstone National Park area. The Shoshone is still locally

pal branch," at a distance of fourteen days' march from the junction of the South Fork with the North Fork of the Shoshone, was a salt cave "and from hence to Spanish Settlements 8 days."[58] These Spanish settlements were on the "river Collarado" in the original Drouillard-Clark maps and on the Rio Grande ("Rio del Norte") in Clark's final version—but the change in rivers was unimportant. For Clark's conjectures on the pyramidal height-of-land were apparently valid, and a well-marked Indian trail led from the Stinking Water to the rivers of New Mexico. The Colter and Drouillard contributions, as interpreted by Clark and symbolized on his master map, had added up to "a remarkable exercise in fictional geography."[59]

The fiction was made more complete by the travels of still another of Lisa's men, Andrew Henry, who crossed over the Continental Divide between the upper Missouri and the Columbia basin in late 1810 and, on Henrys Fork of the Snake River, established (at least temporarily) the first American post west of the Rockies.[60] The route of Henry's crossing has been disputed, and although Clark's map showed a route between the headwaters of the Madison and the sources of the Snake via a "Southern Pass," it is more likely that the crossing was somewhat farther south.[61] The actual location of the pass used by Henry and his men is less important, however, than what Clark made out of it. For in their peregrinations after first crossing the Divide, the Henry party had stumbled on a river which they believed to be part of the Columbia system but after "descending 3 or 4 days they concluded was the Rio del Norte."[62] They retraced their route back up this "Spanish River," crossed over into the Snake, where they wintered, and once again Clark's theories had been vindicated. To the core area containing the upper portions of the Missouri and Rio Grande, the Snake now had to be added, and the pyramidal height-of-land was almost complete.[63] It would become whole when Clark returned to his own experience and added—to complete the

---

known as the "Stinking Water" from the sulphurous fumes which formerly emanated from these springs. A note in Thwaites (VI, 266) describing these springs is obviously based on either Colter or Drouillard information.

58. Clark's copy of the Drouillard map makes this distance eighteen days from the mouth of the Shoshone to the Spanish settlements.

59. Goetzmann, *Exploration and Empire*, p. 25.

60. Hiram M. Chittenden, *A History of the American Fur Trade of the Far West* (reprint ed., 2 vols., Stanford, Calif., 1954), II, 144.

61. The crossing was probably from the upper Yellowstone via the Bannock Trail and the Yellowstone Plateau to the Snake in extreme eastern Idaho (Ralph Ehrenberg, "Sketch of Part of the Missouri & Yellowstone Rivers with a Description of the Country &c.," *Prologue, the Journal of the National Archives*, III (Fall, 1971), 73–78). After the publication of the Biddle *History*, a reviewer of that work who was familiar with Henry's feat commented that the route Henry had discovered was much better than those passes used by Lewis and Clark (Jackson, *Letters*, pp. 324–25, 1).

62. Ehrenberg, "Sketch of Part of the Missouri & Yellowstone," p. 75.

63. Henry was interviewed when he returned to St. Louis, and a report in the *Louisiana Gazette* (Oct. 11, 1811) stated that the passage across the mountains that he had located would make "intercourse with settlements which may be formed on the Columbia, more easy than between those on the heads of the Ohio, and the Atlantic states."

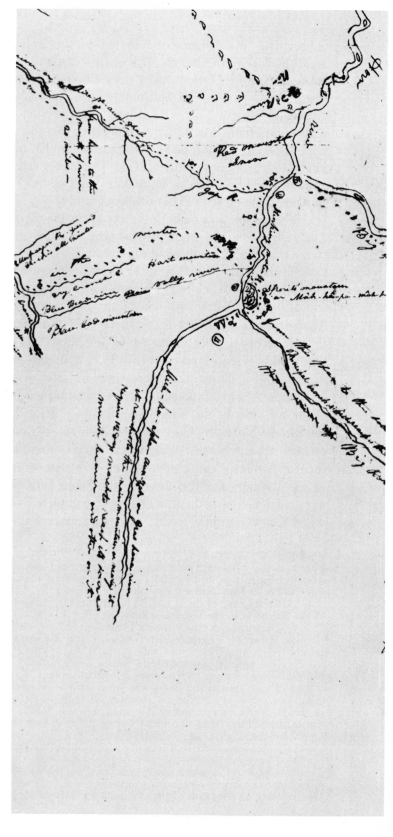

43. Portion of William
Clark's copy of a
George Drouillard map
showing the supposed
route from the upper
Bighorn drainage to the
"Spanish river"
COURTESY,
MISSOURI HISTORICAL
SOCIETY, ST. LOUIS

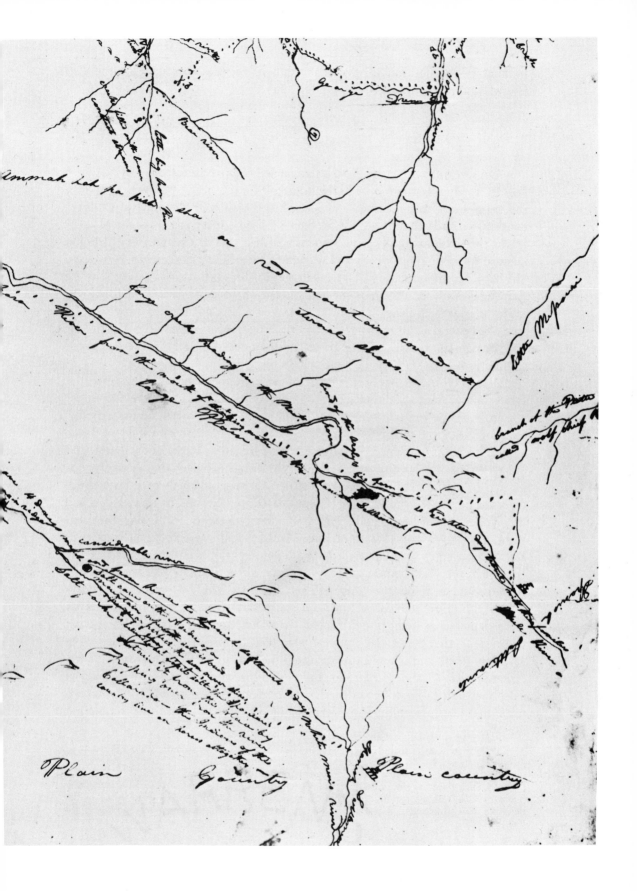

symmetry—the fictitious Multnomah with its sources just west of the Rio Grande and just south of the Snake (fig. 44).

9

On December 20, 1810, Clark forwarded his manuscript map to Nicholas Biddle "to anex as much of it to the book as you think fit."[64] After engraving, the manuscript was returned to Clark,[65] and although the former explorer continually updated and revised his map with new materials from the West,[66] it was the published (1814) version rather than the larger and more detailed manuscript map upon which a new generation of American maps was based (fig. 45). In the rendering of this major contribution to cartography may be seen the clearest indication of the changes the Lewis and Clark Expedition had made in American geographical lore. And in Clark's published map may be seen the general accuracy and character of the new images of the Northwest and the contrast between those views and the ones held prior to the successful completion of the bulk of the expedition's objectives.

Views on the nature and content of western geography held prior to the Lewis and Clark Expedition had been characterized by several key features: a narrow, single ridge of mountains in the interior that were the only mountains between the Mississippi and the Pacific; a core source area in those mountains which spawned the Missouri, the Oregan or River of the West, and the rivers of the Southwest; a number of foreshortened and virtually unknown tributary streams flowing into the Missouri; and a short and coastally confined course for the Oregan (Columbia) River. Several of these views had been modified by Lewis and Clark immediately before and during their expedition. Clark's map, drawn at Fort Mandan, had presented the Rockies as a series of ranges sprawling across almost the entire western portion of the continent, the westernmost ridge lying close to the Pacific. The tributaries of the Missouri were greatly elongated, and rivers such as the Platte and Yellowstone (although their entries into the major stream were shown accurately) were depicted as being much longer than they actually were. The ancient theories of the pyramidal height-of-land were preserved in Clark's Fort Mandan map, and the headwaters of the Missouri, Yellowstone, Platte, Arkansas, Rio Grande, Colorado, and Columbia were represented as being in close proximity. These views of the western interior, derived from the captains' first year of exploration, were changed even more with the completion

64. Jackson, *Letters*, p. 565.

65. Just when the manuscript map was returned to Clark is unknown but he had it in his possession in 1816. In October of that year he wrote to Jefferson, "The map from which the plate was made, is in my possession at this place" (Jackson, *Letters*, p. 624).

66. Such things as the route of Wilson Price Hunt and his party of Astorians, antedating the transmission of the manuscript to Biddle, appear on the original Clark map (now in the Beinecke Rare Books and Manuscript Library, Yale University—the map was published by Yale in 1950).

382

of their journey and the publication of Clark's map illustrating the final contributions of the expedition to western geography (fig. 46).

Of all the alterations in American images of the western part of the continent that emanated from the travels of Lewis and Clark, none were greater or more observable on Clark's map than those pertaining to the mountains of the interior. The simplistic and generalized range of the Stony or Shining or Rocky Mountains gave way to a complex series of mountains and hills, some of which were identified as part of the distinct region of the Rockies and others as outliers of that mighty range or isolated ranges of the Pacific drainage. The hypothetical geography upon which the Passage to India had been predicated for well over a century was eliminated from American geographical thought after Lewis and Clark. A traverse of the mountain region of the Northwest would henceforth be viewed as a mighty accomplishment rather than a minor feat achieved via a simple and short portage between navigable streams.[67]

The easternmost mountain range of the interior was an absolutely new feature in American geographical lore. The existence of the "Black Mountains" or "Black Hills" had been known to adventurers and traders along the upper Missouri since the latter part of the eighteenth century. But when Clark drew his elongated range, running from northwest to southeast and lying between the 105th and 103rd meridians, he became the first cartographer to represent the Black Hills of South Dakota. And in his delineation of those other outlying mountains of the northern Great Plains such as the Moccasin and Judith ranges that lie south of the Missouri (the mountains north of the river—the Bearpaws and Little Rocky Mountains—were, inexplicably, not shown on Clark's map), Clark added to the accuracy of the emerging American view of the Northwest and diminished the older preexploratory notion of the confinement of the interior mountains into a longitudinally narrow north-south strip.

It was in the area of the Rocky Mountains proper where Clark's map made its greatest increments to geographical knowledge, including the first truly definitive cartographic representation of the Continental Divide. Many ranges of the Rockies—primarily those between the Great Falls of the Missouri and the Clearwater River—were drawn as the direct result of field observations during both the Pacific-bound journey and the return trip and were depicted with rather amazing accuracy, considering the actual extent of the captain's field experience. The great east-west extent of the ranges on Clark's 1805 map had been narrowed to a point highly correlative with their actual position, and the positioning of the Montana and Idaho portions of the Rocky Mountains was much closer to reality on the 1814 map than they had formerly been (fig. 47).

67. Note 2 to Appendix III of the Biddle *History* made the nature of the crossing perfectly evident, describing the Lewis and Clark version of the short portage as a total of 340 miles, "200 miles of which is a good road, 140 miles over a tremendous mountain, steep and broken, 60 miles of which is covered several feet deep with snow."

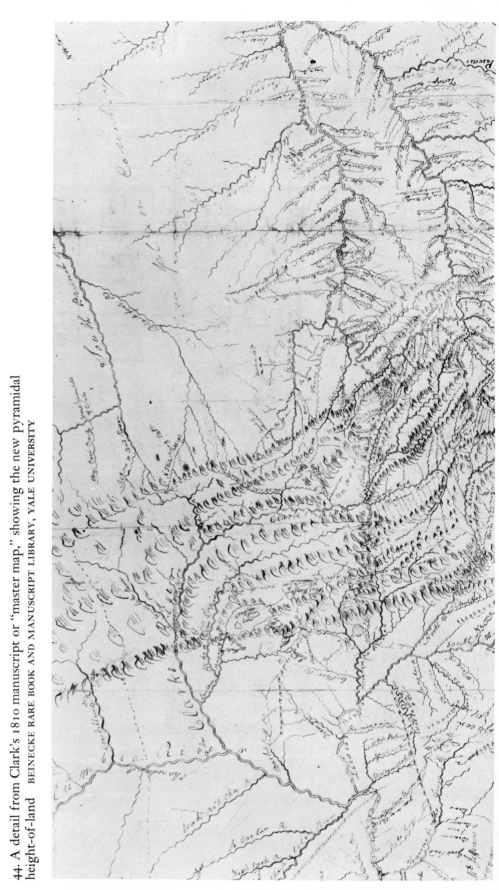

44. A detail from Clark's 1810 manuscript or "master map," showing the new pyramidal height-of-land   BEINECKE RARE BOOK AND MANUSCRIPT LIBRARY, YALE UNIVERSITY

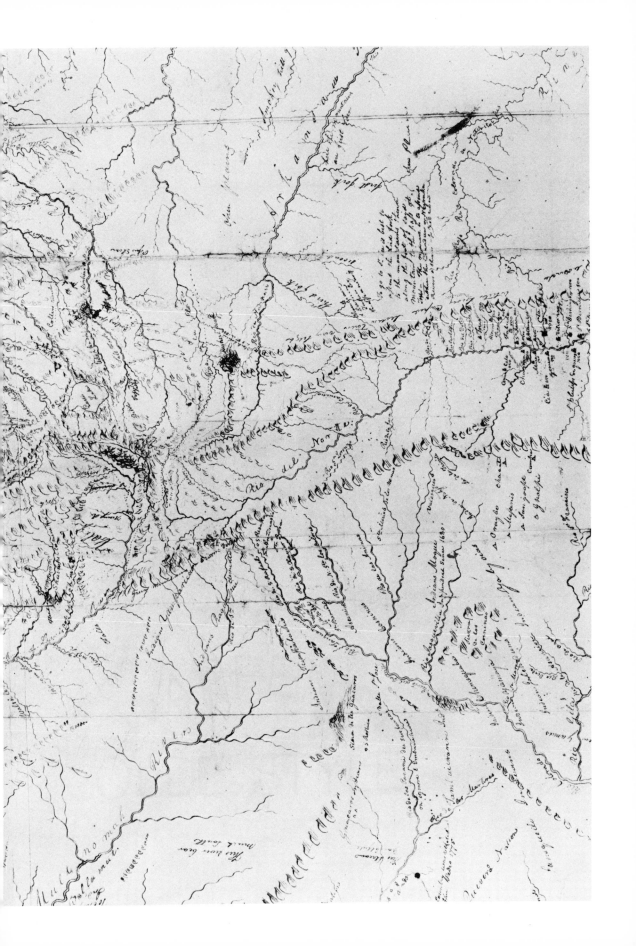

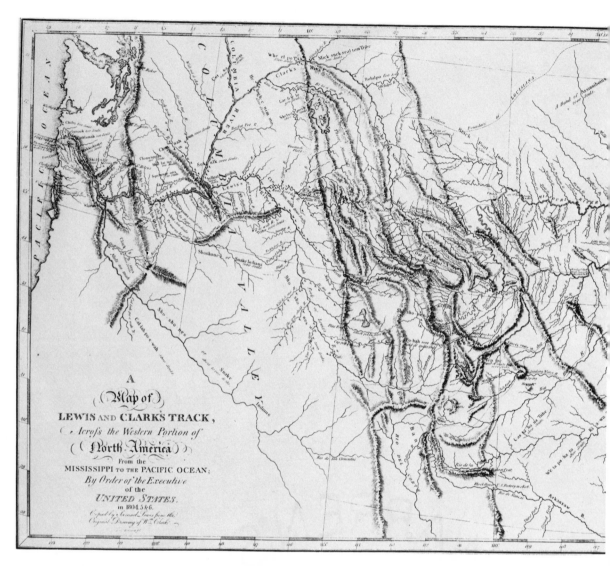

45. Samuel Lewis's copy of Clark's 1810 manuscript. Published in 1814 with the Biddle *History of the Expedition* (Philadelphia)

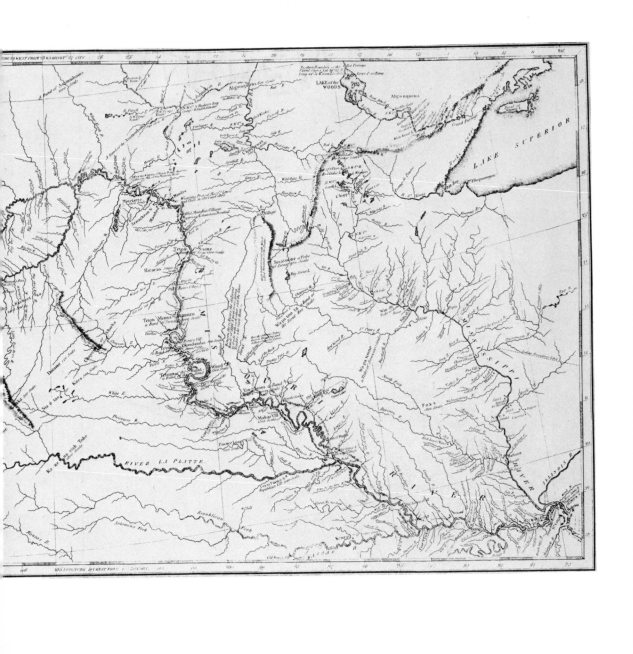

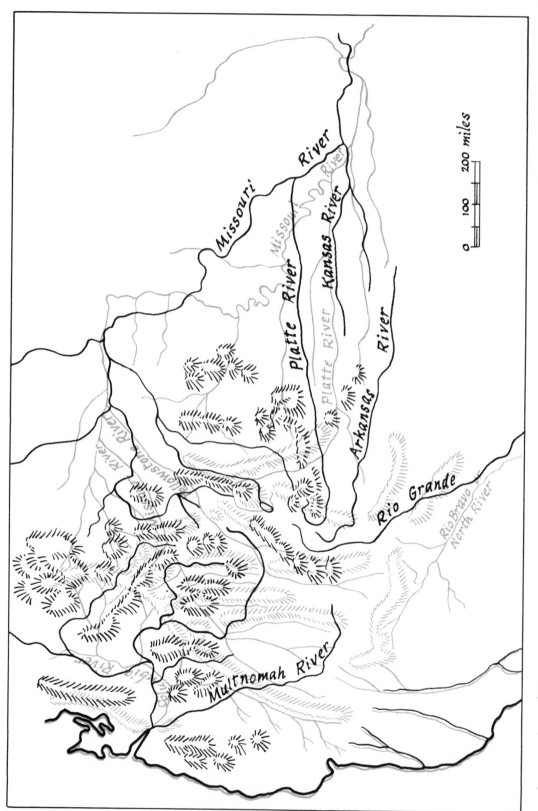

Missouri River

Missouri River

Kansas River

Platte River

Platte River

Arkansas River

Arkansas River

Yellowstone River

Rio Grande

RioBravo or
North River

Multnomah River

0   100   200 miles

46. A comparison of Clark's two most important maps—the one drawn in 1805 at the Mandan villages
and the final 1814 published version of Clark's "master map" of the American West

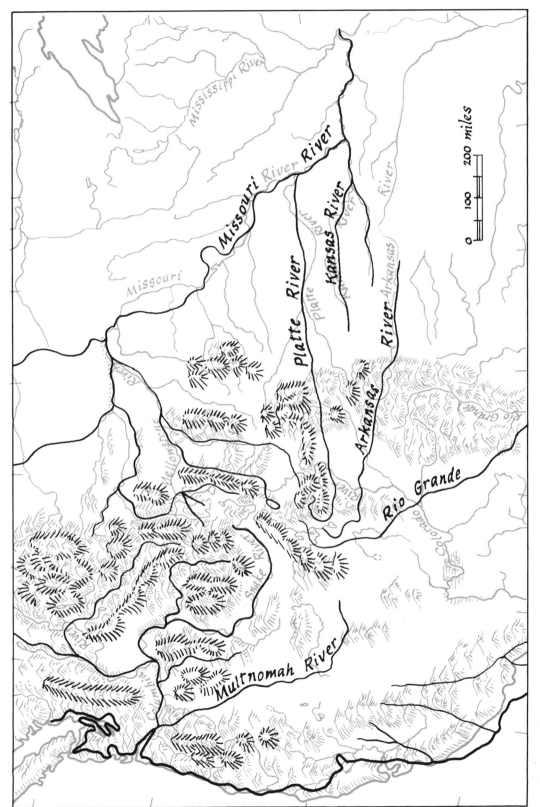

Missouri River River

Mississippi River

Kansas River

Platte River

Platte River

Arkansas River

Arkansas

Missouri

River

Yellowstone

Snake River

River

Multnomah River

Rio Grande

Colorado River

Rio Grande

River

River

200 miles

100

0

47. The 1814 Clark map compared with a modern base map

Some of the ranges of the Rocky Mountains lying south of the expedition's traverse line were also represented with a fair degree of accuracy as a result of the information extracted from the explorations of Colter and Drouillard or put together deductively from data acquired during the course of the expedition from natives. But the farther south of the path of Lewis and Clark, the greater the apparent degree of distortion and misrepresentation of mountainous areas on Clark's chart. As he had done on his Fort Mandan map, Clark expanded known geographical features to fill areas that were as yet unexplored, and the result was the extension of the mountains surrounding the headwaters of the Yellowstone and Bighorn rivers too far south for reality. This error hinged on a conceptual void which was centered on the central portions of the Rocky Mountain system and resulted in a compression of the features of southwestern geography to accommodate the expansion of those of the Northwest.

No such cardinal errors prevailed in Clark's depiction of the mountains west of the Rocky Mountain system, primarily as the result of his more objective approach to that area. Only those ranges directly observed or described in site-specific terms by natives were included in the delineation of ranges of the Pacific side of the Divide, and only three mountainous regions, therefore, were shown for this area. The Horse Heaven and Blue mountains of the Columbian Plain region were included on Clark's chart, and although the former was overemphasized in importance, the positioning of both ranges was fairly accurate. The Cascade range and its major prominences of Rainier, St. Helens, Hood, and Jefferson was, although Clark never did work out the fact that Mt. Adams and Mt. St. Helens were two different peaks, drawn with detailed accuracy—all the more so since here the captains' field observations could be compared and checked against the charts of Vancouver. Finally, the coastal ranges were incorporated into the mountain systems of the Pacific Northwest, and if those ranges appeared to be given an undue emphasis in the published version of Clark's map, the blame can be laid on the cartographic and engraving techniques by which the final map was produced rather than on the captain's actual perception of the importance of the hills along the coast and the lower portions of the valley of the Columbia.

The real significance of Clark's presentation of the mountains between the Rockies and the Pacific does not, however, lie in its general accuracy. Even though the Cascades and the Rockies had been recognized as two distinct mountain systems prior to the expedition, Clark's portrayal of the mountain terrain between the Divide and the Pacific demolished the old myth that the range visible from the shores of the Pacific was "a dependance of the *Stony Mountains*."[68] Two mighty ranges rather than one lay between the upper Missouri and the Great South Sea. And separating those ranges was a physiographic feature that had never appeared before—the Great Columbian Plain. The ancient tales of explorers being able to gaze upon the shining

68. See pp. 173–76 below.

waters of the western ocean from the highest peaks of the Rocky Mountains were finally proved to be fantasy and unfulfilled desire.

10

The modified view of the rivers of western North America illustrated by the Clark map was nearly equal in importance to the new image of western mountains and like that image was characterized by general accuracy and complexity of detail. The most critical transformation of earlier conceptions of rivers was unquestionably Clark's establishment of nearly correct positioning for the headward portions of the Missouri and Columbia, since it had been in the area of the Missouri-Columbia source waters where errors in earlier images had been most apparent. Although the long-accepted notion that the source streams of the Missouri and those of the Columbia sprang from the same vicinity was not destroyed by the Clark map, traditional adherence to the concept of the short portage did not survive after the publication of the chart. For where previous maps had, for the most part, shown the Missouri and Columbia as undifferentiated in terms of size from their sources to their mouths, Clark's map clearly indicated the diminishing in size of streams toward the farthest margins of a drainage basin. Lewis and Clark had learned and had transmitted their experiences as to the nature of mountain streams. Thus both the farthest western sources of the Missouri and the easternmost source waters of the Columbia appeared as small, twisting streams rather than as large and broad navigable waterways as they had earlier been presented. When this visual presentation was viewed in conjunction with the dotted line on the map which traced the expedition's tortuous search for navigable waters and with data from the text of the *History*, the time-honored concept of the simple passage from the Missouri to the Columbia was dealt a fatal stroke.

A more realistic interpretation of the source region of the Missouri and Columbia was far from the only increment in knowledge about the river systems of the Northwest made by the Clark map. Also of cardinal consequence was the vast amount of geographic detail added to the general lore of western North America below the 50th parallel. The map published in 1814 provided a valuable supplement to the Fort Mandan map's data on the Missouri tributaries below the Mandan villages and, through the assimilation of information collected during the second and third summers the expedition had been in the field, added totally new pictures of the feeder streams of the Missouri beyond the Great Bend and on the waters of the Pacific drainage basins.

In only two major instances did the 1814 map deviate from the Fort Mandan map in the portrayal of the Missouri system below the Mandan villages. The first of those exceptions was a vital one, for it bore directly on the southward migration of the conjectural pyramidal height-of-land from the source region of the Missouri and Columbia and Saskatchewan to the source area of the rivers of the Southwest. The 1805 map had shown two major branches of the Platte River, a southern branch heading near the sources of the Arkansas and Rio Grande, and a northern branch rising close to the headwaters of the Bighorn River. Using data based on Pike's map and journals, Clark altered this previous (and more accurate) delineation and showed the Platte as a river with a west-to-east direction from source to mouth and without any major bifurcation.[69] The older concepts of the proximity of the Platte's headwaters to those of the Bighorn, Arkansas, and Rio Grande were preserved, however, and this straight-line river was represented as rising in the same area as all three of those rivers. The core region of river origin theorized by eighteenth-century cosmographers was now in the Southwest.

The second major deviation from the Fort Mandan map was in the 1814 map's depiction of the lengths of the rivers in the Missouri tributary system below the Great Bend. On the Fort Mandan map many of the tributaries of the Missouri between its mouth and the Knife River had been greatly elongated toward the west. The map accompanying the *History* corrected this error, and although the sources of the Platte were still nearly 3° too far west (only a slight diminution of the overextension on the 1805 map), other rivers such as the Kansas, Niobrara, White, and Cheyenne had been shortened from 2° to 4°, thus placing their sources much closer to their actual locations. With the increase in operationally derived data on the area west of the Mandan villages, the need to expand the known features below the Great Bend to fill in the area between the Missouri and the mountains was greatly reduced. The resultant compression of the Missouri's western tributaries below the Knife River to make room for the previously unobserved Yellowstone and Bighorn rivers and for the Rocky Mountains themselves (placed too far west on the Mandan map) brought the portrayal of the river systems of the Great Plains much closer to reality.

It was in the vast country between the Mandan villages and the Pacific, however, where Clark's 1814 map made its greatest modifications of earlier views of the western rivers. The most significant of those conversions were the twin outgrowths of the cartographer's accurate rendering of the Continental Divide's position between the 50th and 43rd parallels: (1) the great western and southern expansion of the Missouri itself that had appeared on the 1805 map was changed drastically, and the 1814 illustration of the course of the Missouri from the upper Jefferson to the Great Bend correlated closely with the physical reality of western geography; (2) the Fort Mandan map's confinement of the Columbia system to a narrow region along the Pacific coast was not retained on the 1814 map and the territory west of the Divide

69. The upper portion of the Platte River on Clark's map was a virtual duplication of the course of the Platte as laid down on Pike's map (see the Pike map between pp. 388 and 389 of vol. I of Jackson, *Journals of Pike*).

that was drained by the Columbia and its tributaries more than doubled in areal extent over that accorded it on the earlier map. Moreover, the courses of at least some of the rivers of the Columbia system were depicted accurately from their heads to their entry into the mighty western river.

In addition to these principal transformations, the Clark 1814 map offered substantial increments to geographical lore by augmenting the detail and texture of the western drainage basins. It is true that the 1805 map had included some details on such important rivers as the Yellowstone and its many tributaries (the Powder, Tongue, Bighorn, and others), the Musselshell, Milk, and Sun rivers, and the Three Forks of the Missouri east of the Divide, while the bifurcation of the Columbia into a northern and southern branch were shown west of the last dividing range. But in spite of the fact that the view the 1814 map presented of the Missouri system beyond the Great Bend was still simplistic and the territory beyond the Divide was still generalized, the 1814 map went far beyond all previous cartographic efforts in elaborating the composition of the Missouri and Columbian systems. The field experiences of two full seasons in the territory west of the Mandan villages plus the lore obtained in the first few years after the expedition's return to civilization had meant that even simplicity and generalization would henceforth be cast in an entirely different mold.

There were some obvious minor distortions in the 1814 representation of the upper Missouri system and the Columbian basin: the basin of the Missouri above the Three Forks was a little out of proportion as the result of an eastward misplacement of the junction of the Gallatin, Madison, and Jefferson rivers; the eastern portions of the Snake drainage were also not drawn quite true to scale; the lengths of the Bighorn and Yellowstone rivers were still somewhat too great; and the White Earth River with its prospective connections with the Saskatchewan was still a stream of myth and fancy, created out of wishful thinking and the geography of hope. By and large, however, the image of western rivers as it appeared on Clark's master map was accurate and—as was the case with the image of western mountains—remarkably so for those portions actually traversed during the expedition. Virtually all of the most important tributaries of the Missouri and Yellowstone were placed with precision, as were the significant feeder streams of "Lewis's River" and "Clark's River" or the Snake and the Clark Fork of the Columbia.[70] Additionally, major lakes such as Yellowstone Lake and Lake Pend Oreille were shown on a map for the first time, and the courses of the vast majority of the two great drainage basins of the Northwest were depicted correctly—including that of the Snake, which had finally achieved its true position of eminence among the tributary rivers of the Columbia.

Its outstanding overall quality notwithstanding, Clark's 1814 map con-

70. Such detail is testimony to the accuracy of the information obtained from Indians and to the captains' ability to absorb Indian information and combine it with their own field observations and intuition.

tained one momentous and erroneous feature of the imagination which marred Clark's otherwise superb geography and distorted images of the West for another thirty years. This was the Multnomah River, arising out of the combination of a misinterpreted Willamette with the pure theories of continental symmetry. South of the Columbia's path across the Columbian Plain there lay a vast area that had to be drained by some river—just as the area south of the Missouri's course across the northern Great Plains was watered by the Yellowstone. The Multnomah was therefore a river of necessity. From its source near the 114th parallel it ripped across a full 9° of longitude to its entry into the Columbia, and it was a mighty river which—in one form or another—bemused a generation of cartographers, geographers, and explorers.[71] Of fateful consequences for later conceptions of the American West, however, was not the Multnomah's length but its source region. For according to Clark's 1814 map it headed in the same general area as did the Yellowstone, Bighorn, Platte, Arkansas, Rio Grande, Colorado, and Snake rivers. It was the final component of a new pyramidal height-of-land through which American commerce might still find its way to the Indies, and therefore was a new Passage to India.[72]

II

The new conception of the Passage was combined, in the images that grew out of the contributions of Lewis and Clark, with the reaffirmation of the Garden concept that was articulated in the text of the *History*. The iridescent vision of an agricultural paradise in the West had, of course, long been a feature of American geographical images, and Lewis's and Clark's descriptions of the lands through which they had passed did little to erode the enthusiastic pre-exploratory views of the bulk of the trans-Missouri West.[73] But in the place of the original uniform Garden of the World, Lewis and Clark offered a more rational and objective interpretation of western land quality. Prior to the expedition, estimates of the potential agricultural productivity of western North America had been based on an overall image of the entire West as a "field of delights! . . . a garden of spices! . . . a paradise of pleasures!"[74] This was a uniform image based on the lack of concrete geographical data derived from direct observation and experience, and after Lewis and Clark its acceptable and popular simplicity was drastically trans-

71. One of the major myths that might have been substantiated by Clark's Multnomah River was that of the Rio San Buenaventura, which, prior to Frémont's explorations, was viewed as draining the country south of the Columbia. Information from late eighteenth-century Spanish explorations of the upper Colorado basin was merged with details from the Lewis and Clark journals, and one of Frémont's objectives was the discovery of such a stream.

72. Allen, "Pyramidal Height-of-Land," p. 396.

73. Bowden, "The Great American Desert and the American Frontier," pp. 52–53.

74. Josiah Morrow, ed., "Tours into Kentucky and the Northwest Territory," *Ohio Archeological and Historical Quarterly*, XVI (1907), 396.

formed. For in the geographical conceptions that emerged from the *History* there was no longer a single West. There were, rather, a number of western regions, and the new images of the prairie lands of the lower Missouri, the Great Plains, the Rockies, the Great Columbian Plain, the Columbian valley, and the Pacific coast signaled an entirely new phase in the development of geographical knowledge about North America.[75]

The territory of the lower Missouri, between St. Louis and the mouth of the Platte, was the area that had figured most prominently in conceptions of land quality before the expedition, primarily because it had been the best-known section of the trans-Missouri West.[76] In the post-exploratory images, the prairie lands continued to form the core of the Garden and the single most important conceptual base for understanding the future of the American agrarian ideal. Throughout the text of the *History*, the prairie lands appeared as a region of sparkling, sunlit, tall-grass meadows, of lovely groves of hardwoods festooned with garlands of wild grape and rose, of vast stretches of "good rich black soil, which is perfectly susceptible of cultivation," of gentle climate and delightful prospects—the "best districts on the Missouri for the purposes of settlers."[77] The Garden of Jefferson's theories and the pastoral ideal still existed, and it was of little consequence that exploration had confined it to a narrower portion of territory than had formerly been assumed.[78] For earlier conceptions of the Garden had been based primarily on hope and desire, as well as the distortions inherent in the adoption by Americans of the landscape descriptions of the chroniclers of French Louisiana; now the dreams of an agrarian utopia in the fertile Northwest could be grounded in the detailed and specific accounts of American explorers.

The prairie lands of the lower Missouri had represented, for many Americans, a known or partly known conceptual environment. Beyond them to the west and north, however, lay the Great Plains with their vast, open expanses of treeless grasslands and their teeming herds of deer, elk, antelope, and bison, a region that was virtually unknown to most Americans prior to the return of Lewis and Clark and the beginning of fur trade along the upper Missouri near the end of the first decade of the nineteenth century. But after the publication of the *History* and other early travel accounts, American notions about the nature of the Great Plains began, for the first time, to crystallize around two basic poles of opinion: the Great Plains as a region of fertile prairies or the Great Plains as a sandy wasteland.

75. This is illustrated nowhere more clearly than on pp. 386–90 of vol. I of the Biddle *History*. Here the country between the Mississippi and the "extreme navigable point of the Missouri" is divided into a series of distinct regions, each having a separate character.

76. This was the area upon which most of the French chronicles of Louisiana had been based and which had dominated the American conceptions of Louisiana in the years immediately preceding the expedition.

77. Biddle, *History*, I, 388.

78. A comparison of the landscape descriptions of the Biddle *History* with the Jefferson "Official Account of Louisiana," published at the time of the Purchase, is most instructive on this point.

If the *History* described the area between the Platte and the Rockies in less glowing terms than those applied to the lower reaches of the Missouri, the overall picture was, nevertheless, of a vast fertile and habitable region. There were powerful obstacles to agricultural settlement in the area—"the almost total lack of timber, and particularly the want of good water, of which there is but a small quantity in the creeks, and even that brackish."[79] But in the pages of the *History* these regional qualities were offset by the fertile soil, animal abundance, and the generally favorable climate of the Plains (perceived as "salubrious" by Lewis and Clark in spite of the persistent high winds and the severe cold of winter). Where other contemporary observers such as Pike compared the treeless plains with "the sandy wastes of Africa" and claimed that they could never be inhabited,[80] Lewis and Clark spoke continually about beautiful plains, delightful tracts of country, handsome prairies, and good land for settlement. And in the American images of the Plains before 1820, it was probably the Lewis and Clark view that was the most acceptable and the most dominant.[81] The Northwest may not have been the uniform Garden of Jefferson's image—but neither was it the uniform Desert of many later nineteenth-century images.

Beyond the Great Plains to the west were "the Great Rocky Mountains," an area which had long remained in mystery and myth and which, after the publication of the *History*, was conceptually transformed more than any other western region. The older notions of the Rockies as mirror images of the Appalachians and as narrow parallel ridges cut by transverse rivers gave way before a newer view of a broad massive upland area of mighty peaks and deep valleys. Unlike the eastern ranges, the Rockies were not rolling and gentle and covered with thick forests. They were, rather, "high mountains whose summits are partially covered with snow, below which the pine is scattered along the sides down to the plain in some places, though the greater part of their surface has no timber and exhibits only a barren soil with no covering except dry parched grass or black rugged rocks."[82] Only in the isolated cases of the "wide and fertile" valleys of the upper Missouri, the Yellowstone, and the Bitterroot were the perceived harshness and barrenness of the "stoney and broken" mountainous region relieved. Nor was the climate as favorable as it had been in the Plains—heat during the day was suffocating, cold during the night almost intolerable, and snows lay on the heights even throughout the summer months. The northern Rockies formed a definite barrier across the path of the march of agricultural civilization.

On the western fringes of the Rocky Mountains, however, was an area deemed suitable for habitation by a farming people. Here, in a strip "several hundred miles in length and about fifty wide," was the prairie country of Idaho, "in all its parts extremely fertile . . . the climate quite as mild, if not

79. Biddle, *History*, I, 390.
80. Smith, *Virgin Land*, pp. 202–03.
81. Bowden, "Perception of the Western Interior," p. 18.
82. Biddle, *History*, I, 313.

milder, than the same parallels of latitude in the Atlantic states."[83] It was a district affording many advantages to settlers and farmers and "if properly cultivated, would yield every object necessary for the subsistence and comfort of civilized man." It was the only such characterization entered in the *History* for the vast tract of country between the upper Missouri and the lower portion of the Columbia, and the attitude of Lewis and Clark toward the Idaho prairies contrasted directly with their opinions on the country immediately to the west.

Bordering the prairie country along its western fringes was the Great Columbian Plain, and in describing this region the *History* came the closest ever to the desert concept. Like the Great Plains east of the Rockies, the Columbian Plain was treeless and level. But the lack of trees was the result of a barren and sterile soil; even the water courses were not bordered by the forest ribbons of the Missouri and its tributaries. The huge herds of game animals so characteristic of the Missouri drainage were absent from the plains of the Columbia, and incorporated in the text of the *History* were tales of hunger and a distasteful, inadequate, and monotonous diet of dried fish and roots. The climate was dry and hot—although in the winter the snows lay chest deep throughout the region—and the winds whipped the sandy soils about, obscuring the horizon and stinging the eyes. If descriptions of the Great Plains of the Missouri retained elements of the Garden, the evaluations of the Great Columbian Plain contained many of the Desert components that would later be applied to a number of areas in the American West.

Between the Columbian Plain and the Pacific there lay areas that, although totally different from the Columbian basin in their environmental characteristics, were also viewed with suspicion and distaste. Both the Cascade range—through which they had passed too rapidly to evaluate properly—and the country bordering on the Pacific were heavily wooded regions, offering immense contrasts to the sterile and treeless plains. But just as the Columbian Plain was adjudged differently than the Great Plains of the Missouri basin, the wooded mountains, hills, and coasts of the Pacific Northwest were viewed in a completely different light from the woodlands of Louisiana Territory. Indeed, beyond the Idaho prairies there was only one "desireable situation for a settlement on the western side of the Rocky mountains,"[84] this being the narrow north-south valley formed by the Cowlitz and Willamette (or Multnomah) rivers flowing south and north respectively into the Columbia. Other than this area, the remainder of the Pacific Northwest coastal zone was damp and disagreeable and choked with the rank growths of timber and underbrush which were not alleviated by the sun-dappled meadowlands and "oak openings" of the lower Missouri.[85] The Northwest was not all garden, and the region which, as both the place and the concept "Oregon," would

83. Biddle, *History*, II, 291.
84. Biddle, *History*, II, 224–25.
85. Brackenridge, *Views of Louisiana*, p. 96.

form the core of later nineteenth-century pastoral images was presented least favorably of all western regions in the official reports of the expedition.

12

The relative proportions of truth or fiction in the landscape evaluations of the *History*, like the varying amounts of accuracy or error inherent in the reappraisals of the potential route to the Pacific, were perhaps of little real consequence. For conceptual geography has as great an influence on thought and action as real geography,[86] and both the geographic fact and the geographic fantasy contained in the *History* and its accompanying map gave the Northwest form and structure, something that could be perceived and understood by the American people. "Henceforth," wrote Bernard DeVoto, "the mind could focus on reality. . . . It was the first report on the West, on the United States over the hill and beyond the sunset, on the province of the American future. . . . It satisfied desire and it created desire: the desire of the westering nation."[87]

For many Americans, the myth of the Passage to India via the Missouri and Columbia rivers had been effectively demolished by the factual reports of Lewis's and Clark's struggle across the Rockies. But for as many others, Clark's revised conception of the pyramidal height-of-land was the "enactment of a myth that embodied the future."[88] The Yellowstone and Bighorn and Platte and Arkansas, those mighty western rivers of Atlantic drainage whose waters mingled with the equally mighty Colorado, Snake, and Multnomah, became, in the new American image, "what the Euphrates, the Oxus, the Phasis, and the Cyrus were to the ancient Romans, lines of communication with eastern Asia, and channels for that rich commerce which, for forty centuries, has created so much wealth and power wherever it has flowed."[89] And although the regional myth of the uniform Garden of the World had been modified to include vast areas that were far from garden-like, much of the Northwest remained a "museum of wonder and value" in the eyes of many nineteenth-cenutry Americans.[90] The exploratory experience of Lewis and Clark had destroyed older versions of the Passage and the Garden. But out of that same experience there emerged newer editions of the ancient myths—the rich commerce of Asia might still flow through the center of a paradise of wealth and beauty, and the grand design of geographical theorists from Columbus to Thomas Jefferson might finally be realized.

86. DeVoto, *Course of Empire*, p. 62.
87. DeVoto, *Journals of Lewis and Clark*, p. lii.
88. Smith, *Virgin Land*, p. 18.
89. *Selections of Editorial Articles from the St. Louis Enquirer, on the Subject of Oregon and Texas, as Originally Published in That Paper in the Years 1818–19; and Written by the Hon. Thomas H. Benton* (St. Louis, 1844), p. 7. Benton claimed to have derived his concepts directly from Jefferson and viewed his efforts toward western expansion as having been inspired directly by the great statesman (Smith, *Virgin Land*, p. 24).
90. Smith, *Virgin Land*, ch. 16.

BIBLIOGRAPHY

ABEL, ANNIE HELOISE. "Mackay's Table of Distances," *Mississippi Valley Historical Review*, X (Mar., 1924).

———. "A New Lewis and Clark Map," *Geographical Review*, I (May, 1916).

———, ed. *Tabeau's Narrative of Loisel's Expedition to the Upper Missouri*. Norman, Okla., 1939.

———. "Trudeau's Description of the Upper Missouri," *Mississippi Valley Historical Review*, VIII (June–Sept., 1921).

ALLEN, JOHN L. "An Analysis of the Exploratory Process: The Lewis and Clark Expedition of 1804–06," *Geographical Review*, LXII (Jan., 1972).

———. "Geographical Knowledge and American Images of the Louisiana Territory," *Western Historical Quarterly*, II (Apr., 1971).

———. "Lewis and Clark on the Upper Missouri: Decision at the Marias," *Montana, the Magazine of Western History*, XXI (Summer, 1971).

———. "Pyramidal Height-of-Land: A Persistent Myth in the Exploration of Western Anglo-America," *International Geography 1972*, I, 395–96.

ANDERSON, SARAH TRAVERS LEWIS. *Lewises, Meriwethers, and Their Kin*. Richmond, Va., 1938.

APPLEMAN, ROY E. "Lewis and Clark: The Route 160 Years After," *Pacific Northwest Quarterly*, LVII (Jan., 1966).

ARMSTRONG, ZELLA. *Who Discovered America?* Chattanooga, 1950.

ARROWSMITH, AARON, AND SAMUEL LEWIS. *A New and Elegant General Atlas of North America*. Boston, 1804.

ASHE, GEOFFREY. *Land to the West*. London, 1962.

AUGER, HELEN. *Passage to Glory: John Ledyard's America*. New York, 1946.

BAKELESS, JOHN, ed. *The Journals of Lewis and Clark*. New York, 1964.

———. *Lewis and Clark, Partners in Discovery*. New York, 1947.

———. "Lewis and Clark's Background for Exploration," *Journal of the Washington Academy of Sciences*, XLIV (Nov., 1954).

BARITZ, LOREN. "The Idea of the West," *American Historical Review*, LXVI (Apr., 1961).

BEAZLEY, C. R. *The Dawn of Modern Geography*. 3 vols. New York, 1949.

BERQUIN-DUVALLON. *Travels in Louisiana and the Floridas*. New York, 1802.

BETTS, EDWIN MORRIS, ed. *Thomas Jefferson's Farm Book*. Memoirs of the American Philosophical Society, XXXV. Princeton, 1953.

———, ed. *Thomas Jefferson's Garden Book, 1766–1824*. Memoirs of the American Philosophical Society, XXII. Philadelphia, 1944.

399

BIDDLE, NICHOLAS, ed. *History of the Expedition under the Command of Captains Lewis and Clark, to the Sources of the Missouri, Thence across the Rocky Mountains and down the River Columbia to the Pacific Ocean. Performed during the years 1804-5-6. By Order of the Government of the United States. Prepared for the Press by Paul Allen Esq.* 2 vols. Philadelphia, 1814.

BILLON, FREDERICK L., ed. *The Annals of St. Louis in Its Territorial Days from 1804 to 1821.* St. Louis, 1888.

BOLTON, HERBERT E., ed. *Pageant in the Wilderness: The Journals of Father Escalante.* Salt Lake City, 1950.

———, ed. *Spanish Exploration in the Southwest.* New York, 1930.

BORLUND, C. H. "American Indian Map-Makers," *Geographical Magazine,* XX (Sept., 1947).

BOSSU, JEAN BERNARD. *Travels through That Part of North America Formerly Called Louisiana.* London, 1771.

BOWDEN, MARTYN J. "The Great American Desert and the American Frontier, 1800-1882: Popular Images of the Plains," in *Anonymous Americans: Explorations in Nineteenth Century Social History,* ed. Temara K. Haraven. Englewood Cliffs, N.J., 1971, pp. 48-79.

———. "The Perception of the Western Interior of the United States 1800-1870," *Proceedings of the Association of American Geographers,* I (1969), 16-21.

BOYD, JULIAN, ed. *The Papers of Thomas Jefferson.* 17 vols. Princeton, 1950-65.

BRACKENRIDGE, HENRY. *Journal of a Voyage up the Missouri in 1811.* Vol. VI of *Early Western Travels,* ed. Reuben Gold Thwaites. Cleveland, 1904.

———. *Views of Louisiana.* Philadelphia, 1814.

BRADBURY, JOHN. *Travels in the Interior of America.* Vol. V of *Early Western Travels,* ed. Reuben Gold Thwaites. Cleveland, 1904.

BREBNER, JOHN BARTLETT. *The Explorers of North America.* London, 1933.

BRETZ, J. HARLAN. "The Channeled Scablands of the Columbia Plateau," *Journal of Geology,* XXXI (Nov.–Dec., 1923).

BRIGGS, HAROLD E. *Frontiers of the Northwest: A History of the Upper Missouri Valley.* New York, 1940.

BRISSOT DE WARVILLE, JACQUES PIERRE. *Nouveaux voyages dans les Etats-Unis de l'Amerique Septentrionale.* Paris, 1791.

BROWN, CHARLES B. "An Address to the Government of the United States on the Cession of Louisiana." Philadelphia, 1803.

BROWN, RALPH HALL. "Jefferson's Notes on Virginia," *Geographical Review,* XXXIII (July, 1943).

BRYCE, GEORGE. *The Remarkable History of the Hudson's Bay Company.* London, 1900.

BURDER, GEORGE. "The Welch Indians," *Magazine of History,* 1797, pp. 80-111.

BURPEE, LAWRENCE J., ed. "The Journal of Anthony Hendry, 1754-55," *Proceedings and Transactions of the Royal Society of Canada,* 3rd ser., II (1908), 307-64.

———, ed. *The Journals and Letters of Pierre Gaultier de Varennes de la Vérendrye and His Sons.* 2 vols. Toronto, 1927.

———. *The Search for the Western Sea.* 2 vols. Toronto, 1908.

BUTEL-DUMONT, GEORGES MARIE. *Mémoires historiques sur la Louisiane.* Paris, 1753.

CAMPBELL, JOHN. *The Spanish Empire in America.* London, 1747.

CARTER, CLARENCE C., ed. *Territorial Papers of the United States.* XIII, Territory of Louisiana-Missouri, 1803-06; XIV, Territory of Louisiana-Missouri, 1806-14. Washington, 1948, 1949.

CARVER, JONATHAN. *Travels through the Interior Parts of North America in the Years 1766, 1767, and 1768.* 3rd ed. London, 1781.

CHARLEVOIX, PIERRE FRANÇOIS XAVIER DE. *Historical Journal.* Reprint ed. New York, 1851.

———. *History and General Description of New France.* Trans. and ed. John Gilmary Shea. 6 vols. New York, 1900.

———. *A Voyage to North America.* 2 vols. Dublin, 1766.

CHINARD, GILBERT, ed. *The Commonplace Book of Thomas Jefferson.* Garden City, N.Y., 1926.

———. "Jefferson and the American Philosophical Society," *Proceedings of the American Philosophical Society,* LXXXVII, no. 3 (1944).

CHITTENDEN, HIRAM M. *A History of the American Fur Trade of the Far West.* Reprint ed. 2 vols. Stanford, Calif., 1954.

———. *Yellowstone National Park.* Cincinnati, 1895.

CHRISTMAN, G. M. "The Mountain Bison," *The American West,* VIII (May, 1971).

CHUINARD, DR. E. G. "The Medical Aspects of the Lewis and Clark Expedition." Friends of the Library, Corvallis, Ore., 1965.

CLARKE, CHARLES G. "The Roster of the Lewis and Clark Expedition," *Oregon Historical Quarterly,* XLV (Dec., 1944).

COLLOT, VICTOR. *A Journey in North America.* London, 1826.

COOK, JAMES. *A Voyage to the Pacific Ocean.* 3 vols. London, 1784.

COUES, ELLIOTT. "An Account of the Various Publications Relating to the Travels of Lewis and Clark, with a Commentary on the Zoological Results of Their Expedition," *Bulletin of the Geological and Geographical Surveys of the Territories,* no. 6, ser. 2 (1876), 417-44.

———, ed. *The Expeditions of Zebulon Montgomery Pike.* 3 vols. Philadelphia, 1895.

———, ed. *History of the Expedition under the Command of Lewis and Clark.* 4 vols. New York, 1893.

———, ed. *New Light on the Early History of the Greater Northwest: The Manuscript Journals of Alexander Henry . . . and of David*

Thompson. 3 vols. New York, 1897.

Cox, Issac Joslin. *The Early Exploration of Louisiana.* University Studies, Cincinnati, 1906.

Coxe, Daniel. *A Description of the English Province of Carolana by the Spaniards Call'd Florida and by the French, La Louisiane.* 2nd ed. London, 1741.

Crawford, Helen. "Sakakawea," *North Dakota Historical Quarterly,* I (Apr., 1927).

Criswell, E. H. *Lewis and Clark: Linguistic Pioneers.* University Studies, Columbia, Mo., 1940.

Cutright, Paul Russell. "Jefferson's Instructions to Lewis and Clark," *Bulletin of the Missouri Historical Society,* XXII (Apr., 1966).

———. *Lewis and Clark: Pioneering Naturalists.* Urbana, Ill., 1969.

———. "Lewis and Clark and Du Pratz," *Bulletin of the Missouri Historical Society,* XXI (Oct., 1964).

———. "Lewis on the Marias—1806," *Montana, the Magazine of Western History,* XVIII (Summer, 1968).

Davidson, Gordon C. *The Northwest Company.* Berkeley, Calif., 1918.

Davidson, Robert. *Geography Epitomized.* Morristown, Pa., 1803.

Davis, Andrew McFarland. "The Journey of Moncacht-Apé," *Proceedings of the American Antiquarian Society,* n.s., II (Apr., 1883).

Davis, Richard Beale. *Intellectual Life in Jefferson's Virginia.* Chapel Hill, N.C., 1964.

Decalves, Don Alonzo. *Travels to the Westward or the Unknown Parts of America.* Keene, N.H., 1794.

Deluzieres, Pierre Delassus. *An Official Account . . . of That Part of Louisiana Which Lies between the Missouri and New Madrid.* Lexington, Ky., 1796.

Denig, Edwin T. "Indian Tribes of the Upper Missouri," ed. J. N. B. Hewitt. *46th Annual Report, Bureau of American Ethnology.* Washington, 1940.

DeVoto, Bernard. *Course of Empire.* Boston, 1952.

———, ed. *The Journals of Lewis and Clark.* Boston, 1953.

Diller, Aubrey. "An Early Account of the Missouri River," *Missouri Historical Review,* XLV (Jan., 1951).

———. "James Mackay's Journey in Nebraska in 1796," *Nebraska History,* XXXVI (Jan., 1955).

———. "Maps of the Missouri River before Lewis and Clark," in *Studies and Essays . . . in Homage to George Sarton.* New York, 1946, pp. 505–19.

———. "A New Map of the Missouri River Drawn in 1795," *Imago Mundi,* XII (1955), 175–80.

Dillon, Richard. *Meriwether Lewis, a Biography.* New York, 1965.

———. "Stephen Long's Great American Desert,"

Proceedings of the American Philosophical Society, CXI, no. 2 (1967).

Dobbs, Arthur. *An Account of the Countries Adjoining to Hudson's Bay in the North-West Part of America.* London, 1744.

Dondore, Dorothy Anne. *The Prairie and the Making of Middle America: Four Centuries of Description.* Reprint ed. New York, 1961.

Douglas, Jesse S. "Lewis Map of 1806," *Military Affairs,* V (Spring, 1941).

Du Pratz, Antoine Simon le Page. *The History of Louisiana, or the Western Parts of Virginia and Carolina; Containing a Description of the Countries That Lie on Both Sides of the River Misisipi.* 2 vols. London, 1763.

Dwight, Nathaniel. *A Short but Comprehensive System of the Geography of the World.* Elizabethtown, N.J., 1801.

Dye, Eva Emery. *The Conquest: The True Story of Lewis and Clark.* Chicago, 1902.

Ehrenberg, Ralph. "Sketch of Part of the Missouri & Yellowstone Rivers with a Description of the Country &c.," *Prologue, the Journal of the National Archives,* III (Fall, 1971).

Eliade, Mircea. "The Yearning for Paradise in Primitive Tradition," *Daedalus,* LXXXVIII (Spring, 1959).

Eliot, T. C., ed. "A Remnant of the Log of the Columbia," *Oregon Historical Quarterly,* XXII (Dec., 1921).

Ellicott, Andrew. *The Journal of Andrew Ellicott.* Philadelphia, 1803.

Emmons, David. *Garden in the Grasslands.* Lincoln, Neb., 1971.

Ewers, John C. "The Indian Trade of the Upper Missouri before Lewis and Clark: An Interpretation," *Bulletin of the Missouri Historical Society,* X (July, 1954).

Ford, Paul Leicester, ed. *Autobiography of Thomas Jefferson, 1743–1790.* New York, 1914.

Forrest, Michael. *Travels through America: A Poem.* Philadelphia, 1793.

Foster, Augustus John. *Jeffersonian America: Notes on the United States of America Collected in the Years 1805–6–7 and 11–12.* Ed. Richard Beale Davis. San Marino, Calif., 1954.

French, Benjamin F., ed. *Historical Collections of Louisiana.* 5 vols. New York, 1846–55.

Friis, Herman R. "Cartographic and Geographic Activities of the Lewis and Clark Expedition," *Journal of the Washington Academy of Sciences,* XLIV (Nov., 1954).

Fritts, H. C. "Tree-Ring Evidence for Climatic Changes in Western North America," *Monthly Weather Review,* XCIII (July, 1965).

Gass, Patrick. *A Journal of the Voyages and Travels of a Corps of Discovery, under the Command of Capt. Lewis and Capt. Clarke of the Army of the United States.* Reprint ed. Minneapolis, 1958.

Gayarré, Charles. *History of Louisiana.* 4 vols. New Orleans, 1903.

GILBERT, E. W. *Exploration of Western America, 1800–1850: An Historical Geography.* Cambridge, Eng., 1933.

GIRAUD, MARCEL. "Étienne Veniard de Bourgmont's Exact Description of Louisiana," *Bulletin of the Missouri Historical Society,* XV (Oct., 1958).

GOETZMANN, WILLIAM H. *Exploration and Empire: The Explorer and the Scientist in the Winning of the American West.* New York, 1966.

GOVAN, THOMAS P. *Nicholas Biddle, Nationalist and Public Banker.* Chicago, 1959.

GREELEY, ARTHUR W. "Jefferson as a Geographer," *National Geographic Magazine,* VII (Aug., 1896).

GUTHRIE, WILLIAM. *A New System of Modern Geography.* Philadelphia, 1794.

HAFEN, LEROY R., AND CARL C. RISTER. *Western America: The Exploration, Settlement, and Development of the Region beyond the Mississippi.* New York, 1941.

HAGUE, ARNOLD. "An Early Map of the Far West," *Science,* X (4 Oct. 1887).

HALLS, JAMES. *A Brief History of the Mississippi Territory.* Salisbury, N.C., 1801.

HAMILTON, RAPHAEL N. "Early Cartography of the Missouri Valley," *American Historical Review,* XXXIX (July, 1934).

HARRIS, BURTON. *John Colter.* New York, 1952.

HARSHBERGER, JOHN W. *The Botanists of Philadelphia and Their Work.* Philadelphia, 1899.

HASTINGS, LANSFORD W. *The Emigrants' Guide to Oregon and California.* Cincinnati, 1845.

HEARNE, SAMUEL. *A Journey from Prince of Wales Fort in Hudson's Bay to the Northern Ocean.* Ed. J. B. Tyrrell. Toronto, 1911.

HEBARD, GRACE RAYMOND. *Sacajawea, a Guide and Interpreter of the Lewis and Clark Expedition with an Account of the Travels of Toussaint Charbonneau, and of Jean Baptiste, the Expedition Papoose.* Glendale, Calif., 1933.

HEITMAN, FRANCIS B., comp. *Historical Register and Dictionary of the United States Army.* 2 vols. Washington, 1903.

HENNEPIN, LOUIS. *Description de la Louisiane.* Paris, 1683.

———. *Nouvelle Decouverte, a New Discovery of a Vast Country in North America.* Trans. and ed. Reuben Gold Thwaites. Chicago, 1903.

HERMANN, PAUL. *The Great Age of Discovery.* New York, 1958.

HILL, JOSEPH J. "Spanish and Mexican Exploration and Trade Northwest from New Mexico into the Great Basin," *Utah Historical Quarterly,* III (Jan., 1930).

HODGE, FREDERICK W., ed. *Spanish Explorers in the Southern United States.* New York, 1908.

HOUCK, LOUIS B. *The Boundaries of the Louisiana Purchase.* St. Louis, 1901.

———, ed. *The Spanish Regime in Missouri.* 2 vols. Chicago, 1909.

HOWAY, FREDERICK W., ed. *Voyages of the "Co-lumbia" to the Northwest Coast.* Boston, 1941.

HUBBARD, JOHN. *The Rudiments of Geography.* Walpole, N.H., 1803.

HUTCHINS, THOMAS. *An Historical Narrative and Topographical Description of Louisiana and West Florida.* Philadelphia, 1784.

———. *A Topographical Description of Louisiana and Western Florida.* London, 1785.

IRVING, WASHINGTON. *Astoria, or Anecdotes of an Enterprise beyond the Rocky Mountains.* New York, 1849.

JACKSON, DONALD, ed. *The Journals of Zebulon Montgomery Pike with Letters and Related Documents.* 2 vols. Norman, Okla., 1966.

———, ed. *Letters of the Lewis and Clark Expedition with Related Documents, 1783–1854.* Urbana, Ill., 1962.

———. "A New Lewis and Clark Map," *Bulletin of the Missouri Historical Society,* XVII (Jan., 1961).

———. "Some Books Carried by Lewis and Clark," *Bulletin of the Missouri Historical Society,* XVI (Oct., 1959).

JAMES, EDWIN. *Account of an Expedition from Pittsburgh to the Rocky Mountains.* 2 vols. Philadelphia, 1823.

JEFFERSON, THOMAS. *Message from the President of the United States Communicating Discoveries Made in Exploring the Missouri, Red River and Washita, by Captains Lewis and Clark, Doctor Sibley, and Mr. Dunbar; with a Statistical Account of the Countries Adjacent.* Washington, 1806.

———. *Notes on the State of Virginia.* London, 1787.

——— et al. *Documents Relating to the Purchase and Exploration of Louisiana.* Philadephia, 1904.

JEFFREYS, THOMAS. *The American Atlas.* London, 1776.

———. *A General Topography of North America and the West Indies.* London, 1768.

———. *The Natural and Civil History of the French Dominions in North and South America.* London, 1760.

———. *The North American and the West Indian Gazeteer.* London, 1776.

JOHANSEN, DOROTHY O. *Empire of the Columbia.* New York, 1967.

JONES, HOWARD MUMFORD. *O Strange New World.* New York, 1964.

JOSEPHY, ALVIN M., JR. *The Indian Heritage of America.* New York, 1968.

———. *The Nez Percé Indians and the Opening of the Northwest.* New Haven, Conn., 1965.

KALM, PEHR. *Travels into North America.* 2 vols. London, 1772.

KELLOGG, LOUISE P., ed. *Early Narrative of the Northwest.* New York, 1917.

———. "The Mission of Jonathan Carver," *Wisconsin Magazine of History,* XII (Dec., 1928).

KINGSTON, C. S. "Sacagawea as a Guide—the Evaluation of a Legend," *Pacific Northwest Quarterly*, XXXV (Jan., 1944).

KOCH, ADRIENNE, AND WILLIAM PEDEN, eds. *The Life and Selected Writings of Thomas Jefferson*. New York, 1944.

LA HARPE, BERNARD DE. *Journal historique de l'etablissement des Français à la Louisiane*. New Orleans, 1831.

LAHONTAN, LOUIS ARMAND, BARON DE. *New Voyages to North America*. 2 vols. London, 1703.

LA PORTE, JOSEPH DE. *Le voyageur français*. Paris, 1769.

LARPENTEUR, CHARLES. *Forty Years a Fur Trader*. Chicago, 1933.

LAVENDER, DAVID. *Land of Giants: The Drive to the Pacific Northwest, 1750–1950*. Garden City, N.Y., 1958.

———. *Westward Vision*. New York, 1963.

LAWSON, MERLIN P. "A Dendroclimatological Interpretation of the Great American Desert," *Proceedings of the Association of American Geographers*, III (1971), 109–14.

LEDYARD, JOHN. *A Journal of Captain Cook's Last Voyage*. Hartford, Conn., 1783.

LE ROUGE, GEORGE LOUIS. *Atlas Americaine Septentrionale*. Paris, 1778.

LEWIS, G. MALCOLM. "Three Centuries of Desert Concepts of the Cis-Rocky Mountain West," *Journal of the West*, IV (July, 1965).

LEWIS, MERIWETHER. *David Thompson and the Lewis and Clark Expedition*. Vancouver, B.C., 1959.

———, and WILLIAM CLARK. *A Statistical View of the Indian Nations Inhabiting the Territory of Louisiana. American State Papers, Indian Affairs*, no. 113, 9th Cong., 1st Sess. Washington, 1806.

LOOS, JOHN LOUIS. "A Biography of William Clark, 1770–1813," unpublished Ph.D. dissertation, Washington University, St. Louis, 1953.

———. "William Clark's Part in the Preparation of the Lewis and Clark Expedition," *Bulletin of the Missouri Historical Society*, X (July, 1954).

LOWENTHAL, DAVID. "Geography, Experience, and Imagination: Toward a Geographical Epistemology," *Annals of the Association of American Geographers*, LI (Sept., 1961).

LUPHER, R. L. "Physiographic Divisions of the Columbia Intermontane Province," *Annals of the Association of American Geographers*, XXXV (Jan., 1945).

LYON, E. WILSON. *Louisiana in French Diplomacy, 1759–1804*. Norman, Okla., 1934.

MACGRUDER, ALLAN B. *Political, Commercial, and Moral Reflections on the Late Cession of Louisiana*. Lexington, Ky., 1803.

MACKENZIE, ALEXANDER. *Voyages from Montreal through the Continent of North America to the Frozen and Pacific Oceans in 1789 and 1793*. Reprint ed. 2 vols. Toronto, 1911.

MALIN, JAMES C. *The Grassland of North America*. 4th printing. Lawrence, Kan., 1961.

MALONE, DUMAS. *Jefferson the Virginian*. Boston, 1948.

MARGRY, PIERRE, ed. *Decouvertes et etablissements des Français dans l'ouest et dans le sud de l'Amerique Septentrionale, 1614–1754*. 6 vols. Paris, 1876–86.

MARTIN, EDWIN T. *Thomas Jefferson, Scientist*. New York, 1952.

MARX, LEO. *The Machine in the Garden: Technology and the Pastoral Ideal in America*. New York, 1964.

MASSON, L. R. *Les bourgeois de la Compagnie du Nord-Quest*. 2 vols. Quebec, 1889.

MAURY, ANNE FONTAINE. *Intimate Virginiana*. Richmond, Va., 1941.

MAURY, JAMES FONTAINE. *Memoirs of a Hugenot Family*. New York, 1912.

———. "Treatise on Practical Education." MS, Manuscript Division, Alderman Library, University of Virginia, Charlottesville.

MEARES, JOHN. *Voyages to the North West Coast of America*. London, 1790.

MEINIG, DONALD W. *The Great Columbian Plain: A Historical Geography, 1805–1910*. Seattle, 1968.

MERK, FREDERICK. *Manifest Destiny and Mission in American History*. New York, 1963.

MICHAUX, ANDRÉ. *Travels into Kentucky, 1793–1796*. Vol. III of *Early Western Travels*, ed. Reuben Gold Thwaites. Cleveland, 1904.

MITCHELL, JOHN. *The Present State of Great Britain and North America*. London, 1755.

MITCHILL, SAMUEL LATHAM. *A Discourse on the Character and Services of Thomas Jefferson, More Especially as a Promoter of Natural and Physical Science*. New York, 1826.

———. "Lewis Map of the Part of North America Which Lies between the 35th and 52st Degrees of North Latitude from the Mississippi and the Upper Lakes to the Pacific Ocean," *Medical Repository*, III (2nd hexade, Nov.–Dec., 1805, Jan., 1806).

MORRIS, RALPH C. "The Notion of a Great American Desert East of the Rockies," *Mississippi Valley Historical Review*, XIII (Sept., 1926).

MORROW, JOSIAH, ed. "Tours into Kentucky and the Northwest Territory," *Ohio Archeological and Historical Quarterly*, XVI (1907), 348–401.

MORSE, JEDEDIAH. *The American Gazeteer*. Boston, 1803.

———. *The American Geography*. 2 vols. London, 1794.

———. *The American Universal Geography*. 5th ed. 2 vols. Boston, 1803.

———. *Geography Made Easy*. Boston, 1804.

Narrative of a Voyage . . . to the Western Continent. Windsor, Conn., 1801.

NASATIR, ABRAHAM P., ed. "An Account of Spanish Louisiana," *Missouri Historical Review*, XXIV (July, 1930).

———. "The Anglo-Spanish Frontier in the Illinois Country during the American Revolution," *Illinois State Historical Society Journal*, XXI (Oct., 1928).

——. "Anglo-Spanish Rivalry on the Upper Missouri," *Mississippi Valley Historical Review*, XVI (Dec., 1929–Mar., 1930).

——, ed. *Before Lewis and Clark: Documents Illustrating the History of the Missouri, 1785–1804.* 2 vols. St. Louis, 1952.

——. "Jacques d'Eglise on the Upper Missouri, 1791–1795," *Mississippi Valley Historical Review*, XIV (Mar., 1927).

——. "John Evans, Explorer and Surveyor," *Missouri Historical Review*, XXV (Oct., 1930–July, 1931).

——. "Spanish Exploration of the Upper Missouri," *Mississippi Valley Historical Review*, XIV (Mar., 1927).

NEWCOMBE, C. F., ed. *Menzie's Journal of Vancouver's Voyages.* Victoria, B.C., 1923.

NUTE, GRACE LEE. "A Peter Pond Map," *Minnesota History*, XIV (Mar., 1933).

OGLESBY, RICHARD. *Manuel Lisa and the Opening of the Missouri Fur Trade.* Norman, Okla., 1963.

OLESON, TRYGGVI J. *Early Voyages and Northern Approaches.* New York, 1964.

OLIVER, JOHN W. "Thomas Jefferson, Scientist," *Scientific Monthly*, LVI (May, 1943).

OSGOOD, ERNEST STAPLES, ed. *The Field Notes of Captain William Clark, 1803–1805.* New Haven, Conn., 1964.

PALAIRET, JOHN. *A Concise Description of the English and French Possessions in North America.* London, 1755.

PAULLIN, C. O., AND JOHN K. WRIGHT. *Atlas of the Historical Geography of the United States.* Washington, 1932.

PERRIN DU LAC, FRANÇOIS MARIE. *Voyages dans les deux Louisianes.* Paris, 1805.

PIKE, MAJOR ZEBULON MONTGOMERY. *An Account of Expeditions to the Sources of the Mississippi, and through the Western Parts of Louisiana.* Philadelphia, 1810.

PINKERTON, JOHN. *Modern Geography.* 2 vols. Philadelphia, 1804.

POHL, FREDERICK J. *Atlantic Crossings before Columbus.* New York, 1961.

POWELL, F. W., ed. *Hall J. Kelley on Oregon.* Princeton, 1932.

POWNALL, THOMAS. *A Topographical Description of North America.* London, 1776.

QUAIFE, MILO M., ed. "Extracts from Capt. McKay's Journal—and Others," *Wisconsin Historical Society Proceedings*, LXIII (1915), 186–210.

——, ed. *The Journals of Captain Meriwether Lewis and Sergeant John Ordway.* Madison, Wis., 1916.

RAMSEY, DAVID. "An Oration on the Cession of Louisiana." Charleston, S.C., 1804.

RAY, VERNE F. "Cultural Relations in the Plateau of Northwestern America," *Publications of the Frederick Webb Hodge Anniversary Publications Fund*, III. Los Angeles, 1939.

——, AND NANCY O. LURIE. "The Contributions of Lewis and Clark to Ethnography," *Journal of the Washington Academy of Sciences*, XLIV (Nov., 1954).

ROBSON, JOSEPH. *An Account of Six Years' Residence in Hudson's Bay.* London, 1752.

ROGERS, ROBERT. *A Concise Account of North America.* London, 1765.

RUSSELL, THOMAS, ed. *Voyages of the Sonora in the Second Bucareli Expedition.* San Francisco, 1920.

SAUER, CARL O. "A Geographic Sketch of Early Man in North America," *Geographical Review*, XXXIV (Oct., 1944).

Selections of Editorial Articles from the St. Louis Enquirer, on the Subject of Oregon and Texas, as Originally Published in That Paper in the Years 1818–19; and Written by the Hon. Thomas H. Benton. St. Louis, 1844.

SHAPELY, HARLOW. "Notes on Thomas Jefferson as a Natural Philosopher," *Proceedings of the American Philosophical Society*, LXXXVII, no. 3 (1944).

SKARSTEN, M. O. *George Drouillard, Hunter and Interpreter for Lewis and Clark and Fur Trader, 1807–1810.* Glendale, Calif., 1964.

SMITH, HENRY NASH. *Virgin Land: The American West in Symbol and Myth.* Cambridge, Mass., 1950.

SMITH, MARIAN W. "The Cultural Development of the Northwest Coast," *Southwestern Journal of Anthropology*, XII (Autumn, 1956).

SOWERBY, E. MILLICENT. *The Library Catalogue of Thomas Jefferson.* 5 vols. Washington, 1952–54.

SPACE, RALPH. "Lewis and Clark through Idaho." Lewiston, Idaho, 1964.

SPARKS, JARED. *Memoirs of the Life and Travels of John Ledyard.* London, 1828.

SPAULDING, KENNETH, ed. *The Fur Hunters of the Far West by Alexander Ross.* Norman, Okla., 1956.

——, ed. *On the Oregon Trail, Robert Stuart's Journal of Discovery.* Norman, Okla., 1953.

SPRAGUE, MARSHALL. *The Great Gates.* Boston, 1964.

STEGNER, WALLACE, ed. *Powell Report on the Lands of the Arid Regions of the United States.* Cambridge, Mass., 1962.

STEVENS, ISSAC I. "Narrative and Final Report of Explorations for a Route for a Pacific Railroad near the Forty-seventh and Forty-ninth Parallels of North Latitude from St. Paul to Puget Sound," *Pacific Railroad Reports*, XII, House and Senate Document series.

——. *Reports of Explorations and Surveys from the Mississippi River to the Pacific Ocean.* Washington, 1859.

STEWART, GEORGE. *Names on the Land.* New York, 1945.

404

STEWART, OMER C. "Fire as the First Great Force Employed by Man," in *Man's Role in Changing the Face of the Earth*, ed. William Thomas. Chicago, 1956, pp. 115–33.

STODDARD, AMOS. *Sketches, Historical and Descriptive of Louisiana*. Philadelphia, 1812.

STORM, COLTON. "Lieutenant Armstrong's Expedition to the Missouri River, 1790," *Mid-America*, XXV (July, 1943).

STRAHORN, R. E. *To the Rockies and Beyond*. Omaha, Neb., 1879.

SURFACE, GEORGE THOMAS. "Thomas Jefferson: A Pioneer Student of American Geography," *American Geographical Society Bulletin*, XLI, no. 12 (1909).

SYLVESTRIS. *Reflections on the Cession of Louisiana to the United States*, Washington, 1803.

TEGGART, FREDERICK J. "Notes Supplementary to Any Edition of Lewis and Clark," *Annual Report of the American Historical Association*, I (1908), 185–95.

THOMAS, ALRFED B., ed. *After Coronado: Documents from the Archives of Spain, Mexico, and New Mexico*. Norman, Okla., 1935.

THORNBURY, WILLIAM D. *Regional Geomorphology of the United States*. New York, 1965.

THWAITES, REUBEN GOLD, ed. *Early Western Travels*. 32 vols. Cleveland, 1904–06.

———, ed. *The Jesuit Relations and Allied Documents*. 72 vols. Cleveland, 1896–1901.

———, ed. *The Original Journals of the Lewis and Clark Expedition*. 8 vols. New York, 1904–05.

TOMKINS, CALVIN. *The Lewis and Clark Trail*. New York, 1965.

TYRRELL, J. B., ed. *David Thompson's Narrative of His Explorations in Western America, 1784–1812*. Toronto, 1916.

———, ed. *Journals of Samuel Hearne and Phillip Turnor*. Toronto, 1934.

———. "Peter Fidler, Trader and Surveyor, 1769–1822," *Proceedings and Transactions of the Royal Society of Canada*, 3rd ser., VII (1913), 117–28.

U.S. CONGRESS. *American State Papers, 1785–1834*. Washington, 1877.

———. *Annals of the 7th–9th Congresses*, XII (1827).

U.S. DEPARTMENT OF STATE. *Papers and Correspondence Bearing upon the Purchase of the Territory of Louisiana*. Washington, 1903.

VANCOUVER, GEORGE. *A Voyage of Discovery to the North Pacific Ocean*. 3 vols. London, 1798.

VANDIVEER, C. A. *The Fur-Trade and Early Western Explorations*. Cleveland, 1929.

VILLIERS, BARON MARC DE, ed. *La decouverte du Missouri*. Paris, 1925.

W. M. P. "A Poem on the Acquisition of Louisiana." Charleston, S.C., 1804.

WAGNER, HENRY RAUP. *The Cartography of the Northwest Coast*. 2 vols. Berkeley, Calif., 1937.

WALKER, THOMAS. *Journal of an Exploration in the Spring of the Year 1750*. Boston, 1888.

WALLACE, W. STEWART, ed. *Documents Relating to the Northwest Company*. Toronto, 1934.

———. "The Pedlars from Quebec," *Canadian Historical Review*, XIII (Dec., 1932).

WARKENTIN, JOHN, ed. *The Western Interior of Canada: A Record of Geographical Discovery, 1612–1917*. Toronto, 1964.

WEBB, WALTER PRESCOTT. *The Great Plains*. New York, 1931.

WEST, HELEN B. "Meriwether Lewis in Blackfeet Country." Museum of the Plains Indian, Browning, Mont., 1964.

WHEAT, CARL IRVING. *Mapping the Transmississippi West, 1540–1861*. 5 vols. Menlo Park, Calif., 1958–62.

WHEELER, OLIN D. *The Trail of Lewis and Clark*. 2 vols. New York, 1904.

WILL, D. W. "Lewis and Clark: Westering Physicians," *Montana, the Magazine of Western History*, XXI (Fall, 1971).

WILL, GEORGE F., AND H. J. SPINDEN. "The Mandan, a Study of Their Culture, Archaeology and Language," *Papers of the Peabody Museum of Archaeology and Ethnology*, III, no. 4 (1906).

WILLIAMS, DAVID. "John Evans' Strange Journey," *American Historical Review*, LIV (Jan.–Apr., 1949).

WINSOR, JUSTIN, ed. *Narrative and Critical History of America*. 8 vols. Boston, 1889.

WINTERBOTHAM, WILLIAM. *An American Atlas*. New York, 1796.

———. *The Historical, Geographical, Commercial and Philosophical View of the American United States*. 4 vols. New York, 1796.

WORKMAN, BENJAMIN. *Elements of Geography*. 9th ed. Philadelphia, 1803.

WRIGHT, JOHN KIRTLAND. *Geographical Lore of the Time of the Crusades*. New York, 1925.

———. *Human Nature in Geography*. Cambridge, Mass., 1966.

———. "Where History and Geography Meet: Recent American Studies in the History of Exploration," *Proceedings of the 8th American Scientific Congress*, IX (1943), 17–23.

WROTH, LAWRENCE C. *The Early Cartography of the Pacific*. New York, 1944.

YATES, TED W. "Since Lewis and Clark," *The American West*, II (Fall, 1965).

INDEX